P9-CDL-272

THE NORTON
ANTHOLOGY OF
CONTEMPORARY FICTION

Second Edition

THE NORTON ANTHOLOGY OF CONTEMPORARY FICTION

Second Edition

R. V. Cassill

Late of Brown University

Joyce Carol Oates

Princeton University

W · W · NORTON & COMPANY

NEW YORK LONDON

Copyright © 1998, 1988 by W. W. Norton & Company, Inc. All rights reserved.
Printed in the United States of America.

The text of this book is composed in Electra
with the display set in Optima
Composition by Maple-Vail Composition Services
Manufacturing by Maple-Vail Book Manufacturing Group
Cover illustration: *Barbeque*, 1982. Oil on canvas, 64 x 100".
Courtesy Eric Fischl.

Library of Congress Cataloging-in-Publication Data
The Norton anthology of contemporary fiction / [selected by]
  R.V. Cassill, Joyce Carol Oates. — 2nd ed.
      p.   cm.
  ISBN 0-393-96833-2 (pbk.)
      1. Short stories, American.   2. American fiction — 20th century.
  I. Cassill, R. V. (Ronald Verlin), 1919– . II. Oates, Joyce
  Carol, 1938– .
  PS648.S5N67   1997
  813'.010805 — dc21   96-51171
                                                                         CIP

W. W. Norton & Company, Inc., 500 Fifth Avenue, New York, N.Y. 10110
www.wwnorton.com

W. W. Norton & Company Ltd., Castle House, 75/76 Wells Street, London W1T 3QT

CONTENTS

INTRODUCTION

Before venturing my scattershot comment on elements of contemporary fiction and its environment, I want to welcome as coeditor Joyce Carol Oates, whose work as a fiction writer, poet, critic, and editor I have so much admired since I began to read her stories and reviewed her novel *Expensive People* in 1968. For many years she has taught in major creative writing programs around the country. It is her combination of teaching and writing experience that has fitted her so well to the tasks of helping to revise this book.

But I would have you take note as well of the obvious fact that she and I are not the only editors who have put the imprint of their sensibility and enthusiasm on the formation of this collection. Every story offered here has been published before—in magazines, collected works, or other anthologies. In all these previous publications, a sifting of innumerable aspects of the contemporary vision was made, the choice of skilled readers who were often themselves writers of short stories and teachers of short fiction. The wisest among them taught us that to keep the literature of the past alive, it must always be renewed by new writing. Each part of their devoted labors helped in coloring the fabric which we acknowledge as the contemporary tapestry of our fiction. And, as must be obvious to all, crediting these echelons of editors does not at all minimize the stellar expression by what Frank O'Connor has called the "lonely voice" of the authors selected by us for this book.

Teachers who used the First Edition of *The Norton Anthology of Contemporary Fiction* passed back their views on which stories should be retained to complement the new titles added here. They also reminded us how many of the authors whose stories we have gathered have been students or teachers in college writing programs—further underlining the way the roots of the short story in our time reach deep into the sensibilities of all of us who assemble on campuses everywhere.

Perhaps it is precisely by validating the collective sensibility of contemporary fiction that we come round, as we must, to the purely singular transaction between one writer and one reader. Only thus will the collective effort prove its worth. Before speaking for an era, the writer must speak person to person.

We may or may not recently have been in a golden age for short fiction. Not much is gained by saying so or denying it. One may well conclude the times have been neither wrong nor right for recent authors. In all events, they have signed with their honor as writers what the times have given them, the precious and the wretched. On the one hand, they have found their voices amid a blab and clatter of media noise unlike anything known before; of the dud eloquence of public discourse in advertising, sports, and manipulative politics; of instant folklore, junk mail, and junk values trickling down through literary and academic decadence; and through cosmetic heroism and the tyrannical buzzwords of received ideas.

In style and content, our writers have often put the worst to good use. That is the mission of art. In a sound-bitten nation of 250 million people on mental tethers that often make them sound like the 250 stragglers in a talk-show audience, what room can we claim for the language of reason and passion? Our best writers had to find their way through clouds of murk. And they must be sought there by the unflaggingly hopeful readers of this student generation.

On the brighter side, there has been a swelling interest in the short story and more publications open to the short story writer than ever before. And the proliferation of writing classes is evidence of vitality, if not of the full enlightenment of which we dream. It is not necessarily the mission of literature in our time to rescue or even to summarize an age, but to speak truly from it. If the writers included here draw little on historic events, it may be said that they need historians less than historians need them. Or that true history is inescapably an ingredient of the discoveries of the imaginative writer.

It might also go without saying that in a time like ours many varieties of subject matter will be found in these pages. The boundaries of experience have been stretched, and old taboos have been replaced by new ones. Not surprisingly, the response of beleaguered people to the creep of cultural change is still the general subject of fiction.

The serious writer is more inclined to regard fashions as subject matter than to cheer for them because they are fashionable. The result is often satire. Young people who are unwillingly goaded to keep abreast of the lightning changes of orthodoxies may have a hard time detecting what *is* ridiculous about them. Therefore, the ironic points of light provided by satire offer fine occasions for classroom discussion. Perhaps the tonic of irony is always in short supply. If so, we may cherish it where it is found, among these stories and others they resemble.

Now, as the millennium slouches to its end, beyond anyone's doubt the world is increasingly urbanized. In America we are a long way from Sherwood Anderson's *Winesburg, Ohio,* and Faulkner's wilderness. The relatively few who remain in rural areas watch the same shows on television as their fellows in the inner cities. They ride snowmobiles and put their thoughts on the internet. The serious writer cannot compete with network journalists who leapfrog the globe in search of what is newsworthy. Yet the latter suffer a disadvantage from which fiction writers are at least partly immune. Journalists write what they have read in the other fellow's newspaper while fiction writers have the freedom to write what they have seen and heard and measured with their own sensibilities. The catchwords of journalism are part of the measured subject matter of fiction. No matter how power and ingenuity try to contain us, with the story we are always on the outside looking in. The range of private experience in this collection ought to encourage students to look into their own school and neighborhood experience when and if they are moved to write. Why should students be reluctant to admit that what goes on around them is fit stuff for writing?

As to the matters of varied style found in the following pages, it may be remarked in general that the passion for a "revolution of the word" has petered out as the century moved on. Still, the experimentalism of earlier decades has left its traces. Students—whether or not they be students in writing classes—will find much to emulate, and class discussions of contemporary styles will be relevant in all literature courses.

Those of you who have used the First Edition will note that in the present one the lists of book publications by each author have been moved from the *Instructor's Handbook* to the main text. This change is small but it expresses a large hope: that all readers who have been stirred and rewarded by some story offered here will go on sooner or later to read more by this author or that, more by those writers who struck them with fear, anticipation, and consuming wonder.

RVC

ACKNOWLEDGMENTS

The editors wish to thank Charles Baxter and George Garrett for their thoughtful reviews of *The Norton Anthology of Contemporary Fiction*, Charles Johnson for his helpful footnotes, as well as: Marcel Cornis-Pope, Virginia Commonwealth University; Henry Hart, College of William and Mary; Nelson Hathcock, St. Xavier University; Laura Wilson Henrikson, Southern Illinois University—Carbondale; Thomas J. Hruska, Northern Michigan University; James Knudsen, University of New Orleans; Patricia Cleary Miller, Rockhurst College; Linda Schafler, Marquette University; N. A. Sherf, North Shore Community College; and John Somer, Emporia State University.

ALICE ADAMS

BARCELONA

In the darkened, uneven cobbled square, in the old quarter of Barcelona, the Barrio Gótico, the middle-aged American couple who walk by appear to be just that: American, middle-aged. The man is tall and bald; his head shines dimly as he and his wife cross the shaft of light from an open doorway. She is smaller, with pale hair; she walks fast to keep up with her husband. She is wearing gold chains, and they, too, shine in the light. She carries a small bag in which there could be—more gold? money? some interesting pills? They pass a young Spaniard lounging in a corner whose face the man for no reason takes note of.

Persis Fox, the woman, is a fairly successful illustrator, beginning to be sought after by New York publishers, but she secs herself as being in most ways a coward, a very fearful person; she is afraid of planes, of high bridges, she is overly worried by the illnesses of children—a rather boring list, as she thinks of it. Some years ago she was afraid that Thad, her husband, who teaches at Harvard, would take off with some student, some dark, sexily athletic type from Texas, possibly. More recently she has been frightened by accounts everywhere of muggings, robberies, rapes. She entirely believes in the likelihood of nuclear war. She can and does lie awake at night with such thoughts, for frozen hours.

However, walking across these darkened cobbles, in the old quarter of Barcelona, toward a restaurant that Cambridge friends have recommended, she is not afraid at all, only interested in what she is seeing: just before the square, an arched and windowed walk up above the alley, now crenellated silhouttes, everywhere blackened old stones. Also, she is hungry, looking forward to the seafood for which this restaurant is famous. And she wishes that Thad would not walk so fast; by now he is about five feet ahead of her, in an alley.

1

In the next instant, though, before she has seen or heard any person approaching, someone is running past her in the dark—but not past; he is beside her, a tall dark boy, grabbing at her purse, pulling its short strap. Persis' first instinct is to let him have it, not because she is afraid—she is not, still not, afraid—but from a conditioned reflex, instructing her to give people what they want: children, her husband.

In the following second a more primitive response sets in, and she cries out, "No!"—as she thinks, Kindergarten, some little boy pulling something away. And next thinks, Not kindergarten. Spain. A thief.

He is stronger, and with a sudden sharp tug he wins; he has pulled the bag from her and run off, as Persis still yells, "No!"—and as (amazingly!) she remembers the word for thief. "LADRÓN!" she cries out. "Ladrón!"

Then suddenly Thad is back (Persis has not exactly thought of him in those seconds), and almost before she has finished saying "He took my bag!" Thad is running toward the square, where the thief went. Thad is running, running—so tall and fast, such a sprint, as though this were a marathon, or Memorial Drive, where he usually runs. He is off into the night, as Persis yells again, "Ladrón!" and she starts out after him.

Persis is wearing low boots (thank God), not heels, and she can hear Thad's whistle, something he does with two fingers in his mouth, intensely shrill, useful for summoning children from ski slopes or beaches as night comes on. Persis, also running, follows the sound. She comes at last to a fairly wide, dimly lit street where Thad is standing, breathing hard.

She touches his arm. "Thad—"

Still intent on the chase, he hardly looks at her. He is not doing this for her; it is something between men. He says, "I think he went that way."

"But Thad—"

The street down which he is pointing, and into which he now begins to stride, with Persis just following—this street's darkness is broken at intervals by the steamy yellow windows of shabby restaurants, the narrow open door of a bar. Here and there a few people stand in doorways, watching the progress of the Americans. Thad sticks his head into the restaurants, the bar. "I don't see him," he reports back each time.

Well, of course not. And of course each time Persis is glad—glad that the boy is hidden somewhere. Gone. Safe, as she and Thad are safe.

They reach the end of the block, when from behind them a voice calls out, in English, not loudly, "Lady, this your bag?"

Thad and Persis turn to see a dark, contemptuous young face, a tall boy standing in a doorway. Not, Thad later assures Persis, and later still their friends—not the thief, whom he saw as they first crossed the square, and would recognize. But a friend of his?

The boy kicks his foot at something on the cobbles, which Thad walks over to pick up, and which is Persis' bag.

"I can't believe it!" she cries out, aware of triteness, as Thad hands over the bag to her. But by now, now that everything is over, she is seriously frightened; inwardly she trembles.

"Well, we got it." Thad speaks calmly, but Persis can hear the pride in his voice, along with some nervousness. He is still breathing hard, but he has begun to walk with his purposeful stride again. "The restaurant must be down here," he tells her.

Astoundingly, it is; after a couple of turns they see the name on a red neon sign, the name of the place they have been told about, where they have made a reservation.

The kitchen seems to be in the front room, next to the bar: all steam and steel, noisy clanging. Smoke and people, glasses rattling, crashing. "I really need a drink." Persis tells Thad, as instead they are led back to a room full of tables, people—many Americans, tourists, all loud and chattering.

At their small table, waiting for wine, with his tight New England smile Thad asks, "Aren't you going to check it? See what's still there?"

Curiously, this has not yet occurred to Persis as something to be done; she has simply clutched the bag. Now, as she looks down at the bag on her lap, it seems shabbier, a battered survivor. Obediently she unsnaps the flap. "Oh good, my passport's here," she tells Thad.

"That's great." He is genuinely pleased with himself—and why should he not be, having behaved with such courage? Then he frowns. "He got all your money?"

"Well no, actually there wasn't any money. I keep it in my pocket. Always, when I go to New York, that's what I do."

Why does Thad look so confused just then? A confusion of emotions is spread across his fair, lined face. He is disappointed, somehow? Upset that he ran after a thief who had stolen a bag containing so little? Upset that Persis, who now goes down to New York on publishing business by herself, has tricks for self-preservation?

Sipping wine, and almost instantly dizzy, light in her head, Persis tries to explain herself. "Men are such dopes," she heedlessly starts. "They always think that women carry everything they own in their bags. Thieves think that, I mean. So I just shove money and credit cards into some pocket. There's only makeup in my bags."

"And your passport." Stern, judicious Thad.

"Oh yes, of course," Persis babbles. "That would have been terrible. We could have spent days in offices."

Gratified, sipping at his wine, Thad says, "I wonder why he didn't take it, actually."

Persis does not say, "Because it's hidden inside my address book"—although quite possibly that was the case. Instead, she says what is also surely true: "Because you scared him. The last thing he expected was someone running after him, and that *whistle*."

Thad smiles, and his face settles into a familiar expression: that of a generally secure, intelligent man, a lucky person, for whom things happen more or less as he would expect them to.

Persis is thinking, and not for the first time, how terrible it must be to be a man, how terrifying. Men are always running, chasing something. And if you are rich and successful, like Thad, you have to hunt down anyone who wants to take away your possessions. Or if you're poor, down on your luck, you might be tempted to chase after a shabby bag that holds nothing of any real value, to snatch such a bag from a foreign woman who is wearing false gold chains that shine and glimmer in the dark.

1984

■   ■   ■

JULIA ALVAREZ

THE RUDY ELMENHURST
STORY

We took turns being the wildest. First one, then another, of us would confess our sins on vacation nights after the parents went to bed, and we had double-checked the hall to make sure there were "no Moors on the coast," an Island expression for the coast being clear. Baby Sister Fifi held that title the longest, though Sandi, with her good looks and many opportunities, gave her some competition. Several times Carla, the responsible eldest, did something crazy. But she always claimed she had done whatever it was she'd done to gain ground for us all. So her reigns of error smacked of good intentions and were never as juicy as Fifi's. To our "Wow, Fifi, how could you?!" Fifi gave us bad-girl grins and the catchphrase from the Alka-Seltzer commercial, "Try it, you'll like it!"

For a brief few giddy years, I was the one with the reputation among my sisters of being the wild one. I suppose it all started at boarding school when I began getting lots of callers, and though none of these beaus lasted long enough to even be called relationships, my sisters mistook volume for vampishness. Back in those days I had what one teacher called "a vivacious personality." I had to look up the word in the dictionary and was relieved to find out it didn't mean I had problems. English was then still a party favor for me—crack open the dictionary, find out if I'd just been insulted, praised, admonished, criticized. Those shy prep school guys at mixers with their endearing long hands and blushing complexions, I could make them laugh. I could make them believe they had really engaged a girl in conversation. There wasn't a Saturday afternoon or Sunday after morning service that I didn't have callers. A bunch of guys from our brother school

5

would come down the hill and hang out in our parlor to get away from their dormitories, maybe sneaking a cigarette or a swig from a flask on the walk over. At our front desk, they had to give a girl's name, and quite a few gave mine. This had nothing to do with my being attractive in any remarkable way. This was vivaciousness through and through.

When I went away to college, my vivaciousness ultimately worked against me. I'd meet someone, conversation would flow, they'd come calling, but pretty soon afterwards, just as my heart was beginning to throw out little tendrils of attachment, they'd leave. I couldn't keep them interested. Why I couldn't keep them interested was pretty simple: I wouldn't sleep with them. By the time I went to college, it was the late sixties, and everyone was sleeping around as a matter of principle. By then, I was a lapsed Catholic, my sisters and I had been pretty well Americanized since our arrival in this country a decade before, so really, I didn't have a good excuse. Why I didn't just sleep with someone as persistent as Rudy Elmenhurst is a mystery I'm exploring here by picking it apart the way we learned to do to each other's poems and stories in the English class where I met Rudolf Brodermann Elmenhurst, the third.

Rudolf Brodermann Elmenhurst, the third, didn't show up until ten minutes or so into the class. I, on the other hand, had been the first to arrive, selecting a place around the seminar table close to the door, but unfortunately since the table was round, equally exposed. Others strolled in, the English jocks at the school. I knew they were special from their jeans and T-shirts, their knowing, ironic looks when obscure works of literature were referred to. The girls didn't all knit during class like education and socio majors. I'd already been writing on my own for a while, but this was my first English class since I'd talked my parents into letting me transfer to this co-ed college last fall.

At my place around the seminar table I unpacked my notebook and every one of the required and recommended texts which I had already bought, stacking them in front of me like my credentials. Most of the other students were too cool to have done anything hasty like purchase the books for the course. The professor walked in, a young guy in a turtleneck and jacket, the uniform of the *with it* professors of the day; he had that edge of the untenured, too eager, too many handouts, too many *please feel frees* on his syllabus, a home number as well as an office number. He called roll, acknowledging most of the other students with nicknames and jokes and remarks, stumbling over my name and smiling falsely at me, a smile I had identified as one flashed on "foreign students" to show them the natives were friendly. I felt profoundly out of place. The only person I seemed to have anything in common with was the absent Rudolf Brodermann Elmenhurst, the third, who also had an odd name and who was out of it because he wasn't there.

We were into the logistics of how to make copies for workshops when a young man walked in, late. He was one of those guys who has just come through a bout of adolescent acne into a scarred, masculine, bad-boy face. A guy to be passed over by the beauties in our class looking for sweethearts. He had an ironic smile on his lips, and—a phrase I haven't heard in a while—bedroom eyes. A guy who would break your heart. But you wouldn't know all this if you went by the sound of his name—which I did, an immigrant's failing, literalism. I assumed he was late because he'd just whizzed in from his small barony somewhere in Austria.

The professor stopped the class. "Rudolf Brodermann Elmenhurst, the third, I presume?" Everybody laughed, this guy too. I admired that from the start, to be able to make such an entrance without blushing and stumbling and arraying the floor with your books and the contents of your pocketbook. He could take a joke, and put on such an ironic self-assured face no one felt bad laughing. The guy looked around and there was a space next to the territory I'd carved out for myself on the table with my pile of books. He came and sat down. I could tell he was looking me over, probably wondering who the hell I was, this intruder upon the sanctuary of English majors.

Class resumed. The professor started explaining again about what all he expected from us in the course. Later, he asked us to write down a response to a little poem he passed around. This guy with a name like a title leaned over and asked if I could lend him a piece of paper and a pen. I felt honored to be the one asked. I tore some pages out of my notebook, then rummaged in my pocketbook for another pen. I looked up with a sorry-eyed expression. "I don't have an extra pen," I whispered, complete sentences for whispers, that's what tells you I was still a greenhorn in this culture. This guy looked at me as if he didn't give a damn about a pen, and I was a fool to think so. It was such an intense look, I felt myself coloring. "That's okay," he mouthed, without really using his voice so I had to lip-read, his full lips puckering as if he were throwing little kisses at me. If I'd known what sexy feelings felt like I would have identified the shiver going down my spine and into my legs. He turned to his other neighbor, who didn't have a pen either. The word went round. Anyone have an extra pen? No one. There was a dearth of pens that day in class.

I sunk my hand back into my pocketbook. I was the proverbially overprepared student; I had to have a standby writing utensil. I felt something promising at the bottom of my purse and pulled it out: it was a teensy pencil from a monogrammed set my mother had given me for Christmas: a box of pencils "my color," red, and inscribed with my so-called name in gold letters: *Jolinda*. (My mother had tried for my own name Yolanda, but the company had substituted the Americanized, southernized *Jolinda*.) *Jolinda*, that's what this pencil used to say. In fact, it was so worn down, only the hook of the *J* was left. We didn't throw things away in my family. I used both sides of a piece of paper. I handed my find over to this guy. He took it and held it up as if to say, "What have we here?" His buddies around us chuckled. I felt shabby for having saved a pencil through so many sharpenings. At the end of class, I fled before he could turn around and give it back to me.

That night there was a knock on my door. I was in my nightgown already, doing our assignment, a love poem in the form of a sonnet. I'd been reading it out loud pretty dramatically, trying to get the accents right, so I felt embarrassed to be caught. I asked who it was. I didn't recognize the name. Rudy? "The guy who borrowed your pencil," the voice said through the closed door. Strange, I thought, ten-thirty at night. I hadn't caught on yet to some of the strategies. "Did I wake you up?" he wanted to know when I opened the door. "No, no," I said, laughing apologetically. This guy I had sworn never to talk to after he had embarrassed me in class, but my politeness-training ran on automatic. I excused myself for not asking him in. "I'm doing my homework." That wasn't an excuse in the circles he ran in. We stood at the door a long moment, he looking over my shoulder into my room for an invitation. "I just came to return your pencil." He held it out, a small red stub in his palm. "Just to return that?" I said, calling his bluff. He grinned, dimples making parenthesis at the corners of his lips as if his smile were a secret between us. "Yeah," he said, and again he had that intent look in his eye, and again he looked over my shoulder. I picked the pencil out of his palm and was glad it had been sharpened to a stub so he couldn't see my name in gold letters inscribed on the side. "Thank you," I said, shifting my weight on my feet and touching the door knob, little moves, polite preliminaries to closing the door.

He spoke up. "Can we have lunch sometime?"

"Sure, we can have lunch, sometime." The way I emphasized *sometime* it was hopeless. I didn't trust this guy, I didn't know how to read him. I had nothing in my vocabulary of human behavior to explain him. Ten minutes late to the first meeting of a class. I knock myself out to get him a pencil and he makes fun. Ten-thirty, he shows up at my door to return it, and asks me to have lunch with him.

"How about tomorrow before class," Rudy said.

"We don't have class tomorrow."

"That gives us time for a long lunch," he answered, real quick on his feet. I couldn't help being impressed. "Okay," I said, shaking my head. "Tomorrow, lunch."

We had lunch the next day, talked until supper, and then had supper. That's the way I remember relationships starting in college — those obsessive marathon beginnings. It was hard to go back to your little dorm room and do your homework after having been so absorbed in someone else. But that's just what I did, I went back and worked on my sonnet. It was a fourteen-line treatise on the nature of love, but the whole time I was writing down my abstractions, I was thinking about how Rudy listened, looking at my mouth, so that it was hard for me to pay attention to what I was saying. How he puckered his lips as if he were kissing each word goodbye. How his hand had touched the small of my back to steer me through a crowd of rowdy frat guys in the dining room. If we admire some people for their originality with words, others for their quirky interesting minds, then Rudy had to be admired for his sexy, instinctive way with his body. He was the kind of guy who could kiss you behind your ear and make you feel like you'd just had kinky sex.

The next day Rudy didn't turn in his sonnet. After class, while I packed up my luggage of schoolbooks, I heard him talking to the professor how he'd gotten stuck and couldn't think of anything. The professor was likable, it was the sixties, not having your creative juices flowing was understandable. Rudy could have until Monday to turn in his sonnet. We spent most of the weekend together, writing it, actually me writing down lines and crossing them off when they didn't scan or rhyme, and Rudy coming up with the ideas. It was the first pornographic poem I'd ever co-written; of course I didn't know it was pornographic until Rudy explained to me all the word plays and double meanings. "The coming of the spring upon the boughs," was the last line. That meant spring was ejaculating green leaves on the trees; the new crocuses were standing stiff on the lawn on account of they were turned on. I was shocked by all of this. I was a virgin, I wasn't one hundred percent sure how sex worked. That anyone should put all of this into a poem, a place I'd reserved for deep feelings and lofty sentiments! I wonder now how much of Rudy's gutsiness was a veiled flirtation with me, who was obviously much taken with words and their meanings. I can't say; like I said, I hadn't learned yet some of the strategies one went through. But I was catching on.

I remember the close of each of those weekend nights as a prolonged farewell. It would start by my noting the time, midnight, one, one-thirty, and saying, "Well, I'm going to bed." Rudy would concur, "Me too," but then, he wouldn't move from his place at the foot of my bed next to my desk where I sat writing. It was a teensy dorm room. If you stood up to open the closet, you'd have to negotiate the desk so you wouldn't end up piled on the bed. "Me too." He smiled that ironic smile of his that always made me feel so foolish. Finally, I would just blurt out, "You've got to go, Rudy." He wouldn't say yes or no, or sorry to have stayed too long. He would just look at me with those bedroom eyes, and stand, as if he wasn't going out the door but coming—in both the old sense of the word and the new I had just learned—coming in from the cold outside for a night of lovemaking with his lady-lay. We stood at the door. Then he leaned over and kissed me behind the ear for goodbye.

It was that weekend too at one of our lingering departure scenes that I learned where he'd gotten his odd, ornate name. He'd had this crusty old grandfather he'd never met, from Germany, who'd left his unborn grandchild a trust fund with the proviso that he be named after the old man. "What if you'd been a girl?" I wondered.

"I wouldn't be having so much fun," Rudy said. By this time the kisses had migrated from behind my ear to my neck. I shivered when he put a necklace of them around me before departing.

Our next workshop, no one understood what my sublimated love sonnet was all about, but Rudy's brought down the house. Suddenly, it seemed to me, not only that the world was full of English majors, but of people with a lot more experience than I had. For the hundredth time, I cursed my immigrant origins. If only I too had been born in Connecticut or Virginia, I too would understand the jokes everyone was making on the last two digits of the year, 1969; I too would be having sex and smoking dope; I too would have suntanned parents who took me skiing in Colorado over Christmas break, and I would say things like "no shit," without feeling like I was imitating someone else.

Rudy and I began seeing each other regularly that spring. Besides class, we ate all our meals together, and on weekends, he'd asked me over to his dormitory for parties in his hall. His dorm was next to mine, the two buildings connected by an underground lounge which would fill weekends with good-natured, clean parties, much monitored by security. The real parties went on in the men's dorms. Mostly guys migrated from one room to another, smoking a little dope, drinking a lot. There were the heavy rooms for dropping acid or taking mushrooms. Candles flickered, incense burned in an unsuccessful attempt to cover the pungent smell of marijuana. The Beatles or Bob Dylan or The Mamas and the Papas blasted from stereos. It was a decadent atmosphere for me whose previous experience of dating had been mixers and parlor calls from boys at prep school. I'd go over to Rudy's, but I would drink only a sip or two of the Dixie cup he offered, and I wouldn't dare touch the drugs. I was less afraid of what they would do to my mind than I was of what Rudy might do to my body while I was under the influence.

He pooh-poohed my fears. For one thing, he said, without my consent, he couldn't do anything. "What about rape?" I asked, I wasn't a total bumpkin. "Jesus Christ," he said, shaking his head, disbelieving what he'd let himself in for with me. "I'm not going to fucking rape you!" I was hurt. I'd never been spoken to that way. If my father had heard a man use such obscenities before his daughters, he would have asked him to step outside where he would have defended my honor. Of course, I would have had to do a lot of explaining afterwards about what I was up to at midnight on a Saturday night in a man's dormitory with a cigarette in one hand and a Dixie cup of cheap wine in the other.

After some time in his buddies' rooms sitting in clusters, guys and their dates, Rudy and I migrated to his room. His bed was a mattress on the floor, the American flag draped over it for a coverlet, which even as a non-native, I thought most disrespectful. We would lie down under it, side by side, cuddling and kissing, Rudy's hand exploring down my blouse. But if he wandered any lower, I'd pull away. "No," I'd say, "don't." "Why not?" he'd challenge, or ironically or seductively or exasperatedly, depending on how much he'd imbibed, smoked, dropped. My own answers varied, depending on my current hangups, that's what Rudy called my refusals, hangups. Mostly I was afraid I'd get pregnant. "From getting felt up?" Rudy said with sarcasm. "Ay, Rudy," I'd plead, "don't say it that way."

"What do you mean, *don't say it that way?* A spade's a spade. This isn't a goddamn poetry class."

Perhaps if Rudy had acted a little more as if lovemaking were a workshop of sorts, things might have moved more swiftly toward his desired conclusion. But the guy had no sense of connotation in bed. His vocabulary turned me off even as I was beginning to acknowledge my body's pleasure. If Rudy had said, *Sweet lady, lay across my big, soft bed and let me touch your dear, exquisite body,* I might have felt up to being felt up. But I didn't want to just be in the sack, screwed, balled, laid, and fucked my first time around with a man.

Rudy did have a honeymoon of patience with me at the start. He must have realized from his having had to explain to me so many references in his sonnet that I didn't know, as he put it, worth shit. To me, vagina, cervix, ovary were synonyms. Via diagrams he introduced me to my anatomy, he drew the little egg going down its hourglass into the sticky pocket of the uterus. He calculated when I'd last had my period, when I'd probably ovulated, whether a certain night was a safe time of the month. "You're not going to get pregnant"—all his lessons ended with the same point. But still I didn't want to sleep with him.

"Why? What's wrong with you, are you frigid or something?"

Now there was a worry. I'd just gotten over worrying I'd get pregnant from proximity, or damned by God should I die at that moment, and now I started wondering if maybe my upbringing had disconnected some vital nerves. "I just don't think it's right yet," I said.

"Jesus, we've been going out a month," Rudy said. "When's it going to be all right?"

"Soon," I promised, as if I knew.

But soon didn't happen soon enough. We had progressed to where I stayed the night, waking up early in the morning, not daring to move for fear I'd wake Rudy up in an amorous mood and end up in an early morning discussion of why not now. I scanned the room, as small as mine. Beside his bed I could see the pad with the hourglass shapes. I touched my belly to make sure I was still intact. On the cinderblock wall opposite the bed, Rudy had put up a bulletin board. There were pennants from his ski teams and photos of his family, all lined up on skis on top of a mountain. His parents looked so young and casual — like classmates. My own old world parents were still an embarrassment at parents' weekend, my father with his thick mustache and three-piece suit and fedora hat, my mother in one of her outfits she bought especially to visit us at school, everything overly matched, patent leather purse and pumps that would go back, once she was home, to plastic storage bags in her closet. I marveled at his youthful parents. No wonder Rudy didn't have hangups, no wonder his high school acne hadn't left him riddled with self-doubt, his name hadn't cowed him. They encouraged him, his parents, to have experiences with girls but to be careful. He had told them he was seeing "a Spanish girl," and he reported they said that should be interesting for him to find out about people from other cultures. It bothered me that they should treat me like a geography lesson for their son. But I didn't have the vocabulary back then to explain even to myself what annoyed me about their remark.

I met them only once right before spring break and ironically at the very close of my relationship with Rudy. What happened was the night before break started, Rudy and I had another one of our showdowns in his bed. Rudy turned on the light and sat up on his mattress, his back against the wall. He was nude — I, in my old long-sleeved flannel nightgown Rudy called a *nungown*. From the moonlight and streetlight coming in through the window, I saw his body beautifully sculpted by light and shadows. I did yearn for him, but I yearned for so much more along with that body, which I must have sensed Rudy would never give me. He was worn down with frustration, he said. I was cruel. I didn't understand that unlike a girl, it was physically painful for guys not to have sex. He thought it was time to call it quits. I was tearful and pleading: I wanted to feel we were serious about each other before we made love. "Serious!" He made a face. "How about fun? Fun, you know?" What did that have to do with this momentous rending of the veil, I wondered. "You mean you don't think sex is fun?" Rudy faced me as if he were finally seeing the root of the problem. "Sure," I lied. "It's fun if it's right." But he shook his head. He had seen through me. "You know," he said, "I thought you'd be hot-blooded, being Spanish and all, and that under all the Catholic bullshit, you'd be really free, instead of all hung up like these cotillion chicks from prep schools. But Jesus, you're worse than a fucking Puritan." I felt stung to the quick. I got up and threw my coat over my nightgown, packed up my clothes, and left the room, half hoping he'd come after me and say he really did love me, he'd wait as long as I needed to after all.

But he didn't slip into my room and under my sheets and hold me tight against the empty, endless night. I hardly slept. I saw what a cold, lonely life awaited me in this country. I would never find someone who would understand my peculiar mix of Catholicism and agnosticism, Hispanic and American styles. Had I been raised with the tradition of stuffed animals, I would have hugged my bear or stuffed dog or rabbit, salting the ragged fur with my tears all night. Instead, I did something that even as a lapsed Catholic I still did for good luck on nights before exams. I opened my drawer and took out the crucifix I kept hidden under my clothes, and I put it under my pillow for the night. This large crucifix had been a "security blanket" I took to bed with me for years after coming to this country. I had slept with it so many nights that finally Jesus had come unglued, and I had to fasten him back on his cross with a rubber band.

Rudy did not come calling the next day. I bumped into him as he was leaving with his parents and I was exiting my dorm to take the taxi to the bus to my parents' in New York. I was sleepy and weepy and did not look back when I felt Rudy's eyes on me. His parents did most of the chatting, talking too slowly to me as if I wouldn't understand native speakers, they complimented me on my "accentless" English and observed that my parents must be so proud of me. When we said goodbye, I did glance up at Rudy, and though I was out in the cold, he was still in the bedroom with the look in his eyes.

After break, I didn't see much of Rudy. He didn't sit by me in class, his workshop poems became unaccountably straightforward and affectionate, out and out love poems. Was he trying to say he really had fallen in love with me? Then why didn't he stop by my room anymore? I started making excuses for him in my head. He had been there, but I wasn't in, and then he was too afraid to leave a note. He was too shy to come sit by me in class. Afraid, shy! Rudolf Brodermann

Elmenhurst, the third! How we lie to ourselves when we've fallen in love with the wrong man.

Of course, I could have sought him out and told him how I felt about him. How I was frightened of sex with a man who called it *getting laid*. But I was still in the mode where the guy did all the courting and seeking out. I kept aloof, I waited, I fantasized, misleading myself. The copies of my poems Rudy handed back had on them brief, inane remarks I read and reread for double meaning. "Good," or "I don't get this line" or "Nice details." My copies of his poems went back to him with long, complimentary comments. I became more and more of a recluse, avoiding our old haunts for fear of running into him. But we rarely bumped into each other, and when we did, he always flashed me his cool, ironic smile and greeted me with an offhand, "How you doing?" I, on the other hand, was bristling with so much feeling, I pretended not to have seen him.

Spring dance approached. I don't know why I still thought Rudy would certainly end up going with me. This was the culminating romantic event of the school year on campus, and it seemed to me in my fantasy mode to be the perfect vehicle for our reconciliation. I played it out in my head. We would dance all night. We would talk and confess how much we had missed each other. I would go back to his dorm room with him. We would make love, my first time, and then, almost as if they were the different positions Rudy had told me about, we would screw and fuck and ball and get laid—all the synonyms Rudy preferred for referring to his sex.

In real life, the day approached, and then the night, and I was still hoping. The dance was in the lounge between the two dorms, and so, when I heard the band start up, I wandered down the stairs to a landing where I could watch, unobserved, the partiers. They were a motley group: the conservative frat guy types in tuxedos and their dates in fancy prom dresses, the new hippies in Indian paisleys, jeans and sneakers, and maybe for flare, an incongruous bow tie. I saw the figures dancing luridly, the lights flashing, the band going. They all seemed so caught up in a rhythm I didn't feel a part of. Then I saw Rudy come into the room, a glass in one hand, no doubt full of something spiked with alcohol or acid. My heart would have fluttered if there had been any time between the initial glimpse of his familiar figure and the sight of another figure clinging to him. I could hardly tell what she looked like, who she was, but by the way they were holding on to each other, leaning into each other's bodies, I knew, first off that she was the beloved of his poems, and second of all the beloved of his bed. Within weeks of breaking up with me! I was crushed. For the second time in our relationship, as a kind of closing frame to our first meeting which had ended in my flight out of the classroom, I fled up the stairs.

There's more to the story. There always is to a true story. About five years later, I was in grad school in upstate New York. I was a poet, a bohemian, et cetera. I'd had a couple of lovers. I was on birth control. I guessed I'd resolved the soul and sin thing by lapsing from my heavy-duty Catholic background, giving up my immortal soul for a blues kind of soul. Funky and low-down, the kind inspired by reading too much Carlos Castaneda and Rilke and Robert Bly and dropping acid with a guy who claimed to be my cosmic mate from a past life. I got this call one night from Rudy. His parents lived just down the road, and he had read that I was at the neighboring university in the Alumni Bulletin. Could he come over to see me? Sure, I said. When? Tonight, he said. Tonight was already about nine-thirty. Up to his same old tricks. But I was taken with the guy's persistence. Sure, I said, come on over.

He came on over. Brought an expensive bottle of wine. At the door, I gave him a friendly hug, but he held on for longer. I got nervous and gabby. His bad boy always drove me to my vivacious good girl. I sat him down in my one chair and started to quiz him on his five years since graduation. He sighed a lot, stretched his legs, cracked his knuckles. Finally, he cut me off, said, Hey, Jesus Christ, I've waited five years, and you look like you've gotten past all your hangups. Let's just fuck. I threw him out. It still offended me that he didn't want to do anything but screw me, get that over with. Catholic or not, I still thought it a sin for a guy to just barge in five years later with a bottle of expensive wine and assume you'd drink out of his hand. A guy who had ditched me, who had haunted my sexual awakening with a night-mare of self-doubt. For a moment as I watched him get in his car and drive away, I felt a flash of that old self-doubt.

On the counter, he had left behind the bottle of wine. I had one of those unserious, cheap, grad school corkscrews. Those days we bought gallon jugs of Gallo with pull-out corks or screwed-on lids. I worked the corkscrew in as far as it would go. I wasn't very good at this. Each time I yanked the screw out, I got a spurt of cork, but the stub remained snug in the bottleneck. Finally, I worked it in so I could see the sharp point of the spiral through the glass neck at the bottom of the cork. I put the bottle between my legs and pulled so hard that not only did I jerk the crumbled cork out but I sprayed myself with expen-sive Bordeaux. "Shit," I thought, "this is not going to wash out." I held the bottle up to my mouth and drew a long messy swallow, as if I were some decadent wild woman who had just dismissed an unsatisfactory lover.

1991

MARGARET ATWOOD

THE MAN FROM MARS

A long time ago Christine was walking through the park. She was still wearing her tennis dress; she hadn't had time to shower and change, and her hair was held back with an elastic band. Her chunky reddish face, exposed with no softening fringe, looked like a Russian peasant's, but without the elastic band the hair got in her eyes. The afternoon was too hot for April; the indoor courts had been steaming, her skin felt poached.

The sun had brought the old men out from wherever they spent the winter: she had read a story recently about one who lived for three years in a manhole. They sat weedishly on the benches or lay on the grass with their heads on squares of used newspaper. As she passed, their wrinkled toadstool faces drifted towards her, drawn by the movement of her body, then floated away again, uninterested.

The squirrels were out too, foraging; two or three of them moved towards her in darts and pauses, eyes fixed on her expectantly, mouths with the rat-like receding chins open to show the yellowed front teeth. Christine walked faster, she had nothing to give them. People shouldn't feed them, she thought, it makes them anxious and they get mangy.

Halfway across the park she stopped to take off her cardigan. As she bent over to pick up her tennis racquet again someone touched her on her freshly-bared arm. Christine seldom screamed; she straightened up suddenly, gripping the handle of her racquet. It was not one of the old men, however: it was a dark-haired boy of twelve or so.

"Excuse me," he said, "I search for Economics Building. It is there?" He motioned towards the west.

Christine looked at him more closely. She had been mistaken: he was not young, just short. He came a little above her shoulder, but

16

then, she was above the average height; "statuesque," her mother called it when she was straining. He was also what was referred to in their family as "a person from another culture;" oriental without a doubt, though perhaps not Chinese. Christine judged he must be a foreign student and gave him her official welcoming smile. In high school she had been president of the United Nations Club; that year her school had been picked to represent the Egyptian delegation at the Mock Assembly. It had been an unpopular assignment—nobody wanted to be the Arabs—but she had seen it through. She had made rather a good speech about the Palestinian refugees.

"Yes," she said, "that's it over there. The one with the flat roof. See it?"

The man had been smiling nervously at her the whole time. He was wearing glasses with transparent plastic rims, through which his eyes bulged up at her as though through a goldfish bowl. He had not followed where she was pointing. Instead he thrust towards her a small pad of green paper and a ballpoint pen.

"You make map," he said.

Christine set down her tennis racquet and drew a careful map. "We are here," she said, pronouncing distinctly. "You go this way. The building is here." She indicated the route with a dotted line and an X. The man leaned close to her, watching the progress of the map attentively; he smelled of cooked cauliflower and an unfamiliar brand of hair grease. When she had finished Christine handed the paper and pen back to him with a terminal smile.

"Wait," the man said. He tore the piece of paper with the map off the pad, folded it carefully and put it in his jacket pocket; the jacket sleeves came down over his wrists and had threads at the edges. He began to write something; she noticed with a slight feeling of revulsion that his nails and the ends of his fingertips were so badly bitten they seemed almost deformed. Several of his fingers were blue from the leaky ballpoint.

"Here is my name," he said, holding the pad out to her.

Christine read an odd assemblage of G's, Y's and N's, neatly printed in block letters. "Thank you," she said.

"You now write your name," he said, extending the pen.

Christine hesitated. If this had been a person from her own culture she would have thought he was trying to pick her up. But then, people from her own culture never tried to pick her up: she was too big. The only one who had made the attempt was the Moroccan waiter at the beer parlor where they sometimes went after meetings, and he had been direct. He had just intercepted her on the way to the Ladies' Room and asked and she said no; that had been that. This man was not a waiter though but a student; she didn't want to offend him. In his culture, whatever it was, this exchange of names on pieces of paper was probably a formal politeness, like saying Thank You. She took the pen from him.

"That is a very pleasant name," he said. He folded the paper and placed it in his jacket pocket with the map.

Christine felt she had done her duty. "Well, goodbye," she said, "it was nice to have met you." She bent for her tennis racquet but he had already stooped and retrieved it and was holding it with both hands in front of him, like a captured banner.

"I carry this for you."

"Oh no, please. Don't bother, I am in a hurry," she said, articulating clearly. Deprived of her tennis racquet she felt weaponless. He started to saunter along the path; he was not nervous at all now, he seemed completely at ease.

"Vous parlez français?"[1] he asked conversationally.

"Oui, un petit peu," she said. "Not very well." How am I going to get my racquet away from him without being rude, she was wondering.

"Mais vous avez un bel accent." His eyes goggled at her through the glasses: was he being flirtatious? She was well aware that her accent was wretched.

"Look," she said, for the first time letting her impatience show, "I really have to go. Give me my racquet please."

He quickened his pace but gave no sign of returning the racquet. "Where are you going?"

"Home," she said. "My house."

"I go with you now," he said hopefully.

"No," she said: she would have to be firm with him. She made a lunge and got a grip on her racquet; after a brief tug of war it came free.

"Goodbye," she said, turning away from his puzzled face and setting off at what she hoped was a discouraging jog-trot. It was like walking away from a growling dog, you shouldn't let on you were frightened. Why should she be frightened anyway? He was only half her size and she had the tennis racquet, there was nothing he could do to her.

Although she did not look back she could tell he was still following. Let there be a streetcar, she thought, and there was one, but it was far down the line, stuck behind a red light. He appeared at her side, breathing audibly, a moment after she reached the stop. She gazed ahead, rigid.

"You are my friend," he said tentatively.

1. Do you speak French? . . . Yes, a little bit. . . . But you have a good accent.

Christine relented: he hadn't been trying to pick her up after all, he was a stranger, he just wanted to meet some of the local people; in his place she would have wanted the same thing.

"Yes," she said, doling him out a smile.

"That is good," he said, "My country is very far."

Christine couldn't think of an apt reply. "That's interesting," she said. "Très intéressant."[2] The streetcar was coming at last; she opened her purse and got out a ticket.

"I go with you now," he said. His hand clamped on her arm above the elbow.

"You . . . stay . . . *here*," Christine said, resisting the impulse to shout but pausing between each word as though for a deaf person. She detached his hand—his hold was quite feeble and could not compete with her tennis biceps—and leapt off the curb and up the streetcar steps, hearing with relief the doors grind shut behind her. Inside the car and a block away she permitted herself a glance out a side window. He was standing where she had left him; he seemed to be writing something on his little pad of paper.

When she reached home she had only time for a snack, and even then she was almost late for the Debating Society. The topic was, "Resolved: That War Is Obsolete." Her team took the affirmative, and won.

Christine came out of her last examination feeling depressed. It was not the exam that depressed her but the fact that it was the last one: it meant the end of the school year. She dropped into the coffee shop as usual, then went home early because there didn't seem to be anything else to do.

"Is that you, dear?" her mother called from the living room. She must have heard the front door close. Christine went in and flopped on the sofa, disturbing the neat pattern of the cushions.

"How was your exam, dear?" her mother asked.

"Fine," said Christine flatly. It had been fine, she had passed. She was not a brilliant student, she knew that, but she was conscientious. Her professors always wrote things like "A serious attempt" and "Well thought out but perhaps lacking in *élan*" on her term papers; they gave her B's, the occasional B+. She was taking Political Science and Economics, and hoped for a job with the Government after she graduated; with her father's connections she had a good chance.

"That's nice."

Christine felt, resentfully, that her mother had only a hazy idea of

2. Very interesting.

what an exam was. She was arranging gladioli in a vase; she had rubber gloves on to protect her hands as she always did when engaged in what she called "housework." As far as Christine could tell her housework consisted of arranging flowers in vases: daffodils and tulips and hyacinths through gladioli, iris and roses, all the way to asters and mums. Sometimes she cooked, elegantly and with chafing-dishes, but she thought of it as a hobby. The girl did everything else. Christine thought it faintly sinful to have a girl. The only ones available now were either foreign or pregnant; their expressions usually suggested they were being taken advantage of somehow. But her mother asked what they would do otherwise, they'd either have to go into a Home or stay in their own countries, and Christine had to agree this was probably true. It was hard anyway to argue with her mother, she was so delicate, so preserved-looking, a harsh breath would scratch the finish.

"An interesting young man phoned today," her mother said. She had finished the gladioli and was taking off her rubber gloves. "He asked to speak with you and when I said you weren't in we had quite a little chat. You didn't tell me about him, dear." She put on the glasses which she wore on a decorative chain around her neck, a signal that she was in her modern, intelligent mood rather than her old-fashioned whimsical one.

"Did he leave his name?" Christine asked. She knew a lot of young men but they didn't often call her, they conducted their business with her in the coffee shop or after meetings.

"He's a person from another culture. He said he would call back later."

Christine had to think a moment. She was vaguely acquainted with several people from other cultures, Britain mostly; they belonged to the Debating Society.

"He's studying Philosophy in Montreal," her mother prompted. "He sounded French."

Christine began to remember the man in the park. "I don't think he's French, exactly," she said.

Her mother had taken off her glasses again and was poking absentmindedly at a bent gladiolus. "Well, he sounded French." She meditated, flowery scepter in hand. "I think it would be nice if you had him to tea."

Christine's mother did her best. She had two other daughters, both of whom took after her. They were beautiful, one was well married already and the other would clearly have no trouble. Her friends consoled her about Christine by saying, "She's not fat, she's just big-boned, it's the father's side," and "Christine is so healthy." Her other daughters had never gotten involved in activities when they were at school, but since Christine could not possibly ever be beautiful even if she took off weight, it was just as well she was so athletic and political, it was a good thing she had interests. Christine's mother tried to encourage her interests whenever possible. Christine could tell when she was making an extra effort, there was a reproachful edge to her voice.

She knew her mother expected enthusiasm but she could not supply it. "I don't know, I'll have to see," she said dubiously.

"You look tired, darling," said her mother. "Perhaps you'd like a glass of milk."

Christine was in the bathtub when the phone rang. She was not prone to fantasy but when she was in the bathtub she often pretended she was a dolphin, a game left over from one of the girls who used to bathe her when she was small. Her mother was being bell-voiced and gracious in the hall; then there was a tap at the door.

"It's that nice young French student, Christine," her mother said.

"Tell him I'm in the bathtub," Christine said, louder than necessary. "He isn't French."

She could hear her mother frowning. "That wouldn't be very polite, Christine. I don't think he'd understand."

"Oh all right," Christine said. She heaved herself out the bathtub, swathed her pink bulk in a towel and splattered to the phone.

"Hello," she said gruffly. At a distance he was not pathetic, he was a nuisance. She could not imagine how he had tracked her down; most likely he went through the phone book, calling all the numbers with her last name until he hit on the right one.

"It is your friend."

"I know," she said, "How are you?"

"I am very fine." There was a long pause, during which Christine had a vicious urge to say, "Well, goodbye then," and hang up; but she was aware of her mother poised figurine-like in her bedroom doorway. Then he said, "I hope you also are very fine."

"Yes," said Christine. She wasn't going to participate.

"I come to tea," he said.

This took Christine by surprise. "You do?"

"Your pleasant mother ask me. I come Thursday, four o'clock."

"Oh," Christine said, ungraciously.

"See you then," he said, with conscious pride of one who has mastered a difficult idiom.

Christine set down the phone and went along the hall. Her mother was in her study, sitting innocently at her writing desk.

"Did you ask him to tea on Thursday?"

"Not exactly, dear," her mother said. "I did mention he might come round to tea *some*time, though."

"Well, he's coming Thursday. Four o'clock."

"What's wrong with that?" her mother said serenely. "I think it's a very nice gesture for us to make. I do think you might try to be a little more cooperative." She was pleased with herself.

"Since you invited him," said Christine, "you can bloody well stick around and help me entertain him. I don't want to be left making nice gestures all by myself."

"Christine *dear*," her mother said, above being shocked. "You ought to put on your dressing gown, you'll catch a chill."

After sulking for an hour Christine tried to think of the tea as a cross between an examination and an executive meeting: not enjoyable, certainly, but to be got through as tactfully as possible. And it *was* a nice gesture. When the cakes her mother had ordered arrived from *The Patisserie* on Thursday morning she began to feel slightly festive; she even resolved to put on a dress, a good one, instead of a skirt and blouse. After all, she had nothing against him, except the memory of the way he had grabbed her tennis racquet and then her arm. She suppressed a quick impossible vision of herself pursued around the living room, fending him off with thrown sofa cushions and vases of gladioli; nevertheless she told the girl they would have tea in the garden. It would be a treat for him, and there was more space outdoors.

She had suspected her mother would dodge the tea, would contrive to be going out just as he was arriving: that way she could size him up and then leave them alone together. She had done things like that to Christine before; her mother carefully mislaid her gloves and located them with a faked murmur of joy when the doorbell rang. Christine relished for weeks afterwards the image of her mother's dropped jaw and flawless recovery when he was introduced: he wasn't quite the foreign potentate her optimistic, veil-fragile mind had concocted.

He was prepared for celebration. He had slicked on so much hair cream that his head seemed to be covered with a tight black patent-leather cap, and he had cut the threads off his jacket sleeves. His orange tie was overpoweringly splendid. Christine noticed however as he shook her mother's suddenly-braced white glove that the ballpoint ink on his fingers was indelible. His face had broken out, possibly in anticipation of the delights in store for him; he had a tiny camera slung over his shoulder and was smoking an exotic-smelling cigarette.

Christine led him through the cool flowery softly-padded living room and out by the French doors into the garden. "You sit here," she said. "I will have the girl bring tea."

This girl was from the West Indies: Christine's parents had been enraptured with her when they were down at Christmas and had brought her back with them. Since that time she had become pregnant, but Christine's mother had not dismissed her. She said she was slightly disappointed but what could you expect, and she didn't see any real difference between a girl who was pregnant before you hired her and one who got that way afterward. She prided herself on her tolerance; also there was a scarcity of girls. Strangely enough, the girl became progressively less easy to get along with. Either she did not share Christine's mother's view of her own generosity, or she felt she had gotten away with something and was therefore free to indulge in contempt. At first Christine had tried to treat her as an equal. "Don't call me 'Miss Christine,' " she had said with an imitation of light, comradely laughter. "What you want me to call you then?" the girl had said, scowling. They had begun to have brief, surly arguments in the kitchen, which Christine decided were like the arguments between one servant and another: her mother's attitude towards each of them was similar, they were not altogether satisfactory but they would have to do.

The cakes, glossy with icing, were set out on a plate and the teapot was standing ready; on the counter the electric kettle boiled. Christine headed for it, but the girl, till then sitting with her elbows on the kitchen table and watching her expressionlessly, made a dash and intercepted her. Christine waited until she had poured the water into the pot. Then, "I'll carry it out, Elvira," she said. She had just decided she didn't want the girl to see her visitor's orange tie; already, she knew, her position in the girl's eyes had suffered because no-one had yet attempted to get *her* pregnant.

"What you think they pay me for, Miss Christine?" the girl said insolently. She swung toward the garden with the tray; Christine trailed her, feeling lumpish and awkward. The girl was at least as big as she was but she was big in a different way.

"Thank you, Elvira," Christine said when the tray was in place. The girl departed without a word, casting a disdainful backward glance at the frayed jacket sleeves, the stained fingers. Christine was now determined to be especially kind to him.

"You are very rich," he said.

"No," Christine protested, shaking her head; "we're not." She had never thought of her family as rich, it was one of her father's sayings that nobody made any money with the Government.

"Yes," he repeated, "You are very rich." He sat back in his lawn chair, gazing about him as though dazed.

Christine set his cup of tea in front of him. She wasn't in the habit of paying much attention to the house or the garden; they were nothing special, far from being the largest on the street; other people took care of them. But now she looked where he was looking, seeing it all as though from a different height: the long expanses, the border flowers blazing in the early-summer sunlight, the flagged patio and walks, the high walls and the silence.

He came back to her face, sighing a little. "My English is not good," he said, "but I improve."

"You do," Christine said, nodding encouragement.

He took sips of his tea, quickly and tenderly as though afraid of injuring the cup. "I like to stay here."

Christine passed him the cakes. He took only one, making a slight face as he ate it; but he had several more cups of tea while she finished the cakes. She managed to find out from him that he had come over on a Church fellowship—she could not decode the denomination— and was studying Philosophy or Theology, or possibly both. She was feeling well-disposed towards him: he had behaved himself, he had caused her no inconvenience.

The teapot was at last empty. He sat up straight in his chair, as though alerted by a soundless gong. "You look this way, please," he said. Christine saw that he had placed his miniature camera on the stone sundial her mother had shipped back from England two years before: he wanted to take her picture. She was flattered, and settled herself to pose, smiling evenly.

He took off his glasses and laid them beside his plate. For a moment she saw his myopic, unprotected eyes turned towards her, with something tremulous and confiding in them she wanted to close herself off from knowing about. Then he went over and did something to the camera, his back to her. The next instant he was crouched beside her, his arm around her waist as far as it could reach, his other hand covering her own hands which she had folded in her lap, his cheek jammed up against hers. She was too startled to move. The camera clicked.

He stood up at once and replaced his glasses, which glittered now with a sad triumph. "Thank you, Miss," he said to her. "I go now." He slung the camera back over his shoulder, keeping his hand on it as though to hold the lid on and prevent escape. "I send to my family; they will like."

He was out the gate and gone before Christine had recovered; then she laughed. She had been afraid he would attack her, she could admit it now, and he had; but not in the usual way. He had raped, *rapeo, rapere, rapui, to seize and carry off*, not herself but her celluloid image, and incidentally that of the silver tea service, which glinted mockingly at her as the girl bore it away, carrying it regally, the insignia, the official jewels.

Christine spent the summer as she had for the past three years: she was the sailing instructress at an expensive all-girls camp near Algonquin Park. She had been a camper there, everything was familiar to her; she sailed almost better than she played tennis.

The second week she got a letter from him, postmarked Montreal and forwarded from her home address. It was printed in block letters on a piece of the green paper, two or three sentences. It began, "I hope you are well," then described the weather in monosyllables and ended, "I am fine." It was signed "Your friend." Each week she got another of these letters, more or less identical. In one of them a color print was enclosed: himself, slightly cross-eyed and grinning hilariously, even more spindly than she remembered him against her billowing draperies, flowers exploding around them like firecrackers, one of his hands an equivocal blur in her lap, the other out of sight; on her own face, astonishment and outrage, as though he was sticking her in the behind with his hidden thumb.

She answered the first letter, but after that the seniors were in training for the races. At the end of the summer, packing to go home, she threw all the letters away.

When she had been back for several weeks she received another of the green letters. This time there was a return address printed at the top which Christine noted with foreboding was in her own city. Every day she waited for the phone to ring; she was so certain his first attempt at contact would be a disembodied voice that when he came upon her abruptly in mid-campus she was unprepared.

"How are you?"

His smile was the same, but everything else about him had deteriorated. He was, if possible, thinner; his jacket sleeves had sprouted a lush new crop of threads, as though to conceal hands now so badly bitten they appeared to have been gnawed by rodents. His hair fell over his eyes, uncut, ungreased; his eyes in the hollowed face, a delicate triangle of skin stretched on bone, jumped behind his glasses like hooked fish. He had the end of a cigarette in the corner of his mouth and as they walked he lit a new one from it.

"I'm fine," Christine said. She was thinking, I'm not going to get involved again, enough is enough, I've done my bit for internationalism. "How are you?"

"I live here now," he said. "Maybe I study Economics."

"That's nice." He didn't sound as though he was enrolled anywhere.

"I come to see you."

Christine didn't know whether he meant he had left Montreal in order to be near her or just wanted to visit her at her house as he had done in the spring; either way she refused to be implicated. They were outside the Political Science building. "I have a class here," she said. "Goodbye." She was being callous, she realized that, but a quick chop was more merciful in the long run, that was what her beautiful sisters used to say.

Afterwards she decided it had been stupid of her to let him find out where her class was. Though a timetable was posted in each of the colleges: all he had to do was look her up and record her every probable movement in block letters on his green notepad. After that day he never left her alone.

Initially he waited outside the lecture rooms for her to come out. She said Hello to him curtly at first and kept on going, but this didn't work; he followed her at a distance, smiling his changeless smile. Then she stopped speaking altogether and pretended to ignore him, but it made no difference, he followed her anyway. The fact that she was in some way afraid of him—or was it just embarrassment?—seemed only to encourage him. Her friends started to notice, asking her who he was and why he was tagging along behind her; she could hardly answer because she hardly knew.

As the weekdays passed and he showed no signs of letting up, she began to jog-trot between classes, finally to run. He was tireless, and had an amazing wind for one who smoked so heavily: he would speed along behind her, keeping the distance between them the same, as though he was a pull-toy attached to her by a string. She was aware of the ridiculous spectacle they must make, galloping across campus, something out of a cartoon short, a lumbering elephant stampeded by a smiling, emaciated mouse, both of them locked in the classic pattern of comic pursuit and flight; but she found that to race made her less nervous than to walk sedately, the skin on the back of her neck crawling with the feel of his eyes on it. At least she could use her muscles. She worked out routines, escapes: she would dash in the front door of the Ladies' Room in the coffee shop and out the back door, and he would lose the trail, until he discovered the other entrance. She would try to shake him by detours through baffling archways and corridors, but he seemed as familiar with the architectural mazes as she was herself. As a last refuge she could head for the women's dormitory and watch from safety as he was skidded to a halt by the receptionist's austere voice: men were not allowed past the entrance.

Lunch became difficult. She would be sitting, usually with other members of the Debating Society, just digging nicely into a sandwich, when he would appear suddenly as though he'd come up through an unseen manhole. She then had the choice of barging out through the crowded cafeteria, sandwich half-eaten, or finishing her lunch with him standing behind her chair, everyone at the table acutely aware of him, the conversation stilting and dwindling. Her friends learned to spot him from a distance; they posted lookouts. "Here he comes," they would whisper, helping her collect her belongings for the sprint they knew would follow.

Several times she got tired of running and turned to confront him. "What do you want?" she would ask, glowering belligerently down at him, almost clenching her fists; she felt like shaking him, hitting him.

"I wish to talk with you."

"Well, here I am," she would say. "What do you want to talk about?"

But he would say nothing; he would stand in front of her, shifting his feet, smiling perhaps apologetically (though she could never pin-point the exact tone of that smile, chewed lips stretched apart over the nicotine-yellowed teeth, rising at the corners, flesh held stiffly in place for an invisible photographer), his eyes jerking from one part of her face to another as though he saw her in fragments.

Annoying and tedious though it was, his pursuit of her had an odd result: mysterious in itself, it rendered her equally mysterious. No-one had ever found Christine mysterious before. To her parents she was a beefy heavyweight, a plodder, lacking in flair, ordinary as bread. To her sisters she was the plain one, treated with an indulgence they did not give to each other: they did not fear her as a rival. To her male friends she was the one who could be relied on. She was helpful and a hard worker, always good for a game of tennis with the athletes among them. They invited her along to drink beer with them so they could get into the cleaner, more desirable Ladies and Escorts side of the beer parlor, taking it for granted she would buy her share of the rounds. In moments of stress they confided to her their problems with women. There was nothing devious about her and nothing interesting.

Christine had always agreed with these estimates of herself. In childhood she had identified with the False Bride[3] or the ugly sister; whenever a story had begun, "Once there was a maiden as beautiful as she was good," she had known it wasn't her. That was just how it was, but it wasn't so bad. Her parents never expected her to be a brilliant social success and weren't overly disappointed when she wasn't. She

3. A recurrent figure in fairy tales.

was spared the maneuvering and anxiety she witnessed among others her age, and she even had a kind of special position among men: she was an exception, she fitted none of the categories they commonly used when talking about girls, she wasn't a cockteaser, a cold fish, an easy lay or a snarky bitch; she was an honorary person. She had grown to share their contempt for most women.

Now however there was something about her that could not be explained. A man was chasing her, a peculiar sort of man, granted, but still a man, and he was without doubt attracted to her, he couldn't leave her alone. Other men examined her more closely than they ever had, appraising her, trying to find out what it was those twitching bespectacled eyes saw in her. They started to ask her out, though they returned from these excursions with their curiosity unsatisfied, the secret of her charm still intact. Her opaque dumpling face, her solid bear-shaped body became for them parts of a riddle no one could solve. Christine knew this and began to use it. In the bathtub she no longer imagined she was a dolphin; instead she imagined she was an elusive water-nixie, or sometimes, in moments of audacity, Marilyn Monroe. The daily chase was becoming a habit; she even looked forward to it. In addition to its other benefits she was losing weight.

All those weeks he had never phoned her or turned up at the house. He must have decided however that his tactics were not having the desired result, or perhaps he sensed she was becoming bored. The phone began to ring in the early morning or late at night when he could be sure she would be there. Sometimes he would simply breathe (she could recognize, or thought she could, the quality of his breathing), in which case she would hang up. Occasionally he would say again that he wanted to talk to her, but even when she gave him lots of time nothing else would follow. Then he extended his range: she would see him on her streetcar, smiling at her silently from a seat never closer than three away; she could feel him tracking her down her own street, though when she would break her resolve to pay no attention and would glance back he would be invisible or in the act of hiding behind a tree or hedge.

Among crowds of people and in daylight she had not really been afraid of him; she was stronger than he was and he had made no recent attempt to touch her. But the days were growing shorter and colder, it was almost November, often she was arriving home in twilight or a darkness broken only by the feeble orange streetlamps. She brooded over the possibility of razors, knives, guns; by acquiring a weapon he could quickly turn the odds against her. She avoided wearing scarves, remembering the newspaper stories about girls who had been strangled by them. Putting on her nylons in the morning gave her a funny feeling. Her body seemed to have diminished, to have become smaller than his.

Was he deranged, was he a sex maniac? He seemed so harmless, yet it was that kind who often went berserk in the end. She pictured those ragged fingers at her throat, tearing at her clothes, though she could not think of herself as screaming. Parked cars, the shrubberies near her house, the driveways on either side of it, changed as she passed them from unnoticed background to sinisterly-shadowed foreground, every detail distinct and harsh: they were places a man might crouch, leap out from. Yet every time she saw him in the clear light of morning or afternoon (for he still continued his old methods of pursuit), his aging jacket and jittery eyes convinced her that it was she herself who was the tormentor, the persecuter. She was in some sense responsible; from the folds and crevices of the body she had treated for so long as a reliable machine was emanating, against her will, some potent invisible odor, like a dog's in heat or a female moth's, that made him unable to stop following her.

Her mother, who had been too preoccupied with the unavoidable fall entertaining to pay much attention to the number of phone calls Christine was getting or to the hired girl's complaints of a man who hung up without speaking, announced that she was flying down to New York for the weekend; her father decided to go too. Christine panicked: she saw herself in the bathtub with her throat slit, the blood drooling out of her neck and running in a little spiral down the drain (for by this time she believed he could walk through walls, could be everywhere at once). The girl would do nothing to help; she might even stand in the bathroom door with her arms folded, watching. Christine arranged to spend the weekend at her married sister's.

When she arrived back Sunday evening she found the girl close to hysterics. She said that on Saturday she had gone to pull the curtains across the French doors at dusk and had found a strangely contorted face, a man's face, pressed against the glass, staring in at her from the garden. She claimed she had fainted and had almost had her baby a month too early right there on the living room carpet. Then she had called the police. He was gone by the time they got there but she had recognized him from the afternoon of the tea; she had informed them he was a friend of Christine's.

They called Monday evening to investigate, two of them; they were very polite, they knew who Christine's father was. Her father greeted them heartily; her mother hovered in the background, fidgeting with her porcelain hands, letting them see how frail and worried she was. She didn't like having them in the living room but they were necessary.

Christine had to admit he'd been following her around. She was relieved he'd been discovered, relieved also that she hadn't been the one to tell, though if he'd been a citizen of the country she would have called the police a long time ago. She insisted he was not dangerous, he had never hurt her.

"That kind don't hurt you," one of the policemen said. "They just kill you. You're lucky you aren't dead."

"Nut cases," the other one said.

Her mother volunteered that the thing about people from another culture was that you could never tell whether they were insane or not because their ways were so different. The policeman agreed with her, deferential but also condescending, as though she was a royal halfwit who had to be humored.

"You know where he lives?" the first policeman asked. Christine had long ago torn up the letter with his address on it; she shook her head.

"We'll have to pick him up tomorrow then," he said. "Think you can keep him talking outside your class if he's waiting for you?"

After questioning her they held a murmured conversation with her father in the front hall. The girl, clearing away the coffee cups, said if they didn't lock him up she was leaving, she wasn't going to be scared half out of her skin like that again.

Next day when Christine came out of her Modern History lecture he was there, right on schedule. He seemed puzzled when she did not begin to run. She approached him, her heart thumping with treachery and the prospect of freedom. Her body was back to its usual size; she felt herself a giantess, self-controlled, invulnerable.

"How are you?" she asked, smiling brightly.

He looked at her with distrust.

"How have you been?" she ventured again. His own perennial smile faded; he took a step back from her.

"This the one?" said the policeman, popping out from behind a notice board like a Keystone Cop and laying a competent hand on the worn jacket shoulder. The other policeman lounged in the background; force would not be required.

"Don't *do* anything to him," she pleaded as they took him away. They nodded and grinned, respectful, scornful. He seemed to know perfectly well who they were and what they wanted.

The first policeman phoned that evening to make his report. Her father talked with him, jovial and managing. She herself was now out of the picture; she had been protected, her function was over.

"What did they *do* to him?" she asked anxiously as he came back into the living room. She was not sure what went on in police stations.

"They didn't do anything to him," he said, amused by her concern. "They could have booked him for Watching and Besetting, they wanted to know if I'd like to proffer charges. But it's not worth a court case: he's got a visa that says he's only allowed in the country as long as he studies in Montreal, so I told them to just ship him up there. If he turns up here again they'll deport him. They went around to his rooming house, his rent's two weeks overdue; the landlady said she was on the point of kicking him out. He seems happy enough to be getting his back rent paid and a free train ticket to Montreal." He paused. "They couldn't get anything out of him though."

"*Out* of him?" Christine asked.

"They tried to find out why he was doing it; following you, I mean." Her father's eyes swept her as though it was a riddle to him also. "They said when they asked him about that he just clammed up. Pretended he didn't understand English. He understood well enough, but he wasn't answering."

Christine thought this was the end, but somehow between his arrest and the departure of the train he managed to elude his escort long enough for one more phone call.

"I see you again," he said. He didn't wait for her to hang up.

Now that he was no longer an embarrassing present reality he could be talked about, he could become an amusing story. In fact he was the only amusing story Christine had to tell, and telling it preserved both for herself and for others the aura of her strange allure. Her friends and the men who continued to ask her out speculated about his motives. One suggested he had wanted to marry her so he could remain in the country; another said that oriental men were fond of well-built women: "It's your Rubens[4] quality."

Christine thought about him a lot. She had not been attracted to him, rather the reverse, but as an idea only he was a romantic figure, the one man who had found her irresistible; though she often wondered, inspecting her unchanged pink face and hefty body in her full-length mirror, just what it was about her that had done it. She avoided whenever it was proposed the theory of his insanity: it was only that there was more than one way of being sane.

But a new acquaintance, hearing the story for the first time, had a different explanation. "So he got you too," he said, laughing. "That has to be the same guy who was hanging around our day camp a year ago this summer. He followed all the girls like that. A short guy, Japanese or something, glasses, smiling all the time."

4. Peter Paul Rubens (1577–1640), Flemish painter known for his full, voluptuous female figures.

"Maybe it was another one," Christine said.

"There couldn't be two of them, everything fits. This was a pretty weird guy."

"What . . . *kind* of girls did he follow?" Christine asked.

"Oh, just anyone who happened to be around. But if they paid any attention to him at first, if they were nice to him or anything, he was unshakeable. He was a bit of a pest, but harmless."

Christine ceased to tell her amusing story. She had been one among many, then. She went back to playing tennis, she had been neglecting her game.

A few months later the policeman who had been in charge of the case telephoned her again.

"Like you to know, Miss, that fellow you were having the trouble with was sent back to his own country. Deported."

"What for?" Christine asked. "Did he try to come back here?" Maybe she had been special after all, maybe he had dared everything for her.

"Nothing like it," the policeman said. "He was up to the same tricks in Montreal but he really picked the wrong woman this time—a Mother Superior of a convent. They don't stand for things like that in Quebec—had him out of here before he knew what happened. I guess he'll be better off in his own place."

"How old was she?" Christine asked, after a silence.

"Oh, around sixty, I guess."

"Thank you very much for letting me know," Christine said in her best official manner. "It's such a relief." She wondered if the policeman had called to make fun of her.

She was almost crying when she put down the phone. What *had* he wanted from her then? A Mother Superior. Did she really look sixty, did she look like a mother? What did convents mean? Comfort, charity? Refuge? Was it that something had happened to him, some intolerable strain just from being in this country; her tennis dress and exposed legs too much for him, flesh and money seemingly available everywhere but withheld from him wherever he turned, the nun the symbol of some final distortion, the robe and the veil reminiscent to his near-sighted eyes of the women of his homeland, the ones he was able to understand? But he was back in his own country, remote from her as another planet; she would never know.

He hadn't forgotten her though. In the spring she got a postcard with a foreign stamp and the familiar block-letter writing. On the front was a picture of a temple. He was fine, he hoped she was fine also, he was her friend. A month later another print of the picture he had taken in the garden arrived, in a sealed manila envelope otherwise empty.

Christine's aura of mystery soon faded; anyway, she herself no longer believed in it. Life became again what she had always expected. She graduated with mediocre grades and went into the Department of Health and Welfare; she did a good job, and was seldom discriminated against for being a woman because nobody thought of her as one. She could afford a pleasant-sized apartment, though she did not put much energy into decorating it. She played less and less tennis; what had been muscle with a light coating of fat turned gradually to fat with a thin substratum of muscle. She began to get headaches.

As the years were used up and the war began to fill the newspapers and magazines, she realized which eastern country he had actually been from. She had known the name but it hadn't registered at the time, it was such a minor place; she could never keep them separate in her mind.

But though she tried, she couldn't remember the name of the city, and the postcard was long gone—had he been from the North or the South, was he near the battle zone or safely far from it? Obsessively she bought the magazines and poured over the available photographs, dead villagers, soldiers on the march, color blowups of frightened or angry faces, spies being executed; she studied maps, she watched the late-night newscasts, the distant country and terrain becoming almost more familiar to her than her own. Once or twice she thought she could recognize him but it was no use, they all looked like him.

Finally she had to stop looking at the pictures. It bothered her too much, it was bad for her; she was beginning to have nightmares in which he was coming through the French doors of her mother's house in his shabby jacket, carrying a packsack and a rifle and a huge bouquet of richly-colored flowers. He was smiling in the same way but with blood streaked over his face, partly blotting out the features. She gave her television set away and took to reading nineteenth-century novels instead; Trollope and Galsworthy were her favorites. When, despite herself, she would think about him, she would tell herself that he had been crafty and agile-minded enough to survive, more or less, in her country, so surely he would be able to do it in his own, where he knew the language. She could not see him in the army, on either side; he wasn't the type, and to her knowledge he had not believed in any particular ideology. He would be something nondescript, something in the background, like herself; perhaps he had become an interpreter.

1977

DONALD BARTHELME

THE INDIAN UPRISING

We defended the city as best we could. The arrows of the Comanches came in clouds. The war clubs of the Comanches clattered on the soft, yellow pavements. There were earthworks along the Boulevard Mark Clark[1] and the hedges had been laced with sparkling wire. People were trying to understand. I spoke to Sylvia. "Do you think this is a good life?" The table held apples, books, long-playing records. She looked up. "No."

Patrols of paras[2] and volunteers with armbands guarded the tall, flat buildings. We interrogated the captured Comanche. Two of us forced his head back while another poured water into his nostrils. His body jerked, he choked and wept. Not believing a hurried, careless, and exaggerated report of the number of casualties in the outer districts where trees, lamps, swans had been reduced to clear fields of fire we issued entrenching tools to those who seemed trustworthy and turned the heavy-weapons companies so that we could not be surprised from that direction. And I sat there getting drunker and drunker and more in love and more in love. We talked.

"Do you know Fauré's 'Dolly'?"

"Would that be Gabriel Fauré?"[3]

"It would."

"Then I know it," she said. "May I say that I play it at certain times, when I am sad, or happy, although it requires four hands."

"How is that managed?"

1. Mark Wayne Clark (1896–1984), American general in charge of allied armies in Italy in World War II. The fictitious squares and streets in this story are named after famous American military officers of that war.
2. Paratroops.
3. Gabriel Urbain Fauré (1845–1924), French organist and composer.

"I accelerate," she said, "ignoring the time signature."

And when they shot the scene in the bed I wondered how you felt under the eyes of the cameramen, grips, juicers, men in the mixing booth:[4] excited? stimulated? And when they shot the scene in the shower I sanded a hollow-core door working carefully against the illustrations in texts and whispered instructions from one who had already solved the problem. I had made after all other tables, one while living with Alice, one while living with Eunice, one while living with Marianne.

Red men in waves like people scattering in a square startled by something tragic or a sudden, loud noise accumulated against the barricades we had made of window dummies, silk, thoughtfully planned job descriptions (including scales for the orderly progress of other colors), wine in demijohns, and robes. I analyzed the composition of the barricade nearest me and found two ashtrays, ceramic, one dark brown and one dark brown with an orange blur at the lip; a tin frying pan; two-liter bottles of red wine; three-quarter-liter bottles of Black & White, aquavit, cognac, vodka, gin, Fad #6 sherry; a hollow-core door in birch veneer on black wrought-iron legs; a blanket, red-orange with faint blue stripes; a red pillow and a blue pillow; a woven straw wastebasket; two glass jars for flowers; corkscrews and can openers; two plates and two cups, ceramic, dark brown; a yellow-and-purple poster; a Yugoslavian carved flute, wood, dark brown; and other items. I decided I knew nothing.

The hospitals dusted wounds with powder the worth of which was not quite established, other supplies having been exhausted early in the first day. I decided I knew nothing. Friends put me in touch with a Miss R., a teacher, unorthodox they said, excellent they said, successful with difficult cases, steel shutters on the windows made the house safe. I had just learned via an International Distress Coupon that Jane had been beaten up by a dwarf in a bar on Tenerife[5] but Miss R. did not allow me to speak of it. "You know nothing," she said, "you feel nothing, you are locked in a most savage and terrible ignorance, I despise you, my boy, *mon cher*,[6] my heart. You may attend but you must not attend now, you must attend later, a day or a week or an hour, you are making me ill. . . ." I nonevaluated these remarks as Korzybski[7] instructed. But it was difficult. Then they pulled back in a feint near the river and we rushed into that sector with a reinforced battalion

---

4. Film technicians: grips are stagehands; juicers are electricians; the mixing booth is where images from various cameras are edited and coordinated.
5. Largest of the Canary Islands, located in the Atlantic.
6. My dear.
7. Alfred Korzybski (1879–1950), American writer on semantics.

hastily formed among the Zouaves[8] and cabdrivers. This unit was crushed in the afternoon of a day that began with spoons and letters in hallways and under windows where men tasted the history of the heart, cone-shaped muscular organ that maintains *circulation of the blood.*

But it is you I want now, here in the middle of this Uprising, with the streets yellow and threatening, short, ugly lances with fur at the throat and inexplicable shell money lying in the grass. It is when I am with you that I am happiest, and it is for you that I am making this hollow-core door table with black wrought-iron legs. I held Sylvia by her bear-claw necklace. "Call off your braves," I said. "We have many years left to live." There was a sort of muck running in the gutters, yellowish, filthy stream suggesting excrement, or nervousness, a city that does not know what it has done to deserve baldness, errors, infidelity. "With luck you will survive until matins," Sylvia said. She ran off down the Rue Chester Nimitz,[9] uttering shrill cries.

Then it was learned that they had infiltrated our ghetto and that the people of the ghetto instead of resisting had joined the smooth, well-coordinated attack with zipguns, telegrams, lockets, causing that portion of the line held by the I.R.A.[1] to swell and collapse. We sent more heroin into the ghetto, and hyacinths, ordering another hundred thousand of the pale, delicate flowers. On the map we considered the situation with its strung-out inhabitants and merely personal emotions. Our parts were blue and their parts were green. I showed the blue-and-green map to Sylvia. "Your parts are green," I said. "You gave me heroin first a year ago,"[2] Sylvia said. She ran off down George C. Marshall Allée,[3] uttering shrill cries. Miss R. pushed me into a large room painted white (jolting and dancing in the soft light, and I was excited! and there were people watching!) in which there were two chairs. I sat in one chair and Miss R. sat in the other. She wore a blue dress containing a red figure. There was nothing exceptional about her. I was disappointed by her plainness, by the bareness of the room, by the absence of books.

The girls of my quarter wore long blue mufflers that reached to their knees. Sometimes the girls hid Comanches in their rooms, the blue mufflers together in a room creating a great blue fog. Block opened the door. He was carrying weapons, flowers, loaves of bread.

---

8. Units of French infantry distinguished by their Algerian uniforms.
9. Chester William Nimitz (1885–1966), commander-in-chief of the U.S. Pacific Fleet during World War II.
1. Irish Republican Army.
2. Parody of line 35 of *The Waste Land* by T. S. Eliot (1888–1965): "You gave me hyacinths first a year ago."
3. George Catlett Marshall (1880–1959), U.S. Army Chief of Staff and designer of the Marshall Plan.

And he was friendly, kind, enthusiastic, so I related a little of the history of torture, reviewing the technical literature quoting the best modern sources, French, German, and American, and pointing out the flies which had gathered in anticipation of some new, cool color.

"What is the situation?" I asked.

"The situation is liquid," he said. "We hold the south quarter and they hold the north quarter. The rest is silence."[4]

"And Kenneth?"

"That girl is not in love with Kenneth," Block said frankly. "She is in love with his coat. When she is not wearing it she is huddling under it. Once I caught it going down the stairs by itself. I looked inside. Sylvia."

Once I caught Kenneth's coat going down the stairs by itself but the coat was a trap and inside a Comanche who made a thrust with his short, ugly knife at my leg which buckled and tossed me over the balustrade through a window and into another situation. Not believing that your body brilliant as it was and your fat, liquid spirit distinguished and angry as it was were stable quantities to which one could return on wires more than once, twice, or another number of times I said: "See the table?"

In Skinny Wainwright[5] Square the forces of green and blue swayed and struggled. The referees ran out on the field trailing chains. And then the blue part would be enlarged, the green diminished. Miss R. began to speak. "A former king of Spain, a Bonaparte, lived for a time in Bordentown, New Jersey. But that's no good." She paused. "The ardor aroused in men by the beauty of women can only be satisfied by God. That is *very* good (it is Valéry)[6] but it is not what I have to teach you, goat, muck, filth, heart of my heart." I showed the table to Nancy. "See the table?" She stuck out her tongue red as a cardinal's hat. "I made such a table once," Block said frankly. "People all over America have made such tables. I doubt very much whether one can enter an American home without finding at least one such table, or traces of its having been there, such as faded places in the carpet." And afterward in the garden the men of the 7th Cavalry played Gabrieli, Albinoni, Marcello, Vivaldi, Boccherini.[7] I saw Sylvia. She wore a yellow ribbon,[8] under a long blue muffler. "Which side are you on," I cried, "after all?"

"The only form of discourse of which I approve," Miss R. said in

4. Hamlet's dying words, *Hamlet*, V.II.
5. Jonathan Mayhew ("Skinny") Wainwright (1883–1953),U.S. Army general.
6. Paul Valéry (1871–1945), French poet and philosopher.
7. Italian composers of the seventeenth and eighteenth centuries. The Seventh Cavalry, commanded by General Custer, was defeated by the Indians at the Little Big Horn.
8. Worn, according to tradition, by the sweethearts of cavalry men in the U.S. Army.

her dry, tense voice, "is the litany. I believe our masters and teachers as well as plain citizens should confine themselves to what can safely be said. Thus when I hear the words pewter, snake, tea, Fad #6 sherry, serviette, fenestration, crown, blue coming from the mouth of some public official, or some raw youth, I am not disappointed. Vertical organization is also possible," Miss R. said, "as in

> pewter
> snake
> tea
> Fad #6 sherry
> serviette
> fenestration
> crown
> blue

I run to liquids and colors," she said, "but you, you may run to something else, my virgin, my darling, my thistle, my poppet, my own. Young people," Miss R. said, "run to more and more unpleasant combinations as they sense the nature of our society. Some people," Miss R. said, "run to conceits or wisdom but I hold to the hard, brown, nutlike word. I might point out that there is enough aesthetic excitement here to satisfy anyone but a damned fool." I sat in solemn silence.

Fire arrows lit my way to the post office in Patton Place[9] where members of the Abraham Lincoln Brigade[1] offered their last, exhausted letters, postcards, calendars. I opened a letter but inside was a Comanche flint arrowhead played by Frank Wedekind[2] in an elegant gold chain and congratulations. Your earring rattled against my spectacles when I leaned forward to touch the soft, ruined place where the hearing aid had been. "Pack it in! Pack it in!" I urged, but the men in charge of the Uprising refused to listen to reason or to understand that it was real and that our water supply had evaporated and that our credit was no longer what it had been, once.

We attached wires to the testicles of the captured Comanche. And I sat there getting drunker and drunker and more in love and more in love. When we threw the switch he spoke. His name, he said, was Gustave Aschenbach.[3] He was born at L——, a country town in the province of Silesia. He was the son of an upper official in the judica-

---

9. George Smith Patton, Jr. (1885–1945), American tank commander in World War II.
1. American contingent of the International Brigade, which fought on the Republican side in the Spanish Civil War, 1936–1939.
2. Frank Wedekind (1864–1918), German dramatist and expressionist writer.
3. Fictitious protagonist of *Death in Venice* by Thomas Mann (1875–1955).

ture, and his forebears had all been officers, judges, departmental func-
tionaries. . . . And you can never touch a girl in the same way more
than once, twice, or another number of times however much you may
wish to hold, wrap, or otherwise fix her hand, or look, or some other
quality, or incident, known to you previously. In Sweden the little
Swedish children cheered when we managed nothing more remarkable than getting off a bus burdened with packages, bread and liver-
paste and beer. We went to an old church and sat in the royal box. The
organist was practicing. And then into the graveyard next to the church.
Here lies Anna Pedersen, a good woman. I threw a mushroom on the
grave. The officer commanding the garbage dump reported by radio
that the garbage had begun to move.

Jane! I heard via an International Distress Coupon that you were
beaten up by a dwarf in a bar on Tenerife. That doesn't sound like you,
Jane. Mostly you kick the dwarf in his little dwarf groin before he can
get his teeth into your tasty and nice-looking leg, don't you, Jane? Your
affair with Harold is reprehensible, you know that, don't you, Jane?
Harold is married to Nancy. And there is Paula to think about (Harold's
kid), and Billy (Harold's other kid). I think your values are peculiar,
Jane! Strings of language extend in every direction to bind the world
into a rushing, ribald whole.

And you can never return to felicities in the same way, the brilliant body, the distinguished spirit recapitulating moments that occur
once, twice, or another number of times in rebellions, or water. The
rolling consensus of the Comanche nation smashed our inner defenses
on three sides. Block was firing a greasegun[4] from the upper floor of a
building designed by Emery Roth & Sons. "See the table?" "Oh, pack
it in with your bloody table!" The city officials were tied to trees. Dusky
warriors padded with their forest tread into the mouth of the mayor.
"Who do you want to be?" I asked Kenneth and he said he wanted to
be Jean-Luc Godard[5] but later when time permitted conversations in
large, lighted rooms, whispering galleries with black-and-white Spanish
rugs and problematic sculpture on calm, red catafalques. The sickness
of the quarrel lay thick in the bed. I touched your back, the white,
raised scars.

We killed a great many in the south suddenly with helicopters
and rockets but we found that those we had killed were children and
more came from the north and from the east and from other places
where there are children preparing to live. "Skin," Miss R. said softly
in the white, yellow room. "This is the Clemency Committee. And

---

4. Slang for a rapid-firing automatic pistol.
5. French New Wave film director (b. 1930).

would you remove your belt and shoelaces." I removed my belt and shoelaces and looked (rain shattering from a great height the prospects of silence and clear, neat rows of houses in the subdivisions) into their savage black eyes, paint, feathers, beads.

1981

■ ■ ■

CHARLES BAXTER

SNOW

Twelve years old, and I was so bored I was combing my hair just for the hell of it. This particular Saturday afternoon, time was stretching out unpleasantly in front of me. I held the comb under the tap and then stared into the bathroom mirror as I raked the wave at the front of my scalp upward so that it would look casual and sharp and perfect. For inspiration I had my transistor radio, balanced on the doorknob, tuned to an AM Top Forty station. But the music was making me jumpy, and instead of looking casual my hair, soaking wet, had the metallic curve of the rear fins of a De Soto. I looked aerodynamic but not handsome. I dropped the comb into the sink and went down the hallway to my brother's room.

Ben was sitting at his desk, crumpling up papers and tossing them into a wastebasket near the window. He was a great shot, particularly when he was throwing away his homework. His stainless-steel sword, a souvenir of military school, was leaning against the bookcase, and I could see my pencil-thin reflection in it as I stood in his doorway. "Did you hear about the car?" Ben asked, not bothering to look at me. He was gazing through his window at Five Oaks Lake.

"What car?"

"The car that went through the ice two nights ago. Thursday. Look. You can see the pressure ridge near Eagle Island."

I couldn't see any pressure ridge; it was too far away. Cars belonging to ice fishermen were always breaking through the ice, but swallowing up a car was a slow process in January, though not in March or April, and the drivers usually got out safely. The clear lake ice reflected perfectly the flat gray sky this drought winter, and we could still see the spiky brown grass on our back lawn. It crackled and crunched whenever I walked on it.

"I don't see it," I said. "I can't see the hole. Where did you hear about this car? Did Pop tell you?"

"No," Ben said. "Other sources." Ben's sources, his network of friends and enemies, were always calling him on the telephone to tell him things. He basked in information. Now he gave me a quick glance. "Holy smoke," he said. "What did you do to your hair?"

"Nothing," I said. "I was just combing it."

"You look like that guy," he said. "The one in the movies."

"Which guy?"

"That Harvey guy."

"Jimmy Stewart?"

"Of course not," he said. "You know the one I mean. Everybody knows that guy. The Harvey guy." When I looked blank, he said, "Never mind. Let's go down to the lake and look at that car. You'd better tell them we're going." He gestured toward the other end of the house.

In the kitchen I informed my parents that I was headed somewhere with my brother, and my mother, chopping carrots for one of her stews, looked up at me and my hair. "Be back by five," she said. "Where did you say you were off to?"

"We're driving to Navarre," I said. "Ben has to get his skates sharpened."

My stepfather's eyebrows started to go up; he exchanged a glance with my mother—the usual pantomime of skepticism. I turned around and ran out of the kitchen before they could stop me. I put on my boots, overcoat, and gloves, and hurried outside to my brother's car, a 1952 Rocket 88. He was already inside. The motor roared.

The interior of the car smelled of gum, cigarettes, wet wool, analgesic balm, and after-shave. "What'd you tell them?" my brother asked.

"I said you were going to Navarre to get your skates sharpened."

He put the car into first gear, then sighed. "Why'd you do that? I have to explain everything to you. Number one: my skates aren't in the car. What if they ask to see them when we get home? I won't have them. That's a problem, isn't it? Number two: when you lie about being somewhere, you make sure you have a friend who's there who can say you *were* there, even if you weren't. Unfortunately, we don't have any friends in Navarre."

"Then we're safe," I said. "No one will say we *weren't* there."

He shook his head. Then he took off his glasses and examined them as if my odd ideas were visible right there on the frames. I was just doing my job, being his private fool, but I knew he liked me and liked to have me around. My unworldliness amused him; it gave him a chance to lecture me. But now, tired of wasting words on me, he turned on the radio. Pulling out onto the highway, he steered the car in his customary way. He had explained to me that only very old or very sick people actually grip steering wheels. You didn't have to hold the wheel to drive a car. Resting your arm over the top of the wheel gave a better appearance. You dangled your hand down, preferably with a cigarette in it, so that the car, the entire car, responded to the mere pressure of your wrist.

"Hey," I said. "Where are we going? This isn't the way to the lake."

"We're not going there first. We're going there second."

"Where are we going first?"

"We're going to Five Oaks. We're going to get Stephanie. Then we'll see the car."

"How come we're getting her?"

"Because she wants to see it. She's never seen a car underneath the ice before. She'll be impressed."

"Does she know we're coming?"

He gave me that look again. "What do they teach you at that school you go to? Of course she knows. We have a date."

"A date? It's three o'clock in the afternoon," I said. "You can't have a date at three in the afternoon. Besides, I'm along."

"Don't argue," Ben said. "Pay attention."

By the time we reached Five Oaks, the heater in my brother's car was blowing out warm air in tentative gusts. If we were going to get Stephanie, his current girlfriend, it was fine with me. I liked her smile—she had an overbite, the same as I did, but she didn't seem self-conscious about it—and I liked the way she shut her eyes when she laughed. She had listened to my crystal radio set and admired my collection of igneous rocks on one of her two visits to our house. My brother liked to bring his girlfriends over to our house because the house was old and large and, my brother said, they would be impressed by the empty rooms and the long hallways and the laundry chutes that dropped down into nowhere. They'd be snowed. Snowing girls was something I knew better than to ask my brother about. You had to learn about it by watching and listening. That's why he had brought me along.

Ben parked outside Stephanie's house and told me to wait in the car. I had nothing to do but look at houses and telephone poles. Stephanie's front-porch swing had rusted chains, and the paint around her house seemed to have blistered in cobweb patterns. One drab lamp with a low-wattage bulb was on near an upstairs window. I could see the lampshade: birds—I couldn't tell what kind—had been painted on it. I adjusted the dashboard clock. It didn't run, but I liked to have it seem accurate. My brother had said that anyone who invented a clock that would really work in a car would become a multimillionaire. Clocks in cars never work, he said, because the mainsprings can't stand the shock of potholes. I checked my wristwatch and yawned. The inside of the front window began to frost over with my breath. I decided that when I grew up I would invent a new kind of timepiece for cars, without springs or gears. At three-twenty I adjusted the clock again. One minute later, my brother came out of the house with Stephanie. She saw me in the car, and she smiled.

I opened the door and got out. "Hi, Steph," I said. "I'll get in the backseat."

"That's okay, Russell," she said, smiling, showing her overbite. "Sit up in front with us."

"Really?"

She nodded. "Yeah. Keep us warm."

She scuttled in next to my brother, and I squeezed in on her right side, with my shoulder against the door. As soon as the car started, she and my brother began to hold hands: he steered with his left wrist over the steering wheel, and she held his right hand. I watched all this, and Stephanie noticed me watching. "Do you want one?" she asked me.

"What?"

"A hand." She gazed at me, perfectly serious. "My other hand."

"Sure," I said.

"Well, take my glove off," she said. "I can't do it by myself."

My brother started chuckling, but she stopped him with a look. I took Stephanie's wrist in my left hand and removed her glove, finger by finger. I hadn't held hands with anyone since second grade. Her hand was not much larger than mine, but holding it gave me an odd sensation, because it was a woman's hand, and where my fingers were bony, hers were soft. She was wearing a bright-green cap, and when I glanced up at it she said, "I like your hair, Russell. It's kind of slummy. You're getting to look dangerous. Is there any gum?"

I figured she meant in the car. "There's some up there on the dashboard," Ben said. His car always had gum in it. It was a museum of gum. The ashtrays were full of cigarette butts and gum, mixed together, and the floor was flecked silver from the foil wrappers.

"I can't reach it," Stephanie said. "You two have both my hands tied down."

"Okay," I said. I reached up with my free hand and took a piece of gum and unwrapped it. The gum was light pink, a sunburn color.

"Now what?" I asked.

"What do you think?" She looked down at me, smiled again, then opened her mouth. I suddenly felt shy. "Come on, Russell," she said. "Haven't you ever given gum to a girl before?" I raised my hand with the gum in it. She kept her eyes open and on me. I reached forward, and just as I got the gum close to her mouth she opened wider, and I slid the gum in over her tongue without even brushing it against her lipstick. She closed and began chewing.

"Thank you," she said. Stephanie and my brother nudged each other. Then they broke out in short quick laughs—vacation laughter. I knew that what had happened hinged on my ignorance, but that I wasn't exactly the butt of the joke and could laugh, too, if I wanted. My palm was sweaty, and she could probably feel it. The sky had turned darker, and I wondered whether, if I was still alive fifty years from now, I would remember any of this. I saw an old house on the side of the highway with a cracked upstairs window, and I thought, that's what I'll remember from this whole day when I'm old—that one cracked window.

Stephanie was looking out at the dry winter fields and suddenly said, "The state of Michigan. You know who this state is for? You know who's really happy in this state?"

"No," I said. "Who?"

"Chickens and squirrels," she said. "They love it here."

My brother parked the car on the driveway down by our dock, and we walked out onto the ice on the bay. Stephanie was stepping awkwardly, a high-center-of-gravity shuffle. "Is it safe?" she asked.

"Sure, it's safe," my brother said. "Look." He began to jump up and down. Ben was heavy enough to be a tackle on his high-school football team, and sounds of ice cracking reverberated all through the bay and beyond into the center of the lake, a deep echo. Already, four ice fishermen's houses had been set up on the ice two hundred feet out—four brightly painted shacks, male hideaways—and I could see tire tracks over the thin layer of sprinkled snow. "Clear the snow and look down into it," he said.

After lowering herself to her knees, Stephanie dusted the snow away. She held her hands to the side of her head and looked. "It's real thick," she said. "Looks a foot thick. How come a car went through?"

"It went down in a channel," Ben said, walking ahead of us and calling backward so that his voice seemed to drift in and out of the wind. "It went over a pressure ridge, and that's all she wrote."

"Did anyone drown?"

He didn't answer. She ran ahead to catch up to him, slipping, losing her balance, then recovering it. In fact I knew that no one had drowned. My stepfather had told me that the man driving the car had somehow—I wasn't sure how a person did this—pulled himself out through the window. Apparently the front end dropped through the ice first, but the car had stayed up for a few minutes before it gradually eased itself into the lake. The last two nights had been very cold, with lows around fifteen below zero, and by now the hole the car had gone through had iced over.

Both my brother and Stephanie were quite far ahead of me, and I could see them clutching at each other, Stephanie leaning against him, and my brother trying out his military-school peacock walk. I attempted this walk for a moment, then thought better of it. The late-afternoon January light was getting very raw: the sun came out for a few seconds, lighting and coloring what there was, then disappeared again, closing up and leaving us in a kind of sour grayness. I wondered if my brother and Stephanie actually liked each other or whether they were friends because they had to be.

I ran to catch up to them. "We should have brought our skates," I said, but they weren't listening to me. Ben was pointing at some clear ice, and Stephanie was nodding.

"Quiet down," my brother said. "Quiet down and listen."

All three of us stood still. Some cloud or other was beginning to drop snow on us, and from the ice underneath our feet we heard a continual chinging and barking as the ice slowly shifted.

"This is exciting," Stephanie said.

My brother nodded, but instead of looking at her he turned slightly to glance at me. Our eyes met, and he smiled.

"It's over there," he said, after a moment. The index finger of his black leather glove pointed toward a spot in the channel between Eagle Island and Crane Island where the ice was ridged and unnaturally clear. "Come on," he said.

We walked. I was ready at any moment to throw myself flat if the ice broke beneath me. I was a good swimmer—Ben had taught me—but I wasn't sure how well I would swim wearing all my clothes. I was absorbent and would probably sink headfirst, like that car.

"Get down," my brother said.

We watched him lowering himself to his hands and knees, and we followed. This was probably something he had learned in military school, this crawling. "We're ambushing this car," Stephanie said, creeping in front of me.

"There it is," he said. He pointed down.

This new ice was so smooth that it reminded me of the thick glass in the Shedd Aquarium, in Chicago. But instead of seeing a loggerhead turtle or a barracuda I looked through the ice and saw this abandoned car, this two-door Impala. It was wonderful to see—white-painted steel filtered by ice and lake water—and I wanted to laugh out of sheer happiness at the craziness of it. Dimly lit but still visible through the murk, it sat down there, its huge trunk and the sloping fins just a bit green in the algae-colored light. This is a joke, I thought, a practical joke meant to confuse the fish. I could see the car well enough to notice its radio-antenna, and the windshield wipers halfway up the front window, and I could see the chrome of the front grille reflecting the dull light that ebbed down to it from where we were lying on our stomachs, ten feet above it.

"That is one unhappy automobile," Stephanie said. "Did anyone get caught inside?"

"No," I said, because no one had, and then my brother said, "Maybe."

I looked at him quickly. As usual, he wasn't looking back at me. "They aren't sure yet," he said. "They won't be able to tell until they bring the tow truck out here and pull it up."

Stephanie said, "Well, either they know or they don't. Someone's down there or not, right?"

Ben shook his head. "Maybe they don't know. Maybe there's a dead body in the backseat of that car. Or in the trunk."

"Oh, no," she said. She began to edge backward.

"I was just fooling you," my brother said. "There's nobody down there."

"What?" She was behind the area where the ice was smooth, and she stood up.

"I was just teasing you," Ben said. "The guy that was in the car got out. He got out through the window."

"Why did you lie to me?" Stephanie asked. Her arms were crossed in front of her chest.

"I just wanted to give you a thrill," he said. He stood up and walked over to where she was standing. He put his arm around her.

"I don't mind normal," she said. "Something could be normal and I'd like that, too." She glanced at me. Then she whispered into my brother's ear for about fifteen seconds, which is a long time if you're watching. Ben nodded and bent forward and whispered something in return, but I swiveled and looked around the bay at all the houses on the shore, and the old amusement park in the distance. Lights were beginning to go on, and, as if that weren't enough, it was snowing. As far as I was concerned, all those houses were guilty, both the houses and the people in them. The whole state of Michigan was guilty—all the adults, anyway—and I wanted to see them locked up.

"Wait here," my brother said. He turned and went quickly off toward the shore of the bay.

"Where's he going?" I asked.

"He's going to get his car," she said.

"What for?"

"He's going to bring it out on the ice. Then he's going to drive me home across the lake."

"That's really stupid!" I said. "That's really one of the dumbest things I ever heard! You'll go through the ice, just like that car down there did."

"No, we won't," she said. "I know we won't."

"How do you know?"

"Your brother understands this lake," she said. "He knows where the pressure ridges are and everything. He just *knows*, Russell. You have to trust him. And he can always get off the ice if he thinks it's not safe. He can always find a road."

"Well, I'm not going with you," I said. She nodded. I looked at her, and I wondered if she might be crazed with the bad judgment my parents had told me all teenagers had. Bad judgment of this kind was starting to interest me; it was a powerful antidote for boredom, which seemed worse.

"You don't want to come?"

"No," I said. "I'll walk home." I gazed up the hill, and in the distance I could see the lights of our house, a twenty-minute walk across the bay.

"Okay," Stephanie said. "I didn't think you'd want to come along." We waited. "Russell, do you think your brother is interested in me?"

"I guess so," I said. I wasn't sure what she meant by "interested." Anybody interested him, up to a point. "He says he likes you."

"That's funny, because I feel like something in the Lost and Found," she said, scratching her boot into the ice. "You know, one of those gloves that don't match anything." She put her hand on my shoulder. "One glove. One left-hand glove, with the thumb missing."

I could hear Ben's car starting, and then I saw it heading down Gallagher's boat landing. I was glad he was driving out toward us, because I didn't want to talk to her this way anymore.

Stephanie was now watching my brother's car. His headlights were on. It was odd to see a car with headlights on out on the ice, where there was no road. I saw my brother accelerate and fishtail the car, then slam on the brakes and do a 360-degree spin. He floored it, revving the back wheels, which made a high, whining sound on the ice, like a buzz saw working through wood. He was having a thrill and soon would give Stephanie another thrill by driving her home across ice that might break at any time. Thrills did it, whatever it was. Thrills led to other thrills.

"Would you look at that," I said.

She turned. After a moment she made a little sound in her throat. I remember that sound. When I see her now, she still makes it—a sign of impatience or worry. After all, she didn't go through the ice in my brother's car on the way home. She and my brother didn't drown, together or separately. Stephanie had two marriages and several children. Recently, she and her second husband adopted a Korean baby. She has the complex dignity of many small-town people who do not resort to alcohol until well after night has fallen. She continues to live in Five Oaks, Michigan, and she works behind the counter at the post office, where I buy stamps from her and gossip, holding up the line, trying to make her smile. She still has an overbite and she still laughs easily, despite the moody expression that comes over her when she relaxes. She has moved back to the same house she grew up in. Even now the exterior paint on that house blisters in cobweb patterns. I keep track of her. She and my brother certainly didn't get married; in fact, they broke up a few weeks after seeing the Chevrolet under ice.

"What are we doing out here?" Stephanie asked. I shook my head. "In the middle of winter, out here on this stupid lake? I'll tell you, Russell, I sure don't know. But I do know that your brother doesn't notice me enough, and I can't love him unless he notices me. You know your brother. You know what he pays attention to. What do I have to do to get him to notice me?"

I was twelve years old. I said, "Take off your shoes."

She stood there, thinking about what I had said, and then, quietly, she bent down and took off her boots, and, putting her hand on my shoulder to balance herself, she took off her brown loafers and her white socks. She stood there in front of me with her bare feet on the ice. I saw in the grayish January light that her toenails were painted. Bare feet with painted toenails on the ice—this was a desperate and beautiful sight, and I shivered and felt my fingers curling inside my gloves.

"How does it feel?" I asked.

"You'll know," she said. "You'll know in a few years."

My brother drove up close to us. He rolled down his window and opened the passenger-side door. He didn't say anything. I watched Stephanie get into the car, carrying her shoes and socks and boots, and then I waved goodbye to them before turning to walk back to our house. I heard the car heading north across the ice. My brother would be looking at Stephanie's bare feet on the floor of his car. He would probably not be saying anything just now.

When I reached our front lawn, I stood out in the dark and looked in through the kitchen window. My mother and stepfather were sitting at the kitchen counter; I couldn't be sure if they were speaking to each other, but then I saw my mother raise her arm in one of her can-you-believe-this gestures. I didn't want to go inside. I wanted to feel cold, so cold that the cold itself became permanently interesting. I took off my overcoat and my gloves. Tilting my head back, I felt some snow fall onto my face. I thought of the word "exposure" and of how once or twice a year deer hunters in the Upper Peninsula died of it, and I bent down and stuck my hand into the snow and frozen grass and held it there. The cold rose from my hand to my elbow, and when I had counted to forty and couldn't stand another second of it, I picked up my coat and gloves and walked into the bright heat of the front hallway.

1990

■   ■   ■

ANN BEATTIE

THE CINDERELLA WALTZ

Milo and Bradley are creatures of habit. For as long as I've known him,
Milo has worn his moth-eaten blue scarf with the knot hanging so low
on his chest that the scarf is useless. Bradley is addicted to coffee and
carries a Thermos with him. Milo complains about the cold, and Bradley is always a little edgy. They come out from the city every Saturday—this is not habit but loyalty—to pick up Louise. Louise is even
more unpredictable than most nine-year-olds; sometimes she waits for
them on the front step, sometimes she hasn't even gotten out of bed
when they arrive. One time she hid in a closet and wouldn't leave with
them.

Today Louise has put together a shopping bag full of things she
wants to take with her. She is taking my whisk and my blue pottery
bowl, to make Sunday breakfast for Milo and Bradley; Beckett's *Happy
Days*,[1] which she has carried around for weeks, and which she looks
through, smiling—but I'm not sure she's reading it; and a coleus growing out of a conch shell. Also, she has stuffed into one side of the
bag the fancy Victorian-style nightgown her grandmother gave her for
Christmas, and into the other she has tucked her octascope.[2] Milo
keeps a couple of dresses, a nightgown, a toothbrush, and extra sneakers and boots at his apartment for her. He got tired of rounding up her
stuff to pack for her to take home, so he has brought some things for
her that can be left. It annoys him that she still packs bags, because
then he has to go around making sure that she has found everything
before she goes home. She seems to know how to manipulate him,
and after the weekend is over she calls tearfully to say that she has left

1. Samuel Beckett (1906–1989), Irish playwright, Nobel Prize winner, and innovator of the
Theater of the Absurd. *Happy Days* is a play published in 1961.
2. Child's optical toy that projects multiple images.

this or that, which means that he must get his car out of the garage and drive all the way out to the house to bring it to her. One time, he refused to take the hour-long drive, because she had only left a copy of Tolkien's *The Two Towers*. The following weekend was the time she hid in the closet.

"I'll water your plant if you leave it here," I say now.

"I can take it," she says.

"I didn't say you couldn't take it. I just thought it might be easier to leave it, because if the shell tips over, the plant might get ruined."

"Okay," she says. "Don't water it today, though. Water it Sunday afternoon."

I reach for the shopping bag.

"I'll put it back on my windowsill," she says. She lifts the plant out and carries it as if it's made of Steuben glass. Bradley bought it for her last month, driving back to the city, when they stopped at a lawn sale. She and Bradley are both very choosy, and he likes that. He drinks French-roast coffee; she will debate with herself almost endlessly over whether to buy a coleus that is primarily pink or lavender or striped.

"Has Milo made any plans for this weekend?" I ask.

"He's having a couple of people over tonight, and I'm going to help them make crepes for dinner. If they buy more bottles of that wine with the yellow flowers on the label, Bradley is going to soak the labels off for me."

"That's nice of him," I say. "He never minds taking a lot of time with things."

"He doesn't like to cook, though. Milo and I are going to cook. Bradley sets the table and fixes flowers in a bowl. He thinks it's frustrating to cook."

"Well," I say, "with cooking you have to have a good sense of timing. You have to coordinate everything. Bradley likes to work carefully and not be rushed."

I wonder how much she knows. Last week, she told me about a conversation she'd had with her friend Sarah. Sarah was trying to persuade Louise to stay around on the weekends, but Louise said she always went to her father's. Then Sarah tried to get her to take her along, and Louise said that she couldn't. "You could take her if you wanted to," I said later. "Check with Milo and see if that isn't right. I don't think he'd mind having a friend of yours occasionally."

She shrugged. "Bradley doesn't like a lot of people around," she said.

"Bradley likes you, and if she's your friend I don't think he'd mind."

She looked at me with an expression I didn't recognize; perhaps she thought I was a little dumb, or perhaps she was just curious to see if I would go on. I didn't know how to go on. Like an adult, she gave a little shrug and changed the subject.

At ten o'clock Milo pulls into the driveway and honks his horn, which makes a noise like a bleating sheep. He knows the noise the horn makes is funny, and he means to amuse us. There was a time just after the divorce when he and Bradley would come here and get out of the car and stand around silently, waiting for her. She knew that she had to watch for them, because Milo wouldn't come to the door. We were both bitter then, but I got over it. I still don't think Milo would have come into the house again, though, if Bradley hadn't thought it was a good idea. The third time Milo came to pick her up after he'd left home, I went out to invite them in, but Milo said nothing. He was standing there with his arms at his sides like a wooden soldier, and his eyes were as dead to me as if they'd been painted on. It was Bradley whom I reasoned with. "Louise is over at Sarah's right now, and it'll make her feel more comfortable if we're all together when she comes in," I said to him, and Bradley turned to Milo and said, "Hey, that's right. Why don't we go in for a quick cup of coffee?" I looked into the back seat of the car and saw his red Thermos there; Louise had told me about it. Bradley meant that they should come in and sit down. He was giving me even more than I'd asked for.

It would be an understatement to say that I disliked Bradley at first. I was actually afraid of him, afraid even after I saw him, though he was slender, and more nervous than I, and spoke quietly. The second time I saw him, I persuaded myself that he was just a stereotype, but someone who certainly seemed harmless enough. By the third time, I had enough courage to suggest that they come into the house. It was embarrassing for all of us, sitting around the table—the same table where Milo and I had eaten our meals for the years we were married. Before he left, Milo had shouted at me that the house was a farce, that my playing the happy suburban housewife was a farce, that it was unconscionable of me to let things drag on, that I would probably kiss him and say, "How was your day, sweetheart?" and that he should bring home flowers and the evening paper. "Maybe I would!" I screamed back. "Maybe it would be nice to do that, even if we were pretending, instead of you coming home drunk and not caring what had happened to me or to Louise all day." He was holding on to the edge of the kitchen table, the way you'd hold on to the horse's reins in a runaway carriage. "I care about Louise," he said finally. That was the most horrible moment. Until then, until he said it that way, I had thought that he was going through something horrible—certainly something was terribly wrong—but that, in his way, he loved me after all. *"You don't love me?"* I had whispered at once. It took us both aback. It was an innocent and pathetic question, and it made him come and put his arms around me in the last hug he ever gave me. "I'm sorry for you," he said, "and I'm sorry for marrying you and causing this, but you know who I love. I told you who I love." "But you were kidding," I said. "You didn't mean it. You were kidding."

When Bradley sat at the table that first day, I tried to be polite and not look at him much. I had gotten it through my head that Milo was crazy, and I guess I was expecting Bradley to be a horrible parody—Craig Russell doing Marilyn Monroe. Bradley did not spoon sugar into Milo's coffee. He did not even sit near him. In fact, he pulled his chair a little away from us, and in spite of his uneasiness he found more things to start conversations about than Milo and I did. He told me about the ad agency where he worked; he is a designer there. He asked if he could go out on the porch to see the brook— Milo had told him about the stream in the back of our place that was as thin as a pencil but still gave us our own watercress. He went out on the porch and stayed there for at least five minutes, giving us a chance to talk. We didn't say one word until he came back. Louise came home from Sarah's house just as Bradley sat down at the table again, and she gave him a hug as well as us. I could see that she really liked him. I was amazed that I liked him too. Bradley had won and I had lost, but he was as gentle and low-key as if none of it mattered. Later in the week, I called him and asked him to tell me if any freelance jobs opened in his advertising agency. (I do a little freelance artwork, whenever I can arrange it.) The week after that, he called and told me about another agency, where they were looking for outside artists. Our calls to each other are always brief and for a purpose, but lately they're not just calls about business. Before Bradley left to scout some picture locations in Mexico, he called to say that Milo had told him that when the two of us were there years ago I had seen one of those big circular bronze Aztec calendars and I had always regretted not bringing it back. He wanted to know if I would like him to buy a calendar if he saw one like the one Milo had told him about.

Today, Milo is getting out of his car, his blue scarf flapping against his chest. Louise, looking out the window, asks the same thing I am wondering: "Where's Bradley?"

Milo comes in and shakes my hand, gives Louise a one-armed hug.

"Bradley thinks he's coming down with a cold," Milo says. "The dinner is still on, Louise. We'll do the dinner. We have to stop at Gristede's when we get back to town, unless your mother happens to have a tin of anchovies and two sticks of unsalted butter."

"Let's go to Gristede's," Louise says. "I like to go there."

"Let me look in the kitchen," I say. The butter is salted, but Milo says that will do, and he takes three sticks instead of two. I have a brainstorm and cut the cellophane on a left-over Christmas present from my aunt—a wicker plate that holds nuts and foil-wrapped triangles of cheese—and sure enough: one tin of anchovies.

"We can go to the museum instead," Milo says to Louise. "Wonderful."

But then, going out the door, carrying her bag, he changes his mind. "We can go to America Hurrah, and if we see something beautiful we can buy it," he says.

They go off in high spirits. Louise comes up to his waist, almost, and I notice again that they have the same walk. Both of them stride forward with great purpose. Last week, Bradley told me that Milo had bought a weather vane in the shape of a horse, made around 1800, at America Hurrah, and stood it in the bedroom, and then was enraged when Bradley draped his socks over it to dry. Bradley is still learning what a perfectionist Milo is and how little sense of humor he has. When we were first married, I used one of our pottery casserole dishes to put my jewelry in, and he nagged me until I took it out and put the dish back in the kitchen cabinet. I remember his saying that the dish looked silly on my dresser because it was obvious what it was and people would think we left our dishes lying around. It was one of the things that Milo wouldn't tolerate, because it was improper.

When Milo brings Louise back on Saturday night they are not in a good mood. The dinner was all right, Milo says, and Griffin and Amy and Mark were amazed at what a good hostess Louise had been, but Bradley hadn't been able to eat.

"Is he still coming down with a cold?" I ask. I was still a little shy about asking questions about Bradley.

Milo shrugs. "Louise made him take megadoses of vitamin C all weekend."

Louise says, "Bradley said that taking too much vitamin C was bad for your kidneys, though."

"It's a rotten climate," Milo says, sitting on the living room sofa, scarf and coat still on. "The combination of cold and air pollution . . ."

Louise and I look at each other, and then back at Milo. For weeks now, he has been talking about moving to San Francisco, if he can find work there. (Milo is an architect.) This talk bores me, and it makes Louise nervous. I've asked him not to talk to her about it unless he's actually going to move, but he doesn't seem to be able to stop himself.

"Okay," Milo says, looking at us both. "I'm not going to say anything about San Francisco."

"*California* is polluted," I say. I am unable to stop myself, either.

Milo heaves himself up from the sofa, ready for the drive back to New York. It is the same way he used to get off the sofa that last year he lived here. He would get up, dress for work, and not even go into the kitchen for breakfast—just sit, sometimes in his coat as he was sitting just now, and at the last minute he would push himself up and go out to the driveway, usually without a good-bye, and get in the car and drive off either very fast or very slowly. I liked it better when he made the tires spin in the gravel when he took off.

He stops at the doorway now, and turns to face me. "Did I take all your butter?" he says.

"No," I say. "There's another stick." I point into the kitchen.

"I could have guessed that's where it would be," he says, and smiles at me.

When Milo comes the next weekend, Bradley is still not with him. The night before, as I was putting Louise to bed, she said that she had a feeling he wouldn't be coming.

"I had that feeling a couple of days ago," I said. "Usually Bradley calls once during the week."

"He must still be sick," Louise said. She looked at me anxiously. "Do you think he is?"

"A cold isn't going to kill him," I said. "If he has a cold, he'll be okay."

Her expression changed; she thought I was talking down to her. She lay back in bed. The last year Milo was with us, I used to tuck her in and tell her that everything was all right. What that meant was that there had not been a fight. Milo had sat listening to music on the phonograph, with a book or the newspaper in front of his face. He didn't pay very much attention to Louise, and he ignored me entirely. Instead of saying a prayer with her, the way I usually did, I would say to her that everything was all right. Then I would go downstairs and hope that Milo would say the same thing to me. What he finally did say one night was "You might as well find out from me as some other way."

"Hey, are you an old bag lady again this weekend?" Milo says now, stooping to kiss Louise's forehead.

"Because you take some things with you doesn't mean you're a bag lady," she says primly.

"Well," Milo says, "you start doing something innocently, and before you know it it can take you over."

He looks angry and acts as though it's difficult for him to make conversation, even when the conversation is full of sarcasm and double entendres.

"What do you say we get going?" he says to Louise.

In the shopping bag she is taking is her doll, which she has not played with for more than a year. I found it by accident when I went to tuck in a loaf of banana bread that I had baked. When I saw Baby Betsy, deep in the bag, I decided against putting the bread in.

"Okay," Louise says to Milo. "Where's Bradley?"

"Sick," he says.

"Is he too sick to have me visit?"

"Good heavens, no. He'll be happier to see you than to see me."

"I'm rooting some of my coleus to give him," she says, "Maybe I'll give it to him like it is, in water, and he can plant it when it roots."

When she leaves the room, I go over to Milo. "Be nice to her," I say quietly.

"I'm nice to her," he says. "Why does everybody have to act like I'm going to grow fangs every time I turn around?"

"You were quite cutting when you came in."

"I was being self-deprecating." He sighs. "I don't really know why I come here and act this way," he says.

"What's the matter, Milo?"

But now he lets me know he's bored with the conversation. He walks over to the table and picks up a *Newsweek* and flips through it. Louise comes back with the coleus in a water glass.

"You know what you could do," I say. "Wet a napkin and put it around that cutting and then wrap it in foil, and put it in water when you get there. That way, you wouldn't have to hold a glass of water all the way to New York."

She shrugs. "This is okay," she says.

"Why don't you take your mother's suggestion," Milo says. "The water will slosh out of the glass."

"Not if you don't drive fast."

"It doesn't have anything to do with my driving fast. If we go over a bump in the road, you're going to get all wet."

"Then I can put on one of my dresses at your apartment."

"Am I being unreasonable?" Milo says to me.

"I started it," I say. "Let her take it in the glass."

"Would you, as a favor, do what your mother says?" he says to Louise.

Louise looks at the coleus and at me.

"Hold the glass over the seat instead of over your lap, and you won't get wet," I say.

"Your first idea was the best," Milo says.

Louise gives him an exasperated look and puts the glass down on the floor, pulls on her poncho, picks up the glass again and says a sullen goodbye to me, and goes out the front door.

"Why is this my fault?" Milo says. "Have I done anything terrible? I—"

"Do something to cheer yourself up," I say, patting him on the back.

He looks as exasperated with me as Louise was with him. He nods his head yes, and goes out the door.

"Was everything all right this weekend?" I ask Louise.

"Milo was in a bad mood, and Bradley wasn't even there on Saturday," Louise says. "He came back today and took us to the Village for breakfast."

"What did you have?"

"I had sausage wrapped in little pancakes and fruit salad and a rum bun."

"Where was Bradley on Saturday?"

She shrugs. "I didn't ask him."

She almost always surprises me by being more grown-up than I give her credit for. Does she suspect, as I do, that Bradley has found another lover?

"Milo was in a bad mood when you two left here yesterday," I say.

"I told him if he didn't want me to come next weekend, just to tell me." She looks perturbed, and I suddenly realize that she can sound exactly like Milo sometimes.

"You shouldn't have said that to him Louise," I say. "You know he wants you. He's just worried about Bradley."

"So?" she says. "I'm probably going to flunk math."

"No, you're not, honey. You got a C-plus on the last assignment."

"It still doesn't make my grade average out to a C."

"You'll get a C. It's all right to get a C."

She doesn't believe me.

"Don't be a perfectionist, like Milo" I tell her. "Even if you got a D, you wouldn't fail."

Louise is brushing her hair—thin, shoulder-length, auburn hair. She is already so pretty and so smart in everything except math that I wonder what will become of her. When I was her age, I was plain and serious and I wanted to be a tree surgeon. I went with my father to the park and held a stethoscope—a real one—to the trunks of trees, listening to their silence. Children seem older now.

"What do you think's the matter with Bradley?" Louise says. She sounds worried.

"Maybe the two of them are unhappy with each other right now."

She misses my point. "Bradley's sad, and Milo's sad that he's unhappy."

I drop Louise off at Sarah's house for supper. Sarah's mother, Martine Cooper, looks like Shelley Winters, and I have never seen her without a glass of Galliano on ice in her hand. She has a strong candy smell. Her husband has left her, and she professes not to care. She has emptied her living room of furniture and put up ballet bars on the walls and dances in a purple leotard to records by Cher and Mac Davis. I prefer to have Sarah come to our house, but her mother is adamant that everything must be, as she puts it, "fifty-fifty." When Sarah visited us a week ago and loved the chocolate pie I had made, I sent two pieces home with her. Tonight, when I left Sarah's house, her mother gave me a bowl of Jell-O fruit salad.

The phone is ringing when I come in the door. It is Bradley.

"Bradley," I say at once, "whatever's wrong, at least you don't have a neighbor who just gave you a bowl of maraschino cherries in green Jell-O with a Reddi Whip flower squirted on top."

"Jesus," he says. "You don't need me to depress you, do you?"

"What's wrong?" I say.

He sighs into the phone. "Guess what?" he says.

"What?"

"I've lost my job."

It wasn't at all what I was expecting to hear. I was ready to hear that he was leaving Milo, and I had even thought that that would serve Milo right. Part of me still wanted him punished for what he did. I was so out of my mind when Milo left me that I used to go over and drink Galliano with Martine Cooper. I even thought seriously about forming a ballet group with her. I would go to her house in the afternoon, and she would hold a tambourine in the air and I would hold my leg rigid and try to kick it.

"That's awful," I say to Bradley. "What happened?"

"They said it was nothing personal—they were laying off three people. Two other people are going to get the ax at the agency within the next six months. I was the first to go, and it was nothing personal. From twenty thousand bucks a year to nothing, and nothing personal, either."

"But your work is so good. Won't you be able to find something again?"

"Could I ask you a favor?" he says. "I'm calling from a phone booth. I'm not in the city. Could I come talk to you?"

"Sure," I say.

It seems perfectly logical that he should come alone to talk—perfectly logical until I actually see him coming up the walk. I can't entirely believe it. A year after my husband has left me, I am sitting with his lover—a man, a person I like quite well—and trying to cheer him up because he is out of work. ("Honey," my father would say, "listen to Daddy's heart with the stethoscope, or you can turn it toward you and listen to your own heart. You won't hear anything listening to a tree." Was my persistence willfulness, or belief in magic? Is it possible that I hugged Bradley at the door because I'm secretly glad he's down-and-out, the way I used to be? Or do I really want to make things better for him?)

He comes into the kitchen and thanks me for the coffee I am making, drapes his coat over the chair he always sits in.

"What am I going to do?" he asks.

"You shouldn't get so upset, Bradley," I say. "You know you're good. You won't have trouble finding another job."

"That's only half of it," he says. "Milo thinks I did this deliberately. He told me I was quitting on him. He's very angry at me. He fights with me, and then he gets mad that I don't enjoy eating dinner. My stomach's upset, and I can't eat anything."

"Maybe some juice would be better than coffee."

"If I didn't drink coffee, I'd collapse," he says.

I pour coffee into a mug for him, coffee into a mug for me.

"This is probably very awkward for you," he says. "That I come here and say all this about Milo."

"What does he mean about you quitting on him?"

"He said . . . he actually accused me of doing badly deliberately, so they'd fire me. I was so afraid to tell him the truth when I was fired that I pretended to be sick. Then I really *was* sick. He's never been angry at me this way. Is this always the way he acts? Does he get a notion in his head for no reason and then pick at a person because of it?"

I try to remember. "We didn't argue much," I say. "When he didn't want to live here, he made me look ridiculous for complaining when I knew something was wrong. He expects perfection, but what that means is that you do things his way."

"I *was*. I never wanted to sit around the apartment, the way he says I did. I even brought work home with me. He made me feel so bad all week that I went to a friend's apartment for the day on Saturday. Then he said I had walked out on the problem. He's a little paranoid. I was listening to the radio, and Carole King was singing 'It's Too Late,' and he came into the study and looked very upset, as though I had planned for the song to come on. I couldn't believe it."

"Whew," I say, shaking my head. "I don't envy you. You have to stand up to him. I didn't do that. I pretended the problem would go away."

"And now the problem sits across from you drinking coffee, and you're being nice to him."

"I know it, I was just thinking we look like two characters in some soap opera my friend Martine Cooper would watch."

He pushes his coffee cup away from him with a grimace.

"But anyway, I like you now," I say. "And you're exceptionally nice to Louise."

"I took her father," he says.

"Bradley—I hope you don't take offense, but it makes me nervous to talk about that."

"I don't take offense. But how can you be having coffee with me?"

"You invited yourself over so you could ask that?"

"Please," he says, holding up both hands. Then he runs his hands through his hair. "Don't make me feel illogical. He does that to me, you know. He doesn't understand it when everything doesn't fall right into line. If I like fixing up the place, keeping some flowers around, therefore I can't like being a working person too, therefore I deliberately sabotage myself in my job." Bradley sips his coffee.

"I wish I could do something for him," he says in a different voice. This is not what I expected, either. We have sounded like two wise adults, and then suddenly he has changed and sounds very tender. I realize the situation is still the same. It is two of them on one side and me on the other, even though Bradley is in my kitchen.

"Come and pick up Louise with me, Bradley," I say. "When you see Martine Cooper, you'll cheer up about your situation."

He looks up from his coffee. "You're forgetting what I'd look like to Martine Cooper," he says.

Milo is going to California. He has been offered a job with a new San Francisco architectural firm. I am not the first to know. His sister, Deanna, knows before I do and mentions it when we're talking on the phone. "It's middle-age crisis," Deanna says sniffily. "Not that I need to tell you." Deanna would drop dead if she knew the way things are. She is scandalized every time a new display is put up in Bloomingdale's window. ("Those mannequins had eyes like an Egyptian princess, and *rags*. I swear to you, they had mops and brooms and ragged gauze dresses on, with whores' shoes—stiletto heels that prostitutes wear.")

I hang up from Deanna's call and tell Louise I'm going to drive to the gas station for cigarettes. I go there to call New York on their pay phone.

"Well, I only just knew," Milo says. "I found out for sure yesterday, and last night Deanna called and so I told her. It's not like I'm leaving tonight."

He sounds elated, in spite of being upset that I called. He's happy in the way he used to be on Christmas morning. I remember him once running into the living room in his underwear and tearing open the gifts we'd been sent by relatives. He was looking for the eight-slice toaster he was sure we'd get. We'd been given two-slice, four-slice, and six-slice toasters, but then we got no more. "Come out, my eight-slice beauty!" Milo crooned, and out came an electric clock, a blender, and an expensive electric pan.

"When are you leaving?" I ask him.

"I'm going out to look for a place to live next week."

"Are you going to tell Louise yourself this weekend?"

"Of course," he says.

"And what are you going to do about seeing Louise?"

"Why do you act as if I don't like Louise?" he says. "I will occasionally come back East, and I will arrange for her to fly to San Francisco on her vacations."

"It's going to break her heart."

"No it isn't. Why do you want to make me feel bad?"

"She's had so many things to adjust to. You don't have to go to San Francisco right now, Milo."

"It happens, if you care, that my own job here is in jeopardy. This is a real chance for me, with a young firm. They really want me. But anyway, all we need in this happy group is to have you bringing in a couple of hundred dollars a month with your graphic work and me destitute and Bradley so devastated by being fired that of course he can't even look for work."

"I'll bet he is looking for a job," I say.

"Yes. He read the want ads today and then fixed a crab quiche."

"Maybe that's the way you like things, Milo, and people respond to you. You forbade me to work when we had a baby. Do you say anything encouraging to him about finding a job, or do you just take it out on him that he was fired?"

There is a pause, and then he almost seems to lose his mind with impatience.

"I can hardly *believe,* when I am trying to find a logical solution to all our problems, that I am being subjected, by telephone, to an unflattering psychological analysis by my ex-wife." He says this all in a rush.

"All right, Milo. But don't you think that if you're leaving so soon you ought to call her, instead of waiting until Saturday?"

Milo sighs very deeply. "I have more sense than to have important conversations on the telephone," he says.

Milo calls on Friday and asks Louise whether it wouldn't be nice if both of us came in and spent the night Saturday and if we all went to brunch together Sunday. Louise is excited. I never go into town with her.

Louise and I pack a suitcase and put it in the car Saturday morning. A cutting of ivy for Bradley has taken root, and she has put it in a little green plastic pot for him. It's heartbreaking, and I hope that Milo notices and has a tough time dealing with it. I am relieved I'm going to be there when he tells her, and sad that I have to hear it at all.

In the city, I give the car to the garage attendant, who does not remember me. Milo and I lived in the apartment when we were first married, and moved when Louise was two years old. When we moved, Milo kept the apartment and sublet it—a sign that things were not going well, if I had been one to heed such a warning. What he said was that if we were ever rich enough we could have the house in Connecticut *and* the apartment in New York. When Milo moved out of the house, he went right back to the apartment. This will be the first time I have visited there in years.

Louise strides in in front of me, throwing her coat over the brass coatrack in the entranceway—almost too casual about being there. She's the hostess at Milo's, the way I am at our house.

He has painted the walls white. There are floor-length white curtains in the living room, where my silly flowered curtains used to hang. The walls are bare, the floor has been sanded, a stereo as huge as a computer stands against one wall of the living room, and there are four speakers.

"Look around," Milo says. "Show your mother around, Louise."

I am trying to remember if I have ever told Louise that I used to live in this apartment. I must have told her, at some point, but I can't remember it.

"Hello," Bradley says, coming out of the bedroom.

"Hi, Bradley," I say. "Have you got a drink?"

Bradley looks sad. "He's got champagne," he says, and looks nervously at Milo.

"No one *has* to drink champagne," Milo says. "There's the usual assortment of liquor."

"Yes," Bradley says. "What would you like?"

"Some bourbon, please."

"Bourbon." Bradley turns to go into the kitchen. He looks different; his hair is different—more wavy—and he is dressed as though it were summer, in straight-legged white pants and black leather thongs.

"I want Perrier water with strawberry juice," Louise says, tagging along after Bradley. I have never heard her ask for such a thing before. At home, she drinks too many Cokes. I am always trying to get her to drink fruit juice.

Bradley comes back with two drinks and hands me one. "Did you want anything?" he says to Milo.

"I'm going to open the champagne in a moment," Milo says. "How have you been this week, sweetheart?"

"Okay," Louise says. She is holding a pale-pink, bubbly drink. She sips it like a cocktail.

Bradley looks very bad. He has circles under his eyes, and he is ill at ease. A red light begins to blink on the phone-answering device next to where Bradley sits on the sofa, and Milo gets out of his chair to pick up the phone.

"Do you really want to talk on the phone right now?" Bradley asks Milo quietly.

Milo looks at him. "No, not particularly," he says, sitting down again. After a moment, the red light goes out.

"I'm going to mist your bowl garden," Louise says to Bradley, and slides off the sofa and goes to the bedroom. "Hey, a little toadstool is growing in here!" she calls back. "Did you put it there, Bradley?"

"It grew from the soil mixture, I guess," Bradley calls back. "I don't know how it got there."

"Have you heard anything about a job?" I ask Bradley.

"I haven't been looking, really," he says. "You know."

Milo frowns at him. "Your choice, Bradley," he says. "I didn't ask you to follow me to California. You can stay here."

"No," Bradley says. "You've hardly made me feel welcome."

"Should we have some champagne—all four of us—and you can get back to your bourbons later?" Milo says cheerfully.

We don't answer him, but he gets up anyway and goes to the kitchen. "Where have you hidden the tulip-shaped glasses, Bradley?" he calls out after a while.

"They should be in the cabinet on the far left," Bradley says.

"You're going with him?" I say to Bradley. "To San Francisco?"

He shrugs and won't look at me. "I'm not quite sure I'm wanted," he says quietly.

The cork pops in the kitchen. I look at Bradley, but he won't look up. His new hairdo makes him look older. I remember that when Milo left me I went to the hairdresser the same week and had bangs cut. The next week, I went to a therapist, who told me it was no good trying to hide from myself. The week after that, I did dance exercise with Martine Cooper, and the week after that the therapist told me not to dance if I wasn't interested in dancing.

"I'm not going to act like this is a funeral," Milo says, coming in with the glasses. "Louise, come in here and have champagne! We have something to have a toast about."

Louise comes into the living room suspiciously. She is so used to being refused even a sip of wine from my glass or her father's that she no longer even asks. "How come I'm in on this?" she asks.

"We're going to drink a toast to me," Milo says.

Three of the four glasses are clustered on the table in front of the sofa. Milo's glass is raised. Louise looks at me, to see what I'm going to say. Milo raises his glass even higher. Bradley reaches for a glass. Louise picks up a glass. I lean forward and take the last one.

"This is a toast to me," Milo says, "because I am going to be going to San Francisco."

It was not a very good or informative toast. Bradley and I sip from our glasses. Louise puts her glass down hard and bursts into tears, knocking the glass over. The champagne spills onto the cover of a big art book about the Unicorn Tapestries. She runs into the bedroom and slams the door.

Milo looks furious. "Everybody lets me know just what my insufficiencies are, don't they?" he says. "Nobody minds expressing himself. We have it all right out in the open."

"He's criticizing me," Bradley murmurs, his head still bowed. "It's because I was offered a job here in the city and I didn't automatically refuse it."

I turn to Milo. "Go say something to Louise, Milo," I say. "Do you think that's what somebody who isn't brokenhearted sounds like?"

He glares at me and stomps into the bedroom, and I can hear him talking to Louise reassuringly. "It doesn't mean you'll *never* see me," he says. "You can fly there, I'll come here. It's not going to be that different."

"You lied!" Louise screams. "You said we were going to brunch."

"We are. We are. I can't very well take us to brunch before Sunday, can I?"

"You didn't say you were going to San Francisco. What *is* San Francisco, anyway?"

"I just said so. I bought us a bottle of champagne. You can come out as soon as I get settled. You're going to like it there."

Louise is sobbing. She has told him the truth, and she knows it's futile to go on.

By the next morning, Louise acts the way I acted—as if everything were just the same. She looks calm, but her face is small and pale. She looks very young. We walk into the restaurant and sit at the table Milo has reserved. Bradley pulls out a chair for me, and Milo pulls out a chair for Louise, locking his finger with hers for a second, raising her arm above her head, as if she were about to take a twirl.

She looks very nice, really. She has a ribbon in her hair. It is cold, and she should have worn a hat, but she wanted to wear the ribbon. Milo has good taste: the dress she is wearing, which he bought for her, is a hazy purple plaid, and it sets off her hair.

"Come with me. Don't be sad," Milo suddenly says to Louise, pulling her by the hand. "Come with me for a minute. Come across the street to the park for just a second, and we'll have some space to dance, and your mother and Bradley can have a nice quiet drink."

She gets up from the table and, looking long-suffering, backs into her coat, which he is holding for her, and the two of them go out. The waitress comes to the table, and Bradley orders three Bloody Marys and a Coke, and eggs Benedict for everyone. He asks the waitress to wait awhile before she brings the food. I have hardly slept at all, and having a drink is not going to clear my head. I have to think of things to say to Louise later, on the ride home.

"He takes so many *chances*," I say. "He pushes things so far with people. I don't want her to turn against him."

"No," he says.

"Why are you going, Bradley? You've seen the way he acts. You know that when you get out there he'll pull something on you. Take the job and stay here."

Bradley is fiddling with the edge of his napkin. I study him. I don't know who his friends are, how old he is, where he grew up, whether he believes in God, or what he usually drinks. I'm shocked that I know so little, and I reach out and touch him. He looks up.

"Don't go," I say quietly.

The waitress puts the glasses down quickly and leaves, embarrassed because she thinks she's interrupted a tender moment. Bradley pats my hand on his arm. Then he says the thing that has always been between us, the thing too painful for me to envision or think about.

"I love him," Bradley whispers.

We sit quietly until Milo and Louise come into the restaurant, swinging hands. She is pretending to be a young child, almost a baby, and I wonder for an instant if Milo and Bradley and I haven't been playing house too—pretending to be adults.

"Daddy's going to give me a first-class ticket," Louise says. "When I go to California we're going to ride in a glass elevator to the top of the Fairman Hotel."

"The Fairmont," Milo says, smiling at her.

Before Louise was born, Milo used to put his ear to my stomach and say that if the baby turned out to be a girl he would put her into glass slippers instead of bootees. Now he is the prince once again. I see them in a glass elevator, not long from now, going up and up, with the people below getting smaller and smaller, until they disappear.

1982

■   ■   ■

T. CORAGHESSAN BOYLE

DESCENT OF MAN

I was living with a woman who suddenly began to stink. It was very difficult. The first time I confronted her she merely smiled. "Occupational hazard," she said. The next time she curled her lip. There were other problems too. Hairs, for instance. Hairs that began to appear on her clothing, sharp and black and brutal. Invariably I would awake to find these hairs in my mouth, or I would glance into the mirror to see them slashing like razor edges across the collars of my white shirts. Then too there was the fruit. I began to discover moldering bits of it about the house—apple and banana most characteristically—but plum and tangelo or even passion fruit and yim-yim were not at all anomalous. These fruit fragments occurred principally in the bedroom, on the pillow, surrounded by darkening spots. It was not long before I located their source: they lay hidden like gems in the long wild hanks of her hair. Another occupational hazard.

Jane was in the habit of sitting before the air conditioner when she came home from work, fingering out her hair, drying the sweat from her face and neck in the cool hum of the machine, fruit bits sifting silently to the carpet, black hairs drifting like feathers. On these occasions the room would fill with the stink of her, bestial and fetid. And I would find my eyes watering, my mind imaging the dark rotting trunks of the rain forest, stained sienna and mandalay and Hooker's green with the excrements dropped from above. My ears would keen with the whistling and crawking of the jungle birds, the screechings of the snot-nosed apes in the branches. And then, slack-faced and tight-boweled, I would step into the bathroom and retch, the sweetness of my own intestinal secrets a balm against the potent hairy stench of her.

One evening, just after her bath (the faintest odor lingered, yet still it was so trenchant I had to fight the impulse to get up and urinate on a tree or a post or something), I lay my hand casually across her belly and was suddenly startled to see an insect flit from its cover, skate up the swell of her abdomen, and bury itself in her navel. "Good Christ," I said.

"Hm?" she returned, peering over the cover of her Yerkish[1] reader.

"That," I said. "That bug, that insect, that vermin."

She sat up, plucked the thing from its cachette, raised it to her lips and popped it between her front teeth. "Louse," she said, sucking. "Went down to the old-age home on Thirteenth Street to pick them up."

I anticipated her: "Not for—?"

"Why certainly, potpie—so Konrad can experience a tangible gratification of his social impulses during the grooming ritual. You know: you scratch my back, I scratch yours."

I lay in bed that night sweating, thinking about Jane and those slippery-fingered monkeys poking away at her, and listening for the lice crawling across her scalp or nestling their bloody little siphons in the tufts under her arms. Finally, about four, I got up and took three Doriden. I woke at two in the afternoon, an insect in my ear. It was only an earwig. I had missed my train, failed to call in at the office. There was a note from Jane: Pick me up at four. Konrad sends love.

The Primate Center stood in the midst of a macadamized acre or two, looking very much like a school building: faded brick, fluted columns, high mesh fences. Finger paintings and mobiles hung in the windows, misshapen ceramics crouched along the sills. A flag raggled at the top of a whitewashed flagpole. I found myself bending to examine the cornerstone: Asa Priff Grammar School, 1939. Inside it was dark and cool, the halls were lined with lockers and curling watercolors, the linoleum gleamed like a shy smile. I stepped into the BOYS' ROOM. The urinals were a foot and a half from the floor. Designed for little people, I mused. Youngsters. Hardly big enough to hold their little peters without the teacher's help. I smiled, and situated myself over one of the urinals, the strong honest scent of Pine-Sol in my nostrils. At that moment the door wheezed open and a chimpanzee shuffled in. He was dressed in shorts, shirt and bow tie. He nodded to me, it seemed, and made a few odd gestures with his hands as he moved up to the urinal beside mine. Then he opened his fly and

---

1. From work of Robert Hearns Yerkes (1875–1956), American psychologist who founded Yale labs of primate biology.

pulled out an enormous slick red organ like a peeled banana. I looked away, embarrassed, but could hear him urinating mightily. The stream hissed against the porcelain like a thunderstorm, rattled the drain as it went down. My own water wouldn't come. I began to feel foolish. The chimp shook himself daintily, zippered up, pulled the plunger, crossed to the sink, washed and dried his hands, and left. I found I no longer had to go.

Out in the hallway the janitor was leaning on his flathead broom. The chimp stood before him gesticulating with manic dexterity: brushing his forehead and tugging his chin, slapping his hands under his armpits, tapping his wrists, his tongue, his ear, his lip. The janitor watched intently. Suddenly—after a particularly virulent flurry—the man burst into laughter, rich braying globes of it. The chimp folded his lip and joined in, adding his weird nasal snickering to the janitor's barrel-laugh. I stood by the door to the BOYS' ROOM in a quandary. I began to feel that it might be wiser to wait in the car—but then I didn't want to call attention to myself, darting in and out like that. The janitor might think I was stealing paper towels or something. So I stood there, thinking to have a word with him after the chimp moved on—with the expectation that he could give me some grassroots insight into the nature of Jane's job. But the chimp didn't move on. The two continued laughing, now harder than ever. The janitor's face was tear-streaked. Each time he looked up the chimp produced a gesticular flurry that would stagger him again. Finally the janitor wound down a bit, and still chuckling, held out his hands, palms up. The chimp flung his arms up over his head and then heaved them down again, rhythmically slapping the big palms with his own. "Right on! Mastuh Konrad," the janitor said, "Right on!" The chimp grinned, then hitched up his shorts and sauntered off down the hall. The janitor turned back to his broom, still chuckling.

I cleared my throat. The broom began a geometrically precise course up the hall toward me. It stopped at my toes, the ridge of detritus flush with the pinions of my wingtips. The janitor looked up. The pupil of his right eye was fixed in the corner, beneath the lid, and the white was red. There was an ironic gap between his front teeth. "Kin ah do sumfin fo yo, mah good man?" he said.

"I'm waiting for Miss Good."

"Ohhh, Miz *Good*," he said, nodding his head. "Fust ah tought yo was thievin paypuh tow-els outen de Boys' Room but den when ah sees yo standin dere rigid as de Venus de Milo ah thinks to mahsef: he is some kinda new sculpture de stoodents done made is what he is." He was squinting up at me and grinning like we'd just come back from sailing around the world together.

"That's a nice broom," I said.

He looked at me steadily, grinning still. "Yo's wonderin what me and Mastuh Konrad was jivin bout up dere, isn't yo? Well, ah tells yo: he was relatin a hoomerous anecdote, de punch line ob which has deep cosmic implications in dat it establishes a common groun between monks and Ho-mo sapiens despite dere divergent ancestries." He shook his head, chortled. "Yes in-deed, dat Mastuh Konrad is quite de wit."

"You mean to tell me you actually understand all that lip-pulling and finger-waving?" I was beginning to feel a nameless sense of out-rage.

"Oh sartinly, mah good man. Dat ASL."

"What?"

"ASL is what we was talkin. A-merican Sign Language. Devel-oped for de deef n dumb. Yo sees, Mastuh Konrad is sumfin ob a genius round here. He can commoonicate de mos esoteric i-deas in bof ASL and Yerkish, re-spond to and translate English, French, Ger-man and Chinese. Fack, it was Miz Good was tellin me dat Konrad is workin right now on a Yerkish translation ob Darwin's *De-scent o Man*. He is mainly into anthro-pology, yo knows, but he has cultivated a in-teress in udder fields too. Dis lass fall he done undertook a Yerkish translation ob Chomsky's *Language and Mind* and Nietzsche's *Jenseits von Gut und Böse*.[2] And dat's some pretty heavy shit, Jackson."

I was hot with outrage. "Stuff," I said. "Stuff and nonsense."

"No sense in feelin personally treatened by Mastuh Konrad's chievements, mah good fellow—yo's got to ree-lize dat he is a genius."

A word came to me: "Bullhonk," I said. And turned to leave.

The janitor caught me by the shirtsleeve. "He is now scorin his turd opera," he whispered. I tore away from him and stamped out of the building.

Jane was waiting in the car. I climbed in, cranked down the sun roof and opened the air vents.

At home I poured a water glass of gin, held it to my nostrils and inhaled. Jane sat before the air conditioner, her hair like a urinal mop, stinking. Black hairs cut the atmosphere, fruit bits whispered to the carpet. Occasionally the tip of my tongue entered the gin. I sniffed and tasted, thinking of plastic factories and turpentine distilleries and rich sulfurous smoke. On my way to the bedroom I poured a second glass.

In the bedroom I sniffed gin and dressed for dinner. "Jane?" I called, "shouldn't you be getting ready?" She appeared in the doorway.

2. "Beyond good and evil."

She was dressed in her work clothes: jeans and sweatshirt. The sweatshirt was gray and hooded. There were yellow stains on the sleeves. I thought of the lower depths of animal cages, beneath the floor meshing. "I figured I'd go like this," she said. I was knotting my tie. "And I wish you'd stop insisting on baths every night—I'm getting tired of smelling like a coupon in a detergent box. It's unnatural. Unhealthy."

In the car on the way to the restaurant I lit a cigar, a cheap twisted black thing like half a pepperoni. Jane sat hunched against her door, unwashed. I had never before smoked a cigar. I tried to start a conversation but Jane said she didn't feel like talking: talk seemed so useless, such an anachronism. We drove on in silence. And I reflected that this was not the Jane I knew and loved. Where, I wondered, was the girl who changed wigs three or four times a day and sported nails like a Chinese emperor?—and where was the girl who dressed like an Arabian bazaar and smelled like the trade winds?

She was committed. The project, the study, grants. I could read the signs: she was growing away from me.

The restaurant was dark, a maze of rocky gardens, pancake-leafed vegetation, black fountains. We stood squinting just inside the door. Birds whistled, carp hissed through the pools. Somewhere a monkey screeched. Jane put her hand on my shoulder and whispered in my ear. "Siamang," she said. At that moment the leaves parted beside us: a rubbery little fellow emerged and motioned us to sit on a bench beneath a wicker birdcage. He was wearing a soiled loincloth and eight or ten necklaces of yellowed teeth. His hair flamed out like a brushfire. In the dim light from the braziers I noticed his nostrils—both shrunken and pinched, as if once pierced straight through. His face was of course inscrutable. As soon as we were seated he removed my socks and shoes, Jane's sneakers, and wrapped our feet in what I later learned were plantain leaves. I started to object—I bitterly resent anyone looking at my feet—but Jane shushed me. We had waited three months for reservations.

The maitre d' signed for us to follow, and led us through a dripping stone-walled tunnel to an outdoor garden where the flagstones gave way to dirt and we found ourselves on a narrow plant-choked path. He licked along like an iguana and we hurried to keep up. Wet fronds slapped back in my face, creepers snatched at my ankles, mud sucked at the plantain leaves on my feet. The scents of mold and damp and long-lying urine hung in the air, and I thought of the men's room at the subway station. It was dark as a womb. I offered Jane my hand, but she refused it. Her breathing was fast. The monkey chatter was loud as a zoo afire. "Far out," she said. I slapped a mosquito on my neck.

A moment later we found ourselves seated at a bamboo table overhung with branch and vine. Across from us sat Dr. and Mrs. U-Hwak-Lo, director of the Primate Center and wife. A candle guttered between them. I cleared my throat, and then began idly tracing my finger around the circular hole cut in the table's center. The Doctor's ears were the size of peanuts. "Glad you two could make it," he said. "I've long been urging Jane to sample some of our humble island fare." I smiled, crushed a spider against the back of my chair. The Doctor's English was perfect, pure Martha's Vineyard—he sounded like Ted Kennedy's insurance salesman. His wife's was weak: "Yes," she said, "nussing cook here, all roar." "How exciting!" said Jane. And then the conversation turned to primates, and the Center.

Mrs. U-Hwak-Lo and I smiled at one another. Jane and the Doctor were already deeply absorbed in a dialogue concerning the incidence of anal retention in chimps deprived of Frisbee coordination during the sensorimotor period. I gestured toward them with my head and arched my eyebrows wittily. Mrs. U-Hwak-Lo giggled. It was then that Jane's proximity began to affect me. The close wet air seemed to concentrate her essence, distill its potency. The U-Hwak-Los seemed unaffected. I began to feel queasy. I reached for the fingerbowl and drank down its contents. Mrs. U-Hwak-Lo smiled. It was coconut oil. Just then the waiter appeared carrying a wooden bowl the size of a truck tire. A single string of teeth slapped against his breastbone as he set the bowl down and slipped off into the shadows. The Doctor and Jane were oblivious—they were talking excitedly, occasionally lapsing into what I took to be ASL, ear- and nose- and lip-picking like a manager and his third-base coach. I peered into the bowl: it was filled to the rim with clean-picked chicken bones. Mrs. U-Hwak-Lo nodded, grinning: "No on-tray," she said. "Appeticer." At that moment a simian screamed somewhere close, screamed like death itself. Jane looked up. "Rhesus," she said.

On my return from the men's room I had some difficulty locating the table in the dark. I had already waded through two murky fountains and was preparing to plunge through my third when I heard Mrs. U-Hwak-Lo's voice behind me. "Here," she said. "Make quick, repass now serve." She took my hand and led me back to the table. "Oh, they're enormously resourceful," the Doctor was saying as I stumbled into my chair, pants wet to the knees. "They first employ a general anesthetic— a distillation of the chu-bok root—and then the chef (who logically doubles as village surgeon) makes a circular incision about the macaque's cranium, carefully peeling back the already-shaven scalp, and staunching the blood flow quite effectively with maura-ro, a highly absorbent powder derived from the tamana leaf. He then removes both the frontal and parietal plates to expose the brain . . ." I looked at Jane: she was rapt. I wasn't really listening. My attention was directed toward what I took to be the main course, which had appeared in my absence. An unsteady pinkish mound now occupied the center of the table, completely obscuring the circular hole—it looked like cherry vanilla yogurt, a carton and a half, perhaps two. On closer inspection I noticed several black hairs peeping out from around its flaccid edges. And thought immediately of the bush-headed maitre d'. I pointed to one of the hairs, remarking to Mrs. U-Hwak-Lo that the rudiments of culinary hygiene could be a little more rigorously observed among the staff. She smiled. Encouraged, I asked her what exactly the dish was. "Much delicacy," she said. "Very rare find in land of Lincoln." At the moment the waiter appeared and handed each of us a bamboo stick beaten flat and sharpened at one end.

". . . then the tribal elders or visiting dignitaries are seated around the table," the Doctor was saying. "The chef has previously of course located the macaque beneath the table, the exposed part of the creature's brain protruding from the hole in its center. After the feast, the lower ranks of the village population divide up the remnants. It's really quite efficient."

"How fascinating!" said Jane. "Shall we try some?"

"By all means . . . but tell me, how has Konrad been coming with that Yerkish epic he's been working up?"

Jane turned to answer, bamboo stick poised: "Oh I'm so glad you asked—I'd almost forgotten. He's finished his tenth book and tells me he'll be doing two more—out of deference to the Miltonic tradition. Isn't that a groove?"

"Yes," said the Doctor, gesturing toward the rosy lump in the center of the table. "Yes it is. He's certainly—and I hope you won't mind the pun—a brainy fellow. Ho-ho."

"Oh, Doctor," Jane laughed, and plunged her stick into the pink. Beneath the table, in the dark, a tiny fist clutched at my pantleg.

I missed work again the following day. This time it took five Doriden to put me under. I had lain in bed sweating and tossing, listening to Jane's quiet breathing, inhaling her fumes. At dawn I dozed off, dreamed briefly of elementary school cafeterias swarming with knickered chimps and weltered with trays of cherry vanilla yogurt, and woke stale-mouthed. Then I took the pills. It was three-thirty when I woke again. There was a note from Jane: Bringing Konrad home for dinner. Vacuum rug and clean toilet.

Konrad was impeccably dressed—long pants, platform wedgies, cufflinks. He smelled of eau de cologne, Jane of used litter. They arrived during the seven o'clock news. I opened the door for them. "Hello Jane," I said. We stood at the door, awkward, silent.

"Well?" she said. "Aren't you going to greet our guest?" "Hello, Konrad" I said. And then: "I believe we met in the boys' room at the Center the other day?" He bowed deeply, straight-faced, his upper lip like a halved cantaloupe. Then he broke into a snicker, turned to Jane and juggled out an impossible series of gestures. Jane laughed. Something caught in my throat. "Is he trying to say something?" I asked. "Oh potpie," she said, "it was nothing—just a little quote from Yeats."

"Yeats?"

"Yes, you know: 'An aged man is but a paltry thing.' "[3]

Jane served watercress sandwiches and animal crackers as hors d'oeuvres. She brought them into the living room on a cut-glass serving tray and set them down before Konrad and me, where we sat on the sofa, watching the news. Then she returned to the kitchen. Konrad plucked up a tiny sandwich and swallowed it like a communion wafer, sucking the tips of his fingers. Then he lifted the tray and offered it to me. I declined. "No, thank you," I said. Konrad shrugged, set the plate down in his lap, and carefully stacked all the sandwiches in its center. I pretended to be absorbed with the news: actually I studied him, half-face. He was filling the gaps in his sandwich-construction with animal crackers. His lower lip protruded, his ears were rubbery, he was balding. With both hands he crushed the heap of crackers and sandwiches together and began kneading it until it took on the consistency of raw dough. Then he lifted the whole thing to his mouth and swallowed it without chewing. There were no whites to his eyes.

Konrad's only reaction to the newscast was a burst of excitement over a war story—the reporter stood against the wasteland of treadless tanks and recoilless guns in Thailand or Syria or Chile; huts were burning, old women weeping. "Wow-wow! Eeeeeeee! Er-er-er-er," Konrad said. Jane appeared in the kitchen doorway, hands dripping. "What is it, Konrad?" she said. He made a series of violent gestures. "Well?" I asked. She translated: 'Konrad says that 'the pig oppressors' genocidal tactics will lead to their mutual extermination and usher in a new golden age . . .' "—here she hesitated, looked up at him to continue (he was springing up and down on the couch, flailing his fists as though they held whips and scourges)—" '. . . of freedom and equality for all, regardless of race, creed, color—or genus.' I wouldn't worry," she added, "it's just his daily slice of revolutionary rhetoric. He'll calm

3. From "Sailing to Byzantium" by William Butler Yeats (1856–1939), Irish poet.

down in a minute—he likes to play Che,[4] but he's basically nonviolent."

Ten minutes later Jane served dinner. Konrad, with remarkable speed and coordination, consumed four cans of fruit cocktail, thirty-two spareribs, half a dozen each of oranges, apples, and pomegranates, two cheeseburgers and three quarts of chocolate malted. In the kitchen, clearing up, I commented to Jane about our guest's prodigious appetite. He was sitting in the other room, listening to *Don Giovanni*,[5] sipping brandy. Jane said that he was a big, active male and that she could attest to his need for so many calories. "How much does he weigh?" I asked. "Stripped," she said, "one eighty-one. When he stands up straight he's four eight and three quarters." I mulled over this information while I scraped away at the dishes, filed them in the dishwasher, neat ranks of blue china. A few moments later I stepped into the living room to observe Jane stroking Konrad's ears, his head in her lap. I stand five seven, one forty-three.

When I returned from work the following day, Jane was gone. Her dresser drawers were bare, the closet empty. There were white rectangles on the wall where her Rousseau[6] reproductions had hung. The top plank of the bookcase was ribbed with the dust-prints of her Edgar Rice Burroughs[7] collection. Her girls' softball trophy, her natural foods cookbook, her oaken cudgel, her moog, her wok: all gone. There were no notes. A pain jabbed at my sternum, tears started in my eyes. I was alone, deserted, friendless. I began to long even for the stink of her. On the pillow in the bedroom I found a fermenting chunk of pineapple. And sobbed.

By the time I thought of the Primate Center the sun was already on the wane. It was dark when I got there. Loose gravel grated beneath my shoes in the parking lot; the flag snapped at the top of its pole; the lights grinned lickerishly from the Center's windows. Inside the lighting was subdued, the building hushed. I began searching through the rooms, opening and slamming doors. The linoleum glowed all the way up the long corridor. At the far end I heard someone whistling "My Old Kentucky Home." It was the janitor. "Howdedo," he said. "Wut kin ah do fo yo at such a inauspicious hour ob de night?"

I was candid with him. "I'm looking for Miss Good."

4. Che Guevara (1928–1967), Cuban revolutionary killed in Bolivia.
5. Opera (1787) by Mozart.
6. Henri Rousseau (1844–1910), French painter.
7. Popular American novelist (1875–1950), author of the Tarzan books.

"Ohhh, she leave bout fo-turdy evy day—sartinly yo should be well apprised ob dat fack."

"I thought she might be working late tonight."

"Noooo, no chance ob dat." He was staring at the floor.

"Mind if I look for myself?"

"Mah good man, ah trusts yo is not intimatin dat ah would diskise de troof . . . far be it fum me to pre-varicate just to proteck a young lady wut run off fum a man dat doan unnerstan her needs nor 'low her to spress de natchrul inclination ob her soul."

At that moment a girlish giggle sounded from down the hall. Jane's girlish giggle. The janitor's right hand spread itself across my chest. 'Ah wooden insinooate mahself in de middle ob a highly sinificant speriment if ah was yo, Jackson," he said, hissing through the gap in his teeth. I pushed by him and started down the corridor. Jane's laugh leaped out again. From the last door on my left. I hurried. Suddenly the Doctor and his wife stepped from the shadows to block the doorway. "Mr. Horne," said the Doctor, arms folded against his chest, "take hold of yourself. We are conducting a series of experiments here that I simply cannot allow you to—"

"A fig for your experiments," I shouted. "I want to speak to my, my—roommate." I could hear the janitor's footsteps behind me. "Get out of my way, Doctor," I said. Mrs. U-Hwak-Lo smiled. I felt panicky. Thought of the Tong Wars. "Is dey a problem here, Doc?" the janitor said, his breath hot on the back of my neck. I broke. Grabbed the Doctor by his elbows, wheeled around and shoved him into the janitor. They went down on thc linoleum like spastic skaters. I applied my shoulder to the door and battered my way in, Mrs. U-Hwak-Lo's shrill in my ear: "You make big missake, Misser!" Inside I found Jane, legs and arms bare, pinching a lab smock across her chest. She looked puzzled at first, then annoyed. She stepped up to me, made some rude gestures in my face. I could hear scrambling in the hallway behind me. Then I saw Konrad—in a pair of baggy BVDs. I grabbed Jane. But Konrad was there in an instant—he hit me like a grill of a Cadillac and I spun across the room, tumbling desks and chairs as I went. I slumped against the chalkboard. The door slammed: Jane was gone. Konrad swelled his chest, swayed toward me, the fluorescent lights hissing overhead, the chalkboard cold against the back of my neck. And I looked up into the black eyes, teeth, fur, rock-ribbed arms.

1974

RON CARLSON

BLAZO

When Burns arrived in Kotzebue,[1] they were shooting the dogs. He'd never been to Alaska before and it seemed without compromise. Weather had kept him in Nome for two days, where he'd seen a saloon fire. He'd been across the street in a shop buying chocolate and bottled water, and the eerie frozen scene mesmerized him. As the flames pulsed from both windows in the sharp wind and the crews sprayed water which caked on the wooden structure instantly as ice, the patrons emerged slowly, their collars up in the weather, drinks in their gloved hands. Burns wasn't drinking. He sipped water and ate chocolate in his hotel room, listening to the wind growl. Then the short hop over to Kotzebue was the roughest flight of his life, the plane pitching and dropping, smacking against the treacherous air. Burns could hear dogs barking in the front hold and they helped. It's a short flight, he thought, and they wouldn't crash with dogs.

In Kotzebue, Burns waited in the small metal terminal until a wizened, leather-faced Inuit came up to him and grinned, showing no teeth, and lifted his suitcase into the back of an orange International pickup. Burns followed the man and got into the truck. The cab was rife with the smell of bourbon and four or five bottles rolled around Burns's feet. The man smiled again, his eyes merry, and drove onto the main road of the village, where they fell behind the sheriff's white truck. There were two men in the back with rifles riding in the cold. Kotzebue was gray under old drifts but the wind had ripped the tops from some of the banks and spread new whiter fans of snow across the road. The high school was letting out and three-wheelers and snow

1. City in northwest Alaska, named for Otto von Kotzebue (1787–1846), navigator who explored the Arctic regions adjacent to the Bering Straits.

machines cruised along the road, both sides, and cut the corners at every crossroad.

Suddenly, the two men in the sheriff's truck stood and raised their rifles, shooting into a field behind the buildings. Each shot twice and then they quickly clambered out of the vehicle as it stopped. One of the men fell to the ice and got back up and followed his partner running into the field.

"What's going on?" Burns asked, but his driver only squinted at him and shook his head slightly. Burns could see the two men standing over a dark form in the snow. He saw one of them shoot again. The man behind the wheel of the sheriff's truck lifted a hand, but Burns's driver did not wave back.

Two streets later, the orange International turned into a narrow off street and stopped in front of an ice-coated trailer. The man unloaded the suitcase and held out four fingers. The way he tapped them made Burns understand.

"Miss Munson will be back at four?"

The man nodded and reached behind Burns and opened the trailer's door. Whiskey, Burns thought, as he watched the man return to the truck and drive off. A thick drift of whiskey moved with the man. As Burns lifted his bag and turned to the iced steps, a black Newfoundland on a chain rose from a doghouse half buried in the snow, shook, and looked up expectantly. It took Burns a moment to recognize the dog, and then he knelt down and ran his hand through the fur. "Molly, you pup," he said. "You grew up." There was a muffled clamor from the roadway and Burns turned to see a passenger fall from a three-wheeler, slide along on his back for ten yards, then climb back on behind the driver. It had begun to snow faintly in the early afternoon, and the tiny dots of frozen snow were sparse in the gloom. Burns scratched the dog again. "Molly," he said. "What happened to Alec?"

In the close warmth of the trailer, Burns again found himself craving food. The cold left him ravenous. In Nome after his daily walks he would fall upon his stash of chocolate like a schoolboy. And now, he barely took time to hang his gear in the small mud room and at the table in the kitchen before he was stuffing the candy into his mouth. It was amusing to be so aware of his body after so many years.

There was a stomping, felt more than heard, and Burns saw light in the entry as the door opened and closed. "Hello!" a man's voice called, and a large bearded man in a blue military parka came into the kitchen, pulling off his glove and extending a hand to Burns. "You picked one hell of a week," the man said, shaking Burns's hand. "Glen Batton. I'm the Forest Service here, and," he added in another tone, "a friend of Julie's."

Burns said his name and Glen Batton went ahead with the weather report about a new Siberian front moving in. "If it cleared, I'd fly you out to Kolvik myself. As is, you'll be lucky to get down to the Co-op for candy." Batton pointed to the candy wrappers on the table. "I'm sorry about your son."

Burns nodded.

"You're from Connecticut."

"Yes. Connecticut."

Glen Batton put his glove back on. "Well, listen, I just wanted to introduce myself and offer my services, though that may be useless. How long are you here?"

"I'm not sure," Burns said. "I need to get out to Kolvik."

"Well, you won't do that," Glen said, moving back to the door. "But have a nice visit. I'll probably see you Friday at the hospital party."

"Why are the police shooting the dogs?"

"Strays," Batton said. "Too many loose dogs raising hell with the teams. Count the dogs in this town sometime." He turned to leave, but came back into the room. "Hey, listen. You may need to know a couple of things." Batton brushed the parka hood off his long hair, "Look, what happened to Alec is a bad deal, but it happens all the time. People don't understand this country. They think they can handle it, but you can't handle it."

"I see," Burns said.

"And I should tell you this." Glen Batton looked quickly away and back. "Julie is a little fragile about this whole deal. Your visit a year after it all happened. We've talked about it. I don't know what your plans are, but you may want to step lightly."

"I will."

"If it gets tight, you can always bunk with me or at the hotel."

"Thank you. I'll remember that," Burns said, holding Glen's look until the bearded man turned and left. Now he wanted a drink, blood sugar or no blood sugar; Burns could feel the call in his gut, his heartbeat, the roof of his mouth. He went to the sink and drew and drank three glasses of water.

Burns heard a fuss outside and then the clatter of claws on the linoleum of the entry and the Newfoundland came bounding in and burrowed his nose into Burns's hand where it hung beside the easy chair in which he slept. He had sat down to read in the small living room and sleep had taken him like an irrefutable force. Now a woman appeared in the entrance, and that was Burns's first thought: She's not a girl. He had last seen his son Alec six years ago when he had graduated college in New Haven. Burns had expected his wife to be a girl.

Julie removed her knee-length lavender parka and the white knit cap and shook her hair, smiling at him. Without meaning to, Burns stared frankly at her in her white nurse's dress. It was the first surprise he'd had since he'd been in Alaska: Julie was a woman, a tall woman with pale blond hair that fell below her shoulders. He stood and took her hand.

"What are you smiling at?" she said, and smiled. "Sit down, Tom. I'm going to call you Tom, okay? I'm glad you're here. How was your flight?" Burns felt things shifting. First all the hunger, and then the nap taking him like a kid, and now this woman in white.

"I fell asleep," he said. "Sorry."

"It's too warm in here." Julie went to the thermostat. "That's the one thing about Alaska. It's too warm all the time. There's no such thing as a little cold. They keep the hospital at eighty degrees. It reminds me of Manhattan that way." She sat on the couch and took off her shoes. "Alec talked about you quite a lot. And so did Helen, but you're quite different than I pictured."

"Oh?"

She stood up, her dress rustling. "You want a drink?"

"Water's fine."

"That's right. I knew that. Sorry." Burns watched her splash some Wild Turkey into a plastic tumbler. "Okay, I'll be right back. I've got to get these stockings off. Yes, from Helen I imagined you'd be a bit wrecked or frumpy, you know, dirty overcoat, greasy hair."

"Bottle of tokay?"

"I'm kidding, but your ex-wife can be a bit severe."

"Helen is a woman with a memory."

Julie went down a short hallway where Burns could see the edge of a bed. When he saw her dress fall upon the bed, he stood and moved to the kitchen sink, poured a glass of water, and tried to see out the frosted window. He felt agitated. He pressed the glass against his lip. He was deeply hungry again and he felt funny about falling asleep. Napping wasn't his custom, but the sweet closed warmth of the trailer and the wind heaving at the structure, rocking it faintly, had just taken him. He had been doing things by will for ten years now, since the first week after his forty-second birthday, and he was known as a measured man who had placed the remaining components of his life back together purposefully. He was a man who didn't feel things instantly, and now there was this person, Julie, whom he instantly felt quite wonderful about, and suddenly his mission seemed strange and he felt far from home.

She returned in a worn pair of brown corduroys and a simple white turtleneck. His room was at the other end of the trailer, and as she laid out some towels, Burns couldn't take his eyes from her.

"Blazo picked you up all right?" she said.

"The talkative soul? The whiskey person?"

As she moved about the room, showing him the bureau and the electric blanket control and the closet, he studied her long arms, her wristwatch, her short unpolished fingernails, the small gold necklace, the rise of her collarbones under the fabric of her pullover.

"He can't talk. He drank some heating fuel years ago. Blazo. He drank some Blazo and doesn't talk, but he's a gem. He is the mechanic to trust in this village."

Julie had pale green eyes and a faint spray of freckles across her nose and forehead. Burns put her at about thirty. He felt like a teenager sneaking looks at her breasts. He hadn't seen a woman in a turtleneck sweater for twenty years. There was an angry red scar on her neck protuding from her shirt, which stunned him at first, and then he realized it was a violin mark. Alec had had one.

Burns heard two concussions from outside and then two more, the distant snapping of gunfire. He held on to the sink and felt the wind pull at the trailer and he thought: Don't touch her. Don't you touch this woman.

For dinner Julie had a white cloth on the kitchen table and Burns tried to eat slowly. "I appreciate your putting me up like this," he said. "I'm genuinely sorry we haven't met until now."

"Tom, don't start apologizing. I mean it. This is Alaska, there isn't room." Julie looked at him squarely. "I understand about the wedding and Alec did too. Believe me. And you were right not to come. It was Helen's show really." She sipped her bourbon, then lifted a finger from the rim and pointed at him. "I'm not kidding."

"I just want to see where he lived out there, where he . . . I missed so much, and now I just want to see what it's like here."

"This is what it's like, dark and windy, lots of accidents."

"I spoke with Helen before I came and she simply wanted you to know that she would love to hear from you and that if you ever needed anything she would help. She was quite sincere."

Julie placed her glass carefully on the table. "I know. We've spoken about the funeral. He wasn't my husband anymore, of course. We were only married the one year. And I hadn't seen him for months. I tried to handle everything I could at this end, but I couldn't go down to the states and get all involved in a world which wasn't there anymore. You went out?"

"I did," Burns said. "I finally went to something."

Burns ate slowly, his hunger a fire that had him on the edge of his chair. He felt oddly alert. "Who found Alec?"

"Glen reported the cabin burn on his return from a caribou count, and the Search and Rescue went out from here. You can see Lloyd tomorrow, the sheriff. It was his men."

They were quiet for a while, Burns eating and watching Molly, chin down on the living-room rug, watch him. All of these things had happened, Alec's wedding, divorce, death, in half a dog's life.

"So, you're Thomas Burns," Julie said, smiling again. "It is just a little weird to see you."

"That's the way everybody seems to be taking it."

"Well, Glen is convinced you're a cop." She pointed at his clean plate. "Still hungry?"

"No," he lied. He stood and set his dishes in the sink. "Is there need for a cop?"

She joined him at the counter and spoke softly. "No. It's an unhappy story, but we've got all the cops we need." She stopped him from clearing the table. "Come on, I'd better take you down to the Tahoe before my students get here. All visitors go to the Tahoe. The largest bar in the Arctic Circle. Even though you don't drink, it's a good walk, and next week in Darien, you can say you've seen it once, tell stories."

Outside in the heavy wind, Burns and Julie shuffled along the hard snowpacked roadway. The dark was gashed by several flaring arc lights above the armory and the high school, new brick buildings built with the first oil surplus money. Several vehicles passed them at close range, snow machines and three-wheelers bulleting by, and as Burns shied from them, he bumped Julie several times, saying, "Sorry, I'm not used to this."

"It's all right. They're not either," she said, pointing to the way the small vehicles cut the corners at every intersection, their paths running across open yards and slicing very close to the buildings. The drivers wouldn't slow down at all around these shortcuts. Burns cringed watching them disappear. They'll be killed, he thought. They'll crash head-on with someone coming the other way and be killed. He and Julie didn't speak in the pressure of the cold. They stopped several times to pick things from the roadway: a scarf, a big leather mitten, and at the corner where they turned for the bar, a loaf of bread, still soft. He found such litter alarming, but Julie only smiled and told him simply, "Bring it along."

The Tahoe was a large metal building which looked like a one-story warehouse. Julie led him up the iced steps and across the wide porch into the big barroom. Inside the door, in the dark, one booth was stacked high with miscellaneous gear: sweaters, hats, and gloves. Julie told him, "Put your treasures right there. It's the lost and found." The vast room was gloomy and crowded. As Burns's eyes adjusted, he saw that the booths were full of Inuit, and though the room was warm and redolent of cigarettes and fur, few people had taken their coats off.

"What would you like?" Julie said.

"I'd like a vanilla shake," Burns said. "This country has got me starved. But I'll take a soda water, anything really."

It was not an animated bar. Burns could see four school board members who were on his flight standing at the bar, talking, but they were the loudest group. The dark clusters of natives huddled around the tables and booths in the room spoke quietly if at all. Even the pool players moved with a kind of lethargy. Burns stood by the end of the bar, his stomach growling as he thawed. He'd been in lots of bars and this was possibly the largest. In the old days, after martinis at his club, he'd hit every hole in the wall on the way to Grand Central, eventually taking the last train to Connecticut, the ride as cloudy and smeared as the windows. He hadn't been a sloppy drunk; he'd been a careful drunk. The word was "serious"—for everything he'd done, really. He was a serious young man, who had married seriously and become a serious attorney, who drank seriously and became a serious drunk. The mistakes he made were serious and now, in the Arctic Circle, he thought of himself in the Tahoe as a serious visitor on a serious mission who did not drink and took his not drinking seriously. He knew how he was perceived and it was a kind of comfort for Burns to have the word to hold on to.

"Welcome to Alaska," Julie said, handing him a glass of sparkling water. "There are no limes." She touched his glass with her own.

"I'd worry if there were."

"You don't drink," she said, sipping her whiskey. "Smart man."

"No. Alec I'm sure told you. I got smart a little late." He sucked on his lip and nodded at her. "I've missed a lot. I'm an *old* man."

"Not quite." She smiled and touched his glass again. "And it is a world of accidents, believe me. Someone just dropped the bread, right? And on the way home we'll find the peanut butter. Lots of things get dropped." She looked at his face appraisingly. "You're still a smart man." Julie waved a hand out over the room. "How do you like the Tahoe, the hub of culture on the frontier?"

"It's big. I spent a lot of time having stronger drinks in smaller places."

"You're a lawyer."

"I am. I was a good lawyer years ago. Now I'm simply highly paid: probate on the Gold Coast. Did Alec say he'd forgiven me for it?"

"Alec always spoke of you in the best terms. You taught him how to sail?"

"One summer a long time ago. I wasn't around much."

Someone, a figure, fell out of a booth across the room and two tablemates stood and lifted the person back into place.

"Will you stay here?" Burns asked her. "In Kotzebue?"

"I'm a nurse. There's a lot of call for that here. I've got a life—and I've got my students."

The walk back to the trailer again awakened in Burns a huge hunger. He had the same feeling he always had when he spoke of his past, honest and diminished, but now he mainly felt hungry. The wind was in their faces and they leaned against it, talking, while Burns felt the chocolate bar in his pocket. Julie spoke of meeting his son their year at Juilliard. "I wasn't their kind of musician," she said, punching the words into the wind. "I was lucky. I'd been lucky with the competitions really. And I didn't really care for all the work. It was nonstop." They could hear dogs barking out in the fields where the teams were staked. Julie took his arm and turned into the narrow, icy lane where her trailer stood. "I like to play—I teach and I still play—but at Juilliard, well," she faced him in the cold dark, her face luminous, "too many *artists.*"

Inside the trailer, Julie's three students plucked at violin strings tuning their instruments. She introduced them to Burns: Tara, Mercy, and Calvin, native kids all about twelve. They sat serious and straight-backed in the living room for the lesson while Julie began leading them through the half hour's exercises. Calvin's eyes kept going sideways to Burns, and Burns could see they were all self-conscious, so he stood and started for his room. Julie stopped and came to him. "Can I get you anything?"

"No, thank you," he said. Taking off his coat had made him impossibly tired. "I'll see you in the morning."

As he climbed into bed he could hear the sliding harmonies of the four violins rise and fall. Alec had started the violin when he was six, the year Helen had taken him and gone back to Ohio, and years later when Alec finished Juilliard, he had gone to Alaska to teach. Burns had never contacted his son when he was studying in New York. In those days guilt had slowed everything Burns did. He had moved his practice to Connecticut by then, and three times Burns had taken the train into the city and walked by the music school, slowing enough to hear the strains of piano or French horn from a window. And then as if scolded by the music, he hurried away. He couldn't cross the street and go in. Now Burns cringed at his cowardice.

Under the heavy blankets in his room, as the wind moaned over the trailer, Burns listened to the violins. He'd eaten his chocolate and was tired to his bones. He could feel the structure moving in the weight of the gusts. It was like being aboard ship.

Later he had heard voices, their timbre, something almost angry, and then he felt the door shut, and the rushing quiet took him again.

Burns woke in the bright morning and heard the white wind. He was disappointed as he wiped at the frost on the inside of his window to see the storm outside, but there was something else: all this weather. He liked this odd place, big on the earth and full of weather. He'd had the same feeling on certain days sailing off St. Johns: the ocean could be a big, unknowable thing there, indifferent to anybody's plans.

Julie had left him a map on the table, a pencil grid of the village with arrows to the sheriff's office and his phone number. At the bottom it said, "I'll be back at five—and then I'd better take you to the hospital party, so everyone can meet the mystery man. It's at seven. J." Beside it was a large sweet roll, which Burns wolfed down with a mug of the cold powdered milk from the fridge. Standing there in his pajamas in the kitchen drinking the thick, cold milk, Burns grinned. He felt like a kid. He was grinning. Powdered milk was better than he had imagined.

Outside, marching sidelong into the killer wind, Burns felt the cold only in his exposed forehead and then not as cold, but as a constriction, a tight band of pain. He walked with his head turned for protection into his parka hood, and the drivers of the snow machines who roared past also drove with their heads turned. It made him stop and move aside several times. He saw several more mittens in the snow, but didn't pick them up. The day, the world, was all wind, even the rustle of his coat was lost in the gale.

The sheriff's office was two long blocks past the Tahoe in a small complex of state and federal buildings, one-story brick cottages linked by covered walkways. The sheriff was waiting for him, but after they shook hands, Burns had to sit down for a moment and rub his forehead while the aching subsided. He'd sat behind his own desk just like this, rubbing his head, unable to talk to some client as a low wave of nausea rinsed through. In those days, while he tried to poison himself with it, drinking pernicious amounts of gin every night, his clients never knew, his business never quivered. When he went down, they didn't find him for a week, and when Helen came to the hospital, she simply said to stop it, that she was fine and would be, but that killing himself would make it worse for everyone. "You've broken me," she said. "I'm taking the baby and going home." And that was that. He was two weeks in the hospital, having almost lost toes to frostbite, and when he came out, he moved the office to New Canaan, dropped everything but probate, and knew—essentially—and this had nothing to do with the drinking—that his life was over. Helen had already taken Alec back to Ohio, where her mother had lived, and a few years later she married Charley, an attorney in Chagrin Falls.

The sheriff's name was Lloyd Right, a man all in khaki, whom Burns liked right away. "Mr. Burns," he said, taking Burns's coat and pointing out the easy chair, "now tell me exactly the objectives of your visit to the frozen north."

He nodded through the tale, his jaw in his fist, and then when Burns finished, Lloyd Right stood and went to the three-drawer file in the corner and pulled out a folder. "It doesn't appear as if Glen Batton or anybody else is going to be able to lift you out there." Right went back to his desk and sat down; placing the folder squarely in front of him. "This weather has been tight for a week, and it's a pity, not that there's much to see, but I understand too well the importance of just being at the scene." Right dialed the phone and then hung up. It rang and he picked up and said, "Jerry, bring us two coffees." He looked at Burns. "You want some coffee, don't you?"

"I do."

"Anyway, Julie told me about you and about Alec's mother. These things are always bad. What I can do for you is tell you what I know, let you read the file. It was an accident, you can tell his mother that. We don't have any photos. But Julie had been by his place and she can describe it to you. You could tell the family that you went out there, that—"

"No, I couldn't," Burns said. "I couldn't do that. You understand. I am the family. I could tell Alec's mother I was here and saw this file and that I spoke to you."

The deputy came in with the coffee, setting the two mugs on the sheriff's desk and backing out. While the office door was open, another officer came in, the cold on him like an odor, a rifle in his hand. "Lloyd, they've seen the stray out at the foothills. You coming?"

"Take Bob. Call me in half an hour," Right said. When the men had left, the sheriff sipped his coffee. "We've got one goddam stray left, and he's a smart one. What a lone dog can do to a staked team. You don't want to see it. Some of our teams are worth thousands; two teams are going down for the Iditarod[2] next month. Do they hear about the Iditarod in Connecticut, Mr. Burns?"

---

2. Sled dog competition.

"They do," Burns said. "You don't think I can get out to Kolvik?"
"I don't. It's too bad. I've been in the site. Alec lived about two miles from the village, south, in the low hills. The cabin had been totally consumed." The sheriff stood and came around his metal desk, sitting on the edge of the short bookshelf near Burns. "You know, even before he left here, something had happened to Alec," he said. "He had a breakdown or something. This is not in the report. But he began acting strange. You can ask Julie about it. We were sorry about it here. What he had done for the music program in the high school in two years was wonderful, and when he dropped out and moved out there sixty miles, well, everybody felt bad. But we see this kind of thing here. A guy moves out and then further out and moves, if he can, to what he sees as the end of the road, the edge, and either he lives there or he doesn't, but he doesn't come back."

Lloyd Right went back and sat behind his desk, working his closed eyes with his fingers for a moment. He went on, "You figure it. He was a fine musician. So, he moves out to Kolvik and starts a trapline. It was just above the cabin in a draw. That's where they found the body. It was a classic case of freezing to death, I mean, he'd taken off his clothes and they were scattered around. It's very common, Mr. Burns, and I would think it's important that you know this was an accident, not suicide. He misjudged the time and was out too long." Lloyd Right stood again and drained his coffee. "We found the dog out there with him. Julie has her."

On the way home, Burns felt his mouth dry with hunger and he went into the small Co-op and bought a bag of chocolate bars. Outside a man had fallen on the steps and Burns and a woman helped the man climb back up. Burns took the back street to Julie's, the wind now pushing him along the pathway. There were fewer close calls with snow machines here, and he ate the candy and walked slowly, his hands thrust deeply into his parka pockets. Then a strange thing happened that scared him so badly he involuntarily ducked and nearly fell. At first Burns thought something had hit him, but then he saw the light change, a sunflash that settled on the village for a second dropping thick blue shadows on the sides of things. It was painfully bright. The sun was out. In the sky Burns could see the contours of individual clouds. Stay there, he thought. Just stay there.

The party that night was held in the hospital recreation room, a small square room lined with blue vinyl couches. The hospital was obviously an old wooden military building that had been superficially redone. There was a new checkerboard linoleum floor, but wooden-framed windows lined each wall. Julie took Burns by the arm and they went around to everybody in the room, thirty or so people: Julie's head nurse, Karen; Lloyd Right and his wife; both deputies; several nurses and two doctors (both women); Glen Batton; the high school principal and his wife; a dozen teachers there; the school board members whom Burns recognized from his flight; a social counselor named Victor (the only Inuit at the party); some guys from the National Guard; and part of the airport staff. Burns wasn't very comfortable. He'd slept all afternoon and his feet hurt and his face felt swollen. But he was keen, too, because the weather had changed—there was talk of a clearing. Jets were coming in from Nome tomorrow.

He stood by the buffet table and ate strips of the salty ham while he filled a small paper plate with deviled eggs. He felt a bit foolish, but he could not move away from the buffet table, eating handfuls of the chips and dip and mixed nuts, nodding at people with his mouth full, smiling, absolutely out of control. When one of the airport personnel came up and said, "So, you're not a cop," Burns just smiled at him too and shook his head, popping another of the tangy eggs into his mouth.

There was a slide show. One of the nurses had been in the Grand Canyon the past summer and showed slides of her river trip. They were good slides, not professional, but full of steep purple rock and shadow. Burns stood behind the couches during the presentation, eating carrot sticks and drinking 7UP, and the Grand Canyon on the hospital wall, the foaming brown river, the two huge yellow rafts, and the travelers in their bikinis and sunglasses all gave him a kind of spin and he finally stopped eating and sat down.

"You're from Connecticut," a woman next to him said. It was Karen, the chief nurse. In the near-dark he saw that she was about his age, a brunette with an aquiline nose, like a pretty schoolteacher.

"Yes, I am," he said. The slide changed and everybody laughed: four naked people holding hands ran toward the river.

"Which one is you, Leslie?" Glen Batton said.

"Dream on, Glen," the projectionist said.

The woman next to Burns, Karen, whispered, "Before we were transferred, we lived in New London for ten years."

Lake Mead appeared as a blue plate under a pale sky. It was the first slide that had a horizontal theme and then the lights clicked on and there was applause. "This year," Leslie said to the group, "we're going to the Everglades and the Keys."

Glen Batton, who had been sitting with Julie, said, "Well, keep your clothes on around the alligators, Leslie."

"That wasn't me."

"Don't listen to him," Julie said. "He's been in Alaska too long."

People were standing up and moving the couches against the walls now, and suddenly the lights went down and a tape began to play a Beatles song that Burns knew, but didn't know the name of, and three couples began to dance. Burns went to the window and holding his hand against the pane, he saw the stars.

"The weather's clearing for a spell." One of the deputies had come up to him.

Burns looked at the man. "Did you find that dog?"

"Not today, but we will."

"How often do you have to do this?"

"Not twice a year. Usually just spring. A lot of dogs are let loose. It's a bad deal."

"Come here," a man said from behind him, taking his arm. It was the counselor, the Inuit, Victor. "I'll show you something." He led Burns past Karen and down the hallway and out the side door into the cold. "Check this." The man pointed over the roof where Burns saw a finger of yellow light run up the sky and fade followed by two pale pink ones that shifted like something seen through a depth of water.

"I've never seen them before," Burns said to the man. His breath rose as white mist.

The man smiled. "Alec hadn't either," he said. "I'm sorry for what happened. He was related to you?"

"He was my son." Now a greenish white washed up the sky and flared in sections as if cooling.

"He was too smart for this place," the man said.

"What do you mean?"

"What would keep him here? All the white guys with their dog teams? Alec was a genius, right? He must be what a genius is."

"Possibly," Burns said. The cold had gone through him and become a pressure in his neck. Now the pink was back, shooting like a crazy beacon into the black.

"You're staying with Julie?"

"Yes," Burns answered, and alerted by something in Victor's voice he added, "Why?"

"Nothing," Victor said, looking up, his hands thrust deep in his pockets. "I could never figure them. Alec and her."

"I see," Burns said. For a moment the sky was black. "She's so . . ." Burns opened the sentence hoping the other man would finish it. He wanted this information.

"I don't know. I shouldn't talk. You'll see that not much up here is what it seems, but they didn't fit. She's too sociable. Maybe that's what I mean."

Suddenly a canopy of blue light came up the sky and then shredded and disappeared.

Someone took Burns's arm and he felt a body next to him. "Aren't you freezing?" Karen said. She shivered against him, hugging his arm with both hands. "It's twenty below." Burns put his arm out and around the woman.

"Do you know what happened to him?" he said to Victor.

"I don't. I took him hunting once, his first year here, before he moved out. He was good people. I never saw somebody so swept away by this place. He loved it all. He was an intense guy all around."

Karen shifted her position, running her arms around Burns's middle and burying her head in his shoulder. "It's cold!" she said, laughing. The night continued to convulse above them, a huge panorama revolving across the horizon. The sharp dry cold sized Burns's skin, his face. The food and the slides were all gone. He was awake.

"What's the weather tomorrow, Victor? Could a person fly somewhere?"

"We'll get one day," Victor said. "Tomorrow you could fly anywhere you want."

Inside, Karen kept his arm, the cold now real in the warm room. Most of the people at the party were dancing, and Burns saw Glen Batton and Julie moving slowly to the music, another song he knew but couldn't identify. He didn't know the name of five songs in the world. It was a wonder to him; he didn't know any songs.

Karen asked him if he wanted to dance and he smiled and said he had to go. She led him back to the coats, which were in the dark entry hall. She handed him his parka, and the way she looked at him, frankly, without any real pity, led him to do something he hadn't done in ten years. He leaned to her and put his free hand around her back and kissed her. She embraced him fully, but without anything frantic, and the dark of the hall and the smell of the coats made him feel like a boy again and now too he was full of resolve about tomorrow as he held her there, lifting her against him. He liked feeling her body and she shifted twice against him, moving so their legs were interwoven, and he heard her moan in the shifting coats, and he did not let go. Then he heard his name. Glen was saying his name.

"Excuse me," Glen said, coming down the dark hallway. They had disengaged by the time he spoke again. "Julie asked me to tell you that I'm willing to take you out to Kolvik tomorrow." Glen was looking at Karen. "The weather's supposed to clear."

"I appreciate that," Burns said. "Are you sure?"

"The weather is going to be splendid." Julie had come up behind him. She saw Burns putting on his coat. "Where are you going?"

"I thought I'd get some rest. Deviled eggs, the Grand Canyon, the northern lights . . . this is a lot for an old man."

"He'd never seen the lights before," Karen said, squeezing Burns's arm.

"Here," Julie said, taking his arm from Karen. "I'll go with you."

"No, please," he said. "I know the way. Please. Stay."

Julie retrieved her coat and pushed Glen back to the party. Karen stood around until she saw that Julie was serious about leaving, and then she took both of Burns's hands and reached up and kissed him quickly, drifting back to the party herself. As he opened the door for Julie and pushed out into the white night, Burns saw Batton watching them.

The night was now still, the first stillness Burns had felt in Alaska, and he felt the weight of the profound chill, the northern sky fringed with erratic blooming light. "Her husband ran the armory here," Julie said. "He was killed loading freight two years ago."

"She stayed."

Julie looked at him. "People stay," she said. "You come out, you don't go back." Julie held his arm all along the crunching snowy road and they didn't speak further, but fell into step like the oldest of friends, and Burns let the night and the cold disappear and he imagined that she was thinking what he was thinking: that tomorrow he would see where Alec died.

At Julie's trailer, the lights were on and two little boys sat at the kitchen table in their stocking feet drawing with crayons. "Well, hello, Timmo," Julie said. "How are you?" Neither boy looked up, but Burns could see their eyes looking around. "Is this your cousin?"

Timmo nodded.

"Well, good. What's he drawing?" The cousin turned his paper a bit so Julie could see the two figures on the sheet. Burns looked at the two brown smudges. The boy traced a line from one to the other. "This is you shooting a caribou, isn't it," Julie said. "And it is very good." The boys smiled to each other. Julie opened the cupboard and put out a plate of graham crackers and poured two glasses of milk. "Now, Timmo," she said, looking at her watch, "at eleven, you must go home." She looked up at Burns. "This is Timmo and his cousin No Name." At this the boys giggled. "Timmo is an artist who comes over some nights. His mother is in the Tahoe." Burns stood there in his coat. He wanted one of the crackers. He wanted them all. He smiled at the beautiful native boys. What a day. He had been warm and cold and hungry. This was all so new.

Julie took her coat off and came over to him. "We'd better go to bed," she said. "You've got a big day ahead, and if we don't leave the room, they'll never eat the crackers."

The next afternoon, in the low white angle of sunlight, Burns walked out to Glen Batton's place, a trailer behind the Forest Service buildings. The light was terrific, knifing at Burns, and he squinted behind his sunglasses.

In the small yard he slipped and fell, and climbing awkwardly back up, saw that he had stumbled across the hindquarters of a caribou lying in the snow. "That's the freezer up here," Glen Batton said from the doorway. "Fresh meat all winter. Hop in the truck, I'll be right there."

Batton seemed in a good mood, quite happy to show Burns all he knew about the small airplane, which was tethered—along with a dozen others—out on the frozen sea. A runway had been freshly bladed through the drifts along the waterfront, and Batton talked Burns through all the preparations he made, taking off the heavy insulated blanket over the motor, checking the oil, freeing the flaps. He had Burns help him push the plane forward a foot, cracking the icy seal between the skis and the snowpack. He opened the passenger door and pointed out the emergency gear under the seat, the food, the cross-country skis, and then he pointed to a small orange box in the back of the small cargo space and said, "Don't worry about that, Mr. Burns. That will start signaling on impact."

And Glen was chatty on the way over to Kolvik, talking to Burns—over the intercom—about his work with the Forest Service. They flew up the river in the sunshine, Batton pointing out the moose and caribou. He explained that for the caribou counts he usually took one of the secretaries and that Julie didn't like that. "Did you ever have a spat with your wife, Mr. Burns?"

"A spat?"

"You know, where she's jealous over something you're doing, although you're totally innocent."

"I guess, sometimes," Burns said, his voice distant on the intercom, sounding small, like what it was: a lie. Helen had never fought with him, never complained. She had been a sweet, happy, confident woman who had—even in their extremity—never fought with him.

"Yeah, well, Julie . . ." Batton said. "That's why she left last night and went home early with you." Batton pointed ahead, where a small herd of caribou moved across the frozen river. "What am I going to do, land out there and screw Denise?"

A haze had come up, like bright smoke, and the plane rippled across the changing sky. Burns was concentrating, trying to see the country as Alec might have seen it.

"We take a lunch and stop for lunch," Glen Batton went on. "But that's lunch. People eat lunch. Right?"

The rest of the flight was different from what Burns could have foreseen. He couldn't get Glen to put down in Kolvik. They came upon the small toss of cabins which was Kolvik and Burns's heart lifted, but then it all changed quickly. There was no strip near the small village, of course, and Glen explained that it wasn't safe to land in the snow so soon after the recent storms. He made one pass by the clearing near where Alec's cabin had been and laid down a pair of tracks with the skis, but then circling he explained to Burns—through the noisy intercom—that it was too soft, too dangerous. Shoulder to shoulder with Glen Batton in the front seat of the smallest plane he'd ever been in, Burns asked again if they couldn't possibly try to land.

"No can do, Mr. Burns," Batton said, his voice tiny through the receiver, sounding miles away. "Too deep, too soft. No one else has been out either. That's where he lived"—Batton dipped the passenger wing steeply and pointed—"below that hill." There was no sign of anything in the perfect snow. They made one more broad circle over the area, seeing several moose in the valley where Alec supposedly had trapped, and then they headed west toward home. Burns felt the little plane rattle in the new headwind, the door flexing against his knee more than it had for the flight out, and he felt a disappointment that replaced hunger in his gut. He'd been so close. He could have jumped from the plane and landed in the drift. From the air, the place where his son lived had looked like all the other terrain they'd seen: snowy hills grown with small pine. Alaska gave up its stories hard. He'd learned nothing.

They had flown quite low on the way out, but now Glen was taking the plane up to three and then four thousand feet. The sun was obscured in the west in a thick roseate mist. Burns was silent, mad at first, feeling cheated, and then resolved simply on what he now knew: he would ask Blazo.

"You spoke to the sheriff," Batton said.

"I did." Even Burns's own voice sounded remote on the intercom. "He was a help."

"And now you've been to Kolvik."

"Not quite, Glen. I've flown over it."

Batton ignored him, resetting some instruments, finally saying, "Did you ever see Russia?"

"I never have."

Batton leveled the plane at five thousand feet and turned it slightly, squinting through the windshield. "You know, it's funny your being here. I wouldn't have walked across the street for my old man and here you've come all the way north to see where your kid died." Burns said nothing. "There." Glen Batton pointed at a faint solid form below the sunset. "That line. That's Russia."

Burns could see the landfall that Batton had indicated, dark and vague beneath the fading rosy dusk, and as the little aircraft was bumped and lifted, he could sense the curvature of the earth from this height. Flying into the lost light made him feel again the sorrow he'd lived by for so long. The little plane descended in rocky strokes, lurching and gliding through the darkening frigid night. The men did not speak, but when the lights of Kotzebue glimmered on the horizon, a settlement in the void, Glen Batton spoke to the airport and then said to Burns: "Look. I know he was your son and he was a good kid, but the end was no good. He was a pain in the ass for everybody. Nearly drove Julie crazy."

Burns just listened. He wasn't mad anymore. He didn't want to argue. The lights of the village grew distinct and Batton circled out over the frozen ocean showing the town as a sweet Christmas decoration, a model, the pools of lamplight on the snowpacked streets.

"And now you're here, starting it all up again. You ought to get the flight to Anchorage tomorrow before this next weather really hits, and let Julie get on with her life."

Burns could see an orange bonfire on the hill at the edge of town and the dark forms of sleds descended the slope. Batton banked sharply, moving for the first time all day with an undue haste, and then leveled, and as the icy runway approached Burns felt the bottom drop out. The plane dipped suddenly, wrenching him up against his seat belt, where he floated for a second before slamming down. His head hit the windscreen and the edge of the console and then he felt the plane riding hard on the ridged ice, shaking him to the spine.

Batton ran the plane to the end of the runway and then wheeled it around to the tie-downs. "Sorry about that," he said. "It's always a little rough, but we hit her pretty hard that time."

Burns's hand was in the blood on his hairline and he could feel the welt rising where his forehead was split.

"You okay?" Batton asked, turning off the plane and climbing down.

"What'd you do to him, Glen? What did you do to Alec?"

With the earphones off everything sounded flat. Batton was fastening the fixed cables to each wing. Burns opened his door and jumped down onto the ice and moved away from the plane. He was dizzy and there seemed to be blood everywhere. Head cuts were like faucets; he'd had plenty playing hockey.

Batton was struggling with the insulation blanket for the engine. "You bleeding?" he said. "Let me see that."

"Were you after Julie before Alec moved?" Burns said.

Batton stopped fastening the snaps on the cover and came around to Burns. It was clear he wanted to hit him. The two men stood between the plane and the pickup on the rough sea ice. "Look," Batton said. "You're a smart guy. Julie said you went to Yale."

"Glen," Burns said, "I didn't come up here for trouble. I came up here to see what Alec saw, something for myself. And now I want to know what you did to him."

Glen came up to Burns and took a handful of his parka shoulder. In the icy light, Burns could see his face, angry and tight, and he felt himself being lifted. He didn't care. He was bleeding. He didn't care what Glen did. Burns saw Batton's eyes flicker over the things he was going to do and then focus on him, "Get in," Glen said finally, letting go of the coat. But Burns backed past the truck and into the dark toward the mounds of ragged plate ice between himself and the village.

Not ten minutes later, Burns found himself on a dark side street disoriented and full of the old dread. He'd just walked and something—the cold, the gash on his head, the iron hardness of the packed roadway, the glimpse of the earth growing dark—had let it all gather in his heart. For years he had thought that the weight of it, the darkest part, was his drinking. He'd wake somewhere sick and feel it around his chest like a cold hand and not be able to swallow. But after he stopped drinking, it didn't lift. It didn't come every day, but when it came as it had tonight, it hit with a force that left him weak.

On their holidays when he and Helen would go to St. Johns, he was drunk by noon, usually, rum was such an easy thing to drink. You could drink it in anything, coffee, juice. You could drink it in milk, for chrissake. You could take warm mouthfuls right from the bottle.

You could drink vodka and bourbon from the bottle too, but not in balmy weather. In the islands it was rum. Manhattan was gin. Airplanes were gin too, the stiff chemical push in the face. Clients were scotch, something that bit and then slid in Burns, he could drink scotch for weeks. He had done it. But his rules were his rules: Manhattan was gin; St. Johns was rum; clients were scotch; and he drank vodka and bourbon those nights when the rules began to float. It was vodka the time he tried to die.

Now Burns felt the goose egg on his forehead. The blood had stopped, but the flesh was too tender to touch. He looked around and couldn't find a landmark. Four or five buildings, warehouses or churches, stood over him. He wasn't sure of the way he'd come and he couldn't tell north from south. He felt drained. He turned around searching for a clue, even a snowbank to sit on, but he could only see how much, how very much, of his own life he had missed.

Between buildings he thought he caught sight of the bonfire on the hill, and then someone took his arm. He looked down at Blazo, his grin showing the missing teeth, a man who by the wrinkles in his brown face could have been a hundred. With a firm grip on Burns's arm, Blazo marched him to the corner, out of the shadows, and pointed at the sledding fire.

"I saw them sledding," Burns said, but Blazo pointed again. A flare of powdery red light rose in the sky and then dissolved as a wave of yellow swelled and faded. "This place," Burns said. He felt dizzy. "These nights. This place is something else." He stepped away from Blazo. "Thanks," he said. "Julie's place is that way, right?"

Blazo nodded. He seemed to be examining Burns's face.

Burns started down the street and then hesitated. "I need to get to Kolvik. Soon. I need to see where Alec Burns lived, where he had a trapline. South of town."

"He was your boy," Blazo said.

Above them, the sky was relentless, the random vast armatures of colored light wheeling up and then vanishing, sometimes printing themselves from nothing on the darkness like bright stains. "He was," Burns whispered. The cold air cut at his nose as he breathed, and he could feel his pulse aching in his wound. "You can talk," Burns said.

"Not really." Blazo quickly pointed down the snowpacked lane, and Burns saw a figure trotting swiftly under the lamplight, a dog, some kind of husky, moving as with purpose. "But we'll go out there," Blazo said. "Tomorrow morning. It's going to snow, but we'll get half a day of good weather."

The trailer was dark. Burns opened the door quietly and heard a strange sound which he then recognized as the violin. He felt the warmth and it made him catch his breath. He almost wept.

As he passed through the mud room without removing his coat, he felt Molly's nose fit into his palm in the dark. His legs were trembling. Julie was playing something sharp, full of energy and angles, it filled the space completely, and Burns saw her as he passed through the living room. She sat on the ottoman in her underwear, playing by the light of two candles. He saw the shine of sweat on her forehead and breastbone, and then he was in his room, suddenly warm himself and pulling at his coat and sweater.

There was a knock at his door, and Julie was there, tying her robe. "Hi," she said. "Sorry about that. . . . What's all this blood?"

"Nothing," he said. He was sitting on the bed. "You play very well."

Julie took his chin in her hand and pulled at the cut with a thumb. "Oh, yes, it's nothing," she said. "Looks like Glen hit you with an ax."

"It was an accident," Burns said quietly. On the warm bed, with his head in a woman's hands, he felt himself letting go. Julie was standing very close. He was a serious and controlled man, and he clenched his jaw, but his eyes welled.

"I'm going to have to stitch this closed, Mr. Tom Burns, or you'll return to the East Coast with a genuine Alaskan tattoo." And in a moment she came back with a warm wet cloth and a small kit. "You want something to eat?"

"No," he said. "I'm all in." He could feel his voice unsteady. "We didn't make it. Glen couldn't land."

Burns leaned back and looked at Julie and he saw her read his face. She stood beside him and put her arm around his neck. Burns held perfectly still. "What are you doing in Alaska? I'm not so sure this is a good idea for you." She began dabbing at his forehead with the cloth.

Then Burns's head began to ache and he could feel her working at the skin with the black thread. He was pulled into the open front of her robe where freckles rose from her cleavage in warm, vertiginous constellations inches from his face and he could smell her skin and the sweet Wild Turkey on her breath. His right ear was full of dried blood and his hearing came and went. He had both of his hands on her hips and he could feel her moving against him, the warmth and pressure of her legs.

"Are you all right," Burns whispered.

He heard her say, "I know what I'm doing."

He had a high hollow feeling and his mouth tasted sweet and dry the way it did before a drunk, and Julie cinched each stitch with three short tugs and this became part of the litany, her shifting breasts, the freckles riding there, his eyes half closed in the warm room, and the steady and expected tug-tug-tug. He ran his hand inside her robe and lifted his face to kiss her. She kissed him back, pausing for a moment to move the dangling needle on its black thread out of their way. She came over onto him on the bed. "Isn't this why you've come?" Her

eyes fixed him as she continued to move with each word: "Isn't it?"
Burns could feel the needle riding in his ear now and Julie lifted it
away. "Watch out for me. I'm not what you think."

"What do I think?"

"You think I'm some coping person. A nurse. Something. I don't
even know anymore what they do in your world, but here we take
comfort where we find it. Glen came after me like a dog in heat. It's
like that, Tom." Julie moved against him and Burns knew she could
feel that he was aroused. "I'm like that."

"No you're not," he said. Even as he heard the words, he realized
he didn't know what he was saying. He'd decided who she was yesterday, standing in her kitchen. The whole journey to Alaska had seemed
mad to him at first, but once he was committed, he'd decided what he
would see. He had written a kind of scenario without knowing it and
now it was coming undone. It was a long moment for Burns, as if he
had dived into the ocean and was waiting to turn and ascend. He was
airless and without will.

Julie had lifted herself and was looking into his eyes, waiting for
something. She looked much older here, harder. When he didn't
move, she said, "You really don't get it, do you."

"What? What is it?" he said to her. "What am I missing? Did Glen
hurt Alec?"

"You're hard to believe, Tom," Julie said, rolling off him and
standing by the bed. "You're too old to be that innocent." She took his
head in her hands once again, but she held it differently. "Yes, Glen
hurt Alec. So did I. So did this place. And probably you did too. Alec
went mad. He did. But when he moved out there, Glen didn't help
him. I know that. They hated each other by then, you can tell that. I
knew he wouldn't land with you. I'm trying to be honest here. What
happened would have happened. Glen didn't kill Alec."

"He didn't save him."

"That's what I'm telling you, Tom." Julie stood back, tugging
sharply at the thread in Burns's forehead, and she looked at him
frankly. "None of us did."

Burns was walking in the snow. So this is where it was, he thought.
He tried to see the valley as Alec might have, and began picking his
way across the meadow. The surface of the snow was crusted and his
snowshoes only cut a few inches with each step. He worked into a
warm rhythm of small steps up the incline, breathing into the gray
afternoon. It was wonderful to move this way after being on the snow
machine all day. The clouds had come down and Burns felt the air
change as he marched. It lifted at him somehow, not a wind but some

quickness that was sharper in his nose, and it grew darker suddenly and he saw the first petals of snow easing down around him.

At the top he turned, breathing hard, and put his hands on his hips to rest. He felt the old high thrill in his chest just like the winter days at Yale, the flasks in the stands at the rink, and crossing campus at midnight wired tight with alcohol, his coat open to the sharp tonic of the air. Now his head was almost against the somber tent of clouds and below him the snow fell as it does at sea, ponderous and invisible at once, disappearing except where it fell on his sleeves, his eyebrows. The snow was falling everywhere.

His knees burned faintly as he stepped along the crest of the hill and descended into the draw where Alec had trapped. Here the small pines were thicker and there were game trails in the snow between the clumps of trees.

The year he quit drinking, that June, he and Alec had sailed from Martha's Vineyard to the Elizabeth Islands and an exhilaration had set in that Burns remembered keenly. Alec had been on loan from Helen. They had anchored off the islands and swum the hundred yards to shore and then lain on the deserted sand, laughing and panting, and the boy had said to him, "This is it, Dad. This is the best day of my life." Burns thought at that time: I am as close to being happy as I will ever be. And he did feel happy, proud to be a good sailing coach and pleased to have captured the Elizabeth Islands on the most beautiful day in the year, but the other thing was always with him. He didn't say it before they stood and began to swim back, but Burns had decided that day to live. He would live.

Halfway up the draw, Burns stopped. This was it. He fell back in the snow, flinging out his arms. He lay there and let his heart pound him deeper. He could hear it crashing in his ears. The pin-dots of snow burned across his forehead, and his arms and legs glowed. Julie was right about Alaska: it was too warm. Burns closed his eyes. This was where Alec died. When he opened them, he stared up into the falling snow until he felt the lift of vertigo. The roaring silence was nicked by a new sound now, the snow machine buzzing closer and then—as he felt the snow fix and himself rise into the sky, weightless—a face appeared above his head.

"Right," he said to Blazo. "I'm coming. One more minute." He caught Blazo's look and added, "Don't worry. I'll get up."

"You and me," Blazo said. "We've been gone a long time already." Blazo's face disappeared, and Burns felt himself again sink into the snow. It was pleasant here, lonely and floating, and Burns stopped trying to sort his thoughts. He was hungry, and pleased to be hungry again. He could feel his feet. His blood seemed very busy. Something had a grip on him. He thought, the world has got ahold of me again. He drew a breath, the air aching in his chest, and he said, "Alec." His voice sounded sure of something. "I've been in the snow here, Alec," he said into the sky. "I've lain on my back in the snow."

1992

■   ■   ■

RAYMOND CARVER

CATHEDRAL

This blind man, an old friend of my wife's, he was on his way to spend the night. His wife had died. So he was visiting the dead wife's relatives in Connecticut. He called my wife from his in-laws'. Arrangements were made. He would come by train, a five-hour trip, and my wife would meet him at the station. She hadn't seen him since she worked for him one summer in Seattle ten years ago. But she and the blind man had kept in touch. They made tapes and mailed them back and forth. I wasn't enthusiastic about his visit. He was no one I knew. And his being blind bothered me. My idea of blindness came from the movies. In the movies, the blind moved slowly and never laughed. Sometimes they were led by seeing-eye dogs. A blind man in my house was not something I looked forward to.

That summer in Seattle she had needed a job. She didn't have any money. The man she was going to marry at the end of the summer was in officers' training school. He didn't have any money, either. But she was in love with the guy, and he was in love with her, etc. She'd seen something in the paper: HELP WANTED—Reading to Blind Man, and a telephone number. She phoned and went over, was hired on the spot. She'd worked with this blind man all summer. She read stuff to him, case studies, reports, that sort of thing. She helped him organize his little office in the county social-service department. They'd become good friends, my wife and the blind man. How do I know these things? She told me. And she told me something else. On her last day in the office, the blind man asked if he could touch her face. She agreed to this. She told me he touched his fingers to every part of her face, her nose—even her neck! She never forgot it. She even tried to write a poem about it. She was always trying to write a poem. She wrote a poem or two every year, usually after something really important had happened to her.

When we first started going out together, she showed me the poem. In the poem, she recalled his fingers and the way they had moved around over her face. In the poem, she talked about what she had felt at the time, about what went through her mind when the blind man touched her nose and lips. I can remember I didn't think much of the poem. Of course, I didn't tell her that. Maybe I just don't understand poetry. I admit it's not the first thing I reach for when I pick up something to read.

Anyway, this man who'd first enjoyed her favors, the officer-to-be, he'd been her childhood sweetheart. So okay. I'm saying that at the end of the summer she let the blind man run his hands over her face, said goodbye to him, married her childhood etc., who was now a commissioned officer, and she moved away from Seattle. But they'd kept in touch, she and the blind man. She made the first contact after a year or so. She called him up one night from an Air Force base in Alabama. She wanted to talk. They talked. He asked her to send him a tape and tell him about her life. She did this. She sent the tape. On the tape, she told the blind man about her husband and about their life together in the military. She told the blind man she loved her husband but she didn't like it where they lived and she didn't like it that he was a part of the military-industrial thing. She told the blind man she'd written a poem about what it was like to be an Air Force officer's wife. The poem wasn't finished yet. She was still writing it. The blind man made a tape. He sent her the tape. She made a tape. This went on for years. My wife's officer was posted to one base and then another. She sent tapes from Moody AFB, McGuire, McConnell, and finally Travis, near Sacramento, where one night she got to feeling lonely and cut off from people she kept losing in that moving-around life. She got to feeling she couldn't go it another step. She went in and swallowed all the pills and capsules in the medicine chest and washed them down with a bottle of gin. Then she got into a hot bath and passed out.

But instead of dying, she got sick. She threw up. Her officer—why should he have a name? he was the childhood sweetheart, and what more does he want?—came home from somewhere, found her, and called the ambulance. In time, she put it all on a tape and sent the tape to the blind man. Over the years, she put all kinds of stuff on tapes and sent the tapes off lickety-split. Next to writing a poem every year, I think it was her chief means of recreation. On one tape, she told the blind man she'd decided to live away from her officer for a time. On another tape, she told him about her divorce. She and I began going out, and of course she told her blind man about it. She told him everything, or so it seemed to me. Once she asked me if I'd like to hear the latest tape from the blind man. This was a year ago. I was on the tape, she said. So I said okay, I'd listen to it. I got us drinks and we settled down in the living room. We made ready to listen. First she inserted the tape into the player and adjusted a couple of dials. Then she pushed a lever. The tape squeaked and someone began to talk in this loud voice. She lowered the volume. After a few minutes of harmless chitchat, I heard my own name in the mouth of this stranger, this blind man I didn't even know! And then this: "From all you've said about him, I can only conclude—" But we were interrupted, a knock at the door, something, and we didn't ever get back to the tape. Maybe it was just as well. I'd heard all I wanted to.

Now this same blind man was coming to sleep in my house.

"Maybe I could take him bowling," I said to my wife. She was at the draining board doing scalloped potatoes. She put down the knife she was using and turned around.

"If you love me," she said, "you can do this for me. If you don't love me, okay. But if you had a friend, any friend, and the friend came to visit, I'd make him feel comfortable." She wiped her hands with the dish towel.

"I don't have any blind friends," I said.

"You don't have *any* friends," she said. "Period. Besides," she said, "goddamn it, his wife's just died! Don't you understand that? The man's lost his wife!"

I didn't answer. She'd told me a little about the blind man's wife. Her name was Beulah. Beulah! That's a name for a colored woman.

"Was his wife a Negro?" I asked.

"Are you crazy?" my wife said. "Have you just flipped or something?" She picked up a potato. I saw it hit the floor, then roll under the stove. "What's wrong with you?" she said. "Are you drunk?"

"I'm just asking," I said.

Right then my wife filled me in with more detail than I cared to know. I made a drink and sat at the kitchen table to listen. Pieces of the story began to fall into place.

Beulah had gone to work for the blind man the summer after my wife had stopped working for him. Pretty soon Beulah and the blind man had themselves a church wedding. It was a little wedding—who'd want to go to such a wedding in the first place?—just the two of them, plus the minister and the minister's wife. But it was a church wedding just the same. It was what Beulah had wanted, he'd said. But even then Beulah must have been carrying the cancer in her glands. After they

had been inseparable for eight years—my wife's word, *inseparable*—
Beulah's health went into a rapid decline. She died in a Seattle hospital room, the blind man sitting beside the bed and holding on to her
hand. They'd married, lived and worked together, slept together—had
sex, sure—and then the blind man had to bury her. All this without
his having ever seen what the goddamned woman looked like. It was
beyond my understanding. Hearing this, I felt sorry for the blind man
for a little bit. And then I found myself thinking what a pitiful life this
woman must have led. Imagine a woman who could never see herself
as she was seen in the eyes of her loved one. A woman who could go
on day after day and never receive the smallest compliment from her
beloved. A woman whose husband could never read the expression on
her face, be it misery or something better. Someone who could wear
makeup or not—what difference to him? She could, if she wanted,
wear green eye-shadow around one eye, a straight pin in her nostril,
yellow slacks and purple shoes, no matter. And then to slip off into
death, the blind man's hand on her hand, his blind eyes streaming
tears—I'm imagining now—her last thought maybe this: that he never
even knew what she looked like, and she on an express to the grave.
Robert was left with a small insurance policy and half of a twenty-peso
Mexican coin. The other half of the coin went into the box with her.
Pathetic.

So when the time rolled around, my wife went to the depot to
pick him up. With nothing to do but wait—sure, I blamed him for
that—I was having a drink and watching the TV when I heard the car
pull into the drive. I got up from the sofa with my drink and went to
the window to have a look.

I saw my wife laughing as she parked the car. I saw her get out of
the car and shut the door. She was still wearing a smile. Just amazing.
She went around to the other side of the car to where the blind man
was already starting to get out. This blind man, feature this, he was
wearing a full beard! A beard on a blind man! Too much, I say. The
blind man reached into the back seat and dragged out a suitcase. My
wife took his arm, shut the car door, and, talking all the way, moved
him down the drive and then up the steps to the front porch. I turned
off the TV. I finished my drink, rinsed the glass, dried my hands. Then
I went to the door.

My wife said, "I want you to meet Robert. Robert, this is my husband. I've told you all about him." She was beaming. She had this
blind man by his coat sleeve.

The blind man let go of his suitcase and up came his hand.

I took it. He squeezed hard, held my hand, and then he let it go.

"I feel like we've already met," he boomed.

"Likewise," I said. I didn't know what else to day. Then I said, "Welcome. I've heard a lot about you." We began to move then, a little group, from the porch into the living room, my wife guiding him by the arm. The blind man was carrying his suitcase in his other hand. My wife said things like, "To your left here, Robert. That's right. Now watch it, there's a chair. That's it. Sit down right here. This is the sofa. We just bought this sofa two weeks ago."

I started to say something about the old sofa. I'd liked that old sofa. But I didn't say anything. Then I wanted to say something else, small-talk, about the scenic ride along the Hudson. How going *to* New York, you should sit on the right-hand side of the train, and coming *from* New York, the left-hand side.

"Did you have a good train ride?" I said. "Which side of the train did you sit on, by the way?"

"What a question, which side!" my wife said. "What's it matter which side?" she said.

"I just asked," I said.

"Right side," the blind man said. "I hadn't been on a train in nearly forty years. Not since I was a kid. With my folks. That's been a long time. I'd nearly forgotten the sensation. I have winter in my beard now," he said. "So I've been told, anyway. Do I look distinguished, my dear?" the blind man said to my wife.

"You look distinguished, Robert," she said. "Robert," she said. "Robert, it's just so good to see you."

My wife finally took her eyes off the blind man and looked at me. I had the feeling she didn't like what she saw. I shrugged.

I've never met, or personally known, anyone who was blind. This blind man was late forties, a heavy set, balding man with stooped shoulders, as if he carried a great weight there. He wore brown slacks, brown shoes, a light-brown shirt, a tie, a sports coat. Spiffy. He also had this full beard. But he didn't use a cane and he didn't wear dark glasses. I'd always thought dark glasses were a must for the blind. Fact was, I wished he had a pair. At first glance, his eyes looked like anyone else's eyes. But if you looked close, there was something different about them. Too much white in the iris, for one thing, and the pupils seemed to move around in the sockets without his knowing it or being able to stop it. Creepy. As I stared at his face, I saw the left pupil turn in toward his nose while the other made an effort to keep in one place. But it was only an effort, for that eye was on the roam without his knowing it or wanting it to be.

I said, "Let me get you a drink. What's your pleasure? We have a little of everything. It's one of our pastimes."

"Bub, I'm a Scotch man myself," he said fast enough in this big voice.

"Right," I said. Bub! "Sure you are. I knew it."

He let his fingers touch his suitcase, which was sitting alongside the sofa. He was taking his bearings. I didn't blame him for that.

"I'll move that up to your room," my wife said.

"No, that's fine," the blind man said loudly. "It can go up when I go up."

"A little water with the Scotch?" I said.

"Very little," he said.

"I knew it," I said.

He said, "Just a tad. The Irish actor, Barry Fitzgerald? I'm like that fellow. When I drink water, Fitzgerald said, I drink water. When I drink whiskey, I drink whiskey." My wife laughed. The blind man brought his hand up under his beard. He lifted his beard slowly and let it drop.

I did the drinks, three big glasses of Scotch with a splash of water in each. Then we made ourselves comfortable and talked about Robert's travels. First the long flight from the West Coast to Connecticut, we covered that. Then from Connecticut up here by train. We had another drink concerning that leg of the trip.

I remembered having read somewhere that the blind didn't smoke because, as speculation had it, they couldn't see the smoke they exhaled. I thought I knew that much and that much only about blind people. But this blind man smoked his cigarette down to the nubbin and then lit another one. This blind man filled his ashtray and my wife emptied it.

When we sat down at the table for dinner, we had another drink. My wife heaped Robert's plate with cube steak, scalloped potatoes, green beans. I buttered him up two slices of bread. I said, "Here's bread and butter for you." I swallowed some of my drink. "Now let us pray," I said, and the blind man lowered his head. My wife looked at me, her mouth agape. "Pray the phone won't ring and the food doesn't get cold," I said.

We dug in. We ate everything there was to eat on the table. We ate like there was no tomorrow. We didn't talk. We ate. We scarfed. We grazed that table. We were into serious eating. The blind man had right away located his foods, he knew just where everything was on his plate. I watched with admiration as he used his knife and fork on the meat. He'd cut two pieces of meat, fork the meat into his mouth, and then go all out for the scalloped potatoes, the beans next, and then he'd tear off a hunk of buttered bread and eat that. He'd follow this up with a big drink of milk. It didn't seem to bother him to use his fingers once in a while, either.

We finished everything, including half a strawberry pie. For a few moments, we sat as if stunned. Sweat beaded on our faces. Finally, we got up from the table and left the dirty plates. We didn't look back. We took ourselves into the living room and sank into our places again. Robert and my wife sat on the sofa. I took the big chair. We had us two or three more drinks while they talked about the major things that had come to pass for them in the past ten years. For the most part, I just listened. Now and then I joined in. I didn't want him to think I'd left the room, and I didn't want her to think I was feeling left out. They talked of things that had happened to them—to them!—these past ten years. I waited in vain to hear my name on my wife's sweet lips: "And then my dear husband came into my life"—something like that. But I heard nothing of the sort. More talk of Robert. Robert had done a little of everything, it seemed, a regular blind jack-of-all-trades. But most recently he and his wife had had an Amway distributorship, from which, I gathered, they'd earned their living, such as it was. The blind man was also a ham radio operator. He talked in his loud voice about conversations he'd had with fellow operators in Guam, in the Philippines, in Alaska, and even in Tahiti. He said he'd have a lot of friends there if he ever wanted to go visit those places. From time to time, he'd turn his blind face toward me, put his hand under his beard, ask me something. How long had I been in my present position? (Three years.) Did I like my work? (I didn't.) Was I going to stay with it? (What were the options?) Finally, when I thought he was beginning to run down, I got up and turned on the TV.

My wife looked at me with irritation. She was heading toward a boil. Then she looked at the blind man and said, "Robert, do you have a TV?"

The blind man said, "My dear, I have two TVs. I have a color set and a black-and-white thing, an old relic. It's funny, but if I turn the TV on, and I'm always turning it on, I turn on the color set. It's funny, don't you think?"

I didn't know what to say to that. I had absolutely nothing to say to that. No opinion. So I watched the news program and tried to listen to what the announcer was saying.

"This is a color TV," the blind man said. "Don't ask me how, but I can tell."

"We traded up a while ago," I said.

The blind man had another taste of his drink. He lifted his beard, sniffed it, and let it fall. He leaned forward on the sofa. He positioned his ashtray on the coffee table, then put the lighter to his cigarette. He leaned back on the sofa and crossed his legs at the ankles.

My wife covered her mouth, and then she yawned. She stretched. She said, "I think I'll go upstairs and put on my robe. I think I'll change into something else. Robert, you make yourself comfortable," she said.

"I'm comfortable," the blind man said.

"I want you to feel comfortable in this house," she said.

"I am comfortable," the blind man said.

After she'd left the room, he and I listened to the weather report and then to the sports roundup. By that time, she'd been gone so long I didn't know if she was going to come back. I thought she might have gone to bed. I wished she'd come back downstairs. I didn't want to be left alone with a blind man. I asked him if he wanted to smoke some dope with me. I said I'd just rolled a number. I hadn't, but I planned to do so in about two shakes.

"I'll try some with you," he said.

"Damn right," I said. "That's the stuff."

I got our drinks and sat down on the sofa with him. Then I rolled us two fat numbers. I lit one and passed it. I brought it to his fingers. He took it and inhaled.

"Hold it as long as you can," I said. I could tell he didn't know the first thing.

My wife came back downstairs wearing her pink robe and her pink slippers.

"What do I smell?" she said.

"We thought we'd have us some cannabis," I said.

My wife gave me a savage look. Then she looked at the blind man and said, "Robert, I didn't know you smoked."

He said, "I do now, my dear. There's a first time for everything. But I don't feel anything yet."

"This stuff is pretty mellow," I said. "This stuff is mild. It's dope you can reason with," I said. "It doesn't mess you up."

"Not much it doesn't, bub," he said, and laughed.

My wife sat on the sofa between the blind man and me. I passed her the number. She took it and toked and then passed it back to me. "Which way is this going?" she said. Then she said, "I shouldn't be smoking this. I can hardly keep my eyes open as it is. That dinner did me in. I shouldn't have eaten so much."

"It was the strawberry pie," the blind man said. "That's what did it," he said, and he laughed his big laugh. Then he shook his head.

"There's more strawberry pie," I said.

"Do you want some more, Robert?" my wife said.

"Maybe in a little while," he said.

We gave our attention to the TV. My wife yawned again. She said, "Your bed is made up when you feel like going to bed, Robert. I know you must have had a long day. When you're ready to go to bed, say so." She pulled his arm. "Robert?"

He came to and said, "I've had a real nice time. This beats tapes, doesn't it?"

I said, "Coming at you," and I put the number between his fingers. He inhaled, held the smoke, and then let it go. It was like he'd been doing it since he was nine years old.

"Thanks, bub," he said. "But I think this is all for me. I think I'm beginning to feel it," he said. He held the burning roach out for my wife.

"Same here," she said. "Ditto. Me, too." She took the roach and passed it to me. "I may just sit here for a while between you two guys with my eyes closed. But don't let me bother you, okay? Either one of you. If it bothers you, say so. Otherwise, I may just sit here with my eyes closed until you're ready to go to bed," she said. "Your bed's made up, Robert, when you're ready. It's right next to our room at the top of the stairs. We'll show you up when you're ready. You wake me up now, you guys, if I fall asleep." She said that and then she closed her eyes and went to sleep.

The news program ended. I got up and changed the channel. I sat back down on the sofa. I wished my wife hadn't pooped out. Her head lay across the back of the sofa, her mouth open. She'd turned so that her robe had slipped away from her legs, exposing a juicy thigh. I reached to draw her robe back over her, and it was then that I glanced at the blind man. What the hell! I flipped the robe open again.

"You say when you want some strawberry pie," I said.

"I will," he said.

I said, "Are you tired? Do you want me to take you up to your bed? Are you ready to hit the hay?"

"Not yet," he said. "No, I'll stay up with you, bub. If that's all right. I'll stay up until you're ready to turn in. We haven't had a chance to talk. Know what I mean? I feel like me and her monopolized the evening." He lifted his beard and he let it fall. He picked up his cigarettes and lighter.

"That's all right," I said. Then I said, "I'm glad for the company."

And I guess I was. Every night I smoked dope and stayed up as long as I could before I fell asleep. My wife and I hardly ever went to bed at the same time. When I did go to sleep, I had these dreams. Sometimes I'd wake up from one of them, my heart going crazy.

Something about the church and the Middle Ages was on the TV. Not your run-of-the-mill TV fare. I wanted to watch something else. I turned to the other channels. But there was nothing on them, either. So I turned back to the first channel and apologized.

"Bub, it's all right," the blind man said. "It's fine with me. Whatever you want to watch is okay. I'm always learning something. Learning never ends. It won't hurt me to learn something tonight. I got ears," he said.

We didn't say anything for a time. He was leaning forward with his head turned at me, his right ear aimed in the direction of the set. Very disconcerting. Now and then his eyelids dropped and then they snapped open again. Now and then he put his fingers into his beard and tugged, like he was thinking about something he was hearing on the television.

On the screen, a group of men wearing cowls was being set upon and tormented by men dressed in skeleton costumes and men dressed as devils. The men dressed as devils wore devil masks, horns, and long tails. This pageant was part of a procession. The Englishman who was narrating the thing said it took place in Spain once a year. I tried to explain to the blind man what was happening.

"Skeletons," he said. "I know about skeletons," he said, and he nodded.

The TV showed this one cathedral. Then there was a long, slow look at another one. Finally, the picture switched to the famous one in Paris,[1] with its flying buttresses and its spires reaching up to the clouds. The camera pulled away to show the whole of the cathedral rising above the skyline.

There were times when the Englishman who was telling the thing would shut up, would simply let the camera move around over the cathedrals. Or else the camera would tour the countryside, men in fields walking behind oxen. I waited as long as I could. Then I felt I had to say something. I said, "They're showing the outside of this cathedral now. Gargoyles. Little statues carved to look like monsters. Now I guess they're in Italy. Yeah, they're in Italy. There's paintings on the walls of this one church."

"Are those fresco paintings, bub?" he asked, and he sipped from his drink.

I reached for my glass. But it was empty. I tried to remember what I could remember. "You're asking me are those frescoes?" I said. "That's a good question. I don't know."

The camera moved to a cathedral outside Lisbon. The differences in the Portuguese cathedral compared with the French and Italian

---

1. Notre Dame de Paris.

were not that great. But they were there. Mostly the interior stuff. Then something occurred to me, and I said, "Something has occurred to me. Do you have any idea what a cathedral is? What they look like, that is? Do you follow me? If somebody says cathedral to you, do you have any notion what they're talking about? Do you know the difference between that and a Baptist church, say?"

He let the smoke dribble from his mouth. "I know they took hundreds of workers fifty or a hundred years to build," he said. "I just heard the man say that, of course. I know generations of the same families worked on a cathedral. I heard him say that, too. The men who began their life's work on them, they never lived to see the completion of their work. In that wise, bub, they're no different from the rest of us, right?" He laughed. Then his eyelids drooped again. His head nodded. He seemed to be snoozing. Maybe he was imagining himself in Portugal. The TV was showing another cathedral now. This one was in Germany. The Englishman's voice droned on. "Cathedrals," the blind man said. He sat up and rolled his head back and forth. "If you want the truth, bub, that's about all I know. What I just said. What I heard him say. But maybe you could describe one to me? I wish you'd do it. I'd like that. If you want to know, I really don't have a good idea."

I stared hard at the shot of the cathedral on the TV. How could I even begin to describe it? But say my life depended on it. Say my life was being threatened by an insane guy who said I had to do it or else.

I stared some more at the cathedral before the picture flipped off into the countryside. There was no use. I turned to the blind man and said, "To begin with, they're very tall." I was looking around the room for clues. "They reach way up. Up and up. Toward the sky. They're so big, some of them, they have to have these supports. To help hold them up, so to speak. These supports are called buttresses. They remind me of viaducts, for some reason. But maybe you don't know viaducts, either? Sometimes the cathedrals have devils and such carved into the front. Sometimes lords and ladies. Don't ask me why this is," I said.

He was nodding. The whole upper part of his body seemed to be moving back and forth.

"I'm not doing so good, am I?" I said.

He stopped nodding and leaned forward on the edge of the sofa. As he listened to me, he was running his fingers through his beard. I wasn't getting through to him, I could see that. But he waited for me to go on just the same. He nodded, like he was trying to encourage me. I tried to think what else to say. "They're really big," I said. "They're massive. They're built of stone. Marble, too, sometimes. In those olden days, when they built cathedrals, men wanted to be close to God. In those olden days, God was an important part of everyone's life. You could tell this from their cathedral-building. I'm sorry," I said, "but it looks like that's the best I can do for you. I'm just no good at it."

"That's all right, bub," the blind man said. "Hey, listen. I hope you don't mind my asking you. Can I ask you something? Let me ask you a simple question, yes or no. I'm just curious and there's no offense. You're my host. But let me ask if you are in any way religious? You don't mind my asking?"

I shook my head. He couldn't see that, though. A wink is the same as a nod to a blind man. "I guess I don't believe in it. In anything. Sometimes it's hard. You know what I'm saying?"

"Sure, I do," he said.

"Right," I said.

The Englishman was still holding forth. My wife sighed in her sleep. She drew a long breath and went on with her sleeping.

"You'll have to forgive me," I said. "But I can't tell you what a cathedral looks like. It just isn't in me to do it. I can't do any more than I've done."

The blind man sat very still, his head down, as he listened to me.

I said, "The truth is, cathedrals don't mean anything special to me. Nothing. Cathedrals. They're something to look at on late-night TV. That's all they are."

It was then that the blind man cleared his throat. He brought something up. He took a handkerchief from his back pocket. Then he said, "I get it, bub. It's okay. It happens. Don't worry about it," he said. "Hey, listen to me. Will you do me a favor? I got an idea. Why don't you find us some heavy paper? And a pen. We'll do something. We'll draw one together. Get us a pen and some heavy paper. Go on, bub, get the stuff," he said.

So I went upstairs. My legs felt like they didn't have any strength in them. They felt like they did after I'd done some running. In my wife's room, I looked around. I found some ballpoints in a little basket on her table. And then I tried to think where to look for the kind of paper he was talking about.

Downstairs, in the kitchen, I found a shopping bag with onion skins at the bottom of the bag. I emptied the bag and shook it. I brought it into the living room and sat down with it near his legs. I moved some things, smoothed the wrinkles from the bag, spread it out on the coffee table.

The blind man got down from the sofa and sat next to me on the carpet.

He ran his fingers over the paper. He went up and down the sides of the paper. The edges, even the edges. He fingered the corners.

"All right," he said. "All right, let's do her."

He found my hand, the hand with the pen. He closed his hand over my hand. "Go ahead, bub, draw," he said. "Draw. You'll see. I'll follow along with you. It'll be okay. Just begin now like I'm telling you. You'll see. Draw," the blind man said.

So I began. First I drew a box that looked like a house. It could have been the house I lived in. Then I put a roof on it. At either end of the roof, I drew spires. Crazy.

"Swell," he said. "Terrific. You're doing fine," he said. "Never thought anything like this could happen in your lifetime, did you, bub? Well, it's a strange life, we all know that. Go on now. Keep it up."

I put in windows with arches. I drew flying buttresses. I hung great doors. I couldn't stop. The TV station went off the air. I put down the pen and closed and opened my fingers. The blind man felt around over the paper. He moved the tips of his fingers over the paper, all over what I had drawn, and he nodded.

"Doing fine," the blind man said.

I took up the pen again, and he found my hand. I kept at it. I'm no artist. But I kept drawing just the same.

My wife opened up her eyes and gazed at us. She sat up on the sofa, her robe hanging open. She said, "What are you doing? Tell me, I want to know."

I didn't answer her.

The blind man said, "We're drawing a cathedral. Me and him are working on it. Press hard," he said to me. "That's right. That's good," he said. "Sure. You got it, bub. I can tell. You didn't think you could. But you can, can't you? You're cooking with gas now. You know what I'm saying? We're going to really have us something here in a minute. How's the old arm?" he said. "Put some people in there now. What's a cathedral without people?"

My wife said, "What's going on? Robert, what are you doing? What's going on?"

"It's all right," he said to her. "Close your eyes now," the blind man said to me.

I did it I closed them just like he said.

"Are they closed?" he said. "Don't fudge."

"They're closed," I said.

"Keep them that way," he said. He said, "Don't stop now. Draw."

So we kept on with it. His fingers rode my fingers as my hand went over the paper. It was like nothing else in my life up to now.

Then he said, "I think that's it. I think you got it," he said. "Take a look. What do you think?"

But I had my eyes closed. I thought I'd keep them that way for a little longer. I thought it was something I ought to do.

"Well?" he said. "Are you looking?"

My eyes were still closed. I was in my house. I knew that. But I didn't feel like I was inside anything.

"It's really something," I said.

1981

■   ■   ■

SANDRA CISNEROS

ONE HOLY NIGHT

*About the truth, if you give it to a person, then he has power over you.
And if someone gives it to you, then they have made themselves your
slave. It is a strong magic. You can never take it back.*
—CHAQ UXMAL PALOQUÍN

He said his name was Chaq. Chaq Uxmal Paloquín. That's what he
told me. He was of an ancient line of Mayan kings. Here, he said,
making a map with the heel of his boot, this is where I come from, the
Yucatán,[1] the ancient cities. This is what Boy Baby said.

It's been eighteen weeks since Abuelita chased him away with the
broom, and what I'm telling you I never told nobody, except Rachel
and Lourdes, who know everything. He said he would love me like a
revolution, like a religion. Abuelita[2] burned the pushcart and sent me
here, miles from home, in this town of dust, with one wrinkled witch
woman who rubs my belly with jade, and sixteen nosy cousins.

I don't know how many girls have gone bad from selling cucum-
bers. I know I'm not the first. My mother took the crooked walk too,
I'm told, and I'm sure my Abuelita has her own story, but it's not my
place to ask.

Abuelita says it's Uncle Lalo's fault because he's the man of the
family and if he had come home on time like he was supposed to and
worked the pushcart on the days he was told to and watched over his
goddaughter, who is too foolish to look after herself, nothing would've
happened, and I wouldn't have to be sent to Mexico. But Uncle Lalo
says if they had never left Mexico in the first place, shame enough
would have kept a girl from doing devil things.

---

1. A city in eastern Mexico, on the Yucatán Peninsula on the Gulf of Mexico.
2. An affectionate term for grandmother, such as Granny.

I'm not saying I'm not bad. I'm not saying I'm special. But I'm not like the Allport Street girls, who stand in doorways and go with men into alleys.

All I know is I didn't want it like that. Not against the bricks or hunkering in somebody's car. I wanted it come undone like gold thread, like a tent full of birds. The way it's supposed to be, the way I knew it would be when I met Boy Baby.

But you must know, I was no girl back then. And Boy Baby was no boy. Chaq Uxmal Paloquín. Boy Baby was a man. When I asked him how old he was he said he didn't know. The past and the future are the same thing. So he seemed boy and baby and man all at once, and the way he looked at me, how do I explain?

I'd park the pushcart in front of the Jewel food store Saturdays. He bought a mango on a stick the first time. Paid for it with a new twenty. Next Saturday he was back. Two mangoes, lime juice, and chili powder, keep the change. The third Saturday he asked for a cucumber spear and ate it slow. I didn't see him after that till the day he brought me Kool-Aid in a plastic cup. Then I knew what I felt for him.

Maybe you wouldn't like him. To you he might be a bum. Maybe he looked it. Maybe. He had broken thumbs and burnt fingers. He had thick greasy fingernails he never cut and dusty hair. And all his bones were strong ones like a man's. I waited every Saturday in my same blue dress. I sold all the mango and cucumber, and then Boy Baby would come finally.

What I knew of Chaq was only what he told me, because nobody seemed to know where he came from. Only that he could speak a strange language that no one could understand, said his name translated into boy, or boy-child, and so it was the street people nicknamed him Boy Baby.

I never asked about his past. He said it was all the same and didn't matter, past and the future all the same to his people. But the truth has a strange way of following you, of coming up to you and making you listen to what it has to say.

Night time. Boy Baby brushes my hair and talks to me in his strange language because I like to hear it. What I like to hear him tell is how he is Chaq, Chaq of the people of the sun, Chaq of the temples, and what he says sounds sometimes like broken clay, and at other times like hollow sticks, or like the swish of old feathers crumbling into dust.

He lived behind Esparza & Sons Auto Repair in a little room that used to be a closet—pink plastic curtains on a narrow window, a dirty cot covered with newspapers, and a cardboard box filled with socks and rusty tools. It was there, under one bald bulb, in the back room of the Esparza garage, in the single room with pink curtains, that he showed me the guns—twenty-four in all. Rifles and pistols, one rusty musket, a machine gun, and several tiny weapons with mother-of-pearl handles that looked like toys. So you'll see who I am, he said, laying them all out on the bed of newspapers. So you'll understand. But I didn't want to know.

The stars foretell everything, he said. My birth. My son's. The boy-child who will bring back the grandeur of my people from those who have broken the arrows, from those who have pushed the ancient stones off their pedestals.

Then he told how he had prayed in the Temple of the Magician years ago as a child when his father had made him promise to bring back the ancient ways. Boy Baby had cried in the temple dark that only the bats made holy. Boy Baby who was man and child among the great and dusty guns lay down on the newspaper bed and wept for a thousand years. When I touched him, he looked at me with the sadness of stone.

You must not tell anyone what I am going to do, he said. And what I remember next is how the moon, the pale moon with its one yellow eye, the moon of Tikal, and Tulum, and Chichén,[3] stared through the pink plastic curtains. Then something inside bit me, and I gave out a cry as if the other, the one I wouldn't be anymore, leapt out.

So I was initiated beneath an ancient sky by a great and mighty heir—Chaq Uxmal Paloquín. I, Ixchel, his queen.

The truth is, it wasn't a big deal. It wasn't any deal at all. I put my bloody panties inside my T-shirt and ran home hugging myself. I thought about a lot of things on the way home. I thought about all the world and how suddenly I became a part of history and wondered if everyone on the street, the sewing machine lady and the *panadería*[4] saleswomen and the woman with two kids sitting on the bus bench didn't all know. *Did I look any different? Could they tell?* We were all the same somehow, laughing behind our hands, waiting the way all women wait, and when we find out, we wonder why the world and a million years made such a big deal over nothing.

I know I was supposed to feel ashamed, but I wasn't ashamed. I wanted to stand on top of the highest building, the top-top floor, and yell, *I know.*

Then I understood why Abuelita didn't let me sleep over at Lourdes's house full of too many brothers, and why the Roman girl in the movies always runs away from the soldier, and what happens when

3. Ancient Mayan cities the remains of which are located in Guatemala and Mexico.
4. Bakery.

the scenes in love stories begin to fade, and why brides blush, and how it is that sex isn't simply a box you check *M* or *F* on in the test we get at school.

I was wise. The corner girls were still jumping into their stupid little hopscotch squares. I laughed inside and climbed the wooden stairs two by two to the second floor rear where me and Abuelita and Uncle Lalo live. I was still laughing when I opened the door and Abuelita asked, Where's the pushcart?

And then I didn't know what to do.

It's a good thing we live in a bad neighborhood. There are always plenty of bums to blame for your sins. If it didn't happen the way I told it, it really could've. We looked and looked all over for the kids who stole my pushcart. The story wasn't the best, but since I had to make it up right then and there with Abuelita staring a hole through my heart, it wasn't too bad.

For two weeks I had to stay home. Abuelita was afraid the street kids who had stolen the cart would be after me again. Then I thought I might go over to the Esparza garage and take the pushcart out and leave it in some alley for the police to find, but I was never allowed to leave the house alone. Bit by bit the truth started to seep out like a dangerous gasoline.

First the nosy woman who lives upstairs from the laundromat told my Abuelita she thought something was fishy, the pushcart wheeled into Esparza & Sons every Saturday after dark, how a man, the same dark Indian one, the one who never talks to anybody, walked with me when the sun went down and pushed the cart into the garage, that once there, and yes we went inside, there where the fat lady named Concha, whose hair is dyed a hard black, pointed a fat finger.

I prayed that we would not meet Boy Baby, and since the gods listen and are mostly good, Esparza said yes, a man like that had lived there but was gone, had packed a few things and left the pushcart in a corner to pay for his last week's rent.

We had to pay $20 before he would give us our pushcart back. Then Abuelita made me tell the real story of how the cart had disappeared, all of which I told this time, except for that one night, which I would have to tell anyway, weeks later, when I prayed for the moon of my cycle to come back, but it would not.

When Abuelita found out I was going to *dar a luz*,[5] she cried until her eyes were little, and blamed Uncle Lalo, and Uncle Lalo blamed

5. Have a baby.

this country, and Abuelita blamed the infamy of men. That is when she burned the cucumber pushcart and called me a *sinvergüenza*[6] because I *am* without shame.

Then I cried too—Boy Baby was lost from me—until my head was hot with headaches and I fell asleep. When I woke up, the cucumber pushcart was dust and Abuelita was sprinkling holy water on my head.

Abuelita woke up early every day and went to the Esparza garage to see if news about that *demonio* had been found, had Chaq Uxmal Paloquín sent any letters, any, and when the other mechanics heard that name they laughed, and asked if we had made it up, that we could have some letters that had come for Boy Baby, no forwarding address, since he had gone in such a hurry.

There were three. The first, addressed "Occupant," demanded immediate payment for a four-month-old electric bill. The second was one I recognized right away—a brown envelope fat with cake-mix coupons and fabric-softener samples—because we'd gotten one just like it. The third was addressed in a spidery Spanish to a Señor C. Cruz, on paper so thin you could read it unopened by the light of the sky. The return address a convent in Tampico.

This was to whom my Abuelita wrote in hopes of finding the man who could correct my ruined life, to ask if the good nuns might know the whereabouts of a certain Boy Baby—and if they were hiding him it would be of no use because God's eyes see through all souls.

We heard nothing for a long time. Abuelita took me out of school when my uniform got tight around the belly and said it was a shame I wouldn't be able to graduate with the other eighth graders.

Except for Lourdes and Rachel, my grandma and Uncle Lalo, nobody knew about my past. I would sleep in the big bed I share with Abuelita same as always. I could hear Abuelita and Uncle Lalo talking in low voices in the kitchen as if they were praying the rosary, how they were going to send me to Mexico, to San Dionisio de Tlaltepango, where I have cousins and where I was conceived and would've been born had my grandma not thought it wise to send my mother here to the United States so that neighbors in San Dionisio de Tlaltepango wouldn't ask why her belly was suddenly big.

I was happy. I liked staying home. Abuelita was teaching me to crochet the way she had learned in Mexico. And just when I had mastered the tricky rosette stitch, the letter came from the convent which gave the truth about Boy Baby—however much we didn't want to hear.

6. Shameless woman.

He was born on a street with no name in a town called Miseria. His father, Eusebio, is a knife sharpener. His mother, Refugia, stacks apricots into pyramids and sells them on a cloth in the market. There are brothers. Sisters too of which I know little. The youngest, a Carmelite, writes me all this and prays for my soul, which is why I know it's all true.

Boy Baby is thirty-seven years old. His name is Chato which means fat-face. There is no Mayan blood.

I don't think they understand how it is to be a girl. I don't think they know how it is to have to wait your whole life. I count the months for the baby to be born, and it's like a ring of water inside me reaching out and out until one day it will tear from me with its own teeth.

Already I can feel the animal inside me stirring in his own uneven sleep. The witch woman says it's the dreams of weasels that make my child sleep the way he sleeps. She makes me eat white bread blessed by the priest, but I know it's the ghost of him inside me that circles and circles, and will not let me rest.

Abuelita said they sent me here just in time, because a little later Boy Baby came back to our house looking for me, and she had to chase him away with the broom. The next thing we hear, he's in the newspaper clippings his sister sends. A picture of him looking very much like stone, police hooked on either arm . . . *on the road to Las Grutas de Xtacumbilxuna, the Caves of the Hidden Girl . . . eleven female bodies . . . the last seven years . . .*

Then I couldn't read but only stare at the little black-and-white dots that make up the face I am in love with.

All my girl cousins here either don't talk to me, or those who do, ask questions they're too young to know *not* to ask. What they want to know really is how it is to have a man, because they're too ashamed to ask their married sisters.

They don't know what it is to lay so still until his sleep breathing is heavy, for the eyes in the dim dark to look and look without worry at the man-bones and the neck, the man-wrist and man-jaw thick and strong, all the salty dips and hollows, the stiff hair of the brow and sour swirl of sideburns, to lick the fat earlobes that taste of smoke, and stare at how perfect is a man.

I tell them, "It's a bad joke. When you find out you'll be sorry."

I'm going to have five children. Five. Two girls. Two boys. And one baby.

The girls will be called Lisette and Maritza. The boys I'll name Pablo and Sandro.

And my baby. My baby will be named Alegre,[7] because life will always be hard.

Rachel says that love is like a big black piano being pushed off the top of a three-story building and you're waiting on the bottom to catch it. But Lourdes says it's not that way at all. It's like a top, like all the colors in the world are spinning so fast they're not colors anymore and all that's left is a white hum.

There was a man, a crazy who lived upstairs from us when we lived on South Loomis. He couldn't talk, just walked around all day with this harmonica in his mouth. Didn't play it. Just sort of breathed through it, all day long, wheezing, in and out, in and out.

This is how it is with me. Love I mean.

1991

■   ■   ■

7. Happy.

ROBERT COOVER

THE BABYSITTER

She arrives at 7:40, ten minutes late, but the children, Jimmy and Bitsy, are still eating supper, and their parents are not ready to go yet. From other rooms come the sounds of a baby screaming, water running, a television musical (no words: probably a dance number—patterns of gliding figures come to mind). Mrs. Tucker sweeps into the kitchen, fussing with her hair, and snatches a baby bottle full of milk out of a pan of warm water, rushes out again. "Harry!" she calls. "The babysitter's here already!"

■   ■   ■

That's My Desire? I'll Be Around?[1] He smiles toothily, beckons faintly with his head, rubs his fast balding pate. Bewitched, maybe? Or, What's the Reason? He pulls on his shorts, gives his hips a slap. The baby goes silent in mid-scream. Isn't this the one who used their tub last time? Who's Sorry Now, that's it.

■   ■   ■

Jack is wandering around town, not knowing what to do. His girlfriend is babysitting at the Tuckers', and later, when she's got the kids in bed, maybe he'll drop over there. Sometimes he watches TV with her when she's babysitting, it's about the only chance he gets to make out a little since he doesn't own wheels, but they have to be careful because most people don't like their sitters to have boyfriends over. Just kissing her makes her nervous. She won't close her eyes because she has to be watching the door all the time. Married people really have it good, he thinks.

1. Titles of popular songs, as are *What's the Reason* and *Who's Sorry Now*.

■   ■   ■

"Hi," the babysitter says to the children, and puts her books on top of the refrigerator. "What's for supper?" The little girl, Bitsy, only stares at her obliquely. She joins them at the end of the kitchen table. "I don't have to go to bed until nine," the boy announces flatly, and stuffs his mouth full of potato chips. The babysitter catches a glimpse of Mr. Tucker hurrying out of the bathroom in his underwear.

■   ■   ■

Her tummy. Under her arms. And her feet. Those are the best places. She'll spank him, she says sometimes. Let her.

■   ■   ■

That sweet odor that girls have. The softness of her blouse. He catches a glimpse of the gentle shadows amid her thighs, as she curls her legs up under her. He stares hard at her. He has a lot of meaning packed into that stare, but she's not even looking. She's popping her gum and watching television. She's sitting right there, inches away, soft, fragrant, and ready: but what's his next move? He notices his buddy Mark in the drugstore, playing the pinball machine, and joins him. "Hey, this mama's cold, Jack baby! She needs your touch!"

■   ■   ■

Mrs. Tucker appears at the kitchen doorway, holding a rolled-up diaper. "Now, don't just eat potato chips, Jimmy! See that he eats his hamburger, dear." She hurried away to the bathroom. The boy glares sullenly at the babysitter, silently daring her to carry out the order. "How about a little of that good hamburger now, Jimmy?" she says perfunctorily. He lets half of it drop to the floor. The baby is silent and a man is singing a love song on the TV. The children crunch chips.

■   ■   ■

He loves her. She loves him. They whirl airily, stirring a light breeze, through a magical landscape of rose and emerald and deep blue. Her light brown hair coils and wisps softly in the breeze, and the soft folds of her white gown tug at her body and then float away. He smiles in a pulsing crescendo of sincerity and song.

■   ■   ■

"You mean she's alone?" Mark asks. "Well, there's two or three kids," Jack says. He slides the coin in. There's a rumble of steel balls tumbling, lining up. He pushes a plunger with his thumb, and one ball pops up in place, hard and glittering with promise. His stare? to say he loves her. That he cares for her and would protect her, would shield her, if need be, with his own body. Grinning, he bends over the ball to take careful aim: he and Mark have studied this machine and have it figured out, but still it's not that easy to beat.

■ ■ ■

On the drive to the party, his mind is partly on the girl, partly on his own high-school days, long past. Sitting at the end of the kitchen table there with his children, she had seemed to be self-consciously arching her back, jutting her pert breasts, twitching her thighs: and for whom if not for him? So she'd seen him coming out of there, after all. He smiles. Yet what could he ever do about it? Those good times are gone, old man. He glances over at his wife, who, readjusting a garter, asks: "What do you think of our babysitter?"

■ ■ ■

He loves her. She loves him. And then the babies come. And dirty diapers and one goddamn meal after another. Dishes. Noise. Clutter. And fat. Not just tight, her girdle actually hurts. Somewhere recently she's read about women getting heart attacks or cancer or something from too-tight girdles. Dolly pulls the car door shut with a grunt, strangely irritated, not knowing why. Party mood. Why is her husband humming, "Who's Sorry Now?" Pulling out of the drive, she glances back at the lighted kitchen window. "What do you think of our babysitter?" she asks. While her husband stumbles all over himself trying to answer, she pulls a stocking tight, biting deeper with the garters.

■ ■ ■

"Stop it!" she laughs. Bitsy is pulling on her skirt and he is tickling her in the ribs. "Jimmy! Don't!" But she is laughing too much to stop him. He leaps on her, wrapping his legs around her waist, and they all fall to the carpet in front of the TV, where just now a man in a tuxedo and a little girl in a flouncy white dress are doing a tapdance together. The babysitter's blouse is pulling out of her skirt, showing a patch of bare tummy: the target. "I'll spank!"

■ ■ ■

Jack pushes the plunger, thrusting up a steel ball, and bends studiously over the machine. "You getting any off her?" Mark asks, and clears his throat, flicks ash from his cigarette. "Well, not exactly, not yet," Jack says, grinning awkwardly, but trying to suggest more than he admits to, and fires. He heaves his weight gently against the machine as the ball bounds off a rubber bumper. He can feel her warming up under his hands, the flippers suddenly coming alive, delicate rapid-fire patterns emerging in the flashing of the lights. 1000 WHEN LIT: *now!* "Got my hand on it, that's about all." Mark glances up from the machine, cigarette dangling from his lip. "Maybe you need some help," he suggests with a wry one-sided grin. "Like maybe together, man, we could do it."

■   ■   ■

She likes the big tub. She uses the Tuckers' bath salts, and loves to sink into the hot fragrant suds. She can stretch out, submerged, up to her chin. It gives her a good sleepy tingly feeling.

■   ■   ■

"What do you think of our babysitter?" Dolly asks, adjusting a garter. "Oh, I hardly noticed," he says "Cute girl. She seems to get along fine with the kids. Why?" "I don't know." His wife tugs her skirt down, glances at a lighted window they are passing, adding: "I'm not sure I trust her completely, that's all. With the baby, I mean. She seems a little careless. And the other time, I'm almost sure she had a boyfriend over." He grins, claps one hand on his wife's broad gartered thigh. "What's wrong with that?" he asks. Still in anklets, too. Bare thighs, no girdles, nothing up there but a flimsy pair of panties and soft adolescent flesh. He's flooded with vague remembrances of football rallies and movie balconies.

■   ■   ■

How tiny and rubbery it is! she thinks, soaping between the boy's legs, giving him his bath. Just a funny jiggly little thing that looks like it shouldn't even be there at all. Is that what all the songs are about?

■   ■   ■

Jack watches Mark lunge and twist against the machine. Got her running now, racked them up. He's not too excited about the idea of Mark fooling around with his girlfriend, but Mark's a cooler operator than he is, and maybe, doing it together this once, he'd get over his own timidity. And if she didn't like it, there were other girls around. If Mark went too far, he could cut him off too. He feels his shoulders tense: enough's enough, man . . . but sees the flesh, too. "Maybe I'll call her later," he says.

■   ■   ■

"Hey, Harry! Dolly! Glad you could make it!" "I hope we're not late." "No, no, you're one of the first, come on in! By golly, Dolly, you're looking younger every day! How do you do it? Give my wife your secret, will you?" He pats her on her girdled bottom behind Mr. Tucker's back, leads them in for drinks.

■   ■   ■

8:00. The babysitter runs water in the tub, combs her hair in front of the bathroom mirror. There's a western on television, so she lets Jimmy watch it while she gives Bitsy her bath. But Bitsy doesn't want a bath. She's angry and crying because she has to be first. The babysitter tells her if she'll take her bath quickly, she'll let her watch television while Jimmy takes his bath, but it does no good. The little girl fights to get out of the bathroom, and the babysitter has to squat with her back against the door and forcibly undress the child. There are better places to babysit. Both children mind badly, and then, sooner or later, the baby is sure to wake up for a diaper change and more bottle. The Tuckers do have a good color TV, though, and she hopes things will be settled down enough to catch the 8:30 program. She thrusts the child into the tub, but she's still screaming and thrashing around. "Stop it now, Bitsy, or you'll wake the baby!" "I have to go potty!" the child wails, switching tactics. The babysitter sighs, lifts the girl out of the tub and onto the toilet, getting her skirt and blouse all wet in the process. She glances at herself in the mirror. Before she knows it, the girl is off the seat and out of the bathroom. "Bitsy! Come back here!"

■   ■   ■

"Okay, that's enough!" Her skirt is ripped and she's flushed and crying. "Who says?" "I do, man!" The bastard goes for her, but she tackles him. They roll and tumble. Tables tip, lights topple, the TV crashes to the floor. He slams a hard right to the guy's gut, clips his chin with a rolling left.

■   ■   ■

"We hope it's a girl." That's hardly surprising, since they already have four boys. Dolly congratulates the woman like everybody else, but she doesn't envy her, not a bit. That's all she needs about now. She stares across the room at Harry, who is slapping backs and getting loud, as usual. He's spreading out through the middle, so why the hell does he have to complain about her all the time? "Dolly, you're looking younger every day!" was the nice greeting she got tonight. "What's your secret?" And Harry: "It's all those calories. She's getting back her baby fat." "Haw haw! Harry, have a heart!"

■   ■   ■

"Get her feet" he hollers at Bitsy, his fingers in her ribs, running over her naked tummy, tangling in the underbrush of straps and strange clothing. "Get her shoes off!" He holds her pinned by pressing his head against her soft chest. "No! No, Jimmy! Bitsy, stop!" But though she kicks and twists and rolls around, she doesn't get up, she can't get up, she's laughing too hard, and the shoes come off, and he grabs a stockinged foot and scratches the sole ruthlessly, and she raises up her legs, trying to pitch him off, she's wild, boy, but he hangs on, and she's laughing, and on the screen there's a rattle of hooves, and he and Bitsy are rolling around and around on the floor in a crazy rodeo of long bucking legs.

■　　■　　■

He slips the coin in. There's a metallic fall and a sharp click as the dial tone begins. "I hope the Tuckers have gone," he says. "Don't worry, they're at our place," Mark says. "They're always the first ones to come and the last ones to go home. My old man's always bitching about them." Jack laughs nervously and dials the number. "Tell her we're coming over to protect her from getting raped," Mark suggests, and lights a cigarette. Jack grins, leaning casually against the door jamb of the phonebooth, chewing gum, one hand in his pocket. He's really pretty uneasy, though. He has the feeling he's somehow messing up a good thing.

■　　■　　■

Bitsy runs naked into the livingroom, keeping a hassock between herself and the babysitter. "Bitsy . . . !" the babysitter threatens. Artificial reds and greens and purples flicker over the child's wet body, as hooves clatter, guns crackle, and stagecoach wheels thunder over rutted terrain. "Get outa the way, Bitsy!" the boy complains. "I can't see!" Bitsy streaks past and the babysitter chases, cornering the girl in the back bedroom. Bitsy throws something that hits her softly in the face: a pair of men's undershorts. She grabs the girl scampering by, carries her struggling to the bathroom, and with a smart crack on her glistening bottom, pops her back into the tub. In spite, Bitsy peepees in the bathwater.

■　　■　　■

Mr. Tucker stirs a little water into his bourbon and kids with his host and another man, just arrived, about their golf games. They set up a match for the weekend, a threesome looking for a fourth. Holding his drink in his right hand, Mr. Tucker swings his left through the motion of a tee-shot. "You'll have to give me a stroke a hole," he says. "I'll give you a stroke!" says his host: "Bend over!" Laughing, the other man asks. "Where's your boy Mark tonight?" "I don't know," replies the host, gathering up a trayful of drinks. Then he adds in a low growl: "Out chasing tail probably." They chuckle loosely at that, then shrug in commiseration and return to the living room to join their women.

▪   ▪   ▪

Shades pulled. Door locked. Watching the TV. Under a blanket maybe. Yes, that's right, under a blanket. Her eyes close when he kisses her. Her breasts, under both their hands, are soft and yielding.

▪   ▪   ▪

A hard blow to the belly. The face. The dark beardy one staggers, the lean-jawed sheriff moves in, but gets a spurred boot in his face. The dark one hurls himself forward, drives his shoulder into the sheriff's hard midriff, her own tummy tightens, withstands, as the sheriff smashes the dark man's nose, slams him up against a wall, slugs him again! and again! The dark man grunts rhythmically, backs off, then plunges suicidally forward—her own knees draw up protectively—the sheriff staggers! caught low! but instead of following through, the other man steps back—a pistol! the dark one has a pistol! the sheriff draws! shoots from the hip! explosions! she clutches her hands between her thighs—no! the sheriff spins! wounded! the dark man hesitates, aims, her legs stiffen toward the set, the sheriff rolls desperately in the straw, fires: dead! the dark man is dead! groans, crumples, his pistol drooping in his collapsing hand, dropping, he drops. The sheriff, spent, nicked, watches weakly from the floor where he lies. Oh, to be whole! to be good and strong and right! to embrace and be embraced by harmony and wholeness! The sheriff, drawing himself painfully up on one elbow, rubs his bruised mouth with the back of his other hand.

▪   ▪   ▪

"Well, we just sorta thought we'd drop over," he says, and winks broadly at Mark. "Who's we?" "Oh, me and Mark here." "Tell her, good thing like her, gotta pass it around," whispers Mark, dragging on his smoke, then flicking the butt over under the pinball machine. "What's that?" she asks. "Oh, Mark and I were just saying, like two's company, three's an orgy," Jack says, and winks again. She giggles. "Oh Jack!" Behind her, he can hear shouts and gunfire. "Well, okay, for just a little while, if you'll both be good." Way to go, man.

▪   ▪   ▪

Probably some damn kid over there right now. Wrestling around on the couch in front of his TV. Maybe he should drop back to the house. Just to check. None of that stuff, she was there to do a job! Park the car a couple doors down, slip in the front door before she knows it. He sees the disarray of clothing, the young thighs exposed to the flickering television light, hears his baby crying. "Hey, what's going on here! Get outa here, son, before I call the police!" Of course, they haven't really been doing anything. They probably don't even know how. He stares benignly down upon the girl, her skirt rumpled loosely around her thighs. Flushed, frightened, yet excited, she stares back at him. He smiles. His finger touches a knee, approaches the hem. Another couple arrives. Filling up here with people. He wouldn't be missed. Just slip out, stop back casually to pick up something or other he forgot, never mind what. He remembers that the other time they had this babysitter, she took a bath in their house. She had a date afterwards, and she'd come from cheerleading practice or something. Aspirin maybe. Just drop quietly and casually into the bathroom to pick up some aspirin. "Oh, excuse me, dear! I only . . . !" She gazes back at him, astonished, yet strangely moved. Her soft wet breasts rise and fall in the water, and her tummy looks pale and ripply. He recalls that her pubic hairs, left in the tub, were brown. Light brown.

■   ■   ■

She's no more than stepped into the tub for a quick bath, when Jimmy announces from outside the door that he has to go to the bathroom. She sighs: just an excuse, she knows. "You'll have to wait." The little nuisance. "I can't wait." "Okay, then come ahead, but I'm taking a bath." She supposes that will stop him, but it doesn't. In he comes. She slides down into the suds until she's eye-level with the edge of the tub. He hesitates. "Go ahead, if you have to," she says, a little awkwardly, "but I'm not getting out." "Don't look," he says. She: "I will if I want to."

■   ■   ■

She's crying. Mark is rubbing his jaw where he's just slugged him. A lamp lies shattered. "Enough's enough, Mark! Now get outa here!" Her skirt is ripped to the waist, her bare hip bruised. Her panties lie on the floor like a broken balloon. Later, he'll wash her wounds, help her dress, he'll take care of her. Pity washes through him, giving him a sudden hard-on. Mark laughs at it, pointing. Jack crouches, waiting, ready for anything.

■   ■   ■

Laughing, they roll and tumble. Their little hands are all over her, digging and pinching. She struggles to her hands and knees, but Bitsy leaps astride her neck, bowing her head to the carpet. "Spank her,

Jimmy!" His swats sting: is her skirt up? The phone rings. "The cavalry to the rescue!" she laughs, and throws them off to go answer.

▩   ▩   ▩

Kissing Mark, her eyes closed, her hips nudge toward Jack. He stares at the TV screen, unsure of himself, one hand slipping cautiously under her skirt. Her hand touches his arm as though to resist, then brushes on by to rub his leg. This blanket they're under was a good idea. "Hi! This is Jack!"

▩   ▩   ▩

Bitsy's out and the water's running. "Come on, Jimmy, your turn!" Last time, he told her he took his own baths, but she came in anyway. "I'm not gonna take a bath," he announces, eyes glued on the set. He readies for the struggle. "But I've already run your water. Come on, Jimmy, please!" He shakes his head. She can't make him, he's sure he's as strong as she is. She sighs. "Well, it's up to you. I'll use the water myself then," she says. He waits until he's pretty sure she's not going to change her mind, then sneaks in and peeks through the keyhole in the bathroom door: just in time to see her big bottom as she bends over to stir in the bubblebath. Then she disappears. Trying to see as far down as the keyhole will allow, he bumps his head on the knob. "Jimmy, is that you?" "I—I have to go to the bathroom!" he stammers.

▩   ▩   ▩

Not actually in the tub, just getting in. One foot on the mat, the other in the water. Bent over slightly, buttocks flexed, teats swaying, holding on to the edge of the tub. "Oh, excuse me! I only wanted . . . !" He passes over her astonishment, the awkward excuses, moves quickly to the part where he reaches out to—"What on earth are you doing, Harry?" his wife asks, staring at his hand. His host, passing, laughs. "He's practicing his swing for Sunday, Dolly, but it's not going to do him a damn bit of good!" Mr. Tucker laughs, sweeps his right hand on through the air as though lifting a seven-iron shot onto the green. He makes a *dok!* sound with his tongue. "In there!"

▩   ▩   ▩

"No, Jack, I don't think you'd better." "Well, we just called, we just, uh, thought we'd, you know, stop by for a minute, watch television for thirty minutes, or, or something." "Who's we?" "Well, Mark's here, I'm with him, and he said he'd like to, you know, like if it's all right, just—" "Well, it's *not* all right. The Tuckers said no." "Yeah, but if we only—" "And they seemed awfully suspicious about last time." "Why? We didn't—I mean, I just thought—" "No, Jack, and that's period." She hangs up. She returns to the TV, but the commercial is on. Anyway, she's missed most of the show. She decides maybe she'll take a quick bath. Jack might come by anyway, it'd make her mad, that'd be the end as far as he was concerned, but if he should, she doesn't want to be all sweaty. And besides, she likes the big tub the Tuckers have.

       ■   ■   ■

He is self-conscious and stands with his back to her, his little neck flushed. It takes him forever to get started, and when it finally does come, it's just a tiny trickle. "See, it was just an excuse," she scolds, but she's giggling inwardly at the boy's embarrassment. "You're just a nuisance, Jimmy." At the door, his hand on the knob, he hesitates, staring timidly down on his shoes. "Jimmy?" She peeks at him over the edge of the tub, trying to keep a straight face, as he sneaks a nervous glance back over his shoulder. "As long as you bothered me," she says, "you might as well soap my back."

       ■   ■   ■

"The aspirin . . ." They embrace. She huddles in his arms like a child. Lovingly, paternally, knowledgeably, he wraps her nakedness. How compact, how tight and small her body is! Kissing her ear, he stares down past her rump at the still clear water. "I'll join you," he whispers hoarsely.

       ■   ■   ■

She picks up the shorts Bitsy threw at her. Men's underwear. She holds them in front of her, looks at herself in the bedroom mirror. About twenty sizes too big for her, of course. She runs her hand inside the opening in front, pulls out her thumb. How funny it must feel!

       ■   ■   ■

"Well, man, I say we just go rape her," Mark says flatly, and swings his weight against the pinball machine. "Uff! Ahh! Get in there, you mother! Look at that! Hah! Man, I'm gonna turn this baby over!" Jack is embarrassed about the phone conversation. Mark just snorted in disgust when he hung up. He cracks down hard on his gum, angry that he's such a chicken. "Well, I'm game if you are," he says coldly.

       ■   ■   ■

8:30 "Okay, come on, Jimmy, it's time." He ignores her. The western gives way to a spy show. Bitsy, in pajamas, pads into the living room. "No, Bitsy, it's time to go to bed." "You said I could watch!" the girl whines, and starts to throw another tantrum. "But you were too slow and it's late. Jimmy, you get in that bathroom, and right now!" Jimmy stares sullenly at the set, unmoving. The babysitter tries to catch the opening scene of the television program so she can follow it later, since Jimmy gives himself his own baths. When the commercial interrupts, she turns off the sound, stands in front of the screen. "Okay, into the tub, Jimmy Tucker, or I'll take you in there and give you your bath myself!" "Just try it," he says, "and see what happens."

■   ■   ■

They stand outside, in the dark, crouched in the bushes, peeking in. She's on the floor, playing with the kids. Too early. They seem to be tickling her. She gets to her hands and knees, but the little girl leaps on her head, pressing her face to the floor. There's an obvious target, and the little boy proceeds to beat on it. "Hey, look at that kid go!" whispers Mark, laughing and snapping his fingers softly. Jack feels uneasy out here. Too many neighbors, too many cars going by, too many people in the world. That little boy in there is one up on him, though: he's never thought about tickling her as a starter.

■   ■   ■

His little hand, clutching the bar of soap, lathers shyly a narrow space between her shoulderblades. She is doubled forward against her knees, buried in rich suds, pecking at him over the edge of her shoulder. The soap slithers out of his grip and plunks into the water. "I . . . I dropped the soap," he whispers. She: "Find it."

■   ■   ■

"I dream of Jeannie with the light brown pubic hair!"[2] "Harry! Stop that! You're drunk!" But they're laughing, they're all laughing, damn! he's feeling pretty goddamn good at that, and now he just knows he needs that aspirin. Watching her there, her thighs spread for him, on the couch, in the tub, hell, on the kitchen table for that matter, he tees off on Number Nine, and—whap!—swats his host's wife on the bottom. "Hole in one!" he shouts. "Harry!" Why can't his goddamn wife Dolly ever get happy-drunk instead of sour-drunk all the time? "Gonna be tough Sunday, old buddy!" "You're pretty tough right now, Harry," says his host.

■   ■   ■

The babysitter lunges forward, grabs the boy by the arms and hauls him off the couch, pulling two cushions with him, and drags him toward the bathroom. He lashes out, knocking over an endtable full of

2. Parody of actual song title, *I Dream of Jeannie with the Light Brown Hair.*

magazines and ashtrays. "You leave my brother alone!" Bitsy cries and grabs the sitter around the waist. Jimmy jumps on her and down they all go. On the silent screen, there's a fade-in to a dark passageway in an old apartment building in some foreign country. She kicks out and somebody falls between her legs. Somebody else is sitting on her face. "Jimmy! Stop that!" the babysitter laughs, her voice muffled.

░   ░   ░

She's watching television. All alone. It seems like a good time to go in. Just remember: really, no matter what she says, she wants it. They're standing in the bushes, trying to get up the nerve. "We'll tell her to be good," Mark whispers, "and if she's not good, we'll spank her." Jack giggles softly, but his knees are weak. She stands. They freeze. She looks right at them. "She can't see us." Mark whispers tensely. "Is she coming out?" "No," says Mark, "She's going into—that must be the bathroom!" Jack takes a deep breath, his heart pounding. "Hey, is there a window back there?" Mark asks.

░   ░   ░

The phone rings. She leaves the tub, wrapped in a towel. Bitsy gives a tug on the towel. "Hey, Jimmy, get the towel!" she squeals. "Now stop that, Bitsy!" the babysitter hisses, but too late: with one hand on the phone, the other isn't enough to hang on to the towel. Her sudden nakedness awes them and it takes them a moment to remember about tickling her. By then, she's in the towel again. "I hope you got a good look," she says angrily. She feels chilled and oddly a little frightened. "Hello?" No answer. She glances at the window—is somebody out there? Something, she saw something, and a rustling—footsteps?

░   ░   ░

"Okay, I don't care, Jimmy, don't take a bath," she says irritably. Her blouse is pulled out and wrinkled, her hair is all mussed, and she feels sweaty. There's about a million things she'd rather be doing than babysitting with these two. Three: at least the baby's sleeping. She knocks on the overturned endtable for luck, rights it, replaces the magazines and ashtrays. The one thing that really makes her sick is a dirty diaper. "Just go on to bed." "I don't have to go to bed until nine," he reminds her. Really, she couldn't care less. She turns up the volume on the TV, settles down on the couch, poking her blouse back into her skirt, pushing her hair out of her eyes. Jimmy and Bitsy watch from the floor. Maybe, once they're in bed, she'll take a quick bath. She wishes Jack would come by. The man, no doubt the spy, is following a woman, but she doesn't know why. The woman passes another man. Something seems to happen, but it's not clear what. She's probably already missed too much. The phone rings.

▩   ▩   ▩

Mark is kissing her. Jack is under the blanket, easing her panties down over her squirming hips. Her hand is in his pants, pulling it out, pulling it toward her, pulling it hard. She knew just where it was! Mark is stripping, too. God, it's really happening! he thinks with a kind of pious joy, and notices the open door. "Hey! What's going on here?"

▩   ▩   ▩

He soaps her back, smooth and slippery under his hand. She is doubled over, against her knees, between his legs. Her light brown hair, reaching to her gleaming shoulders, is wet at the edges. The soap slips, falls between his legs. He fishes for it, finds it, slips it behind him. "Help me find it," he whispers in her ear. "Sure Harry," says his host, going around behind him. "What'd you lose?"

▩   ▩   ▩

Soon be nine, time to pack the kids off to bed. She clears the table, dumps paper plates and leftover hamburgers into the garbage, puts glasses and silverware into the sink, and the mayonnaise, mustard, and ketchup in the refrigerator. Neither child has eaten much supper finally, mostly potato chips and ice cream, but it's really not her problem. She glances at the books on the refrigerator. Not much chance she'll get to them, she's already pretty worn out. Maybe she'd feel better if she had a quick bath. She runs water into the tub, tosses in bubblebath salts, undresses. Before pushing down her panties, she stares for a moment at the smooth silken panel across her tummy, fingers the place where the opening would be if there were one. Then she steps quickly out of them, feeling somehow ashamed, unhooks her brassiere. She weighs her breasts in the palms of her hands, watching herself in the bathroom mirror, where, in the open window behind her, she sees a face. She screams.

▩   ▩   ▩

She screams: "Jimmy! Give me that!" "What's the matter?" asks Jack on the other end. "Jimmy! Give me my towel! Right now!" "Hello? Hey, are you still there?" "I'm sorry, Jack," she says, panting. "You caught me in the tub. I'm just wrapped in a towel and these silly kids grabbed it away!" "Gee, I wish I'd been there!" "Jack—!" "To protect you, I mean." "Oh, sure," she says, giggling. "Well, what do you think, can I come over and watch TV with you?" "Well, not right this min-

ute," she says. He laughs lightly. He feels very cool. "Jack?" "Yeah?"
"Jack, I . . . I think there's somebody outside the window!"

■   ■   ■

She carries him, fighting all the way, to the tub, Bitsy pummeling her
in the back and kicking her ankles. She can't hang on to him and
undress him at the same time. "I'll throw you in, clothes and all, Jimmy
Tucker!" she gasps. "You better not!" he cries. She sits on the toilet
seat, locks her legs around him, whips his shirt up over his head before
he knows what's happening. The pants are easier. Like all little boys
his age, he has almost no hips at all. He hangs on desperately to his
underpants, but when she succeeds in snapping these down out of his
grip, too, he gives up, starts to bawl, and beats her wildly in the face
with his fists. She ducks her head, laughing hysterically, oddly
entranced by the spectacle of that pale little thing down there, bobbing
and bouncing rubberlike about the boy's helpless fury and anguish.

■   ■   ■

"Aspirin? Whaddaya want aspirin for, Harry? I'm sure they got aspirin
here, if you—" "Did I say aspirin? I meant uh, my glasses. And, you
know, I thought, well, I'd sorta check to see if everything was okay at
home." Why the hell is it his mouth feels like it's got about six sets of
teeth packed in there, and a tongue the size of that liverwurst his host's
wife is passing around? "Whaddaya want your glasses for, Harry? I don't
understand you at all!" "Aw, well, honey, I was feeling kind of dizzy or
something, and I thought—" "Dizzy is right. If you want to check on
the kids, why don't you just call on the phone?"

■   ■   ■

They can tell she's naked and about to get into the tub, but the bathroom window is frosted glass, and they can't see anything clearly. "I got
an idea," Mark whispers. "One of us goes and calls her on the phone,
and the other watches when she comes out." "Okay, but who calls?"
"Both of us, we'll do it twice. Or more."

■   ■   ■

Down forbidden alleys. Into secret passageways. Unlocking the world's
terrible secrets. Sudden shocks: a trapdoor! a fall! or the stunning
report of a rifle shot, the *whaaii-ii-ing!* of the bullet biting concrete by
your ear! Careful! Then edge forward once more, avoiding the light,
inch at a time, now a quick dash for an open doorway—*look out!*
there's a knife! a struggle! no! the long blade glistens! jerks! thrusts!
stabbed! No, no, it missed! The assailant's down, yes! the spy's on top,

pinning him, a terrific thrashing about, the spy rips off the assailant's mask: *a woman!*

■　■　■

Fumbling behind her, she finds it, wraps her hand around it, tugs. "Oh!" she gasps, pulling her hand back quickly, her ears turning crimson. "I . . . I thought it was the soap!" He squeezes her close between his thighs, pulls her back toward him, one hand sliding down her tummy between her legs. I Dream of Jeannie—"I have to go to the bathroom!" says someone outside the door.

■　■　■

She's combing her hair in the bathroom when the phone rings. She hurries to answer it before it wakes the baby. "Hello, Tuckers." There's no answer. "Hello?" A soft click. Strange. She feels suddenly alone in the big house, and goes in to watch TV with the children.

■　■　■

"Stop it!" she screams, "Please stop!" She's on her hands and knees, trying to get up, but they're too strong for her. Mark holds her head down. "Now, baby, we're gonna teach you how to be a nice girl," he says coldly, and nods at Jack. When she's doubled over like that, her skirt rides up her thighs to the leg bands of her panties. "C'mon, man, go! This baby's cold! She needs your touch!"

■　■　■

Parks the car a couple blocks away. Slips up to the house, glances in his window. Just like he's expected. Her blouse is off and the kid's shirt is unbuttoned. He watches, while slowly, clumsily, childishly, they fumble with each other's clothes. My God, it takes them forever. "Some party!" "You said it!" When they're more or less naked, he walks in. "Hey! What's going on here?" They go white as bleu cheese. Haw haw! "What's the little thing you got sticking out there, boy?" "Harry, behave yourself!" No, he doesn't let the kid get dressed, he sends him home bareassed. "Bareassed!" He drinks to that. "Promises, promises," says his host's wife. "I'll mail you your clothes, son!" He gazes down on the naked little girl on his couch. "Looks like you and me, we got a little secret to keep, honey," he says coolly. "Less you wanna go home the same way your boyfriend did!" He chuckles at his easy wit, leans down over her, and unbuckles his belt. "Might as well make it two secrets, right?" "What in God's name are you talking about, Harry?" He staggers out of there, drink in hand, and goes to look for his car.

■   ■   ■

"Hey! What's going on here?" They huddle half-naked under the blanket, caught utterly unawares. On television: the clickety-click of frightened running feet on foreign pavements. Jack is fumbling for his shorts, tangled somehow around his ankles. The blanket is snatched away. "On your feet there!" Mr. Tucker, Mrs. Tucker, and Mark's mom and dad, the police, the neighbors, everybody comes crowding in. Hopelessly, he has a terrific erection. So hard it hurts. Everybody stares down at it.

■   ■   ■

Bitsy's sleeping on the floor. The babysitter is taking a bath. For more than an hour now, he'd had to use the bathroom. He doesn't know how much longer he can wait. Finally, he goes to knock on the bathroom door. "I have to use the bathroom." "Well, come ahead, if you have to." "Not while you're in there." She sighs loudly. "Okay, okay, just a minute," she says, "but you're a real nuisance, Jimmy!" He's holding on, pinching it as tight as he can. "*Hurry!*" He holds his breath, squeezing shut his eyes. No. Too late. At last, she opens the door. "Jimmy!" "I *told* you to hurry!" he sobs. She drags him into the bathroom and pulls his pants down.

■   ■   ■

He arrives just in time to see her emerge from the bathroom, wrapped in a towel, to answer the phone. His two kids sneak up behind her and pull the towel away. She's trying to hang onto the phone and get the towel back at the same time. It's quite a picture. She's got a sweet ass. Standing there in the bushes, pawing himself with one hand, he lifts his glass with the other and toasts her sweet ass, which his son now swats. Haw haw, maybe that boy's gonna shape up, after all.

■   ■   ■

They're in the bushes, arguing about their next move, when she comes out of the bathroom, wrapped in a towel. They can hear the baby crying. Then it stops. They see her running, naked, back to the bathroom like she's scared or something. "I'm going in after her, man, whether you're with me or not!" Mark whispers, and he starts out of the bushes. But just then, a light comes sweeping up through the yard, as a car swings in the drive. They hit the dirt, hearts pounding. "Is it the cops?" "I don't know!" "Do you think they saw us?" "Sshh!" A man comes staggering up the walk from the drive, a drink in his hand, stumbles on in the kitchen door and then straight into the bathroom. "It's Mr. Tucker!" Mark whispers. A scream. "Let's get outa here, man!"

■ ■ ■

9:00. Having missed most of the spy show anyway and having little else to do, the babysitter has washed the dishes and cleaned the kitchen up a little. The books on the refrigerator remind her of her better intentions, but she decides that first she'll see what's next on TV. In the living room, she finds little Bitsy sound asleep on the floor. She lifts her gently, carries her into her bed, and tucks her in. "Okay, Jimmy, it's nine o'clock, I've let you stay up, now be a good boy." Sullenly, his sleepy eyes glued still to the set, the boy backs out of the room toward his bedroom. A drama comes on. She switches channels. A ballgame and a murder mystery. She switches back to the drama. It's a love story of some kind. A man married to an aging invalid wife, but in love with a younger girl. "Use the bathroom and brush your teeth before going to bed, Jimmy!" she calls, but as quickly regrets it, for she hears the baby stir in its crib.

■ ■ ■

Two of them are talking about mothers they've salted away in rest homes. Oh boy, that's just wonderful, this is one helluva party. She leaves them to use the john, takes advantage of the retreat to ease her girdle down awhile, get a few good deep breaths. She has this picture of her three kids carting her off to a rest home. In a wheelbarrow. That sure is something to look forward to, all right. When she pulls her girdle back up, she can't seem to squeeze into it. The host looks in. "Hey, Dolly, are you all right?" "Yeah, I just can't get into my damn girdle, that's all." "Here, let me help."

■ ■ ■

She pulls them on, over her own, standing in front of the bedroom mirror, holding her skirt bundled up around the waist. About twenty sizes too big for her, of course. She pulls them tight from behind, runs her hand inside the opening in front, pulls out her thumb. "And what a good boy am I!" She giggles: how funny it must feel! Then, in the mirror, she sees him: in the doorway behind her, sullenly watching. "Jimmy! You're supposed to be in bed!" "Those are my daddy's!" the boys says. "I'm gonna tell!"

■ ■ ■

"Jimmy!" She drags him into the bathroom and pulls his pants down. "Even your shoes are wet! Get them off!" She soaps up a warm washcloth she's had with her in the bathtub, scrubs him from the waist down with it. Bitsy stands in the doorway, staring. "Get out! Get out!"

the boy screams at his sister. "Go back to bed, Bitsy. It's just an accident." "Get out!" The baby wakes and starts to howl.

■ ■ ■

The young lover feels sorry for her rival, the invalid wife; she believes
the man has a duty toward the poor woman and and insists she is
willing to wait. But the man argues that he also has a duty toward
himself: his life, too, is short, and he could not love his wife now even
were she well. He embraces the young girl feverishly; she twists away
in anguish. The door opens. They stand there grinning, looking devilish, but pretty silly at the same time. "Jack! I thought I told you not to
come!" She's angry, but she's also glad in a way she was beginning to
feel a little too alone in the big house, with the children all sleeping.
She should have taken that bath, after all. "We just came by to see if
you were being a good girl," Jack says and blushes. The boys glance at
each other nervously.

■ ■ ■

She's just sunk down into the tubful of warm fragrant suds, ready for a
nice long soaking, when the phone rings. Wrapping a towel around
her, she goes to answer: no one there. But now the baby's awake and
bawling. She wonders if that's Jack bothering her all the time. If it is,
brother, that's the end. Maybe it's the end anyway. She tries to calm
the baby with the half-empty bottle, not wanting to change it until
she's finished her bath. The bathroom's where the diapers go dirty, and
they make it stink to high heaven. "Shush, shush!" she whispers, rocking the crib. The towel slips away, leaving an airy empty tingle up and
down her backside. Even before she stoops for the towel, even before
she turns around, she knows there's somebody behind her.

■ ■ ■

"We just came by to see if you were being a good girl," Jack says,
grinning down at her. She's flushed and silent, her mouth half open.
"Lean over," says Mark amiably. "We'll soap your back, as long as we're
here." But she just huddles there, down in the suds, staring up at them
with big eyes.

■ ■ ■

"Hey! What's going on here?" It's Mr. Tucker, stumbling through the
door with a drink in his hand. She looks up from the TV. "What's the
matter, Mr. Tucker?" "Oh, uh, I'm sorry, I got lost—no, I mean, I
had to get some aspirin. Excuse me!" And he rushes past her into the

bathroom, caroming off the living room door jamb on the way. The baby awakes.

■ ■ ■

"Okay, get off her, Mr. Tucker!" "Jack!" she cries, "what are *you* doing here?" He stares hard at them a moment: so that's where it goes. Then, as Mr. Tucker swings heavily off, he leans into the bastard with a hard right to the belly. Next thing he knows, though, he's got a face full of an old man's fist. He's not sure, as the lights go out, if that's his girlfriend screaming or the baby . . .

■ ■ ■

Her host pushes down on her fat fanny and tugs with all his might on her girdle, while she bawls on his shoulder: "I don't *wanna* go to a rest home!" "Now, now, take it easy, Dolly, nobody's gonna make you—" "Ouch! Hey, you're hurting!" "You should buy a bigger girdle, Dolly." "You're telling me?" Some other guy pokes his head in. "Whatsa-matter? Dolly fall in?" "No, she fell out. Give me a hand."

■ ■ ■

By the time she's chased Jack and Mark out of there, she's lost track of the program she's been watching on television. There's another woman in the story now for some reason. That guy lives a very complicated life. Impatiently, she switches channels. She hates ballgames, so she settles for the murder mystery. She switches just in time, too: there's a dead man sprawled out on the floor of what looks like an office or a study or something. A heavyset detective gazes up from his crouch over the body. "He's been strangled." Maybe she'll take that bath, after all.

■ ■ ■

She drags him into the bathroom and pulls his pants down. She soaps up a warm washcloth she's had in the tub with her, but just as she reaches between his legs, it starts to spurt, spraying her arms and hands. "Oh, Jimmy! I thought you were done!" she cries, pulling him toward the toilet and aiming it into the bowl. How moist and rubbery it is! And you can turn it every which way. How funny it must feel!

■ ■ ■

"Stop it!" she screams. "Please stop!" She's on her hands and knees and Jack is holding her head down. "Now we're gonna teach you how to be a nice girl," Mark says and lifts her skirt. "Well, I'll be damned!" "What's the matter?" asks Jack, his heart pounding. "Look at this big pair of men's underpants she's got on!" "Those are my daddy's!" Jimmy, watching them from the doorway. "I'm gonna tell!"

■   ■   ■

People are shooting at each other in the murder mystery, but she's so mixed up, she doesn't know which ones are the good guys. She switches back to the love story. Something seems to have happened, because now the man is kissing his invalid wife tenderly. Maybe she's finally dying. The baby wakes, begins to scream. Let it. She turns up the volume on the TV.

■   ■   ■

Leaning down over her, unbuckling his belt. It's all happening just like he's known it would. Beautiful! The kid is gone, though his pants, poor lad, remain. "Looks like you and me, we got a secret to keep, child!" But he's cramped on the couch and everything is too slippery and small. "Lift your legs up, honey. Put them around my back." But instead, she screams. He rolls off, crashing to the floor. There they all come, through the front door. On television, somebody is saying: "Am I a burden to you, darling?" "Dolly! My God! Dolly, I can explain . . . !"

■   ■   ■

The game of the night is Get Dolly Tucker Back in Her Girdle Again. They've got her down on her belly in the living room and the whole damn crowd is working on her. Several of them are stretching the girdle, while others try to jam the fat inside. "I think we made a couple inches on this side! Roll her over!" Harry?

■   ■   ■

She's just stepped into the tub, when the phone rings, waking the baby. She sinks down in the suds, trying not to hear. But that baby doesn't cry, it screams. Angrily, she wraps a towel around herself, stamps peevishly into the baby's room, just letting the phone jangle. She tosses the baby down on its back, unpins its diapers hastily, and gets yellowish baby stool all over her hands. Her towel drops away. She turns to find Jimmy staring at her like a little idiot. She slaps him in the face with her dirty hand, while the baby screams, the phone rings, and nagging voices argue on the TV. There are better things she might be doing.

■   ■   ■

What's happening? Now there's a young guy in it. Is he after the young girl or the old invalid? To tell the truth, it looks like he's after the same man the women are. In disgust, she switches channels. "The strangler again," growls the fat detective, hands on hips, staring down at the body of a half-naked girl. She's considering either switching back to the love story or taking a quick bath, when a hand suddenly clutches her mouth.

■　　■　　■

"You're both chicken," she says, staring up at them. "But what if Mr. Tucker comes home?" Mark asks nervously.

■　　■　　■

How did he get here? He's standing pissing in his own goddamn bathroom, his wife is still back at the party, the three of them are, like good kids, sitting in there in the living room watching TV. One of them is his host's boy Mark. "It's a good murder mystery, Mr. Tucker," Mark said, when he came staggering in on them a minute ago. "Sit still!" he shouted, "I am just home for a moment!" Then whump thump on into the bathroom. Long hike for a wee-wee, Mister. But something keeps bothering him. Then it hits him: the girl's panties hanging like a broken balloon from the rabbit-ear antennae on the TV! He barges back in there, giving his shoulder a helluva crack on the living room door jamb on the way—but they're not hanging there any more. Maybe he's only imagined it. "Hey, Mr. Tucker," Mark says flatly. "Your fly's open."

■　　■　　■

The baby's dirty. Stinks to high heaven. She hurries back to the living room, hearing sirens and gunshots. The detective is crouched peering in. Already, she's completely lost. The baby screams at the top of its lungs. She turns up the volume. But it's all confused. she hurries back in there, claps an angry hand to the baby's mouth. "Shut up!" she cries. She throws the baby down on its back, starts to unpin the diaper, as the baby tunes up again. The phone rings. She answers it, one eye on the TV. "What?" The baby cries so hard it starts to choke. Let it. "I said, hi, this is Jack!" Then it hits her: oh no! The diaper pin!

■　　■　　■

"The aspirin . . ." But she's already in the tub. Way down in the tub. Staring at him through the water. Her tummy looks pale and ripply. He hears sirens, people on the porch.

■　　■　　■

Jimmy gets up to the bathroom and gets his face slapped and smeared with baby poop. Then she hauls him off to the bathroom, yanks off his pajamas, and throws him into the tub. That's okay, but next she gets naked and acts like she's gonna get in the tub, too. The baby's screaming and the phone's ringing like crazy and in walks his dad. Saved! he thinks, but, no, his dad grabs him right back out of the tub and whales the dickens out of him no questions asked, while she watches, then sends him—*whack!*—back to bed. So he's lying there, wet and dirty and naked and sore, and he still has to go to the bathroom, and outside his window he hears two older guys talking. "Listen, you know where to do it if we get her pinned?" "No! Don't you?"

◼   ◼   ◼

"Yo ho heave ho! *Ugh!*" Dolly's on her back and they're working on the belly side. Somebody got the great idea of buttering her down first. Not to lose the ground they've gained, they've shot it inside with a basting syringe. But now suddenly there's this big tug-of-war under way between those who want to stuff her in and those who want to let her out. Something rips, but she feels better. The odor of hot butter makes her think of movie theaters and popcorn. "Hey, has anybody seen Harry?" she asks. "Where's Harry?"

◼   ◼   ◼

Somebody's getting chased. She switches back to the love story, and now the man's back kissing the young lover again. What's going on? She gives it up, decides to take a quick bath. She's just stepping into the tub, one foot in, one foot out, when Mr. Tucker walks in. "Oh, excuse me! I only wanted some aspirin . . ." She grabs for a towel, but he yanks it away. "Now, that's not how it's supposed to happen, child," he scolds. "Please! Mr. Tucker . . . !" He embraces her savagely, his calloused old hands clutching roughly at her backside. "Mr. Tucker!" she cries, squirming. "Your wife called—!" He's pushing something between her legs, hurting her. She slips, they both slip—something cold and hard slams her in the back, cracks her skull, she seems to be sinking into a sea . . .

◼   ◼   ◼

They've got her over the hassock, skirt up and pants down. "Give her a little lesson there, Jack baby!" The television lights flicker and flash over her glossy flesh, 1000 WHEN LIT. Whack! Slap! Bumper to bumper! He leans into her, feeling her come alive.

◼   ◼   ◼

The phone rings, waking the baby. "Jack, is that you? Now, you listen to me—" "No, dear, this is Mrs. Tucker. Isn't the TV awfully loud?"

"Oh, I'm sorry, Mrs. Tucker! I've been getting—" "I tried to call you before, but I couldn't hang on. To the phone, I mean. I'm sorry, dear." "Just a minute, Mrs. Tucker, the baby's—" "Honey, listen! Is Harry there? Is Mr. Tucker there, dear?"

▪   ▪   ▪

"Stop it!" she screams and claps a hand over the baby's mouth. "Stop it! Stop it! *Stop it!*" Her other hand is full of baby stool and she's afraid she's going to be sick. The phone rings. "No!" she cries. She's hanging on to the baby, leaning woozily away, listening to the phone ring. "Okay, okay," she sighs, getting ahold of herself. But when she lets go of the baby, it isn't screaming any more. She shakes it. Oh no . . .

▪   ▪   ▪

"Hello?" No answer. Strange. She hangs up and, wrapped only in a towel, stares out the window at the cold face staring in—she screams!

▪   ▪   ▪

She screams, scaring the hell out of him. He leaps out of the tub, glances up at the window she's gaping at just in time to see two faces duck away, then slips on the bathroom tiles, and crashes to his ass, whacking his head on the sink on the way down. She stares down at him, trembling, a towel over her narrow shoulders. "Mr. Tucker! Mr. Tucker, are you all right . . . ?" Who's Sorry Now? Yessir, who's back is breaking with each . . . He stares up at the little tufted locus of all his woes, and passes out, dreaming of Jeannie . . .

▪   ▪   ▪

The phone rings. "Dolly! It's for you!" "Hello?" "Hello, Mrs. Tucker?" "Yes, speaking." "Mrs. Tucker, this is the police calling . . ."

▪   ▪   ▪

It's cramped and awkward and slippery, but he's pretty sure he got it in her, once anyway. When he gets the suds out of his eyes, he sees her staring up at them. Through the water. "Hey, Mark! Let her up!"

▪   ▪   ▪

Down in the suds. Feeling sleepy. The phone rings, starling her. Wrapped in a towel, she goes to answer. "No, he's not here, Mrs. Tucker." Strange. Married people act pretty funny sometimes. The baby is awake and screaming. Dirty, a real mess. Oh boy, there's a lot of things she'd rather be doing than babysitting in this madhouse. She decides to wash the baby off in her own bathwater. She removes her towel, unplugs the tub, lowers the water level so the baby can sit. Glancing back over her shoulder, she sees Jimmy staring at her. "Go back to bed, Jimmy." "I have to go to the bathroom." "Good grief, Jimmy! It looks like you already have!" The phone rings. She doesn't bother with the towel—what can Jimmy see he hasn't already seen?—and goes to answer. "No, Jack, and that's final." Sirens, on the TV, as the police move in. But wasn't that the channel with the love story? Ambulance maybe. Get this over with so she can at least catch the news. "Get those wet pajamas off, Jimmy, and I'll find clean ones. Maybe you better get in the tub, too." "I think something's wrong with the baby," he says. "It's down in the water and it's not swimming or anything."

▪ ▪ ▪

She's staring up at them from the rug. They slap her. Nothing happens. "You just tilted her, man!" Mark says softly. "We gotta get outa here!" Two little kids are standing wideeyed in the doorway. Mark looks hard at Jack. "No, Mark, they're just little kids . . . !" "We gotta, man, or we're dead."

▪ ▪ ▪

"Dolly! My God! Dolly, I can explain!" She glowers down at them, her ripped girdle around her ankles. "What the four of you are doing in the bathtub with *my* babysitter?" she says sourly. "I can hardly wait!"

▪ ▪ ▪

Police sirens wail, lights flash. "I heard the scream!" somebody shouts. "There were two boys!" "I saw a man!" "She was running with the baby!" "My God!" somebody screams "they're *all* dead!" Crowds come running. Spotlights probe the bushes.

▪ ▪ ▪

"Harry, where the hell you been?" his wife whines, glaring blearily up at him from the carpet. "I can explain," he says. "Hey, whatsamatter, Harry?" his host asks, smeared with butter for some goddamn reason. "You look like you just seen a ghost!" Where did he leave his drink? Everybody's laughing, everybody except Dolly, whose cheeks are streaked with tears. "Hey, Harry, you won't let them take me to a rest home, will you, Harry?"

▪ ▪ ▪

10:00. The dishes done, children to bed, her books read, she watches the news on television. Sleepy. The man's voice is gentle, soothing.

She dozes—awakes with a start: a babysitter? Did the announcer say something about a babysitter?

◼   ▦   ▦

"Just want to catch the weather," the host says, switching on the TV. Most of the guests are leaving, but the Tuckers stay to watch the news. As it comes on, the announcer is saying something about a babysitter. The host switches channels. "They got a better weatherman on four," he explains. "Wait!" says Mrs. Tucker. "There was something about a babysitter . . . !" The host switches back. "Details have not yet been released by the police," the announcer says. "Harry, maybe we'd better go . . ."

▦   ▦   ▦

They stroll casually out of the drugstore, run into a buddy of theirs. "Hey! Did you hear about the babysitter?" the guy asks. Mark grunts, glances at Jack. "Got a smoke?" he asks the guy.

▦   ▦   ▦

"I think I hear the baby screaming!" Mrs. Tucker cries, running across the lawn from the drive.

▦   ▦   ▦

She wakes, startled, to find Mr. Tucker hovering over her. "I must have dozed off!" she exclaims. "Did you hear the news about the babysitter?" Mr. Tucker asks. "Part of it," she says, rising. "Too bad, wasn't it?" Mr. Tucker is watching the report of the ball scores and golf tournaments. "I'll drive you home in just a minute, dear," he says. "Why, how nice!" Mrs. Tucker exclaims from the kitchen. "The dishes are all done!"

▦   ▦   ▦

"What can I say, Dolly?" the host says with a sigh, twisting the buttered strands of her ripped girdle between his fingers. "Your children are murdered, your husband gone, a corpse in your bathtub, and your house is wrecked. I'm sorry. But what can I say?" On the TV, the news is over, and they're selling aspirin. "Hell, I don't know," she says. "Let's see what's on the late late movie."

1969

▦   ▦   ▦

MARK COSTELLO

MURPHY'S XMAS

I

Murphy's drunk on the bright verge of still another Christmas and a car door slams. Then he's out in the headlights and in bed waking up the next afternoon with Annie kissing his crucified right fist. It's blue and swollen, and when he tries to move it, it tingles, it chimes and Annie says, How did you hurt your hand? Did you hit somebody?

Murphy waits while that question fades on her mouth, then the room glitters and he sniffs the old fractured acid of remorse asking: Was I sick?

Yes.

Where?

On the floor. And you fell out of bed twice. It was so terrible I don't think I could stand it if it happened again promise me you won't get drunk anymore, Glover had to teach both of your classes this morning you frighten me when you're this way and you've lost so much weight you should have seen yourself last night lying naked on the floor like something from a concentration camp in your own vomit you were so white you were blue

is the color of Annie's eyes as Murphy sinks into the stars and splinters of the sheets with her, making love to her and begging her forgiveness which she gives and gives until Murphy can feel her shy skeleton waltzing away with his in a fit of ribbons, the bursting bouquets of a Christmas they are going to spend apart and

bright the next morning they rise in sweet sorrow to part for Christmas; she to her parents' home in Missouri, he to haunted Illinois.

Murphy holds her head in his hands and whispers: I can't leave you. I won't be able to sleep. I know I won't. I'll get sick. I need you Annie.

She squeezes his shoulders, kisses his cheeks and tells him he can do it. It's only for two weeks. Goodbye. And be careful. Driving.

The door slams, the windows rattle and Annie walking through the snow is no bigger than her cello which she holds to her shoulder, a suitcase bangs against her left knee and the door opens and there's Glover jangling the keys of his Volkswagen, offering again to drive Murphy's family into Illinois for him.

Stricken by swerving visions of his son strewn across the wet December roadside, his toys and intestines glistening under the wheels of semi trucks, Murphy says no, he will drive and as he takes the proffered keys, Glover says: Is Annie gone already? I was supposed to give her a cello lesson before she left

then he leaves, the door slams and Murphy hates him, his Byronesque[1] limp through the snow, his cello and his Volkswagen and sobriety. Rubbing his right fist, Murphy goes to the kitchen and drains a can of beer. Then he packs his bag and lights out for his abandoned home.

II

Now the trunks are tied down and the Volkswagen is overladen and they roll out of Kansas into Missouri with the big wind knocking them all over the road while vigilant Murphy fights the wheel and grins at the feather touches of his 5-year-old son, who kisses his neck and romps in the back seat, ready for Christmas.

In Mexico, Missouri, his wife looks at his swollen right fist and says: Tsk-tsk. You haven't grown up yet have you. Who did you hit this time?

Into the face of her challenge, Murphy blows blue cigarette smoke.

When they cross the Mighty Mississippi at Hannibal, she looks up at the old, well-kept houses, pats her swollen stomach and says: Maybe I could come here to live, to have my baby.

Murphy's son rushes into the crack of her voice. And he doesn't stop asking him to come back and be his daddy again until Murphy takes Dexamyl to keep awake and it is dark and his son is asleep and the Volkswagen hops and shudders over the flat mauve stretches of Illinois.

At Springfield, where they stop to take on gas, the fluorescent light of the filling station is like the clap of a blue hand across the face.

1. In the melodramatic, picturesque manner of George Gordon, Lord Byron (1788–1824), English Romantic poet.

Murphy's son wakes and his wife says: This is where President Lincoln lived and is buried.

Where?

In a tomb. Out there.

She points a finger past his nose and Murphy makes a promise he knows he can't keep. I know what. Do you want to hear a poem, Michael?

With his son at the back of his neck all snug in a car that he should never have presumed to borrow, he drives through Springfield trying to remember "When Lilacs Last in the Dooryard Bloom'd."[2] But he can't get past the first stanza. Three times he repeats "O powerful western fallen star," and then goes on in prose about the coffin moving across the country with the pomp of the inloop'd flags, through cities draped in black until his son is asleep again and

that coffin becomes his wife's womb and from deep in its copious satin Murphy hears the shy warble of the fetus: *you are my father, you are my father*, the throat bleeds, the song bubbles. Murphy is afraid enough to fight. He looks at his wife and remembers the wily sunlight of conception, the last time he made love to her amid the lace iron and miniature American flags of the Veterans Cemetery (it's the quietest place I know to talk, she said) while the crows slipped across the sun like blue razor blades and the chatter of their divorce sprang up around them

stone and pine, lilac and star, the cedars dusk and dim: *well it's final then, we're definitely going to get a divorce?* Murphy said *yes*, for good? *yes* and his wife caught him by the hip as he turned away *well it's almost dark now so why don't we just lie down and fuck once more for old time's sake here on the grass come on there are pine needles and they're soft.*

Did you take your pill?

Yes

Ok, but no strings attached and

3½ months later Murphy is informed that he is going to be a father again and again, hurray, whoopee now

Murphy drives across slippery Illinois hearing a carol of death until the singer so shy becomes a child he will never hold or know, and the sweet chant of its breath gets caught in the whine of the tires as he imagines holding the child and naming it and kissing it, until it falls asleep on his shoulder—*how could you have tricked me this way? how could you have done it?*

That question keeps exploding behind. Murphy's eyes, and when

---

2. Poem by Walt Whitman commemorating the death of President Lincoln.

they hit his wife' hometown, he stops the car in front of a tavern and
says: I can't do it.

What?

Face your parents.

He gets out: I'll wait here. Come back when you're unloaded.

His wife says *wait a minute*, and Murphy slams the door. He walks
under the glittering Budweiser sign and she screams: I can't drive. I
don't even know how to get this thing in reverse . . .

Push down.

Child!

Murphy hovers over the car: *I'm not a child!* and the motor roars,
and the gears grind, and the Volkswagen hops and is dead. A red light
flashes on in the middle of the speedometer and Murphy turns to the
wakening face of 5-year-old Michael: Are we at Grandma's yet Daddy?

He slams his swollen right fist into his left palm: Yes we are!

Then he gets in and takes the wheel. And he drives them all the
way home.

But he doesn't stop there. Murphy roars northwest out of Illinois
into Iowa in search of friends and gin he can't find. Then he bangs
back across the Mississippi, cuts down the heart of Illinois, and holes
up in the YMCA in his wife's hometown, within visiting distance of
his son.

Whom he loves and doesn't see. He keeps telling himself: *I think
I'll surprise Michael and take him to the park this afternoon*, then he
races down to the gym to run in circles and spit against the walls. He
sits in the steam room, watches the clock and slaps his stomach, which
is flat, but on the blink. To ease his pain, he drinks milk and eats
cottage cheese and yogurt and calls Annie long distance in Missouri:
God I love you and miss your body Annie I haven't slept for two days

and she says: Guess what?

What?

Glover was through town and gave me a cello lesson, he's a great
guy his

gifts are stunning and relentless, he limps off to take your classes
when you're too drunk to stand up in the morning—his hair is
scrubbed, his skin cherubic, his wrists are opal and delicate; right now
Murphy would like to seize them and break them off. Instead he says:
Is he still in town?

"Who?

Glover.

Heavens no, he just stopped through for about two hours are you
all right?

Yes. Listen Annie I love you

Murphy slams the phone down and bounds back upstairs to his room in the YMCA to sit alone while his cottage cheese and yogurt cartons fill up with snow on the window ledge and he imagines Annie back in their rooms in Kansas. When she walks across the floor her heels ring against the walls and every morning Murphy hears her before he sees her standing at the stove, her hair dark, her earrings silver, her robe wine, her thighs so cool, and the pearl flick of her tongue is like a beak when she kisses him

Murphy tastes unbelievable mint and blood and

imagines Glover limping across the floor of the living room with two glasses of gin in his hands. The betrayal is dazzling and quick. Bending under Glover's tongue, Annie whispers *no, no,* and as she goes down in their bed, her fingers make star-shaped wrinkles in the sheets

Murphy slams his fist down on his YMCA windowsill. Then popping them like white bullwhips over his head, he stuffs his towels and clothes into his bag, and lights out of there on lustrous Highway 47. The night is prodigal, the inane angels of the radio squawk out their thousand songs of Christmas and return. Bearing down on the wheel, Murphy murders the memory of Annie and Glover with the memory of his father, whom he has betrayed to old age, the stars and stripes of the U.S. Mail.

Composing them on the back of his American Legion 40 *and* 8 stationery, Murphy's father sends quick notes By Air to his grandson saying: I was feeling pretty low x until I got the pictures you drew for me Michael boy x then I bucked up x God bless you x I miss you x give my love to your daddy x who

unblessed and rocking in the slick crescents of Dexamyl and fatigue, is on his way home for still another Christmas. Now as he drives, he notes the dim absence of birds on the telephone lines, and thinking of the happy crows that Michael draws with smiles in their beaks, Murphy sees his father stumbling under the sign of the cross, crossing himself again and again on the forehead and lips, crossing himself on his tie clasp, wandering in a listless daze across the front lawn with a rake in his hands, not knowing whether to clean the gutter along the street or pray for his own son, who has sunk so low out in Kansas.

It is just dawning when Murphy breaks into the mauve and white outskirts of his dear dirty Decatur where billboards and *Newport* girls[3] in turquoise are crowned by the bursting golden crosses of Murphy's high school then

3. Advertisements for Newport cigarettes.

he's home. Pulled up and stopped in his own driveway. And sitting there with his hands crossed in his lap he feels agog like a Buddhistic time bomb about to go off, about to splinter and explode inside the dry sleep of his parents, the tears will smoulder, the braying angels of insomnia will shatter around the childless Christmas tree, there will be a fire, it will sputter and run up the walls and be Murphy's fault. Sitting there he feels hearts beginning to pump in the palms of his hands and he doesn't want to let anybody die

as he knocks on the dry oaken door of his parents' home and is welcomed with open arms and the sun rising behind his back

Inside the sockets of his mother's eyes, there are mauve circles and they have had the living room walls painted turquoise. Murphy blinks, shakes his father's hands, and his mother leads him into the kitchen.

There he drinks milk, eats cottage cheese and kisses his mother's hands. She cries and wants him to eat a big breakfast. With tears in her eyes, she offers him bacon, eggs, cornbread, coffee, butterchunk sweet rolls and Brazil-nuts. When Murphy shakes his head she says: I think you're making the biggest mistake of your life, I think you'll live to regret it. Patricia is a lovely girl, you have a wonderful son and another child on the way. Isn't there any hope of you getting back together? I pray night and day and can't get little Michael off my mind. What's ever going to happen to him and the new child? Oh I wish I were twenty years younger

After breakfast they go shopping, and for his Christmas present Murphy picks out three packs of stainless steel razor blades and a pair of black oxford basketball shoes. Then he slips off for a workout at his high school gym. The basketball team is practicing and Murphy runs in wide circles around them, not bothering a soul.

Left to himself that afternoon, he drinks rum and eggnog and plays with the remote controls of the color television set. Then he roams the house and neighborhood and everything has changed. The sheets of his bed are blue. On the walls, where once there were newspaper photographs of himself in high school basketball uniform, there are now purple paintings of Jesus Christ kneeling on rocks in the Garden of Gethsemane.[4] Every place he looks, in corniced frames of diminishing size, there are color photographs of Murphy in tight-collared military attire. As he looks, the photographs get smaller and smaller and there is always a snub-nosed statue of St. Francis of Assisi[5] standing there, to measure himself by.

---

4. The garden where Christ prayed before the Crucifixion (Mark 14:32).
5. St. Francis (1182?–1226), founder of the Franciscan order, was known for his humility and his love of all living creatures.

Up and down the blocks, birds bang in and out of bird feeders. The withering neighbors have put up fences within fences within fences. Half-drunk, Murphy keeps hitting the wrong switches and floodlights glare from the roof of the garage and light up the whole backyard. All night long his father keeps paying the encroaching negro carolers not to sing. Finally Murphy gets up from the sofa, and smiling, announces that he's going out. Taking his rum and eggnog with him, he sits in the Volkswagen and drinks until 3 o'clock in the morning. Then he gets out, vomits on the curb and goes back inside

Where his mother is awake in a nightgown of shriveled violet, with yellow spears of wheat sewn into the shoulders like cross-staves of static lightning about to go off and how
will Murphy hold her when she stops him on the carpet outside his bedroom door to tell him that she loves him, that he will always be her son no matter what happens she is so sorry that he had to leave his wife and children for
a mere girl, it is unbelievable that
in his hands her small skull buzzes and even before she mentions the fact of Annie, Murphy is holding Annie's skull in his hands and the sinking wings of his mother's sweet shoulders are Annie's shoulders in his mother's nightgown sinking: What are you talking about?
That girl you're living with. She called tonight
on Christmas Eve
Murphy hears the old familiar bells of his father's fury gonging
Your father answered, he was furious
Mother I'm not living with anyone
Michael I know you are

then the small lightning of her nightgown begins to strike across her shoulders and she is sobbing against his throat and Murphy is in bed holding his lie like a sheet up to his chin: Mother I told you I'm not living with anyone
Stroking his leg through the blankets, she disregards the crocked insomnia of his eyes, and makes him promise to try to sleep: Do you promise now?
Yes, Mother, I promise
and she leaves him sleepless between the blue sheets with Christ kneeling on the wall, the scent of his mother's handcream on the back of his neck and he hears her alone in her room coughing like a wife he has lost at last and picking at her rosary beads all night long
There is no sleep
or peace on earth. But with the muzzy dawn Murphy rises and goes to church with his parents. In the choir loft, the organs shudder;

in his pew Murphy shivers and sniffs the contrition of Christmastide. All around him the faithful kneel in candle smoke and pray; all day long Murphy kneels and shuffles around trying to get Annie *long distance*, trying to tell her *never to call him at home again.* Then at 7 P.M. the phone rings and Murphy's simmering 70-year-old father answers it hissing: Long distance, for you

By the time Murphy hangs up, his father is dizzy. He staggers through the rooms slamming doors while Murphy's mother follows him whispering: Mike your blood pressure, your blood pressure

Then in the living room they face each other: The bitch! Calling here on Christmas Day! The little bitch!

Murphy turns to his mother and says, *I'm leaving* and his father spins him by the shoulder: You're not leaving, *I* am!

They both leave. Murphy by the back, his father by the front. Storm doors slam, crucifixes rattle on the walls. Murphy's father rounds the corner and screams: Come back here!

His voice is higher than Murphy has ever heard it, and the wind pulls at their clothes while they walk toward each other, his father in a slanting stagger, his overcoat too big for him, his eyes filled with tears.

I'm an old man. I'm dying. You won't see me again. Go back to your family, don't abandon your son.

Murphy reaches for his shoulder and says *Dad I can't* and his father slaps his hand away

Michael Murphy. You have a son named *Michael Murphy* and you tell me you can't go back to him?

Murphy lifts his hand and starts to speak, but his father screams: Phony! You're a phon*eee*, do you hear me?

They are at the door and Murphy's mother, in grief and her nightgown, pulls them in. His father stumbles to the wall and hits it: You phony. You ought to be in Vietnam!

Murphy's laughter is curdled and relieved. He slaps his hands together and screams: That's it, that's it!

Then he spins and bolts toward the back door, with his mother screaming: Michael! Where are you going?

To Vietnam, god damn it! To Vietnam

Which isn't far. 150 miles north. From a motel room deep in her own hometown, Murphy calls his wife and when he asks her to come over she says: Why *should* I come over?

You know why. I'm going out of my mind.

Be my guest.

Click

She opens the door during half-time of a TV football game and neither of them says a word as their clothes fly in slurred arcs onto the bed. Then standing naked in front of her, Murphy hunches up with holy quietude and smiles and breathes as he holds a glass of gin and tonic to her lips and she drinks and smiles as the lime skin nudges her teeth and she nods when she's had enough. While her mouth is still cool, Murphy kisses her tongue and gums and wants to push the bed against the wall and then to drive all the other guests to insomniac rack and ruin by humping and banging the bed with wet good health against the wall all afternoon but

his wife is sunk in an older despair. She runs her fingers up the vapid stack of Murphy's spine and says: You *are* handsome. I love to touch you.

Bare-chested Murphy turns on it, and the quick trick of her flattery gets them into bed, where to the pelvic thud of the innerspring she sucks on the spare skin of his collarbone and says: Tell me that you love me. You don't have to mean it. Just say it . . .

Murphy would like to but he can't. Both memory and flesh legislate against him. He looks down, and like painted furniture his wife's ribs now seem chipped by a thousand kicks; when he takes them in his mouth, her nipples taste as tight and deprived as walnuts; within the pregnant strop of her stomach against his, Murphy can feel the delicate strophes of Annie's waist, and moving like a pale liar before his wife's bared teeth, he remembers the beginning of the end of their marriage; the masks, mirrors and carrots that began to sprout around their bed like a bitter, 2 A.M. Victory garden,[6] one that Murphy had planted all by himself and was going to pick and shake in his wife's face on the sparkling, sacrosanct morning that he left for good and ever. Caught in the dowdy mosaics of their bedroom mirror, they would get down on their hands and knees and as the orange joke of a carrot disappeared between her legs, his wife would turn and ask, *who are you?* and Murphy would smile down from behind his mask and say: *who are you?* Then his smile would rot in his opened mouth, and Murphy *became* his impersonations; he played and moaned within an adultery so hypothetical it stunk and smoked the bedroom ceiling up like the induced death of love between them *Harder, Oh Harder* now Murphy and his father are standing outside the motel room window looking in at Murphy's marriage like peeping toms and his father is ordering Murphy back into the bed but Murphy resists and all of his reasons are rosy and shrill like a schoolboy he screams: *I wouldn't swap Annie for anybody, do you hear me, not anybody* and his father, in tears and death, screams: *Not for your son? Not for Michael Murphy? I'm*
Coming

6. Garden planted to supplement food supply in World War II.

and Murphy opens his eyes to endure his wife's orgasm like a slap across the face *Oh Thank You God, Oh Thank You.*

Thanking her with whispers and pecks about the neck and ears, Murphy sweeps his wife out into the brittle December afternoon and bright the next morning he picks up his son to take him home, 150 miles south, to his grandmother. Michael's raucous teeth glitter in the rearview mirror of the VW, and as they rattle into Decatur, Murphy loves him so much, he can't stop or share him with anybody just yet: I know what Michael. Do you want to go to the zoo before we go to Grandma's? Yes

he does. Right now. And Murphy, full of grins and flapdoodle, takes him there. He buys Michael a bag of popcorn, and as he goes back to the car to flick off the headlights, he turns to see the popcorn falling in white, jerky sprays among the ducks and geese.

The whole pause at the zoo is that way: spendthrift, inaugural and loving. Murphy squats and shows Michael how to feed the steaming billy goat with his bare hands. He flinches and giggles at the pink pluck of his lips, then they race over to look through the windows at the pacing leopards. Bare-handed and standing there, Murphy wonders how he would defend his son against a leopard. He can feel his fists and forearms being ripped away, but also he can feel his son escaping into the dusk and dim of the elm trees that surround the zoo.

Then he gets zany and amid giggles and protests, Murphy drives the borrowed VW up over the curb and through the park to Grandmother's house they go with the radio blaring: help I need somebody's help then

suddenly it's darker and cooler and their smiles are whiter when the subject changes like a slap across the face to

Michael's dreams. Five years old in a fatherless house, he sleeps alone and dreams of

snow. Murphy pulls him into the front seat, sets him on his lap and turns off the radio. Holding him too tight, he says: what kind of snow Michael?

You know. The kind that falls.

What do you dream?

That it's covering me up.

Then Michael begins to cry and says: I want somebody to sleep with me tonight and tomorrow night. I want *you* to sleep with me Daddy.

Murphy does. Three nights they stay in his parents' house and Murphy sleeps between the blue sheets while Michael sucks his thumb and urinates the first night against Murphy's leg, giving him the chance to be patient father loving his son he carries him to the bathroom with sure avowals and tender kisses: That's all right Michael boy, Dad will take care of you

Always?

Always

and Murphy's mother is there in her nightgown in the stark light of the bedroom changing the sheets, putting down towels, kissing her grandson, wishing she were twenty years younger

In the lilac morning quick with clouds and sunlight, Murphy and his mother and son go uptown. Standing in front of laughing mirrors in the Buster Brown Shoe Store, Murphy and Michael grow fat and skinny and tall and short together, then go to see Pinnochio not in the belly of a whale

but in the outer space of sure death and forgiveness, they eat silver sno-cones and Murphy is finally able to eat steak while his father roams through the rooms presenting his grandson with a plastic pistol on the barrel of which an assassin's scope has been mounted.

Compounding that armament with love, he displays, on the last afternoon, Murphy's basketball clippings. Spreading them out for his grandson on the bed, he whispers, smiles and gloats until 5-year-old Michael can't help himself. He walks over to Murphy and says: Grandpa says you were a great basketball player and played on TV

is that right Daddy?

That's right Michael, then they

are leaving. Clasping his toys to him, Michael cries pained and formal tears. Murphy stands on the curb, the wind in his eyes, and the apologies are yet to be made. Overhead the streetlight clangs and they are standing on the same corner where Murphy used to sit under the streetlight at night on the orange fire hydrant twirling his rosary beads like a black propeller over his head waiting for his parents to come home and light up the dark rooms with their voices and cigarettes then

he would see their headlights coming up the street and he would rise and put away his rosary beads to greet them now

he takes off his gloves and puts out his right hand to his father and says: Dad, I'm sorry.

When his apology cracks the air, his mother begins to cry. Grateful for that cue, his father takes his hand and says Goodbye, good luck, God bless you

III

Out there in Kansas the next afternoon, under a sere and benedictory sun, Murphy's Christmas comes to an end. He tools west away from home and the holidays, southwest toward the snaggled conclusion of still another New Year. His family rides in a swarm of shredded Kleenex, Cracker Jack, and terror referred

is terror refined: like the crucial envoy of his grandfather, Michael, sweet assassin, holds his plastic pistol to the base of Murphy's skull and says: Daddy? Why don't you come back and be my daddy?

Terse and perspirate, Murphy's wife takes a swipe at the pistol, but Michael moves out of her reach, and keeping it trained on the back of his father's skull, he repeats his question: Why don't you come back Daddy?

Before he can think or excuse himself, Murphy says, *Because.*

Because why?

Because Mommy and I fight.

You're not fighting now.

In tears and on her knees, Murphy's wife lunges into the back seat and disarms her son. But he begins to cry and find his ultimatum: Daddy

I'm too shy to have a new daddy, I want you to be my daddy, and if you won't come back and be my daddy

I'm going to kill you.

The moment of his threat is considered. And then it is foregone. Out of his fist and index finger, Michael makes a pistol and a patricide: Bang, bang, bang

you're dead Daddy

you're dead

Coffin that passes through lanes and streets, Volkswagen that blows and rattles under the new snow's perpetual clang, here, Murphy hands over his sprig of lilac and return, his modicum of rage and disbelief.

Certain that his son's aim was shy and hypothetical, he stops the Volkswagen in front of his apartment, flicks off the headlights, slams the door and hears the

dual squawk of tuned and funereal cellos

their notes curdle the snow, splinter the windows with a welcome so baroque and sepulchral, Murphy can't stand it. Roaring toward the door, he imagines Annie and Glover sitting on stiff-backed chairs, their cellos between their legs, their innocence arranged by Bach, certified by

the diagonal churn of their bows on string, the spiny octagons of their music stands, the opal bone and nylon of Annie's knees. Murphy rattles the door with his fist, and for a moment their music needles his rage, then squeaks to a stop. In turquoise slacks and sweater, with a

smile brimful of tears and teeth so bright, Annie throws open the door
and how

will Murphy return her kiss, while blurred in the corner of his
eye, Glover scurries, gathering up his cello and his music: *Happy New
Year did the car run all right* he takes the proffered keys and

guilty of nothing but his embarrassment

he says *don't mention it* as he leaves, slams out the door, and

left in the rattled vacuum of that departure, Murphy has no one
to beat up or murder, no one on whom to avenge his Christmas; he is
left with only the echo of the music, a suspicion founded on nothing
but a cherub's limp and hustle through the chiming snow.

In bed, Annie is a sweet new anatomy of hope and extinction. She
kisses him, the *Newport* flood of her hair gets in his eyes and Murphy
cracks an elegiac and necessary joke: *Annie you'll never leave me for
Glover will you?* She tells him not to be silly then

Murphy kisses her, and in a rush of flesh and new avowals, he
puts everything into his lovemaking but his

heart

which hangs unbelievable and dead in his ribs, all shot to smither-
eens by Michael.

Outside the new snow falls and inside it is over. Annie is asleep
in his arms and Murphy lies sleepless on a numb and chiming cross of
his own making. On the walls there are no praying Christs, the turquoise Gethsemanes of Decatur are gone forever. The clock drones,
the womb whirs, the shy trill of his wife's gestation comes to Murphy
through the pines like Michael calling to him: *Sleep with me tonight
and tomorrow night Daddy* the cradle's eloquence depends on pain, it
is sewn in lilacs and shocks of wheat. Shy charlatan, Murphy sneaks
up to me and in a roomfull of white, white sunlight, he looks in at his
newborn child, and cannot look away or kid himself, his fatherhood is
the fatherhood

of cottage cheese, the retreating footprints of snow and yogurt up
his father's spine, the borrowed Volkswagen that will never run out of
gas or plastic pistols. Then the dry bells of the furnace begin to hiss
against Murphy's ankles, and he hears the whistling pines, the clangor-
ous tombstones of the Veterans Cemetery. Flapping their arms like
downed angels in the middle of winter, Murphy and Annie make love
and forgive each other until their ears and eyesockets fill up with snow

then Michael stands over them, takes aim at Murphy and

makes his final declaration: Bang

bang, bang

you're dead Daddy
you're dead

IV
And for the first time in his life, Murphy lies there and knows it.

1973

▪   ▪   ▪

ANDRE DUBUS

A FATHER'S STORY

My name is Luke Ripley, and here is what I call my life: I own a stable of thirty horses, and I have young people who teach riding, and we board some horses too. This is in northeastern Massachusetts. I have a barn with an indoor ring, and outside I've got two fenced-in rings and a pasture that ends at a woods with trails. I call it my life because it looks like it is, and people I know call it that, but it's a life I can get away from when I hunt and fish, and some nights after dinner when I sit in the dark in the front room and listen to opera. The room faces the lawn and the road, a two-lane country road. When cars come around the curve northwest of the house, they light up the lawn for an instant, the leaves of the maple out by the road and the hemlock closer to the window. Then I'm alone again, or I'd appear to be if someone crept up to the house and looked through a window: a big-gutted grey-haired guy, drinking tea and smoking cigarettes, staring out at the dark woods across the road, listening to a grieving soprano.

My real life is the only one nobody talks about anymore, except Father Paul LeBoeuf, another old buck. He has a decade on me: he's sixty-four, a big man, bald on top with grey at the sides; when he had hair, it was black. His face is ruddy, and he jokes about being a whiskey priest,[1] though he's not. He gets outdoors as much as he can, goes for a long walk every morning, and hunts and fishes with me. But I can't get him on a horse anymore. Ten years ago I could badger him into a trail ride! I had to give him a western saddle, and he'd hold the pommel and bounce through the woods with me, and be sore for days. He's looking at seventy with eyes that are younger than many I've seen in people in their twenties. I do not remember ever feeling the way they

1. Vernacular term for a priest addicted to alcohol.

seem to; but I was lucky, because even as a child I knew that life would try me, and I must be strong to endure, though in those early days I expected to be tortured and killed for my faith, like the saints I learned about in school.

Father Paul's family came down from Canada, and he grew up speaking more French than English, so he is different from the Irish priests who abound up here. I do not like to make general statements, or even to hold general beliefs, about people's blood, but the Irish do seem happiest when they're dealing with misfortune or guilt, either their own or somebody's else's, and if you think you're not a victim of either one, you can count on certain Irish priests to try to change your mind. On Wednesday nights Father Paul comes to dinner. Often he comes on other nights too, and once, in the old days when we couldn't eat meat on Fridays, we bagged our first ducks of the season on a Friday, and as we drove home from the marsh, he said: For the purposes of Holy Mother Church, I believe a duck is more a creature of water than land, and is not rightly meat. Sometimes he teases me about never putting anything in his Sunday collection, which he would not know about if I hadn't told him years ago. I would like to believe I told him so we could have a philosophical talk at dinner, but probably the truth is I suspected he knew, and I did not want him to think I so loved money that I would not even give his church a coin on Sunday. Certainly the ushers who pass the baskets know me as a miser.

I don't feel right about giving money for buildings, places. This starts with the Pope, and I cannot respect one of them till he sells his house and everything in it, and that church too, and uses the money to feed the poor. I have rarely, and maybe never, come across saintliness, but I feel certain it cannot exist in such a place. But I admit, also, that I know very little, and maybe the popes live on a different plane and are tried in ways I don't know about. Father Paul says his own church, St. John's, is hardly the Vatican. I like his church: it is made of wood, and has a simple altar and crucifix, and no padding on the kneelers. He does not have to lock its doors at night. Still it is a place. He could say Mass in my barn. I know this is stubborn, but I can find no mention by Christ of maintaining buildings, much less erecting them of stone or brick, and decorating them with pieces of metal and mineral and elements that people still fight over like barbarians. We had a Maltese woman taking riding lessons, she came over on the boat when she was ten, and once she told me how the nuns in Malta used to tell the little girls that if they wore jewelry, rings and bracelets and necklaces, in purgatory snakes would coil around their fingers and wrists and throats. I do not believe in frightening children or telling them lies, but if those nuns saved a few girls from devotion to things, maybe they were right. That Maltese woman laughed about it, but I noticed she wore only a watch, and that with a leather strap.

The money I give to the church goes in people's stomachs, and on their backs, down in New York City. I have no delusions about the worth of what I do, but I feel it's better to feed somebody than not. There's a priest in Times Square giving shelter to runaway kids, and some Franciscans who run a bread line; actually it's a morning line for coffee and a roll, and Father Paul calls it the continental breakfast for winos and bag ladies. He is curious about how much I am sending, and I know why: he guesses I send a lot, he has said probably more than tithing, and he is right; he wants to know how much because he believes I'm generous and good, and he is wrong about that; he has never had much money and does not know how easy it is to write a check when you have everything you will ever need, and the figures are mere numbers, and represent no sacrifice at all. Being a real Catholic is too hard; if I were one, I would do with my house and barn what I want the Pope to do with his. So I do not want to impress Father Paul, and when he asks me how much, I say I can't let my left hand know what my right is doing.

He came on Wednesday nights when Gloria and I were married, and the kids were young; Gloria was a very good cook (I assume she still is, but it is difficult to think of her in the present), and I liked sitting at the table with a friend who was also a priest. I was proud of my handsome and healthy children. This was long ago, and they were all very young and cheerful and often funny, and the three boys took care of their baby sister, and did not bully or tease her. Of course they did sometimes, with that excited cruelty children are prone to, but not enough so that it was part of her days. On the Wednesday after Gloria left with the kids and a U-Haul trailer, I was sitting on the front steps, it was summer, and I was watching cars go by on the road, when Father Paul drove around the curve and into the driveway. I was ashamed to see him because he is a priest and my family was gone, but I was relieved too. I went to the car to greet him. He got out smiling, with a bottle of wine, and shook my hand, then pulled me to him, gave me a quick hug, and said: 'It's Wednesday, isn't it? Let's open some cans.'

With arms about each other we walked to the house, and it was good to know he was doing his work but coming as a friend too, and I thought what good work he had. I have no calling. It is for me to keep horses.

In that other life, anyway. In my real one I go to bed early and sleep well and wake at four forty-five, for an hour of silence. I never want to get out of bed then, and every morning I know I can sleep for another four hours, and still not fail at any of my duties. But I get up, so have come to believe my life can be seen in miniature in that struggle in the dark of morning. While making the bed and boiling water for coffee, I talk to God: I offer Him my day, every act of my body and spirit, my thoughts and moods, as a prayer of thanksgiving, and for Gloria and my children and my friends and two women I made love with after Gloria left. This morning offertory is a habit from my boyhood in a Catholic school; or then it was a habit, but as I kept it and grew older it became a ritual. Then I say the Lord's Prayer, trying not to recite it, and one morning it occurred to me that a prayer, whether recited or said with concentration, is always an act of faith.

I sit in the kitchen at the rear of the house and drink coffee and smoke and watch the sky growing light before sunrise, the trees of the woods near the barn taking shape, becoming single pines and elms and oaks and maples. Sometimes a rabbit comes out of the treeline, or is already sitting there, invisible till the light finds him. The birds are awake in the trees and feeding on the ground, and the little ones, the purple finches and titmice and chickadees, are at the feeder I rigged outside the kitchen window; it is too small for pigeons to get a purchase. I sit and give myself to coffee and tobacco that get me brisk again, and I watch and listen. In the first year or so after I lost my family, I played the radio in the mornings. But I overcame that, and now I rarely play it at all. Once in the mail I received a questionnaire asking me to write down everything I watched on television during the week they had chosen. At the end of those seven days I wrote in *The Wizard of Oz* and returned it. That was in winter and was actually a busy week for my television, which normally sits out the cold months without once warming up. Had they sent the questionnaire during baseball season, they would have found me at my set. People at the stables talk about shows and performers I have never heard of, but I cannot get interested; when I am in the mood to watch television, I go to a movie or read a detective novel. There are always good detective novels to be found, and I like remembering them next morning with my coffee.

I also think of baseball and hunting and fishing, and of my children. It is not painful to think about them anymore, because even if we had lived together, they would be gone now, grown into their own lives, except Jennifer. I think of death too, not sadly, or with fear, though something like excitement does run through me, something more quickening than the coffee and tobacco. I suppose it is an intense interest, and an outright distrust: I never feel certain that I'll be here watching birds eating at tomorrow's daylight. Sometimes I try to think of other things, like the rabbit that is warm and breathing but not there till twilight. I feel on the brink of something about the life of the senses, but either am not equipped to go further or am not interested enough to concentrate. I have called all of this thinking, but it is not, because it is unintentional; what I'm really doing is feeling the day, in silence, and that is what Father Paul is doing too on his five-to-ten-mile walks.

When the hour ends I take an apple or carrot and I go to the stable and tack up a horse. We take good care of these horses, and no one rides them but students, instructors, and me, and nobody rides the horses we board unless an owner asks me to. The barn is dark and I turn on lights and take some deep breaths, smelling the hay and horses and their manure, both fresh and dried, a combined odor that you either like or you don't. I walk down the wide space of dirt between stalls, greeting the horses, joking with them about their quirks, and choose one for no reason at all other than the way it looks at me that morning. I get my old English saddle that has smoothed and darkened through the years, and go into the stall, talking to this beautiful creature who'll swerve out of a canter if a piece of paper blows in front of him, and if the barn catches fire and you manage to get him out he will, if he can get away from you, run back into the fire, to his stall. Like the smells that surround them, you either like them or you don't. I love them, so am spared having to try to explain why I feed one the carrot or apple and tack up and lead him outside, where I mount, and we go down the driveway to the road and cross it and turn northwest and walk, then trot then canter to St. John's.

A few cars are on the road, their drivers looking serious about going to work. It is always strange for me to see a woman dressed for work so early in the morning. You know how long it takes them, with the makeup and hair and clothes, and I think of them waking in the dark of winter or early light of other seasons, and dressing as they might for an evening's entertainment. Probably this strikes me because I grew up seeing my father put on those suits he never wore on weekends or his two weeks off, and so am accustomed to the men, but when I see these women I think something went wrong, to send all those dressed-up people out on the road when the dew hasn't dried yet. Maybe it's because I so dislike getting up early, but am also doing what I choose to do, while they have no choice. At heart I am lazy, yet I find such peace and delight in it that I believe it is a natural state, and in what looks like my laziest periods I am closet to my center. The ride to St. John's is fifteen minutes. The horses and I do it in all weather; the road is well plowed in winter, and there are only a few days a year when ice makes me drive the pickup. People always look at someone on horseback, and for a moment their faces change and many drivers and I wave to each other. Then at St. John's, Father Paul and five or six regulars and I celebrate the Mass.

Do not think of me as a spiritual man whose every thought during those twenty-five minutes is at one with the words of the Mass. Each morning I try, each morning I fail, and know that always I will be a creature who, looking at Father Paul and the altar, and uttering prayers, will be distracted by scrambled eggs, horses, the weather, and memories and daydreams that have nothing to do with the sacrament I am about to receive. I can receive, though: the Eucharist, and also, at Mass and at other times, moments and even minutes of contemplation. But I cannot achieve contemplation, as some can; and so, having to face and forgive my own failures, I have learned from them both the necessity and wonder of ritual. For ritual allows those who cannot will themselves out of the secular to perform the spiritual, as dancing allows the tongue-tied man a ceremony of love. And, while my mind dwells on breakfast, or Major or Duchess tethered under the church eave, there is, as I take the Host from Father Paul and place it on my tongue and return to the pew, a feeling that I am thankful I have not lost in the forty-eight years since my first Communion. At its center is excitement; spreading out from it is the peace of certainty. Or the certainty of peace. One night Father Paul and I talked about faith. It was long ago, and all I remember is him saying: Belief is believing in God; faith is believing that God believes in you. That is the excitement, and the peace; then the Mass is over, and I go into the sacristy and we have a cigarette and chat, the mystery ends, we are two men talking like any two men on a morning in America, about baseball, plane crashes, presidents, governors, murders, the sun, the clouds. Then I go to the horse and ride back to the life people see, the one in which I move and talk, and most days I enjoy it.

It is late summer now, the time between fishing and hunting, but a good time for baseball. It has been two weeks since Jennifer left, to drive home to Gloria's after her summer visit. She is the only one who still visits; the boys are married and have children, and sometimes fly up for a holiday, or I fly down or west to visit one of them. Jennifer is twenty, and I worry about her the way fathers worry about daughters but not sons. I want to know what she's up to, and at the same time I don't. She looks athletic, and she is: she swims and runs and of course rides. All my children do. When she comes for six weeks in summer, the house is loud with girls, friends of hers since childhood, and new ones. I am glad she kept the girl friends. They have been young company for me and, being with them, I have been able to gauge her growth between summers. On their riding days, I'd take them back to the house when their lessons were over and they had walked the horses and put them back in the stalls, and we'd have lemonade or Coke, and cookies if I had some, and talk until their parents came to drive them home. One year their breasts grew, so I wasn't startled when I saw Jennifer in July. Then they were driving cars to the stable, and beginning to look like young women, and I was passing out beer and ashtrays and they were talking about college.

When Jennifer was here in summer, they were at the house most days. I would say generally that as they got older they became quieter, and though I enjoyed both, I sometimes missed the giggles and shouts. The quiet voices, just low enough for me not to hear from wherever I was, rising and falling in proportion to my distance from them, frightened me. Not that I believed they were planning or recounting anything really wicked, but there was a female seriousness about them, and it was secretive, and of course I thought: love, sex. But it was more than that: it was womanhood they were entering, the deep forest of it, and no matter how many women and men too are saying these days that there is little difference between us, the truth is that men find their way into that forest only on clearly marked trails, while women move about in it like birds. So hearing Jennifer and her friends talking so quietly, yet intensely, I wanted very much to have a wife.

But not as much as in the old days, when Gloria had left but her presence was still in the house as strongly as if she had only gone to visit her folks for a week. There were no clothes or cosmetics, but potted plants endured my neglectful care as long as they could, and slowly died; I did not kill them on purpose, to exorcise the house of her, but I could not remember to water them. For weeks, because I did not use it much, the house was as neat as she had kept it, though dust layered the order she had made. The kitchen went first: I got the dishes in and out of the dishwasher and wiped the top of the stove, but did not return cooking spoons and pot holders to their hooks on the wall, and soon the burners and oven were caked with spillings, the refrigerator had more space and was spotted with juices. The living room and my bedroom went next; I did not go into the children's rooms except on bad nights when I went from room to room and looked and touched and smelled, so they did not lose their order until a year later when the kids came for six weeks. It was three months before I ate the last of the food Gloria had cooked and frozen: I remember it was a beef stew, and very good. By then I had four cookbooks, and was boasting a bit, and talking about recipes with the women at the stables, and looking forward to cooking for Father Paul. But I never looked forward to cooking at night only for myself, though I made myself do it; on some nights I gave in to my daily temptation, and took a newspaper or detective novel to a restaurant. By the end of the second year, though, I had stopped turning on the radio as soon as I woke in the morning, and was able to be silent and alone in the evening too, and then I enjoyed my dinners.

It is not hard to live through a day, if you can live through a moment. What creates despair is the imagination, which pretends there is a future, and insists on predicting millions of moments, thousands of days, and so drains you that you cannot live the moment at hand. That is what Father Paul told me in those first two years, on some of the bad nights when I believed I could not bear what I had to: the most painful loss was my children, then the loss of Gloria, whom I still loved despite or maybe because of our long periods of sadness that rendered us helpless, so neither of us could break out of it to give a hand to the other. Twelve years later I believe ritual would have healed us more quickly than the repetitive talks we had, perhaps even kept us healed. Marriages have lost that, and I wish I had known then what I know now, and we had performed certain acts together every day, no matter how we felt, and perhaps then we could have subordinated feeling to action, for surely that is the essence of love. I know this from my distractions during Mass, and during everything else I do, so that my actions and feelings are seldom one. It does happen every day, but in proportion to everything else in a day, it is rare, like joy. The third most painful loss, which became second and sometimes first as months passed, was the knowledge that I could never marry again, and so dared not even keep company with a woman.

On some of the bad nights I was bitter about this with Father Paul, and I so pitied myself that I cried, or nearly did, speaking with damp eyes and breaking voice. I believe that celibacy is for him the same trial it is for me, not of the flesh, but the spirit: the heart longing to love. But the difference is he chose it, and did not wake one day to a life with thirty horses. In my anger I said I had done my service to love and chastity, and I told him of the actual physical and spiritual pain of practicing rhythm: nights of striking the mattress with a fist, two young animals lying side by side in heat, leaving the bed to pace, to smoke, to curse, and too passionate to question, for we were so angered and oppressed by our passion that we could see no further than our loins. So now I understand how people can be enslaved for generations before they throw down their tools or use them as weapons, the form of their slavery—the cotton fields, the shacks and puny cupboards and untended illnesses—absorbing their emotions and thoughts until finally they have little or none at all to direct with clarity and energy at the owners and legislators. And I told him of the trick of passion and its slaking: how during what we had to believe were safe periods, though all four children were conceived at those times, we were able with some coherence to question the tradition and reason and justice of the law against birth control, but not with enough conviction to soberly act against it, as though regular satisfaction in bed tempered our revolutionary as well as our erotic desires. Only when abstinence drove us hotly away from each other did we receive an urge so strong it lasted all the way to the drugstore and back; but always, after release, we threw away the remaining condoms; and after going through this a few times, we knew what would happen, and from then on we submitted to the calendar she so precisely marked on the bedroom wall. I told him that living two lives each month, one as celibates, one as lovers, made us tense and short-tempered, so we snapped at each other like dogs.

To have endured that, to have reached a time when we burned slowly and could gain from bed the comfort of lying down at night with one who loves you and whom you love, could for weeks on end go to bed tired and peacefully sleep after a kiss, a touch of the hands, and then to be thrown out of the marriage like a bundle from a moving freight car, was unjust, was intolerable, and I could not or would not muster the strength to endure it. But I did, a moment at a time, a day, a night, except twice, each time with a different woman and more than a year apart, and this was so long ago that I clearly see their faces in my memory, can hear the pitch of their voices, and the way they pronounced words, one with a Massachusetts accent, one midwestern, but I feel as though I only heard about them from someone else. Each rode at the stables and was with me for part of an evening, one was badly married, one divorced, so none of us was free. They did not understand this Catholic view, but they were understanding about my having it, and I remained friends with both of them until the married one left her husband and went to Boston, and the divorced one moved to Maine. After both those evenings, those good women, I went to Mass early while Father Paul was still in the confessional, and received his absolution. I did not tell him who I was, but of course he knew, though I never saw it in his eyes. Now my longing for a wife comes only once in a while, like a cold: on some late afternoons when I am alone in the barn, then I lock up and walk to the house, daydreaming, then suddenly look at it and see it empty, as though for the first time, and all at once I'm weary and feel I do not have the energy to broil meat, and I think of driving to a restaurant, then shake my head and go on to the house, the refrigerator, the oven; and some mornings when I wake in the dark and listen to the silence and run my hand over the cold sheet beside me; and some days in summer when Jennifer is here.

Gloria left first me, then the Church, and that was the end of religion for the children, though on visits they went to Sunday Mass with me, and still do, out of a respect for my life that they manage to keep free of patronage. Jennifer is an agnostic, though I doubt she would call herself that, any more than she would call herself any other name that implied she had made a decision, a choice, about existence, death, and God. In truth she tends to pantheism, a good sign, I think; but not wanting to be a father who tells his children what they ought to believe, I do not say to her that Catholicism includes pantheism, like onions in a stew. Besides, I have no missionary instincts and do not believe everyone should or even could live with the Catholic faith. It is Jennifer's womanhood that renders me awkward. And womanhood now is frank, not like when Gloria was twenty and there were symbols: high heels and cosmetics and dresses, a cigarette, a cocktail. I am glad that women are free now of false modesty and all its attention paid the flesh; but, still, it is difficult to see so much of your daughter, to hear her talk as only men and bawdy women used to, and most of all to see in her face the deep and unabashed sensuality of women, with no tricks of the eyes and mouth to hide the pleasure she feels at having a strong young body. I am certain, with the way things are now, that she has very happily not been a virgin for years. That does not bother me. What bothers me is my certainty about it, just from watching her walk across a room or light a cigarette or pour milk on cereal.

She told me all of it, waking me that night when I had gone to sleep listening to the wind in the trees and against the house, a wind so strong that I had to shut all but the lee windows, and still the house cooled; told it to me in such detail and so clearly that now, when she has driven the car to Florida, I remember it all as though I had been a passenger in the front seat, or even at the wheel. It started with a movie, then beer and driving to the sea to look at the waves in the night and the wind, Jennifer and Betsy and Liz. They drank a beer on the beach and wanted to go in naked but were afraid they would drown in the high surf. They bought another six-pack at a grocery store in New Hampshire, and drove home. I can see it now, feel it: the three girls and the beer and the ride on country roads where pines curved in the wind and the big deciduous trees swayed and shook as if they might leap from the earth. They would have some windows partly open so they could feel the wind; Jennifer would be playing a cassette, the music stirring them, as it does the young, to memories of another time, other people and places in what is for them the past.

She took Betsy home, then Liz, and sang with her cassette as she left the town west of us and started home, a twenty-minute drive on the road that passes my house. They had each had four beers, but now there were twelve empty bottles in the bag on the floor at the passenger seat, and I kept focusing on their sound against each other when the car shifted speeds or changed directions. For I want to understand that one moment out of all her heart's time on earth, and whether her history had any bearing on it, or whether her heart was then isolated from all it had known, and the sound of those bottles urged it. She was just leaving the town, accelerating past a nightclub on the right, gaining speed to climb a long, gradual hill, then she went up it, singing, patting the beat on the steering wheel, the wind loud through her few inches of open window, blowing her hair as it did the high branches alongside the road, and she looked up at them and watched the top of the hill for someone drunk or heedless coming over it in part of her lane. She crested to an open black road, and there he was a bulk, a blur, a thing running across her headlights, and she swerved left and her foot went for the brake and was stomping air above its pedal when she hit him, saw his legs and body in the air, flying out of her light, into the dark. Her brakes were screaming into the wind, bottles clinking in the fallen bag, and with the music and wind inside the car was his sound, already a memory but as real as an echo, that car-shuddering thump as though she had struck a tree. Her foot was back on the accelerator. Then she shifted gears and pushed it. She ejected the cassette and closed the window. She did not start to cry until she knocked on my bedroom door, then called: "Dad?"

Her voice, her tears, broke through my dream and the wind I heard in my sleep, and I stepped into jeans and hurried to the door, thinking harm, rape, death. All were in her face, and I hugged her and pressed her cheek to my chest and smoothed her blown hair, then led her, weeping, to the kitchen and sat her at the table where still she could not speak, nor look at me; when she raised her face it fell forward again, as of its own weight, into her palms. I offered tea and she shook her head, so I offered beer twice, then she shook her head, so I offered whiskey and she nodded. I had some rye that Father Paul and I had not finished last hunting season, and I poured some over ice and set it in front of her and was putting away the ice but stopped and got another glass and poured one for myself too, and brought the ice and bottle to the table where she was trying to get one of her long menthols out of the pack, but her fingers jerked like severed snakes, and I took the pack and lit one for her and took one for myself. I watched her shudder with her first swallow of rye, and push hair back from her face, it is auburn and gleamed in the overhead light, and I remember how beautiful she looked riding a sorrel; she was smoking fast, then the sobs in her throat stopped, and she looked at me and said it, the words coming out with smoke: I hit somebody. With the *car*.

Then she was crying and I was on my feet, moving back and forth, looking down at her, asking *Who? Where? Where?* She was pointing at the wall over the stove, jabbing her fingers and cigarette at it, her other hand at her eyes, and twice in horror I actually looked at the wall. She finished the whiskey in a swallow and I stopped pacing and asking and poured another, and either the drink or the exhaustion of tears quieted her, even the dry sobs, and she told me; not as I tell it now, for that was later as again and again we relived it in the kitchen or living room, and, if in daylight, fled it on horseback out on the trails through the woods and, if at night, walked quietly around in the moonlit pasture, walked around and around it, sweating through our clothes. She told it in bursts, like she was a child again, running to me, injured from play. I put on boots and a shirt and left her with the bottle and her streaked face and a cigarette twitching between her fingers, pushed the door open against the wind, and eased it shut. The wind squinted and watered my eyes as I leaned into it and went to the pickup.

When I passed St. John's I looked at it, and Father Paul's little white rectory in the rear, and wanted to stop, wished I could as I could if he were simply a friend who sold hardware or something. I had forgotten my watch but I always know the time within minutes, even when a sound or dream or my bladder wakes me in the night. It was nearly two; we had been in the kitchen about twenty minutes; she had hit him around one-fifteen. Or her. The road was empty and I drove between blowing trees; caught for an instant in my lights, they seemed to be in panic. I smoked and let hope play its tricks on me: it was neither man nor woman but an animal, a goat or calf or deer on the road; it was a man who had jumped away in time, the collision of metal and body glancing not direct, and he had limped home to nurse bruises and cuts. Then I threw the cigarette and hope both out the window and prayed that he was alive, while beneath that prayer, a reserve deeper in my heart, another one stirred: that if he were dead, they would not get Jennifer.

From our direction, east and a bit south, the road to that hill and the nightclub beyond it and finally the town is, for its last four or five miles, straight through farming country. When I reached that stretch I slowed the truck and opened my window for the fierce air; on both sides were scattered farmhouses and barns and sometimes a silo, looking not like shelters but like unsheltered things the wind would flatten. Corn bent toward the road from a field on my right, and always something blew in front of me: paper, leaves, dried weeds, branches. I slowed approaching the hill, and went up it in second, staring through my open window at the ditch on the left side of the road, its weeds alive, whipping, a mad dance with the trees above them. I went over the hill and down and, opposite the club, turned right onto a side street of houses, and parked there, in the leaping shadows of trees. I walked back across the road to the club's parking lot, the wind behind me, lifting me as I strode, and I could not hear my boots on pavement. I walked up the hill, on the shoulder, watching the branches above me, hearing their leaves and the creaking trunks and the wind. Then I was at the top, looking down the road and at the farms and fields; the night was clear, and I could see a long way; clouds scudded past the half-moon and stars, blown out to sea.

I started down, watching the tall grass under the trees to my right, glancing into the dark of the ditch, listening for cars behind me; but as soon as I cleared one tree, its sound was gone, its flapping leaves and rattling branches far behind me, as though the greatest distance I had at my back was a matter of feet, while ahead of me I could see a barn two miles off. Then I saw her skid marks: short, and going left and downhill, into the other lane. I stood at the ditch, its weeds blowing; across it were trees and their moving shadows, like the clouds. I stepped onto its slope, and it took me sliding on my feet, then rump, to the bottom, where I sat still, my body gathered to itself, lest a part of me should touch him. But there was only tall grass, and I stood, my shoulders reaching the sides of the ditch, and I walked uphill, wishing for the flashlight in the pickup, walking slowly, and down in the ditch I could hear my feet in the grass and on the earth, and kicking cans and bottles. At the top of the hill I turned and went down, watching the ground above the ditch on my right, praying my prayer from the truck again, the first one, the one I would admit, that he was not dead, was in fact home, and began to hope again, memory telling me of lost pheasants and grouse I had shot, but they were small and the colors of their home, while a man was either there or not; and from that memory I left where I was and while walking in the ditch under the wind was in the deceit of imagination with Jennifer in the kitchen telling her she had hit no one, or at least had not badly hurt anyone, when I realized he could be in the hospital now and I would have to think of a way to check there, something to say on the phone. I see now that, once hope returned, I should have been certain what it prepared me for: ahead of me, in high grass and the shadows of trees, I saw his shirt. Or that is all my mind would allow itself: a shirt, and I stood looking at it for the moments it took my mind to admit the arm and head and the dark length covered by pants. He lay face down, the arm I could see near his side, his head turned from me, on its cheek.

"Fella?" I said. I had meant to call, but it came out quiet and high, lost inches from my face in the wind. Then I said, 'Oh God,' and felt Him in the wind and the sky moving past the stars and moon and the field around me, but only watching me as He might have watched

Cain or Job, I did not know which, and I said it again, and wanted to sink to the earth and weep till I slept there in the weeds. I climbed, scrambling up the side of the ditch, pulling at clutched grass, gained the top on hands and knees, and went to him like that, panting, moving through the grass as high and higher than my face, crawling under that sky, making sounds too, like some animal, there being no words to let him know I was here with him now. He was long; that is the word that came to me, not tall. I kneeled beside him, my hands on my legs. His right arm was by his side, his left arm straight out from the shoulder, but turned, so his palm was open to the tree above us. His left cheek was cleanshaven, his eye closed, and there was no blood. I leaned forward to look at his open mouth and saw the blood on it, going down into the grass. I straightened and looked ahead at the wind blowing past me through grass and trees to a distant light, and I stared at the light, imagining someone awake out there, wanting someone to be, a gathering of old friends, or someone alone listening to music or painting a picture, then I figured it was a night light at a farmyard whose house I couldn't see. *Going,* I thought. *Still going.* I leaned over again and looked at dripping blood.

So I had to touch his wrist, a thick one with a watch and expansion band that I pushed up his arm, thinking *he's left-handed,* my three fingers pressing his wrist, and all I felt was my tough fingertips on that smooth underside flesh and small bones, then relief, then certainty. But against my will, or only because of it, I still don't know, I touched his neck, ran my fingers down it as if petting, then pressed, and my hand sprang back as from fire. I lowered it again, held it there until it felt that faint beating that I could not believe. There was too much wind. Nothing could make a sound in it. A pulse could not be felt in it, nor could mere fingers in that wind feel the absolute silence of a dead man's artery. I was making sounds again; I grabbed his left arm and his waist, and pulled him toward me, and that side of him rose, turned, and I lowered him to his back, his face tilted up toward the tree that was groaning, the tree and I the only sounds in the wind. Turning my face from his, looking down the length of him at his sneakers, I placed my ear on his heart, and heard not that but something else, and I clamped a hand over my exposed ear, heard something liquid and alive, like when you pump a well and after a few strokes you hear air and water moving in the pipe, and I knew I must raise his legs and cover him and run to a phone, while still I listened to his chest, thinking *raise with what? cover with what?* and amid the liquid sound I heard the heart, then lost it, and pressed my ear against bone, but his chest was quiet, and I did not know when the liquid had stopped, and do not know now when I heard air, a faint rush of it, and whether under my ear or at his mouth or whether I heard it at all. I straightened and looked at the light, dim and yellow. Then I touched his throat, looking him full in the face. He was blond and young. He could have been sleeping in the shade of a tree, but for the smear of blood from his mouth to his hair, and the night sky, and the weeds blowing against his head, and the leaves shaking in the dark above us.

I stood. Then I kneeled again and prayed for his soul to join in peace and joy all the dead and living; and, doing so, confronted my first sin against him, not stopping for Father Paul, who could have given him the last rites, and immediately then my second one, or, I saw then, my first, not calling an ambulance to meet me there, and I stood and turned into the wind, slid down the ditch and crawled out of it, and went up the hill and down it, across the road to the street of houses whose people I had left behind forever, so that I moved with stealth in the shadows to my truck.

When I came around the bend near my house, I saw the kitchen light at the rear. She sat as I had left her, the ashtray filled, and I looked at the bottle, felt her eyes on me, felt what she was seeing too: the dirt from my crawling. She had not drunk much of the rye. I poured some in my glass, with the water from melted ice, and sat down and swallowed some and looked at her and swallowed some more, and said: 'He's dead.'

She rubbed her eyes with the heels of her hands, rubbed the cheeks under them, but she was dry now.

'He was probably dead when he hit the ground. I mean, that's probably what killed—'

'Where was he?'

'Across the ditch, under a tree.'

'Was he—did you see his face?'

'No, Not really. I just felt. For life, pulse. I'm going out to the car.'

'What for? Oh.'

I finished the rye, and pushed back the chair, then she was standing too.

'I'll go with you.'

'There's no need.'

'I'll go.'

I took a flashlight from a drawer and pushed open the door and held it while she went out. We turned our faces from the wind. It was like on the hill, when I was walking, and the wind closed the distance behind me: after three or four steps I felt there was no house back there. She took my hand, as I was reaching for hers. In the garage we let go, and squeezed between the pickup and her little car, to the front of it, where we had more room, and we stepped back from the grill and I shone the light on the fender, the smashed headlight turned into it, the concave chrome staring to the right, at the garage wall.

'We ought to get the bottles,' I said.

She moved between the garage and the car, on the passenger side, and had room to open the door and lift the bag. I reached out, and she gave me the bag and backed up and shut the door and came around the car. We sidled to the doorway, and she put her arm around my waist and I hugged her shoulders.

'I thought you'd call the police,' she said.

We crossed the yard, faces bowed from the wind, her hair blowing away from her neck, and in the kitchen I put the bag of bottles in the garbage basket. She was working at the table: capping the rye and putting it away, filling the ice tray, washing the glasses, emptying the ashtray, sponging the table.

'Try to sleep now,' I said.

She nodded at the sponge circling under her hand, gathering ashes. Then she dropped it in the sink and, looking me full in the face, as I had never seen her look, as perhaps she never had, being for so long a daughter on visits (or so it seemed to me and still does: that until then our eyes had never seriously met), she crossed to me from the sink and kissed my lips, then held me so tightly I lost balance, and would have stumbled forward had she not held me so hard.

I sat in the living room, the house darkened, and watched the maple and the hemlock. When I believed she was asleep I put on *La Boheme*,[2] and kept it at the same volume as the wind so it would not wake her. Then I listened to *Madame Butterfly*, and in the third act had to rise quickly to lower the sound: the wind was gone. I looked at the still maple near the window, and thought of the wind leaving farms and towns and the coast, going out over the sea to die on the waves. I smoked and gazed out the window. The sky was darker, and at daybreak the rain came. I listened to *Tosca*, and at six-fifteen went to the kitchen where Jennifer's purse lay on the table, a leather shoulder-purse crammed with the things of an adult woman, things she had begun accumulating only a few years back, and I nearly wept, thinking of what sandy foundations they were: driver's license, credit card, disposable lighter, cigarettes, checkbook, ballpoint pen, cash, cosmetics, comb, brush, Kleenex, these the rite of passage from childhood, and I took one of them—her keys—and went out, remembering a jacket and hat when the rain struck me, but I kept going to the car, and squeezed and lowered myself into it, pulled the seat belt over my shoulder and

---

2. This and the two titles just below are operas by Giacomo Puccini (1858–1924).

fastened it and backed out, turning in the drive, going forward into the road, toward St. John's and Father Paul.

Cars were on the road, the workers, and I did not worry about any of them noticing the fender and light. Only a horse distracted them from what they drove to. In front of St. John's is a parking lot; at its far side, past the church and at the edge of the lawn, is an old pine, taller than the steeple now. I shifted to third, left the road, and, aiming the right headlight at the tree, accelerated past the white blur of church, into the black trunk growing bigger till it was all I could see, then I rocked in that resonant thump she had heard, had felt, and when I turned off the ignition it was still in my ears, my blood, and I saw the boy flying in the wind. I lowered my forehead to the wheel. Father Paul opened the door, his face white in the rain.

'I'm all right.'

'What happened?'

'I don't know. I fainted.'

I got out and went around to the front of the car, looked at the smashed light, the crumpled and torn fender.

'Come to the house and lie down.'

'I'm all right.'

'When was your last physical?'

'I'm due for one. Let's get out of this rain.'

'You'd better lie down.'

'No. I want to receive.'

That was the time to say I want to confess, but I have not and will not. Though I could now, for Jennifer is in Florida, and weeks have passed, and perhaps now Father Paul would not feel that he must tell me to go to the police. And, for that very reason, to confess now would be unfair. It is a world of secrets, and now I have one from my best, in truth my only, friend. I have one from Jennifer too, but that is the nature of fatherhood.

Most of that day it rained, so it was only in early evening, when the sky cleared, with a setting sun, that two little boys, leaving their confinement for some play before dinner, found him. Jennifer and I got that on the local news, which we listened to every hour, meeting at the radio, standing with cigarettes, until the one at eight o'clock; when she stopped crying, we went out and walked on the wet grass, around the pasture, the last of sunlight still in the air and trees. His name was Patrick Mitchell, he was nineteen years old, was employed by CETA,[3] lived at home with his parents and brother and sister. The

---

3. Comprehensive Employment and Training Act—a government program to assist people into the job market.

paper next day said he had been at a friend's house and was walking home, and I thought of that light I had seen, then knew it was not for him; he lived on one of the streets behind the club. The paper did not say then, or in the next few days, anything to make Jennifer think he was alive while she was with me in the kitchen. Nor do I know if we— I—could have saved him.

In keeping her secret from her friends, Jennifer had to perform so often, as I did with Father Paul and at the stables, that I believe the acting, which took more of her than our daylight trail rides and our night walks in the pasture, was her healing. Her friends teased me about wrecking her car. When I carried her luggage out to the car on that last morning, we spoke only of the weather for her trip—the day was clear, with a dry cool breeze—and hugged and kissed, and I stood watching as she started the car and turned it around. But then she shifted to neutral and put on the parking brake and unclasped the belt, looking at me all the while, then she was coming to me, as she had that night in the kitchen, and I opened my ams.

I have said I talk with God in the mornings, as I start my day, and sometimes I sit with coffee, looking at the birds, and the woods. Of course He has never spoken to me, but that is not something I require. Nor does He need to. I know Him, as I know the part of myself that knows Him, that felt Him watching from the wind and the night as I knelt over the dying boy. Lately I have taken to arguing with Him, as I can't with Father Paul, who, when he hears my monthly confession, has not heard and will not hear anything of failure to do all that one can to save an anonymous life, of injustice to a family in their grief, of deepening their pain at the chance and mystery of death by giving them nothing—no one—to hate. With Father Paul I feel lonely about this, but not with God. When I received the Eucharist while Jennifer's car sat twice-damaged, so redeemed, in the rain, I felt neither loneliness nor shame, but as though He were watching me, even from my tongue, intestines, blood, as I have watched my sons at times in their young lives when I was able to judge but without anger, and so keep silent while they, in the agony of their youth, decided how they must act; or found reasons, after their actions, for what they had done. Their reasons were never as good or as bad as their actions, but they needed to find them, to believe they were living by them, instead of the awful solitude of the heart.

I do not feel the peace I once did: not with God, nor the earth, or anyone on it. I have begun to prefer this state, to remember with fondness the other one as a period of peace I neither earned nor deserved. Now in the mornings while I watch purple finches driving larger titmice from the feeder, I say to Him: I would do it again. For when she knocked on my door, then called me, she woke what had flowed dormant in my blood since her birth, so that what rose from the bed was not a stable owner or a Catholic or any other Luke Ripley I had lived with for a long time, but the father of a girl.

And He says: I am a Father too.

Yes, I say, as You are a Son Whom this morning I will receive; unless You kill me on the way to church, then I trust You will receive me. And as a Son You made Your plea.

Yes, He says, but I would not lift the cup.

True, and I don't want You to lift it from me either. And if one of my sons had come to me that night, I would have phoned the police and told them to meet us with an ambulance at the top of the hill.

Why? Do you love them less?

I tell Him no, it is not that I love them less, but that I could bear the pain of watching and knowing my sons' pain, could bear it with pride as they took the whip and nails. But You never had a daughter and, if You had, You could not have borne her passion.

So, He says, you love her more than you love Me.

I love her more than I love truth.

Then you love in weakness, He says.

As You love me, I say, and I go with an apple or carrot out to the barn.

1983

■   ■   ■

STUART DYBEK

PET MILK

Today I've been drinking instant coffee and Pet milk, and watching it snow. It's not that I enjoy the taste especially, but I like the way Pet milk swirls in the coffee. Actually, my favorite thing about Pet milk is what the can opener does to the top of the can. The can is unmistakable—compact, seamless looking, its very shape suggesting that it could condense milk without any trouble. The can opener bites in neatly, and the thick liquid spills from the triangular gouge with a different look and viscosity than milk. Pet milk isn't *real* milk. The color's off, to start with. There's almost something of the past about it, like old ivory. My grandmother always drank it in her coffee. When friends dropped over and sat around the kitchen table, my grandma would ask, "Do you take cream and sugar?" Pet milk was the cream.

There was a yellow plastic radio on her kitchen table, usually tuned to the polka station, though sometimes she'd miss it by half a notch and get the Greek station instead, or the Spanish, or the Ukrainian. In Chicago, where we lived, all the incompatible states of Europe were pressed together down at the staticky right end of the dial. She didn't seem to notice, as long as she wasn't hearing English. The radio, turned low, played constantly. Its top was warped and turning amber on the side where the tubes were. I remember the sound of it on winter afternoons after school, as I sat by her table watching the Pet milk swirl and cloud in the steaming coffee, and noticing, outside her window, the sky doing the same thing above the railroad yard across the street.

And I remember, much later, seeing the same swirling sky in tiny liqueur glasses containing a drink called a King Alphonse: the crème de cacao rising like smoke in repeated explosions, blooming in kaleidoscopic clouds through the layer of heavy cream. This was in the Pilsen, a little Czech restaurant where my girlfriend, Kate, and I would go sometimes in the evening. It was the first year out of college for both of us, and we had astonished ourselves by finding real jobs—no more waitressing or pumping gas, the way we'd done in school. I was investigating credit references at a bank, and she was doing something slightly above the rank of typist for Hornblower & Weeks, the investment firm. My bank showed training films that emphasized the importance of suitable dress, good grooming, and personal neatness, even for employees like me, who worked at the switchboard in the basement. Her firm issued directives on appropriate attire—skirts, for instance, should cover the knees. She had lovely knees.

Kate and I would sometimes meet after work at the Pilsen, dressed in our proper business clothes and still feeling both a little self-conscious and glamorous, as if we were impostors wearing disguises. The place had small, round oak tables, and we'd sit in a corner under a painting called "The Street Musicians of Prague" and trade future plans as if they were escape routes. She talked of going to grad school in Europe; I wanted to apply to the Peace Corps. Our plans for the future made us laugh and feel close, but those same plans somehow made anything more than temporary between us seem impossible. It was the first time I'd ever had the feeling of missing someone I was still with.

The waiters in the Pilsen wore short black jackets over long white aprons. They were old men from the old country. We went there often enough to have our own special waiter, Rudi, a name he pronounced with a rolled R. Rudi boned our trout and seasoned our salads, and at the end of the meal he'd bring the bottle of crème de cacao from the bar, along with two little glasses and a small pitcher of heavy cream, and make us each a King Alphonse right at our table. We'd watch as he'd fill the glasses halfway up with the syrupy brown liqueur, then carefully attempt to float a layer of cream on top. If he failed to float the cream, we'd get that one free.

"Who was King Alphonse anyway, Rudi?" I sometimes asked, trying to break his concentration, and if that didn't work I nudged the table with my foot so the glass would jiggle imperceptibly just as he was floating the cream. We'd usually get one on the house. Rudi knew what I was doing. In fact, serving the King Alphonses had been his idea, and he had also suggested the trick of jarring the table. I think it pleased him, though he seemed concerned about the way I'd stare into the liqueur glass, watching the patterns.

"It's not a microscope," he'd say. "Drink."

He liked us, and we tipped extra. It felt good to be there and to be able to pay for a meal.

Kate and I met at the Pilsen for supper on my twenty-second birthday. It was May, and unseasonably hot. I'd opened my tie. Even before looking at the dinner menu, we ordered a bottle of Mumm's and a dozen oysters apiece. Rudi made a sly remark when he brought the oysters on platters of ice. They were freshly opened and smelled of the sea. I'd heard people joke about oysters being aphrodisiac but never considered it anything but a myth—the kind of idea they still had in the old country.

We squeezed on lemon, added dabs of horseradish, slid the oysters into our mouths, and then rinsed the shells with champagne and drank the salty, cold juice. There was a beefy-looking couple eating schnitzel at the next table, and they stared at us with the repugnance that public oyster-eaters in the Midwest often encounter. We laughed and grandly sipped it all down. I was already half tipsy from drinking too fast, and starting to feel filled with a euphoric, aching energy. Kate raised a brimming oyster shell to me in a toast: "To the Peace Corps!"

"To Europe!" I replied, and we clunked shells.

She touched her wineglass to mine and whispered, "Happy birthday," and then suddenly leaned across the table and kissed me.

When she sat down again, she was flushed. I caught the reflection of her face in the glass-covered "The Street Musicians of Prague" above our table. I always loved seeing her in mirrors and windows. The reflections of her beauty startled me. I had told her that once, and she seemed to fend off the compliment, saying, "That's because you've learned what to look for," as if it were a secret I'd stumbled upon. But, this time, seeing her reflection hovering ghostlike upon an imaginary Prague was like seeing a future from which she had vanished. I knew I'd never meet anyone more beautiful to me.

We killed the champagne and sat twining fingers across the table. I was sweating. I could feel the warmth of her through her skirt under the table and I touched her leg. We still hadn't ordered dinner. I left money on the table and we steered each other out a little unsteadily.

"Rudi will understand," I said.

The street was blindingly bright. A reddish sun angled just above the rims of the tallest buildings. I took my suit coat off and flipped it over my shoulder. We stopped in the doorway of a shoe store to kiss.

"Let's go somewhere," she said.

My roommate would already be home at my place, which was closer. Kate lived up north, in Evanston. It seemed a long way away.

We cut down a side street, past a fire station, to a small park, but its gate was locked. I pressed close to her against the tall iron fence. We could smell the lilacs from a bush just inside the fence, and when I jumped for an overhanging branch my shirt sleeve hooked on a fence spike and tore, and petals rained down on us as the sprig sprang from my hand.

We walked to the subway. The evening rush was winding down; we must have caught the last express heading toward Evanston. Once the train climbed from the tunnel to the elevated tracks, it wouldn't stop until the end of the line, on Howard. There weren't any seats together, so we stood swaying at the front of the car, beside the empty conductor's compartment. We wedged inside, and I clicked the door shut.

The train rocked and jounced, clattering north. We were kissing, trying to catch the rhythm of the ride with our bodies. The sun bronzed the windows on our side of the train. I lifted her skirt over her knees, hiked it higher so the sun shone off her thighs, and bunched it around her waist. She wouldn't stop kissing. She was moving her hips to pin us to each jolt of the train.

We were speeding past scorched brick walls, gray windows, back porches outlined in sun, roofs, and treetops—the landscape of the El I'd memorized from subway windows over a lifetime of rides: the podiatrist's foot sign past Fullerton; the bright pennants of Wrigley Field, at Addison; ancient hotels with TRANSIENTS WELCOME signs on their flaking back walls; peeling and graffiti-smudged billboards; the old cemetery just before Wilson Avenue. Even without looking, I knew almost exactly where we were. Within the compartment, the sound of our quick breathing was louder than the clatter of tracks. I was trying to slow down, to make it all last, and when she covered my mouth with her hand I turned my face to the window and looked out.

The train was braking a little from express speed, as it did each time it passed a local station. I could see blurred faces on the long wooden platform watching us pass—businessmen glancing up from folded newspapers, women clutching purses and shopping bags. I could see the expression on each face, momentarily arrested, as we flashed by. A high school kid in shirt sleeves, maybe sixteen, with books tucked under one arm and a cigarette in his mouth, caught sight of us, and in the instant before he disappeared he grinned and started to wave. Then he was gone, and I turned from the window, back to Kate, forgetting everything—the passing stations, the glowing late sky, even the sense of missing her—but that arrested wave stayed with me. It was as if I were standing on that platform, with my schoolbooks and a smoke, on one of those endlessly accumulated afternoons after school when I stood almost outside of time simply waiting for a train, and I thought how much I'd have loved seeing someone like us streaming by.

1981

▪   ▪   ▪

LOUISE ERDRICH

SAINT MARIE

(1934)

Marie Lazarre

So when I went there, I knew the dark fish must rise. Plumes of radiance had soldered on me. No reservation girl had ever prayed so hard. There was no use in trying to ignore me any longer. I was going up there on the hill with the black robe women. They were not any lighter than me. I was going up there to pray as good as they could. Because I don't have that much Indian blood. And they never thought they'd have a girl from this reservation as a saint they'd have to kneel to. But they'd have me. And I'd be carved in pure gold. With ruby lips. And my toenails would be little pink ocean shells, which they would have to stoop down off their high horse to kiss.

I was ignorant. I was near age fourteen. The length of sky is just about the size of my ignorance. Pure and wide. And it was just that— the pure and wideness of my ignorance—that got me up the hill to Sacred Heart Convent and brought me back down alive. For maybe Jesus did not take my bait, but them Sisters tried to cram me right down whole.

You ever see a walleye strike so bad the lure is practically out its back end before you reel it in? That is what they done with me. I don't like to make that low comparison, but I have seen a walleye do that once. And it's the same attempt as Sister Leopolda made to get me in her clutch.

I had the mail-order Catholic soul you get in a girl raised out in the bush, whose only thought is getting into town. For Sunday Mass is the only time my aunt brought us children in except for school, when we were harnessed. Our soul went cheap. We were so anxious to get there we would have walked in on our hands and knees. We just craved going to the store, slinging bottle caps in the dust, making fool eyes at each other. And of course we went to church.

Where they have the convent is on top of the highest hill, so that from its windows the Sisters can be looking into the marrow of the town. Recently a windbreak was planted before the bar "for the purposes of tornado insurance." Don't tell me that. That poplar stand was put up to hide the drinkers as they get the transformation. As they are served into the beast of their burden. While they're drinking, that body comes upon them, and then they stagger or crawl out the bar door, pulling a weight they can't move past the poplars. They don't want no holy witness to their fall.

Anyway, I climbed. That was a long-ago day. There was a road then for wagons that wound in ruts to the top of the hill where they had their buildings of painted brick. Gleaming white. So white the sun glanced off in dazzling display to set forms whirling behind your eyelids. The face of God you could hardly look at. But that day it drizzled, so I could look all I wanted. I saw the homelier side. The cracked whitewash and swallows nesting in the busted ends of caves. I saw the boards sawed the size of broken windowpanes and the fruit trees, stripped. Only the tough wild rhubarb flourished. Goldenrod rubbed up their walls. It was a poor convent. I didn't see that then but I know that now. Compared to others it was humble, ragtag, out in the middle of no place. It was the end of the world to some. Where the maps stopped. Where God had only half a hand in the creation. Where the Dark One had put in thick bush, liquor, wild dogs, and Indians.

I heard later that the Sacred Heart Convent was a catchall place for nuns that don't get along elsewhere. Nuns that complain too much or lose their mind. I'll always wonder now, after hearing that, where they picked up Sister Leopolda. Perhaps she had scarred someone else, the way she left a mark on me. Perhaps she was just sent around to test her Sister's faith, here and there, like the spot-checker in a factory. For she was the definite most-hard trial to anyone's endurance, even when they started out with veils of wretched love upon their eyes.

I was that girl who thought the black hem of her garment would help me rise. Veils of love which was only hate petrified by longing— that was me. I was like those bush Indians who stole the holy black hat of a Jesuit and swallowed little scraps of it to cure their fevers. But the hat itself carried smallpox and was killing them with belief. Veils of faith! I had this confidence in Leopolda. She was different. The other Sisters had long ago gone blank and given up on Satan. He slept for them. They never noticed his comings and goings. But Leopolda kept track of him and knew his habits, minds he burrowed in, deep spaces where he did. She knew as much about him as my grandma, who called him by other names and was not afraid.

In her class, Sister Leopolda carried a long oak pole for opening high windows. It had a hook made of iron on one end that could jerk a patch of your hair out or throttle you by the collar—all from a distance. She used this deadly hook-pole for catching Satan by surprise. He could have entered without your knowing it—through your lips or your nose or any one of your seven openings—and gained your mind. But she would see him. That pole would brain you from behind. And he would gasp, dazzled, and take the first thing she offered, which was pain.

She had a stringer of children who could only breathe if she said the word. I was the worst of them. She always said the Dark One wanted me most of all, and I believed this. I stood out. Evil was a common thing I trusted. Before sleep sometimes he came and whispered conversation in the old language of the bush. I listened. He told me things he never told anyone but Indians. I was privy to both worlds of his knowledge. I listened to him, but I had confidence in Leopolda. She was the only one of the bunch he even noticed.

There came a day, though, when Leopolda turned the tide with her hook-pole.

It was a quiet day with everyone working at their desks, when I heard him. He had sneaked into the closets in the back of the room. He was scratching around, tasting crumbs in our pockets, stealing buttons, squirting his dark juice in the linings and the boots. I was the only one who heard him, and I got bold. I smiled. I glanced back and smiled and looked up at her sly to see if she had noticed. My heart jumped. For she was looking straight at me. And she sniffed. She had a big stark bony nose stuck to the front of her face for smelling out brimstone and evil thoughts. She had smelled him on me. She stood up. Tall, pale, a blackness leading into the deeper blackness of the slate wall behind her. Her oak pole had flown into her grip. She had seen me glance at the closet. Oh, she knew. She knew just where he was. I watched her watch him in her mind's eye. The whole class was watching now. She was staring, sizing, following his scuffle. And all of a sudden she tensed down, posed on her bent kneesprings, cocked her arm back. She threw the oak pole singing over my head, through my braincloud. It cracked through the thin wood door of the back closet, and the heavy pointed hook drove through his heart. I turned. She'd speared her own black rubber overboot where he'd taken refuge in the tip of her darkest toe.

Something howled in my mind. Loss and darkness. I understood. I was to suffer for my smile.

He rose up hard in my heart. I didn't blink when the pole cracked. My skull was tough. I didn't flinch when she shrieked in my ear. I only shrugged at the flowers of hell. He wanted me. More than anything he craved me. But then she did the worst. She did what broke my mind to her. She grabbed me by the collar and dragged me, feet flying, through the room and threw me in the closet with her dead black overboot. And I was there. The only light was a crack beneath the door. I asked the Dark One to enter into me and boost my mind. I asked him to restrain my tears, for they was pushing behind my eyes. But he was afraid to come back there. He was afraid of her sharp pole. And I was afraid of Leopolda's pole for the first time, too. I felt the cold hook in my heart. How it could crack through the door at any minute and drag me out, like a dead fish on a gaff, drop me on the floor like a gunshot squirrel.

I was nothing. I edged back to the wall as far as I could. I breathed the chalk dust. The hem of her full black cloak cut against my cheek. He had left me. Her spear could find me any time. Her keen ears would aim the hook into the beat of my heart.

What was that sound?

It filled the closet, filled it up until it spilled over, but I did not recognize the crying wailing voice as mine until the door cracked open, brightness, and she hoisted me to her camphor-smelling lips.

"He *wants* you," she said. "That's the difference. I give you love."

Love. The black hook. The spear singing through the mind. I saw that she had tracked the Dark One to my heart and flushed him out into the open. So now my heart was an empty nest where she could lurk.

Well, I was weak. I was weak when I let her in, but she got a foothold there. Hard to dislodge as the year passed. Sometimes I felt him—the brush of dim wings—but only rarely did his voice compel. It was between Marie and Leopolda now, and the struggle changed. I began to realize I had been on the wrong track with the fruits of hell. The real way to overcome Leopolda was this: I'd get to heaven first. And then, when I saw her coming, I'd shut the gate. She'd be out! That is why, besides the bowing and the scraping I'd be dealt, I wanted to sit on the altar as a saint.

To this end, I went up on the hill. Sister Leopolda was the consecrated nun who had sponsored me to come there.

"You're not vain," she said. "You're too honest, looking into the mirror, for that. You're not smart. You don't have the ambition to ' clear. You have two choices. One, you can marry a no-good Ir bear his brats, die like a dog. Or two, you can give yourself to ⌐

"I'll come up there," I said, "but not because of what yⁿ

I could have had any damn man on the reservation at the time. And I could have made him treat me like his own life. I looked good. And I looked white. But I wanted Sister Leopolda's heart. And here was the thing: sometimes I wanted her heart in love and admiration. Sometimes. And sometimes I wanted her heart to roast on a black stick.

She answered the back door where they had instructed me to call. I stood there with my bundle. She looked me up and down.

"All right," she said finally. "Come in."

She took my hand. Her fingers were like a bundle of broom straws, so thin and dry, but the strength of them was unnatural. I couldn't have tugged loose if she was leading me into rooms of white-hot coal. Her strength was a kind of perverse miracle, for she got it from fasting herself thin. Because of this hunger practice her lips were a wounded brown and her skin deadly pale. Her eye sockets were two deep lashless hollows in a taut skull. I told you about the nose already. It stuck out far and made the place her eyes moved even deeper, as if she stared out the wrong end of a gun barrel. She took the bundle from my hands and threw it in the corner.

"You'll be sleeping behind the stove, child."

It was immense, like a great furnace. There was a small cot close behind it.

"Looks like it could get warm there," I said.

"Hot. It does."

"Do I get a habit?"

I wanted something like the thing she wore. Flowing black cotton. Her face was strapped in white bandages, and a sharp crest of starched white cardboard hung over her forehead like a glaring beak. If possible, I wanted a bigger, longer, whiter beak than hers.

"No," she said, grinning her great skull grin. "You don't get one yet. Who knows, you might not like us. Or we might not like you."

But she had loved me, or offered me love. And she had tried to hunt the Dark One down. So I had this confidence.

"I'll inherit your keys from you," I said.

She looked at me sharply, and her grin turned strange. She hissed, taking in her breath. Then she turned to the door and took a key from her belt. It was a giant key, and it unlocked the larder where the food was stored.

Inside there was all kinds of good stuff. Things I'd tasted only once or twice in my life. I saw sticks of dried fruit, jars of orange peel, spice like cinnamon. I saw tins of crackers with ships painted on the side. I saw pickles. Jars of herring and the rind of pigs. There was cheese, a big brown block of it from the thick milk of goats. And besides that there was the everyday stuff, in great quantities, the flour and the coffee.

It was the cheese that got to me. When I saw it my stomach hollowed. My tongue dripped. I loved that goat-milk cheese better than anything I'd ever ate. I stared at it. The rich curve in the buttery cloth.

"When you inherit my keys," she said sourly, slamming the door in my face, "you can eat all you want of the priest's cheese."

Then she seemed to consider what she'd done. She looked at me. She took the key from her belt and went back, sliced a hunk off, and put it in my hand.

"If you're good you'll taste this cheese again. When I'm dead and gone," she said.

Then she dragged out the big sack of flour. When I finished that heaven stuff she told me to roll my sleeves up and begin doing God's labor. For a while we worked in silence, mixing up the dough and pounding it out on stone slabs.

"God's work," I said after a while. "If this is God's work, then I've done it all my life."

"Well, you've done it with the Devil in your heart then," she said. "Not God."

"How do you know?" I asked. But I knew she did. And I wished I had not brought up the subject.

"I see right into you like a clear glass," she said. "I always did."

"You don't know it," she continued after a while, "but he's come around here sulking. He's come around here brooding. You brought him in. He knows the smell of me, and he's going to make a last ditch try to get you back. Don't let him." She glared over at me. Her eyes were cold and lighted. "Don't let him touch you. We'll be a long time getting rid of him."

So I was careful. I was careful not to give him an inch. I said a rosary, two rosaries, three, underneath my breath. I said the Creed. I said every scrap of Latin I knew while we punched the dough with our fists. And still, I dropped the cup. It rolled under that monstrous iron stove, which was getting fired up for baking.

And she was on me. She saw he'd entered my distraction.

"Our good cup," she said. "Get it out of there, Marie."

I reached for the poker to snag it out from beneath the stove. But I had a sinking feel in my stomach as I did this. Sure enough, her long arm darted past me like a whip. The poker lighted in her hand.

"Reach," she said. "Reach with your arm for that cup. And when your flesh is hot, remember that the flames you feel are only one fraction of the heat you will feel in his hellish embrace."

She always did things this way, to teach you lessons. So I wasn't surprised. It was playacting, anyway, because a stove isn't very hot underneath right along the floor. They aren't made that way. Otherwise a wood floor would burn. So I said yes and got down on my stomach and reached under. I meant to grab it quick and jump up again, before she could think up another lesson, but here it happened. Although I groped for the cup, my hand closed on nothing. That cup was nowhere to be found. I heard her step toward me, a slow step. I heard the creak of thick shoe leather, the little *plat* as the folds of her heavy skirts met, a trickle of fine sand sifting, somewhere, perhaps in the bowels of her, and I was afraid. I tried to scramble up, but her foot came down lightly behind my ear, and I was lowered. The foot came down more firmly at the base of my neck, and I was held.

"You're like I was," she said. "He wants you very much."

"He doesn't want me no more," I said. "He had his fill. I got the cup!"

I heard the valve opening, the hissed intake of breath, and knew that I should not have spoke.

"You lie," she said. "You're cold. There is a wicked ice forming in your blood. You don't have a shred of devotion for God. Only wild cold dark lust. I know it. I know how you feel. I see the beast . . . the beast watches me out of your eyes sometimes. Cold."

The urgent scrape of metal. It took a moment to know from where. Top of the stove. Kettle. Lessons. She was steadying herself with the iron poker. I could feel it like pure certainty, driving into the wood floor. I would not remind her of pokers. I heard the water as it came, tipped from the spout, cooling as it fell but still scalding as it struck. I must have twitched beneath her foot, because she steadied me, and then the poker nudged up beside my arm as if to guide. "To warm your cold ash heart," she said. I felt how patient she would be. The water came. My mind went dead blank. Again. I could only think the kettle would be cooling slowly in her hand. I could not stand it. I bit my lip so as not to satisfy her with a sound. She gave me more reason to keep still.

"I will boil him from your mind if you make a peep," she said, "by filling up your ear."

Any sensible fool would have run back down the hill the minute Leopolda let them up from under her heel. But I was snared in her black intelligence by then. I could not think straight. I had prayed so hard I think I broke a cog in my mind. I prayed while her foot squeezed my throat. While my skin burst. I prayed even when I heard the wind come through, shrieking in the busted bird nests. I didn't stop when pure light fell, turning slowly behind my eyelids. God's face. Even that did not disrupt my continued praise. Words came. Words came from nowhere and flooded my mind.

Now I could pray much better than any one of them. Than all of them full force. This was proved. I turned to her in a daze when she let me up. My thoughts were gone, and yet I remember how surprised I was. Tears glittered in her eyes, deep down, like the sinking reflection in a well.

"It was so hard, Marie," she gasped. Her hands were shaking. The kettle clattered against the stove. "But I have used all the water up now. I think he is gone."

"I prayed," I said foolishly. "I prayed very hard."

"Yes," she said. "My dear one, I know."

We sat together quietly because we had no more words. We let the dough rise and punched it down once. She gave me a bowl of mush, unlocked the sausage from a special cupboard, and took that in to the Sisters. They sat down the hall, chewing their sausage, and I could hear them. I could hear their teeth bite through their bread and meat. I couldn't move. My shirt was dry but the cloth stuck to my back, and I couldn't think straight. I was losing the sense to understand how her mind worked. She'd gotten past me with her poker and I would never be a saint. I despaired. I felt I had no inside voice, nothing to direct me, no darkness, no Marie. I was about to throw that cornmeal mush out to the birds and make a run for it, when the vision rose up blazing in my mind.

I was rippling gold. My breasts were bare and my nipples flashed and winked. Diamonds tipped them. I could walk through panes of glass. I could walk through windows. She was at my feet, swallowing the glass after each step I took. I broke through another and another. The glass she swallowed ground and cut until her starved insides were only a subtle dust. She coughed. She coughed a cloud of dust. And then she was only a black rag that flapped off, snagged in bobwire, hung there for an age, and finally rotted into the breeze.

I saw this, mouth hanging open, gazing off into the flagged boughs of trees.

"Get up!" she cried. "Stop dreaming. It is time to bake."

Two other Sisters had come in with her, wide women with hands like paddles. They were evening and smoothing out the firebox beneath the great jaws of the oven.

"Who is this one?" they asked Leopolda. "Is she yours?"

"She is mine," said Leopolda. "A very good girl."

"What is your name?" one asked me.

"Marie."

"Marie. Star of the Sea."

"She will shine," said Leopolda, "when we have burned off the dark corrosion."

The others laughed, but uncertainly. They were mild and sturdy French, who did not understand Leopolda's twisted jokes, although they muttered respectfully at things she said. I knew they wouldn't believe what she had done with the kettle. There was no question. So I kept quiet.

"*Elle est docile,*"[1] they said approvingly as they left to starch the linens.

"Does it pain?" Leopolda asked me as soon as they were out the door.

I did not answer. I felt sick with the hurt.

"Come along," she said.

The building was wholly quiet now. I followed her up the narrow staircase into a hall of little rooms, many doors. Her cell was the quietest, at the very end. Inside, the air smelled stale, as if the door had not been opened for years. There was a crude straw mattress, a tiny bookcase with a picture of Saint Francis hanging over it, a ragged palm, a stool for sitting on, a crucifix. She told me to remove my blouse and sit on the stool. I did so. She took a pot of salve from the bookcase and began to smooth it upon my burns. Her hands made slow, wide circles, stopping the pain. I closed my eyes. I expected to see blackness. Peace. But instead the vision reared up again. My chest was still tipped with diamonds. I was walking through windows. She was chewing up the broken litter I left behind.

"I am going," I said. "Let me go."

But she held me down.

"Don't go," she said quickly. "Don't. We have just begun."

I was weakening. My thoughts were whirling pitifully. The pain had kept me strong, and as it left me I began to forget it; I couldn't hold on. I began to wonder if she'd really scalded me with the kettle. I could not remember. To remember this seemed the most important thing in the world. But I was losing the memory. The scalding. The pouring. It began to vanish. I felt like my mind was coming off its hinge, flapping in the breeze, hanging by the hair of my own pain. I wrenched out of her grip.

"He was always in you," I said. "Even more than in me. He wanted you even more. And now he's got you. Get thee behind me!"

I shouted that, grabbed my shirt, and ran through the door throw-

1. She is docile.

ing the cloth on my body. I got down the stairs and into the kitchen, even, but no matter what I told myself, I couldn't get out the door. It wasn't finished. And she knew I would not leave. Her quiet step was immediately behind me.

"We must take the bread from the oven now," she said.

She was pretending nothing happened. But for the first time I had gotten through some chink she'd left in her darkness. Touched some doubt. Her voice was so low and brittle it cracked off at the end of her sentence.

"Help me, Marie," she said slowly.

But I was not going to help her, even though she had calmly buttoned the back of my shirt up and put the big cloth mittens in my hands for taking out the loaves. I could have bolted for it then. But I didn't. I knew that something was nearing completion. Something was about to happen. My back was a wall of singing flame. I was turning. I watched her take the long fork in one hand, to tap the loaves. In the other hand she gripped the black poker to hook the pans.

"Help me," she said again, and I thought, Yes, this is part of it. I put the mittens on my hands and swung the door open on its hinges. The oven gaped. She stood back a moment, letting the first blast of heat rush by. I moved behind her. I could feel the heat at my front and at my back. Before, behind. My skin was turning to beaten gold. It was coming quicker than I thought. The oven was like the gate of a personal hell. Just big enough and hot enough for one person, and that was her. One kick and Leopolda would fly in headfirst. And that would be one-millionth of the heat she would feel when she finally collapsed in his hellish embrace.

Saints know these numbers.

She bent forward with her fork held out. I kicked her with all my might. She flew in. But the outstretched poker hit the back wall first, so she rebounded. The oven was not so deep as I had thought.

There was a moment when I felt a sort of thin, hot disappointment, as when a fish slips off the line. Only I was the one going to be lost. She was fearfully silent. She whirled. Her veil had cutting edges. She had the poker in one hand. In the other she held that long sharp fork she used to tap the delicate crusts of loaves. Her face turned upside down on her shoulders. Her face turned blue. But saints are used to miracles. I felt no trace of fear.

If I was going to be lost, let the diamonds cut! Let her eat ground glass!

"Bitch of Jesus Christ!" I shouted. "Kneel and beg! Lick the floor!"

That was when she stabbed me through the hand with the fork, then took the poker up alongside my head, and knocked me out.

It must have been a half an hour later when I came around. Things were so strange. So strange I can hardly tell it for delight at the remembrance. For when I came around this was actually taking place. I was being worshiped. I had somehow gained the altar of a saint.

I was lying back on the stiff couch in the Mother Superior's office. I looked around me. It was as though my deepest dream had come to life. The Sisters of the convent were kneeling to me. Sister Bonaventure. Sister Dympna. Sister Cecilia Saint-Claire. The two French with hands like paddles. They were down on their knees. Black capes were slung over some of their heads. My name was buzzing up and down the room, like a fat autumn fly lighting on the tips of their tongues between Latin, humming up the heavy blood-dark curtains, circling their little cosseted heads. Marie! Marie! A girl thrown in a closet. Who was afraid of a rubber overboot. Who was half overcome. A girl who came in the back door where they threw their garbage. Marie! Who never found the cup. Who had to eat their cold mush. Marie! Leopolda had her face buried in her knuckles. Saint Marie of the Holy Slops! Saint Marie of the Bread Fork! Saint Marie of the Burnt Back and Scalded Butt!

I broke out and laughed.

They looked up. All holy hell burst loose when they saw I'd woke. I still did not understand what was happening. They were watching, talking, but not to me.

"The marks . . ."

"She has her hand closed."

"*Je ne peux pas voir.*"

I was not stupid enough to ask what they were talking about. I couldn't tell why I was lying in white sheets. I couldn't tell why they were praying to me. But I'll tell you this: it seemed entirely natural. It was me. I lifted up my hand as in my dream. It was completely limp with sacredness.

"Peace be with you."

My arm was dried blood from the wrist down to the elbow. And it hurt. Their faces turned like flat flowers of adoration to follow that hand's movements. I let it swing through the air, imparting a saint's blessing. I had practiced. I knew exactly how to act.

They murmured. I heaved a sigh, and a golden beam of light suddenly broke through the clouded window and flooded down directly on my face. A stroke of perfect luck! They had to be convinced.

Leopolda still knelt in the back of the room. Her knuckles were crammed halfway down her throat. Let me tell you, a saint has senses honed keen as a wolf. I knew that she was over my barrel now. How it happened did not matter. The last thing I remembered was how she flew from the oven and stabbed me. That one thing was most certainly true.

"Come forward, Sister Leopolda." I gestured with my heavenly wound. Oh, it hurt. It bled when I reopened the slight heal. "Kneel beside me," I said.

She kneeled, but her voice box evidently did not work, for her mouth opened, shut, opened, but no sound came out. My throat clenched in noble delight I had read of as befitting a saint. She could not speak. But she was beaten. It was in her eyes. She stared at me now with all the deep hate of the wheel of devilish dust that rolled wild within her emptiness.

"What is it you want to tell me?" I asked. And at last she spoke.

"I have told my Sisters of your passion," she managed to choke out. "How the stigmata . . . the marks of the nails . . . appeared in your palm and you swooned at the holy vision. . . ."

"Yes," I said curiously.

And then, after a moment, I understood.

Leopolda had saved herself with her quick brain. She had witnessed a miracle. She had hid the fork and told this to the others. And of course they believed her, because they never knew how Satan came and went or where he took refuge.

"I saw it from the first," said the large one who put the bread in the oven. "Humility of the spirit. So rare in these girls."

"I saw it, too," said the other one with great satisfaction. She sighed quietly. "If only it was me."

Leopolda was kneeling bolt upright, face blazing and twitching, a barely held fountain of blasting poison.

"Christ has marked me," I agreed.

I smiled the saint's smirk into her face. And then I looked at her. That was my mistake.

For I saw her kneeling there. Leopolda with her soul like a rubber overboot. With her face of a starved rat. With the desperate eyes drowning in the deep wells of her wrongness. There would be no one else after me. And I would leave. I saw Leopolda kneeling within the shambles of her love.

My heart had been about to surge from my chest with the blackness of my joyous heat. Now it dropped. I pitied her. I pitied her. Pity twisted in my stomach like that hook-pole was driven through me. I was caught. It was a feeling more terrible than any amount of boiling water and worse than being forked. Still, still, I could not help what I did. I had already smiled in a saint's mealy forgiveness. I heard myself speaking gently.

"Receive the dispensation of my sacred blood," I whispered.

But there was no heart in it. No joy when she bent to touch the floor. No dark leaping. I fell back into the white pillows. Blank dust was whirling through the light shafts. My skin was dust. Dust my lips. Dust the dirty spoons on the ends of my feet.

Rise up! I thought. Rise up and walk! There is no limit to this dust!

1984, 1993

■   ■   ■

RICHARD FORD

ROCK SPRINGS

Edna and I had started down from Kalispell, heading for Tampa–St. Pete where I still had some friends from the old glory days who wouldn't turn me in to the police. I had managed to scrape with the law in Kalispell over several bad checks—which is a prison crime in Montana. And I knew Edna was already looking at her cards and thinking about a move, since it wasn't the first time I'd been in law scrapes in my life. She herself had already had her own troubles, losing her kids and keeping her ex-husband, Danny, from breaking in her house and stealing her things while she was at work, which was really why I had moved in in the first place, that and needing to give my little daughter, Cheryl, a better shake in things.

I don't know what was between Edna and me, just beached by the same tides when you got down to it. Though love has been built on frailer ground than that, as I well know. And when I came in the house that afternoon, I just asked her if she wanted to go to Florida with me, leave things where they sat, and she said, "Why not? My datebook's not that full."

Edna and I had been a pair eight months, more or less man and wife, some of which time I had been out of work, and some when I'd worked at the dog track as a lead-out and could help with the rent and talk sense to Danny when he came around. Danny was afraid of me because Edna had told him I'd been in prison in Florida for killing a man, though that wasn't true. I had once been in jail in Tallahassee for stealing tires and had gotten into a fight on the county farm where a man had lost his eye. But I hadn't done the hurting, and Edna just wanted the story worse than it was so Danny wouldn't act crazy and make her have to take her kids back, since she had made a good adjustment to not having them, and I already had Cheryl with me. I'm not a violent person and would never put a man's eye out, much less kill someone. My former wife, Helen, would come all the way from Wai- kiki Beach to testify to that. We never had violence, and I believe in crossing the street to stay out of trouble's way. Though Danny didn't know that.

But we were half down through Wyoming, going toward I-80 and feeling good about things, when the oil light flashed on in the car I'd stolen, a sign I knew to be a bad one.

I'd gotten us a good car, a cranberry Mercedes I'd stolen out of an ophthalmologist's lot in Whitefish, Montana. I stole it because I thought it would be comfortable over a long haul, because I thought it got good mileage, which it didn't, and because I'd never had a good car in my life, just old Chevy junkers and used trucks back from when I was a kid swamping citrus with Cubans.

The car made us all high that day. I ran the windows up and down, and Edna told us some jokes and made faces. She could be lively. Her features would light up like a beacon and you could see her beauty, which wasn't ordinary. It all made me giddy, and I drove clear down to Bozeman, then straight on through the park to Jackson Hole. I rented us the bridal suite in the Quality Court in Jackson and left Cheryl and her little dog, Duke, sleeping while Edna and I drove to a rib barn and drank beer and laughed till after midnight.

It felt like a whole new beginning for us, bad memories left behind and a new horizon to build on. I got so worked up, I had a tattoo done on my arm that said FAMOUS TIMES, and Edna bought a Bailey hat with an Indian feather band and a little turquoise-and-silver bracelet for Cheryl, and we made love on the seat of the car in the Quality Court parking lot just as the sun was burning up on the Snake River, and everything seemed then like the end of the rainbow.

It was that very enthusiasm, in fact, that made me keep the car one day longer instead of driving it into the river and stealing another one, like I should've done and *had* done before.

Where the car went bad there wasn't a town in sight or even a house, just some low mountains maybe fifty miles away or maybe a hundred, a barbed wire fence in both directions, hardpan prairie, and some hawks riding the evening air seizing insects.

I got out to look at the motor, and Edna got out with Cheryl and the dog to let them have a pee by the car. I checked the water and checked the oil stick, and both of them said perfect.

"What's that light mean, Earl?" Edna said. She had come and stood by the car with her hat on. She was just sizing things up for herself.

"We shouldn't run it," I said. "Something's not right in the oil."

She looked around at Cheryl and Little Duke, who were peeing on the hardtop side-by-side like two little dolls, then out at the mountains, which were becoming black and lost in the distance. "What're we doing?" she said. She wasn't worried yet, but she wanted to know what I was thinking about.

"Let me try it again."

"That's a good idea," she said, and we all got back in the car.

When I turned the motor over, it started right away and the red light stayed off and there weren't any noises to make you think something was wrong. I let it idle a minute, then pushed the accelerator down and watched the red bulb. But there wasn't any light on, and I started wondering if maybe I hadn't dreamed I saw it, or that it had been the sun catching an angle off the window chrome, or maybe I was scared of something and didn't know it.

"What's the matter with it, Daddy?" Cheryl said from the backseat. I looked back at her, and she had on her turquoise bracelet and Edna's hat set back on the back of her head and that little black-and-white Heinz dog on her lap. She looked like a little cowgirl in the movies.

"Nothing, honey, everything's fine now," I said.

"Little Duke tinkled where I tinkled," Cheryl said, and laughed.

"You're two of a kind," Edna said, not looking back. Edna was usually good with Cheryl, but I knew she was tired now. We hadn't had much sleep, and she had a tendency to get cranky when she didn't sleep. "We oughta ditch this damn car first chance we get," she said.

"What's the first chance we got?" I asked, because I knew she'd been at the map.

"Rock Springs, Wyoming," Edna said with conviction. "Thirty miles down this road." She pointed out ahead.

I had wanted all along to drive the car into Florida like a big success story. But I knew Edna was right about it, that we shouldn't take crazy chances. I had kept thinking of it as my car and not the ophthalmologist's, and that was how you got caught in these things.

"Then my belief is we ought to go to Rock Springs and negotiate ourselves a new car," I said. I wanted to stay upbeat, like everything was panning out right.

"That's a great idea," Edna said, and she leaned over and kissed me hard on the mouth.

"That's a great idea," Cheryl said. "Let's pull on out of here right now."

The sunset that day I remember as being the prettiest I'd ever seen. Just as it touched the rim of the horizon, it all at once fired the air into jewels and red sequins the precise likes of which I had never seen before and haven't seen since. The West has it all over everywhere for sunsets, even Florida, where it's supposedly flat but where half the time trees block your view.

"It's cocktail hour," Edna said after we'd driven awhile. "We ought to have a drink and celebrate something." She felt better thinking we were going to get rid of the car. It certainly had dark troubles and was something you'd want to put behind you.

Edna had out a whiskey bottle and some plastic cups and was measuring levels on the glove-box lid. She liked drinking, and she liked drinking in the car, which was something you got used to in Montana, where it wasn't against the law, but where, strangely enough, a bad check would land you in Deer Lodge Prison for a year.

"Did I ever tell you I once had a monkey?" Edna said, setting my drink on the dashboard where I could reach it when I was ready. Her spirits were already picked up. She was like that, up one minute and down the next.

"I don't think you ever did tell me that," I said. "Where were you then?"

"Missoula," she said. She put her bare feet on the dash and rested the cup on her breasts. "I was waitressing at the AmVets. This was before I met you. Some guy came in one day with a monkey. A spider monkey. And I said, just to be joking, 'I'll roll you for that monkey.' And the guy said, 'Just one roll?' And I said, 'Sure.' He put the monkey down on the bar, picked up the cup, and rolled out boxcars. I picked it up and rolled out three fives. And I just stood there looking at the guy. He was just some guy passing through, I guess a vet. He got a strange look on his face—I'm sure not as strange as the one I had—but he looked kind of sad and surprised and satisfied all at once. I said, 'We can roll again.' But he said, 'No, I never roll twice for anything.' And he sat and drank a beer and talked about one thing and another for a while, about nuclear war and building a stronghold somewhere up in the Bitterroot, whatever it was, while I just watched the monkey, wondering what I was going to do with it when the guy left. And pretty soon he got up and said, 'Well, good-bye, Chipper'—that was this monkey's name, of course. And then he left before I could say anything. And the monkey just sat on the bar all that night. I don't know what made me think of that, Earl. Just something weird. I'm letting my mind wander."

"That's perfectly fine," I said. I took a drink of my drink. "I'd never own a monkey," I said after a minute. "They're too nasty. I'm sure Cheryl would like a monkey, though, wouldn't you, honey?" Cheryl was down on the seat playing with Little Duke. She used to talk about monkeys all the time then. "What'd you ever do with that monkey?" I said, watching the speedometer. We were having to go slower now because the red light kept fluttering on. And all I could do to keep it off was go slower. We were going maybe thirty-five and it was an hour before dark, and I was hoping Rock Springs wasn't far away.

"You really want to know?" Edna said. She gave me a quick glance, then looked back at the empty desert as if she was brooding over it.

"Sure," I said. I was still upbeat. I figured I could worry about breaking down and let other people be happy for a change.

"I kept it a week." And she seemed gloomy all of a sudden, as if she saw some aspect of the story she had never seen before. "I took it home and back and forth to the AmVets on my shifts. And it didn't cause any trouble. I fixed a chair up for it to sit on, back of the bar, and people liked it. It made a nice little clicking noise. We changed its name to Mary because the bartender figured out it was a girl. Though I was never really comfortable with it at home. I felt like it watched me too much. Then one day a guy came in, some guy who'd been in Vietnam, still wore a fatigue coat. And he said to me, 'Don't you know that a monkey'll kill you? It's got more strength in its fingers than you got in your whole body.' He said people had been killed in Vietnam by monkeys, bunches of them marauding while you were asleep, killing you and covering you with leaves. I didn't believe a word of it, except that when I got home and got undressed I started looking over across the room at Mary on her chair in the dark watching me. And I got the creeps. And after a while I got up and went out to the car, got a length of clothesline wire, and came back in and wired her to the doorknob through her little silver collar, then went back and tried to sleep. And I guess I must've slept the sleep of the dead—though I don't remember it—because when I got up I found Mary had tipped off her chair-back and hanged herself on the wire line. I'd made it too short."

Edna seemed badly affected by that story and slid low in the seat so she couldn't see out over the dash. "Isn't that a shameful story, Earl, what happened to that poor little monkey?"

"I see a town! I see a town!" Cheryl started yelling from the back seat, and right up Little Duke started yapping and the whole car fell into a racket. And sure enough she had seen something I hadn't, which was Rock Springs, Wyoming, at the bottom of a long hill, a little glowing jewel in the desert with I-80 running on the north side and the black desert spread out behind.

"That's it, honey," I said. "That's where we're going. You saw it first."

"We're hungry," Cheryl said. "Little Duke wants some fish, and I want spaghetti." She put her arms around my neck and hugged me.

"Then you'll just get it," I said. "You can have anything you want. And so can Edna and so can Little Duke." I looked over at Edna, smiling, but she was staring at me with eyes that were fierce with anger. "What's wrong?" I said.

"Don't you care anything about that awful thing that happened to me?" Her mouth was drawn tight, and her eyes kept cutting back at Cheryl and Little Duke, as if they had been tormenting her.

"Of course I do," I said. "I thought that was an awful thing." I didn't want her to be unhappy. We were almost there, and pretty soon we could sit down and have a real meal without thinking somebody might be hurting us.

"You want to know what I did with that monkey?" Edna said.

"Sure I do," I said.

"I put her in a green garbage bag, put it in the trunk of my car, drove to the dump, and threw her in the trash." She was staring at me darkly, as if the story meant something to her that was real important but that only she could see and that the rest of the world was a fool for.

"Well, that's horrible," I said. "But I don't see what else you could do. You didn't mean to kill it. You'd have done it differently if you had. And then you had to get rid of it, and I don't know what else you could have done. Throwing it away might seem unsympathetic to somebody, probably, but not to me. Sometimes that's all you can do, and you can't worry about what somebody else thinks." I tried to smile at her, but the red light was staying on if I pushed the accelerator at all, and I was trying to gauge if we could coast to Rock Springs before the car gave out completely. I looked at Edna again. "What else can I say?" I said.

"Nothing," she said, and stared back at the dark highway. "I should've known that's what you'd think. You've got a character that leaves something out, Earl. I've known that a long time."

"And yet here you are," I said. "And you're not doing so bad. Things could be a lot worse. At least we're all together here."

"Things could always be worse," Edna said. "You could go to the electric chair tomorrow."

"That's right," I said. "And somewhere somebody probably will. Only it won't be you."

"I'm hungry," said Cheryl. "When're we gonna eat? Let's find a motel. I'm tired of this. Little Duke's tired of it too."

Where the car stopped rolling was some distance from the town, though you could see the clear outline of the interstate in the dark with Rock Springs lighting up the sky behind. You could hear the big tractors hitting the spacers in the overpass, revving up for the climb to the mountains.

I shut off the lights.

"What're we going to do now?" Edna said irritably, giving me a bitter look.

"I'm figuring it," I said. "It won't be hard, whatever it is. You won't have to do anything."

"I'd hope not," she said and looked the other way.

Across the road and across a dry wash a hundred yards was what looked like a huge mobile-home town, with a factory or a refinery of some kind lit up behind it and in full swing. There were lights on in a lot of the mobile homes, and there were cars moving along an access road that ended near the freeway overpass a mile the other way. The lights in the mobile homes seemed friendly to me, and I knew right then what I should do.

"Get out," I said, opening my door.

"Are we walking?" Edna said.

"We're pushing."

"I'm not pushing." Edna reached up and locked her door.

"All right," I said. "Then you just steer."

"You're pushing us to Rock Springs, are you, Earl? It doesn't look like it's more than about three miles."

"I'll push," Cheryl said from the back.

"No, hon. Daddy'll push. You just get out with Little Duke and move out of the way."

Edna gave me a threatening look, just as if I'd tried to hit her. But when I got out she slid into my seat and took the wheel, staring angrily ahead straight into the cottonwood scrub.

"Edna can't drive that car," Cheryl said from out in the dark. "She'll run it in the ditch."

"Yes, she can, hon. Edna can drive it as good as I can. Probably better."

"No she can't," Cheryl said. "No she can't either." And I thought she was about to cry, but she didn't.

I told Edna to keep the ignition on so it wouldn't lock up and to steer into the cottonwoods with the parking lights on so she could see. And when I started, she steered it straight off into the trees, and I kept pushing until we were twenty yards into the cover and the tires sank in the soft sand and nothing at all could be seen from the road.

"Now where are we?" she said, sitting at the wheel. Her voice was tired and hard, and I knew she could have put a good meal to use. She had a sweet nature, and I recognized that this wasn't her fault but mine. Only I wished she could be more hopeful.

"You stay right here, and I'll go over to that trailer park and call us a cab," I said.

"What cab?" Edna said, her mouth wrinkled as if she'd never heard anything like that in her life.

"There'll be cabs," I said, and tried to smile at her. "There's cabs everywhere."

"What're you going to tell him when he gets here? Our stolen car broke down and we need a ride to where we can steal another one? That'll be a big hit, Earl."

"I'll talk," I said. "You just listen to the radio for ten minutes and then walk on out to the shoulder like nothing was suspicious. And you and Cheryl act nice. She doesn't need to know about this car."

"Like we're not suspicious enough already, right?" Edna looked up at me out of the lighted car. "You don't think right, did you know that, Earl? You think the world's stupid and you're smart. But that's not how it is. I feel sorry for you. You might've *been* something, but things just went crazy someplace."

I had a thought about poor Danny. He was a vet and crazy as a shit-house mouse, and I was glad he wasn't in for all this. "Just get the baby in the car," I said, trying to be patient. "I'm hungry like you are."

"I'm tired of this," Edna said. "I wish I'd stayed in Montana."

"Then you can go back in the morning," I said. "I'll buy the ticket and put you on the bus. But not till then."

"Just get on with it, Earl." She slumped down in the seat, turning off the parking lights with one foot and the radio on with the other.

The mobile-home community was as big as any I'd ever seen. It was attached in some way to the plant that was lighted up behind it, because I could see a car once in a while leave one of the trailer streets, turn in the direction of the plant, then go slowly into it. Everything in the plant was white, and you could see that all the trailers were painted white and looked exactly alike. A deep hum came out of the plant, and I thought as I got closer that it wouldn't be a location I'd ever want to work in.

I went right to the first trailer where there was a light, and knocked on the metal door. Kids' toys were lying in the gravel around the little wood steps, and I could hear talking on TV that suddenly went off. I heard a woman's voice talking, and then the door opened wide.

A large Negro woman with a wide, friendly face stood in the doorway. She smiled at me and moved forward as if she was going to come out, but she stopped at the top step. There was a little Negro boy behind her peeping out from behind her legs, watching me with his eyes half closed. The trailer had that feeling that no one else was inside, which was a feeling I knew something about.

"I'm sorry to intrude," I said. "But I've run up on a little bad luck tonight. My name's Earl Middleton."

The woman looked at me, then out into the night toward the freeway as if what I had said was something she was going to be able to see. "What kind of bad luck?" she said, looking down at me again.

"My car broke down out on the highway," I said. "I can't fix it myself, and I wondered if I could use your phone to call for help."

The woman smiled down at me knowingly. "We can't live without cars, can we?"

"That's the honest truth," I said.

"They're like our hearts," she said, her face shining in the little bulb light that burned beside the door. "Where's your car situated?"

I turned and looked over into the dark, but I couldn't see anything because of where we'd put it. "It's over there," I said. "You can't see it in the dark."

"Who all's with you now?" the woman said. "Have you got your wife with you?"

"She's with my little girl and our dog in the car," I said. "My daughter's asleep or I would have brought them."

"They shouldn't be left in the dark by themselves," the woman said and frowned. "There's too much unsavoriness out there."

"The best I can do is hurry back." I tried to look sincere, since everything except Cheryl being asleep and Edna being my wife was the truth. The truth is meant to serve you if you'll let it, and I wanted it to serve me. "I'll pay for the phone call," I said. "If you'll bring the phone to the door I'll call from right here."

The woman looked at me again as if she was searching for a truth of her own, then back out into the night. She was maybe in her sixties, but I couldn't say for sure. "You're not going to rob me, are you, Mr. Middleton?" She smiled like it was a joke between us.

"Not tonight," I said, and smiled a genuine smile. "I'm not up to it tonight. Maybe another time."

"Then I guess Terrel and I can let you use our phone with Daddy not here, can't we, Terrel? This is my grandson, Terrel Junior, Mr. Middleton." She put her hand on the boy's head and looked down at him. "Terrel won't talk. Though if he did he'd tell you to use our phone. He's a sweet boy." She opened the screen for me to come in.

The trailer was a big one with a new rug and a new couch and a living room that expanded to give the space of a real house. Something good and sweet was cooking in the kitchen, and the trailer felt like it was somebody's comfortable new home instead of just temporary. I've lived in trailers, but they were just snailbacks with one room and no toilet, and they always felt cramped and unhappy— though I've thought maybe it might've been me that was unhappy in them.

There was a big Sony TV and a lot of kids' toys scattered on the floor. I recognized a Greyhound bus I'd gotten for Cheryl. The phone was beside a new leather recliner, and the Negro woman pointed for me to sit down and call and gave me the phone book. Terrel began fingering his toys and the woman sat on the couch while I called, watching me and smiling.

There were three listings for cab companies, all with one number different. I called the numbers in order and didn't get an answer until the last one, which answered with the name of the second company. I said I was on the highway beyond the interstate and that my wife and family needed to be taken to town and I would arrange for a tow later. While I was giving the location, I looked up the name of a tow service to tell the driver in case he asked.

When I hung up, the Negro woman was sitting looking at me with the same look she had been staring with into the dark, a look that seemed to want truth. She was smiling, though. Something pleased her and I reminded her of it.

"This is a very nice home," I said, resting in the recliner, which felt like the driver's seat of the Mercedes, and where I'd have been happy to stay.

"This isn't *our* house, Mr. Middleton," the Negro woman said. "The company owns these. They give them to us for nothing. We have our own home in Rockford, Illinois."

"That's wonderful," I said.

"It's never wonderful when you have to be away from home, Mr. Middleton, though we're only here three months, and it'll be easier when Terrel Junior begins his special school. You see, our son was killed in the war, and his wife ran off without Terrel Junior. Though you shouldn't worry. He can't understand us. His little feelings can't be hurt." The woman folded her hands in her lap and smiled in a satisfied way. She was an attractive woman, and had on a blue-and-pink floral dress that made her seem bigger than she could've been, just the right woman to sit on the couch she was sitting on. She was good nature's picture, and I was glad she could be, with her little brain-damaged boy, living in a place where no one in his right mind would want to live a minute. "Where do *you* live, Mr. Middleton?" she said politely, smiling in the same sympathetic way.

"My family and I are in transit," I said. "I'm an ophthalmologist, and we're moving back to Florida, where I'm from. I'm setting up practice in some little town where it's warm year-round. I haven't decided where."

"Florida's a wonderful place," the woman said. "I think Terrel would like it there."

"Could I ask you something?" I said.

"You certainly may," the woman said. Terrel had begun pushing his Greyhound across the front of the TV screen, making a scratch that no one watching the set could miss. "Stop that, Terrel Junior," the woman said quietly. But Terrel kept pushing his bus on the glass, and she smiled at me again as if we both understood something sad. Except I knew Cheryl would never damage a television set. She had respect for nice things, and I was sorry for the lady that Terrel didn't. "What did you want to ask?" the woman said.

"What goes on in that plant or whatever it is back there beyond these trailers, where all the lights are on?"

"Gold," the woman said and smiled.

"It's what?" I said.

"Gold," the Negro woman said, smiling as she had for almost all the time I'd been there. "It's a gold mine."

"They're mining gold back there?" I said, pointing.

"Every night and every day." She smiled in a pleased way.

"Does your husband work there?" I said.

"He's the assayer," she said. "He controls the quality. He works three months a year, and we live the rest of the time at home in Rockford. We've waited a long time for this. We've been happy to have our grandson, but I won't say I'll be sorry to have him go. We're ready to start our lives over." She smiled broadly at me and then at Terrel, who was giving her a spiteful look from the floor. "You said you had a daughter," the Negro woman said. "And what's her name?"

"Irma Cheryl," I said. "She's named for my mother."

"That's nice. And she's healthy, too. I can see it in your face." She looked at Terrel Junior with pity.

"I guess I'm lucky," I said.

"So far you are. But children bring you grief, the same way they bring you joy. We were unhappy for a long time before my husband got his job in the gold mine. Now, when Terrel starts to school, we'll be kids again." She stood up. "You might miss your cab, Mr. Middleton," she said, walking toward the door, though not to be forcing me out. She was too polite. "If we can't see your car, the cab surely won't be able to."

"That's true." I got up off the recliner, where I'd been so comfortable. "None of us have eaten yet, and your food makes me know how hungry we probably all are."

"There are fine restaurants in town, and you'll find them," the Negro woman said. "I'm sorry you didn't meet my husband. He's a wonderful man. He's everything to me."

"Tell him I appreciate the phone," I said. "You saved me."

"You weren't hard to save," the woman said. "Saving people is what we were all put on earth to do. I just passed you on to whatever's coming to you."

"Let's hope it's good," I said, stepping back into the dark.

"I'll be hoping, Mr. Middleton. Terrel and I will both be hoping."

I waved to her as I walked out into the darkness toward the car where it was hidden in the night.

The cab had already arrived when I got there. I could see its little red-and-green roof lights all the way across the dry wash, and it made me worry that Edna was already saying something to get us in trouble, something about the car or where we'd come from, something that would cast suspicion on us. I thought, then, how I never planned things well enough. There was always a gap between my plan and what happened, and I only responded to things as they came along and hoped I wouldn't get in trouble. I was an offender in the law's eyes. But I always *thought* differently, as if I weren't an offender and had no intention of being one, which was the truth. But as I read on a napkin once, between the idea and the act a whole kingdom lies. And I had a hard time with my acts, which were oftentimes offender's acts, and my ideas, which were as good as the gold they mined there where the bright lights were blazing.

"We're waiting for you, Daddy," Cheryl said when I crossed the road. "The taxicab's already here."

"I see, hon," I said, and gave Cheryl a big hug. The cabdriver was sitting in the driver's seat having a smoke with the lights on inside. Edna was leaning against the back of the cab between the taillights, wearing her Bailey hat. "What'd you tell him?" I said when I got close.

"Nothing," she said. "What's there to tell?"

"Did he see the car?"

She glanced over in the direction of the trees where we had hid the Mercedes. Nothing was visible in the darkness, though I could hear Little Duke combing around in the underbrush tracking something, his little collar tinkling. "Where're we going?" she said. "I'm so hungry I could pass out."

"Edna's in a terrible mood," Cheryl said. "She already snapped at me."

"We're tired, honey," I said. "So try to be nicer."

"She's never nice," Cheryl said.

"Run go get Little Duke," I said. "And hurry back."

"I guess *my* questions come last here, right?" Edna said.

I put my arm around her. "That's not true."

"Did you find somebody over there in the trailers you'd rather stay with? You were gone long enough."

"That's not a thing to say," I said. "I was just trying to make things look right, so we don't get put in jail."

"So *you* don't, you mean." Edna laughed a little laugh I didn't like hearing.

"That's right. So I don't," I said. "I'd be the one in Dutch." I stared out at the big, lighted assemblage of white buildings and white lights beyond the trailer community, plumes of white smoke escaping up into the heartless Wyoming sky, the whole company of buildings looking like some unbelievable castle, humming away in a distorted dream. "You know what all those buildings are there?" I said to Edna, who hadn't moved and who didn't really seem to care if she ever moved anymore ever.

"No. But I can't say it matters, because it isn't a motel and it isn't a restaurant."

"It's a gold mine," I said, staring at the gold mine, which, I knew now, was a greater distance from us than it seemed, though it seemed huge and near, up against the cold sky. I thought there should've been a wall around it with guards instead of just the lights and no fence. It seemed as if anyone could go in and take what they wanted, just the way I had gone up to that woman's trailer and used the telephone, though that obviously wasn't true.

Edna began to laugh then. Not the mean laugh I didn't like, but a laugh that had something caring behind it, a full laugh that enjoyed a joke, a laugh she was laughing the first time I laid eyes on her, in Missoula in the East Gate Bar in 1979, a laugh we used to laugh together when Cheryl was still with her mother and I was working steady at the track and not stealing cars or passing bogus checks to merchants. A better time all around. And for some reason it made me laugh just hearing her, and we both stood there behind the cab in the dark, laughing at the gold mine in the desert, me with my arm around her and Cheryl out rustling up Little Duke and the cabdriver smoking in the cab and our stolen Mercedes-Benz, which I'd had such hopes for in Florida, stuck up to its axle in sand, where I'd never get to see it again.

"I always wondered what a gold mine would look like when I saw it," Edna said, still laughing, wiping a tear from her eye.

"Me too," I said. "I was always curious about it."

"We're a couple of fools, aren't we, Earl?" she said, unable to quit laughing completely. "We're two of a kind."

"It might be a good sign, though," I said.

"How could it be? It's not our gold mine. There aren't any drive-up windows." She was still laughing.

"We've seen it," I said, pointing. "That's it right there. It may mean we're getting closer. Some people never see it at all."

"In a pig's eye, Earl," she said. "You and me see it in a pig's eye." And she turned and got in the cab to go.

The cabdriver didn't ask anything about our car or where it was, to mean he'd noticed something queer. All of which made me feel like we had made a clean break from the car and couldn't be connected with it until it was too late, if ever. The driver told us a lot about Rock Springs while he drove, that because of the gold mine a lot of people had moved there is just six months, people from all over, including New York, and that most of them lived out in the trailers. Prostitutes from New York City, who he called "B-girls," had come into town, he said, on the prosperity tide, and Cadillacs with New York plates cruised the little streets every night, full of Negroes with big hats who ran the women. He told us that everybody who got in his cab now wanted to know where the women were, and when he got our call he almost didn't come because some of the trailers were brothels operated by the mine for engineers and computer people away from home. He said he got tired of running back and forth out there just for vile business. He said that 60 *Minutes* had even done a program about Rock Springs and that a blow-up had resulted in Cheyenne, though nothing could be done unless the boom left town. "It's prosperity's fruit," the driver said. "I'd rather be poor, which is lucky for me."

He said all the motels were sky-high, but since we were a family he could show us a nice one that was affordable. But I told him we wanted a first-rate place where they took animals, and the money didn't matter because we had had a hard day and wanted to finish on a high note. I also knew that it was in the little nowhere places that the police look for you and find you. People I'd known were always being arrested in cheap hotels and tourist courts with names you'd never heard of before. Never in Holiday Inns or TraveLodges.

I asked him to drive us to the middle of town and back out again so Cheryl could see the train station, and while we were there I saw a pink Cadillac with New York plates and a TV aerial being driven slowly by a Negro in a big hat down a narrow street where there were just bars and a Chinese restaurant. It was an odd sight, nothing you could ever expect.

"There's your pure criminal element," the cabdriver said and seemed sad. "I'm sorry for people like you to see a thing like that.

We've got a nice town here, but there're some that want to ruin it for everybody. There used to be a way to deal with trash and criminals, but those days are gone forever."

"You said it," Edna said.

"You shouldn't let it get *you* down," I said to him. "There's more of you than them. And there always will be. You're the best advertisement this town has. I know Cheryl will remember you and not *that* man, won't you, honey?" But Cheryl was asleep by then, holding Little Duke in her arms on the taxi seat.

The driver took us to the Ramada Inn on the interstate, not far from where we'd broken down. I had a small pain of regret as we drove under the Ramada awning that we hadn't driven up in a cranberry-colored Mercedes but instead in a beat-up old Chrysler taxi driven by an old man full of complaints. Though I knew it was for the best. We were better off without that car; better, really, in any other car but that one, where the signs had turned bad.

I registered under another name and paid for the room in cash so there wouldn't be any questions. On the line where it said "Representing" I wrote "Ophthalmologist" and put "M.D." after the name. It had a nice look to it, even though it wasn't my name.

When we got to the room, which was in the back where I'd asked for it, I put Cheryl on one of the beds and Little Duke beside her so they'd sleep. She'd missed dinner, but it only meant she'd be hungry in the morning, when she could have anything she wanted. A few missed meals don't make a kid bad. I'd missed a lot of them myself and haven't turned out completely bad.

"Let's have some fried chicken," I said to Edna when she came out of the bathroom. "They have good fried chicken at Ramadas, and I noticed the buffet was still up. Cheryl can stay right here, where it's safe, till we're back."

"I guess I'm not hungry anymore," Edna said. She stood at the window staring out into the dark. I could see out the window past her some yellowish foggy glow in the sky. For a moment I thought it was the gold mine out in the distance lighting the night, though it was only the interstate.

"We could order up," I said. "Whatever you want. There's a menu on the phone book. You could just have a salad."

"You go ahead," she said. "I've lost my hungry spirit." She sat on the bed beside Cheryl and Little Duke and looked at them in a sweet way and put her hand on Cheryl's cheek just as if she'd had a fever. "Sweet little girl," she said. "Everybody loves you."

"What do you want to do?" I said. "I'd like to eat. Maybe I'll order up some chicken."

"Why don't you do that?" she said. "It's your favorite." And she smiled at me from the bed.

I sat on the other bed and dialed room service. I asked for chicken, garden salad, potato and a roll, plus a piece of hot apple pie and iced tea. I realized I hadn't eaten all day. When I put down the phone I saw that Edna was watching me, not in a hateful way or a loving way, just in a way that seemed to say she didn't understand something and was going to ask me about it.

"When did watching me get so entertaining?" I said and smiled at her. I was trying to be friendly. I knew how tired she must be. It was after nine o'clock.

"I was just thinking how much I hated being in a motel without a car that was mine to drive. Isn't that funny? I started feeling like that last night when that purple car wasn't mine. That purple car just gave me the willies, I guess, Earl."

"One of those cars *outside* is yours," I said. "Just stand right there and pick it out."

"I know," she said. "But that's different, isn't it?" She reached and got her blue Bailey hat, put it on her head, and set it way back like Dale Evans. She looked sweet. "I used to like to go to motels, you know," she said. "There's something secret about them and free—I was never paying, of course. But you felt safe from everything and free to do what you wanted because you'd made the decision to be there and paid that price, and all the rest was the good part. Fucking and everything, you know." She smiled at me in a good-natured way.

"Isn't that the way this is?" I was sitting on the bed, watching her, not knowing what to expect her to say next.

"I don't guess it is, Earl," she said and stared out the window. "I'm thirty-two and I'm going to have to give up on motels. I can't keep that fantasy going anymore."

"Don't you like this place?" I said and looked around at the room. I appreciated the modern paintings and the lowboy bureau and the big TV. It seemed like a plenty nice enough place to me, considering where we'd been.

"No, I don't," Edna said with real conviction. "There's no use in my getting mad at you about it. It isn't your fault. You do the best you can for everybody. But every trip teaches you something. And I've learned I need to give up on motels before some bad thing happens to me. I'm sorry."

"What does that mean?" I said, because I really didn't know what she had in mind to do, though I should've guessed.

"I guess I'll take that ticket you mentioned," she said, and got up and faced the window. "Tomorrow's soon enough. We haven't got a car to take me anyhow."

"Well, that's a fine thing," I said, sitting on the bed, feeling like I was in shock. I wanted to say something to her, to argue with her, but I couldn't think what to say that seemed right. I didn't want to be mad at her, but it made me mad.

"You've got a right to be mad at me, Earl," she said, "but I don't think you can really blame me." She turned around and faced me and sat on the windowsill, her hands on her knees. Someone knocked on the door, and I just yelled for them to set the tray down and put it on the bill.

"I guess I *do* blame you," I said, and I was angry. I thought about how I could've disappeared into that trailer community and hadn't, had come back to keep things going, had tried to take control of things for everybody when they looked bad.

"Don't. I wish you wouldn't," Edna said and smiled at me like she wanted me to hug her. "Anybody ought to have their choice in things if they can. Don't you believe that, Earl? Here I am out here in the desert where I don't know anything, in a stolen car, in a motel room under an assumed name, with no money of my own, a kid that's not mine, and the law after me. And I have a choice to get out of all of it by getting on a bus. What would you do? I know exactly what you'd do."

"You think you do," I said. But I didn't want to get into an argument about it and tell her all I could've done and didn't do. Because it wouldn't have done any good. When you get to the point of arguing, you're past the point of changing anybody's mind, even though it's supposed to be the other way, and maybe for some classes of people it is, just never mine.

Edna smiled at me and came across the room and put her arms around me where I was sitting on the bed. Cheryl rolled over and looked at us and smiled, then closed her eyes, and the room was quiet. I was beginning to think of Rock Springs in a way I knew I would always think of it, a lowdown city full of crimes and whores and disappointments, a place where a woman left me, instead of a place where I got things on the straight track once and for all, a place I saw a gold mine.

"Eat your chicken, Earl," Edna said. "Then we can go to bed. I'm tired, but I'd like to make love to you anyway. None of this is a matter of not loving you, you know that."

Sometime late in the night, after Edna was asleep, I got up and walked outside into the parking lot. It could've been anytime because there was still the light from the interstate frosting the low sky and the big red Ramada sign humming motionlessly in the night and no light at all in the east to indicate it might be morning. The lot was full of cars all nosed in, a couple of them with suitcases strapped to their roofs and their trunks weighed down with belongings the people were taking someplace, to a new home or a vacation resort in the mountains. I had laid in bed a long time after Edna was asleep, watching the Atlanta Braves on television, trying to get my mind off how I'd feel when I saw that bus pull away the next day, and how I'd feel when I turned around and there stood Cheryl and Little Duke and no one to see about them but me alone, and that the first thing I had to do was get hold of some automobile and get the plates switched, then get them some breakfast and get us all on the road to Florida, all in the space of probably two hours, since that Mercedes would certainly look less hid in the daytime than the night, and word travels fast. I've always taken care of Cheryl myself as long as I've had her with me. None of the women ever did. Most of them didn't even seem to like her, though they took care of me in a way so that I could take care of her. And I knew that once Edna left, all that was going to get harder. Though what I wanted most to do was not think about it just for a little while, try to let my mind go limp so it could be strong for the rest of what there was. I thought that the difference between a successful life and an unsuccessful one, between me at that moment and all the people who owned the cars that were nosed into their proper places in the lot, maybe between me and that woman out in the trailers by the gold mine, was how well you were able to put things like this out of your mind and not be bothered by them, and maybe, too, by how many troubles like this one you had to face in a lifetime. Through luck or design they had all faced fewer troubles, and by their own characters, they forgot them faster. And that's what I wanted for me. Fewer troubles, fewer memories of trouble.

I walked over to a car, a Pontiac with Ohio tags, one of the ones with bundles and suitcases strapped to the top and a lot more in the trunk, by the way it was riding. I looked inside the driver's window. There were maps and paperback books and sunglasses and the little plastic holders for cans that hang on the window wells. And in the back there were kids' toys and some pillows and a cat box with a cat sitting in it staring up at me like I was the face of the moon. It all looked familiar to me, the very same things I would have in my car if I had a car. Nothing seemed surprising, nothing different. Though I had a funny sensation at that moment and turned and looked up at the windows along the back of the motel. All were dark except two. Mine and another one. And I wondered, because it seemed funny, what would you think a man was doing if you saw him in the middle of the night looking in the windows of cars in the parking lot of the Ramada Inn? Would you think he was trying to get his head cleared? Would you think he was trying to get ready for a day when trouble would come down on him? Would you think his girlfriend was leaving him? Would you think he had a daughter? Would you think he was anybody like you?

1987

▪   ▪   ▪

GABRIEL GARCÍA MÁRQUEZ

A VERY OLD MAN WITH ENORMOUS WINGS

Translated by Gregory Rabassa

On the third day of rain they had killed so many crabs inside the house that Pelayo had to cross his drenched courtyard and throw them into the sea, because the newborn child had a temperature all night and they thought it was due to the stench. The world had been sad since Tuesday. Sea and sky were a single ash-gray thing and the sands of the beach, which on March nights glimmered like powdered light, had become a stew of mud and rotten shellfish. The light was so weak at noon that when Pelayo was coming back to the house after throwing away the crabs, it was hard for him to see what it was that was moving and groaning in the rear of the courtyard. He had to go very close to see that it was an old man, a very old man, lying face down in the mud, who, in spite of his tremendous efforts, couldn't get up, impeded by his enormous wings.

Frightened by that nightmare, Pelayo ran to get Elisenda, his wife, who was putting compresses on the sick child, and he took her to the rear of the courtyard. They both looked at the fallen body with mute stupor. He was dressed like a ragpicker. There were only a few faded hairs left on his bald skull and very few teeth in his mouth, and his pitiful condition of a drenched great-grandfather had taken away any sense of grandeur he might have had. His huge buzzard wings, dirty and half-plucked, were forever entangled in the mud. They looked at him so long and so closely that Pelayo and Elisenda very soon overcame their surprise and in the end found him familiar. Then they dared speak to him, and he answered in an incomprehensible dialect with a strong sailor's voice. That was how they skipped over the inconvenience of the wings and quite intelligently concluded that he was a lonely castaway from some foreign ship wrecked by the storm. And yet, they called in a neighbor woman who knew everything about life and death to see him, and all she needed was one look to show them their mistake.

"He's an angel," she told them. "He must have been coming for the child, but the poor fellow is so old that the rain knocked him down."

On the following day everyone knew that a flesh-and-blood angel was held captive in Pelayo's house. Against the judgment of the wise neighbor woman, for whom angels in those times were the fugitive survivors of a celestial conspiracy, they did not have the heart to club him to death. Pelayo watched over him all afternoon from the kitchen, armed with his bailiff's club, and before going to bed he dragged him out of the mud and locked him up with the hens in the wire chicken coop. In the middle of the night, when the rain stopped, Pelayo and Elisenda were still killing crabs. A short time afterward the child woke up without a fever and with a desire to eat. Then they felt magnanimous and decided to put the angel on a raft with fresh water and provisions for three days and leave him to his fate on the high seas. But when they went out into the courtyard with the first light of dawn, they found the whole neighborhood in front of the chicken coop having fun with the angel, without the slightest reverence, tossing him things to eat through the openings in the wire as if he weren't a supernatural creature but a circus animal.

Father Gonzaga arrived before seven o'clock, alarmed at the strange news. By that time onlookers less frivolous than those at dawn had already arrived and they were making all kinds of conjectures concerning the captive's future. The simplest among them thought that he should be named mayor of the world. Others of sterner mind felt that he should be promoted to the rank of five-star general in order to win all wars. Some visionaries hoped that he could be put to stud in order to implant on earth a race of winged wise men who could take charge of the universe. But Father Gonzaga, before becoming a priest, had been a robust woodcutter. Standing by the wire, he reviewed his catechism in an instant and asked them to open the door so that he could take a close look at that pitiful man who looked more like a huge decrepit hen among the fascinated chickens. He was lying in a corner drying his open wings in the sunlight among the fruit peels and breakfast leftovers that the early risers had thrown him. Alien to the impertinences of the world, he only lifted his antiquarian eyes and murmured something in his dialect when Father Gonzaga went into the chicken coop and said good morning to him in Latin. The parish priest had his first suspicion of an impostor when he saw that he did not understand the language of God or know how to greet His ministers. Then he noticed that seen close up he was much too human: he had an unbearable smell of the outdoors, the back side of his wings was strewn with parasites and his main feathers had been mistreated by terrestrial winds, and nothing about him measured up to the proud dignity of angels. Then he came out of the chicken coop and in a brief sermon warned the curious against the risks of being ingenuous. He reminded them that the devil had the bad habit of making use of carnival tricks in order to confuse the unwary. He argued that if wings were not the essential element in determining the difference between a hawk and an airplane, they were even less so in the recognition of angels. Nevertheless, he promised to write a letter to his bishop so that the latter would write to his primate so that the latter would write to the Supreme Pontiff in order to get the final verdict from the highest courts.

His prudence fell on sterile hearts. The news of the captive angel spread with such rapidity that after a few hours the courtyard had the bustle of a marketplace and they had to call in troops with fixed bayonets to disperse the mob that was about to knock the house down. Elisenda, her spine all twisted from sweeping up so much marketplace trash, then got the idea of fencing in the yard and charging five cents admission to see the angel.

The curious came from far away. A traveling carnival arrived with a flying acrobat who buzzed over the crowd several times, but no one paid any attention to him because his wings were not those of an angel but, rather, those of a sidereal[1] bat. The most unfortunate invalids on earth came in search of health: a poor woman who since childhood had been counting her heartbeats and had run out of numbers; a Portuguese man who couldn't sleep because the noise of the stars disturbed him; a sleep-walker who got up at night to undo the things he had done while awake; and many others with less serious ailments. In the midst of that shipwreck disorder that made the earth tremble, Pelayo and Elisenda were happy with fatigue, for in less than a week they had crammed their rooms with money and the line of pilgrims waiting their turn to enter still reached beyond the horizon.

The angel was the only one who took no part in his own act. He spent his time trying to get comfortable in his borrowed nest, befuddled by the hellish heat of the oil lamps and sacramental candles that had been placed along the wire. At first they tried to make him eat

1. Relating to stars or constellations.

some mothballs, which, according to the wisdom of the wise neighbor woman, were the food prescribed for angels. But he turned them down, just as he turned down the papal lunches that the penitents brought him, and they never found out whether it was because he was an angel or because he was an old man that in the end he ate nothing but eggplant mush. His only supernatural virtue seemed to be patience. Especially during the first days, when the hens pecked at him, searching for the stellar parasites that proliferated in his wings, and the cripples pulled out feathers to touch their defective parts with, and even the most merciful threw stones at him, trying to get him to rise so they could see him standing. The only time they succeeded in arousing him was when they burned his side with an iron for branding steers, for he had been motionless for so many hours that they thought he was dead. He awoke with a start, ranting in his hermetic language and with tears in his eyes, and he flapped his wings a couple of times, which brought on a whirlwind of chicken dung and lunar dust and a gale of panic that did not seem to be of this world. Although many thought that his reaction had been one not of rage but of pain, from then on they were careful not to annoy him, because the majority understood that his passivity was not that of a hero taking his ease but that of a cataclysm in repose.

Father Gonzaga held back the crowd's frivolity with formulas of maidservant inspiration while awaiting the arrival of a final judgment on the nature of the captive. But the mail from Rome showed no sense of urgency. They spent their time finding out if the prisoner had a navel, if his dialect had any connection with Aramaic, how many times he could fit on the head of a pin, or whether he wasn't just a Norwegian with wings. Those meager letters might have come and gone until the end of time if a providential event had not put an end to the priest's tribulations.

It so happened that during those days, among so many other carnival attractions, there arrived in town the traveling show of the woman who had been changed into a spider for having disobeyed her parents. The admission to see her was not only less than the admission to see the angel, but people were permitted to ask her all manner of questions about her absurd state and to examine her up and down so that no one would ever doubt the truth of her horror. She was a frightful tarantula the size of a ram and with the head of a sad maiden. What was most heart-rending, however, was not her outlandish shape but the sincere affliction with which she recounted the details of her misfortune. While still practically a child she had sneaked out of her parents' house to go to a dance, and while she was coming back through the woods after having danced all night without permission, a fearful thunderclap rent the sky in two and through the crack came the lightning bolt of brimstone that changed her into a spider. Her only nourishment came from the meatballs that charitable souls chose to toss into her mouth. A spectacle like that, full of so much human truth and with such a fearful lesson, was bound to defeat without even trying that of a haughty angel who scarcely deigned to look at mortals. Besides, the few miracles attributed to the angel showed a certain mental disorder, like the blind man who didn't recover his sight but grew three new teeth, or the paralytic who didn't get to walk but almost won the lottery, and the leper whose sores sprouted sunflowers. Those consolation miracles, which were more like mocking fun, had already ruined the angel's reputation when the woman who had been changed into a spider finally crushed him completely. That was how Father Gonzaga was cured forever of his insomnia and Pelayo's courtyard went back to being as empty as during the time it had rained for three days and crabs walked through the bedrooms.

The owners of the house had no reason to lament. With the money they saved they built a two-story mansion with balconies and gardens and high netting so that crabs wouldn't get in during the winter, and with iron bars on the windows so that angels wouldn't get in. Pelayo also set up a rabbit warren close to town and gave up his job as bailiff for good, and Elisenda bought some satin pumps with high heels and many dresses of iridescent silk, the kind worn on Sunday by the most desirable women in those times. The chicken coop was the only thing that didn't receive any attention. If they washed it down with creolin and burned tears of myrrh inside it every so often, it was not in homage to the angel but to drive away the dungheap stench that still hung everywhere like a ghost and was turning the new house into an old one. At first, when the child learned to walk, they were careful that he not get too close to the chicken coop. But then they began to lose their fears and got used to the smell, and before the child got his second teeth he'd gone inside the chicken coop to play, where the wires were falling apart. The angel was no less standoffish with him than with other mortals, but he tolerated the most ingenious infamies with the patience of a dog who had no illusions. They both came down with chicken pox at the same time. The doctor who took care of the child couldn't resist the temptation to listen to the angel's heart, and he found so much whistling in the heart and so many sounds in his kidneys that it seemed impossible for him to be alive. What surprised him most, however, was the logic of his wings. They seemed so natural on that completely human organism that he couldn't understand why other men didn't have them too.

When the child began school it had been some time since the

sun and rain had caused the collapse of the chicken coop. The angel went dragging himself about here and there like a stray dying man. They would drive him out of the bedroom with a broom and a moment later find him in the kitchen. He seemed to be in so many places at the same time that they grew to think that he'd been duplicated, that he was reproducing himself all through the house, and the exasperated and unhinged Elisenda shouted that it was awful living in that hell full of angels. He could scarcely eat and his antiquarian eyes had also become so foggy that he went about bumping into posts. All he had left were the bare cannulae[2] of his last feathers. Pelayo threw a blanket over him and extended him the charity of letting him sleep in the shed; and only then did they notice that he had a temperature at night, and was delirious with the tongue twisters of an old Norwegian. That was one of the few times they became alarmed, for they thought he was going to die and not even the wise neighbor woman had been able to tell them what to do with dead angels.

And yet he not only survived his worst winter, but seemed improved with the first sunny days. He remained motionless for several days in the farthest corner of the courtyard, where no one would see him, and at the beginning of December some large, stiff feathers began to grow on his wings, the feathers of a scarecrow, which looked more like another misfortune of decrepitude. But he must have known the reason for those changes, for he was quite careful that no one should notice them, that no one should hear the sea chanteys that he sometimes sang under the stars. One morning Elisenda was cutting some bunches of onions for lunch when a wind that seemed to come from the high seas blew into the kitchen. Then she went to the window and caught the angel in his first attempts at flight. They were so clumsy that his fingernails opened a furrow in the vegetable patch and he was on the point of knocking the shed down with the ungainly flapping that slipped on the light and couldn't get a grip on the air. But he did manage to gain altitude. Elisenda let out a sigh of relief, for herself and for him, when she saw him pass over the last houses, holding himself up in some way with the risky flapping of a senile vulture. She kept watching him even when she was through cutting the onions and she kept on watching until it was no longer possible for her to see him, because then he was no longer an annoyance in her life but an imaginary dot on the horizon of the sea.

1955, first English translation 1971

▪   ▪   ▪

---

2. The tubular parts of feathers that attach to a body.

GEORGE GARRETT

AN EVENING PERFORMANCE

For several weeks, maybe a month or so, there she stood, a plump woman in a sequined one-piece bathing suit, poised on a stylized tower which rose into the very clouds, like Jacob's dreamy ladder,[1] with here and there around it a few birds in tense swift V's, and below, far, far below, there was a tub, flaming and terrible, into which she was surely going to plunge. Beneath in fiery letters was printed: ONE OF THE FABULOUS WONDERS OF MODERN TIMES / STELLA THE HIGH DIVER / SHE DIVES ONE HUNDRED FEET / INTO A FLAMING CAULDRON.

These posters had appeared mysteriously one Monday morning, and they were everywhere, on store windows, on the sides of buildings, on telephone and light poles, tacked to green trees; and you can believe they caused a stir. The children on the way to school (for it was just the beginning of the school year) bunched around them in excited clusters—staring at her buxom magnificence, wondering at her daring—and buzzed about it all day long like a hive of disturbed bees. By midmorning grumbling adults were ripping the posters down from windows and buildings, and a couple of policemen went up and down the main street and some of the side streets, taking them off telephone and light poles. But there were so many! And it was such a mystery. Lurid and unsettling as a blast of trumpets, they had come nevertheless in the night as silently as snow.

It would be later, much later, that the night counterman at the Paradise Diner on the outskirts of town, beyond the last glare of filling stations and the winking motels and the brilliant inanity of used-car lots—where, no matter how carnival-colorful with flags and whirligigs, no matter how brightly lit, the rows of cars stood lonesome like sad

1. Biblical: far from home, Jacob dreamed of a ladder to heaven. Genesis 28:10–22.

wooden horses from some carousel set out to graze—it would be later when he would remember that the man, the angry little man with the limp, had stopped there for coffee that same night that the posters had appeared.

In spite of all effort, a few of the posters remained, tantalizing in their vague promise of a future marvel, teased by the wind and the weather, faded by the still summer-savage sun and the first needling rains of autumn, the red letters blurring and dribbling away, fuzzy now as if they had been written by a shaking finger in something perishable like blood. Talked about for a while—and there were those who swore they remembered seeing such a thing and certainly those who had heard of it, a subject of some debate and even a little sermonizing in certain of the more fundamentalist churches, where amusement is, by definition, nearly equivalent to vice—the promise faded with the posters. There were few who hoped that Stella would ever dive there, fewer still who believed in her coming. It seemed, after all, only another joke of some kind, pointless, mirthless, and in a strange way deeply distressing.

Then one evening in late October with the weather now as cool and gray as wash water the truck came and parked in the field by the old Fairgrounds. At first it was nothing to take much notice of, merely a big, battered truck and pretty soon an Army surplus squad tent, sprouting (sagging in a most unmilitary, careless way) like a khaki mushroom beside it.

And there were people.

There were three of them. There was the man, gimpy (his left leg might have been wooden), his face puckered and fierce and jowly and quizzical like a Boston bulldog, his eyes glazed and almost lightless like the little button eyes of a doll; fierce and tired he seemed, spoke in mutters, showing from time to time a ruined mouth with teeth all awry and at all angles like an old fence; and sometimes around the town, shopping for groceries at the Supermarket, once taking a load of dirty clothes to the Washeteria, buying cigarettes and aspirins and comic books at the drugstore, and busily sorting out bolts and nuts and screws and clamps and brackets at the hardware store (for what?), he talked to himself, a harsh, steady, and indecipherable monotone. There was the little girl, a frail thing made entirely of glazed china with altogether unlikely eyes and hair as bright as new pennies, like a shower of money, richly brushed and shining and worn long to her waist. She wore white always, starched and ironed and fabulously clean; and the women had to wonder how her mother (?)—the woman anyhow—living in a sagging tent and a worn-out truck managed that. The little girl was heard to answer to the name of Angel and did not play with the other children who sometimes, after school, gathered in shrill clots around the tent and the truck to stare until the terrible man came out, limping, waving a pick handle, and chased them away.

The woman was an equal curiosity. She was short, broad-shouldered, wide-hipped, huge-handed, sturdy as a man. Her hair, dyed redder than you'd care to believe, was cut in a short bowl. She appeared to be in early middle age, though she might easily have been old—she wore such savage makeup, wild, accented, slanted eyes, a mouth of flame, and always two perfectly round spots of red like dying roses on her high cheekbones. Still, she had a smile that was a glory and she smiled often. She was not heard to speak to anyone and when she was talked to she smiled and stared, uncomprehending. It was not long before everyone knew she was a mute; it was proved when she was seen to communicate with the man, her hands as swift as wings and not a word.

The truth came out like a jack-in-the-box in a week or so. One fine morning the man had unloaded an enormous pile of boards and pipes beside the truck, and by noon he had erected in the center of the field what seemed to be the beginning of a good-size drilling derrick.

"For oil?" That was the joke around town before a few prominent men and a policeman went out there in cars, parked at the edge of the field, and walked to where he was working. He paid them no mind at all as they straggled toward him, and, as they drew near, they could see that he was sweat-soaked and working at his task with an unbecoming fury, all in hasty, jerky gestures like a comedian in a silent movie. He did not stop his work until they spoke to him.

"What are you trying to do here?" the policeman said.

The man spat and put his heavy wrench on the ground.

"What the hell does it look like I'm doing?" he said and someone giggled. "I'm putting up the tower."

"What kind of a tower?"

"The tower for Stella," the man said, sighing between his teeth. "How can she dive without a tower? That's logic, ain't it?"

"Oh," the policeman said. "You got to have a license to put on any kind of a exhibition around here."

The lame man lowered his head, seemed to shrink and sag like a slowly deflating balloon, and muttered to himself. Finally he raised his head and looked at them, and they could see the tears glisten in his eyes.

"How much do the license cost?" he said.

"Twenty-five dollars."

"We don't have to do the dive," the man said. "We got a lots of tricks. I can put up just a little bit of a trapeze and Angel can do things that would make your eyes pop out of your head. If worse come to worst we don't have to build nothing at all. If I have to I can stand on the back end of the truck and swallow swords and fire and Angel and Stella can dance."

"Any kind of exhibition costs twenty-five dollars for the license."

The man shrugged and hung his head again.

"Don't you have the money?"

He shook his head, but still would not look at them.

"Well, what the hell?" the policeman said. "You better take that tower down and get on out of town. We got a law—"

"Wait a minute," a merchant said. "You aim to sell tickets, don't you?"

The man nodded.

"If you put on the high drive, I reckon you may get as many as a thousand to see it, counting kids and all. What kind of a price do you charge?"

When the man looked up again, he had his ruined smile for them all. "Two bits a head," he said. "We got a roll of tickets printed up and everything."

The merchant made a hasty calculation. "All right," he said. "I'll tell you what I'll do. I'll get your license for you and you cut me in for half of what you take."

"*Half?*" the man said. "Half is too much. That's a dirty shame. It ain't hardly worth it for half. Besides, the high dive is dangerous."

"Take it or leave it."

"All right," the man said. "I can't do nothing but take it."

"Tell you what else I'll do," the merchant said. "I got a nigger boy helps me down to the store. I'll send him to help you put that tower up. How soon can you put on the show?"

"Tomorrow evening if the weather's good."

While they were standing there talking the woman had come across the field from the tent and stood holding the hand of the little girl, smiling her wonderful smile. She seemed to have not the least notion of what was going on, but as they walked away they saw that she had turned on the man, unsmiling, and as he shook and shook his head, her hands flashed at him like the wings of a wild bird in a cage.

All that day the tower grew and by noon of the next day it was finished. It stood not nearly so tall as the cloud- and bird-troubled structure on the posters, but menacingly high, a rickety skeleton that swayed a little in the light breeze. All the way to the top there was a rope ladder and on the top a small platform with an extended plank for a diving board. At the foot of the tower the lame man had created a large wooden and canvas tank into which he and the woman and the

Negro who worked for the merchant poured buckets of water, drawn from a public spigot, all afternoon, until it was filled about to the depth of a tall man. There was a large GI can of gasoline nearby. The lame man rigged up a string of colored lights and two large searchlights intended to focus on the diver at the top. He set up a card table at the corner where the main road turned into the Fairgrounds. He put up a few of the posters on the poles and the side of the truck, and by mid-afternoon everything was ready.

Then the weather turned. The wind came from the north, steady, and with a thin rain like cold needles. The tower moved with the wind and shone with wet. The woman and the little girl stayed in the tent. The lame man stood at the card table, with a newspaper on his head to keep off the rain, waiting for the first customers to arrive.

Just at dark the merchant arrived. There was a good crowd, equal at least to their expectation, gathered in a ring around the tower, standing in raincoats and underneath umbrellas, silently waiting.

"Well," the merchant said, "it looks like we did all right irregardless of the weather."

"Yeah," the man replied. "Except she don't want to do it."

"What's that?"

"I mean it's too risky at a time like this."

"You should have thought of that before," the merchant said. "If you don't go through with it now, no telling what might happen."

"Oh, we'll give them a show," the man said. "I'll swallow swords if I have to. We'll do something."

"She's got to dive," the merchant said, "Or else you got a case of fraud on your hands."

After that the two of them went into the tent. Inside the woman was sitting on an Army cot, wrapped up in man's bathrobe, and the little girl was beside her. It was cold and damp and foul in the tent. The merchant winced at the smell of it.

"Tell her she's got to do it."

The lame man waved his hands in deft code to her. She moved her hands slowly in reply and, smiling, shook her head. Outside the people had started to clap their hands in unison.

"She says it's too dangerous. It's dangerous anyhow, but on a night like this—"

"Come on," the merchant said. "It can't be that bad. There must be a trick to it."

The lame man shook his head.

"No, sir," he said. "It ain't no trick to it. It's the most dangerous activity in the world. She don't like to do it one bit."

"That's a fine thing," the merchant said. "Just fine and dandy. If she don't like it, why the hell do you put up posters and build towers and sell tickets, that's what I'd like to know."

"Somebody's got to do it. If it wasn't us, it would just have to be somebody else."

"Oh my God!" the merchant said, throwing up his hands. "Now you listen here. If you don't get the show going in five minutes, I'll have you all slapped right in the jail. Five minutes."

He opened the flap of the tent and went out into the dark and the chill rain. He could hear the little girl crying and the lame man muttering to himself.

Almost at once the lame man followed him. He started up the truck and turned on all the lights. Then the woman appeared in her outsize bathrobe and wearing now a white bathing cap. She walked to the foot of the power and leaned against it, one hand clutching a rung of the rope ladder, smiling.

"Ladies and gentlemen," the lame man said. "You are about to witness a performance that defies the laws of nature and science. This little lady you see before you is fixing to climb to the top of the tower. There, at that terrible altitude, she's going to stand and dive into a flaming tank of water that's barely six feet deep. You won't believe your eyes. It's marvel of the modern world. 'How does she do it?' some of you will ask. Now some show people will give you all kinds of fancy reasons for how and why they do their work. They'll tell you they learned it from the wise men of the East. They'll tell you about magicians and dreams and the Secrets of the Ancient World. Not us. The way that Stella does this dive is skill, skill pure and simple. When Stella climbs that tower and dives into the flames she's doing something anyone could do who has the heart and the skill and the nerve for it. That's what's different and special about our show. When Stella sails through the air and falls in the fire and comes up safe and smiling, she is the living and breathing proof of the boundless possibility of all mankind. It should make you happy. It should make you glad to be alive."

"Let's get on with it," someone shouted, and the crowd hollered and whistled.

"All right, we won't give you no special buildup," the lame man continued in an even voice. "We just say, there it is. See for yourself. And without further ado I give you Stella, the high diver."

He touched her. She removed the bathrobe and, opening her arms wide, showed herself, pale and stocky in the tight bathing suit with the winking sequins. Then she turned and began to climb the rope ladder. It was a perilous ascent and the ladder swung with the weight of her. When she reached the top, she rested, kneeling on the platform; then she stood up and unhitched the rope ladder and it fell away in a limp curve like a dead snake.

The crowd gasped.

"Do you see?" the lame man shouted. "Now there's no other way to get down except by diving!"

He hobbled over to the tank and sloshed gasoline on top of the water. He stood back and looked up at her. She stood on the diving plank and looked down. The tower rattled and moved in the wind and she seemed very small and far away. She stood on the end of the plank looking down, then she signaled to the man. He lit the gasoline and jumped back awkwardly as the flames shot up. Just at that instant she dived. Soaring and graceful, her arms wide apart, she seemed for a breathless time to hang at that great height in the wind, caught in the brilliant snare of the searchlights. Then she seemed to fold into herself like a fan and straight and swift as a thrown spear she descended, plummeting into the tank with a great and sparkling flash of fire and water.

There was a hushed moment while the crowd waited to see if she was still alive, but then she emerged, climbed out of the tank smiling, and showed herself to them, damp and unscathed. She put on her bathrobe and hurried back to the tent. Some of the people began to leave, but many stood gazing at the tower and the vacant tank. The lame man switched off the lights and followed after her, disappearing into the tent.

The merchant entered the tent. The three of them, sitting in a row along the edge of the cot, were eating something out of a can. A red lantern glared at their feet.

"Is that all?" the merchant said. "I mean is that all there is to it?"

The man nodded.

"Kind of brief, don't you think, for two bits a head?"

"That's all there is to it," the man said. "She could have killed herself. Ain't that enough for one evening? They ought to be glad."

The merchant looked at her. She was eating from the can and seemed as happy as could be.

"Can't you swallow some swords or something? We want everybody to feel they got their money's worth."

"Goddamnit, they did!" the lame man said. "They got all they're going to."

The merchant tried to persuade him to do something more, but he continued to refuse. So the merchant took his share of the money and left them. Soon the rest of the people left too.

The next morning the three of them were gone. The tower was gone, the truck, the tent, and they might never have been there at all, for all the trace they left. Except for the dark spots on the grass where the flaming water had splashed, except for a few posters remaining (and they were not true to fact or life), there was no trace of them.

But if the evening performance had been brief, it remained with them, haunting, a long time afterwards. Some of the preachers continued to denounce it as the work of the devil himself. The drunkards and tellers of tall tales embroidered on it and exaggerated it and preserved it until the legend of that high dive was like a beautiful tapestry before which they might act out their lives, strangely dwarfed and shamed. The children pestered and fidgeted and wanted to know when the three would come again.

A wise man said it had been a terrible thing.

"It made us all sophisticated," he said. "We can't be pleased by any ordinary marvels anymore—tightrope walkers, fire-eaters, pretty girls being fired out of cannons. It's going to take a regular apocalypse to make us raise our eyebrows again."

He was almost right, as nearly correct as a man could hope to be. How could he even imagine that more than one aging, loveless woman slept better ever after, smiled as she dreamed herself gloriously descending for all the world to see from a topless tower into a lake of flame?

1985

■   ■   ■

WILLIAM H. GASS

IN THE HEART OF THE HEART
OF THE COUNTRY

A Place

So I have sailed the seas and come . . .
$\qquad$ to B . . .[1]

a small town fastened to a field in Indiana. Twice there have been twelve hundred people here to answer to the census. The town is outstandingly neat and shady, and always puts its best side to the highway. On one lawn there's even a wood or plastic iron deer.

You can reach us by crossing a creek. In the spring the lawns are green, the forsythia is singing, and even the railroad that guts the town has straight bright rails which hum when the train is coming, and the train itself has a welcome horning sound.

Down the back streets the asphalt crumbles into gravel. There's Westbrook's, with the geraniums, Horsefall's, Mott's. The sidewalk shatters. Gravel dust rises like breath behind the wagons. And I am in retirement from love.

Weather

In the Midwest, around the lower Lakes, the sky in the winter is heavy and close, and it is a rare day, a day to remark on, when the sky lifts and allows the heart up. I am keeping count, and as I write this page, it is eleven days since I have seen the sun.

My House

There's a row of headless maples behind my house, cut to free the passage of electric wires. High stumps, ten feet tall, remain, and I

---

1. Allusion to "Sailing to Byzantium" by William Butler Yeats, Irish poet (1856–1939).

climb these like a boy to watch the country sail away from me. They are ordinary fields, a little more uneven than they should be, since in the spring they puddle. The topsoil's thin, but only moderately stony. Corn is grown one year, soybeans another. At dusk starlings darken the single tree—a larch—which stands in the middle. When the sky moves, fields move under it. I feel, on my perch, that I've lost my years. It's as though I were living at last in my eyes, as I have always dreamed of doing, and I think then I know why I've come here: to see, and so to go out against new things—oh god how easily—like air in a breeze. It's true there are moments—foolish moments, ecstasy on a tree stump—when I'm all but gone, scattered I like to think like seed, for I'm the sort now in the fool's position of having love left over which I'd like to lose; what good is it now to me, candy ungiven after Halloween?

A Person

There are vacant lots on either side of Billy Holsclaw's house. As the weather improves, they fill with hollyhocks. From spring through fall, Billy collects coal and wood and puts the lumps and pieces in piles near his door, for keeping warm is his one work. I see him most often on mild days sitting on his doorsill in the sun. I notice he's squinting a little, which is perhaps the reason he doesn't cackle as I pass. His house is the size of a single garage, and very old. It shed its paint with its youth, and its boards are a warped and weathered gray. So is Billy. He wears a short lumpy faded black coat when it's cold, otherwise he always goes about in the same loose, grease-spotted shirt and trousers. I suspect his galluses were yellow once, when they were new.

Wires

These wires offend me. Three trees were maimed on their account, and now these wires deface the sky. They cross like a fence in front of me, enclosing the crows with the clouds. I can't reach in, but like a stick, I throw my feelings over. What is it that offends me? I am on my stump, I've built a platform there and the wires prevent my going out. The cut trees, the black wires, all the beyond birds therefore anger me. When I've wormed through a fence to reach a meadow, do I ever feel the same about the field?

The Church

The church has a steeple like the hat of a witch, and five birds, all doves, perch in its gutters.

My House

Leaves move in the windows. I cannot tell you yet how beautiful it is, what it means. But they do move. They move in the glass.

Politics
. . . for all those not in love.

I've heard Batista described as a Mason. A farmer who'd seen him in Miami made this claim. He's as nice a fellow as you'd ever want to meet. Of Castro, of course, no one speaks.

For all those not in love there's law: to rule . . . to regulate . . . to rectify. I cannot write the poetry of such proposals, the poetry of politics, though sometimes—often—always now—I am in that uneasy peace of equal powers which makes a State; then I communicate by passing papers, proclamations, orders, through my bowels. Yet I was not a State with you, nor were we both together any Indiana. A squad of Pershing Rifles at the moment, I make myself Right Face! Legislation packs the screw of my intestines. Well, king of the classroom's king of the hill. You used to waddle when you walked because my sperm between your legs was draining to a towel. Teacher, poet, folded lover—like the politician, like those drunkards, ill, or those who faucet-off while pissing heartily to preach upon the force and fullness of that stream, or pause from vomiting to praise the purity and passion of their puke—I chant, I beg, I orate, I command, I sing—

Come back to Indiana—not too late!
(Or will you be a ranger to the end?)
Good-bye . . . Good-bye . . . oh, I shall always wait
 You, Larry, traveler—
  stranger,
   son,
    —my friend—[2]

my little girl, my poem by heart, my self, my childhood.

But I've heard Batista described as a Mason. That dries up my pity, melts my hate. Back from the garage where I have overheard it, I slap the mended fender of my car to laugh, and listen to the metal stinging tartly in my hand.

People
Their hair in curlers and their heads wrapped in loud scarves, young mothers, fattish in trousers, lounge about in the speedwash, smoking cigarettes, eating candy, drinking pop, thumbing magazines, and screaming at their children above the whir and rumble of the machines.

At the bank a young man freshly pressed is letting himself in with a key. Along the street, delicately teetering, many grandfathers move

2. Quote from "Indiana" by Hart Crane (1899–1932), American poet.

in a dream. During the murderous heat of summer, they perch on window ledges, their feet dangling just inside the narrow shelf of shade the store has made, staring steadily into the street. Where their consciousness has gone I can't say. It's not in the eyes. Perhaps it's diffuse, all temperature and skin, like an infant's, though more mild. Near the corner there are several large overalled men employed in standing. A truck turns to be weighed on the scales at the Feed and Grain. Images drift on the drugstore window. The wind has blown the smell of cattle into town. Our eyes have been driven in like the eyes of the old men. And there's no one to have mercy on us.

Vital Data

There are two restaurants here and a tearoom, two bars, one bank, three barbers, one with a green shade with which he blinds his window, two groceries, a dealer in Fords, one drug, one hardware, and one appliance store, several that sell feed, grain, and farm equipment, an antique shop, a poolroom, a laundromat, three doctors, a dentist, a plumber, a vet, a funeral home in elegant repair the color of a buttercup, numerous beauty parlors which open and shut like night-blooming plants, a tiny dime and department store of no width but several floors, a hutch, home-made, where you can order, after lying down or squirming in, furniture that's been fashioned from bent lengths of stainless tubing, glowing plastic, metallic thread, and clear shellac, an American Legion Post and a root beer stand, little agencies for this and that: cosmetics, brushes, insurance, greeting cards and garden produce—anything—sample shoes—which do their business out of hats and satchels, over coffee cups and dissolving sugar, a factory for making paper sacks and pasteboard boxes that's lodged in an old brick building bearing the legend OPERA HOUSE, still faintly golden, on its roof, a library given by Carnegie, a post office, a school, a railroad station, fire station, lumberyard, telephone company, welding shop, garage . . . and spotted through the town from one end to the other in a line along the highway, gas stations to the number five.

Education

In 1833, Colin Goodykoontz, an itinerant preacher, with a name from a fairytale, summed up the situation in one Indiana town this way:

> Ignorance and her squalid brood. A universal dearth of intellect. Total abstinence from literature is very generally practiced. . . . There is not a scholar in grammar or geography, or a *teacher capable* of *instructing* in them, to my knowledge. . . . Others are supplied a few months of the year with the most antiquated & unreasonable forms of teaching

reading, writing & cyphering. . . . Need I stop to remind you of the host of loathsome reptiles such a stagnant pool is fitted to breed. Croaking jealousy; bloated bigotry; coiling suspicion; wormish blindness; crocodile malice!

Things have changed since then, but in none of the respects mentioned.

Business

One side section of street is blocked off with sawhorses. Hard, thin, bitter men in blue jeans, cowboy boots and hats, untruck a dinky carnival. The merchants are promoting themselves. There will be free rides, raucous music, parades and coneys, pop, popcorn, candy, cones, awards and drawings, with all you can endure of pinch, push, bawl, shove, shout, scream, shriek, and bellow. Children pedal past on decorated bicycles, their wheels a blur of color, streaming crinkled paper and excited dogs. A little later, there's a pet show for a prize—dogs, cats, birds, sheep, ponies, goats—none of which wins. The whirlabouts whirl about. The Ferris wheel climbs dizzily into the sky as far as a tall man on tiptoe might be persuaded to reach, and the irritated operators measure the height and weight of every child with sour eyes to see if they are safe for the machines. An electrical megaphone repeatedly trumpets the names of the generous sponsors. The following day they do not allow the refuse to remain long in the street.

My House, This Place, and Body

I have met with some mischance, wings withering, as Plato says obscurely, and across the breadth of Ohio, like heaven on a table, I've fallen as far as the poet, to the sixth sort of body, this house in B, in Indiana, with its blue and gray bewitching windows, holy magical insides. Great thick evergreens protect its entry. And I live *in*.

Lost in the corn rows, I remember feeling just another stalk, and thus this country takes me over in the way I occupy myself when I am well . . . completely—to the edge of both my house and body. No one notices, when they walk by, that I am brimming in the doorways. My house, this place, and body, I've come in mourning to be born in. To anybody else it's pretty silly: love. Why should I feel a loss? How am I bereft? She was never mine; she was a fiction, always a golden tomgirl, barefoot, with an adolescent's slouch and a boy's taste for sports and fishing, a figure out of Twain, or worse, in Riley.[3] Age cannot be kind.

3. James Whitcomb Riley (1849–1910), American poet who wrote sentimental depictions of rural life.

There's little hand-in-hand here . . . not in B. No one touches except in rage. Occasionally girls will twine their arms about each other and lurch along, school out, toward home and play. I dreamed my lips would drift down your back like a skiff on a river. I'd follow a vein with the point of my finger, hold your bare feet in my naked hands.

The Same Person

Billy Holsclaw lives alone—how alone it is impossible to fathom. In the post office he talks greedily to me about the weather. His head bobs on a wild flood of words, and I take this violence to be a measure of his eagerness for speech. He badly needs a shave, coal dust has layered his face, he spits when he speaks, and his fingers pick at his tatters. He wobbles out in the wind when I leave him, a paper sack mashed in the fold of his arm, the leaves blowing past him, and our encounter drives me sadly home to poetry—where there's no answer. Billy closes his door and carries coal or wood to his fire and closes his eyes, and there's simply no way of knowing how lonely and empty he is or whether he's as vacant and barren and loveless as the rest of us are—here in the heart of the country.

Weather

For we're always out of luck here. That's just how it is—for instance in the winter. The sides of the buildings, the roofs, the limbs of the trees are gray. Streets, sidewalks, faces, feelings—they are gray. Speech is gray, and the grass where it shows. Every flank and front, each top is gray. Everything is gray: hair, eyes, window glass, the hawkers' bills and touters' posters, lips, teeth, poles and metal signs—they're gray, quite gray. Cars are gray. Boots, shoes, suits, hats, gloves are gray. Horses, sheep, and cows, cats killed in the road, squirrels in the same way, sparrows, doves, and pigeons, all are gray, everything is gray, and everyone is out of luck who lives here.

A similar haze turns the summer sky milky, and the air muffles your head and shoulders like a sweater you've got caught in. In the summer light, too, the sky darkens a moment when you open your eyes. The heat is pure distraction. Steeped in our fluids, miserable in the folds of our bodies, we can scarcely think of anything but our sticky parts. Hot cyclonic winds and storms of dust crisscross the country. In many places, given an indifferent push, the wind will still coast for miles, gathering resource and edge as it goes, cunning and force. According to the season, paper, leaves, field litter, seeds, snow, fill up the fences. Sometimes I think the land is flat because the winds have leveled it, they blow so constantly. In any case, a gale can grow in a field of corn that's as hot as a draft from hell, and to receive it is one of the most dismaying experiences of this life, though the smart of the same wind in winter is more humiliating, and in that sense even worse. But in the spring it rains as well, and the trees fill with ice.

Place

Many small Midwestern towns are nothing more than rural slums, and this community could easily become one. Principally, during the first decade of the century, though there were many earlier instances, well-to-do farmers moved to town and built fine homes to contain them in their retirement. Others desired a more social life, and so lived in, driving to their fields like storekeepers to their business. These houses are now dying like the bereaved who inhabit them; they are slowly losing their senses—deafness, blindness, forgetfulness, mumbling, an insecure gait, an uncontrollable trembling has overcome them. Some kind of Northern Snopes[4] will occupy them next: large-familied, Catholic, Democratic, scrambling, vigorous, poor; and since the parents will work in larger, nearby towns, the children will be loosed upon themselves and upon the hapless neighbors much as the fabulous Khan[5] loosed his legendary horde. These Snopes will undertake make-shift repairs with materials that other people have thrown away; paint halfway round their house, then quit; almost certainly maintain an ugly loud cantankerous dog and underfeed a pair of cats to keep the rodents down. They will collect piles of possibly useful junk in the back yard, park their cars in the front, live largely leaning over engines, give not a hoot for the land, the old community, the hallowed ways, the established clans. Weakening widow ladies have already begun to hire large rude youths from families such as these to rake and mow and tidy the grounds they will inherit.

People

In the cinders at the station, boys sit smoking steadily in darkened cars, their arms bent out the windows, white skirts glowing behind the glass. Nine o'clock is the best time. They sit in a line facing the highway—two or three or four of them—idling their engines. As you walk by a machine may growl at you or a pair of headlights flare up briefly. In a moment one will pull out, spinning cinders behind it, to stalk impatiently up and down the dark streets or roar half a mile into the country before returning to its place in line and pulling up.

4. The Snopes clan from William Faulkner's fiction has come to stand for trashy no-good people of all regions.
5. Genghis Khan (1162–1227) was the Mongol conqueror of Asia and Eastern Europe.

My House, My Cat, My Company

I must organize myself. I must, as they say, pull myself together, dump this cat from my lap, stir—yes, resolve, move, do. But do what? My will is like the rosy dust-like light in this room: soft, diffuse, and gently comforting. It lets me do . . . anything . . . nothing. My ears hear what they happen to; I eat what's put before me; my eyes see what blunders into them; my thoughts are not thoughts, they are dreams. I'm empty or I'm full . . . depending; and I cannot choose. I sink my claws in Tick's fur and scratch the bones of his back until his rear rises amorously. Mr. Tick, I murmur, I must organize myself. I must pull myself together. And Mr. Tick rolls over on his belly, all ooze.

I spill Mr. Tick when I've rubbed his stomach. Shoo. He steps away slowly, his long tail rhyming with his paws. How beautifully he moves, I think; how beautifully he accepts. So I rise and wander from room to room, up and down, gazing through most of my forty-one windows. How well this house receives its loving, too. Let out like Mr. Tick, my eyes sink in the shrubbery. I am not here; I've passed the glass, passed second-story spaces, flown by branches, brilliant berries, to the ground, grass high in seed and leafage every season; and it is the same as when I passed above you in my aged, ardent body; it's, in short, a kind of love; and I am learning to restore myself, my house, my body, by paying court to gardens, cats, and running water, and with neighbors keeping company.

Mrs. Desmond is my right-hand friend; she's eighty-five. A thin white mist of hair, fine and tangled, manifests the climate of her mind. She is habitually suspicious, fretful, nervous. Burglars break in at noon. Children trespass. Even now they are shaking the pear tree, stealing rhubarb, denting lawn. Flies caught in the screen and numbed by frost awake in the heat to buzz and scrape the metal cloth and frighten her, though she is deaf to me, and consequently cannot hear them. Boards creak, the wind whistles across the chimney mouth, drafts cruise like fish through the hollow rooms. It is herself she hears, her own flesh failing, for only death will preserve her from those daily chores she climbs like stairs, and all that anxious waiting. Is it now, she wonders. No? Then: is it now?

We do not converse. She visits me to talk. My task to murmur. She talks about her grandson, her daughter who lives in Delphi, her sister or her husband—both gone—obscure friends—dead—obscurer aunts and uncles—lost—ancient neighbors, members of her church or of her clubs—passed or passing on; and in this way she brings the ends of her life together with a terrifying rush: she is a girl, a wife, a mother, widow, all at once. All at once—appalling—but I believe it; I wince in expectation of the clap. Her talk's a fence—a shade drawn, window fastened, door that's locked—for no one dies taking tea in a kitchen; and as her years compress and begin to jumble, I really believe in the brevity of life; I sweat in my wonder; death is the dog down the street, the angry gander, bedroom spider, goblin who's come to get her; and it occurs to me that in my listening posture I'm the boy who suffered the winds of my grandfather with an exactly similar politeness, that I am, right now, all my ages, out in elbows, as angular as badly stacked cards. Thus was I, when I loved you, every man I could be, youth and child—far from enough—and you, so strangely ambiguous a being, met me, heart for spade, play after play, the whole run of our suits.

Mr. Tick, you do me honor. You not only lie in my lap, but you remain alive there, coiled like a fetus. Through your deep nap, I feel you hum. You are, and are not, a machine. You are alive, alive exactly, and it means nothing to you—much to me. You are a cat—you cannot understand—you are a cat so easily. Your nature is not something you must rise to. You, not I, live in: in house, in skin, in shrubbery. Yes. I think I shall hat my head with a steeple; turn church; devour people. Mr. Tick, though, has a tail he can twitch, he need not fly his Fancy. Claws, not metrical schema, poetry his paws; while smoothing . . . smoothing . . . smoothing roughly, his tongue laps its neatness. O Mr. Tick, I know you; you are an electrical penis. Go on now, shoo. Mrs. Desmond doesn't like you. She thinks you will tangle yourself in her legs and she will fall. You murder her birds, she knows, and walk upon her roof with death in your jaws. I must gather myself together for a bound. What age is it I'm at right now, I wonder. The heart, don't they always say, keeps the true time. Mrs. Desmond is knocking. Faintly, you'd think, but she pounds. She's brought me a cucumber. I believe she believes I'm a woman. Come in, Mrs. Desmond, thank you, be my company, it looks lovely, and have tea. I'll slice it, crisp, with cream, for luncheon, each slice as thin as me.

Politics

O all ye isolate and separate powers, Sing! Sing, and sing in such a way that from a distance it will seem a harmony, a Strindberg play, a friendship ring . . . so happy—happy, happy, happy—as here we go hand in handling, up and down. Our union was a singing, though we were silent in the songs we sang like single notes are silent in a symphony. In no sense sober, we barbershopped together and never heard the discords in our music or saw ourselves as dirty, cheap, or silly. Yet cats have worn out better shoes than those thrown through our love songs at us. Hush. Be patient—prudent—politic. Still, Cleveland killed you, Mr. Crane. Were you not politic enough and fond of being beaten? Like a piece of sewage, the city shat you from its stem three hundred miles from history—beyond the loving reach of sailors.[6] Well, I'm not a poet who puts Paris to his temple in his youth to blow himself from Idaho, or—fancy that—Missouri. My god, I said, this is my country, but must my country go so far as Terre Haute or Whiting, go so far as Gary?

When the Russians first announced the launching of their satellite, many people naturally refused to believe them. Later others were outraged that they had sent a dog around the earth. I wouldn't want to take that mutt from out that metal flying thing if he's still living when he lands, our own dog catcher said; anybody knows you shut a dog up by himself to toss around the first thing he'll be setting on to do you let him out is bite somebody.

This Midwest. A dissonance of parts and people, we are a consonance of Towns. Like a man grown fat in everything but heart, we overlabor; our outlook never really urban, never rural either, we enlarge and linger at the same time. As Alice both changed and remained in her story. You are a blond. I put my hand upon your belly; feel it tremble from my trembling. We always drive large cars in my section of the country. How could you be a comfort to me now?

More Vital Data

The town is exactly fifty houses, trailers, stores, and miscellaneous buildings long, but in places no streets deep. It takes on width as you drive south, always adding to the east. Most of the dwellings are fairly spacious farm houses in the customary white, with wide wraparound porches and tall narrow windows, though there are many of the grander kind—fretted, scalloped, turreted, and decorated with clapboards set at angles or on end, with stained-glass windows at the stair landings and lots of wrought iron full of fancy curls—and a few of these look like castles in their rarer brick. Old stables serve as garages now, and the lots are large to contain them and the vegetable and flower gardens which, ultimately, widows plant and weed and then entirely disappear in. The shade is ample, the grass is good, the sky a glorious fall violet; the apple trees are heavy and red, the roads are calm and empty; corn has sifted from the chains of tractored wagons to speckle the streets with gold and with the russet fragments of the cob, and a man would be a fool who wanted, blessed with this, to live anywhere else in the world.

6. Hart Crane committed suicide by jumping from a ship. A homosexual, he associated considerably with sailors.

Education

Buses like great orange animals move through the early light to school. There the children will be taught to read and warned against Communism. By Miss Janet Jakes. That's not her name. Her name is Helen something—Scott or James. A teacher twenty years. She's now worn fine and smooth, and has a face, Wilfred says, like a mail-order ax. Her voice is hoarse, and she has a cough. For she screams abuse. The children stare, their faces blank. This is the thirteenth week. They are used to it. You will all, she shouts, you will all draw pictures of me. No. She is a Mrs.—someone's missus. And in silence they set to work while Miss Jakes jabs hairpins in her hair. Wilfred says an ax, but she has those rimless tinted glasses, graying hair, an almost dimpled chin. I must concentrate. I must stop making up things. I must give myself to life; let it mold me: that's what they say in *Wisdom's Monthly Digest* every day. Enough, enough—you've been at it long enough; and the children rise formally a row at a time to present their work to her desk. No, she wears rims; it's her chin that's dimpleless. Well, it will take more than a tablespoon of features to sweeten that face. So she grimly shuffles their sheets, examines her reflection crayoned on them. I would not dare . . . allow a child . . . to put a line around me. Though now and then she smiles like a nick in the blade, in the end these drawings depress her. I could not bear it—how can she ask?—that anyone . . . draw me. Her anger's lit. That's why she does it: flame. There go her eyes; the pink in her glasses brightens, dims. She is a pumpkin, and her rage is breathing like the candle in. No, she shouts, no—the cartoon trembling—no, John Mauck, John Stewart Mauck, this will not do. The picture flutters from her fingers. You've made me too muscular.

I work on my poetry. I remember my friends, associates, my students, by their names. Their names are Maypop, Dormouse, Upsydaisy. Their names are Gladiolus, Callow Bladder, Prince and Princess Oleo, Hieronymous, Cardinal Mummum, Mr. Fitchew, The Silken Howdah, Spot. Sometimes you're Tom Sawyer, Huckleberry Finn; it is perpetually summer; your buttocks are my pillow; we are adrift on a raft; your back is our river. Sometimes you are Major Barbara, sometimes a goddess who kills men in battle, sometimes you are soft like a shower of water; you are bread in my mouth.

I do not work on my poetry. I forget my friends, associates, my students, and their names: Gramophone, Blowgun, Pickle, Serenade . . . Marge the Barge, Arena, Uberhaupt . . . Doctor Dildoe, The Fog Machine. For I am now in B, in Indiana: out of job and out of patience, out of love and time and money, out of bread and out of body, in a temper, Mrs. Desmond, out of tea. So shut your fist up, bitch, you bag of death; go bang another door; go die, my dearie. Die, life-deaf old lady. Spill your breath. Fall over like a frozen board. Gray hair grows from the nose of your mind. You are a skull already—*memento mori*[7]— the foreskin retracts from your teeth. Will your plastic gums last longer than your bones, and color their grinning? And is your twot still hazel-hairy, or are you bald as a ditch? . . . bitch . . . . . . bitch . . . . bitch. I wanted to be famous, but you bring me age—my emptiness. Was it *that* which I thought would balloon me above the rest? Love? where are you? . . . love me. I want to rise so high, I said, that when I shit I won't miss anybody.

Business

For most people, business is poor. Nearby cities have siphoned off all but a neighborhood trade. Except for feed and grain and farm supplies, you stand a chance to sell only what runs out to buy. Chevrolet has quit, and Frigidaire. A locker plant has left its afterimage. The lumber-yard has been, so far, six months about its going. Gas stations change hands clumsily, a restaurant becomes available, a grocery closes. One day they came and knocked the cornices from the watch repair and pasted campaign posters on the windows. Torn across, by now, by boys, they urge you still to vote for half an orange beblazoned man who as a whole one failed two years ago to win at his election. Everywhere, in this manner, the past speaks, and it mostly speaks of failure. The empty stores, the old signs and dusty fixtures, the debris in alleys, the flaking paint and rusty gutters, the heavy locks and sagging boards: they say the same disagreeable things. What do the sightless windows see, I wonder, when the sun throws a passerby against them? Here a stair unfolds toward the street—dark, rickety, and treacherous—and I always feel, as I pass it, that if I just went carefully up and turned the corner at the landing, I would find myself out of the world. But I've never had the courage.

That Same Person

The weeds catch up with Billy. In pursuit of the hollyhocks, they rise in coarse clumps all around the front of his house. Billy has to stamp down a circle by his door like a dog or cat does turning round to nest up, they're so thick. What particularly troubles me is that winter will find the weeds still standing stiff and tindery to take the sparks which Billy's little mortarless chimney spouts. It's true that fires are fun here. The town whistle, which otherwise only blows for noon (and there's no noon on Sunday), signals the direction of the fire by the length and

---

7. Remember that you will die.

number of its blasts, the volunteer firemen rush past in their cars and trucks, houses empty their owners along the street every time like an illustration in a children's book. There are many bikes, too, and barking dogs, and sometimes—halleluiah—the fire's right here in town—a vacant lot of weeds and stubble flaming up. But I'd rather it weren't Billy or Billy's lot or house. Quite selfishly, I want him to remain the way he is—counting his sticks and logs, sitting on his sill in the soft early sun—though I'm not sure what his presence means to me . . . or to anyone. Nevertheless, I keep wondering whether, given time, I might not someday find a figure in our language which would serve him faithfully, and furnish his poverty and loneliness richly out.

Wires

Where sparrows sit like fists. Doves fly the steeple. In mist the wires change perspective, rise and twist. If they led to you, I would know what they were. Thoughts passing often, like the starlings who flock these fields at evening to sleep in the trees beyond, would form a family of paths like this; they'd foot down the natural height of air to just about a bird's perch. But they do not lead to you.

> Of whose beauty it was sung
> She shall make the old man young.

They fasten me.

If I walked straight on, in my present mood, I would reach the Wabash. It's not a mood in which I'd choose to conjure you. Similes dangle like baubles from me. This time of year the river is slow and shallow, the clay banks crack in the sun, weeds surprise the sandbars. The air is moist and I am sweating. It's impossible to rhyme in this dust. Everything—sky, the cornfield, stump, wild daisies, my old clothes and pressless feelings—seem fabricated for installment purchase. Yes. Christ. I am suffering a summer Christmas; and I cannot walk under the wires. The sparrows scatter like handfuls of gravel. Really, wires are voices in thin strips. They are words wound in cables. Bars of connection.

Weather

I would rather it were the weather that was to blame for what I am and what my friends and neighbors are—we who live here in the heart of the country. Better the weather, the wind, the pale dying snow . . . the snow—why not the snow? There's never much really, not around the lower Lakes anyway, not enough to boast about, not enough to be useful. My father tells how the snow in the Dakotas would sweep to the roofs of the barns in the old days, and he and his friends could sled on the crust that would form because the snow was so fiercely driven. In Bemidji trees have been known to explode. That would be something—if the trees in Davenport or Francisville or Cardondale or Niles were to go blam some winter—blam! blam! blam! all the way down the gray, cindery, snow-sick streets.

A cold fall rain is blackening the trees or the air is like lilac and full of parachuting seeds. Who cares to live in any season but his own? Still I suspect the secret's in this snow, the secret of our sickness, if we could only diagnose it, for we are all dying like the elms in Urbana. This snow—like our skin it covers the country. Later dust will do it. Right now—snow. Mud presently. But it is snow without any laughter in it, a pale gray pudding thinly spread on stiff toast, and if that seems a strange description, it's accurate all the same. Of course soot blackens everything, but apart from that, we are never sufficiently cold here. The flakes as they come, alive and burning, we cannot retain, for if our temperatures fall, they rise promptly again, just as, in the summer, they bob about in the same feckless way. Suppose though . . . suppose they were to rise some August, climb and rise, and then hang in the hundreds like a hawk through December, what a desert we could make of ourselves—from Chicago to Cairo, from Hammond to Columbus—what beautiful Death Valleys.

Place
I would rather it were the weather. It drives us in upon ourselves—an unlucky fate. Of course there is enough to stir our wonder anywhere: there's enough to love, anywhere, if one is strong enough, if one is diligent enough, if one is perceptive, patient, kind enough—whatever it takes; and surely it's better to live in the country, to live on a prairie by a drawing of rivers, in Iowa or Illinois or Indiana, say, than in any city, in any stinking fog of human beings, in any blooming orchard of machines. It ought to be. The cities are swollen and poisonous with people. It ought to be better. Man has never been a fit environment for man—for rats, maybe, rats do nicely, or for dogs or cats and the household beetle.

And how long the street is, nowadays. These endless walls are fallen to keep back the tides of earth. Brick could be beautiful but we have covered it gradually with gray industrial vomits. Age does not make concrete genial and asphalt is always—like America—twenty-one, until it breaks up in crumbs like stale cake. The brick, the asphalt, the concrete, the dancing signs and garish posters, the feed and excrement of the automobile, the litter of its inhabitants: they compose, they decorate, they line our streets, and there is nowhere, nowadays, our streets can't reach.

A man in the city has no natural thing by which to measure himself. His parks are potted plants. Nothing can live and remain free where he resides but the pigeon, starling, sparrow, spider, cockroach, mouse, moth, fly and weed, and he laments the existence of even these and makes his plans to poison them. The zoo? There *is* the zoo. Through its bars the city man stares at the great cats and dully sucks his ice. Living, alas, among men and their marvels, the city man supposes that his happiness depends on establishing, somehow, a special kind of harmonious accord with others. The novelists of the city, of slums and crowds, they call it love—and break their pens.

Wordsworth feared the accumulation of men in cities. He foresaw their "degrading thirst after outrageous stimulation," and some of their hunger for love. Living in a city, among so many, dwelling in the heat and tumult of incessant movement, a man's affairs are touch and go— that's all. It's not surprising that the novelists of the slums, the cities, and the crowds, should find that sex is but a scratch to ease a tickle, that we're most human when we're sitting on the john, and that the justest image of our life is in full passage through the plumbing.

> The man, immur'd in cities, still retains
> His inborn inextinguishable thirst
> Of rural scenes, compensating his loss
> By supplemental shifts, the best he may.

Come into the country, then. The air nimbly and sweetly recommends itself unto our gentle senses. Here, growling tractors tear the earth. Dust roils up behind them. Drivers sit jouncing under bright umbrellas. They wear refrigerated hats and steer by looking at the tracks they've cut behind them, their transistors blaring. Close to the land, are they? good companions to the soil? Tell me: do they live in harmony with the alternating seasons?

It's a lie of old poetry. The modern husbandman uses chemicals from cylinders and sacks, spike-ball-and-claw machines, metal sheds, and cost accounting. Nature in the old sense does not matter. It does not exist. Our farmer's only mystical attachment is to parity. And if he does not realize that cows and corn are simply different kinds of chemical engine, he cannot expect to make a go of it.

It isn't necessary to suppose our cows have feelings; our neighbor hasn't as many as he used to have either; but think of it this way a moment, you can correct for the human imputations later: how would it feel to nurse those strange tentacled calves with their rubber, glass, and metal lips, their stainless eyes?

Aunt Pet's still able to drive the car—a high square Ford—even though she walks with difficulty and a stout stick. She has a watery gaze, a smooth plump face despite her age, and jet black hair in a bun. She has the slowest smile of anyone I ever saw, but she hates dogs, and not very long ago cracked the back of one she cornered in her garden. To prove her vigor she will tell you this, her smile breaking gently while she raises the knob of her stick to the level of your eyes.

House, My Breath and Window
My window is a grave, and all that lies within it's dead. No snow is falling. There's no haze. It is not still, not silent. Its images are not an animal that waits, for movement is no demonstration. I have seen the sea slack, life bubble through a body without a trace, its spheres impervious as soda's. Downwound, the whore at wagtag clicks and clicks. Leaves wiggle. Grass sways. A bird chirps, pecks the ground. An auto wheel in penning circles keeps its rigid spokes. These images are stones; they are memorials. Beneath this sea lies sea: god rest it . . . rest the world beyond my window, me in front of my reflection, above this page, my shade. Death is not so still, so silent, since silence implies a falling quiet, stillness a stopping, containing, holding in; for death is time in a clock, like Mr. Tick, electric . . . like wind through a windup poet. And my blear floats out to visible against the, glass, befog its country and bespill myself. The mist lifts slowly from the fields in the morning. No one now would say: the Earth throws back its covers; it is rising from sleep. Why is the feeling foolish? The image is too Greek. I used to gaze at you so wantonly your body blushed. Imagine: wonder: that my eyes could cause such flowering. Ah, my friend, your face is pale, the weather cloudy; a street has been felled through your chin, bare trees do nothing, houses take root in their rectangles, a steeple stands up in your head. You speak of loving; then give me a kiss. The pane is cold. On icy mornings the fog rises to greet me (as you always did); the barns and other buildings, rather than ghostly, seem all the more substantial for looming, as if they grew in themselves while I watched (as you always did). Oh, my approach, I suppose, was like breath in a rubber monkey. Nevertheless, on the road along the Wabash in the morning, though the trees are sometimes obscured by fog, their reflection floats serenely on the river, reasoning the banks, the sycamores in French rows. Magically, the world tips. I'm led to think that only those who grow down live (which will scarcely win me twenty-five from *Wisdom's Monthy Digest*), but I find I write that only those who live down grow; and what I write, I hold, whatever I really

248 · WILLIAM H. GASS

know. My every world's inverted, or reversed—or I am. I held you, too, that way. You were so utterly provisional, subject to my change. I could inflate your bosom with a kiss, disperse your skin with gentleness, enter your vagina from within, and make my love emerge like a fresh sex. The pane is cold. Honesty is cold, my inside lover. The sun looks, through the mist, like a plum on the tree of heaven, or a bruise on the slope of your belly. Which? The grass crawls with frost. We meet on this window, the world and I, inelegantly, swimmers of the glass; and swung wrong way round to one another, the world seems in. The world—how grand, how monumental, grave and deadly, that word is: the world, my house and poetry. All poets have their inside lovers. Wee penis does not belong to me, or any of this foggery. It is *his* property which he's thrust through what's womanly of me to set down this. These wooden houses in their squares, gray streets and fallen sidewalks, standing trees, your name I've written sentimentally across my breath into the whitening air, pale birds: they exist in me now because of him. I gazed with what intensity . . . A bush in the excitement of its roses could not have bloomed so beautifully as you did then. It was a look I'd like to give this page. For that is poetry: to bring within about, to change.

Politics

Sports, politics, and religion are the three passions of the badly educated. They are the Midwest's open sores. Ugly to see, a source of constant discontent, they sap the body's strength. Appalling quantities of money, time, and energy are wasted on them. The rural mind is narrow, passionate, and reckless on these matters. Greed, however shortsighted and direct, will not alone account for it. I have known men, for instance, who for years have voted squarely against their interests. Nor have I ever noticed that their surly Christian views prevented them from urging forward the smithereening, say, of Russia, China, Cuba, or Korea. And they tend to back their country like they back their local team: they have a fanatical desire to win; yelling is their forte; and if things go badly, they are inclined to sack the coach. All in all, then, Birch[8] is a good name. It stands for the bigot's stick, the wild-child-tamer's cane.

Forgetfulness—is that their object?

Oh, I was new, I thought. A fresh start; new cunt, new climate, and new country—there you were, and I was pioneer, and had no history. That language hurts me, too, my dear. You'll never hear it.

8. Allusion to the John Birch Society, a right-wing political group.

Final Vital Data

The Modern Homemakers' Demonstration Club. The Prairie Home Demonstration Club. The Night-outer's Home Demonstration Club. The IOOF, FFF, VFW, WCTU, WSCS, 4-H, 40 and 8, Psi Iota Chi, and PTA. The Boy and Girl Scouts, Rainbows, Masons, Indians and Rebekah Lodge. Also the Past Noble Grand Club of the Rebekah Lodge. As well as the Moose and the Ladies of the Moose. The Elks, the Eagles, the Jaynettes and the Eastern Star. The Women's Literary Club, the Hobby Club, the Art Club, the Sunshine Society, the Dorcas Society, the Pythian Sisters, the Pilgrim Youth Fellowship, the American Legion, the American Legion Auxiliary, the American Legion Junior Auxiliary, the Garden Club, the Bridge for Fun Club, the What-can-you-do? Club, the Get Together Club, the Coterie Club, the Worthwhile Club, the Let's Help Our Town Club, the No Name Club, the Forget-me-not Club, the Merry-go-round Club . . .

Education

Has a quarter disappeared from Paula Frosty's pocket book? Imagine the landscape of that face: no crayon could engender it; soft wax is wrong; thin wire in trifling snips might do the trick. Paula Frosty and Christopher Roger accuse the pale and splotchy Cheryl Pipes. But Miss Jakes, I *saw* her. Miss Jakes is so extremely vexed she snaps her pencil. What else is missing? I appoint you a detective, John: search her desk. Gum, candy, paper, pencils, marble, round eraser—whose? A thief. I can't watch her all the time, I'm here to teach. Poor pale fossetted Cheryl, it's determined, can't return the money because she took it home and spent it. Cindy, Janice, John, and Pete—you four who sit around her—you will be detectives this whole term to watch her. A thief. In all my time. Miss Jakes turns, unfists, and turns again. I'll handle you, she cries. To think. A thief. In all my years. Then she writes on the blackboard the name of Cheryl Pipes and beneath that the figure twenty-five with a large sign for cents. Now Cheryl, she says, this won't be taken off until you bring that money out of home, out of home straight up to here, Miss Jakes says, tapping her desk.

Which is three days.

Another Person

I was raking leaves when Uncle Halley introduced himself to me. He said his name came from the comet, and that his mother had borne him prematurely in her fright of it. I thought of Hobbes,[9] whom fear of the Spanish Armada had hurried into birth, and so I believed Uncle

9. Thomas Hobbes (1588–1679), English philosopher.

Halley to honor the philosopher, though Uncle Halley is a liar, and neither the one hundred twenty-nine nor the fifty-three he ought to be. That fall the leaves had burned themselves out on the trees, the leaf lobes had curled, and now they flocked noisily down the street and were broken in the wires of my rake. Uncle Halley was himself (like Mrs. Desmond and history generally) both deaf and implacable, and he shooed me down his basement stairs to a room set aside there for stacks of newspapers reaching to the ceiling, boxes of leaflets and letters and programs, racks of photo albums, scrapbooks, bundles of rolled-up posters and maps, flags and pennants and slanting piles of dusty magazines devoted mostly to motoring and the Christian ethic. I saw a bird cage, a tray of butterflies, a bugle, a stiff straw boater and all kinds of tassels tied to a coat tree. He still possessed and had on display the steering lever from his first car, a linen duster, driving gloves and goggles, photographs along the wall of himself, his friends, and his various machines, a shell from the first war, a record of "Ramona" nailed through its hole to a post, walking sticks and fanciful umbrellas, shoes of all sorts (his baby shoes, their counters broken, were held in sorrow beneath my nose—they had not been bronzed, but he might have them done someday before he died, he said), countless boxes of medals, pins, beads, trinkets, toys, and keys (I scarcely saw—they flowed like jewels from his palms), pictures of downtown when it was only a path by the railroad station, a brightly colored globe of the world with a dent in Poland, antique guns, belt buckles, buttons, souvenir plates and cups and saucers (I can't remember all of it—I won't), but I recall how shamefully, how rudely, how abruptly, I fled, a good story in my mouth but death in my nostrils; and how afterward I busily, righteously, burned my leaves as if I were purging the world of its years. I still wonder if this town—its life, and mine now—isn't really a record like the one of "Ramona" that I used to crank around on my grandmother's mahogany Victrola through lonely rainy days as a kid.

The First Person

Billy's like the coal he's found: spilled, mislaid, discarded. The sky's no comfort. His house and his body are dying together. His windows are boarded. And now he's reduced to his hands. I suspect he has glaucoma. At any rate he can scarcely see, and weeds his yard of rubble on his hands and knees. Perhaps he's a surgeon cleansing a wound or an ardent and tactile lover. I watch, I must say, apprehensively. Like mine-war detectors, his hands graze in circles ahead of him. Your nipples were the color of your eyes. Pebble. Snarl of paper. Length of twine. He leans down closely, picks up something silvery, holds it near his nose. Foil? cap? coin? He has within him—what, I wonder? Does he know more now because he fingers everything and has to sniff to see? It would be romantic cruelty to think so. He bends the down on your arms like a breeze. You wrote me: something is strange when we don't understand. I write in return: I think when I loved you I fell to my death.

Billy, I could read to you from Beddoes,[1] he's your man perhaps; he held with dying, freed his blood of its arteries; and he said that there were many wretched love-ill fools like me lying alongside the last bone of their former selves, as full of spirit and speech, nonetheless, as Mrs. Desmond, Uncle Halley and the Ferris wheel, Aunt Pet, Miss Jakes, Ramona or the megaphone; yet I reverse him finally, Billy, on no evidence but braggadocio, and I declare that though my inner organs were devoured long ago, the worm which swallowed down my parts still throbs and glows like a crystal palace.

Yes, you were younger. I was Uncle Halley, the museum man and infrequent meteor. Here is my first piece of ass. They weren't so flat in those days, had more round, more juice. And over here's the sperm I've spilled, nicely jarred and clearly labeled. Look at this tape like lengths of intestine where I've stored my spew, the endless worm of words I've written, a hundred million emissions or more: oh I was quite a man right from the start; even when unconscious in my cradle, from crotch to cranium, I was erectile tissue; tough mostly, after the manner approved by Plato, I had intercourse by eye. Never mind, old Holsclaw, you are blind. We pull down darkness when we go to bed; put out like Oedipus the actually offending organ, and train our touch to lies. All cats are gray, says Mr. Tick; so under cover of glaucoma you are sack gray too, and cannot be distinguished from a stallion.

I must pull myself together, get a grip, just as they say, but I feel spilled, bewildered, quite mislaid. I did not restore my house to its youth, but to its age. Hunting, you hitch through the hollyhocks. I'm inclined to say you aren't half the cripple I am, for there is nothing left of me but mouth. However, I resist the impulse. It is another lie of poetry. My organs are all there, though it's there where I fail—a the roots of my experience. Poet of the spiritual, Rilke,[2] weren't you? yet that's what you said. Poetry, like love, is—in and out—a physical caress. I can't tolerate any more of my sophistries about spirit, mind, and breath. Body equals being, and if your weight goes down, you are the less.

1. Thomas Beddoes (1803–1849), English dramatist.
2. Rainer Maria Rilke (1875–1926), Austrian poet.

Household Apples

I knew nothing about apples. Why should I? My country came in my childhood, and I dreamed of sitting among the blooms like the bees. I failed to spray the pear tree too. I doubled up under them at first, admiring the sturdy low branches I should have pruned, and later I acclaimed the blossoms. Shortly after the fruit formed there were falls—not many—apples the size of goodish stones which made me wobble on my ankles when I walked about the yard. Sometimes a piece crushed by a heel would cling on the shoe to track the house. I gathered a few and heaved them over the wires. A slingshot would have been splendid. Hard, an unattractive green, the worms had them. Before long I realized the worms had them all. Even as the apples reddened, lit their tree, they were being swallowed. The birds preferred the pears, which were small—sugar pears I think they're called—with thick skins of graying green that ripen on toward violet. So the fruit fell, and once I made some applesauce by quartering and paring hundreds; but mostly I did nothing, left them, until suddenly, overnight it seemed, in that ugly late September heat we often have in Indiana, my problem was upon me.

My childhood came in the country. I remember, now, the flies on our snowy luncheon table. As we cleared away they would settle, fastidiously scrub themselves and stroll to the crumbs to feed where I would kill them in crowds with a swatter. It was quite a game to catch them taking off. I struck heavily since I didn't mind a few stains; they'd wash. The swatter was a square of screen bound down in red cloth. It drove no air ahead of it to give them warning. They might have thought they'd flown headlong into a summered window. The faint pink dot where they had died did not rub out as I'd supposed, and after years of use our luncheon linen would faintly, pinkly, speckle.

The country became my childhood. Flies braided themselves on the flypaper in my grandmother's house. I can smell the bakery and the grocery and the stables and the dairy in that small Dakota town I knew as a kid; knew as I dreamed I'd know your body, as I've known nothing, before or since; knew as the flies knew, in the honest, unchaste sense: the burned house, hose-wet, which drew a mist of insects like the blue smoke of its smolder, and gangs of boys, moist-lipped, destructive as its burning. Flies have always impressed me; they are so persistently alive. Now they were coating the ground beneath my trees. Some were ordinary flies; there were the large blue-green ones; there were swarms of fruit flies too, and the red-spotted scavenger beetle; there were a few wasps, several sorts of bees and butterflies— checkers, sulphurs, monarchs, commas, question marks—and delicate dragonflies . . . but principally houseflies and horseflies and bottleflies,

flies and more flies in clusters around the rotting fruit. They loved the pears. Inside, they fed. If you picked up a pear, they flew, and the pear became skin and stem. They were everywhere the fruit was: in the tree still—apples like a hive for them—or where the fruit littered the ground, squashing itself as you stepped ... there was no help for it. The flies droned, feasting on the sweet juice. No one could go near the trees; I could not climb; so I determined at last to labor like Hercules. There were fruit baskets in the barn. Collecting them and kneeling under the branches, I began to gather remains. Deep in the strong rich smell of the fruit, I began to hum myself. The fruit caved in at the touch. Glistening red apples, my lifting disclosed, had families of beetles, flies, and bugs, devouring their rotten undersides. There were streams of flies; there were lakes and cataracts and rivers of flies, seas, and oceans. The hum was heavier, higher, than the hum of the bees when they came to the blooms in the spring, though the bees were there, among the flies, ignoring me—ignoring everyone. As my work went on and juice covered my hands and arms, they would form a sleeve, black and moving, like knotty wool. No caress could have been more indifferently complete. Still I rose fearfully, ramming my head in the branches, apples bumping against me before falling, bursting with bugs. I'd snap my hand sharply but the flies would cling to the sweet. I could toss a whole cluster into a basket from several feet. As the pear or apple lit, they would explosively rise, like monads[3] for a moment, windowless, certainly, with respect to one another, sugar their harmony. I had to admit, though, despite my distaste, that my arm had never been more alive, oftener or more gently kissed. Those hundreds of feet were light. In washing them off, I pretended the hose was a pump. What have I missed? Childhood is a lie of poetry.

The Church

Friday night. Girls in dark skirts and white blouses sit in ranks and scream in concert. They carry funnels loosely stuffed with orange and black paper which they shake wildly, and small megaphones through which, as drilled, they direct and magnify their shouting. Their leaders, barely pubescent girls, prance and shake and whirl their skirts above their bloomers. The young men, leaping, extend their arms and race through puddles of amber light, their bodies glistening. In a lull, though it rarely occurs, you can hear the squeak of tennis shoes against the floor. Then the yelling begins again, and then continues; fathers, mothers, neighbors joining in to form a single pulsing ululation—a cry of the whole community—for in this gymnasium each body becomes

3. Simple, single-celled organism.

the bodies beside it, pressed as they are together, thigh to thigh, and the same shudder runs through all of them, and runs toward the same release. Only the ball moves serenely through this dazzling din. Obedient to law, it scarcely speaks but caroms quietly and lives at peace.

Business

It is the week of Christmas and the stores, to accommodate the rush they hope for, are remaining open in the evening. You can see snow falling in the cones of the street lamps. The roads are filling—undisturbed. Strings of red and green lights droop over the principal highway, and the water tower wears a star. The windows of the stores have been bedizened. Shamelessly they beckon. But I am alone, leaning against a pole—no ... there is no one in sight. They're all at home, perhaps by their instruments, tuning in on their evenings, and like Ramona, tirelessly playing and replaying themselves. There's a speaker perched in the tower, and through the boughs of falling snow and over the vacant streets, it drapes the twisted and metallic strains of a tune that can barely be distinguished—yes, I believe it's one of the jolly ones, it's "Joy to the World." There's no one to hear the music but myself, and though I'm listening, I'm no longer certain. Perhaps the record's playing something else.

1968

■   ■   ■

THE WIZARD

"Hey, look at that! You know what that is?" the Wizard says. "That's a goddamn red-winged blackbird. Miss Watts saw four of 'em last week at her feeder. You know what that means?"

Rensselaer blinks and checks his jockstrap, where he has stuffed two small brown packages. He is an unbelievably skinny twelve-year-old with a dreamy smile and a fine, caramel-colored face. It makes the older boy's face look almost blue.

" 'Spring,' asshole."

"Where is the old witch?" Rensselaer asks mildly. They are in Miss Watts's back yard, but she isn't around and he can't feel her little beady eyes creeping out at them from a window.

"She's at Boston City Hospital right this goddamn minute. She's got a dropped bladder and they're tying the whole thing up," the Wizard says.

"Miss Watts is crippled," he told Rensselaer the year before. "Walks with a cane, but she ain't old. She sees you buying or selling, she hit you with a cane. Wham! Broke Bama Aguilar's windshield. Ain't afraid of nobody! She teaches eighth grade. She was my last teacher. She say, 'George Albert, you have a gift for numbers. You don't need prealgebra. You don't need *pre* anything.' We finished these two books, her and me. One was the tenth-grade math book and one was a little green book, *Amusements in Mathematics*. It was full of weird stuff. It told about this one guy, Fibonacci.[1] Fibonacci figured, if he put a pair of rabbits in a box, how many pairs of babies from that first pair would be made in a year if every month each pair had a new pair that could

1. Leonardo Fibonacci (ca. 1170–after 1240), Italian mathematician.

make babies when it was two months old. It goes: 1 2 3 5 8 13 21 34 55, like that. The rabbits are immortal."

He does not know why he does this, explains stuff like this to Rensselaer, whose soft smile may well have roots in retardation. But Rensselaer, though inappropriate in age and intelligence, is a friend, and the Wizard is now in a zone between friends, between the possibilities of friendship. At sixteen, he has become a dealing power on Homestead Street, and so not a child. He is no man, though he is wily and moving up.

"Miss Watts told about hundreds of things," the Wizard says. "The Constitution. Goiter belts. She told about Monticello, Jefferson's mansion. And I know I got to see that place. I sold two kilos in four days and took a Trailways bus. Just me. I brought her back a pen with a little plastic Monticello floatin' inside.

"What a place. That dude *hid* everything. He hid the slave quarters under the house. He had dumbwaiters, little chimneys for food to go up and down, hot food coming up from the kitchen and revolving doors so he don't have to be bothered with servants while he is conversing in his dining room. He just pulled the food out of the walls and stuck in the dirty plates.

"He had a chair with this arm. An extension. You copy something small, trace it over with a pen, but the pen is attached to a rod and a lot of crap and then to another pen, which is making a huge fucking picture of the same thing you are at that moment drawing little.[2] Goddamn! You look up at this dial over the doorway *inside*, and it tells you the wind, where it's coming from and how strong, *outside*. He had a clock that could tell the time any which way. All the hours, days, months, and moons. And flowers! Yellow tulips like a blanket. 'Herbs.' Miss Watts liked her pen. She say, 'What do you know!' tiltin' it to make the little house float."

Corinna Watts lives at 49 Homestead. Homestead is a heavy dealing street that still has a few crazy genteel pockets. In between is a quarter mile of empty, boarded-up houses with hundreds of places to deal and disappear. Miss Watts owns her house. She has a small garden in the back. That's how the Wizard met her outside school. He was checking out the flowers. Actually, he and another kid were setting up their scales,[3] just chickenshit stuff in the sixth grade, and they noticed all these flowers on the other side of the fence. Roses. They picked off a couple and started throwing them at each other.

2. A pantograph.
3. For weighing drugs for sale.

She came out waving these huge scissors and they grabbed their stuff and ran. But she yelled, "Come back! Come back! You boys like flowers? Here!" she held up the scissors. "Pick yourselves some." They looked at each other and put their stuff in the grass and crept back and took the scissors and thanked her and she went inside. They picked every flower she had. Some they just knocked the tops off, swatting them with the closed blades. Whap! Whap! Whap! When she came out, they ran. She stood with her arms hanging in the middle of that little headless garden. It looked like a war zone.

Walking up Humboldt, the Wizard didn't feel so great. He twisted a few gas caps off parked cars and dropped them into the drain at the corner, but he didn't feel any better. They finished their packages behind Baby Lyle's Deli and split. Walking home, he felt an itch in his collar and it was the tiny head of a rose caught inside. It was tight like a little umbrella, with no smell because it was still shut. He split it open with his nails and felt the hundreds of pink, silky layers, like a little body not born.

The next day, he took the MBTA to Quincy Market and bought two boxes of flowers from a ripoff plant store under a glass dome. He made fifty bucks off Earl Johnson for a crack delivery and he took it, the whole thing, and bought these red flowers in flat boxes. They at least looked like something; the roses this guy had were just sticks in pots with pictures of roses stuck on. The guy said it wasn't the season for roses. You pay and wait for them to *appear* from these sticks. He couldn't believe people bought that line. He took the red ones. Salvia, the guy called them. He took them back on the MBTA, these two flat boxes taking up four seats, with all these old farts standing. He enjoyed it. He shuffled down the back alley with a box on each shoulder. He waited a while to see if anyone was around and then cut into Miss Watts's yard and took out Selma's soup spoon and began to dig. He put the plants in carefully, not in rows but in spirals of 'increasing radii.' When he finished the little spirals, he took a pail by the basement steps and ran some water in it but she heard that. She came leaping out, swinging her cane. It came down like lead, and he thought she broke his back. He grabbed it up where it was high, ready to slam down again, only she froze, her arm in the air, her eyes bouncing around the ground.

"Salvia," she said softly. "My Lord."

The salvia didn't do so hot, but the Wizard came by regularly to take care of it. He lived eleven houses down, at number 28.

"A perfect number," he said to Rensselaer the night he moved in his stuff.

"What's so perfect?" the child asked.

"Twenty-eight is the sum of its own divisors, if you count one but don't count *it*. It's the second perfect number."

"What's the first?" Rensselaer asked, smiling wide.

"Six. Your IQ."

Number 28 is a three-story building with six apartments, the Wizard's and the other five which are boarded up. It has no electricity and no phone, "just sunlight and direct communication," he says, although he does have two little battery lamps from Kmart. He has a sleeping bag, an impressive collection of *Penthouses*, a bear statue in a bathrobe with holes in his paws for toothbrushes that Selma bought him, and a giant ficus tree he also got at Kmart and which is amazingly healthy. When it gets too cool for the tree, he covers it with plastic garbage bags and tapes it and moves back to his mother's. He doesn't live with Selma unless it's freezing. "Her house is shit-dirty both ways," he says. "Crap all over, and dealing round the clock. When I lived there, I went to school a lot. It was a fucking relief.

"At school I got ninety-ninth percentile in 'conceptual mathematical ability.' I did out of sight in the ERBs, these five days of tests of which days I did not miss one. I am 'bright.' Bright like a nuclear bomb."

The Wizard's real name is George Albert Cantrell. Earl calls him the Wizard because he can figure street price in a flash. "You got to figure your flat cost," the Wizard says, "then things like bail money, dealing time lost if you're picked up, runners, eyes. This is not easy, it's fucking calculus. It is also work under pressure. Earl is thirty-two years old but he don't go nowhere without me no more. We never carry much. 'We light,' he says, 'we are two feathers.' Earl weighs about 250 pounds. He's got this huge smile, his whole face gets into the act. But he's a mean son of a bitch. Even if he is my brother, which he ain't. Not by the latest which Selma tells me. But Selma, she is a great storyteller."

Earl is always polite to certain people. To Bama, his main supply. And to people like Miss Watts. He teaches school, too, and he is good at it. "This is a good place," he says to the new payroll of baby runners. "We should take care of it. No molesting innocent people. Keep a nice clean street. We are doing business and we don't need no crap. We deal clean and we move. Don't hurt nobody. They our cover. They our 'ticket.' These are Queen Elizabeths," he says to the small child Toussaint, handing him a bunch of bright pink roses in cellophane with a twenty-dollar bill for delivery. "They for Miss Watts. *I* give them to her, she crack my skull!" he laughs. "You say they from Mr. Earl Johnson. Then run."

The Wizard and Earl really didn't know each other, even though they were half-brothers, or fourths or something, and then one day Earl's up at Anne Marie's, his "mother-in-law's" dealing, and the Wizard sees 5-0 come down the street, and then another car, slow, the wrong way, and he checks and sees Earl's got nobody looking out so he runs up and says, "The Man's coming down both ways." Earl streaks out, he is big but he can move, then he comes back fast and shoves the Wizard a hundred. So they get to know each other.

Miss Watts doesn't speak of Earl. Her time, she says, is not to be wasted on shit. She talks about other things. "Out of the blue," the Wizard says, "I am watering the salvia, which later I found out was too much and rotting the roots and killing them but she just let me do it because I believe she likes to see me. I am in many ways entertaining, and out of the blue she looks up from her aluminum chair and her Sunday *Globe* and says, 'George Albert, you take the Secondary School Admission Test. Take it three, four times till you get the hang. We get you into Alden Hill. That school is this island,' she says, 'in the jungle of life.' That was one of her expressions, 'the jungle of life.' She says things like 'the jungle of life' and 'with the help of God and eighty-five policemen,' and, when she looks in a mirror sometime she say, 'I look like the wreck of the *Hesperus*,[4] which I believed for a long time was some prehistoric animal, but it turns out to be a fucking boat."

"Miss Watts says take this test. I say, 'Miss Watts, I don't mind. How do I take it?' And I take it. I go to school, another school, on a Saturday morning and blow my brains out over this fucking long test. You go in with two number 2 pencils—it has to say number 2 on the side of the pencils or you can't use them. You can't take food, no 'artificial aids' like calculators or calculator watches, my jacket has thirteen because people sometimes like a little extra and I had not yet hit the street, so I left the jacket on and I was *warm*. There was this dude watchin' everybody all the time. One girl, fat, white, was crying. She was getting her test wet. She had big breasts and no bra and a little girl dress and I said, I whispered, 'Hey baby, don't do that, you get your test all wet,' and the guy almost threw me out. I didn't do so good that time. Miss Watts, she says take it again, so I do. And a third time. 'That's enough!' she say. The score I got was, you know, in outer space.

"Alden Hill *is* a fucking hill. Green. All these big brick buildings and neat little paths at the top. It has great 'sports facilities,' big flat

4. Allusion to *The Wreck of the Hesperus* by popular American poet Henry Wadsworth Longfellow (1807–1882).

fields where you play games that needs tons of 'equipment,' which means the place is ass-deep in cash. It's got extremely smart, rich students. Miss Watts set me up for the interview. The junior high sent my record and she set me up. They had this Chinese kid show me around. It was funny they picked a Chinese. They got brothers there, too. Black and beautiful as me, jackets and ties you'd put on a corpse, big blue book bags with the name of the school all over. You wonder how the fuck they got there. They'd have to be airlifted from Homestead. But, as the man says, they 'do.' We ate lunch in this room entirely of natural wood, even the ceiling. Gordon Ho plays the violin and lacrosse. Lacrosse is this Indian game with big salad spoons. I stuck around and watched the practice in which he was pretty lousy and then I tried it. I did all right. I got the walk for it, and I got the run.

"The Hill gets tons of money from everywhere because it does a fucking good job as a school. After you finish you are made. You just slide cross the river to Harvard, I mean your ass is greased forever. You're a lawyer, you get the richest, evilest cases. You be a business man, you got yourself a direct South American pipeline. You got yourself an education.

"Ho dropped me at Admissions and this guy Crosby interviewed me. He sat on the side of his desk. Friendly. Sly. Ask you nothing right out. A cruisin' shark. He says, 'We encourage inner city boys.' Then he zones in. 'George, what kind of a boy would you say you are?'

"I don't know how to answer this.

" 'You've been out of school this year. What do you do with your time?'

"I decide to tell the truth, but not about working for Earl which takes up most of my time. I tell him about 'Miss Watts days.' And these exist. She used to actually come, but lately she don't. She's got this bladder and we just get started and I have to bring her back. So I have Miss Watts days without her.

"I tell Crosby about Miss Watts days. I go to the aquarium a lot. It's this gigantic tube of water standing on end with a ramp wrapped around it so you can look in at the fish as you climb up. The fish look out. At eleven o'clock and four this guy in a rubber suit jumps in and feeds them. He even feeds the sharks. The fish don't eat each other. And that's amazing. I mean all these fish, natural enemies, and they just cruise around looking at the people. They don't 'molest' each other. They got so much fucking food, they don't need to. They're bored.

"I get to the aquarium on the T. You can get anywhere in Boston on the T. 'Boston is a cultural mecca,' Miss Watts says. 'Walk in! Walk on in like you strut into my garden and whack my flowers!' I do.

"I find you can cruise into some pretty good places. For instance, you can get off at Central Square and cut into MIT. I found this out when I ran stuff to a candy factory next door. You can walk right into those big stone buildings. You carry a book and look like you're late for something. Sometimes, you can actually walk into rooms where guys are working and they don't give a shit. That's how I met Stoltz. I stepped out of a hall when all these Japs come walking towards me and then I was in this big room. I mean *big*. The ceiling was about thirty feet high and it had these extremely shiny aluminum pillars every-where. I hear music, a twinkly music like the kind they play for Rensselaer's sister when she dances at BoJo's, and then it stops. *No one* is there. I mean, this is a really big room with only me in it and then this twinkly music that just stops. I start to leave and the music starts again. When I stop, it stops. A light comes on but only over me. I start walking again and the light follows me and the twinkly music starts and I walk real fast and the music goes crazy and the light turns red. I freeze. It all stops. I tap one foot. The music jangs once. So then I go into my moves. I jive slow, and then I take off. I leap and scrouch down and come up wild, and the room is filled with this Martian music. I stop and head for the door and this white guy comes out, really *white*, like somebody who lives in the dark all the time. He says, 'Wow. Wow. I didn't know it could do that.' It turns out this is art. The music and lights are connected to the fucking floor. He shows me my moves on video and I look spectacular. It's 'audio kinetic art.' Some of the stuff is great, but some is shit. I mean, one whole room is some-body's 'dream,' right? I check in with Stoltz every once in a while, though. He is a patient dude.

"I also touch down also at BoJo's and the Fine Arts, usually on the same day because you can change lines easy at the Combat Zone[5] and head out Huntington Avenue to the museum. The museum is this palace. Outside they got a stone Indian on a horse with his arms spread out and his face looking up at the sky, a natural six-time loser. They got thousands of pictures and museum cops who don't do anything but let you float along. The thing I like about this place is, after you come out, you can be anywhere, sleeping, eating, and still know the stuff is there if you want to go back and check it out again. Sometimes they get new stuff which stays for only a little while so you got to look good. There is one thing I always check out when I go. It is a picture called *The Fantastic Beast*. It is an 'etching,' a drawing of a monster. But a goddamn genius monster. It's from the Bible. When I saw it the first time, I'm turning this corner by the Egyptian stuff, and there it is, like

---

5. District of Boston where vice is more or less tolerated.

an enemy you see in the street. It was all the crap in the world in a face. The eyes were good eyes that look like they know you and maybe even love you, but the lips could kiss you or eat you. There are these little Walkmen you rent that tell you about the picture, only Wiley, the black dude in a brown uniform who rents them, give me mine free. I listen for the part coming up about *The Fantastic Beast*, but it don't say much. Early Renaissance, some other stuff. I didn't use the box again because it wrecks looking. Your ears take the energy from your eyes, I find.

"Wiley is a friendly man. He looks old, but when he laughs he looks young. 'Nobody know how old a black man is,' he says. 'I can be a senior citizen at the movies, and I still got the moves for sweet young ass.' He knows a lot about art. He's got his favorite stuff too. His favorite thing of all is a room. It's a big empty room they got on the second floor. All polished wood, soft and quiet. The whole ceiling is carved and set in like it belongs, but it don't. It belongs in Japan. They got houses like this in Japan with nothing in them. Except they're filled up with something. They're filled up with 'quiet.' On the sides of this room they got huge cardboard pictures, folded and standing up, each one bigger than ten men shoulder to shoulder. There's a bench in the middle of the room with nobody ever on it and I sit there sometimes and jiggle numbers for the evening action. One cardboard has a warrior chasing another on horseback, with armor like you wouldn't believe. He makes Robocop look like Mickey Mouse. The guy he's chasing is crossing a river and you can see by his expression and the swirly lines in the water that that river is fuckin' movin'! You think, 'Sucker! You're caught! If the guy behind don't get you, the river will.' The first time, I walked all the way out of that room and down the stairs and outside to the T stop and then I come back and look at that guy in the river again. And he don't look afraid. He looks like he knows something. And then I don't know which one is chasing which, for he looks like he's just waiting in that river for the other dude to follow. Now *that's* a picture. I told Miss Watts about it. She says there is this movie at Coolidge Corner, that if I like that picture I should see this movie. We go. It turns out to be one hell of a movie. It's about an old Jap king who decides to be nice to his sons because he's getting old and so he 'abdicates' before dying, to let them all sort of get their feet wet in ruling, and they go nuts.[6] It doesn't sound like a good story, but it is. Especially in the beginning, when everything is real quiet. There is a long time when you just look at all these green mountains with wind blowing in the grass and these horsemen, quiet, looking, looking,

---

6. *Ran* (1985), a Japanese film adapted from Shakespeare's *King Lear*, directed by Akira Kurosawa (b. 1910).

and you wonder what the fuck they're looking for but you know it's
something because you hear weird Stoltz[7]-type music in the background. And then the whole thing explodes because this animal, this
fucking monster, a wild boar, busts out of the grass and the horsemen
charge after it, even this old guy who is a very good horseback rider. It
is really not Japanese at all, Miss Watts says. It is a story by 'Shakespeare.' She give me the book and I try a couple of pages but it don't
make sense. It's in another language with just bits of English thrown
in, although I can see the guy is no dope.

"I tell Crosby about the aquarium and the museum and some of
the other places I go and he listens and I think it's going OK, but then
he hits me again with a bunch of those 'loose' questions.

" 'Look, Mr. Crosby,' " I say finally. 'What do you want to know?
Am I a smart boy? Yes I am. Am I a good boy? I am a good boy, but I
don't take no shit.'

"He looks out the window. 'Good in what way, George?'

"I look out, too, 'It depends. Just good or good *at*. When I'm good,
I know it. I can say, "I am being good right now," and I think if you
can say that, I mean if you *know* that, I don't think you really are.
'Good.' Not like Rensselaer Charles is good, I think. He's good and he
don't know it. It's just like breathin' to him. Like when he stood up
and yelled to me, he knew Bama's gorillas were coming across Franklin
Field just a hundred yards behind, and he stands up, *stands up* in that
purple shirt with the singing raisins and yells to me. 'That's good,' I
think to myself. 'And fucking stupid.'

" 'What are you good *at*?' Crosby asks.

" 'Mathematics, reading, auto mechanics . . .' Pussy, I might add.
Whistlin'. I am, in fact, an extremely good whistler.

" 'In that order?' he says.

" 'All equal. I'm Superman.' I get up and walk to the door. 'What
are you good at, Mr. Crosby? It sure as hell isn't interviewing.' But I
don't say that either, because at the door, or half behind it, I see it. A
picture of a man, young, with half his arm exposed, the skin is lifted
back, and all the veins and muscles inside are drawn perfect. His face,
or half a face because the rest isn't drawn, is beautiful, like a woman's,
and I know in the whole world the same fucking guy made it that
made *The Beast*.

" 'Dürer,'[8] Crosby says. 'One of his earlier drawings. It was given
to the school by the Alden family. There's another outside the infir-
mary. Do you like it?'

" 'Yeah. But not as much as some of his other stuff.'

---

7. Probably a reference to Robert Stolz (1880–1975), Austrian composer.
8. Albrecht Dürer (1471–1528), German painter and printmaker.

"His eyes light up. He's kind of leaning over me, his arm high up on the door. 'What else do you like?'

" *The Fantastic Beast,*' I say.

"He looks pink and happy. 'A masterpiece,' he whispers."

Miss Watts got the call. The Wizard walked up those rickety back steps and she opened the door and yanked him in and he had to hold her shoulders to stop her from jumping. "They like you fine! You are *in!*" she yelled. "Full scholarship! They say they just hope they can keep up the caliber of your education!" They "juked," she called it, holding on to him and jumping up and down like a monkey. Afterwards, he put her to bed like an old baby. He felt somehow great and no one to tell but this old baby.

He planned to work solid with Earl the five months before school started. You couldn't live on a scholarship and he wasn't going to screw things up by dealing at the Hill. Earl would ask it, demand it in his pig way when he found out. But by then, he figured, he could handle Earl.

By then, Earl might not even be around. He was doing some pretty stupid things. He was doing almost all his business in one place, for one thing. Anne Marie's had already been busted twice, and an apartment busted three times could be padlocked. Most regulars moved before this happened, but Anne Marie couldn't move anywhere.

"How the hell she gonna move with that tribe?" the Wizard asked, but Earl just said to meet him. The Wizard didn't like Anne Marie's for another reason. He didn't like the 'atmosphere.' The family was pure women, a hundred percent. All kinds of women. There were Shirley and her baby and La Toya, Daryl's baby girl, back to roost, and Francine and Kendra, who went to hairdressing school now and then. Six fucking women. Daryl, Anne Marie's only boy, was caught dealing, and they were "upgrading" the project so a known dealer could not visit his mama, and she had to sign that he wouldn't and she did that.

Anne Marie was everything in life a female could be. She was sweet and she was mean as hell. She was skinny like sticks in her arms and legs, and fat, really big, round her middle. She was—but only in the soft light coming up from the courtyard around ten in the morning in her old rose robe—pretty. She had a magic. She could get real funny in the blackest times. When Daryl was hit she was so sad, she looked at the cop who came in the morning and told her about Daryl at the door. He told her and she died. Then she made the fucking cop laugh. He told her about Daryl and she died for a while in the doorway and then turned around and made him laugh. She was a daughter and a mother and a grandmother and a sister, but she was no friend. Sometimes she was a shrieking witch and sometimes she was an angel of light. The only thing she always was, was tired. She was, to her older daughters, Shirley and Francine, disappearing in bits, like an old screw doll. All that would be left some morning, Shirley felt, was Anne Marie's raging heart in her ashtray on the kitchen table. Yet in that dim debacle of a life of hers, she had one ironbound claim to fame: She had never killed a child. No baby ever started in her or in one of hers was ever cut out. Anne Marie held on to that like a rope thrown to a drowning man and none of her children was going to wrench it from her hands. There were filthy diapers everywhere.

Shirley is usually not home when the Wizard shows up to wait for Earl. This time she is, but she looks like she's leaving. Tall, hair down to her ass. Looks like a model. She's Earl's girl, and has one baby by him—yet another girl, the five hundredth or something. Georgia Delight. That is a gorgeous name, and the kid is too. Dark and gorgeous like a bug-eyed doll. Earl bought her a huge pink bear almost as big as himself last Christmas. When he was carrying it up the stairs, it looked like this gorilla and giant bear come up fighting.

Earl likes to give presents. On Shirley's birthday, he gave her a fifty-thousand-volt sting gun in a blue velvet box. She said, "What the hell am I supposed to do with this? Earrings! You give a girl *jewelry*, asshole!" Only Shirley can talk to Earl like this.

"Hey, baby," he says, the phone wedged into his bull neck. "You're mine. Sooner or later you'll need it." He reaches over and wiggles her ear. Earl is accurate. He's connected direct with a Miami supply, and that is a jumping game.

"Watch Delight for me, baby," Shirley says to the Wizard. And she is gone.

He finds *Square One* on the tube, a program he likes, and sits down with Delight, who is balled up at her end of the sofa. Delight's "inner home" in the apartment is the maroon sofa or the right-hand corner of it, where she is usually asleep or looking at the tube or somewhere in between. She doesn't get up, at two, to go to the bathroom. She smells all the time like Delight.

A bunch of colored triangles dance around the screen and fall into a dazzling design. "Tessa-laaation" peels out on a salsa beat.

"Hey, little bean bag," the Wizard says, grabbing the tiny wrists, gently jamming his nose into hers. "You are looking at a 'secret yuppie.' Soon nobody gonna see nothing but my fucking dust." Delight laughs and reaches for his nose and he pulls her, smell and all, into his lap. He liked watching TV with this baby. He thinks, holding her wondrous warmth, and then rejects the revelation with bitterness, that his only friends in the world are an old woman and a retarded boy and this baby. Earl arrives with his customer. His stupidity is becoming phenomenal.

Half the time, he doesn't show at all. There is one time the Wizard came up and the place was totally deserted. This was good. It is the way it's supposed to be, professionally speaking. Even Delight is not in her corner. "What would happen," he thinks, switching on the TV and easing into the sofa, "to that baby *outside?* Her skin would split. Fresh air and sunlight would shatter her insides with surprise."

Little mousy sounds come from the bedroom. He checks in and sees Delight in one bed and in the other, wide-eyed, spaced out, is Francine, a baby face on a long woman's body with butterflies on her panties. "Hey, Wizard," she says. Delight makes small, cranky sounds, curling up like an elbow noodle and spiking out. Two pillows keep her from falling on the floor.

"She's all right," Francine says, "she'll go back to sleep. Come here, baby. Sit down." He does. And through, above, and below Delight's murmurings, her tiny wails and fitful sleep, he gets to know Francine. Later, easing down the stairs, away from that universe of women, he reflects on how there might now be another exotically named star, shining just for him, already pressing against those butterfly wings with a steady beat.

"You fucking going to do the right thing," Earl says. It's the day after Christmas and he is holding a beer. His watch, a present from Shirley, is bleeping, bleeping red.

"What's the right thing?" the Wizard asks politely, raising his eyebrows. "A sting gun? A hundred-pound pink bear?"

Earl's face levels menacingly. Then it suddenly cracks into its wide smile. "You got balls, my man."

Francine is carrying a little ball. She carries it every Tuesday and Thursday morning to hairdressing class and then over to Bama Aguilar's, who pats it afterwards for good luck. She likes hairdressing, but she also carries an ad in her curler case for the Ryco Travel Agent School in Brighton. She is an ambitious child. She is quick and can predict most things, but she is mildly amazed at the Wizard. He is a baby boy who makes a hell of a lot of money. There is no reason not to tuck him under her wing. But he resists like a full-grown son of a bitch.

"Do you believe I am that fucking dumb!" he says when she tells him. "You get rid of it, maybe it's mine. Only way." Yet even as he hurls this at her, he knows, in rising despair, that Francine will be true to Anne Marie, that preserver of life.

"It's no fucking deal," Francine says. She has a lovely, easy smile. "There's Delight's clothes and her playpen which she'll outgrow soon. Nothing will change. If you put up regular. And you do, baby," she kneads him softly. "You do."

He does not. His last run to Miami with Earl is in late August and he gets back to Homestead on a broiling Saturday afternoon and visits no one, not Francine or Selma or Miss Watts, distributing no wealth. He climbs the stairs with his three white shirts and two dead ties in a shopping bag and opens the door to that cool, boarded-up apartment, and finds that the essence of death is air. The ficus is a brown cornstalk. He crumples a leaf and fills a thin shaft of light with golden motes.

On Monday, climbing Anne Marie's ammonia-scented stairwell, that endless spiral of information and gratification, he is told that the family is not at home. They're all down at J. Arnold Moon & Sons, where Delight has gone and gotten her baby hair done up in four white plastic barrettes and a pink nylon party dress smoothed down in a satin-lined box. Moon's, a cockeyed, gaily austere funeral home at the corner of Columbia Avenue, is packed. He pushes through the crowd but seems to get nowhere, then suddenly stares down at a doll in a shoebox. He passes back, underwater, not breathing, into the sudden, merciful jolt of daylight and traffic.

Shirley is standing on a patch of grass. "The little bitch should have complained!" she screams. Earl has her arms pinned. It was true, he thinks: If they couldn't hear her, how could they know? Those stupid little "mumbles"! Francine waddles down the stairs behind him in high heels and a shiny black dress and Shirley lunges for her. "You were in the next fucking bed! Day in, day out!"

The patch of grass in front of Moon's is the same homogeneous green of the grass on the Hill. The Wizard's sneakers leave soft half-moons as he traverses, scanning the future. Francine's ball, this "Julep Jill" or "Spring Fantana," for these are names she has considered, will be placed in Delight's playpen and Francine will be her own first customer in the travel business. He knows this. Yet it is not "Julep Jill" or "Spring Fantana" or even "Shannon Hussein" he sees, but Delight, aglow with fever, her small sounds rising, and all he wants in the world is to get that elbow-noodle body in his arms and run.

Miss Watts is not in her chair. He does not expect her to be. Twice she has gone to the hospital for her rotting bladder, and now they've got her in some kind of home. The aluminum chair is there, open and jammed into the earth like always, its dirty white and green webbing loose at the back. He sits in it and looks around. The yard looks good. He pays Rensselaer to take care of it. He pays him an insane amount, same as a courier. He would like to keep Rensselaer in this yard forever.

The next day he finds it, he is good at finding things in this city, a concrete, convalescent bunker across from Franklin Park. He has three of her Magenta Queens in waxed paper. A fat woman in a dirty uniform lets him in and suspiciously parks him outside a little room with four beds. He finds her in the one behind the door. It looks like they made a dummy Miss Watts out of her old green sweater and a dried peach for her head. She looks at him, a long look with nothing in it, but he sits down anyway and begins to talk. He talks and talks, like he has never talked before to anyone. He can actually watch himself talking, but he can't stop. He talks about everything: Francine, Selma, Earl, Crosby, everything except Delight. He circles round that baby like a rock in a stream. He knows Miss Watts is listening because every once in a while her mouth does a little jerk. She looks "light," as if something has all but eaten her up inside, but when she speaks, it flops to the floor and slithers under the door.

"You are a shining star!" she says with amazing volume and venom. "Stick to your plan!" This explosion caves her in or maybe kills her. Through the blinds, he watches Franklin Park disappear in the oncoming night.

"A baby," Miss Watts says, her eyes closed. "Most precious, precious thing." At the T, he is still holding the Magenta Queens. He vows he will never go back.

But the next time is better. Miss Watts has managed to concentrate a nut of energy, enough to sustain almost five minutes of her original self. "They will remove me, George Albert," she says calmly. "Don't look for me. There's no point. I won't be there. I'm not even here!" Her face looks almost cheerful. "Right now I'm in my chair in my yard and the sun is shining and you are rotting the roots of my salvia. I can see the little rainbows in the spray from your can. I can be any goddamned place I want!"

He rises, smiling.

"You'll do the right thing," she says, a claw grasps his wrist hard, painfully. "And it sure as hell isn't supporting some whore."

Sometimes the Wizard liked to think that he was physically made up of a lot of little clocks. Ping, ping. Clocks for dealing, when and how much, where, the time to expand, when to pull back, sit tight, move again. Ping. Time to fertilize the ficus. The ping he heard was a new one. He had set that clock five months before, the alarm for the first day of class. He rose in the darkness and put on the white shirt and dead tie and jacket and pants and softly flopped down the stairs into the silent, almost beautiful street.

He got to the Hill just before dawn, and he pulled his jacket together and sat down. The air was cool and amazingly still, like sitting under a big blue bell, and he lay back and closed his eyes. After a while, a soft shaft of light glided up the slope, gilding his hands, then his face. A car door slammed.

Five or six boys passed by, their voices melding into the early light. He sat up and watched half a dozen more cars pull up, then he got up and walked back down the narrow path, out across St. Francis Avenue and down to the T.

The train was jammed with early commuters. He stood in the middle of the car, not having to brace himself on anything, supported upright and propelled along at roaring speed. He changed at Park and took an emptier car west. Wiley would not be working today. He didn't want to run into him anyway. He would wait until the glass doors opened and climb up to the second floor and walk down the long corridor, past the store and cafeteria and the Egyptian stuff in cases, and look at it, its several horns and teeth, its stupid, menacing, ardent eyes, the consummate genius of the hand that drew it, and know he didn't have to see it again. He could remember it. He could draw it perfectly from memory. If he had Jefferson's chair, he could draw it as big as it really was. And it was enormous, bigger than the world.

1989

■   ■   ■

TOM HAWKINS

PUTTING A CHILD TO BED

Jane stripped the spread from the bed, undoing the careful tucks and folds she'd put there in the morning when she'd remade the bed after the child. With two hands she unfurled a light wool blanket and let it fall across the expanse of the mattress. Then she turned back the top of the sheet.

The nine-year-old stood in his pajama bottoms maneuvering a tennis ball with his bare feet as if he were playing soccer. He was a middle-sized child, lean but not especially thin, so moderately proportioned it was hard to tell if he would always be so, or if growth would take some surprising turn, stalling him into a short man or making him tall, or muscular, or in some other way distinct.

"Why don't you get in?" Jane said. Without replying, the boy went through a flurry of footwork with the tennis ball that evidently ended with a scoring kick. Then he pulled on his pajama shirt, acknowledging his mother's request. He did the bottom buttons of his shirt, and she did the top two, turning down the collar and smoothing it flat.

"Come on," she persisted.

The boy jumped and landed sitting up on the pillow, then shoved his feet full length under the covers and lay all the way down, his body still stiff and wide-awake from activity.

"Do you want to say prayers?" his mother asked.

"Maybe not tonight."

"You had your water, right?"

He nodded and looked down at where his feet formed two hills under the covers. "What day is it?"

"Tuesday, I think."

"You didn't ever say about the hamster, when I asked you on Saturday."

270

"I don't know yet," she said, then saw his face darken. "They're sort of like rabbits? Or are they like guinea pigs?"

"Oh, no," he said, holding up his index fingers to show length. "They're very small. Almost as small as mice." She noticed the imaginary hamster grew just a little bit as he held it there for her examination.

"Where would we keep it? In a cage?"

"In a cage with a wheel for exercise."

"I don't know what the landlady would say. There's bound to be an odor."

"Oh, no," the boy said. "No odor."

"No odor?" She frowned.

"Very little odor," he said.

"Well, the animal with the cage and a table for the cage—that would be maybe ten or twelve dollars. You don't have that much in your sock, do you?" The boy kept his savings in the toe of a sock which he knotted for safekeeping and stored in his dresser drawer.

"No," he said. There was a small rush of anger, tension around the mouth, the hint of a blush, and a swipe with his hand to put his hair out of his eyes. She'd pointed out his weakness and made a baby of him; for this same anger, she'd given up kissing him good night. Her impulse was to cuddle or flatter him, but she drew back and let him fight it out.

"Ten or twelve dollars is a lot of money. I'm still not sure about the landlady. We've got to have a place to live, and we can't move every few months. It's too hard on me. I'll think it over. I really will. If I think we can do it, maybe I can get it for your birthday. Is that too long to wait?"

She may as well have said no. On his scale of time, what happened in several months was of no importance. At that range, a dental appointment was tolerable. Gradually though, with the wish put out of reach, he balanced his disappointment and came back to himself from his anticipation.

"Hamsters eat lettuce," he explained.

"Oh? What else do they eat?"

"Seeds of different kinds. You can't feed them meat or they bite," he said. He checked his mother's face quickly.

"But only if you make the mistake and feed them meat."

"I wouldn't want to be bitten," Jane said, "not even by a hamster."

"A boy at school had two hamsters. They had two litters. He had twelve hamsters, but the mother hamster ate two, so he only has eight little ones and the two big ones."

"They sound sort of awful," Jane said.

"But we'd just have the one."

"Wouldn't it get sort of lonely living alone?"

"We'd keep it company."

"We'll see. Listen, I've got to do the dishes yet. You go to sleep. I'm tired. Too much about hamsters. You warm enough?"

The boy nodded, wrapping the blankets around his shoulders. He drew his knees up so he was half-curled around his warmth.

"You'd really like one. We'd never feed it meat. They eat very little."

Jane stood up and went to the door. The boy peered from where his head was almost beneath the covers. "Dream about something besides hamsters," she joked. "Good night now."

She switched out the light. The boy added something about the cleanliness of hamsters, but his voice was drowsy and she didn't answer.

The dishes in the kitchen were scraped and stacked. Jane ran the water over her hand waiting for it to warm. The pipes whistled. She picked up a plate in one hand, soaping the dish brush with the other. She washed the dishes, taking care not to make much noise.

1989

■   ■   ■

IN THE CEMETERY WHERE AL JOLSON IS BURIED

"Tell me things I won't mind forgetting," she said. "Make it useless stuff or skip it."

I began. I told her insects fly through rain, missing every drop, never getting wet. I told her no one in America owned a tape recorder before Bing Crosby did. I told her the shape of the moon is like a banana—you see it looking full, you're seeing it end-on.

The camera made me self-conscious and I stopped. It was trained on us from a ceiling mount—the kind of camera banks use to photograph robbers. It played our image to the nurses down the hall in Intensive Care.

"Go on, girl," she said, "you get used to it."

I had my audience. I went on. Did she know that Tammy Wynette had changed her tune? Really. That now she sings "Stand By Your Friends"? Paul Anka did it too, I said. Does "You're Having Our Baby." He got sick of all that feminist bitching.

"What else?" she said. "Have you got something else?"

Oh yes. For her I would always have something else.

"Did you know when they taught the first chimp to talk, it lied? When they asked her who did it on the desk, she signed back Max, the janitor. And when they pressed her, she said she was sorry, that it was really the project director. But she was a mother, so I guess she had her reasons."

"Oh, that's good," she said. "A parable."

"There's more about the chimp," I said. "But it will break your heart."

"No thanks," she says, and scratches at her mask.

We look like good-guy outlaws. Good or bad, I am not used to the mask yet. I keep touching the warm spot where my breath, thank God, comes out. She is used to hers. She only ties the strings on top. The other ones—a pro by now—she lets hang loose.

We call this place the Marcus Welby Hospital. It's the white one with the palm trees under the opening credits of all those shows. A Hollywood hospital, though in fact it is several miles west. Off camera, there is a beach across the street.

She introduces me to a nurse as "the Best Friend." The impersonal article is more intimate. It tells me that *they* are intimate, my friend and her nurse.

"I was telling her we used to drink Canada Dry Ginger Ale and pretend we were in Canada."

"That's how dumb *we* were," I say.

"You could be sisters," the nurse says.

So how come, I'll bet they are wondering, it took me so long to get to such a glamorous place? But do they ask?

They do not ask.

Two months, and how long is the drive?

The best I can explain it is this—I have a friend who worked one summer in a mortuary. He used to tell me stories. The one that really got to me was not the grisliest, but it's the one that did. A man wrecked his car on 101 going south. He did not lose consciousness. But his arm was taken down to the wet bone—and when he looked at it—it scared him to death. I mean, he died.

So I didn't dare look any closer. But now I'm doing it—and hoping I won't be scared to death.

She shakes out a summer-weight blanket, showing a leg you did not want to see. Except for that, you look at her and understand the law that requires *two* people to be with the body at all times.

"I thought of something," she says. "I thought of it last night. I think there is a real and present need here. You know," she says, "like for someone to do it for you when you can't do it yourself. You call them up whenever you want—like when push comes to shove."

She grabs the bedside phone and loops the cord around her neck.

"Hey," she says, "the End o' the Line."

She keeps on, giddy with something. But I don't know with what.

"The giveaway was the solarium," she says. "That's where Marcus Welby broke the news to his patients. Then here's the real doctor suggesting we talk in the solarium. So I knew I was going to die.

"I can't remember," she says, "what does Kübler-Ross[1] say comes after Denial?"

It seems to me Anger must be next. Then Bargaining, Depression, and so on and so forth. But I keep my guesses to myself.

"The only thing is," she says, "is where's Resurrection? God knows I want to do it by the book. But she left out Resurrection."

She laughs, and I cling to the sound the way someone dangling above a ravine holds fast to the thrown rope.

We could have cried then, but when we didn't, we couldn't.

"Tell me," she says, "about that chimp with the talking hands. What do they do when the thing ends and the chimp says, 'I don't want to go back to the zoo'?"

When I don't say anything, she says, "OK—then tell me another animal story. I like animal stories. But not a sick one—I don't want to know about all the Seeing Eye dogs going blind."

No, I would not tell her a sick one.

"How about the hearing-ear dogs?" I say. "They're not going deaf, but they are getting very judgmental. For instance, there's this golden retriever in Jersey, he wakes up the deaf mother and drags her into the daughter's room because the kid has got a flashlight and is reading under the covers."

"Oh, you're killing me," she says. "Yes, you're definitely killing me."

"They say the smart dog obeys, but the smarter dog knows when to *dis*obey."

"Yes," she says, "the smarter *anything* knows when to disobey. Now, for example."

She is flirting with the Good Doctor, who has just appeared. Unlike the Bad Doctor, who checks the I.V. drip before saying good morning, the Good Doctor says things like "God didn't give epileptics a fair shake." He awards himself points for the cripples he could have hit in the parking lot. Because the Good Doctor is a little in love with her he says maybe a year. He pulls a chair up to her bed and suggests I might like to spend an hour on the beach.

"Bring me something back," she says. "Anything from the beach. Or the gift shop. Taste is no object."

The doctor slowly draws the curtain around her bed.

"Wait!" she cries.

I look in at her.

"Anything," she says, "except a magazine subscription."

---

1. Elizabeth Kübler-Ross (b. 1926), author of popular books on death and dying.

The doctor turns away.
I watch her mouth laugh.

What seems dangerous often is not—black snakes, for example, or clear-air turbulence. While things that just lie there, like this beach, are loaded with jeopardy. A yellow dust rising from the ground, the heat that ripens melons overnight—this is earthquake weather. You can sit here braiding the fringe on your towel and the sand will all of a sudden suck down like an hourglass. The air roars. In the cheap apartments onshore, bathtubs fill themselves and gardens roll up and over like green waves. If nothing happens, the dust will drift and the heat deepen till fear turns to desire. Nerves like that are only bought off by catastrophe.

"It never happens when you're thinking about it," she observed once.

"Earthquake, earthquake, earthquake," she said.

"Earthquake, earthquake, earthquake," I said.

Like the aviaphobe who keeps the plane aloft with prayer, we kept it up till an aftershock cracked the ceiling.

That was after the big one in '72. We were in college; our dormitory was five miles from the epicenter. When the ride was over and my jabbering pulse began to slow, she served five parts champagne to one part orange juice and joked about living in Ocean View, Kansas. I offered to drive her to Hawaii on the new world psychics predicted would surface the next time, or the next.

I could not say that now—next. *Whose* next? she could ask.

Was I the only one who noticed that the experts had stopped saying *if* and now spoke of *when?* Of course not; the fearful ran to thousands. We watched the traffic of Japanese beetles for deviation. Deviation might mean more natural violence.

I wanted her to be afraid with me, but she said, "I don't know. I'm just not."

She was afraid of nothing, not even of flying.

I have this dream before a flight where we buckle in and the plane moves down the runway. It takes off at thirty-five miles an hour, and then we're airborne, skimming the tree tops. Still, we arrive in New York on time. It is so pleasant. One night I flew to Moscow this way.

She flew with me once. That time she flew with me she ate macadamia nuts while the wings bounced. She knows the wing tips can bend thirty feet up and thirty feet down without coming off. She believes it. She trusts the laws of aerodynamics. My mind stampedes. I can almost accept that a battleship floats, and everybody knows steel sinks.

I see fear in her now and am not going to try to talk her out of it. She is right to be afraid.

After a quake, the six o'clock news airs a film clip of first-graders yelling at the broken playground per their teacher's instructions.

"*Bad* earth!" they shout, because anger is stronger than fear.

But the beach is standing still today. Everyone on it is tranquilized, numb or asleep. Teenaged girls rub coconut oil on each other's hard-to-reach places. They smell like macaroons. They pry open compacts like clamshells; mirrors catch the sun and throw a spray of white rays across glazed shoulders. The girls arrange their wet hair with silk flowers the way they learned in *Seventeen*. They pose.

A formation of low-riders[2] pulls over to watch with a six-pack. They get vocal when the girls check their tan lines. When the beer is gone, so are they—flexing their cars on up the boulevard.

Above this aggressive health are the twin wrought-iron terraces, painted flamingo pink, of the Palm Royale. Someone dies there every time the sheets are changed. There's an ambulance in the driveway, so the remaining residents line the balconies, rocking and not talking, one-upped.

The ocean they stare at is dangerous, and not just the undertow. You can almost see the slapping tails of sand sharks keeping cruising bodies alive.

If she looked, she could see this, some of it, from her window. She would be the first to say how little it takes to make a thing all wrong.

There was a second bed in the room when I returned. For two beats I didn't get it. Then it hit me like an open coffin.

She wants every minute, I thought. She wants my life.

"You missed Gussie," she said.

Gussie is her parents' 300-pound narcoleptic maid. Her attacks often come at the ironing board. The pillowcases in that family are all bordered with scorch.

"It's a hard trip for her," I said. "How is she?"

"Well, she didn't fall asleep, if that's what you mean. Gussie's great—you know what she said? She said, 'Darlin' just keep prayin', down on your knees.' "

---

2. Rebuilt, underslung cars.

She shrugged. "See anybody good?"

"No," I said, "just the new Charlie's Angel. And I saw Cher's car down near the Arcade."

"Cher's car is worth *three* Charlie's Angels," she said, "What else am I missing?"

"It's earthquake weather," I told her.

"The best thing to do about earthquakes," she said, "is not to live in California."

"That's useful," I said. "You sound like Reverend Ike: "The best thing to do for the poor is not be one of them.' "

We're crazy about Reverend Ike.

I noticed her face was bloated.

"You know," she said, "I feel like hell. I'm about to stop having fun."

"The ancients have a saying," I said. " 'There are times when the wolves are silent; there are times when the moon howls.' "

"What's that, Navajo?"

"Palm Royale lobby graffiti," I said. "I bought a paper there. I'll read to you."

"Even though I care about nothing?" she said.

I turned to page three, to a UPI filler datelined Mexico City. I read her "Man Robs Bank with Chicken," about a man who bought a barbecued chicken at a stand down the block from a bank. Passing the bank, he got the idea. He walked in and approached a teller. He pointed the brown paper bag at her and she handed over the day's receipts. It was the smell of barbecue sauce that eventually led to his capture.

The story made her hungry, she said, so I took the elevator down six floors to the cafeteria and brought back all the ice cream she wanted. We lay side by side, adjustable beds cranked up for optimal TV viewing, littering the sheets with Good Humor wrappers, picking toasted almonds out of the gauze. We were Lucy and Ethel, Mary and Rhoda in extremis. The blinds were closed to keep light off the screen.

We watched a movie starring men we used to think we wanted to sleep with. Hers was a tough cop out to stop mine, a vicious rapist who went after cocktail waitresses.

"This is a good movie," she said, when snipers felled them both.

I missed her already; my straight man, my diary.

A Filipino nurse tiptoed in and gave her an injection. She removed the pile of Popsicle sticks from the nightstand—enough to splint a small animal.

The injection made us sleepy—me in the way I picked up her inflection till her mother couldn't tell us apart on the phone. We slept.

I dreamed she was a decorator, come to furnish my house. She worked in secret, singing to herself. When she finished, she guided me proudly to the door. "How do you like it?" she asked, easing me inside.

Every beam and sill and shelf and knob was draped in black bunting, with streamers of black crepe looped around darkened mirrors.

"I have to go home," I said when she woke up.

She thought I meant home to her house in the Canyon, and I had to say No, *home* home. I twisted my hands in the hackneyed fashion of people in pain. I was supposed to offer something. The Best Friend. I could not even offer to come back.

I felt weak and small and failed. Also exhilarated. I had a convertible in the parking lot. Once out of that room, I would drive it too fast down the coast highway through the crab-smelling air. A stop in Malibu for sangria. The music in the place would be sexy and loud. They would serve papaya and shrimp and watermelon ice. After dinner I would pick up beach boys. I would shimmer with life, buzz with heat, vibrate with health, stay up all night with one and then the other.

Without a word, she yanked off her mask and threw it on the floor. She kicked at the blankets and moved to the door. She must have hated having to pause for breath and balance before slamming out of Isolation, and out of the second room, the one where you scrub and tie on the white masks.

A voice shouted her name in alarm, and people ran down the corridor. The Good Doctor was paged over the intercom. I opened the door and the nurses at the station stared hard, as if this flight had been my idea.

"Where is she?" I asked, and they nodded to the supply closet.

I looked in. Two nurses were kneeling beside her on the floor, talking to her in low voices. One held a mask over her nose and mouth, the other rubbed her back in slow circles. The nurses glanced up to see if I was the doctor, and when they saw I wasn't, they went back to what they were doing.

"There, there, honey," they cooed.

On the morning she was moved to the cemetery, the one where Al Jolson is buried, I enrolled in a Fear of Flying class. "What is your worst fear?" The instructor asked, and I answered, "That I will finish this course and still be afraid."

I sleep with a glass of water on the nightstand so I can see by its level if the coastal earth is trembling or if the shaking is still me.

What do I remember? I remember only the useless things I hear—that Bob Dylan's mother invented Wite-out, that twenty-three people must be in a room before there is a fifty-fifty chance two will have the same birthdate. Who cares whether or not it's true? In my head there are bath towels swaddling this stuff. Nothing else seeps through.

I review those things that will figure in the retelling: a kiss through surgical gauze, the pale hand correcting the position of the wig. I noted these gestures as they happened, not in any retrospect. Though I don't know why looking *back* should show us more than looking *at*. It is just possible I will say I stayed the night. And who is there that can say I did not?

Nothing else gets through until I think of the chimp, the one with the talking hands.

In the course of the experiment, that chimp had a baby. Imagine how her trainers must have thrilled when the mother, without prompting, began to sign to the newborn. Baby, drink milk. Baby, play ball. And when the baby died, the mother stood over the body, her wrinkled hands moving with animal grace, forming again and again the words, Baby, come hug, Baby, come hug, fluent now in the language of grief.

1985

PAM HOUSTON

COWBOYS ARE MY WEAKNESS

I have a picture in my mind of a tiny ranch on the edge of a stand of pine trees with some horses in the yard. There's a woman standing in the doorway in cutoffs and a blue chambray work shirt and she's just kissed her tall, bearded, and soft-spoken husband goodbye. There's laundry hanging outside and the morning sun is filtering through the tree branches like spiderwebs. It's the morning after a full moon, and behind the house the deer have eaten everything that was left in the garden.

If I were a painter, I'd paint that picture just to see if the girl in the doorway would turn out to be me. I've been out west ten years now, long enough to call it my home, long enough to know I'll be here forever, but I still don't know where that ranch is. And even though I've had plenty of men here, some of them tall and nearly all of them bearded, I still haven't met the man who has just walked out of the painting, who has just started his pickup truck, whose tire marks I can still see in the sandy soil of the drive.

The west isn't a place that gives itself up easily. Newcomers have to sink into it slowly, to descend through its layers, and I'm still descending. Like most easterners, I started out in the transitional zones, the big cities and the ski towns that outsiders have set up for their own comfort, the places so often referred to as "the best of both worlds." But I was bound to work my way back, through the land, into the small towns and beyond them. That's half the reason I wound up on a ranch near Grass Range, Montana; the other half is Homer.

I've always had this thing about cowboys, maybe because I was born in New Jersey. But a real cowboy is hard to find these days, even in the west. I thought I'd found one on several occasions, I even at one time thought Homer was a cowboy, and though I loved him like crazy for a while and in some ways always will, somewhere along the line I had to face the fact that even though Homer looked like a cowboy, he was just a capitalist with a Texas accent who owned a horse.

Homer's a wildlife specialist in charge of a whitetail deer management project on the ranch. He goes there every year to observe the deer from the start of the mating season in late October until its peak in mid-November. It's the time when the deer are most visible, when the bucks get so lusty they lose their normal caution, when the does run around in the middle of the day with their white tails in the air. When Homer talked me into coming with him, he said I'd love the ranch, and I did. It was sixty miles from the nearest paved road. All of the buildings were whitewashed and plain. One of them had been ordered from a 1916 Sears catalogue. The ranch hands still rode horses, and when the late-afternoon light swept the grainfields across from headquarters, I would watch them move the cattle in rows that looked like waves. There was a peace about the ranch that was uncanny and might have been complete if not for the eight or nine hungry barn cats that crawled up your legs if you even smelled like food, and the exotic chickens of almost every color that fought all day in their pens.

Homer has gone to the ranch every year for the last six, and he has a long history of stirring up trouble there. The ranch hands watch him sit on the hillside and hate him for the money he makes. He's slept with more than one or two of their wives and girlfriends. There was even some talk that he was the reason the ranch owner got divorced.

When he asked me to come with him I knew it would be me or somebody else and I'd heard good things about Montana so I went. There was a time when I was sure Homer was the man who belonged in my painting and I would have sold my soul to be his wife, or even his only girlfriend. I'd come close, in the spring, to losing my mind because of it, but I had finally learned that Homer would always be separate, even from himself, and by the time we got to Montana I was almost immune to him.

Homer and I live in Fort Collins, Colorado, most of the year, in houses that are exactly one mile apart. He's out of town as often as not, keeping track of fifteen whitetail deer herds all across the West. I go with him when he lets me, which is lately more and more. The herds Homer studies are isolated by geography, given plenty of food in bad winters, and protected from hunters and wolves. Homer is working on reproduction and genetics, trying to create, in the wild, super-bucks bigger and tougher than elk. The Montana herd has been his most successful, so he spends the long mating season there. Under his care the bucks have shown incredible increases in antler mass, in body weight, and in fertility.

The other scientists at the university that sponsors Homer respect him, not only for his success with the deer, but for his commitment to observation, for his relentless dedication to his hours in the field. They also think he is eccentric and a bit overzealous.

At first I thought he just liked to be outdoors, but when we got to the ranch his obsession with the deer made him even more like a stranger. He was gone every day from way before sunrise till long after dark. He would dress all in camouflage, even his gloves and socks, and sit on the hillsides above where the deer fed and watch, making notes a few times an hour, changing position every hour or two. If I went with him I wasn't allowed to move except when he did, and I was never allowed to talk. I'd try to save things up for later that I thought of during the day, but by the time we got back to our cabin they seemed unimportant and Homer liked to eat his dinner in front of the TV. By the time we got the dishes done it was way past Homer's bedtime. We were making love less and less, and when we did, it was always from behind.

The ranch owner's name was David, and he wasn't what you'd think a Montana ranch owner would be. He was a poet, and a vegetarian. He listened to Andreas Vollenweider[1] and drank hot beverages with names like Suma and Morning Rain. He wouldn't let the ranch hands use pesticides or chemicals, he wouldn't hire them if they smoked cigarettes. He undergrazed the ranch by about fifty percent, so the organic grain was belly-high to a horse almost everywhere.

David had an idea about recreating on his forty thousand acres the Great Plains that only the Indians and the first settlers had seen. He wasn't making a lot of money ranching, but he was producing the fattest, healthiest, most organic Black Angus cattle in North America. He was sensitive, thoughtful, and kind. He was the kind of man I always knew I should fall in love with, but never did.

Homer and David ate exactly one dinner a week together, which I always volunteered to cook. Homer was always polite and full of incidental conversation and much too quick to laugh. David was quiet and sullen and so restrained that he was hard to recognize.

The irreconcilable differences between Homer and me had been revealing themselves one at a time since late summer. In early November I asked him what he wanted to do on Thanksgiving, and he said he'd like most of all to stay on the ranch and watch the does in heat.

---

1. Austrian "New Age" musician and composer (b. 1953).

Homer was only contracted to work on the ranch until the Sunday before Thanksgiving. When he asked me to come with him he told me we would leave the ranch in plenty of time to have the holidays at home.

I was the only child in a family that never did a lot of celebrating because my parents couldn't plan ahead. They were sun worshipers, and we spent every Thanksgiving in a plane on the way to Puerto Rico, every Christmas in a car on Highway 95, heading for Florida. What I remember most from those days is Casey Kasem's Christmas shows, the long-distance dedications, "I'll be home for Christmas" from Bobby D. in Spokane to Linda S. in Decatur. We never had hotel reservations and the places we wound up in had no phones and plastic mattress covers and triple locks on the doors. Once we spent Christmas night parked under a fluorescent streetlight, sleeping in the car.

I've spent most of the holidays in my adult life making up for those road trips. I spend lots of money on hand-painted ornaments. I always cook a roast ten pounds bigger than anything we could possibly eat.

Homer thinks my enthusiasm about holidays is childish and self-serving. To prove it to me, last Christmas morning he set the alarm for six-thirty and went back to his house to stain a door. This year I wanted Thanksgiving in my own house. I wanted to cook a turkey we'd be eating for weeks.

I said, "Homer, you've been watching the deer for five weeks now. What else do you think they're gonna do?"

"You don't know anything about it," he said. "Thanksgiving is the premium time. Thanksgiving," he shook one finger in the air, "is the height of the rut."

David and I drank tea together, and every day took walks up into the canyon behind ranch headquarters. He talked about his ex-wife, Carmen, about the red flowers that covered the canyon walls in June, about imaging away nuclear weapons. He told me about the woman Homer was sleeping with on the ranch the year before, when I was back in Colorado counting days till he got home. She was the woman who took care of the chickens, and David said that when Homer left the ranch she wrote a hundred love songs and made David listen while she sang them all.

"She sent them on a tape to Homer," David said, "and when he didn't call or write, she went a little nuts. I finally told her to leave the ranch. I'm not a doctor, and we're a long way from anywhere out here."

From the top of the canyon we could see Homer's form blending with the trees on the ridge above the garden, where the deer ate organic potatoes by the hundreds of pounds.

"I understand if he wasn't interested anymore," David said. "But I can't believe even he could ignore a gesture that huge."

We watched Homer crawl along the ridge from tree to tree. I could barely distinguish his movements from what the wind did to the tall grass. None of the deer below him even turned their heads.

"What is it about him?" David said, and I knew he was looking for an explanation about Carmen, but I'd never even met her and I didn't want to talk about myself.

"Homer's always wearing camouflage," I said. "Even when he's not."

The wind went suddenly still and we could hear, from headquarters, the sounds of cats fighting, a hen's frantic scream, and then, again, the cats.

David put his arm around me. "We're such good people," he said. "Why aren't we happy?"

One day when I got back from my walk with David, Homer was in the cabin in the middle of the day. He had on normal clothes and I could tell he'd shaved and showered. He took me into the bedroom and climbed on top of me frontwards, the way he did when we first met and I didn't even know what he did for a living.

Afterwards he said, "We didn't need a condom, did we?" I counted the days forward and backward and forward again. Homer always kept track of birth control and groceries and gas mileage and all the other things I couldn't keep my mind on. Still, it appeared to be exactly ten days before my next period.

"Yes," I said. "I think we did."

Homer has never done an uncalculated thing in his life, and for a moment I let myself entertain the possibility that his mistake meant that somewhere inside he wanted to have a baby with me, that he really wanted a family and love and security and the things I thought everybody wanted before I met Homer. On the other hand, I knew that one of the ways I had gotten in trouble with Homer, and with other men before him, was by inventing thoughts for them that they'd never had.

"Well," he said. "In that case we better get back to Colorado before they change the abortion laws."

Sometimes the most significant moments of your life reveal themselves to you even as they are happening, and I knew in that moment that I would never love Homer the same way again. It wasn't so much that not six months before, when I had asked Homer what we'd do if I got pregnant, he said we'd get married and have a family. It wasn't even that I was sure I wanted a baby. It wasn't even that I thought there was going to be a baby to want.

It all went back to the girl in the log cabin, and how the soft-spoken man would react if she thought she was going to have a baby. It would be winter now, and snowing outside the windows warm with yellow light. He might dance with the sheepdog on the living-room floor, he might sing the theme song from *Father Knows Best*, he might go out and do a swan dive into the snow.

I've been to a lot of school and read a lot of thick books, but at my very core there's a made-for-TV-movie mentality I don't think I'll ever shake. And although there's a lot of doubt in my mind about whether or not an ending as simple and happy as I want is possible anymore in the world, it was clear to me that afternoon that it wasn't possible with Homer.

Five o'clock the next morning was the first time I saw the real cow-boy. He was sitting in the cookhouse eating cereal and I couldn't make myself sleep next to Homer so I'd been up all night wandering around.

He was tall and thin and bearded. His hat was white and ratty and you could tell by looking at his stampede strap that it had been made around a campfire after lots of Jack Daniel's. I'd had my fingers in my hair for twelve hours and my face was breaking out from too much stress and too little sleep and I felt like such a greaseball that I didn't say hello. I poured myself some orange juice, drank it, rinsed the glass, and put it in the dish drainer. I took one more look at the cowboy, and walked back out the door, and went to find Homer in the field.

Homer's truck was parked by a culvert on the South Fork road, which meant he was walking the brush line below the cliffs that used to be the Blackfeet buffalo jumps. It was a boneyard down there, the place where hundreds of buffalo, chased by the Indians, had jumped five hundred feet to their death, and the soil was extremely fertile. The grass was thicker and sweeter there than anywhere on the ranch, and Homer said the deer sucked calcium out of the buffalo bones. I saw Homer crouched at the edge of a meadow I couldn't get to without being seen, so I went back and fell asleep in the bed of his truck.

It was hunting season, and later that morning Homer and I found a deer by the side of the road that had been poached but not taken. The poacher must have seen headlights or heard a truck engine and gotten scared.

I lifted the back end of the animal into the truck while Homer picked up the antlers. It was a young buck, two and a half at the oldest, but it would have been a monster in a few years, and I knew Homer was taking the loss pretty hard.

We took it down to the performance center, where they weigh the organic calves. Homer attached a meat hook to its antlers and hauled it into the air above the pickup.

"Try and keep it from swinging," he said. And I did my best, considering I wasn't quite tall enough to get a good hold, and its blood was bubbling out of the bullet hole and dripping down on me.

That's when the tall cowboy, the one from that morning, walked out of the holding pen behind me, took a long slow look at me trying to steady the back end of the dead deer, and settled himself against the fence across the driveway. I stepped back from the deer and pushed the hair out of my eyes. He raised one finger to call me over. I walked slow and didn't look back at Homer.

"Nice buck," he said. "Did you shoot it?"

"It's a baby," I said. "I don't shoot animals. A poacher got it last night."

"Who was the poacher?" he said, and tipped his hat just past my shoulder toward Homer.

"You're wrong," I said. "You can say a lot of things about him, but he wouldn't poach a deer."

"My name's Montrose T. Coty," he said. "Everyone calls me Monte."

I shook his hand. "Everyone calls you Homer's girlfriend," he said, "but I bet that's not your name."

"You're right," I said, "it's not."

I turned to look at Homer. He was taking measurements off the hanging deer: antler length, body length, width at its girth.

"Tonight's the Stockgrowers' Ball in Grass Range," Monte said. "I thought you might want to go with me."

Homer was looking into the deer's hardened eyeballs. He had its mouth open, and was pulling on its tongue.

"I have to cook dinner for Homer and David," I said. "I'm sorry. It sounds like fun."

In the car on the way back to the cabin, Homer said, "What was that all about?"

I said, "Nothing," and then I said, "Monte asked me to the Stockgrowers' Ball."

"The Stockgrowers' Ball?" he said. "Sounds like a great time. What do stockgrowers do at a ball?" he said. "Do they dance?"

I almost laughed with him until I remembered how much I loved to dance. I'd been with Homer chasing whitetail so long that I'd forgotten that dancing, like holidays, was something I loved. And I started to wonder just then what else being with Homer had made me forget.

Hadn't I, at one time, spent whole days listening to music? Wasn't there a time when I wanted, more than anything, to buy a sailboat? And didn't I love to be able to go outdoors and walk anywhere I wanted, and to make, if I wanted, all kinds of noise?

I wanted to blame Homer, but I realized then it was more my fault than his. Because even though I'd never let the woman in the chambray work shirt out of my mind I'd let her, in the last few years, become someone different, and she wasn't living, anymore, in my painting. The painting she was living in, I saw, belonged to somebody else.

"So what did you tell him?" Homer said.

"I told him I'd see if you'd cook dinner," I said.

I tried to talk to Homer before I left. First I told him that it wasn't a real date, that I didn't even know Monte, and really I was only going because I didn't know if I'd ever have another chance to go to a Stockgrowers' Ball. When he didn't answer at all I worked up to saying that maybe it was a good idea for me to start seeing other people. That maybe we'd had two different ideas all along and we needed to find two other people who would better meet our needs. I told him that if he had any opinions I wished he'd express them to me, and he thought for a few minutes and then he said,

"Well, I guess we have Jimmy Carter to thank for all the trouble in Panama."

I spent the rest of the day getting ready for the Stockgrowers' Ball. All I'd brought with me was some of Homer's camouflage and blue jeans, so I wound up borrowing a skirt that David's ex-wife had left behind, some of the chicken woman's dress shoes that looked ridiculous and made my feet huge, and a vest that David's grandfather had been shot at in by the Plains Indians.

Monte had to go into town early to pick up ranch supplies, so I rode in with his friends Buck and Dawn, who spent the whole drive telling me what a great guy Monte was, how he quit the rodeo circuit to make a decent living for himself and his wife, how she'd left without saying goodbye not six months before.

They told me that he'd made two thousand dollars in one afternoon doing a Wrangler commercial. That he'd been in a laundromat on his day off and the director had seen him through the window, had gone in and said, "Hey, cowboy, you got an hour? You want to make two thousand bucks?"

"Ole Monte," Buck said. "He's the real thing."

After an hour and a half of washboard road we pulled into the dance hall just on our edge of town. I had debated about wearing the cowboy hat I'd bought especially for my trip to Montana, and was thankful I'd decided against it. It was clear, once inside, that only the men wore hats, and only dress hats at that. The women wore high heels and stockings and in almost every case hair curled away from their faces in great airy rolls.

We found Monte at a table in the corner, and the first thing he did was give me a corsage, a pink one, mostly roses that couldn't have clashed more with my rust-colored blouse. Dawn pinned it on me, and I blushed, I suppose, over my first corsage in ten years, and a little old woman in spike heels leaned over and said, "Somebody loves you!" just loud enough for Monte and Buck and Dawn to hear.

During dinner they showed a movie about a cattle drive. After dinner a young enthusiastic couple danced and sang for over an hour about cattle and ranch life and the Big Sky, a phrase which since I'd been in Montana had seemed perpetually on the tip of everybody's tongue.

After dinner the dancing started, and Monte asked me if I knew how to do the Montana two-step. He was more than a foot taller than me, and his hat added another several inches to that. When we stood on the dance floor my eyes came right to the place where his silk scarf disappeared into the shirt buttons on his chest. His big hands were strangely light on me and my feet went the right direction even though my mind couldn't remember the two-step's simple form.

"That's it," he said into the part in my hair. "Don't think. Just let yourself move with me."

And we were moving together, in turns that got tighter and tighter each time we circled the dance floor. The songs got faster and so did our motion until there wasn't time for anything but the picking up and putting down of feet, for the swirling colors of Carmen's ugly skirt, for breath and sweat and rhythm.

I was farther west than I'd ever imagined, and in the strange, nearly flawless synchronization on the dance floor I knew I could be a Montana ranch woman, and I knew I could make Monte my man. It had taken me ten years, and an incredible sequence of accidents, but that night I thought I'd finally gotten where I'd set out to go.

The band played till two and we danced till three to the jukebox. Then there was nothing left to do but get in the car and begin the two-hour drive home.

First we talked about our horses. It was the logical choice, the only thing we really had in common, but it only lasted twenty minutes.

I tried to get his opinion on music and sailing, but just like a cowboy, he was too polite for me to tell anything for sure.

Then we talked about the hole in my vest that the Indians shot, which I was counting on, and half the reason I wore it.

The rest of the time we just looked at the stars.

I had spent a good portion of the night worrying about what I was going to say when Monte asked me to go to bed with him. When he pulled up between our two cabins he looked at me sideways and said,

"I'd love to give you a great big kiss, but I've got a mouthful of chew."

I could hear Homer snoring before I got past the kitchen.

Partly because I didn't like the way Monte and Homer eyed each other, but mostly because I couldn't bear to spend Thanksgiving watching does in heat, I loaded my gear in my truck and got ready to go back to Colorado.

On the morning I left, Homer told me that he had decided that I was the woman he wanted to spend the rest of his life with after all, and that he planned to go to town and buy a ring just as soon as the rut ended.

He was sweet on my last morning on the ranch, generous and attentive in a way I'd never seen. He packed me a sack lunch of chicken salad he mixed himself, and he went out to my car and dusted off the inch of snow that had fallen in our first brush with winter, overnight. He told me to call when I got to Fort Collins, he even said to call collect, but I suppose one of life's big tricks is to give us precisely the thing we want, two weeks after we've stopped wanting it, and I couldn't take Homer seriously, even when I tried.

When I went to say goodbye to David he hugged me hard, said I was welcome back on the ranch anytime. He said he enjoyed my company and appreciated my insight. Then he said he liked my perfume and I wondered where my taste in men had come from, I wondered whoever taught me to be so stupid about men.

I knew Monte was out riding the range, so I left a note on his car thanking him again for the dancing and saying I'd be back one day and we could dance again. I put my hat on, that Monte had never got to see, and rolled out of headquarters. It was the middle of the day, but I saw seven bucks in the first five miles, a couple of them giants, and when I slowed down they just stood and stared at the truck. It was the height of the rut and Homer said that's how they'd be, love-crazed and fearless as bears.

About a mile before the edge of ranch property, I saw something that looked like a lone antelope running across the skyline, but antelope are almost never alone, so I stopped the car to watch. As the figure came closer I saw it was a horse, a big chestnut, and it was carrying a rider at a full gallop, and it was coming right for the car.

I knew it could have been any one of fifty cowboys employed on the ranch, and yet I've learned to expect more from life than that, and so in my heart I knew it was Monte. I got out of the car and waited, pleased that he'd see my hat most of all, wondering what he'd say when I said I was leaving.

He didn't get off his horse, which was sweating and shaking so hard I thought it might die while we talked.

"You on your way?" he said.

I smiled and nodded. His chaps were sweat-soaked, his leather gloves worn white.

"Will you write me a letter?" he said.

"Sure," I said.

"Think you'll be back this way?" he asked.

"If I come back," I said, "will you take me dancing?"

"Damn right," he said, and a smile that seemed like the smile I'd been waiting for my whole life spread wide across his face.

"Then it'll be sooner than later," I said.

He winked and touched the horse's flank with his spurs and it hopped a little on the takeoff and then there was just dirt flying while the high grass swallowed the horse's legs. I leaned against the door of my pickup truck watching my new cowboy riding off toward where the sun was already low in the sky and the grass shimmering like nothing I'd ever seen in the mountains. And for a minute I thought we were living inside my painting, but he was riding away too fast to tell. And I wondered then why I had always imagined my cowboy's truck as it was leaving. I wondered why I hadn't turned the truck around and painted my cowboy coming home.

There's a story—that isn't true—that I tell about myself when I first meet someone, about riding a mechanical bull in a bar. In the story, I stay on through the first eight levels of difficulty, getting thrown on level nine only after dislocating my thumb and winning my boyfriend, who was betting on me, a big pile of money. It was something I said in a bar one night, and I liked the way it sounded so much I kept telling it. I've been telling it for so many years now, and in such scrupulous detail, that it has become a memory and it's hard for me to remember that it isn't true. I can smell the smoke and beer-soaked carpets, I can hear the cheers of all the men. I can see the bar lights blur and spin, and I can feel the cold iron buck between my thighs, the painted saddle slam against my tailbone, the surprise and pain when my thumb extends too far and I let go. It's a good story, a story that holds my listeners' attention, and although I consider myself almost pathologically honest, I have somehow allowed myself this one small lie.

And watching Monte ride off through the long grains, I thought about the way we invent ourselves through our stories, and in a similar way, how the stories we tell put walls around our lives. And I think that may be true about cowboys. That there really isn't much truth in my saying cowboys are my weakness; maybe, after all this time, it's just something I've learned how to say.

I felt the hoofbeats in the ground long after Monte's white shirt and ratty hat melded with the sun. When I couldn't even pretend to feel them anymore, I got in the car and headed for the hard road.

I listened to country music the whole way to Cody, Wyoming. The men in the songs were all either brutal or inexpressive and always sorry later. The women were victims, every one. I started to think about coming back to the ranch to visit Monte, about another night dancing, about another night wanting the impossible love of a country song, and I thought:

This is not my happy ending.

This is not my story.

1992

■　　　■　　　■

CHARLES JOHNSON

KWOON

David Lewis' martial-arts *kwoon*[1] was in a South Side Chicago neighborhood so rough he nearly had to fight to reach the door. Previously,
it had been a dry cleaner's, then a small Thai restaurant, and although
he Lysol-scrubbed the buckled linoleum floors and burned jade
incense for the Buddha before each class, the studio was a blend of
pungent odors, the smell of starched shirts and the tang of cinnamon
pastries riding alongside the sharp smell of male sweat from nightly
workouts. For five months, David had bivouacked on the back-room
floor after his students left, not minding the clank of presses from the
print shop next door, the noisy garage across the street or even the two-
grand bank loan needed to renovate three rooms with low ceilings and
leaky pipes overhead. This was his place, earned after ten years of
training in San Francisco and his promotion to the hard-won title of
sifu.[2]
    As his customers grunted through Tuesday-night warm-up exer-
cises, then drills with Elizabeth, his senior student (she'd been a dancer
and still had the elasticity of Gumby), David stood off to one side to
watch, feeling the force of their *kiais*[3] vibrate in the cavity of his chest,
interrupting them only to correct a student's stance. On the whole, his
students were a hopeless bunch, a Franciscan test of his patience.
Some came to class on drugs; one, Wendell Miller, a retired cook
trying to recapture his youth, was the obligatory senior citizen; a few
were high school dropouts, orange-haired punks who played in rock

1. A place where one studies martial arts or meditation, a hall (Chinese).
2. Teacher (Chinese).
3. Literally, "spirit shout," the shout made when one throws a punch, mainly to concentrate
that punch and force air from the lungs (Japanese).

293

bands with names like Plastic Anus. But David did not despair. He believed he was duty bound to lead them, like the Pied Piper, from Sylvester Stallone movies to a real understanding of the martial arts as a way that prepared the young, through discipline and large doses of humility, to be of use to themselves and others. Accordingly, his sheet of rules said no high school student could be promoted unless he kept a B average, and no dropouts were allowed through the door until they signed up for their G.E.D. exam; if they got straight A's, he took them to dinner. Anyone caught fighting outside his school was suspended. David had been something of a punk himself a decade earlier, pushing nose candy in Palo Alto, living on barbiturates and beer before his own teacher helped him see, to David's surprise, that in his spirit he had resources greater than anything in the world outside. The master's picture was just inside the door, so all could bow to him when they entered David's school. Spreading the style was his rationale for moving to the Midwest, but the hidden agenda, David believed, was an inward training that would make the need for conflict fall away like a chrysalis. If nothing else, he could make their workouts so tiring none of his students would have any energy left for getting into trouble.

Except, he thought, for Ed Morgan.

He was an older man, maybe 40, with a bald spot and razor burns that ran from just below his ears to his throat. This was his second night at the studio, but David realized Morgan knew the calisthenics routine and basic punching drills cold. He'd been in other schools. Any fool could see that, which meant the new student had lied on his application about having no formal training. Unlike David's regular students, who wore the traditional white Chinese T-shirt and black trousers, Morgan had changed into a butternut running suit with black stripes on the sleeves and pants legs. David had told him to buy a uniform the week before, during his brief interview. Morgan refused. And David dropped the matter, noticing that Morgan had pecs and forearms like Popeye. His triceps could have been lifted right off Marvin Hagler.[4] He was thick as a tree, even top-heavy, in David's opinion, and he stood half a head taller than the other students. He didn't *have* a suit to fit Morgan. And Morgan moved so fluidly David caught himself frowning, a little frightened, for it was as though the properties of water and rock had come together in one creature. Then he snapped himself back, laughed at his silliness, looked at the clock—only half an hour of class remained—then clapped his hands loudly. He popped his fin-

---

4. Marvin Hagler (b. 1952), American boxer, middleweight titleholder in the 1980s known for his devastating punches.

gers on his left hand, then his right, as his students, eager for his advice, turned to face him.

"We should do a little sparring now. Pair up with somebody your size. Elizabeth, you work with the new students."

"*Sifu?*"

It was Ed Morgan.

David paused, both lips pressed together.

"If you don't mind, I'd like to spar with you."

One of David's younger students, Toughie, a Filipino boy with a falcon emblazoned on his arm, elbowed his partner, who wore his hair in a stiff Mohawk, and both said, "Uh-oh." David felt his body flush hot, sweat suddenly on his palms like a sprinkling of salt water, though there was no whiff of a challenge, no disrespect in Morgan's voice. His speech, in fact, was as soft and gently syllabled as a singer's. David tried to laugh:

"You sure you want to try me?"

"Please." Morgan bowed his head, which might have seemed self-effacing had he not been so tall and still looking down at David's crown. "It would be a privilege."

Rather than spar, his students scrambled back, nearly falling over themselves to form a circle, as if to ring two gun fighters from opposite ends of town. David kept the slightest of smiles on his lips, even when his mouth tired, to give the impression of masterful indifference—he was, after all, *sifu* here, wasn't he? A little sparring would do him good. Wouldn't it? Especially with a man the size of Morgan. Loosen him up, so to speak.

He flipped his red sash behind him and stepped lower into a cat stance, his weight on his rear leg, his lead foot light and lifted slightly, ready to whip forward when Morgan moved into range.

Morgan was not so obliging. He circled left, away from David's lead leg, then did a half step of broken rhythm to confuse David's sense of distance, and then, before he could change stances, flicked a jab at David's jaw. If his students were surprised, David didn't know, for the room fell away instantly, dissolving as his adrenaline rose and his concentration closed out everything but Morgan—he always needed to get hit once before he got serious—and only he and the other existed, both in motion but pulled out of time, the moment flickerish, fibrous and strangely two-dimensional, yet all too familiar to fighters, perhaps to men falling from heights, to motorists microseconds before a head-on collision, these minutes a spinning mosaic of crescent kicks, back fists and flurry punches that, on David's side, failed. All his techniques fell short of Morgan, who, like a shadow—or Mephistopheles—simply dematerialized before they arrived.

The older man shifted from boxing to *wu*-style *ta'i chi Chuan*.[5] From this he flowed into *pa kua*,[6] then Korean karate: style after style, a blending of a dozen cultures and histories in one blink of an eye after another. With one move, he tore away David's sash. Then he called out each move in Mandarin as he dropped it on David, bomb after bomb, as if this were only an exhibition exercise.

On David's face, blossoms of blood opened like orchids. He knew he was being hurt; two ribs felt broken, but he wasn't sure. He thanked God for endorphins—a body's natural painkiller. He'd not touched Morgan once. Outclassed as he was, all he could do was ward him off, stay out of his way—then not even that when a fist the size of a cantaloupe crashed straight down, driving David to the floor, his ears ringing then, and legs outstretched like a doll's. He wanted to stay down forever but sprang to his feet, sweat stinging his eyes, to salvage one scrap of dignity. He found himself facing the wrong way. Morgan was behind him, his hands on his hips, his head thrown back. Two of David's students laughed.

It was Elizabeth who pressed her sweat-moistened towel under David's bloody nose. Morgan's feet came together. He wasn't even winded. "Thank you, *Sifu*." Mockery, David thought, but his head banged too badly to be sure. The room was still behind heat waves, though sounds were coming back, and now he could distinguish one student from another. His sense of clock time returned. He said, "You're a good fighter, Ed."

Toughie whispered, "No shit, *bwana*.[7]

The room suddenly leaned vertiginously to David's left; he bent his knees a little to steady his balance. "But you're still a beginner in this system." Weakly, he lifted his hand, then let it fall. "Go on with class. Elizabeth, give everybody a new lesson."

"David, I think class is over now."

Over? He thought he knew what that meant. "I guess so. Bow to the master."

His students bowed to the portrait of the school's founder.

"Now to each other."

Again, they bowed, but this time to Morgan.

"Class dismissed."

Some of his students were whooping, slapping Morgan on his back as they made their way to the hallway in back to change. Eliza-

---

5. "Grand Ultimate Fist," one of the principal internal martial arts and the most popular martial art in the world.
6. An internal martial art. There are three of these: the other two are *tai chi chuan* and *hsing-i*.
7. African term for "boss" or "leader."

beth, the only female, stayed behind to let them shower and dress. Both she and the youngest student, Mark, a middle school boy with skin as smooth and pale as a girl's, looked bewildered, uncertain what this drubbing meant.

David limped back to his office, which also was his bedroom, separated from the main room only by a curtain. There, he kept equipment: free weights, a heavy bag on which he'd taped a snapshot of himself—for who else did he need to conquer?—and the rowing machine Elizabeth avoided, calling it Instant Abortion. He sat down for a few seconds at his unvarnished kneehole desk bought cheap at a Salvation Army outlet, then rolled onto the floor, wondering what he'd done wrong. Would another *sifu*, more seasoned, simply have refused to spar with a self-styled beginner?

After a few minutes, he heard them leaving, a couple of students begging Morgan to teach them, and really, this was too much to bear. David, holding his side, his head pulled in, limped back out. "Ed," he coughed, then recovered. "Can I talk to you?"

Morgan checked his watch, a diamond-studded thing that doubled as a stop watch and a thermometer, and probably even monitored his pulse. Half its cost would pay the studio's rent for a year. He dressed well, David saw. Like a retired champion, everything tailored, nothing off the rack. "I've got an appointment, *Sifu*. Maybe later, OK?"

A little dazed, David, swallowing the rest of what he wanted to say, gave a headshake. "OK."

Just before the door slammed, he heard another boy say, "Lewis ain't no fighter, man. He's a dancer." He lay down again in his office, too sore to shower, every muscle tender, strung tight as catgut, searching with the tip of his tongue for broken teeth.

As he was stuffing toilet paper into his right nostril to stop the bleeding, Elizabeth, dressed now in high boots and a baggy coat and slacks, stepped behind the curtain. She'd replaced her contacts with owl-frame glasses that made her look spinsterish. "I'm sorry—he was wrong to do that."

"You mean win?"

"It wasn't supposed to be a real fight! He tricked you. Anyone can score, like he did, if they throw out all the rules."

"Tell him that." Wincing, he rubbed his shoulder. "Do you think anybody will come back on Thursday?" She did not answer. "Do you think I should close the school?" David laughed, bleakly. "Or just leave town?"

"David, you're a good teacher. A *sifu* doesn't always have to win, does he? It's not about winning, is it?"

No sooner had she said this than the answer rose between them.

Could you be a doctor whose every patient died? A credible mathematician who couldn't count? By the way the world and, more important, his students reckoned things, he was a fraud. Elizabeth hitched the strap on her workout bag, which was big enough for both of them to climb into, higher on her shoulder. "Do you want me to stick around?"

"No."

"You going to put something on that eye?"

Through the eye Morgan hadn't closed, she looked flattened, like a coin, her skin flushed and her hair faintly damp after a workout, so lovely David wanted to fall against her, blend with her—disappear. Only, it would hurt now to touch or be touched. And, unlike some teachers he knew, his policy was to take whatever he felt for a student—the erotic electricity that sometimes arose—and transform it into harder teaching, more time spent on giving them their money's worth. Besides, he was always broke; his street clothes were old enough to be in elementary school: a 30-year-old man no better educated than Toughie or Mark, who'd concentrated on shop in high school. Elizabeth was another story: a working mother, a secretary on the staff at the University of Illinois at Chicago, surrounded all day by professors who looked young enough to be graduate students. A job sweet as this, from David's level, seemed high-toned and secure. What could he offer Elizabeth? Anyway, this might be the last night he saw her, if she left with the others, and who could blame her? He studied her hair, how it fell onyx-black and abundant, like some kind of blessing over and under her collar, which forced Elizabeth into the unconscious habit of tilting her head just so and flicking it back with her fingers, a gesture of such natural grace it made his chest ache. She was so much lovelier than she knew. To his surprise, a line from *Psalms* came to him, "I will praise thee, for I am fearfully and wonderfully made." Whoever wrote that, he thought, meant it for her.

He looked away. "Go on home."

"We're having class on Thursday?"

"You paid until the end of the month, didn't you?"

"I paid for six months, remember?"

He did—she was literally the one who kept the light bill paid. "Then we'll have class."

All that night and half the next day David stayed horizontal, hating Morgan. Hating himself more. It took him hours to stop shaking. That night it rained. He fended off sleep, listening to the patter with his full attention, hoping its music might have something to tell him. Twice he belched up blood, then a paste of phlegm and hamburger pulp. Jesus, he thought, distantly, I'm sick. By nightfall, he was able to sit awhile and take a little soup, but he could not stand. Both his legs ballooned so tightly in his trousers he had to cut the cloth with scissors and peel it off like strips of bacon. Parts of his body were burning, refusing to obey him. He reached into his desk drawer for Morgan's application and saw straightaway that Ed Morgan couldn't spell. David smiled ruefully, looking for more faults. Morgan listed his address in Skokie, his occupation as a merchant marine, and provided no next of kin to call in case of emergencies.

That was all, and David for the life of him could not see that night, or the following morning, how he could face anyone in the studio again. Painfully, he remembered his promotion a year earlier. His teacher had held a ceremonial Buddhist candle, the only light in his darkened living room in a house near the Mission District[8] barely bigger than a shed. David, kneeling, held a candle, too. "The light that was given to me," said his teacher, repeating an invocation two centuries old, "I now give to you." He touched his flame to the wick of David's candle, passing the light, and David's eyes burned with tears. For the first time in his life, he felt connected to cultures and people he'd never seen—to traditions larger than himself.

His high school instructors had dismissed him as unteachable. Were they right? David wondered. Was he made of wood too flimsy ever to amount to anything? Suddenly, he hated those teachers, as well as the ones at Elizabeth's school, but only for a time, hatred being so sharp an emotion, like the business end of a bali-song knife, he could never hang on to it for long—perhaps that was why he failed as a fighter—and soon he felt nothing, only numbness. As from a great distance, he watched himself sponge-bathe in the sink, dress himself slowly and prepare for Thursday's class, the actions previously fueled by desire, by concern over consequences, by fear of outcome, replaced now by something he could not properly name, as if a costly operation once powered by coal had reverted overnight to the water wheel.

When six o'clock came and only Mark, Wendell, and Elizabeth showed, David telephoned a few students, learning from parents, roommates and live-in lovers that none were home. With Morgan, he suspected. So that's who he called next.

"Sure," said Morgan. "A couple are here. They just wanted to talk."

"They're missing class."

"I didn't ask them to come."

Quietly, David drew breath deeply just to see if he could. It hurt,

8. A poor section of San Francisco.

so he stopped, letting his wind stay shallow, swirling at the top of his lungs. He pulled a piece of dead skin off his hand. "Are you coming back?"

"I don't see much point in that, do you?"

In the background he could hear voices, a television and beer cans being opened. "You've fought professionally, haven't you?"

"That was a long time ago—overseas. Won two, lost two, then I quit," said Morgan. "It doesn't count for much."

"Did you teach?"

"Here and there. Listen," he said, "why did you call?"

"Why did you en*roll?*"

"I've been out of training. I wanted to see how much I remembered. What do you want me to say? I won't come back, all right? What do you want from me, Lewis?"

He did not know. He felt the stillness of his studio, a similar stillness in himself, and sat quiet so long he could have been posing for a portrait. Then:

"You paid for a week in advance. I owe you another lesson."

Morgan snorted. "In what—Chinese ballet?"

"Fighting," said David. "A private lesson in *budo.*[9] I'll keep the studio open until you get here." And then he hung up.

Morgan circled the block four times before finding a parking space across from Lewis' school. Why hurry? Ten, maybe 15 minutes he waited, watching the open door, wondering what the boy (and he was a boy to Morgan's eye) wanted. He'd known too many kids like this one. They took a few classes, promoted themselves to seventh *dan,*[1] then opened a storefront *dojo*[2] that was no better than a private stage, a theater for the ego, a place where they could play out fantasies of success denied them on the street, in school, in dead-end jobs. They were phony, Morgan thought, like almost everything in the modern world, which was a subject he could spend hours deriding, though he seldom did, his complaints now being tiresome even to his own ears. *Losers,* he thought, who strutted around in fancy Oriental costumes, refusing to spar or show their skill. "Too advanced for beginners," they claimed, or, "My *sensei*[3] made me promise not to show that to anyone." Hogwash. He could see through that shit. All over America he'd seen

9. The art of fighting (Japanese).
1. Referring to "rank," as in fifth dan or fifth level of achievement (Japanese); applies to ranks above black belt.
2. Same as "kwoon": a place to study fighting (Japanese).
3. Teacher, or "one who has gone before" (Japanese).

them, and India, too, where they weren't called fakirs[4] for nothing. And they'd made him suffer. They made him pay for the "privilege" of their teachings. In 20 years as a merchant marine, he'd been in as many schools in Europe, Japan, Korea and Hong Kong, submitting himself to the lunacy of illiterate fak(e)irs—men who claimed they could slay an opponent with their breath or *ch'i*[5]—and simply because his hunger to learn was insatiable. So he had no rank anywhere. He could tolerate no "master" 's posturing long enough to ingratiate himself into the inner circles of any school—though 80 percent of these fly-by-night *dojos* bottomed out inside a year. And, hell, he was a bilge rat, never in any port long enough to move up in rank. Still, he had killed men. It was depressingly easy. Killed them in back alleys in Tokyo with blows so crude no master would include such inelegant means among "traditional" techniques.

More hogwash, thought Morgan. He'd probably done the boy good by exposing him. His own collarbones had been broken twice, each leg three times, all but two fingers smashed, and his nose reshaped so often he couldn't remember its original contours. On wet nights, he had trouble breathing. But why complain? You couldn't make an omelet without breaking a few eggs.

And yet, Morgan thought, squinting at the door of the school, there was a side to Lewis he'd liked. At first, he had felt comfortable, as if he had at last found the *kwoon* he'd been looking for. True, Lewis had come on way too cocky when asked to spar, but what could you expect when he was hardly older than the high school kids he was teaching? And maybe teaching them well, if he was really going by that list of rules he handed out to beginners. And it wasn't so much that Lewis was a bad fighter, only that he, Morgan, was about five times better because whatever he lacked now in middle age—flexibility and youth's fast reflexes—he more than made up for in size and experience, which was a polite word for dirty tricks. Give Lewis a few more years, a little more coaching in the combat strategies Morgan could show him, and he might become a champion.

But who did he think he was fooling? Things never worked out that way. There was always too much ego in it. Something every *sifu* figured he had to protect, or save face about. A lesson in *budo?* Christ, he'd nearly killed this kid, and there he was, barking on the telephone like Saddam Hussein before the bombing started, even begging for the ground war to begin. And that was just all right, if a showdown—a

---

4. "Fakir": an Indian holy man.
5. Inner spirit or life force (Chinese); also means internal energy.

duel—was what he wanted. Morgan set his jaw and stepped onto the pavement of the parking lot. However things went down, he decided, the consequences would be on Lewis—it would be *his* call.

Locking his car, then double-checking each door (this was a rough neighborhood, even by Morgan's standards), he crossed the street, carrying his workout bag under his arm, the last threads of smog-filtered twilight fading into darkness, making the door of the *kwoon* a bright portal chiseled from blocks of glass and cement. A few feet from the entrance, he heard voices. Three students had shown. Most of the class had not. The two who had visited him weren't there. He'd lectured them on his experience of strangling an assailant in Kyoto, and Toughie had gone quiet, looked edgy (fighting didn't seem like fun then) and uneasy. Finally, they left, which was fine with Morgan. He didn't want followers. Sycophants made him sick. All he wanted was a teacher he could respect.

Inside the school's foyer, he stopped, his eyes tracking the room. He never entered closed spaces too quickly or walked near corners or doorways on the street. Toward the rear, by a rack filled with halberds and single-edged broadswords, a girl about five, with piles of ebony hair and blue eyes like splinters of the sky, was reading a dog-eared copy of *The Cat in the Hat.* This would be the child of the class leader, he thought, bowing quickly at the portrait of the school's founder. But why bring her here? It cemented his contempt for this place, more a daycare center than a *kwoon.* Still, he bowed a second time to the founder. Him he respected. Where were such grand old stylists when you needed them? He did not see Lewis, or any other student until, passing the curtained office, Morgan whiffed food cooking on a hot plate and, parting the curtain slightly, he saw Wendell, who would never in this life learn to fight, stirring and seasoning a pot of couscous. He looked like that children's toy, Mr. Potato Head. Morgan wondered, Why did David Lewis encourage the man? Just to take his money? He passed on, feeling his tread shake the floor, into the narrow hall where a few hooks hung for clothing, and found Elizabeth with her left foot on a low bench, lacing the wrestling shoes she wore for working out.

"Excuse me," he said. "I'll wait until you're finished."

Their eyes caught for a moment.

"I'm done now." She kicked her bag under the bench, squeezed past Morgan by flattening herself to the wall, as if he had a disease, then spun round at the entrance and looked squarely at him. "You know something?"

"What?"

"You're wrong. Just *wrong.*"

"I don't know what you're talking about."

"The hell you don't! David may not be the fighter, the killer, you are, but he *is* one of the best teachers in this system."

Morgan smirked. "Those who can't do, teach, eh?"

She burned a look of such hatred at Morgan he turned his eyes away. When he looked back, she was gone. He sighed. He'd seen that look on so many faces, yellow, black, and white, after he'd punched them in. It hardly mattered anymore. Quietly, he suited up, stretched his arms wide and padded barefoot back onto the main floor, prepared to finish this, if that was what Lewis wanted, for why else would he call?

But at first he could not catch sight of the boy. The others were standing around him in a circle, chatting, oddly like chess pieces shielding an endangered king. His movements were jerky and Chaplinesque, one arm around Elizabeth, the other braced on Wendell's shoulder. Without them, he could not walk until his bruised ankles healed. He was temporarily blind in one blackened, beefed-over eye. And since he could not tie his own sash, Mark was doing it for him. None of them noticed Morgan, but in the school's weak light, he could see blue welts he'd raised like crops on Lewis' cheeks and chest. That, and something else. The hands of the others rested on Lewis' shoulder, his back, as if he belonged to them, no matter what he did or didn't do. Weak as Lewis looked now, even the old cook Wendell could blow him over, and somehow it didn't matter if he was beaten every round, or missed class, or died. The others were the *kwoon*. It wasn't his school. It was theirs. Maybe brought together by the boy, Morgan thought, but now a separate thing living beyond him. To prove the system, the teaching here, false, he would have to strike down every one of them. And still he would have touched nothing.

"Ed," Lewis said, looking over Mark's shoulder. "When we were sparring, I saw mistakes in your form, things someone better than me might take advantage of. I'd like to correct them, if you're ready."

"What things?" His head snapped back. "What mistakes?"

"I can't match your reach," said Lewis, "but someone who could, getting inside your guard, would go for your groin or knee. It's the way you stand, probably a blend of a couple of styles you learned somewhere. But they don't work together. If you do this," he added, torquing his leg slightly so that his thigh guarded his groin, "the problem is solved."

"Is that why you called me?"

"No, there's another reason."

Morgan tensed; he should have known. "You do some warm-up exercises we've never seen. I like them. I want you to lead class tonight, if that's OK, so the others can learn them, too." Then he laughed. "I think I should warm the bench tonight."

Before he could reply, Lewis limped off, leaning on Mark, who led him back to his office. The two others waited for direction from Morgan. For a moment, he shifted his weight uncertainly from his right foot to his left, pausing until his tensed shoulders relaxed and the tight fingers on his right hand, coiled into a fist, opened. Then he pivoted toward the portrait of the founder. "Bow to the master." They bowed. "Now to our teacher." They did so, bowing toward the curtained room, with Morgan, a big man, bending deepest of all.

1991

THE BLACK LIGHTS

Commander Andy Hawkins, chief psychiatrist of the neuropsych ward at Camp Pendleton, received the inevitable nickname Eaglebeak, or Eagle, early in his first tour in Vietnam when a crazy Marine attacked him out of the clear blue and bit off his nose. It became a serious medical event when Commander Hawkins developed a resistant staph infection in his sinuses, which quickly spread to his brain—a danger that is always present with face wounds. To complicate matters, Hawkins was allergic to the first antibiotics administered to him and went into anaphylactic shock. When that was finally controlled, his kidneys shut down, and he had to be placed on dialysis, as the infection continued to run rampant through his system. Hawkins developed a raging fever and had to be wrapped in ice blankets for two days, and weeks later, after his kidneys and immune system kicked in again, he came down with hepatitis B and nearly died from that. He resigned his commission, quit doctoring altogether for a time, and went to the Menninger Foundation in Kansas, where he did some work—work on himself. He wanted to regain some compassion for his fellow man before trying to go back into private practice, but his dreams of a successful civilian career were destroyed by the fact that he had no nose. He wore a tin nose, complete with a head strap, crafted by a Vietnamese peasant, and it made him an object of ridicule, led to a divorce from his wife, and prompted him to rejoin the Navy, where it didn't really matter that much what you looked like if you had enough rank. It mattered socially—at the Officers' Club and so on—but not on the job.

Commander Hawkins started out with a plastic prosthetic nose, but it was easily detectable, so he decided to make the best of a bad situation by wearing the tin nose and being up front about it. He was always quick to point out that he, more than anyone, realized how absurd his condition was, and in doing so he attenuated in part the sniggering he was subjected to for wearing a tin nose. What bothered him more was what he imagined people said about it in private. He became a virtual paranoid in this regard.

I was sent to Pendleton's neuropsych facility—that bleak, austere nuthouse—some weeks after defending my title as the 1st Marine Division Middleweight Champ in a boxing smoker at Camp Las Pulgas. I lost on a KO. My injuries resulted in a shocking loss of weight, headaches, double vision, and strange, otherworldly spells. EEG readings taken at the hospital indicated that I had a lesion on my left temporal lobe from a punch to the temple that had put me out cold for over an hour. I was a boxer with over a hundred and fifty fights, and I had taken a lot of shots, but this last punch was the hardest I had ever received and the first punch ever to put me down. I had seen stars before from big punches; I had seen pinwheels; but after that shot to the temple I saw the worst thing you ever see in boxing—I saw the black lights.

There I sat in a corner of the dayroom on the kelly-green floor tiles, dressed in a uniform of pajamas and bathrobe, next to a small, tightly coiled catatonic named Joe, who wore a towel on his shoulder. Here in this corner—the most out-of-the-way place in the ward—was one of the few windows. Occasionally a Marine would freak out and bolt for the window, jump up on the sill, shake the security screen, and scream "I want to die!" or "I can't take it anymore, let me out of this motherfucker!" At these times Joe would actually move a little. By that I mean he would tilt to the left to give the screamer a little space. Except for me and one of the corpsmen, Joe would not let anyone touch him or feed him or change him.

As I said, Joe wore a towel on his shoulder. He drooled constantly, and he would grunt in gratitude when I dabbed his mouth dry. Joe gave off a smell. Schizophrenics give off a smell, and you get used to it. Sometimes, however, it would get so bad that I could swear I saw colors coming off Joe—shades of blue, red, and violet—and to get away from it I would get up and walk over to the wall-mounted cigarette lighter, a spiral electrical device much like the cigarette lighters in cars. The staff didn't trust us with open flames or razor blades.

Sitting next to Joe, I would chain smoke Camels until the Thorazine and phenobarbital that Eagle had prescribed to contain my agitated restlessness got to be too much and I fell into heavy, unpleasant dreams, or I had a fit and woke up on the tile with piss and shit in my pants—alone, neglected, a pariah. The same corpsman who changed

Joe would change me. The others would let you lie in your filth until the occasional doctor or nurse came in and demanded that they take action.

I was having ten to twenty spells a day during my first month, and I was so depressed that I refused to talk to anyone, especially when some of the fits marched into full-blown grand-mal seizures, which caused me much shame and confusion. I refused to see the buddies from my outfit who came by to visit me, and I did not answer my mail or take calls from my family. But as I got used to the Thorazine I began to snap out of my fits quicker. I began to shave and brush my teeth, and mingle with the rest of the neuropsych population. With Eagle as my living example, I had decided I would make the best of a bad situation; I would adjust to it and get on with my life.

As a rule, there were about thirty men in our ward—the Security Ward, where they kept the craziest, most volatile marines in all of Pendleton. Eagle seemed to regard me as super-volatile, although I was anything but at the time. He always kept me at arm's length, but he would get right in and mix with really dangerous, really spooky whacked-out freaks. I figured he was afraid of me because of my history as a recon marine with three tours in Nam, or because I had been a boxer. But he was a doctor, and his professional fear made me wonder about myself.

One day a great big black man named Gothia came into the ward. I had been there about two months, and this was the first new admission I had witnessed. He was extra-big, extra-black, extra-muscular, and extra-crazy. Gothia was into a manic episode and talking fast: there was a Buick waiting outside with a general in it, and he and Gothia were going to fly off to the Vatican, where the pope urgently awaited Gothia's expertise concerning the impending apocalypse. He kept repeating, "It's going to come like a thief in the night—a thief in the night!" until he had everyone half believing that the end of the world was at hand. I immediately liked Gothia. He made things interesting in the ward. As my hair got long, Gothia arranged with the other brothers to give me a hair treatment, a kind of pompadour. It looked like shit, but I was flattered to be admitted into the company of the brothers, which was difficult, my being white and a sergeant and a lifer and all.

A few weeks after he arrived, Gothia bolted unseen up the fence in the exercise yard, did the Fosbury Flop over the barbed wire that topped it, and returned with a six-pack of cold malt liquor. I drank three as fast as possible on an empty stomach and had my first cheap satori[1]—though whether it was epilepsy or the blast from the alcohol

1. A state of spiritual enlightenment sought in Zen Buddhism.

is difficult to say. As I finished a fourth can of the malt liquor, sitting against the fence in the warmth of the golden sun, I realized that everything was for the best. Years later, I read a passage from Nietzsche that articulated what I felt in that fifteen-second realization: "Becoming is justified . . . war is a means to achieve balance. . . . Is the world full of guilt, injustice, contradiction and suffering? Yes, cries Heraclitus,[2] but only for the limited man who does not see the total design; not for the contuitive God; for him all contradiction is harmonized."

Weird. Sleeping in the neuropsych ward at night, I sensed the presence of a very large rabbit under my bunk. A seven-foot rabbit with brown fur and skin sores, who took long, raking breaths. I didn't want to do it, but I had to keep getting out of bed to look. Gothia, who never slept, finally came over and asked me what was the matter, and when I told him about the rabbit he chuckled sympathetically. "Hey, man, there's no *rabbit*. Just take it easy and get some rest, baby. Can you dig it? Rabbit. Shit." But by and by my compulsive rabbit checks got on his nerves, until one night he came over to my bed and said, "I told you there was no rabbit under the bed. If you don't stop this shit, I am going to pinch you." He said it louder than he meant to, and the corpsman on watch came over with his flashlight and told Gothia that if he didn't get to bed he was going to write him up. I lay in the darkness and waited and listened to the rabbit breathe like an asthmatic until I had to check again, whereupon Gothia popped up in his bed and pointed his finger at me and shouted, "There ain't no goddamn rabbit, goddamn it! Knock that shit off!"

I shouted back at him. "It's that rabbit on the Br'er Rabbit molasses jar. That rabbit with buckles on his shoes! Bow tie. Yaller teeth! Yaller! Yaller!" For causing such a commotion we were both shot up, and put in isolation rooms. It was my first experience with a straitjacket, and I nearly lost it. I forced myself to lie still, and it seemed that my brain was filled with sawdust and that centipedes, roaches, and other insects were crawling through it. I could taste brown rabbit fur in my teeth. I had a horror that the rabbit would come in the room, lie on my face, and suffocate me.

After my day of isolation, a brig rat, a white marine named Rouse, came up to me and said, "Hey—you can tell me—you're faking this shit so you can get out of the service, aren't you?" Rouse, an S-1 clerk-typist, a "Remington raider" who had picked up a heroin habit in Saigon, had violet slash marks on his arms, and liked to show me a razorblade half he had in his wallet. He offered to let me use it and often

2. Greek philosopher (ca. 540–480 B.C.) known for his thesis that life is "atoms in the void."

suggested that we use it together. Rouse had a lot of back pay saved up and ordered candy and cigarettes from the commissary, and innumerable plastic airplanes to assemble. He always claimed to have nasal congestion and ordered Vicks Inhalers, which at that time contained Benzedrine. Rouse would break them open and swallow the cottons and then pour airplane glue on a washcloth and roll it into a tube and suck on it. I got high with Rouse once by doing this, but the Benzedrine made me so restless that I begged Thorazine from the guys who used to cheek it and then spit it out after meds were issued.

Actually, Rouse was wrong about me: I didn't have anything to hide, and I wasn't faking anything. At the time, I didn't want out. I intended to make the Marine Corps my home. At group-therapy sessions I reasonably insisted that mine was a straightforward case of epilepsy, and for this I was ridiculed by inmate enemies and the medical staff alike. When I saw I was getting nowhere, I refused to speak at the group-therapy sessions at all, and I spent a month sitting sullenly, listening to everyone argue over an old record-player one of the residents had brought in to spice up the dayroom. The blacks liked Smokey Robinson and the Miracles; the war vets were big on the Doors, the Rolling Stones, and CCR. I started getting fat from inactivity—fat, although the food was cold and tasted lousy, and in spite of the fact that I fasted on Fridays, because Thursday's dinner was always rabbit. The thought of eating rabbit after a night of sensing the molasses rabbit under my bed gasping for air, and hearing the air whistle between his yellow teeth as he sucked desperately to live—the sight of fried rabbit put me off food for a solid day.

When I had been on the ward about six months and my fits were under better control, a patient named Chandler was admitted. Chandler was a college graduate. His degree was in French. He had joined the Marine Corps to become a fighter pilot but quickly flunked out of flight school and was left with a six-year enlistment as a grunt, which was unbearable to him. I wasn't sure if he was going out of his way to camp things up so he could get a Section Eight discharge,[3] or if he always acted like a fairy. No one held it against him. In fact, a number of the borderline patients quickly became devotees of his and were swishing around with limp wrists, putting on skits and whatnot, and smoking Chandler's cigarette of choice—Salem. Rouse was the first to join in with Chandler by wearing scarves, kerchiefs, and improvised makeup. Rouse even changed his name to Tallulah.

But Chandler wasn't just some stupid fairy. He was erudite, well

3. An honorable discharge for psychiatric reasons.

read, and well mannered. He had been to Europe. Chandler turned me on to Kafka and Paul Valéry. He knew how to work the library system, and soon I found that as long as I had a good book I did not mind the ward half as much.

Under Chandler's influence, Gothia somehow became convinced that he was Little Richard. After about the five hundredth time I heard Gothia howl, "It's Saturday night and I just got paid," and Chandler respond, "That's better, but try and put a little more pizzazz in your delivery!" I was glad to see Gothia go. They transferred him to a long-term-care psychiatric facility in North Carolina. In truth, Gothia was pretty good as Little Richard. He was better at it than Chandler was at Bette Davis or Marlene Dietrich—although at that time I had never seen Marlene Dietrich and had no basis for comparison.

Overwhelmed by boredom one afternoon in the dayroom, as we watched Chandler execute yet another "grand entrance" (a little pivot with a serious lip pout and a low and sultry "Hello, darling"), I confided to Rouse that I suspected Eagle of being a "closet" faggot, and shortly afterward I was called into the Eagle's den for a rare appointment. Obviously Rouse had snitched on me. I told Eagle that I thought he was a homosexual because he had surfing posters in his office, and I watched him scribble three pages of notes about this. Eagle's desk was cramped, and his office was hot in spite of a pair of twelve-inch portable fans beating like they could use a couple of shots of lightweight motor oil, and I began to perspire heavily as I watched Eagle write. He was a spectacle—a tall man, cadaverously thin, with his long, angular legs crossed tightly at the knees, his ass perched on the front edge of his chair as he chain-smoked with one hand, flicking ashes into a well-filled ashtray on his desk while he scribbled at the notepad on his lap with his other hand; turning pages, lighting fresh cigarettes off the butts of old ones, scribbling, flipping the pad, seemingly oblivious of me until he looked up and confronted me with that incredible tin nose. "Do you realize that you are sweating?"

"It's hot."

"It's hot," he repeated. He looked down at his notepad and proceeded to write a volume.

By now I was drenched with sweat, having something very much like a panic attack. Without looking up, Eagle said, "You're hyperventilating."

Everything was getting swirly. Eagle dashed out his cigarette and reached into a drawer, withdrawing a stained paper sack from McDonald's. "Here," he said. "Breathe into this."

I took the bag and started breathing into it. "It isn't working," I said between breaths.

"Just give it a minute. Have you ever done this before? Hyperventilated?"

"Oh, God, no." I felt like I was dying.

Eagle pushed himself back in his chair and placed his hands on his knees. "There's more at work here than just a seizure disorder," he said. "I'm seeing some psychopathology."

"It's that fucking nose," I said, gasping. "I'm freaking out."

"You don't like the nose?" Eagle said. "Well, how do you think I feel about the nose? What am I supposed to do, go off on some island like Robinson Crusoe and hide?"

"I didn't mean that," I said. "It's just—"

"It's just too fucking weird, isn't it, Sergeant?"

"Yes, sir," I said. "Not normally, I mean, but I'm on all this medicine. You've got to cut back my dosage. I can't handle it."

"I'll make you a deal. I'm going to cut you back if you do something for me."

The paper bag finally started to work, and everything began to settle down. "What?"

Eagle removed a notepad and pencil from his desk. "Take this. I want you to jot down your feelings every day. This is just between you and me. I mean, it can be anything. If you were a kind of breakfast cereal, for instance, what would you be? Would you be—oatmeal? Would you be—mush? Would you be—FrankenBerries? Would you be—Count Chocula?" Eagle reclined in his chair, extracted a Lucky Strike, and lit it—with the same effeminate gestures, I noted, that Chandler used to light his Salems. Eagle had very broad shoulders for such a thin man. The sleeves of his tropical uniform were rolled up past his elbows. He brushed what few strands of hair he had back across his shiny pate. It was impossible to ignore his nose. He looked like an enormous carrion bird, and although I knew I could break him in pieces, he terrified me. He took a deep drag and exhaled through his thin nose. "Would you be—a Wheatie?"

"Don't try to fuck with my head!" I protested, crushing the McDonald's sack. I got up and stalked out of Eagle's office, but that night, when I went to bed, I found the notepad and pencil on top of my footlocker.

To disprove Eagle's theory that I was borderline psycho, I began to write what I thought were mundane and ordinary things in the diary, things which I thought proved my mental health, e.g., "A good day. Read. Played volleyball and had a good time smoking with the brothers. Picked up a lot of insight in group. Favorite breakfast: Shit on a Shingle. Two hundred push-ups. Happy, happy, happy!" I found such a release in writing that I started a diary of my own—a real one, a secret one, which I recently glanced through, noting that the quality of my penmanship was very shaky.

JANUARY 11, 1975: Sick.
JANUARY 13, 1975: Sick. Managed to read from Schopenhauer.
JANUARY 15, 1975: Borrowed some reading glasses and read Cioran. Sickness unto death. Better in the evening. Constipated. Food here is awful. There are bugs crawling on the wall and through the sawdust that is my brain. My personality is breaking down? I am having a nervous breakdown? Curiously I don't have the "stink" of schizophrenia.
MARCH 14, 1975: Vertigo. Double vision. Sick. Can't eat.
MARCH 18, 1975: There is a smell. A mousy smell.
APRIL 34, 2007: *I am a boxer dog of championship lineage dating back to the late nineteenth century, when the breed was brought to a high point of development in Germany. I have a short, clean brindle coat involving a pattern of black stripes over a base coat of golden fawn. At seventy-five pounds, I am considered large for a female. My muzzle is broad and gracefully carried, giving balance and symmetry to my head. In repose or when I am deep in thought my face is the very picture of dignified nobility.*
APRIL 40: *My under jaw is somewhat longer than the upper jaw and is turned up at the end, as it should be. The jaw projects just enough to afford a maximum of grasping power and holding power (but without the exaggeration and underbite you sometimes see in poorly bred or inbred boxers). Once my jaws are clamped on something it cannot escape.*

My entire muzzle is black. My nose is completely black, the nostrils wide and flaring. My eyes are of a deep brown and are set deeply in the skull. I do not have that liquid, soft expression you see in spaniels, but rather assertive eyes that can create a menacing and baleful effect when I am irritable. This is particularly the case when I fix my piercing stare on its target. I can burn a hole through steel and escape this Mickey Mouse jail anytime I want, and I will as soon as I get my rest. Arf!
APRIL 55: *Before my accident I was a circus performer with the simple-minded animal consciousness of the here-and-now. That I had been a great hero of the circus—the dog shot from cannons, the dog that dove from fifty-foot platforms into shallow barrels of water, the dog that rode galloping stallions bareback—that I was Boris, the Great One, a celebrated hero of Mother Russia, beloved by my countrymen meant . . . nothing to me.*

Eagle has me back in his little office, and he confronts me not only with my fake diary but with my real one as well. I'm pissed that they've been rummaging through my personal gear.

"Let me get this straight. You say you were this circus dog in Russia, and you got a brain injury when you were *shot from a cannon?*"

"I forgot to wear my safety helmet."

"So a famous neurosurgeon put your brains back together and sent you to a health spa—"

"Only the VIPs went there. Nikita K. was there. I knew him. Dancers from the Bolshoi. Army generals. KGB officials. Chess champions."

"And you . . . a dog?"

"I wasn't *just* a dog. I was the Rin Tin Tin of Russia."

"You're pretty bright and well informed. How can you know all this kind of thing?"

"Because it's true," I said.

"How would you like it if I sent you to the brig?"

"Fine. The brig would be fine. I'm a howlin' wolf. Put me in a cage or let me go."

Eagle drummed his fingers on his desk, changing pace. "Tell me something. What does this old saying mean to you? 'People who live in glass houses shouldn't throw stones'?" Finger drumming. "Well?"

"I don't know—"

" 'A rolling stone gathers no moss.' What does that mean?"

"Don't know."

Eagle began to write furiously.

"Why would anyone live in a glass house? It would be hot," I said. "And everyone could see you."

"I hear you like to read Kafka. That's heavy stuff for a young guy. You're pretty bright. Have you ever read any books on abnormal psychology?"

"Hey, man, just let me out of this motherfucker. I'm going down in this place. Put me in a normal ward and let me see a real doctor."

"I'll give it some thought. In the meantime, I'd like you to check this out," Eagle said, clapping me on the shoulder. He handed me a copy of *Love Against Hate*, by Karl Menninger.

STARLOG, JANUFEB, 2010: "Gate is straight/Deep and wide/Break on through to the other side. . . ."

There was an old piano in the dayroom. When a Marine freaked out and broke the record-player, Chandler started playing the piano day and night—driving me crazy. "Canadian Sunset" over and over and over again! One night I rubbed cigarette ashes all over myself for camouflage, crawled into the dayroom recon style, and snapped off the little felt hammers inside the piano. Shoulda seen the look on Chandler's face when he sat down to play. This was not insane behavior. I knew I was not really insane. I was just a garden-variety epileptic temporarily off my game. Thrown a little by the war. I laughed and said to

Chandler, "Hey man, what's the sound of one hand clapping?"

After I put the piano out of commission, I noticed Chandler was losing weight. They had him on some new medication. He quit camping around and took a troubled leap into the darkness of his own soul. He grew quiet and started sitting in the corner with catatonic Joe. A black Marine, a rotund and powerful murderer from South Carolina named Bobby Dean Steele, was admitted to the ward for observation, and he began to dominate. Despite the charges pending against him, he was buoyant and cheerful. He walked over to Joe's corner a lot and would say, "Joe-be-doe, what's happening? What's the matter, man? You saw some bad shit in the Nam, didn't you? Well, that's okay. We're going to fix you up—not those doctors, but us, the jarheads. We'll help you. I know you can hear me. Go easy, man."

Bobby Dean Steele gave Joe back rubs and wiped his face and in a matter of a few days was leading him around the ward in a rigid, shuffle-step fashion. The patients began to rally around Joe, and soon everyone was giving him hugs and reassuring him. One of the corpsmen warned me that catatonics often snap out of their rigid stupors to perform sudden acts of extreme violence. It was a catatonic who had bitten off Eagle's nose, he said.

For a brief period during Bobby Dean Steele's tenure, my temporal-lobe visions jumped more and more into grand-mal seizures. Just before the fits, instead of having other-worldly spells, I felt only fear and would see the black lights of boxing. I was having very violent fits. In one of these I bit my tongue nearly in half, and for two weeks I sat in Joe's corner with Chandler, overloaded on anticonvulsants. My corpsman came by with a little spray bottle and sprayed my tongue. It had swollen so much that I could not shut my mouth, and it stank. It stank worse than schizophrenia, and even the schizophrenics complained. Bobby Dean Steele and I got into a fist-fight over the tongue, and I was amazed at my ability to spring into action, since I felt nearly comatose when he came over to the corner and started jawing at me, kicking at me with his shower shoes. I got up punching and dropped him with a left hook to the jaw. The sound of his huge body hitting the tile was like that of a half-dozen rotten melons dropped on concrete. Bobby Dean Steele had to be helped to the seclusion room, but I was not required to go there, nor was I shot up. I guess it was because my tongue made me look miserable enough.

When Bobby Dean Steele came out of isolation, he was so heavily loaded on Thorazine that his spunk was gone, and without his antics and good cheer there was suddenly no "character" on the ward. Joe, who had seemed to be coming out of his catatonia, reverted back to it, but rather than seeking out his corner, he assumed and maintained impossible positions of waxy flexibility wherever he happened to be. It was like some kind of twisted yoga. I had heard that Joe had been at Khe Sanh[4] during the siege and, like Jake Barnes in *The Sun Also Rises*, received a groin wound—that he had lost his coconuts. I often wonder why that is considered such a terrible thing. I brought this up and was roundly put down. Better to lose your sight, arms, legs, hearing, said Rouse. Only Chandler, who rarely spoke up anymore, agreed with me. "If there was a hot-fudge sundae on one side of the room and a young Moroccan stud with a cock like a bronze sculpture on the other," he said, "I'd make for the ice cream."

Eagle came to Chandler's rescue, just as he had bailed me out for a while with the diary idea. Eagle appointed Chandler his clerk, and in a few weeks Chandler began to put on weight. As a clerk, he was allowed to leave the ward under the escort of one of the corpsmen. Invariably he went into Oceanside to the bookstores or to restaurants to gorge on big meals. He brought me delicious food in doggie bags, and books: Dostoyevski, Spinoza, Sartre—the writers he insisted I read—and the lighter stuff I preferred. I was reading a lot and having fewer seizures; I had begun to get better. Chandler was better, too, and up to his old mischief. He constantly mimicked his new boss, and his devastating imitations were so accurate that they actually made me realize how much I respected Eagle, who had the advantages of a good education and presumably had a history of confidence and self-esteem, but now, with his tin nose, had been cut adrift from the human race. The humiliation of epilepsy had unmanned me, and I felt empathy for the doctor. At least I looked like a human being. According to Chandler, Eagle had no friends. Chandler also told me that Eagle would get drunk and remove his tin nose and bellow, "I am the Phantom of the Opera. Ah ha ha ha!"

Patients came and went, and time passed—I had been in the nuthouse for fourteen months. I was becoming one of the senior patients on the ward. We got very good meals on the anniversary of the founding of the Marine Corps, on Thanksgiving, at Christmas. In fact, at Christmas, entertainment was brought in. I remember a set of old geezers who constituted a Dixieland band. They did not play that well, but it made for a welcome break in the routine of med calls, of shower shoes flip-flopping across the kelly-green tiles, of young men freaking out at the security screen near Joe's corner, of people getting high on airplane glue and Vicks Inhalers, of people trying to kill themselves by putting their heads in plastic bags, of the long nights in the ward with

4. A region in Vietnam.

the bed springs squealing from incessant masturbation, punctuated by nightmares and night terrors and cries of "Incoming!," of the same cold starchy meals over and over again, of a parched mouth from drug dehydration and too many cigarettes, of a life without hope.

When the band took a rest between sets, two old farts, one white and one black, played a banjo duet of "Shanty Town" that brought tears to my eyes. Then a group of square dancers came in. They were miserable-looking middle-aged types in Western getups, the women with fat legs. You could sense their apprehension, and I realized that I had forgotten how frightening someone like Bobby Dean Steele, who had been copping an attitude of late, wearing an Afro and a pair of black gloves, must have seemed to people like them. Once the music began, however, the misery was erased from their faces and replaced by a hypnotic expression as they mechanically went through their paces. From my folding chair, swooning on phenobarbital, overly warm from all the body heat, I was in agony until I saw—with a rare and refined sense of objectivity—that their sufferings and miseries vanished in their dancing, as they fell into the rhythm of the music and the singsong of the caller's instructions. And for a moment I saw myself as well; I saw myself as if from on high, saw the pattern of my whole life with a kind of geometrical precision, like the pattern the dancers were making, and it seemed there was a perfect rightness to it all.

One day after chow, Bobby Dean Steele was summoned to the meds kiosk by one of the doctors, and a corpsman buzzed a pair of enormous brig chasers through the heavy steel door of the ward. They cuffed Bobby Dean Steele, while the resident on duty shrugged his shoulders and told Steele that he was being transferred back to the brig to stand General Court-Martial for three counts of murder in the second degree. It had been decided, Chandler informed us, that Bobby Dean Steele was not especially crazy—at least not according to observation, the MMPI, and the Rorschach. Chandler told us that Steele would end up doing twenty years hard labor in a federal prison.

My own departure was somewhat different. Eagle called me into his office and said, "I'm sending you home. Don't ask me whether you're cured or not. I don't know. I do know you were an outstanding Marine, and I have processed papers for a full disability pension. Good luck to you, Sergeant."

"Thank you." I was dumbfounded.

"When you get home, find yourself a good neurologist. . . . And keep your ass out of the boxing ring."

"Yes, sir."

As I turned to leave, Eagle saluted me. I returned the salute proudly, and I heard his booming, operatic laugh start up after I pulled his door shut behind me.

The next morning I collected over nine thousand dollars in back pay and I went out to the bus stop with my seabag on my shoulder. A master sergeant came by, and I asked him what time the bus came. He told me that I could not leave the base until I got a No. 1 haircut and I told him to forget it, that I was a civilian. A moment later a jeep pulled over and a captain with an MP band on his sleeve hopped out. I showed him my discharge papers, the jump wings on my set of blues, the Navy Cross and the two Silvers, and he said, "Big fucking deal. You got a General Discharge, Sergeant. A psychiatric discharge, Sergeant. I want you off this base immediately."

"Well give me a ride and I'll be glad to get off the motherfucker," I said. I was beginning to see cockroaches crawling through the wet sawdust inside my skull, and I kept wiping my nose for fear they would run out and brush across my lips.

"You're a psycho," the master sergeant said. "Go out there and wreak havoc and mayhem on the general population, and good riddance."

"You could cut me some slack," I said. "I was a real Marine, not some rear-echelon blowhard, and by the way, fuck the Corps. Eat the apple, and fuck the Corps. I curse the day I ever joined this green motherfucker."

"I want you off this base and I want you to hump it off this base," the master sergeant said.

"You mean I don't have to get a haircut after all?" I said in my best nellie voice.

"Fucking hit the road, Marine. Haight-Ashbury[5] is that way."

"Well, fuck you," I said.

"And fuck you. Go fuck yourself."

I threw my seabag down and was about to fight when a Marine in a beatup T-bird pulled over to the bus stop and asked me if I needed a lift. Without another word I tossed my seabag in his backseat and hopped into the car. Before I could say thanks he hit me up for five bucks in gas money. "It's twenty-three miles to Oceanside," he said. "And I'm runnin' on empty. I ain't even got a spare tire, no jack, no nothing." He looked at me and laughed, revealing a mouth filled with black cavities. He said, "Hey, man, you wouldn't happen to have a cigarette, would you?" I handed him my pack. "Hey, thanks," he said.

"That's all right," I said.

---

5. A district in San Francisco notorious for "hippie culture" and drug use.

He lit the cigarette and took a deep drag. "You want to hear some strange shit?"

"Why not?" I said.

"I just got six, six, and a kick." The Marine took another pull off the cigarette and said, "Six months in the brig, six months without pay, and a Bad Conduct Discharge."

"What did you do?" I asked. I was trying to stop the vision of bugs.

"AWOL," he said. "Which is what I'm doing now. I ain't going to do no six months in the fucking brig, man. I did two tours in Nam. I don't deserve this kind of treatment. You want to know something?"

"What's that?"

"I stole this fucking car. Hot-wired the motherfucker."

"Far out," I said. "Which way you going?"

"As far as five bucks in gas will take me."

"I got a little money. Drive me to Haight-Ashbury?"

"Groovy. What are you doing, man, picking your nose?"

"Just checking for cockroaches," I said weakly. I was afraid I was going to have a fit, and I began to see the black lights—they were coming on big time, but I fought them off. "What was your MOS?"

"Oh-three-eleven, communications. I packed a radio over in I Corps. Three Purple Hearts and three Bronze Stars with valor. That's why I ain't doing six months in no brig. I just hope the 'P. waves us through at the gate. I don't want no high-speed chases." The Marine lit another of my cigarettes from the butt of the first one. "Hey, man, were you in the war? You look like you got some hard miles on you. Were you in the war? Did you just get out? You're not going AWOL, too—that ain't no regulation haircut. Man, you got a headful of hair. On the run? How about it? Were you in the war? You got that thousand-yard stare, man. Hey, man, stop picking your nose and tell me about it."

Arf!

"Goddammit, are you zoned or what?"

Bow wow!

"I can't believe this shit. That motherfucker 'P. at the gate is pulling me over. Look at that. Can you believe this shit? They never pull you over at this gate, not at this time of day—and I haven't got any identification. Shit! Buckle up your seat belt, nose-pickin' man, we are gonna motate. This fucking Ford has got a blower on the engine and it can boogie. Haight-Ashbury, here we come or we die tryin'. Save us some of that free love! Just hope you get some of that free lovin'—save me some of that *good* pussy!"

The Marine slammed his foot down full on the accelerator. The T-bird surged like a rocket and blew by the guard post, snapping off the wooden crossbar. For a moment I felt like I was back in the jungle again, a savage in greasepaint, or back in the boxing ring, a primal man—kill or be killed. It was the best feeling. It was ecstasy. The bugs vanished. My skull contained gray matter again. I looked back at the MP in the guard post making a frantic call on the telephone. But the crazy Marine at the wheel told me not to worry, he knew the back roads.

1993

▪   ▪   ▪

JAMAICA KINCAID

GIRL

Wash the white clothes on Monday and put them on the stone heap; wash the color clothes on Tuesday and put them on the clothesline to dry; don't walk barehead in the hot sun; cook pumpkin fritters in very hot sweet oil; soak your little cloths right after you take them off; when buying cotton to make yourself a nice blouse, be sure that it doesn't have gum on it, because that way it won't hold up well after a wash; soak salt fish overnight before you cook it; is it true that you sing benna[1] in Sunday school?; always eat your food in such a way that it won't turn someone else's stomach; on Sundays try to walk like a lady and not like the slut you are so bent on becoming; don't sing benna in Sunday school; you mustn't speak to wharf-rat boys, not even to give directions; don't eat fruits on the street—flies will follow you; *but I don't sing benna on Sundays at all and never in Sunday school*; this is how to sew on a button; this is how to make a buttonhole for the button you have just sewed on; this is how to hem a dress when you see the hem coming down and so to prevent yourself from looking like the slut I know you are so bent on becoming; this is how you iron your father's khaki shirt so that it doesn't have a crease; this is how you iron your father's khaki pants so that they don't have a crease; this is how you grow okra—far from the house, because okra tree harbors red ants; when you are growing dasheen, make sure it gets plenty of water or else it makes your throat itch when you are eating it; this is how you sweep a corner; this is how you sweep a whole house; this is how you sweep a yard; this is how you smile to someone you don't like very much; this is how you smile to someone you don't like at all; this is how you smile to someone you like completely; this is how you set a

1. Calypso songs.

table for tea; this is how you set a table for dinner; this is how you set a table for dinner with an important guest; this is how you set a table for lunch; this is how you set a table for breakfast; this is how to behave in the presence of men who don't know you very well, and this way they won't recognize immediately the slut I have warned you against becoming; be sure to wash every day, even if it is with your own spit; don't squat down to play marbles—you are not a boy, you know; don't pick people's flowers—you might catch something; don't throw stones at blackbirds, because it might not be a blackbird at all; this is how to make a bread pudding; this is how to make doukona; this is how to make pepper pot; this is how to make a good medicine for a cold; this is how to make a good medicine to throw away a child before it even becomes a child; this is how to catch a fish; this is how to throw back a fish you don't like, and that way something bad won't fall on you; this is how to bully a man; this is how a man bullies you; this is how to love a man, and if this doesn't work there are other ways, and if they don't work don't feel too bad about giving up; this is how to spit up in the air if you feel like it, and this is how to move quick so that it doesn't fall on you; this is how to make ends meet; always squeeze bread to make sure it's fresh; *but what if the baker won't let me feel the bread?*; you mean to say that after all you are really going to be the kind of woman who the baker won't let near the bread?

1983

WILLIAM KOTZWINKLE

FOLLOW THE EAGLE

Johnny Eagle climbed onto his 750-cubic-centimeter Arupa motorcycle and roared out of the Navaho Indian Reservation, followed by the Mexican, Domingo, on a rattling Japanese cycle stolen from a Colorado U law student.

Up the morning highway they rode toward the Colorado River, half-drunk and full-crazy in the sunlight, Eagle's slouch hat brim bent in the wind, Domingo's long black moustaches trailing in the air.

Yes, thought Eagle, wheeling easy over the flat land, yes indeed. And they came to Navaho Canyon where they shut down their bikes. Mist from the winding river far below rose up through the scarred plateau and the air was still.

Eagle and Domingo wheeled their bikes slowly to the edge of the Canyon. Domingo got off and threw a stone across the gorge. It struck the far wall, bounced, echoed, fell away in silence.

"Long way to the other side, man," he said, looking at Eagle.

Eagle said nothing, sat on his bike, staring across the gaping crack in the earth.

Domingo threw another stone, which cleared the gap, kicking up a little cloud of dust on top of the other cliff. "How fast you got to go— hunnert, hunnert twenty-five?"

Eagle spit into the canyon and tromped the starter of his bike.

"When you goin', man?" shouted Domingo over the roar.

"Tomorrow!"

That night was a party for Johnny Eagle on the Reservation. He danced with Red Wing in the long house, pressed her up against a corner. Medicine Man came by, gave Eagle a cougar tooth. "I been talkin' to it, Eagle," he said.

"Thanks, man," said Eagle and he put it around his neck and took Red Wing back to his shack, held her on the falling porch in the moonlight, looked at the moon over her shoulder.

She lay on his broken bed, hair undone on his ragged pillow, her buckskin jacket on the floor. Through the open window came music from the party, guitar strings and a drum head and Domingo singing.

Uncle John have everything he need

"Don't go tomorrow," said Red Wing, unbuttoning Eagle's cowboy shirt.

"Gitchimanito[1] is watchin' out for me, baby," said Eagle, and he mounted her, riding bareback, up the draw, slow, to the drumbeat. His eyes were closed but he saw her tears, like silver beads, and he rode faster and shot his arrow through the moon.

"Oh, Johnny," she moaned, quivering beneath him, "don't go," and he felt her falling away, down the waving darkness.

They lay, looking out through the window. He hung the cat's tooth around her neck. "Stay with me," she said, holding him till dawn, and he rose up while she was sleeping. The Reservation was grey, the shacks crouching in the dawn light.

Eagle shook Domingo out of his filthy bed. The Mexican crawled across the floor, looking for his sombrero, and they walked across the camp to the garage where the pickup truck was stowed with Eagle's bike.

Eagle pulled the cycle off the kickstand and they rolled it up a wooden ramp into the back of the truck, then slid the ramp in the truck, roped it down, and drove quietly off the Reservation.

They went down the empty highway, Domingo at the wheel, Eagle slouched in the corner by the door. "Why you doin' this, man?" asked the Mexican, not looking at Eagle.

Eagle's hat was over his eyes. He slept a little, nodding with the bounces in and out of a dream. His head dropped against the cold window. The truck was stopped.

Eagle stepped down onto the silent mesa. *My legs shakin*, he thought and went round to the back of the truck, where Domingo was letting down the ramp. Eagle touched the cold handlebars of the bike and stopped shaking. They wheeled the cycle to the ground.

"I know a chick," said Domingo. They pushed the ramp to the edge of the canyon. "—with a fantastic ass—" They faced the ramp to

1. The Great Spirit.

the misty hole, bracing it with cinder blocks. "She lives down in Ensenada, man, whattya say we go down there?"

Eagle climbed onto the bike, turned over the motor, breaking the morning stillness. He circled slowly, making bigger circles until the motor was running strong, then drove over to Domingo at the edge of the ramp.

"*Buena suerte, amigo!*"[2] shouted the Mexican over the roaring engine.

"On the other side!" called Eagle, and drove away from the ramp, fifty, a hundred, two, three, four hundred yards. He turned, lined the bike up with the ramp. A white chicken fluttered in his stomach. Domingo waved his black hat.

In neutral, Eagle gunned the big Arupa engine, once, twice, and engaging first gear spun out toward the ramp.

The sun was rising, the speedometer climbing as he shifted into second gear, fifty, sixty, seventy, eighty miles an hour. Eagle burned across the table land toward Navaho Canyon, into third gear, ninety, a hundred, had jumped twelve cars on this bike, had no job, saw Domingo from the corner of his eye, was going one twenty-five and that was it as he hit the ramp and sailed his ass off into space.

The cycle whined above the mist, floating like a thunder clap, and Johnny Eagle in his slouch hat rode lightly as an arrow, airborne in the glory of the moment as a sunbeam struck him in his arc of triumph, then his sunset came upon him and he saw the flaw in his life story, *one fifty, man, not one twenty-five*, as the far cliff for which he hungered came no closer, seemed to mock him through the mist, was impossible, always had been, and his slouch hat blew away.

Don't go, Johnny.

He strained to lift his falling horse, to carry her above the morning, to fly with her between his legs, rupturing several muscles in his passion and then as he fell for certain just clung sadly with the morning rising up his asshole, poor balls groaning Johnny Eagle, falling down Navaho Canyon, the geological formations quite apparent as the mist was clearing from the rock.

"SO LONG, MAN!" he shouted, with quite a way to go, falling like a regular comet, smoke and fire out the tailpipe as the bike turned slowly over, plunging through the hollow entry. Jesus Christ my blood is boiling there goes the engine.

He fell quietly, hissing through the mist, dreaming it was still dawn on Red Wing's red-brown thighs.

Johnny, don't go. O.K. babe I'll stay here.

2. "Good luck, friend!"

But he saw the real rocks rushing past him.

I uster dance. Neck down in the fender. She held me in my screw-loose, Johnny Eagle, be my old man, babe I'm crazy and mus' go to Gitchegumee.[3]

Down in Ensenada man

Domingo falling to the barroom laughing with his knife blade bloody, my look at that terra cotter there like faces in the Canyon, Sheriff you kin let us out now, won't do no harm. There goes my shoes man where am I.

A *fantastic*

Water lick rock. Thousand fist pound my brain out. Crack me, shell me, awful snot death crap death hunnert bucks that bike death cost me black death o no Colorado do not take me.

Yes I took you Johnny Eagle

Wham the arrow crossed the morning. I am shot from out my body whooooooooooooooo the endless sunrise.

Some time later a fledgling eagle was hatched by an old white-headed fierce-beaked queen of the Canyon. She pushed the little eagle into space where he learned to soar, crying *kyreeeee*, high above the morning, turning in the mist upon the wind.

And Domingo, riding down to Ensenada, to see the girl in Ensenada, crossed the border singing

> *He saw Aunt Mary comin' an'*
> *He duck back in the alley*

1971

■   ■   ■

3. Place of the spirits.

URSULA K. LE GUIN

THE NEW ATLANTIS

Coming back from my Wilderness Week I sat by an odd sort of man in the bus. For a long time we didn't talk; I was mending stockings and he was reading. Then the bus broke down a few miles outside Gresham. Boiler trouble, the way it generally is when the driver insists on trying to go over thirty. It was a Supersonic Superscenic Deluxe Longdistance coal-burner, with Home Comfort, that means a toilet, and the seats were pretty comfortable, at least those that hadn't yet worked loose from their bolts, so everybody waited inside the bus; besides, it was raining. We began talking, the way people do when there's a breakdown and a wait. He held up his pamphlet and tapped it—he was a dry-looking man with a school-teacherish way of using his hands—and said, "This is interesting. I've been reading that a new continent is rising from the depths of the sea."

The blue stockings were hopeless. You have to have something besides holes to darn onto. "Which sea?"

"They're not sure yet. Most specialists think the Atlantic. But there's evidence it may be happening in the Pacific, too."

"Won't the oceans get a little crowded?" I said, not taking it seriously. I was a bit snappish, because of the breakdown and because those blue stockings had been good warm ones.

He tapped the pamphlet again and shook his head, quite serious. "No," he said. "The old continents are sinking, to make room for the new. You can see that that is happening."

You certainly can. Manhattan Island is now under eleven feet of water at low tide, and there are oyster beds in Ghirardelli Square.[1]

"I thought that was because the oceans are rising from polar melt."

1. A fancy shopping area in San Francisco.

He shook his head again. "That is a factor. Due to the greenhouse effect of pollution, indeed Antarctica may become inhabitable. But climatic factors will not explain the emergence of the new—or, possibly, very old—continents in the Atlantic and Pacific." He went on explaining about continental drift, but I liked the idea of inhabiting Antarctica and daydreamed about it for a while. I thought of it as very empty, very quiet, all white and blue, with a faint golden glow northward from the unrising sun behind the long peak of Mount Erebus.[2] There were a few people there; they were very quiet, too, and wore white tie and tails. Some of them carried oboes and violas. Southward the white land went up in a long silence toward the Pole.

Just the opposite, in fact, of the Mount Hood Wilderness Area.[3] It had been a tiresome vacation. The other women in the dormitory were all right, but it was macaroni for breakfast, and there were so many organized sports. I had looked forward to the hike up to the National Forest Preserve, the largest forest left in the United States, but the trees didn't look at all the way they do in the postcards and brochures and Federal Beautification Bureau advertisements. They were spindly, and they all had little signs on saying which union they had been planted by. There were actually a lot more green picnic tables and cement Men's and Women's than there were trees. There was an electrified fence all around the forest to keep out unauthorized persons. The forest ranger talked about mountain jays, "bold little robbers," he said, "who will come and snatch the sandwich from your very hand," but I didn't see any. Perhaps because that was the weekly Watch Those Surplus Calories! Day for all the women, and so we didn't have any sandwiches. If I'd seen a mountain jay I might have snatched the sandwich from his very hand, who knows. Anyhow it was an exhausting week, and I wished I'd stayed home and practiced, even though I'd have lost a week's pay because staying home and practicing the viola doesn't count as planned implementation of recreational leisure as defined by the Federal Union of Unions.

When I came back from my Antarctican expedition, the man was reading again, and I got a look at his pamphlet; and that was the odd part of it. The pamphlet was called "Increasing Efficiency in Public Accountant Training Schools," and I could see from the one paragraph I got a glance at that there was nothing about new continents emerging from the ocean depths in it—nothing at all.

Then we had to get out and walk on into Gresham, because they had decided that the best thing for us all to do was get onto the Greater

2. Peak on the west coast of Antarctica.
3. Mount Hood is the highest point in Oregon.

Portland Area Rapid Public Transit Lines, since there had been so many breakdowns that the charter bus company didn't have any more buses to send out to pick us up. The walk was wet, and rather dull, except when we passed the Cold Mountain Commune. They have a wall around it to keep out unauthorized persons, and a big neon sign out front saying COLD MOUNTAIN COMMUNE and there were some people in authentic jeans and ponchos by the highway selling macramé belts and sandcast candles and soybean bread to the tourists. In Gresham, I took the 4:40 GPARPTL Superjet Flyer train to Burnside and East 230th, and then walked to 217th and got the bus to the Goldschmidt Overpass, and transferred to the shuttlebus, but it had boiler trouble, so I didn't reach the downtown transfer point until ten after eight, and the buses go on a once-an-hour schedule at eight o'clock, so I got a meatless hamburger at the Longhorn Inch-Thick Steak House Dinerette and caught the nine o'clock bus and got home about ten. When I let myself into the apartment I flipped the switch to turn on the lights, but there still weren't any. There had been a power outage in West Portland for three weeks. So I went feeling about for the candles in the dark, and it was a minute or so before I noticed that somebody was lying on my bed.

I panicked, and tried again to turn the lights on.

It was a man, lying there in a long thin heap. I thought a burglar had got in somehow while I was away and died. I opened the door so I could get out quick or at least my yells could be heard, and then I managed not to shake long enough to strike a match, and lighted the candle, and came a little closer to the bed.

The light disturbed him. He made a sort of snorting in his throat and turned his head. I saw it was a stranger, but I knew his eyebrows, then the breadth of his closed eyelids, then I saw my husband.

He woke up while I was standing there over him with the candle in my hand. He laughed and said still half-asleep, "Ah, Psyche! From the regions which are holy land."[4]

Neither of us made much fuss. It was unexpected, but it did seem so natural for him to be there, after all, much more natural than for him not to be there, and he was too tired to be very emotional. We lay there together in the dark, and he explained that they had released him from the Rehabilitation Camp early because he had injured his back in an accident in the gravel quarry, and they were afraid it might get worse. If he died there it wouldn't be good publicity abroad, since there have been some nasty rumors about deaths from illness in the

---

4. From the better known of two poems called "To Helen" by Edgar Allan Poe. Psyche, in classical mythology, was a princess of remarkable beauty, beloved by Cupid.

Rehabilitation Camps and the Federal Medical Association Hospitals; and there are scientists abroad who have heard of Simon, since somebody published his proof of Goldbach's Hypothesis in Peking. So they let him out early, with eight dollars in his pocket, which is what he had in his pocket when they arrested him, which made it, of course, fair. He had walked and hitched home from Coeur D'Alene, Idaho, with a couple of days in jail in Walla Walla[5] for being caught hitchhiking. He almost fell asleep telling me this, and when he had told me, he did fall asleep. He needed a change of clothes and a bath but I didn't want to wake him. Besides, I was tired, too. We lay side by side and his head was on my arm. I don't suppose that I have ever been so happy. No; was it happiness? Something wider and darker, more like knowledge, more like the night: joy.

It was dark for so long, so very long. We were all blind. And there was the cold, a vast, unmoving, heavy cold. We could not move at all. We did not move. We did not speak. Our mouths were closed, pressed shut by the cold and by the weight. Our eyes were pressed shut. Our limbs were held still. Our minds were held still. For how long? There was no length of time; how long is death? And is one dead only after living, or before life as well? Certainly we thought, if we thought anything, that we were dead; but if we had ever been alive, we had forgotten it.

There was a change. It must have been the pressure that changed first, although we did not know it. The eyelids are sensitive to touch. They must have been weary of being shut. When the pressure upon them weakened a little, they opened. But there was no way for us to know that. It was too cold for us to feel anything. There was nothing to be seen. There was black.

But then—"then," for the event created time, created before and after, near and far, now and then—"then" there was the light. One light. One small, strange light that passed slowly, at what distance we could not tell. A small, greenish white, slightly blurred point of radiance, passing.

Our eyes were certainly open, "then," for we saw it. We saw the moment. The moment is a point of light. Whether in darkness or in the field of all light, the moment is small, and moves, but not quickly. And "then" it is gone.

It did not occur to us that there might be another moment. There was no reason to assume that there might be more than one. One was marvel enough: that in all the field of the dark, in the cold, heavy, dense, moveless, timeless, placeless, boundless black, there should have

5. City in Washington.

occurred, once, a small slightly blurred, moving light! Time need be created only once, we thought.

But we were mistaken. The difference between one and more than one is all the difference in the world. Indeed, that difference is the world.

The light returned.

The same light, or another one? There was no telling.

But, "this time," we wondered about the light: Was it small and near to us, or large and far away? Again there was no telling; but there was something about the way it moved, a trace of hesitation, a tentative quality, that did not seem proper to anything large and remote. The stars, for instance. We began to remember the stars.

The stars had never hesitated.

Perhaps the noble certainty of their gait had been a mere effect of distance. Perhaps in fact they had hurtled wildly, enormous furnace-fragments of a primal bomb thrown through the cosmic dark; but time and distance soften all agony. If the universe, as seems likely, began with an act of destruction, the stars we had used to see told no tales of it. They had been implacably serene.

The planets, however . . . We began to remember the planets. They had suffered certain changes both of appearance and of course. At certain times of the year Mars would reverse its direction and go backward through the stars. Venus had been brighter and less bright as she went through her phases of crescent, full, and wane. Mercury had shuddered like a skidding drop of rain on the sky flushed with daybreak. The light we now watched had that erratic, trembling quality. We saw it, unmistakably, change direction and go backward. It then grew smaller and fainter; blinked—an eclipse?—and slowly disappeared.

Slowly, but not slowly enough for a planet.

Then—the third "then"!—arrived the indubitable and positive Wonder of the World, the Magic Trick, watch now, watch, you will not believe your eyes, mama, mama, look what I can do—

Seven lights in a row, proceeding fairly rapidly, with a darting movement, from left to right. Proceeding less rapidly from right to left, two dimmer, greenish lights. Two-lights halt, blink, reverse course, proceed hastily and in a wavering manner from left to right. Seven-lights increase speed, and catch up. Two-lights flash desperately, flicker, and are gone.

Seven-lights hang still for some while, then merge gradually into one streak, veering away, and little by little vanish into the immensity of the dark.

But in the dark now are growing other lights, many of them: lamps, dots, rows, scintillations—some near at hand, some far. Like the stars, *yes, but not stars. It is not the great Existences we are seeing, but only the little lives.*

In the morning Simon told me something about the Camp, but not until after he had had me check the apartment for bugs. I thought at first he had been given behavior mod and gone paranoid. We never had been infested. And I'd been living alone for a year and a half; surely they didn't want to hear me talking to myself? But he said, "They may have been expecting me to come here."

"But they let you go free!"

He just lay there and laughed at me. So I checked everywhere we could think of. I didn't find any bugs, but it did look as if somebody had gone through the bureau drawers while I was away in the Wilderness. Simon's papers were all at Max's so that didn't matter. I made tea on the Primus,[6] and washed and shaved Simon with the extra hot water in the kettle—he had a thick beard and wanted to get rid of it because of the lice he had brought from Camp—and while we were doing that he told me about the Camp. In fact he told me very little, but not much was necessary.

He had lost about twenty pounds. As he only weighed 140 to start with, this left little to go on with. His knees and wrist bones stuck out like rocks under the skin. His feet were all swollen and chewed-looking from the Camp boots; he hadn't dared take the boots off, the last three days of walking, because he was afraid he wouldn't be able to get them back on. When he had to move or sit up so I could wash him, he shut his eyes.

"Am I really here?" he asked. "Am I here?"

"Yes," I said. "You are here. What I don't understand is how you got here."

"Oh, it wasn't bad so long as I kept moving. All you need is to know where you're going—to have someplace to go. You know, some of the people in Camp, if they'd let them go, they wouldn't have had that. They couldn't have gone anywhere. Keeping moving was the main thing. See, my back's all seized up, now."

When he had to get up to go to the bathroom he moved like a ninety-year-old. He couldn't stand straight, but was all bent out of shape, and shuffled. I helped him put on clean clothes. When he lay down on the bed again, a sound of pain came out of him, like tearing thick paper. I went around the room putting things away. He asked me to come sit by him and said I was going to drown him if I went on

6. Simple camp stove.

crying. "You'll submerge the entire North American continent," he said. I can't remember what he said, but he made me laugh finally. It is hard to remember things Simon says, and hard not to laugh when he says them. This is not merely the partiality of affection: He makes everybody laugh. I doubt that he intends to. It is just that a mathematician's mind works differently from other people's. Then when they laugh, that pleases him.

It was strange, and it is strange, to be thinking about "him," the man I have known for ten years, the same man, while "he" lay there changed out of recognition, a different man. It is enough to make you understand why most languages have a word like "soul." There are various degrees of death, and time spares us none of them. Yet something endures, for which a word is needed.

I said what I had not been able to say for a year and a half: "I was afraid they'd brainwash you." He said, "Behavior mod is expensive. Even just the drugs. They save it mostly for the VIPs. But I'm afraid they got a notion I might be important after all. I got questioned a lot the last couple of months. About my 'foreign contacts.' " He snorted. "The stuff that got published abroad, I suppose. So I want to be careful and make sure it's just a Camp again next time, and not a Federal Hospital."

"Simon, were they . . . are they cruel, or just righteous?"

He did not answer for a while. He did not want to answer. He knew what I was asking. He knew by what thread hangs hope, the sword, above our heads.

"Some of them . . ." he said at last, mumbling.

Some of them had been cruel. Some of them had enjoyed their work. You cannot blame everything on society.

"Prisoners, as well as guards," he said.

You cannot blame everything on the enemy.

"Some of them, Belle," he said with energy, touching my hand, "some of them, there were men like gold there—"

The thread is tough; you cannot cut it with one stroke.

"What have you been playing?" he asked.

"Forrest, Schubert."

"With the quartet?"

"Trio, now. Janet went to Oakland with a new lover."

"Ah, poor Max."

"It's just as well, really. She isn't a good pianist."

I make Simon laugh, too, though I don't intend to. We talked until it was past time for me to go to work. My shift since the Full Employment Act last year is ten to two. I am an inspector in a recycled paper bag factory. I have never rejected a bag yet; the electronic inspector catches all the defective ones first. It is a rather depressing job. But it's only four hours a day, and it takes more time than that to go through all the lines and physical and mental examinations, and fill out all the forms, and talk to all the welfare counselors and inspectors every week in order to qualify as Unemployed, and then line up every day for the ration stamps and the dole. Simon thought I ought to go to work as usual. I tried to, but I couldn't. He had felt very hot to the touch when I kissed him goodbye. I went instead and got a black-market doctor. A girl at the factory had recommended her, for an abortion, if I ever wanted one without going through the regulation two years of sex-depressant drugs the fed-meds make you take when they give you an abortion. She was a jeweler's assistant in a shop on Alder Street, and the girl said she was convenient because if you didn't have enough cash you could leave something in pawn at the jeweler's as payment. Nobody ever does have enough cash, and of course credit cards aren't worth much on the black market.

The doctor was willing to come at once, so we rode home on the bus together. She gathered very soon that Simon and I were married, and it was funny to see her look at us and smile like a cat. Some people love illegality for its own sake. Men, more often than women. It's men who make laws, and enforce them, and break them, and think the whole performance is wonderful. Most women would rather just ignore them. You could see that this woman, like a man, actually enjoyed breaking them. That may have been what put her into an illegal business in the first place, a preference for the shady side. But there was more to it than that. No doubt she'd wanted to be a doctor, too; and the Federal Medical Association doesn't admit women into the medical schools. She probably got her training as some other doctor's private pupil, under the counter. Very much as Simon learned mathematics, since the universities don't teach much but Business Administration and Advertising and Media Skills anymore. However she learned it, she seemed to know her stuff. She fixed up a kind of homemade traction device for Simon very handily and informed him that if he did much more walking for two months he'd be crippled the rest of his life, but if he behaved himself he'd just be more or less lame. It isn't the kind of thing you'd expect to be grateful for being told, but we both were. Leaving, she gave me a bottle of about two hundred plain white pills, unlabeled. "Aspirin," she said. "He'll be in a good deal of pain off and on for weeks."

I looked at the bottle. I had never seen aspirin before, only the Super-Buffered Pane-Gon and the Triple-Power N-L-G-Zic and the Extra-Strength Apansprin with the miracle ingredient more doctors recommend, which the fed-meds always give you prescriptions for, to be filled at your FMA-approved private enterprise friendly drugstore at the low, low prices established by the Pure Food and Drug Administration in order to inspire competitive research.

"Aspirin," the doctor repeated. "The miracle ingredient more doctors recommend." She cat-grinned again. I think she liked us because we were living in sin. That bottle of black-market aspirin was probably worth more than the old Navajo bracelet I pawned for her fee.

I went out again to register Simon as temporarily domiciled at my address and to apply for Temporary Unemployment Compensation ration stamps for him. They only give them to you for two weeks and you have to come every day; but to register him as Temporarily Disabled meant getting the signatures of two fed-meds, and I thought I'd rather put that off for a while. It took three hours to go through the lines and get the forms he would have to fill out, and to answer the 'crats' questions about why he wasn't there in person. They smelled something fishy. Of course it's hard for them to prove that two people are married and aren't just adultering if you move now and then and your friends help out by sometimes registering one of you as living at their address; but they had all the back files on both of us and it was obvious that we had been around each other for a suspiciously long time. The State really does make things awfully hard for itself. It must have been simpler to enforce the laws back when marriage was legal and adultery was what got you into trouble. They only had to catch you once. But I'll bet people broke the law just as often then as they do now.

The lantern-creatures came close enough at last that we could see not only their light, but their bodies in the illumination of their light. They were not pretty. They were dark colored, most often a dark red, and they were all mouth. They ate one another whole. Light swallowed light, all swallowed together in the vaster mouth of the darkness. They moved slowly, for nothing, however small and hungry, could move fast under that weight, in that cold. Their eyes, round with fear, were never closed. Their bodies were tiny and bony behind the gaping jaws. They wore queer, ugly decorations on their lips and skulls: fringes, serrated wattles, featherlike fronds, gauds, bangles, lures. Poor little sheep of the deep pastures! Poor ragged, hunchjawed dwarfs squeezed to the bone by the weight of the darkness, chilled to the bone by the cold of the darkness, tiny monsters burning with bright hunger, who brought us back to life!

Occasionally, in the wan, sparse illumination of one of the lantern-creatures, we caught a momentary glimpse of other, large, unmoving shapes: the barest suggestion, off in the distance, not of a wall, nothing so solid and certain as a wall, but of a surface, an angle . . . Was it there?

Or something would glitter, faint, far off, far down. There was no use trying to make out what it might be. Probably it was only a fleck of sediment, mud or mica, disturbed by a struggle between the lantern-creatures, flickering like a bit of diamond dust as it rose and settled slowly. In any case, we could not move to go see what it was. We had not even the cold, narrow freedom of the lantern-creatures. We were immobilized, borne down, still shadows among the half-guessed shadow walls. Were we there?

The lantern-creatures showed no awareness of us. They passed before us, among us, perhaps even through us—it was impossible to be sure. They were not afraid, or curious.

Once something a little larger than a hand came crawling near, and for a moment we saw quite distinctly the clean angle where the foot of a wall rose from the pavement, in the glow cast by the crawling creature, which was covered with a foliage of plumes, each plume dotted with many tiny, bluish points of light. We saw the pavement beneath the creature and the wall beside it, heartbreaking in its exact, clear linearity, its opposition to all that was fluid, random, vast, and void. We saw the creature's claws, slowly reaching out and retracting like small stiff fingers, touch the wall. Its plumage of light quivering, it dragged itself along and vanished behind the corner of the wall.

So we knew that the wall was there; and that it was an outer wall, a housefront, perhaps, or the side of one of the towers of the city.

We remembered the towers. We remembered the city. We had forgotten it. We had forgotten who we were; but we remembered the city, now.

When I got home, the FBI had already been there. The computer at the police precinct where I registered Simon's address must have flashed it right over to the computer at the FBI building. They had questioned Simon for about an hour, mostly about what he had been doing during the twelve days it took him to get from the Camp to Portland. I suppose they thought he had flown to Peking or something. Having a police record in Walla Walla for hitchhiking helped him establish his story. He told me that one of them had gone to the bathroom. Sure enough I found a bug stuck on the top of the bathroom doorframe. I left it, as we figured it's really better to leave it when you know you have one, than to take it off and then never be sure they haven't planted another one you don't know about. As Simon said, if we felt we had to say something unpatriotic we could always flush the toilet at the same time.

I have a battery radio—there are so many work stoppages because of power failures, and days the water has to be boiled, and so on, that you really have to have a radio to save wasting time and dying of typhoid—and he turned it on while I was making supper on the Primus. The six o'clock All-American Broadcasting Company news announcer announced that peace was at hand in Uruguay, the president's confidential aide having been seen to smile at a passing blonde as he left the 613th day of the secret negotiations in a villa outside Katmandu. The war in Liberia[7] was going well; the enemy said they had shot down seventeen American planes but the Pentagon said we had shot down twenty-two enemy planes, and the capital city—I forget its name, but it hasn't been inhabitable for seven years anyway—was on the verge of being recaptured by the forces of freedom. The police action in Arizona was also successful. The Neo-Birch insurgents in Phoenix could not hold out much longer against the massed might of the American army and air force, since their underground supply of small tactical nukes from the Weathermen[8] in Los Angeles had been cut off. Then there was an advertisement for Fed-Cred cards, and a commercial for the Supreme Court: "Take your legal troubles to the Nine Wise Men!" Then there was something about why tariffs had gone up, and a report from the stock market, which had just closed at over two thousand, and a commercial for U.S. Government canned water, with a catchy little tune: "Don't be sorry when you drink/It's not as healthy as you think/Don't you think you really ought to/ Drink cooool, puu-uure U.S.G. water?"—with three sopranos in close harmony on the last line. Then, just as the battery began to give out and his voice was dying away into a faraway tiny whisper, the announcer seemed to be saying something about a new continent emerging.

"What was that?"

"I didn't hear," Simon said, lying with his eyes shut and his face pale and sweaty. I gave him two aspirins before we ate. He ate little, and fell asleep while I was washing the dishes in the bathroom. I had been going to practice, but a viola is fairly wakeful in a one-room apartment. I read for a while instead. It was a best-seller Janet had given me when she left. She thought it was very good, but then she likes Franz Liszt too. I don't read much since the libraries were closed down, it's too hard to get books; all you can buy is best-sellers. I don't remember the title of this one, the cover just said "Ninety Million Copies in Print!!!" It was about small-town sex life in the last century, the dear old 1970s when there weren't any problems and life was so

---

7. Liberia is a West African country; Katmandu is the capital of Nepal, at the foot of the Himalayas.
8. Polar opposites on the political spectrum of the 1960s. The Weathermen was an extreme left-wing youth organization, while the John Birch Society (apparent forerunner of the "Neo-Birch insurgents") was very conservative.

simple and nostalgic. The author squeezed all the naughty thrills he could out of the fact that all the main characters were married. I looked at the end and saw that all the married couples shot each other after all their children became schizophrenic hookers, except for one brave pair that divorced and then leapt into bed together with a clear-eyed pair of government-employed lovers for eight pages of healthy group sex as a brighter future dawned. I went to bed then, too. Simon was hot, but sleeping quietly. His breathing was like the sound of soft waves far away, and I went out to the dark sea on the sound of them.

I used to go out to the dark sea, often, as a child, falling asleep. I had almost forgotten it with my waking mind. As a child all I had to do was stretch out and think, "the dark sea . . . the dark sea . . ." and soon enough I'd be there, in the great depths, rocking. But after I grew up it only happened rarely, as a great gift. To know the abyss of the darkness and not to fear it, to entrust oneself to it and whatever may arise from it—what greater gift?

We watched the tiny lights come and go around us, and doing so, we gained a sense of space and of direction—near and far, at least, and higher and lower. It was that sense of space that allowed us to become aware of the currents. Space was no longer entirely still around us, suppressed by the enormous pressure of its own weight. Very dimly we were aware that the cold darkness moved, slowly, softly, pressing against us a little for a long time, then ceasing, in a vast oscillation. The empty darkness flowed slowly along our unmoving unseen bodies; along them, past them; perhaps through them; we could not tell.

Where did they come from, those dim, slow, vast tides? What pressure or attraction stirred the deeps to these slow drifting movements? We could not understand that; we could only feel their touch against us, but in straining our sense to guess their origin or end, we became aware of something else: something out there in the darkness of the great currents: sounds. We listened. We heard.

So our sense of space sharpened and localized to a sense of place. For sound is local, as sight is not. Sound is delimited by silence; and it does not rise out of the silence unless it is fairly close, both in space and in time. Though we stand where once the singer stood we cannot hear the voice singing; the years have carried it off on their tides, submerged it. Sound is a fragile thing, a tremor, as delicate as life itself. We may see the stars, but we cannot hear them. Even were the hollowness of outer space an atmosphere, an ether that transmitted the waves of sound, we could not hear the stars; they are too far away. At most if we listened we might hear our own sun, all the mighty, roiling, exploding storm of its burning, as a whisper at the edge of hearing.

A sea wave laps one's feet: It is the shock wave of a volcanic eruption on the far side of the world. But one hears nothing.

A red light flickers on the horizon: It is the reflection in smoke of a city on the distant mainland, burning. But one hears nothing.

Only on the slopes of the volcano, in the suburbs of the city, does one begin to hear the deep thunder, and the high voices crying.

Thus, when we became aware that we were hearing, we were sure that the sounds we heard were fairly close to us. And yet we may have been quite wrong. For we were in a strange place, a deep place. Sound travels fast and far in the deep places, and the silence there is perfect, letting the least noise be heard for hundreds of miles.

And these were not small noises. The lights were tiny, but the sounds were vast: not loud, but very large. Often they were below the range of hearing, long slow vibrations rather than sounds. The first we heard seemed to us to rise up through the currents from beneath us: immense groans, sighs felt along the bone, a rumbling, a deep uneasy whispering.

Later, certain sounds came down to us from above, or borne along the endless levels of the darkness, and these were stranger yet, for they were music. A huge calling, yearning music from far away in the darkness, calling not to us. Where are you? I am here.

Not to us.

They were the voices of the great souls, the great lives, the lonely ones, the voyagers. Calling. Not often answered. Where are you? Where have you gone?

But the bones, the keels and girders of white bones on icy isles of the South, the shores of bones did not reply.

Nor could we reply. But we listened, and the tears rose in our eyes, salt, not so salt as the oceans, the world-girdling deep bereaved currents, the abandoned roadways of the great lives; not so salt, but warmer.

I am here. Where have you gone?

No answer.

Only the whispering thunder from below.

But we knew now, though we could not answer, we knew because we heard, because we felt, because we wept, we knew that we were; and we remembered other voices.

Max came the next night. I sat on the toilet lid to practice, with the bathroom door shut. The FBI men on the other end of the bug got a solid half hour of scales and doublestops, and then a quite good performance of the Hindemith[9] unaccompanied viola sonata. The

9. Paul Hindemith (1895–1963), German composer and violinist.

bathroom being very small and all hard surfaces, the noise I made was really tremendous. Not a good sound, far too much echo, but the sheer volume was contagious, and I played louder as I went on. The man up above knocked on his floor once; but if I have to listen to the weekly All-American Olympic Games at full blast every Sunday morning from his TV set, then he has to accept Paul Hindemith coming up out of his toilet now and then.

When I got tired I put a wad of cotton over the bug, and came out of the bathroom half-deaf. Simon and Max were on fire. Burning, unconsumed. Simon was scribbling formulae in traction, and Max was pumping his elbows up and down the way he does, like a boxer, and saying "The e-lec-tron emis-sion . . ." through his nose, with his eyes narrowed, and his mind evidently going light-years per second faster than his tongue, because he kept beginning over and saying "The e-lec-tron emis-sion . . ." and pumping his elbows.

Intellectuals at work are very strange to look at. As strange as artists. I never could understand how an audience can sit there and look at a fiddler rolling his eyes and biting his tongue, or a horn player collecting spit, or a pianist like a black cat strapped to an electrified bench, as if what they *saw* had anything to do with the music.

I damped the fires with a quart of black-market beer—the legal kind is better, but I never have enough ration stamps for beer; I'm not thirsty enough to go without eating—and gradually Max and Simon cooled down. Max would have stayed talking all night, but I drove him out because Simon was looking tired.

I put a new battery in the radio and left it playing in the bathroom, and blew out the candle and lay and talked with Simon; he was too excited to sleep. He said that Max had solved the problems that were bothering them before Simon was sent to Camp, and had fitted Simon's equations to (as Simon put it) the bare facts, which means they have achieved "direct energy conversion." Ten or twelve people have worked on it at different times since Simon published the theoretical part of it when he was twenty-two. The physicist Ann Jones had pointed out right away that the simplest practical application of the theory would be to build a "sun tap," a device for collecting and storing solar energy, only much cheaper and better than the U.S.G. Sola-Hee-tas that some rich people have on their houses. And it would have been simple only they kept hitting the same snag. Now Max has got around the snag.

I said that Simon published the theory, but that is inaccurate. Of course he's never been able to publish any of his papers, in print; he's not a federal employee and doesn't have a government clearance. But it did get circulated in what the scientists and poets call Sammy's-dot,[1] that is, just handwritten or hectographed. It's an old joke that the FBI arrests everybody with purple fingers, because they have either been hectographing Sammy's-dots, or they have impetigo.

Anyhow, Simon was on top of the mountain that night. His true joy is in the pure math; but he had been working with Clara and Mac and the others in this effort to materialize the theory for ten years, and a taste of material victory is a good thing, once in a lifetime.

I asked him to explain what the sun tap would mean to the masses, with me as a representative mass. He explained that it means we can tap solar energy for power, using a device that's easier to build than a jar battery. The efficiency and storage capacity are such that about ten minutes of sunlight will power an apartment complex like ours, heat and lights and elevators and all, for twenty-four hours; and no pollution, particulate, thermal, or radioactive. "There isn't any danger of using up the sun?" I asked. He took it soberly—it was a stupid question, but after all not so long ago people thought there wasn't any danger of using up the earth—and said no, because we wouldn't be pulling out energy, as we did when we mined and lumbered and split atoms, but just using the energy that comes to us anyhow: as the plants, the trees and grass and rosebushes, always have done. "You could call it Flower Power,"[2] he said. He was high, high up on the mountain, ski-jumping in the sunlight.

"The State owns us," he said, "because the corporative State has a monopoly on power sources, and there's not enough power to go around. But now, anybody could build a generator on their roof that would furnish enough power to light a city."

I looked out the window at the dark city.

"We could completely decentralize industry and agriculture. Technology could serve life instead of serving capital. We could each run our own life. Power is power! . . . The State is a machine. We could unplug the machine, now. Power corrupts; absolute power corrupts absolutely.[3] But that's true only when there's a price on power. When groups can keep the power to themselves; when they can use physical power-to in order to exert spiritual power-over; when might makes right. But if power is free? If everybody is equally mighty? Then everybody's got to find a better way of showing that he's right. . . ."

"That's what Mr. Nobel[4] thought when he invented dynamite," I said. "Peace on earth."

1. Punning reference to *Samizdat*, a circuit of underground publications in the Soviet Union in the 1960s–70s.
2. Youth slogan in the 1960s.
3. Said by Lord Acton (1834–1902), English historian.
4. Alfred Nobel (1833–1896), inventor of dynamite and donor of Nobel Prizes.

He slid down the sunlit slope a couple of thousand feet and stopped beside me in a spray of snow, smiling. "Skull at the banquet," he said, "finger writing on the wall. Be still! Look, don't you see the sun shining on the Pentagon,[5] all the roofs are off, the sun shines at last into the corridors of power. . . . And they shrivel up, they wither away. The green grass grows through the carpets of the Oval Room, the Hot Line[6] is disconnected for nonpayment of the bill. The first thing we'll do is build an electrified fence outside the electrified fence around the White House. The inner one prevents unauthorized persons from getting in. The outer one will prevent authorized persons from getting out. . . ."

Of course he was bitter. Not many people come out of prison sweet.

But it was cruel, to be shown this great hope, and to know that there was no hope for it. He did know that. He knew it right along. He knew that there was no mountain, that he was skiing on the wind.

The tiny lights of the lantern-creatures died out one by one, sank away. The distant lonely voices were silent. The cold, slow currents flowed, vacant, only shaken from time to time by a shifting in the abyss.

It was dark again, and no voice spoke. All dark, dumb, cold.

Then the sun rose.

It was not like the dawns we had begun to remember: the change, manifold and subtle, in the smell and touch of the air; the hush that, instead of sleeping, wakes, holds still, and waits; the appearance of objects, looking gray, vague, and new, as if just created—distant mountains against the eastern sky, one's own hands, the hoary grass full of dew and shadow, the fold in the edge of a curtain hanging by the window—and then, before one is quite sure that one is indeed seeing again, that the light has returned, that day is breaking, the first, abrupt, sweet stammer of a waking bird. And after that the chorus, voice by voice: This is my nest, this is my tree, this is my egg, this is my day, this is my life, here I am, here I am, hurray for me! I'm here!—No, it wasn't like that at all, this dawn. It was completely silent, and it was blue.

In the dawns that we had begun to remember, one did not become aware of the light itself, but of the separate objects touched by the light, the things, the world. They were there, visible again, as if visibility were their own property, not a gift from the rising sun.

In this dawn, there was nothing but the light itself. Indeed there was not even light, we would have said, but only color: blue.

5. Building in Arlington, Va., containing most of the United States Defense offices.
6. The Oval Room in the United States President's office; the Hot Line was a system for emergency communication between the American President and Soviet authorities.

There was no compass bearing to it. It was not brighter in the east. There was no east or west. There was only up and down, below and above. Below was dark. The blue light came from above. Brightness fell. Beneath, where the shaking thunder had stilled, the brightness died away through violet into blindness.

We, arising, watched light fall.

In a way it was more like an ethereal snowfall than like a sunrise. The light seemed to be in discrete particles, infinitesimal flecks, slowly descending, faint, fainter than fleeks of fine snow on a dark night, and tinier; but blue. A soft, penetrating blue tending to the violet, the color of the shadows in an iceberg, the color of a streak of sky between gray clouds on a winter afternoon before snow: faint in intensity but vivid in hue: the color of the remote, the color of the cold, the color farthest from the sun.

On Saturday night they held a scientific congress in our room. Clara and Max came, of course, and the engineer Phil Drum and three others who had worked on the sun tap. Phil Drum was very pleased with himself because he had actually built one of the things, a solar cell, and brought it along. I don't think it had occurred to either Max or Simon to build one. Once they knew it could be done they were satisfied and wanted to get on with something else. But Phil unwrapped his baby with a lot of flourish, and people made remarks like, "Mr. Watson, will you come here a minute," and "Hey, Wilbur, you're off the ground!" and "I say, nasty mould you've got there, Alec, why don't you throw it out?" and "Ugh, ugh, burns, burns, wow, ow," the latter from Max, who does look a little pre-Mousterian.[7] Phil explained that he had exposed the cell for one minute at four in the afternoon up in Washington Park during a light rain. The lights were back on on the West Side since Thursday, so we could test it without being conspicious.

We turned off the lights, after Phil had wired the table-lamp cord to the cell. He turned on the lamp switch. The bulb came on, about twice as bright as before, at its full forty watts—city power of course was never full strength. We all looked at it. It was a dime-store table with a metallized gold base and a white plasticloth shade.

"Brighter than a thousand suns,"[8] Simon murmured from the bed.

7. The remarks parody the first communication on a telephone by its inventor, Alexander Graham Bell (1847–1922); Wilbur Wright (1867–1912), who with his brother Orville (1871–1948), built the craft in which the first powered flight through air was made; Sir Alexander Fleming (1881–1955), discoverer of penicillin; and the first man to discover fire. Mousterians were Paleolithic cave dwellers in France.

8. A reference to the first atomic explosion.

"Could it be," said Clara Edmonds, "that we physicists have known sin[9]—and have come out the other side?"

"It really wouldn't be any good at all for making bombs with," Max said dreamily.

"Bombs," Phil Drum said with scorn. "Bombs are obsolete. Don't you realize that we could move a mountain with this kind of power? I mean pick up Mount Hood, move it, and set it down. We could thaw Antarctica, we could freeze the Congo. We could sink a continent. Give me a fulcrum and I'll move the world.[1] Well, Archimedes, you've got your fulcrum. The sun."

"Christ," Simon said, "the radio, Belle!"

The bathroom door was shut and I had put cotton over the bug, but he was right; if they were going to go ahead at this rate there had better be some added static. And though I liked watching their faces in the clear light of the lamp—they all had good, interesting faces, well worn, like the handles of wooden tools or the rocks in a running stream—I did not much want to listen to them talk tonight. Not because I wasn't a scientist, that made no difference. And not because I disagreed or disapproved or disbelieved anything they said. Only because it grieved me terribly, their talking. Because they couldn't rejoice aloud over a job done and a discovery made, but had to hide there and whisper about it. Because they couldn't go out into the sun.

I went into the bathroom with my viola and sat on the toilet lid and did a long set of sautillé exercises. Then I tried to work at the Forrest trio, but it was too assertive. I played the solo part from *Harold in Italy*,[2] which is beautiful, but it wasn't quite the right mood either. They were still going strong in the other room. I began to improvise.

After a few minutes in E-minor the light over the shaving mirror began to flicker and dim; then it died. Another outage. The table lamp in the other room did not go out, being connected with the sun, not with the twenty-three atomic fission plants that power the Greater Portland Area. Within two seconds somebody had switched it off, too, so that we shouldn't be the only window in the West Hills left alight; and I could hear them rooting for candles and rattling matches. I went on improvising in the dark. Without light, when you couldn't see all the hard shiny surfaces of things, the sound seemed softer and less muddled. I went on, and it began to shape up. All the laws of harmonies sang together when the bow came down. The strings of the viola were the cords of my own voice, tightened by sorrow, tuned to the pitch of

9. Paraphrase of statement by J. Robert Oppenheimer, one of the scientists who perfected the atomic bomb.
1. Said by Archimedes (287–212 B.C.), Greek mathematician and inventor.
2. Symphony by Hector Berlioz (1803–1869).

joy. The melody created itself out of air and energy, it raised up the valleys, and the mountains and hills were made low, and the crooked straight, and the rough places plain. And the music went out to the dark sea and sang in the darkness, over the abyss.

When I came out they were all sitting there and none of them was talking. Max had been crying. I could see little candle flames in the tears around his eyes. Simon lay flat on the bed in the shadows, his eyes closed. Phil Drum sat hunched over, holding the solar cell in his hands.

I loosened the pegs, put the bow and the viola in the case, and cleared my throat. It was embarrassing. I finally said, "I'm sorry."

One of the women spoke: Rose Abramski, a private student of Simon's, a big shy woman who could hardly speak at all unless it was in mathematical symbols. "I saw it," she said. "I saw it. I saw the white towers, and the water streaming down their sides, and running back down to the sea. And the sunlight shining in the streets, after ten thousand years of darkness."

"I heard them," Simon said, very low, from the shadow. "I heard their voices."

"Oh, Christ! Stop it!" Max cried out, and got up and went blundering out into the unlit hall, without his coat. We heard him running down the stairs.

"Phil," said Simon, lying there, "could we raise up the white towers, with our lever and our fulcrum?"

After a long silence Phil Drum answered, "We have the power to do it."

"What else do we need?" Simon said. "What else do we need, besides power?"

Nobody answered him.

The blue changed. It became brighter, lighter, and at the same time thicker: impure. The ethereal luminosity of blue-violet turned to turquoise, intense and opaque. Still we could not have said that everything was now turquoise-colored, for there were still no things. There was nothing, except the color of turquoise.

The change continued. The opacity became veined and thinned. The dense, solid color began to appear translucent, transparent. Then it seemed as if we were in the heart of a sacred jade, or the brilliant crystal of a sapphire or an emerald.

As at the inner structure of a crystal, there was no motion. But there was something, now, to see. It was as if we saw the motionless, elegant inward structure of the molecules of a precious stone. Planes and angles appeared about us, shadowless and clear in that even, glowing, blue-green light.

These were the walls and towers of the city, the streets, the windows, the gates.

We knew them, but we did not recognize them. We did not dare to recognize them. It had been so long. And it was so strange. We had used to dream, when we lived in this city. We had lain down, nights, in the rooms behind the windows, and slept, and dreamed. We had all dreamed of the ocean, of the deep sea. Were we not dreaming now?

Sometimes the thunder and tremor deep below us rolled again, but it was faint now, far away; as far away as our memory of the thunder and the tremor and the fire and the towers falling, long ago. Neither the sound nor the memory frightened us. We knew them.

The sapphire light brightened overhead to green, almost green-gold. We looked up. The tops of the highest towers were hard to see, glowing in the radiance of light. The streets and doorways were darker, more clearly defined.

In one of those long, jewel-dark streets something was moving—something not composed of planes and angles, but of curves and arcs. We all turned to look at it, slowly, wondering as we did so at the slow ease of our own motion, our freedom. Sinuous, with a beautiful flowing, gathering, rolling movement, now rapid and now tentative, the thing drifted across the street from a blank garden wall to the recess of a door. There, in the dark blue shadow, it was hard to see for a while. We watched. A pale blue curve appeared at the top of the doorway. A second followed, and a third. The moving thing clung or hovered there, above the door, like a swaying knot of silvery cords or a boneless hand, one arched finger pointing carelessly to something above the lintel of the door, something like itself, but motionless—a carving. A carving in jade light. A carving in stone.

Delicately and easily the long curving tentacle followed the curves of the carved figure, the eight petal-limbs, the round eyes. Did it recognize its image?

The living one swung suddenly, gathered its curves in a loose knot, and darted away down the street, swift and sinuous. Behind it a faint cloud of darker blue hung for a minute and dispersed, revealing again the carved figure above the door: the sea-flower, the cuttlefish, quick, great-eyed, graceful, evasive, the cherished sign, carved on a thousand walls, worked into the design of cornices, pavements, handles, lids of jewel boxes, canopies, tapestries, tabletops, gateways.

Down another street, about the level of the first-floor windows, came a flickering drift of hundreds of motes of silver. With a single motion all turned toward the cross street, and glittered off into the dark blue shadows.

There were shadows, now.

We looked up, up from the flight of silverfish, up from the streets where the jade-green currents flowed and the blue shadows fell. We moved and looked up, yearning, to the high towers of our city. They stood, the fallen towers. They glowed in the ever-brightening radiance, not blue or blue-green, up there, but gold. Far above them lay a vast, circular, trembling brightness: the sun's light on the surface of the sea.

We are here. When we break through the bright circle into life, the water will break and stream white down the white sides of the towers, and run down the steep streets back into the sea. The water will glitter in dark hair, on the eyelids of dark eyes, and dry to a thin white film of salt.

We are here.

Whose voice? Who called to us?

He was with me for twelve days. On January 28 the 'crats came from the Bureau of Health, Education and Welfare and said that since he was receiving Unemployment Compensation while suffering from an untreated illness, the government must look after him and restore him to health, because health is the inalienable right of the citizens of a democracy. He refused to sign the consent forms, so the chief health officer signed them. He refused to get up, so two of the policemen pulled him up off the bed. He started to try to fight them. The chief health officer pulled his gun and said that if he continued to struggle he would shoot him for resisting welfare, and arrest me for conspiracy to defraud the government. The man who was holding my arms behind my back said they could always arrest me for unreported pregnancy with intent to form a nuclear family.[3] At that Simon stopped trying to get free. It was really all he was trying to do, not to fight them, just to get his arms free. He looked at me, and they took him out.

He is in the federal hospital in Salem. I have not been able to find out whether he is in the regular hospital or the mental wards.

It was on the radio again yesterday, about the rising land masses in the South Atlantic and the Western Pacific. At Max's the other night I saw a TV special explaining about geophysical stresses and subsidence and faults. The U.S. Geodetic Service is doing a lot of advertising around town, the most common one is a big billboard that says IT'S NOT OUR FAULT! with a picture of a beaver pointing to a schematic map that shows how even if Oregon has a major earthquake and subsidence

---

3. Parents and children regarded as a unit.

as California did last month, it will not affect Portland, or only the
western suburbs perhaps. The news also said that they plan to halt the
tidal waves in Florida by dropping nuclear bombs where Miami was.
Then they will reattach Florida to the mainland with landfill. They
are already advertising real estate for housing developments on the
landfill. The president is staying at the Mile High White House in
Aspen, Colorado. I don't think it will do him much good. Houseboats
down on the Willamette are selling for $500,000. There are no trains
or buses running south from Portland, because all the highways were
badly damaged by the tremors and landslides last week, so I will have
to see if I can get to Salem on foot. I still have the rucksack I bought
for the Mount Hood Wilderness Week. I got some dry lima beans and
raisins with my Federal Fair Share Super Value Green Stamp minimal
ration book for February—it took the whole book—and Phil Drum
made me a tiny camp stove powered with the solar cell. I didn't want
to take the Primus, it's too bulky, and I did want to be able to carry the
viola. Max gave me a half pint of brandy. When the brandy is gone I
expect I will stuff this notebook into the bottle and put the cap on tight
and leave it on a hillside somewhere between here and Salem. I like
to think of it being lifted up little by little by the water, and rocking,
and going out to the dark sea.

Where are you?
We are here. Where have you gone?

1975

DAVID MADDEN

NO TRACE

Gasping for air, his legs weak from the climb up the stairs, Ernest stopped outside the room, surprised to find the door wide open, almost sorry he had made it before the police. An upsurge of nausea, a wave of suffocation forced him to suck violently for breath as he stepped into Gordon's room—his *own* two decades before.

Tinted psychedelic emerald, the room looked like a hippie pad posing for a photograph in *Life*, but the monotonous electronic frenzy he heard was the seventeen-year locusts, chewing spring leaves outside. He wondered whether the sedative had so dazed him that he had stumbled into the wrong room. No, now, as every time in his own college years when he had entered this room, what struck him first was the light falling through the leaded, green-stained windowglass. As the light steeped him in the ambience of the early fortics, it simultaneously illuminated the artifacts of the present. Though groggy from the sedative, he experienced, intermittently, moments of startling clarity when he saw each object separately.

Empty beer can pyramids.

James Dean, stark poster photograph.

Records leaning on orange crate.

Life-sized redheaded girl, banjo blocking her vagina, lurid color.

Rolltop desk, swivel chair, typewriter.

Poster photograph of a teen-age hero he didn't recognize.

Large CORN FLAKES carton.

Ernest recognized nothing, except the encyclopedias, as Gordon's. Debris left behind when Gordon's roommate ran away. Even so, knowing Gordon, Ernest had expected the cleanest room in DeLozier Hall, vacant except for suitcases sitting in a neat row, awaiting the end-of-ceremonies dash to the car. He shut the door quietly, listening to an automatic lock catch, as if concealing not just the few possible incriminating objects he had come to discover but the entire spectacle of a room startlingly overpopulated with objects, exhibits, that might bear witness, like archeological unearthings, to the life lived there.

He glanced into the closet. Gordon's suitcases did not have the look of imminent departure. Clothes hung, hangers crammed tightly together, on the rack above. The odor emanating from the closet convulsed him slightly, making him shut his eyes, see Gordon raise his arm, the sleeve of his gown slip down, revealing his white arm, the grenade in his hand. Shaking his head to shatter the image, Ernest opened his eyes.

Turning abruptly from the closet, he moved aimlessly about the room, distracted by objects that moved toward him. He had to hurry before someone discovered the cot downstairs empty, before police came to lock up Gordon's room. The green light drew him to the window where the babel of locusts was louder. Through the antique glass, he saw, as if under water, the broken folding chairs below, parodying postures into which the explosion had thrown the audience. The last of the curiosity seekers, turning away, trampling locusts, left three policemen alone among knocked over chairs.

I AM ANONYMOUS/HELP ME. Nailed, buttons encrusted the windowframe. SUPPORT MENTAL HEALTH OR I'LL KILL YOU. SNOOPY FOR PRESIDENT. As he turned away, chalked, smudged lettering among the buttons drew him back: DOCTOR SPOCK IS AN ABORTIONIST. After his roommate ran away, why hadn't Gordon erased that? Jerking his head away from the buttons again, Ernest saw a ballpoint pen sticking up in the desk top. On a piece of paper, the title "The Theme of Self-hatred in the Works of—", the rest obscured by a blue circular, a message scrawled in lipstick across it: GORDY BABY, LET ME HOLD SOME BREAD FOR THIS CAUSE, MY OLD LADY IS SENDING ME A CHECK NEXT WEEK. THE CARTER. The circular pleaded for money for the Civil Liberties Union. Ernest shoved it aside, but "The Theme of Self-hatred in the Works of—" broke off anyway. Gordon's blue scrapbook, green in the light, startled him. Turning away, Ernest noticed *Revolution in a Revolution?* A *Tolkien Reader, Boy Scout Handbook* in a bookcase.

As he stepped toward the closet, something crunching harshly underfoot made him jump back. Among peanut shells, brown streaks in the green light. Gordon tracking smashed guts of locusts. Fresh streaks, green juices of leaves acid-turned to slime. He lifted one foot, trying to look at the sole of his shoe, lost balance, staggered backward, let himself drop on the edge of a cot. If investigators compared the stains—. Using his handkerchief, he wiped the soles. Dying and dead locusts. *The Alumni Bulletin* had reported, had littered the campus paths for weeks. Everywhere, the racket of their devouring machinery, the reek of their putrefaction when they fell, gorged. Sniffing his lapels, he inhaled the stench of locusts and sweat, saw flecks of—. He shut his eyes, raked breath into his lungs, lay back on the cot.

Even as he tried to resist the resurgent power of the sedative, Ernest felt his exhausted mind and body sink into sleep. When sirens woke him, he thought for a moment he still lay on the bare mattress in the room downstairs, listening to the siren of that last ambulance. The injured, being carried away on stretchers, passed by him again. The Dean of Men had hustled Ernest into a vacated room, and sent to his house nearby for a sedative. Sinking into sleep, seeing the grenade go off again and again until the explosions became tiny, receding, mute puffs of smoke, Ernest had suddenly imagined Lydia's face when he would have to telephone her about Gordon, and the urgency of being prepared for the police had made him sit up in the bed. The hall was empty, everyone seemed to be outside, and he had sneaked up the narrow back stairway to Gordon's room.

Wondering which cot was Gordon's, which his roommate's, and why *both* had recently been slept in, Ernest sat up and looked along the wooden frame for the cigarette burn he had deliberately made the day before his own commencement when he and his roommate were packing for home. As he leaned across the cot, looking for the burn, his hand grazed a stiff yellow spot on the sheet. The top sheet stuck to the bottom sheet. An intuition of his son's climactic moment in an erotic dream the night before—the effort to keep from crying choked him. "I advocate—." Leaping away from the cot, he stopped, reeling, looked up at a road sign that hung over the door: DRIVE SLOWLY, WE LOVE OUR KIDS. Somewhere an unprotected street. What's-his-name's fault. *His* junk cluttered the room.

Wondering what the suitcases would reveal, Ernest stepped into the closet. Expecting them to be packed, he jerked up on them and jolted himself, they were so light. He opened them anyway. Crumbs of dirt, curls of lint. Gordon's clothes, that Lydia had helped him select, or sent him as birthday or Easter presents, hung in the closet, pressed. Fetid clothes Gordon's roommate—Carter, yes, Carter—had left behind dangled from hooks, looking more like costumes. A theatrical black leather jacket, faded denim pants, a wide black belt, ruby studs, a jade velvet cape, and, on the floor, boots and sandals. In a dark corner leaned the hooded golf clubs Ernest had handed down to Gordon, suspecting he would never lift them from the bag. "You don't like to hunt," he had blurted out one evening. "You don't like to fish. You don't get excited about football. Isn't there *something* we could do together?" "We could just sit and talk." They had ended up watching the Ed Sullivan Show.

Ernest's hand, paddling fish-like among the clothes in the dim closet, snagged on a pin that fastened a price tag to one of the suits he had bought Gordon for Christmas. Though he knew from Lydia that no girl came regularly on weekends from Melbourne's sister college to visit Gordon, surely he had had some occasion to wear the suit. Stacked on the shelf above: shirts, the cellophane packaging unbroken. His fingers inside one of the cowboy boots, Ernest stroked leather that was still flesh soft. Imagining Lydia's hysteria at the sight of Gordon, he saw a mortician handling Gordon's body, sorting, arranging pieces, saw not Gordon's, but the body of one of his clients on view, remembering how awed he had been by the miracle of skill that had put the man back together only three days after the factory explosion. Ernest stroked a damp polo shirt, unevenly stained pale green in the wash, sniffled it, realizing that Carter's body could not have left an odor that lasting. Now he understood what had disturbed him about Gordon's clothes, showing, informal and ragged, under the skirt of the black gown, at the sleeves, at the neck, as he sat on the platform, waiting to deliver the valedictory address.

Gripping the iron pipe that held hangers shoved tightly together, his body swinging forward as his knees sagged, Ernest let the grenade explode again. Gentle, almost delicate, Gordon suddenly raises his voice above the nerve-wearying shrill of the seventeen-year locusts that encrust the barks of the trees, a voice that had been too soft to be heard except by the men on the platform whose faces expressed shock—at *what* Ernest still did not know—and as that voice screams, a high-pitched nasal screech like brass, "I advocate a total revolution!" Gordon's left arm raises a grenade, holds it out before him, eclipsing his still-open mouth, and in his right hand, held down stiff at his side, the pin glitters on his finger. Frightened, raring back, as Ernest himself does, in their seats, many people try to laugh the grenade off as a bold but imprudent rhetorical gesture.

Tasting again Gordon's blood on his mouth, Ernest thrust his face between smothering wool coats, retched again, vomited at last.

As he tried to suck air into his lungs, gluey bands of vomit strangled him, lack of oxygen smothered him. Staggering backward out of the closet, he stood in the middle of the room, swaying. Avoiding Gordon's, he lowered himself carefully onto the edge of Carter's cot by the closet. He craved air but the stained-glass window, the only window in this corner room, wouldn't open, a disadvantage that came with the privilege of having the room with the magnificent light. The first time he had seen the room since his own graduation—he and Lydia had brought Gordon down to begin his freshman year—he had had to heave breath up from dry lungs to tell Gordon about the window. Early in the nineteenth century when DeLozier Hall was the entire school— and already one of the finest boys' colleges in the midwest—this corner room and the two adjacent comprised the chapel. From the fire that destroyed DeLozier Hall in 1938, three years before Ernest himself arrived as a freshman, only this window was saved. Except for the other chapel windows, DeLozier had been restored, brick by brick, exactly as it was originally. "First chance you get, go look in the cemetery at the grave of the only victim of the fire—nobody knows who it was, so the remains were never claimed. Probably somebody just passing through." He had deliberately saved that to leave Gordon with something interesting to think about. From the edge of the cot, he saw the bright eruption of vomit on Gordon's clothes.

The chapel steeple chimed four o'clock. The racket of the locusts' mandibles penetrated the room as if carried in through the green light. Photosynthesis. Chlorophyll. The D+ in biology that wrecked his average.

Rising, he took out his handkerchief and went into the closet. When the handkerchief was sopping wet, he dropped it into a large beer carton, tasting again the foaming beer at his lips, tingling beads on his tongue in the hot tent on the lawn as the ceremonies were beginning. He had reached the green just as the procession was forming: "You've been accepted by Harvard Grad School." Gordon had looked at him without a glimmer of recognition—Ernest had assumed that the shrilling of the locusts had drowned out his voice—then led his classmates toward the platfom.

Ernest was standing on a dirty tee shirt. He finished the job with that, leaving a corner to wipe his hands on, then he dropped it, also, into the carton.

He sat on the edge of the cot again, afraid to lie back on the mattress, sink into the gulley Carter had made over the four years and fall asleep. He only leaned back, propped on one arm. Having collected himself, he would make a thorough search, to prepare himself for whatever the police would find, tag, then show him for final identification. An exhibit of shocks. The police might even hold him responsible somehow—delinquently ignorant of his son's habits, associates. They might even find something that would bring in the FBI—membership in some radical organization. What was *not* possible in a year like this? He had to arm himself against interrogation. "What sort of boy was your son?" "Typical, average, normal boy in every way. Ask my wife." But how many times had he read that in newspaper accounts of monstrous crimes? What did it mean anymore to be normal?

Glancing around the room, on the verge of an unsettling realization, Ernest saw a picture of Lydia leaning on Carter's rolltop desk.
Even in shadow, the enlarged snapshot he had taken himself was radi-
ant. A lucid April sunburst in the budding trees behind her, bleached
her green dress white, made her blond hair look almost platinum.
Clowning, she had kicked out one foot, upraising and spreading her
arms, and when her mouth finished yelling "Spring!" he had snapped
her dimpled smile. On the campus of Melbourne's sister college Briar-
heath, locusts riddled those same trees, twenty years taller, forty miles
from where he sat, while Lydia languished in bed alone—a mysterious
disease, a lingering illness. Then the shunned realization came, made
him stand up as though he were an intruder. On this cot, or perhaps
the one across the room, he had made love to Lydia—that spring, the
first and only time before their marriage. In August, she had discovered
that she was pregnant. Gordon had never for a moment given them
cause to regret that inducement to marriage. But Lydia's cautionary
approach to sexual relations had made Gordon an only child.

Glancing around the room he hoped to discover a picture of himself. Seeing none, he sat down again. Under his thumb, he felt a rough
texture on the wooden frame of the cot. The cigarette burn he had
made himself in 1945. Then *this* had been Gordon's cot. Of course.
By his desk. Flinging back the sheets, Ernest found nothing.

He crossed the room to Carter's cot where a dimestore reproduction of a famous painting of Jesus hung on the wall. Jerking hard to
unstick the sheets, he lay bare Carter's bed. Twisted white sweat socks
at the bottom. He shook them out. Much too large for Gordon. But
Carter, then Gordon, had worn them with Carter's cowboy boots. Gordon had been sleeping in Carter's bed. Pressing one knee against the
edge of the cot, Ernest leaned over and pushed his palms against the
wall to examine closely what it was that had disturbed him about
the painting. Tiny holes like acne scars in Jesus' upturned face. Ernest
looked up. Ragged, feathered darts hung like bats from the ceiling.
Someone had printed in Gothic script on the bottom white border:
J. C. BLOWS. Using his fingernails, Ernest scraped at the edge of the
tape, pulled carefully, but white wall paint chipped off, exposing the
wallpaper design that dated back to his own life in the room. He
stopped, aware that he had only started his search, that if he took this
painting, he might be inclined to take other things. His intention, he
stressed again to himself, was only to investigate, to be forewarned, not
to search and destroy. But already he had the beer carton containing
Carter's, or Gordon's, tee shirt and his own handkerchief to dispose of.
He let the picture hang, one edge curling over, obscuring the lettering.

Backing into the center of the room, one leg painfully asleep, Ernest looked at the life-sized girl stuck to the wall with masking tape, holding a banjo over her vagina, the neck of it between her breasts, tip of her tongue touching one of the tuning knobs. His eye on a sticker stuck to the pane, he went to the window again: FRUIT OF THE LOOM 100% VIRGIN COTTON. More buttons forced him to read: WAR IS GOOD BUSINESS, INVEST YOUR SON. How would the police separate Carter's from Gordon's things? FLOWER POWER. He would simply tell them that Carter had left his junk behind when he bolted. But Gordon's failure to discard some of it, at least the most offensive items, bewildered Ernest. One thing appeared clear: living daily since January among Carter's possessions, Gordon had worn Carter's clothes, slept in Carter's bed.

From the ceiling above the four corners of the room hung the blank faces of four amplifiers, dark mouths gaping. Big Brother is listening. 1984. Late Show. Science fiction bored Ernest. Squatting, he flipped through records leaning in a Sunkist orange crate. MILES DAVIS/ THE GRATEFUL DEAD/LEADBELLY/THE BEATLES, their picture x-ed out/ MANTOVANI/THE MAMAS AND THE PAPAS/THE LOVING SPOONFUL. He was wasting time—Carter's records couldn't be used against Gordon. But then he found Glenn Miller's "In the Mood" and "Moonlight Serenade," a 78-rpm collector's item he had given Gordon. "Soothing background music for test-cramming time." TOM PAXTON/THE MOTHERS OF INVENTION/1812 OVERTURE (Gordon's?)/THE ELECTRONIC ERA/JOAN BAEZ/CHARLIE PARKER/BARTOK.

Rising, he saw a poster he had not glimpsed before, stuck to the wall with a bowie knife, curled inward at its four corners: a color photograph of a real banana rising like a finger out of the middle of a cartoon fist.

Over the rolltop desk hung a guitar, its mouth crammed full of wilted roses. The vomit taste in his own mouth made Ernest retch. Hoping Carter had left some whiskey behind, he quickly searched the rolltop desk, and found a Jack Daniel's bottle in one of the cubbyholes. Had Gordon taken the last swallow himself this morning just before stepping out of this room?

Finding a single cigarette in a twisted package, Ernest lit it, quickly snuffed it in a hubcap used as an ashtray. The smell of fresh smoke would make the police suspicious. Recent daily activity had left Carter's desk a shambles. Across the room, Gordon's desk was merely a surface, strewn with junk. The Royal portable typewriter he had given Gordon for Christmas his freshman year sat on Carter's desk, the capital lock key set.

Among the papers on Carter's desk, Ernest searched for Gordon's notes for his speech. Ernest had been awed by the way Gordon prepared his senior project in high school—very carefully, starting with an outline, going through three versions, using cards, dividers, producing a forty-page research paper on Wordsworth. Lydia had said, "Why Ernest, he's been that way since junior high, worrying about college." On Carter's desk, Ernest found the beginnings of papers on Dryden, *The Iliad, Huckleberry Finn.* While he had always felt contentment in Gordon's perfect social behavior and exemplary academic conduct and achievements, sustained from grammar school right on through college, Ernest had sometimes felt, but quickly dismissed, a certain dismay. In her presence, Ernest agreed with Lydia's objections to Gordon's desire to major in English, but alone with him, he had told Gordon, "Satisfy yourself first of all." But he couldn't tell Gordon that he had pretended to agree with his mother to prevent her from exaggerating her suspicion that their marriage had kept him from switching to English himself after he got his B.S. in Business Administration. Each time she brought up the subject, Ernest wondered for weeks what his life would have been like had he become an English professor. As he hastily surveyed the contents of the desk, he felt the absence of the papers Gordon had written that had earned A's, helping to qualify him, as the student with the highest honors, to give the valedictory address.

Handling chewed pencils made Ernest sense the taste of lead and wood on his own tongue. He noticed a CORN FLAKES box but was distracted by a ball-point pen that only great force could have thrust so firmly into the oak desk. The buffalo side of a worn nickel leaned against a bright Kennedy half-dollar. Somewhere under this floor lay a buffalo nickel he had lost himself through a crack. Perhaps Gordon or Carter had found it. He unfolded a letter. It thanked Carter for his two-hundred-dollar contribution to a legal defense fund for students who had gone, without permission, to Cuba. Pulling another letter out of a pigeonhole, he discovered a bright gold piece resembling a medal. Trojan contraceptive. His own brand before Lydia became bedridden. Impression of it still on his wallet—no, that was the *old* wallet he carried as a senior. The letter thanked Carter for his inquiry about summer work with an organization sponsored by SNCC.[1] In another pigeonhole, he found a letter outlining Carter's duties during a summer voter campaign in Mississippi. "As for the friend you mention, we don't believe it would be in our best interests to attempt to persuade him to join in our work. If persuasion is desirable, who is more strategically situated than you, his own roommate?" Marginal scrawl in pencil: "This is the *man* talking, Baby!"

---

1. Student Nonviolent Coordinating Committee, a national radical student group.

As he rifled through the numerous letters, folded hastily and slipped or stuffed into pigeonholes, Ernest felt he was getting an overview of liberal and left-wing activities, mostly student-oriented, over the past five years, for Carter's associations began in high school. He lifted his elbow off Gordon's scrapbook—birthday present from Lydia—and flipped through it. Newspaper photo of students at a rally, red ink enringing a blurred head, a raised fist. Half full: clippings of Carter's activities. AP photo: Carter, bearded, burning his draft card. But no creep—handsome, hair and smile like Errol Flynn in "The Sea Hawk." Looking around at the poster photograph he hadn't recognized when he came in, Ernest saw Carter, wearing a Gestapo billcap, a monocle, an opera cape, black tights, Zorro boots, carrying a riding crop. When Ernest first noticed the ads—"Blow Yourself Up"—he had thought it a good deal at $2.99. Had Gordon given the scrapbook to Carter, or had he cut and pasted the items himself?

Ernest shoved the scrapbook aside and reached for a letter. "Gordy, This is just to tell you to save your tears over King.[2] We all wept over JFK our senior year in high school, and we haven't seen straight since. King just wasn't where the action's at. Okay, so I told you different a few months ago! How come you're always light years behind *me?* Catch up! Make the leap! I'm dumping all these creeps that try to play a rigged game. Look at Robert! I think I'm beginning to understand Oswald and Speck and Whitman.[3] They're the *real* individuals! They work alone while we run together like zebras. But, on the other hand, maybe the same cat did *all* those jobs. And maybe Carter knows who. Sleep on *that* one, Gordy, Baby." Boot camp. April 5. Suddenly, the first day back from Christmas vacation, Carter had impulsively walked out of this room. "See America first! Then the world!" That much Gordon had told them when Ernest and Lydia telephoned at Easter, made uneasy by his terse letter informing them that he was remaining on campus to "watch the locusts emerge from their seventeen-year buried infancy into appalling one-week adulthood," adding, parenthetically, that he had to finish his honors project. Marriage to Lydia had prevented Ernest's desire, like Carter's, to see the world. Not "prevented." Postponed perhaps. A vice-president of a large insurance company might hope to make such a dream come true—if only after he retired. Deep in a pigeonhole, Ernest found a snapshot of Gordon, costumed for a part in *Tom Sawyer*—one of the kids who saunter by in the whitewashing scene. False freckles. He had

2. Martin Luther King Jr. (1929–1968).
3. Lee Harvey Oswald assassinated President Kennedy. Richard Speck and Charlie Whitman were notorious mass murderers.

forgotten. On the back, tabs of fuzzy black paper—ripped out of the scrapbook.

Mixed in with Carter's were Lydia's letters. "Gordon Precious, You Promised—" Feverish eyes. Bed rashes. Blue Cross. Solitude. Solitaire. "Sleep, Lydia." Finding none of his own letters, Ernest remembered writing last week from his office, and the sense of solitude on the fifteenth floor, where he had seemed the only person stirring, came back momentarily. Perhaps in some drawer or secret compartment all his letters to Gordon (few though they had been) and perhaps other little mementos—his sharp-shooter's medal and the Korean coin that he had given Gordon, relics of his three years in the service, and matchbooks from the motels where he and Gordon had stayed on occasional weekend trips—were stored. Surely, somewhere in the room, he would turn up a picture of himself. He had always known that Gordon preferred his mother, but had he conscientiously excluded his father from his life, eliminating all trace? No, he shouldn't jump to conclusions. He had yet to gather and analyze all the evidence. Thinking in those terms about what he was doing, Ernest realized that not only was he going to destroy evidence to protect Gordon's memory as much as possible and shield Lydia, he was now deliberately searching for fragments of a new Gordon, hoping to know and understand him, each discovery destroying the old Gordon who would now always remain a stranger.

But he didn't have time to move so slowly, like a slow-motion movie. Turning quickly in Carter's swivel chair, Ernest bent over the large CORN FLAKES box, brimful of papers that had been dropped, perhaps tossed into it. Gordon's themes, including his honors thesis in a stiff black binder: "ANGUISH, SPIRITUAL AND PHYSICAL IN GERARD MANLEY HOPKINS' POETRY. Approved by: Alfred Hansen, Thorne Halpert (who had come to Melbourne in Ernest's own freshman year), Richard Kelp, John Morton." In red pencil at the bottom, haphazard scrawls, as if they were four different afterthoughts: "Disapproved by: Jason Carter, Gordon Foster, Lydia Foster, Gerard Manley Hopkins." Up the left margin, in lead pencil: "PISS ON ALL OF YOU!" Ernest saw Gordon burning the box in the community dump on the edge of the village.

Ernest stepped over to Gordon's desk, seeking some sort of perspective, some evidence of Gordon's life before he moved over to the rolltop desk and mingled his own things with Carter's. The gray steel drawers were empty. Not just empty. Clean. Wiped clean with a rag—a swipe in the middle drawer had dried in a soapy pattern of broken beads of moisture. Ernest saw there an image: a clean table that made him feel the presence behind him of another table where Gordon now, in pieces, lay. Under dirty clothes slung aside lay stacks of books and old newspapers, whose headlines of war, riot, murder, assassinations, negotiations seemed oddly remote in this room. The portable tape recorder Ernest had given Gordon last fall to help him through his senior year. He pressed the LISTEN button. Nothing. He pressed the REWIND, LISTEN. ". . . defy analysis. But let's examine this passage from Aristotle's 'De Interpretatione': 'In the case of that which is or which has taken place, propositions, whether positive or negative, must be true or false.' " "What did he say?" Someone whispering. "I didn't catch it." (Gordon's voice?) "Again, in the case of a pair of contraries—contradictories, that is. . . ." The professor's voice slipped into a fizzing silence. "I'm recording your speech, son," he had written to Gordon last week, "so your mother can hear it." But Ernest had forgotten his tape recorder.

The headline of a newspaper announced Charlie Whitman's sniper slaying of twelve people from the observation tower of the University administration building in Austin, Texas. But that was two summers past. Melbourne had no summer school. Folded, as though mailed. Had Carter sent it to Gordon from—Where *was* Carter from? Had Gordon received it at home?

A front page news photo showed a Buddhist monk burning on a Saigon street corner. Ernest's sneer faded in bewilderment as he saw that the caption identified an American woman burning on the steps of the Pentagon. Smudged pencil across the flames: THE MOTHER OF US ALL. Children bereft, left to a father, perhaps no father even. Ernest tried to remember the name of one of his clients, an English professor, who shot himself a week after the assassination of Martin Luther King. No note. Any connection? His wife showed Ernest the Student Guide to Courses—one anonymous, thus sexless, student's evaluation might have been a contributing factor: "This has got to be the most boring human being on the face of the earth." Since then, Ernest had tried to make his own presentations at company meetings more entertaining. Lately, many cases of middle-aged men who had mysteriously committed suicide hovered on the periphery of Ernest's consciousness. It struck him now that in every case, he had forgotten most of the "sensible" explanations, leaving nothing but mystery. Wondering whether those men had seen something in the eyes of their children, even their wives, that Ernest himself had been blind to, he shuddered but did not shake off a sudden clenching of muscles in his shoulders. "When the cause of death is legally ruled as suicide," he had often written, "the company is relieved of its obligations to—" Did Gordon *know* the grenade would explode? Or did he borrow it, perhaps steal it from a museum, and then did it, like the locusts, seventeen years dormant, suddenly come alive? Ernest had always been lukewarm about gun

controls, but now he would insist on a thorough investigation to deter-
mine where Gordon purchased the grenade. Dealer in war surplus?
Could they *prove* he meant it to go off? "When the cause of death is
legally ruled—" Horrified that he was thinking so reflexively like an
insurance executive, Ernest slammed his fist into his groin, and staggered back into the bed Gordon had abandoned.

His eyes half-opened, he saw his cigarette burn again on the
wooden frame beside his hand. He recalled Gordon's vivid letter home
the first week of his freshman year: "My roommate turns my stomach
by the way he dresses, talks, acts, eats, sleeps." Ernest had thought that
a boy so different from Gordon would be good for him, so his efforts,
made at Lydia's fretful urgings, to have Carter replaced, or to have
Gordon moved, were slapdash. He very much wanted his son to go
through Melbourne in his old room. Books on Gordon's desk at the
foot of the cot caught his attention. Some dating from junior high,
these were all Gordon's, including the Great Books, with their marvel-
ous Syntopicon.[4] As the swelling pain in his groin subsided, Ernest
stood up, hovering over the books.

A frayed copy of *Winnie the Pooh* startled him. "To Ernest, Christmas, 1928. All my love, Grandmother." The year he learned to write,
Gordon had printed his own name in green crayon across the top of
the next page. As Ernest leafed through the book, nostalgia eased his
nerves. Penciled onto Winnie the Pooh was a gigantic penis extending
across the page to Christopher Robin, who was bending over a daisy.
"Damn you, Carter!" Ernest slammed it down—a pillar of books
slurred, tumbled onto the floor. He stood still, staring into the green
light, trying to detect the voices of people who might have heard in the
rooms below. Ernest heard only the locusts in the light. A newspaper
that had fallen leaned and sagged like a tent: Whitman's face looked
up from the floor, two teeth in his high school graduation smile
blacked out, a pencil-drawn tongue flopping out of his mouth. His
name was scratched out and YOU AND ME, BABY was lettered in. Ernest
kicked at the newspaper, twisted his heel into Whitman's face, and the
paper rose up around his ankles like a yellowed flower, soot-dappled.

Ernest backed into the swivel chair, turned, rested his head in his
hands on the rolltop desk, and breathed in fits and starts. He wanted
to throw the hubcap ashtray through the stained-glass window and feel
the spring air rush in upon his face and fill and stretch his lungs.
Cigarillo butts, scorched Robert Burns bands, cigarette butts. Marijuana? He sniffed, but realized he couldn't recognize it if it *were*.

---

4. Two-volume index to the ideas appearing in the Great Books that constitute a curriculum
at the University of Chicago. Index edited by Mortimer Adler (b. 1902).

Was there nothing in the room but pale emanations of Carter's gradual transformation of Gordon? Closing his eyes, trying to conjure up Gordon's face, he saw, clearly, only Carter's smile, like a weapon, in the draft-card-burning photograph. *Wanting* to understand Gordon, he had only a shrill scream of defiance, an explosion, and this littered room with which to begin. He imagined the mortician, fitting pieces together, an arm on a drain board behind him. And when he was finished, what would he have accomplished? In the explosion, Gordon had vacated his body, and now the pieces had stopped moving, but the objects in his room twitched when Ernest touched them. Taking a deep breath, he inhaled the stench of spit and tobacco. He shoved the hubcap aside, and stood up.

Bending his head sideways, mashing his ear against his shoulder, Ernest read the titles of books crammed into cinderblock and pineboard shelves between Carter's cot and the window: *120 Days of Sodom*, the Marquis de Sade/*Autobiography of Malcolm X*/*The Postman Always Rings Twice*, James M. Cain/*Mein Kampf*—. He caught himself reading title and authors aloud in a stupor. Silently, his lips still moving, he read: *Boy Scout Handbook*. Though he had never been a scout, Ernest had agreed with Lydia that, like a fraternity, it would be good for Gordon in future life. *Freedom Now*, Max Reiner/*Nausea*, Jean-Paul Sartre/*Atlas Shrugged*, Ayn Rand/*The Scarlet Letter*. Heritage, leatherbound edition he had given Gordon for his sixteenth birthday. He had broken in the new Volkswagen, a surprise graduation present, driving it down. Late for the ceremonies, he had parked it, illegally, behind DeLozier Hall so it would be there when he and Gordon brought the suitcases and his other belongings down. *Castro's Cause*, Harvey Kreyborg/*Notes from Underground*, Dostoyevski/*Lady Chatterley's Lover*, Ernest's own copy. Had Gordon sneaked it out of the house? Slumping to his knees, he squinted at titles he had been unable to make out: Carter had cynically shelved Ernest's own copy of *Profiles in Courage*, passed on to Gordon, next to *Oswald Resurrected* by Eugene Federogh.

There was a book with a library number on its spine. He would have to return that. The Gordon he had known would have done so before commencement. Afraid the police might come in suddenly and catch him there, Ernest rose to his feet. Glancing through several passages, highlighted with a yellow magic-marker, he realized that he was reading about "anguish, spiritual and physical, in Gerard Manley Hopkins' poetry." He rooted through the CORN FLAKES box again, took out Gordon's honors thesis. Flipping through the pages, he discovered a passage that duplicated, verbatim, a marked passage in the book. No footnote reference. The bibliography failed to cite the book that he held in his hand and now let drop, along with the honors thesis, into the beer carton onto Carter's fouled tee shirt and Ernest's handkerchief.

Why had he cheated? He never had before. Or had he plagiarized *all* those papers, from junior high on up to this one? No, surely, this time only. Ernest himself had felt the pressure in his senior year, and most of the boys in his fraternity had cheated when they really *had* to. Now he felt compelled to search thoroughly, examine everything carefully. The police had no right to invade a dead boy's privacy and plunge his invalid mother into grief.

In Carter's desk drawers, Ernest searched more systematically among letters and notes, still expecting to discover an early draft of Gordon's unfinished speech; perhaps it would be full of clues. He might even find the bill of sale for the grenade. Across the naked belly of a girl ripped from a magazine was written: "Gordy—" Carter had even renamed, rechristened Gordon. "Jeff and Conley and I are holding a peace vigil in the cold rain tonight, all night. Bring us a fresh jar of water at midnight. And leave your goddamn middle-class mottos in the room. Love, Carter."

A letter from Fort Jackson, South Carolina, April 20, 1968. "Dear Gordon, I am being shipped to Vietnam. I will never see you again. I have not forgotten what you said to me that night in our room across the Dark Gulf between our cots. As always, Carter." Without knowing what Carter meant, Ernest knew that gulf himself. He had tried to bridge it, touch Scott, his own roommate, whose lassitude about life's possibilities often provoked Ernest to wall-pounding rage. He had finally persuaded Scott to take a trip West with him right after graduation. Scott's nonchalant withdrawal at the last minute was so dispiriting that Ernest had accepted his father's offer of a summer internship with the insurance company as a claim adjustor.

A 1967 letter described in detail the march on the Pentagon. "What are you doing down there, you little fink? You should be up here with the rest of us. My brothers have been beaten by the cops. I'm not against the use of napalm in *some* instances. Just don't let me get my hands on any of it when those pig sonofabitches come swinging their sticks at us. We're rising up all over the world, Baby—or didn't you know it, with your nose in Chaucer's tales. Melbourne is about due to be hit so you'd better decide who's side you're on. I heard about this one campus demonstration where somebody set fire to this old fogey's life-long research on some obscure hang-up of his. I can think of a few at Melbourne that need shaking up." Ernest was shocked, then surprised at himself for being shocked. He wondered how Gordon had felt.

As Ernest pulled a postcard out of a pigeonhole, a white capsule rolled out into his hand. For a common cold, or LSD? He stifled an impulse to swallow it. By chance escape what chance might reveal. He flipped the capsule against the inside of the CORN FLAKES box and it popped like a cap pistol. Comic postcard—outhouse, hillbillies—mailed from Alabama, December 12, 1966. "Gordy, Baby, Wish you were here. You sure as hell ain't all *there!* Love, till death do us part, Carter." In several letters, Carter fervently attempted to persuade Gordon to abandon his "middle-class Puritan Upforcing" and embrace the cause of world brotherhood, which itself embraced all other great causes of "our time." But even through the serious ones ran a trace of self-mockery. He found Carter's draft notice, his *own* name crossed out, Gordon's typed in. Across the body of the form letter, dated February 1, 1968, was printed in Gothic script: NON SERVIUM.[5]

As Ernest reached for a bunch of postcards, he realized that he was eager not only to discover more about Gordon, but to assemble into some shape the fragments of Carter's life. A series of postcards with cryptic, taunting messages traced Carter's trail over the landscape of America, from early January to the middle of March, 1968. From Carmel, California, a view of a tower and cypress trees: "Violence is the sire of all the world's values."[6] Ernest remembered the card Gordon sent him from Washington, D.C., when he was in junior high: "Dear Dad, Our class went to see Congress but they were closed. Our teacher got mad. She dragged us all to the Smithsonian and showed us Lindbergh's airplane. It was called THE SPIRIT OF ST. LOUIS. I didn't think it looked so hot. Mrs. Landis said she saved the headlines when she was in high school. Did you? Your son, Gordon."

Ernest found a night letter from Lynn, Massachusetts. "Dear Gordon, Remembering that Jason spoke of you so often and so fondly, his father and I felt certain that you would not want to learn through the newspapers that our dear son has been reported missing in action. While no one can really approve in his heart of this war, Jason has always been the sort of boy who believed in dying for his convictions. We know that you will miss him. He loved you as though you were his own brother. Affectionate regards, Grace and Harold Carter." June 1, 1968, three days ago.

Trembling, Ernest sought more letters from Carter. One from boot camp summed up, in wild, impassioned prose, Carter's opinions on civil rights, the war, and "the American Dream that's turned into a nightmare." In another, "God is dead and buried on LBJ's ranch" dispensed with religion and politics, "inseparable." May 4, 1968: "Dear

5. "I will not serve."
6. From the poem "The Bloody Sire" by Robinson Jeffers (1887–1962).

Gordy, We are in the jungle now, on a search and destroy mission. You have to admire some of these platoon leaders. I must admit I enjoy watching them act out their roles as all-American tough guys. They have a kind of style, anyway. In here you don't have time to analyze your thoughts. But I just thought a word or two written at the scene of battle might bring you the smell of smoke." Ernest sniffed the letter, uncertain whether the faint smell came from the paper.

He pulled a wadded letter out of a pigeonhole where someone had stuffed it. As he unwadded the note, vicious ballpoint pen markings wove a mesh over the words: "Gordon, I'm moving in with Conley. Pack my things and set them in the hall. I don't even want to *enter* that room again. What you said last night made me sick. I've lived with you for three and a half years because I was always convinced that I could save your soul. But after last night, I know it's hopeless. Carter." Across the "Dark Gulf" between their beds, what could *Gordon* have said to shock Carter? Had Gordon persuaded him to stay after all? Or was it the next day that Carter had "impulsively" run away? Ernest searched quickly through the rest of the papers, hoping no answer existed, but knowing that if one did and he failed to find it, the police wouldn't fail.

"Gordy, Baby, Everything you read is lies! I've been in the field three weeks now. My whole life's search ends here, in this burning village, where I'm taking time to write to you. Listen, Baby, this is life! This is what it's all about. In the past weeks I've personally set fire to thirty-seven huts belonging to Viet Cong sympathizers. Don't listen to those sons-of-bitches who whine and gripe and piss and moan about the war. This is a *just* war. We're on the *right* side. This place has opened my eyes and heart, baby. With the bullets and the blood all around, you see things clearer. Words! To hell with words! All these beady-eyed little bastards understand is *bullets*, and a knife now and then. These bastards killed my buddy, a Black boy by the name of Bird. The greatest guy that ever lived. Well, there's ten Viet Cong that ain't alive today because of what they did to my buddy, and there'll be another hundred less Viet Cong if I can persuade them to send me out after I'm due to be pulled back. Yesterday, I found a Viet Cong in a hut with his goddamn wife and kids. I turned the flame thrower on the sons-of-bitches and when the hut burned down, I pissed on the hot ashes. I'm telling you all this to open your eyes, mister. This is the way it really is. Join your ass up, get over here where you belong. Forget everything I ever said to you or wrote to you before. I have seen the light. The future of the world will be decided right here. And I will fight until the last Viet Cong is dead. Always, your friend, Carter." May 21, 1968, two weeks ago.

Trying to feel as Gordon had felt reading this letter, feeling nothing, Ernest remembered Gordon's response to a different piece of information some kid in grammar school dealt him when he was eleven. Having informed Gordon that Santa Claus was a lie, he added the observation that nobody ever knows who his real father and mother are. Just as Ernest stepped into the house from the office, Gordon had asked: "Are you my real father?" In the living room where colored lights blazed on the tree, Lydia was weeping. It took two months to rid Gordon of the fantasy that he had been adopted. Or had he simply stopped interrogating them? But how did a man know *anything*? Did that professor ever suspect that one day in print he would be labeled "the most boring man on the face of the earth?" Did Carter ever sense he would end up killing men in Vietnam? Did Gordon ever suspect that on his graduation day . . . ?

Now the day began to make sense. After Carter's letter from Vietnam, reversing everything he had preached to Gordon, Gordon had let his studies slide, and then the plagiarism had just happened, the way things will, because how could he really care anymore? Then did the night letter from Carter's mother shock him into pulling the grenade pin? Was "I advocate a total revolution!" Gordon's *own* climax to the attitude expressed in Carter's Vietnam letter? Or did the *old* Carter finally speak through Gordon's mouth? These possibilities made sense, but Ernest felt nothing.

His foot kicked a metal wastebasket under Carter's desk. Squatting, he pulled it out, and sitting again in the swivel chair, began to unwad several letters. "Dear Dad—" The rest blank. "Dear Dad—" Blank. "Dear Dad—" Blank. "Dear Father—" Blank. "Dear Dad—" Blank.

Ernest swung around in Carter's chair, rocked once, got to his feet, stood in the middle of the room, his hands dangling in front of him, the leaded moldings of the window cast black wavy lines over his suit, the green light stained his hands, his heart beat so fast he became aware that he was panting. Like a dog. His throat felt dry, his tongue swollen, eyes burning from reading in the oblique light. Dark spots of sweat on the floor. "Gordon. Gordon. Gordon."

Whatever Gordon had said in his valedictory address, Ernest knew that certain things in this room would give the public the wrong image of his son. Or perhaps—he faced it—the right image. Wrong or right, it would incite the disease in Lydia's body to riot and she would burn. He rolled the desk top down and began stuffing things into the beer carton. When it was full, he emptied the contents of the CORN FLAKES box onto the desk, throwing only the honors thesis back into it. When he jerked the bowie knife out of the wall, the banana poster fell. He scraped at the clotting vomit on the clothes hanging in the closet, and wiped the blade on the sole of his shoe. Then he filled the CORN FLAKES box with letters and other incriminating objects.

He opened the door and looked out. The hall was dim and deserted. The surviving seniors had gone home, though some must have lingered behind with wounded classmates, teachers, parents. The police would still be occupied with traffic. The back staircase was dark. He stacked the beer carton on top of the CORN FLAKES box, lifted both in his arms, and started to back out the door. But under the rolltop desk in a bed of lint lay a piece of paper that, even wadded up, resembled a telegram. Setting the boxes down, the cardboard already dark brown where he had pressed his forehead, Ernest got on his knees and reached under the desk. Without rising, he unwadded the paper. URGENT YOU RENEW SUBSCRIPTION TO TIME AT STUDENT RATE. STOP. WORLD NEWS AT YOUR FINGERTIPS. STOP. Mock telegram technique, special reply pencil enclosed.

The boxes were heavier as Ernest lifted them again and backed out the door, almost certain that the grenade had not been a rhetorical flourish. Bracing the boxes against the wall, lifting his knee under them, Ernest quickly reached out, pulled at the door knob. When the door slammed, locked, startling him, he grabbed the boxes as they almost tipped over into the stairwell.

He had to descend very slowly. The narrow staircase curved twice before it reached the basement. His shoulder slid along the wall as he went down, carefully, step by step. The bottom of the box cut into his palms, sweat tickled his spine, and his thighs chafed each other as sweat dried on his flesh. He saw nothing until he reached the basement where twilight coming through the window of the door revealed the furnace. As he fumbled for the doorknob, already the devouring locusts jangled in his ears like a single note quivering relentlessly on a violin.

Locusts had dropped from the ivy onto the black hood of the Volkswagen, parked up tight against the building. He opened the trunk, set the boxes inside, closed the lid, locked it.

As he got in behind the wheel, a glimpse of the cemetery behind the dormitory made him recall the grave that had so awed him during his freshman year. From where he sat, turning the ignition key, the larger tombs of the historic dead obscured the small white stone, but he had not forgotten the epitaph: HERE LIES AN UNIDENTIFIED VICTIM OF THE FIRE THAT RAZED DELOZIER HALL. May 16, 1938. Since all the Melbourne students had been accounted for, he (or perhaps she) must have been a visitor.

Pulling off the highway, he drove along a dirt trail, new grass sprouting between the wheel ruts. Here, as visible evidence testified,

Melbourne students brought the girls who came down from Briar-heath. Parked, he let dusk turn to dark.

Then he left the woods, lights dimmed until he got onto the highway. On the outskirts of the town, looking at this distance like a village erected in one of those elaborate electric train sets, he turned onto a cinder road and stopped at a gate, got out, lifted the latch, drove through, then went back and closed the gate.

Headlights off, he eased over the soft, sooty dirt road, the rough bushes on each side a soft gray blur, into the main lot, where the faculty and other townspeople dumped junk and garbage.

The smell made him aware of the taste at the back of his mouth, the stench of burning rubber and plastic and dead animals made his headache pound more fiercely, his left eyelid beat like a pulse.

He unlocked the trunk, lifted out the CORN FLAKES box, and stumbled in the dark over tin cans and broken tools and springs and tires, set the box down, then went back and got the other box.

The boxes weren't far enough into the dump. He dragged them, one with each hand, backwards, up and over the rough terrain, stumbling, cutting his hands on rusty cans and nails in charred wood, thinking of tetanus, of Lydia without him.

Standing up, he sucked in the night air, feeling a dewy freshness mingled with the acrid smoke and fumes. He reached into his pocket for his lighter. His thumb began to hurt as he failed repeatedly to make the flint catch.

A bright beam shot out over the dump, another several yards beside it, then another—powerful flashlights—and as he crouched to avoid the lights, rifle fire shattered the silence over the dump. Reaching out, grabbing the cardboard flaps to keep his balance, Ernest squatted beside his boxes.

"Get that son-of-a-bitch, Doc!"

Twisting his neck around, Ernest saw the beam swing and dip through oily smoke coiling out of the debris and stop on a rat, crouched on a fire-blackened ice-box door. It started to run. But the slick porcelain allowed its feet no traction.

1970

■   ■   ■

LOVE LIFE

Opal lolls in her recliner, wearing the Coors cap her niece Jenny brought her from Colorado. She fumbles for the remote-control paddle and fires a button. Her swollen knuckles hurt. On TV, a boy is dancing in the street. Some other boys dressed in black are banging guitars and drums. This is her favorite program. It is always on, night or day. The show is songs, with accompanying stories. It's the music channel. Opal never cared for stories—she detests those soap operas her friends watch—but these fascinate her. The colors and the costumes change and flow with the music, erratically, the way her mind does these days. Now the TV is playing a song in which all the boys are long-haired cops chasing a dangerous woman in a tweed cap and a checked shirt. The woman's picture is in all their billfolds. They chase her through a cold-storage room filled with sides of beef. She hops on a motorcycle, and they set up a roadblock, but she jumps it with her motorcycle. Finally, she slips onto a train and glides away from them, waving a smiling goodbye.

On the table beside Opal is a Kleenex box, her glasses case, a glass of Coke with ice, and a cut-glass decanter of clear liquid that could be just water for the plants. Opal pours some of the liquid into the Coke and sips slowly. It tastes like peppermint candy, and it feels soothing. Her fingers tingle. She feels happy. Now that she is retired, she doesn't have to sneak into the teachers' lounge for a little swig from the jar in her pocketbook. She still dreams algebra problems, complicated quadratic equations with shifting values and no solutions. Now kids are using algebra to program computers. The kids in the TV stories remind her of her students at Hopewell High. Old age could have a grandeur about it, she thinks now as the music surges through her, if only it weren't so scary.

But she doesn't feel lonely, especially now that her sister Alice's girl, Jenny, has moved back here, to Kentucky. Jenny seems so confident, the way she sprawls on the couch, with that backpack she carries everywhere. Alice was always so delicate and feminine, but Jenny is enough like Opal to be her own daughter. She has Opal's light, thin hair, her large shoulders and big bones and long legs. Jenny even has a way of laughing that reminds Opal of her own laughter, the boisterous scoff she always saved for certain company but never allowed herself in school. Now and then Jenny lets loose one of those laughs and Opal is pleased. It occurs to her that Jenny, who is already past thirty, has left behind a trail of men, like that girl in the song. Jenny has lived with a couple of men, here and there. Opal can't keep track of all of the men Jenny has mentioned. They have names like John and Skip and Michael. She's not in a hurry to get married, she says. She says she is going to buy a house trailer and live in the woods like a hermit. She's full of ideas, and she exaggerates. She uses the words "gorgeous," "adorable," and "wonderful" interchangeably and persistently.

Last night, Jenny was here, with her latest boyfriend. Randy Newcomb. Opal remembers when he sat in the back row in her geometry class. He was an ordinary kid, not especially smart, and often late with his lessons. Now he has a real-estate agency and drives a Cadillac. Jenny kissed him in front of Opal and told him he was gorgeous. She said the placemats were gorgeous, too.

Jenny was asking to see those old quilts again. "Why do you hide away your nice things, Aunt Opal?" she said. Opal doesn't think they're that nice, and she doesn't want to have to look at them all the time. Opal showed Jenny and Randy Newcomb the double-wedding-ring quilt, the star quilt, and some of the crazy quilts, but she wouldn't show them the craziest one—the burial quilt, the one Jenny kept asking about. Did Jenny come back home just to hunt up that old rag? The thought makes Opal shudder.

The doorbell rings. Opal has to rearrange her comforter and magazines in order to get up. Her joints are stiff. She leaves the TV blaring a song she knows, with balloons and bombs in it.

At the door is Velma Shaw, who lives in the duplex next to Opal. She has just come home from her job at Shop World. "Have you gone out of your mind, Opal?" cries Velma. She has on a plum-colored print blouse and a plum skirt and a little green scarf with a gold pin holding it down. Velma shouts, "You can hear that racket clear across the street!"

"Rock and roll is never too loud," says Opal. This is a line from a song she has heard.

Opal releases one of her saved-up laughs, and Velma backs away.

Velma is still trying to be sexy, in those little color-coordinated outfits she wears, but it is hopeless, Opal thinks with a smile. She closes the door and scoots back to her recliner.

Opal is Jenny's favorite aunt. Jenny likes the way Opal ties her hair in a ponytail with a ribbon. She wears muumuus and socks. She is tall and only a little thick in the middle. She told Jenny that middle-age spread was caused by the ribs expanding and that it doesn't matter what you eat. Opal kids around about "old Arthur"—her arthritis, visiting her on damp days.

Jenny has been in town six months. She works at the courthouse, typing records—marriages, divorces, deaths, drunk-driving convictions. Frequently, the same names are on more than one list. Before she returned to Kentucky, Jenny was waitressing in Denver, but she was growing restless again, and the idea of going home seized her. Her old rebellion against small-town conventions gave way to curiosity.

In the South, the shimmer of the heat seems to distort everything, like old glass with impurities in it. During her first two days there, she saw two people with artificial legs, a blind man, a man with hooks for hands, and a man without an arm. It seemed unreal. In a parking lot, a pit bull terrier in a Camaro attacked her from behind the closed window. He barked viciously, his nose stabbing the window. She stood in the parking lot, letting the pit bull attack, imagining herself in an arena, with a crowd watching. The South makes her nervous. Randy Newcomb told her she had just been away too long. "We're not as countrified down here now as people think," he said.

Jenny has been going with Randy for three months. The first night she went out with him, he took her to a fancy place that served shrimp flown in from New Orleans, and then to a little bar over in Hopkinsville. They went with Kathy Steers, a friend from work, and Kathy's husband, Bob. Kathy and Bob weren't getting along and they carped at each other all evening. In the bar, an attractive, cheerful woman sang requests for tips, and her companion, a blind man, played the guitar. When she sang, she looked straight at him, singing to him, smiling at him reassuringly. In the background, men played pool with their girlfriends, and Jenny noticed the sharp creases in the men's jeans and imagined the women ironing them. When she mentioned it, Kathy said she took Bob's jeans to the laundromat to use the machine there that puts knifelike creases in them. The men in the bar had two kinds of women with them: innocent-looking women with pastel skirts and careful hairdos, and hard-looking women without makeup, in T-shirts and jeans. Jenny imagined that each type could be either a girlfriend or a wife. She felt odd. She was neither type. The singer sang

"Happy Birthday" to a popular regular named Will Ed, and after the set she danced with him, while the jukebox took over. She had a limp, as though one leg were shorter than the other. The leg was stiff under her jeans, and when the woman danced Jenny could see that the leg was not real.

"There, but for the grace of God, go I," Randy whispered to Jenny. He squeezed her hand, and his heavy turquoise ring dug into her knuckle.

"Those quilts would bring a good price at an estate auction," Randy says to Jenny as they leave her aunt's one evening and head for his real-estate office. They are in his burgundy Cadillac. "One of those star quilts used to bring twenty-five dollars. Now it might run three hundred."

"My aunt doesn't think they're worth anything. She hides all her nice stuff, like she's ashamed of it. She's got beautiful dresser scarves and starched doilies she made years ago. But she's getting a little weird. All she does is watch MTV."

"I think she misses the kids," Randy says. Then he bursts out laughing. "She used to put the fear of God in all her students! I never will forget the time she told me to stop watching so much television and read some books. It was like an order from God Almighty. I didn't dare not do what she said. I read *Crime and Punishment*. I never would have read it if she hadn't shamed me into it. But I appreciated that. I don't even remember what *Crime and Punishment* was about, except there was an ax murderer in it."

"That was basically it," Jenny says. "He got caught. Crime and punishment—just like any old TV show."

Randy touches some controls on the dashboard and Waylon Jennings starts singing. The sound system is remarkable. Everything Randy owns is quality. He has been looking for some land for Jenny to buy—a couple of acres of woods—but so far nothing on his listings has met with his approval. He is concerned about zoning and power lines and frontage. All Jenny wants is a remote place where she can have a dog and grow some tomatoes. She knows that what she really needs is a better car, but she doesn't want to go anywhere.

Later, at Randy's office, Jenny studies the photos of houses on display, while he talks on the telephone to someone about dividing up a sixty-acre farm into farmettes. His photograph is on several certificates on the wall. He has a full, well-fed face in the pictures, but he is thinner now and looks better. He has a boyish, endearing smile, like Dennis Quaid, Jenny's favorite actor. She likes his smile. It seems so innocent, as though he would do anything in the world for someone he cared about. He doesn't really want to sell her any land. He says he is afraid she will get raped if she lives alone in the woods.

"I'm impressed," she says when he slams down the telephone. She points to his new regional award for the fastest-growing agency of the year.

"Isn't that something? Three branch offices in a territory this size—I can't complain. There's a lot of turnover in real estate now. People are never satisfied. You know that? That's the truth about human nature." He laughs. "That's the secret of my success."

"It's been two years since Barbara divorced me," he says later, on the way to Jenny's apartment. "I can't say it hasn't been fun being free, but my kids are in college, and it's like starting over. I'm ready for a new life. The business has been so great, I couldn't really ask for more, but I've been thinking—Don't laugh, please, but what I was thinking was if you want to share it with me, I'll treat you good. I swear."

At a stoplight, he paws at her hand. On one corner is the Pepsi bottling plant, and across from it is the Broad Street House, a restaurant with an old-fashioned statue of a jockey out front. People are painting the black faces on those little statues white now, but this one has been painted bright green all over. Jenny can't keep from laughing at it.

"I wasn't laughing at you—honest!" she says apologetically. "That statue always cracks me up."

"You don't have to give me an answer now."

"I don't know what to say."

"I can get us a real good deal on a house," he says. "I can get any house I've got listed. I can even get us a farmette, if you want trees so bad. You won't have to spend your money on a piece of land."

"I'll have to think about it." Randy scares her. She likes him, but there is something strange about his energy and optimism. Everyone around her seems to be bursting at the seams, like that pit bull terrier.

"I'll let you think on it," he says, pulling up to her apartment. "Life has been good to me. Business is good, and my kids didn't turn out to be dope fiends. That's about all you can hope for in this day and time."

Jenny is having lunch with Kathy Steers at the Broad Street House. The iced tea is mixed with white grape juice. It took Jenny a long time to identify the flavor, and the Broad Street House won't admit it's grape juice. Their iced tea is supposed to have a mystique about it, probably because they can't sell drinks in this dry county. In the daylight, the statue out front is the color of the Jolly Green Giant.

People confide in Jenny, but Jenny doesn't always tell things back.

It's an unfair exchange, though it often goes unnoticed. She is curious, eager to hear other people's stories, and she asks more questions than is appropriate. Kathy's life is a tangle of deceptions. Kathy stayed with her husband, Bob, because he had opened his own body shop and she didn't want him to start out a new business with a rocky marriage, but she acknowledges now it was a mistake.

"What about Jimmy and Willette?" Jenny asks. Jimmy and Willette are the other characters in Kathy's story.

"That mess went on for months. When you started work at the office, remember how nervous I was? I thought I was getting an ulcer." Kathy lights a cigarette and blows at the wall. "You see, I didn't know what Bob and Willette were up to, and they didn't know about me and Jimmy. That went on for two years before you came. And when it started to come apart—I mean, we had *hell!* I'd say things to Jimmy and then it would get back to Bob because Jimmy would tell Willette. It was an unreal circle. I was pregnant with Jason and you get real sensitive then. I thought Bob was screwing around on me, but it never dawned on me it was with Willette."

The fat waitress says, "Is everything all right?"

Kathy says, "No, but it's not your fault. Do you know what I'm going to do?" she asks Jenny.

"No, what?"

"I'm taking Jason and moving in with my sister. She has a sort of apartment upstairs. Bob can do what he wants to with the house. I've waited too long to do this, but it's time. My sister keeps the baby anyway, so why shouldn't I just live there?"

She puffs the cigarette again and levels her eyes at Jenny. "You know what I admire about you? You're so independent. You say what you think. When you started work at the office, I said to myself, 'I wish I could be like that.' I could tell you had been around. You've inspired me. That's how come I decided to move out."

Jenny plays with the lemon slice in the saucer holding her iced-tea glass. She picks a seed out of it. She can't bring herself to confide in Kathy about Randy Newcomb's offer. For some reason, she is embarrassed by it.

"I haven't spoken to Willette since September third," says Kathy.

Kathy keeps talking, and Jenny listens, suspicious of her interest in Kathy's problems. She notices how Kathy is enjoying herself. Kathy is looking forward to leaving her husband the same way she must have enjoyed her fling with Jimmy, the way she is enjoying not speaking to Willette.

"Let's go out and get drunk tonight," Kathy says cheerfully. "Let's celebrate my decision."

"I can't. I'm going to see my aunt this evening. I have to take her some booze. She gives me money to buy her vodka and peppermint schnapps, and she tells me not to stop at the same liquor store. She says she doesn't want me to get a reputation for drinking! I have to go all the way to Hopkinsville to get it."

"Your aunt tickles me. She's a pistol."

The waitress clears away the dishes and slaps down dessert menus. They order chocolate pecan pie, the day's special.

"You know the worst part of this whole deal?" Kathy says. "It's the years it takes to get smart. But I'm going to make up for lost time. You can bet on that. And there's not a thing Bob can do about it."

Opal's house has a veranda. Jenny thinks that verandas seem to imply a history of some sort—people in rocking chairs telling stories. But Opal doesn't tell any stories. It is exasperating, because Jenny wants to know about her aunt's past love life, but Opal won't reveal her secrets. They sit on the veranda and observe each other. They smile, and now and then roar with laughter over something ridiculous. In the bedroom, where she snoops after using the bathroom, Jenny notices the layers of old wallpaper in the closet, peeling back and spilling crumbs of gaudy ancient flower prints onto Opal's muumuus.

Downstairs, Opal asks, "Do you want some cake, Jenny?"

"Of course. I'm crazy about your cake, Aunt Opal."

"I didn't beat the egg whites long enough. Old Arthur's visiting again." Opal flexes her fingers and smiles. "That sounds like the curse. Girls used to say they had the curse. Or they had a visitor." She looks down at her knuckles shyly. "Nowadays, of course, they just say what they mean."

The cake is delicious—an old-fashioned lemon chiffon made from scratch. Jenny's cooking ranges from English-muffin mini-pizzas to brownie mixes. After gorging on the cake, Jenny blurts out, "Aunt Opal, aren't you sorry you never got married? Tell the truth, now."

Opal laughs. "I was talking to Ella Mae Smith the other day—she's a retired geography teacher?—and she said, 'I've got twelve great-great-grandchildren, and when we get together I say, "Law me, look what I started!" ' " Opal mimics Ella Mae Smith, giving her a mindless, chirpy tone of voice. "Why, I'd have to use quadratic equations to count up all the people that woman has caused," she goes on. "All with a streak of her petty narrow-mindedness in them. I don't call that a contribution to the world." Opal laughs and sips from her glass of schnapps. "What about you, Jenny? Are you ever going to get married?"

"Marriage is outdated. I don't know anybody who's married and happy."

Opal names three schoolteachers she has known who have been married for decades.

"But are they really happy?"

"Oh, foot, Jenny! What you're saying is why are *you* not married and why are *you* not happy. What's wrong with little Randy Newcomb? Isn't that funny? I always think of him as little Randy."

"Show me those quilts again, Aunt Opal."

"I'll show you the crazies but not the one you keep after me about."

"OK, show me the crazies."

Upstairs, her aunt lays crazy quilts on the bed. They are bright-colored patches of soft velvet and plaids and prints stitched together with silky embroidery. Several pieces have initials embroidered on them. The haphazard shapes make Jenny imagine odd, twisted lives represented in these quilts.

She says, "Mom gave me a quilt once, but I didn't appreciate the value of it and I washed it until it fell apart."

"I'll give you one of these crazies when you stop moving around," Opal says. "You couldn't fit it in that backpack of yours." She polishes her glasses thoughtfully. "Do you know what those quilts mean to me?"

"No, what?"

"A lot of desperate old women ruining their eyes. Do you know what I think I'll do?"

"No, what?"

"I think I'll take up aerobic dancing. Or maybe I'll learn to ride a motorcycle. I try to be modern."

"You're funny, Aunt Opal. You're hilarious."

"Am I gorgeous, too?"

"Adorable," says Jenny.

After her niece leaves, Opal hums a tune and dances a stiff little jig. She nestles among her books and punches her remote-control paddle. Years ago, she was allowed to paddle students who misbehaved. She used a wooden paddle from a butter churn, with holes drilled in it. The holes made a satisfying sting. On TV, a 1950s convertible is out of gas. This is one of her favorites. It has an adorable couple in it. The girl is wearing bobby socks and saddle oxfords, and the boy has on a basketball jacket. They look the way children looked before the hippie element took over. But the boy begins growing cat whiskers and big cat ears, and then his face gets furry and leathery, while the girl screams bloody murder. Opal sips some peppermint and watches his face change. The red and gold of his basketball jacket are the Hopewell school colors. He chases the girl. Now he has grown long claws.

The boy is dancing energetically with a bunch of ghouls who have escaped from their coffins. "Grisly ghouls are closing in to seal your doom," Vincent Price says in the background. The girl is very frightened. The ghouls are so old and ugly. That's how kids see us, Opal thinks. She loves this story. She even loves the credits: "Scary Music by Elmer Bernstein." This is a story with a meaning. It suggests all the feelings of terror and horror that must be hidden inside young people. And inside, deep down, there really are monsters. An old person waits, a nearly dead body that can still dance.

Opal pours another drink. She feels relaxed, her joints loose like a dancer's now.

Jenny is so nosy. Her questions are so blunt. Did Opal ever have a crush on a student? Only once or twice. She was in her twenties then, and it seemed scandalous. Nothing happened—just daydreams. When she was thirty, she had another attachment to a boy, and it seemed all right then, but it was worse again at thirty-five, when another pretty boy stayed after class to talk. After that, she kept her distance.

But Opal is not wholly without experience. There have been men, over the years, though nothing like the casual affairs Jenny has had. Opal remembers a certain motel room in Nashville. She was only forty. The man drove a gray Chrysler Imperial. When she was telling about him to a friend, who was sworn to secrecy, she called him "Imperial," in a joking way. She went with him because she knew he would take her somewhere, in such a fine car, and they would sleep together. She always remembered how clean and empty the room was, how devoid of history and association. In the mirror, she saw a scared woman with a pasty face and a shrimpy little man who needed a shave. In the morning he went out somewhere and brought back coffee and orange juice. They had bought some doughnuts at the new doughnut shop in town before they left. While he was out, she made up the bed and put her things in her bag, to make it as neat as if she had never been there. She was fully dressed when he returned, with her garter belt and stockings on, and when they finished the doughnuts she cleaned up all the paper and the cups and wiped the crumbs from the table by the bed. He said, "Come with me and I'll take you to Idaho." "Why Idaho?" she wanted to know, but his answer was vague. Idaho sounded cold, and she didn't want to tell him how she disliked his scratchy whiskers and the hard, powdery doughnuts. It seemed unkind of her, but if he had been nicer-looking, without such a demanding dark beard, she might have gone with him to Idaho in that shining Imperial. She hadn't even given him a chance, she thought later. She had been so scared. If anyone from school had seen her at that motel, she could have lost her job. "I need a woman," he had said. "A woman like you."

On a hot Saturday afternoon, with rain threatening, Jenny sits under a tent on a folding chair while Randy auctions off four hundred acres of woods on Lake Barkley. He had a road a bulldozed into the property, and he divided it up into lots. The lakefront lots are going for as much as two thousand an acre, and the others are bringing up to a thousand. Randy has several assistants with him, and there is even a concession stand, offering hot dogs and cold drinks.

In the middle of the auction, they wait for a thundershower to pass. Sitting in her folding chair under a canopy reminds Jenny of graveside services. As soon as the rain slacks up, the auction continues. In his cowboy hat and blue blazer, Randy struts around with a microphone as proudly as a banty rooster. With his folksy chatter, he knows exactly how to work the crowd. "Y'all get yourselves a cold drink and relax now and just imagine the fishing you'll do in this dreamland. This land is good for vacation, second home, investment—heck, you can just park here in your camper and live. It's going to be paradise when that marina gets built on the lake there and we get some lots cleared."

The four-hundred-acre tract looks like a wilderness. Jenny loves the way the sun splashes on the water after the rain, and the way it comes through the trees, hitting the flickering leaves like lights on a disco ball. A marina here seems farfetched. She could pitch a tent here until she could afford to buy a used trailer. She could swim at dawn, the way she did on a camping trip out West, long ago. All of a sudden, she finds herself bidding on a lot. The bidding passes four hundred, and she sails on, bidding against a man from Missouri who tells the people around him that he's looking for a place to retire.

"Sold to the young lady with the backpack," Randy says when she bids six hundred. He gives her a crestfallen look, and she feels embarrassed.

As she waits for Randy to wind up his business after the auction, Jenny locates her acre from the map of the plots of land. It is along a gravel road and marked off with stakes tied with hot-pink survey tape. It is a small section of the woods—her block on the quilt, she thinks. These are her trees. The vines and underbrush are thick and spotted with raindrops. She notices a windfall leaning on a maple, like a lover dying in its arms. Maples are strong, she thinks, but she feels like getting an ax and chopping that windfall down, to save the maple. In the distance, the whining of a speedboat cuts into the day.

They meet afterward at Randy's van, his mobile real-estate office, with a little shingled roof raised in the center to look rustic. It looks like an outhouse on wheels. A painted message on the side says, "REALITY IS REAL ESTATE." As Randy plows through the mud on the new road, Jenny apologizes. Buying the lot was like laughing at the statue at the wrong moment—something he would take the wrong way, an insult to his attentions.

"I can't reach you," he says. "You say you want to live out in the wilderness and grow your own vegetables, but you act like you're somewhere in outer space. You can't grow vegetables in outer space. You can't even grow them in the woods unless you clear some ground."

"I'm looking for a place to land."

"What do I have to do to get through to you?"

"I don't know. I need more time."

He turns onto the highway, patterned with muddy tire tracks from the cars at the auction. "I said I'd wait, so I guess I'll have to," he says, flashing his Dennis Quaid smile. "You take as long as you want to, then. I learned my lesson with Barbara. You've got to be understanding with the women. That's the key to a successful relationship." Frowning, he slams his hand on the steering wheel. "That's what they tell me, anyhow."

Jenny is having coffee with Opal. She arrived unexpectedly. It's very early. She looks as though she has been up all night.

"Please show me your quilts," Jenny says. "I don't mean your crazy quilts. I want to see that special quilt. Mom said it had the family tree."

Opal spills coffee in her saucer. "What is wrong with young people today?" she asks.

"I want to know why it's called a burial quilt," Jenny says. "Are you planning to be buried in it?"

Opal wishes she had a shot of peppermint in her coffee. It sounds like a delicious idea. She starts toward the den with the coffee cup rattling in its saucer, and she splatters drops on the rug. Never mind it now, she thinks, turning back.

"It's just a family history," she says.

"Why's it called a burial quilt?" Jenny asks.

Jenny's face is pale. She has blue pouches under her eyes and blue eye shadow on her eyelids.

"See that closet in the hall?" Opal says. "Get a chair and we'll get the quilt down."

Jenny stands on a kitchen chair and removes the quilt from beneath several others. It's wrapped in blue plastic and Jenny hugs it closely as she steps down with it.

They spread it out on the couch, and the blue plastic floats off somewhere, Jenny looks like someone in love as she gazes at the quilt. "It's gorgeous," she murmurs. "How beautiful."

"Shoot!" says Opal. "It's ugly as homemade sin."

Jenny runs her fingers over the rough textures of the quilt. The quilt is dark and somber. The backing is a heavy gray gabardine, and the nine-inch-square blocks are pieced of smaller blocks of varying shades of gray and brown and black. They are wools, apparently made from men's winter suits. On each block is an appliquéd off-white tombstone—a comical shape, like Casper the ghost. Each tombstone has a name and date on it.

Jenny recognizes some of the names. Myrtle Williams. Voris Williams. Thelma Lee Freeman. The oldest gravestone is "Eulalee Freeman 1857–1900." The shape of the quilt is irregular, a rectangle with a clumsy foot sticking out from one corner. The quilt is knotted with yarn, and the edging is open, for more blocks to be added.

"Eulalee's daughter started it," says Opal. "But that thing has been carried through this family like a plague. Did you ever see such horrible old dark colors? I pieced on it some when I was younger, but it was too depressing. I think some of the kinfolks must have died without a square, so there may be several to catch up on."

"I'll do it," says Jenny. "I could learn to quilt."

"Traditionally, the quilt stops when the family name stops," Opal says. "And since my parents didn't have a boy, that was the end of the Freeman line on this particular branch of the tree. So the last old maids finish the quilt." She lets out a wild cackle. "Theoretically, a quilt like this could keep going till doomsday."

"Do you care if I have this quilt?" asks Jenny.

"What would you do with it? It's too ugly to put on a bed and too morbid to work on."

"I think it's kind of neat," says Jenny. She strokes the rough tweed. Already it is starting to decay, and it has moth holes. Jenny feels tears start to drip down her face.

"Don't you go putting my name on that thing," her aunt says.

Jenny has taken the quilt to her apartment. She explained that she is going to study the family tree, or that she is going to finish the quilt. If she's smart, Opal thinks, she will let Randy Newcomb auction it off. The way Jenny took it, cramming it into the blue plastic, was like snatching something that was free. Opal feels relieved, as though she has pushed the burden of that ratty old quilt onto her niece. All those miserable, cranky women, straining their eyes, stitching on those dark scraps of material.

For a long time, Jenny wouldn't tell why she was crying, and when she started to tell, Opal was uncomfortable, afraid she'd be required to tell something comparable of her own, but as she listened she found herself caught up in Jenny's story. Jenny said it was a man. That was always the case, Opal thought. It was five years earlier. A man Jenny knew in a place by the sea. Opal imagined seagulls, pretty sand. There were no palm trees. It was up North. The young man worked with Jenny in a restaurant with glass walls facing the ocean. They waited on tables and collected enough tips to take a trip together near the end of the summer. Jenny made it sound like an idyllic time, waiting on tables by the sea. She started crying again when she told about the trip, but the trip sounded nice. Opal listened hungrily, imagining the young man, thinking that he would have had handsome, smooth cheeks, and hair that fell attractively over his forehead. He would have had good manners, being a waiter. Jenny and the man, whose name was Jim, flew to Denver, Colorado, and they rented a car and drove around out West. They visited the Grand Canyon and Yellowstone and other places Opal had heard about. They grilled salmon on the beach, on another ocean. They camped out in the redwoods, trees so big they hid the sky. Jenny described all these scenes, and the man sounded like a good man. His brother had died in Vietnam and he felt guilty that he had been the one spared, because his brother was a swimmer and could have gone to the Olympics. Jim wasn't athletic. He had a bad knee and hammertoes. He slept fitfully in the tent, and Jenny said soothing things to him, and she cared about him, but by the time they had curved northward and over to Yellowstone the trip was becoming unpleasant. The romance wore off. She loved him, but she couldn't deal with his needs. One of the last nights they spent together, it rained all night long. He told her not to touch the tent material, because somehow the pressure of a finger on the nylon would make it start to leak at that spot. Lying there in the rain, Jenny couldn't resist touching a spot where water was collecting in a little sag in the top of the tent. The drip started then, and it grew worse, until they got so wet they had to get in the car. Not long afterward, when they ran short of money, they parted. Jenny got a job in Denver. She never saw him again.

Opal listened eagerly to the details about grilling the fish together, about the zip-together sleeping bags and setting up the tent and washing themselves in the cold stream. But when Jenny brought the story up to the present, Opal was not prepared. She felt she had been dunked in the cold water and left gasping. Jenny said she had heard a couple of times through a mutual friend that Jim had spent some time in Mexico. And then, she said, this week she had begun thinking about him, because of all the trees at the lake, and she had an overwhelming desire to see him again. She had been unfair, she knew now. She telephoned the friend, who had worked with them in the restaurant by the sea. He hadn't known where to locate her, he said, and so he couldn't tell her that Jim had been killed in Colorado over a year ago. His four-wheel-drive had plunged off a mountain curve.

"I feel some trick has been played on me. It seems so unreal." Jenny tugged at the old quilt, and her eyes darkened. "I was in Colorado, and I didn't even know he was there. If I still knew him, I would know how to mourn, but now I don't know how. And it was over a year ago. So I don't know what to feel."

"Don't look back, hon," Opal said, hugging her niece closely. But she was shaking, and Jenny shook with her.

Opal makes herself a snack, thinking it will pick up her strength. She is very tired. On the tray, she places an apple and a paring knife and some milk and cookies. She touches the remote-control button, and the picture blossoms. She was wise to buy a large TV, the one listed as the best in the consumer magazine. The color needs a little adjustment, though. She eases up the volume and starts peeling the apple. She has a little bump on one knuckle. In the old days, people would take the family Bible and bust a cyst like that with it. Just slam it hard.

On the screen, a Scoutmaster is telling a story to some Boy Scouts around a campfire. The campfire is only a fireplace, with electric logs. Opal loses track of time, and the songs flow together. A woman is lying on her stomach on a car hood in a desert full of gas pumps. TV sets crash. Smoke emerges from an eyeball. A page of sky turns like a page in a book. Then, at a desk in a classroom, a cocky blond kid with a pack of cigarettes rolled in the sleeve of his T-shirt is singing about a sexy girl with a tattoo on her back who is sitting on a commode and smoking a cigarette. In the classroom, all the kids are gyrating and snapping their fingers to wild music. The teacher at the blackboard with her white hair in a bun looks disapproving, but the kids in the class don't know what's on her mind. The teacher is thinking about how, when the bell rings, she will hit the road to Nashville.

1990

■   ■   ■

SUSAN MINOT

LUST

Leo was from a long time ago, the first one I ever saw nude. In the spring before the Hellmans filled their pool, we'd go down there in the deep end, with baby oil, and like that. I met him the first month away at boarding school. He had a halo from the campus light behind him. I flipped.

Roger was fast. In his illegal car, we drove to the reservoir, the radio blaring, talking fast, fast, fast. He was always going for my zipper. He got kicked out sophomore year.

By the time the band got around to playing "Wild Horses," I had tasted Bruce's tongue. We were clicking in the shadows on the other side of the amplifier, out of Mrs. Donovan's line of vision. It tasted like salt, with my neck bent back, because we had been dancing so hard before.

Tim's line: "I'd like to see you in a bathing suit." I knew it was his line when he said the exact same thing to Annie Hines.

You'd go on walks to get off campus. It was raining like hell, my sweater as sopped as a wet sheep. Tim pinned me to a tree, the woods light brown and dark brown, a white house half-hidden with the lights already on. The water was as loud as a crowd hissing. He made certain comments about my forehead, about my cheeks.

We started off sitting at one end of the couch and then our feet were squished against the armrest and then he went over to turn off the TV and came back after he had taken off his shirt and then we slid onto the floor and he got up again to close the door, then came back to me, a body waiting on the rug.

You'd try to wipe off the table or to do the dishes and Willie would untuck your shirt and get his hands up under in front, standing behind you, making puffy noises in your ear.

He likes it when I wash my hair. He covers his face with it and if I start to say something, he goes, "Shush."

For a long time, I had Philip on the brain. The less they noticed you, the more you got them on the brain.

My parents had no idea. Parents never really know what's going on, especially when you're away at school most of the time. If she met them, my mother might say, "Oliver seems nice" or "I like that one" without much of an opinion. If she didn't like them, "He's a funny fellow, isn't he?" or "Johnny's perfectly nice but a drink of water." My father was too shy to talk to them at all, unless they played sports and he'd ask them about that.

The sand was almost cold underneath because the sun was long gone. Eben piled a mound over my feet, patting around my ankles, the ghostly surf rumbling behind him in the dark. He was the first person I ever knew who died, later that summer, in a car crash. I thought about it for a long time.

"Come here," he says on the porch.
I go over to the hammock and he takes my wrist with two fingers.
"What?"
He kisses my palm then directs my hand to his fly.

Songs went with whichever boy it was. "Sugar Magnolia" was Tim, with the line "Rolling in the rushes/down by the riverside." With "Darkness Darkness," I'd picture Philip with his long hair. Hearing "Under my Thumb" there'd be the smell of Jamie's suede jacket.

We hid in the listening rooms during study hall. With a record cover over the door's window, the teacher on duty couldn't look in. I came out flushed and heady and back at the dorm was surprised how red my lips were in the mirror.

One weekend at Simon's brother's, we stayed inside all day with the shades down, in bed, then went out to Store 24 to get some ice cream. He stood at the magazine rack and read through MAD while I got butterscotch sauce, craving something sweet.

I could do some things well. Some things I was good at, like math or painting or even sports, but the second a boy put his arm around me, I forget about wanting to do anything else, which felt like a relief at first until it became like sinking into a muck.

It was different for a girl.

When we were little, the brothers next door tied up our ankles. They held the door of the goat house and wouldn't let us out till we showed them our underpants. Then they'd forget about being after us and when we played whiffleball, I'd be just as good as them.

Then it got to be different. Just because you have on a short skirt, they yell from the cars, slowing down for a while and if you don't look, they screech off and call you a bitch.

"What's the matter with me?" they say, point-blank.
Or else, "Why won't you go out with me? I'm not asking you to get married," about to get mad.
Or it'd be, trying to be reasonable, in a regular voice, "Listen, I just want to have a good time."
So I'd go because I couldn't think of something to say back that wouldn't be obvious, and if you go out with them, you sort of have to do something.

I sat between Mack and Eddie in the front seat of the pickup. They were having a fight about something. I've a feeling about me.

Certain nights you'd feel a certain surrender, maybe if you'd had wine. The surrender would be forgetting yourself and you'd put your nose to his neck and feel like a squirrel, safe, at rest, in a restful dream. But then you'd start to slip from that and the dark would come in and there'd be a cave. You make out the dim shape of the windows and feel yourself become a cave, filled absolutely with air, or with a sadness that wouldn't stop.

Teenage years. You know just what you're doing and don't see the things that start to get in the way.

Lots of boys, but never two at the same time. One was plenty to keep you in a state. You'd start to see a boy and something would rush over you like a fast storm cloud and you couldn't possibly think of anyone else. Boys took it differently. Their eyes perked up at any little number that walked by. You'd act like you weren't noticing.

The joke was that the school doctor gave out the pill like aspirin. He didn't ask you anything. I was fifteen. We had a picture of him in assembly, holding up an IUD shaped like a T. Most girls were on the pill, if anything, because they couldn't handle a diaphragm. I kept the dial in my top drawer like my mother and thought of her each time I tipped out the yellow tablets in the morning before chapel.

If they were too shy, I'd be more so. Andrew was nervous. We stayed up with his family album, sharing a pack of Old Golds. Before it got light, we turned on the TV. A man was explaining how to plant seedlings. His mouth jerked to the side in a tic. Andrew thought it was a riot and kept imitating him. I laughed to be polite. When we finally dozed off, he dared to put his arm around me but that was it.

You wait till they come to you. With half fright, half swagger, they stand one step down. They dare to touch the button on your coat then lose their nerve and quickly drop their hand so you—you'd do anything for them. You touch their cheek.

The girls sit around in the common room and talk about boys, smoking their heads off.
"What are you complaining about?" says Jill to me when we talk about problems.
"Yeah," says Giddy. "You always have a boyfriend."
I look at them and think, As if.

I thought the worst thing anyone could call you was a cock-teaser. So, if you flirted, you had to be prepared to go through with it. Sleeping with someone was perfectly normal once you had done it. You didn't really worry about it. But there were other problems. The problems had to do with something else entirely.

Mack was during the hottest summer ever recorded. We were renting a house on an island with all sorts of other people. No one slept during the heat wave, walking around the house with nothing on which we were used to because of the nude beach. In the living room, Eddie lay on top of a coffee table to cool off. Mack and I, with the bedroom door open for air, sweated and sweated all night.

"I can't take this," he said at 3 A.M. "I'm going for a swim." He and some guys down the hall went to the beach. The heat put me on edge. I sat on a cracked chest by the open window and smoked and smoked till I felt even worse, waiting for something—I guess for him to get back.

One was on a camping trip in Colorado. We zipped our sleeping bags together, the coyotes' hysterical chatter far away. Other couples murmured in other tents. Paul was up before sunrise, starting a fire for breakfast. He wasn't much of a talker in the daytime. At night, his hand leafed about in the hair at my neck.

There'd be times when you overdid it. You'd get carried away. All the next day, you'd be in a total fog, delirious, absent-minded, crossing the street and nearly getting run over.

The more girls a boy has, the better. He has a bright look, having reaped fruits, blooming. He stalks around, sure-shouldered, and you have the feeling he's got more in him, a fatter heart, more stories to tell. For a girl, with each boy it's like a petal gets plucked each time.

Then you start to get tired. You begin to feel diluted, like watered-down stew.

Oliver came skiing with us. We lolled by the fire after everyone had gone to bed. Each creak you'd think was someone coming downstairs. The silver-loop bracelet he gave me had been a present from his girlfriend before.

On vacations, we went skiing, or you'd go south if someone invited you. Some people had apartments in New York that their families hardly ever used. Or summer houses, or older sisters. We always managed to find some place to go.

We made the plan at coffee hour. Simon snuck out and met me at Main Gate after lights-out. We crept to the chapel and spent the night in the balcony. He tasted like onions from a submarine sandwich.

The boys are one of two ways: either they can't sit still or they don't move. In front of the TV, they won't budge. On weekends they play touch football while we sit on the sidelines, picking blades of grass to chew on, and watch. We're always watching them run around. We shiver in the stands, knocking our boots together to keep our toes warm and they whizz across the ice, chopping their sticks around the puck. When they're in the rink, they refuse to look at you, only eyeing each other beneath low helmets. You cheer for them but they don't look up, even if it's a face-off when nothing's happening, even if they're doing drills before any game has started at all.

Dancing under the pink tent, he bent down and whispered in my ear. We slipped away to the lawn on the other side of the hedge. Much later, as he was leaving the buffet with two plates of eggs and sausage, I saw the grass stains on the knees of his white pants.

Tim's was shaped like a banana, with a graceful curve to it. They're all different. Willie's like a bunch of walnuts when nothing was happening, another's as thin as a thin hot dog. But it's like faces; you're never really surprised.

Still, you're not sure what to expect.

I look into his face and he looks back. I look into his eyes and they look back at mine. Then they look down at my mouth so I look at his mouth, then back to his eyes then, backing up, at his whole face. I think, Who? Who are you? His head tilts to one side.
I say, "Who are you?"
"What do you mean?"
"Nothing."
I look at his eyes again, deeper. Can't tell who he is, what he thinks.
"What?" he says. I look at his mouth.
"I'm just wondering," I say and go wandering across his face. Study the chin line. It's shaped like a persimmon.
"Who are you? What are you thinking?"
He says, "What the hell are you talking about?"

Then they get mad after when you say enough is enough. After, when it's easier to explain that you don't want to. You wouldn't dream of saying that maybe you weren't really ready to in the first place.

Gentle Eddie. We waded into the sea, the waves round and plowing in, buffalo-headed, slapping our thighs. I put my arms around his freckled shoulders and he held me up, buoyed by the water, and rocked me like a sea shell.

I had no idea whose party it was, the apartment jam-packed, stepping over people in the hallway. The room with the music was practically empty, the bare floor, me in red shoes. This fellow slides onto one knee and takes me around the waist and we rock to jazzy tunes, with my toes pointing heavenward, and waltz and spin and dip to "Smoke Gets in Your Eyes" or "I'll Love You Just for Now." He puts his head to my chest, runs a sweeping hand down my inside thigh and we go loose-limbed and sultry and as smooth as silk and I stamp my red heels and he takes me into a swoon. I never saw him again after that but I thought, I could have loved that one.

You wonder how long you can keep it up. You begin to feel like you're showing through, like a bathroom window that only lets in grey light, the kind you can't see out of.

They keep coming around. Johnny drives up at Easter vacation from Baltimore and I let him in the kitchen with everyone sound asleep. He has friends waiting in the car.

"What are you crazy? It's pouring out there," I say.

"It's okay," he says. "They understand."

So he gets some long kisses from me, against the refrigerator, before he goes because I hate those girls who push away a boy's face as if she were made out of Ivory soap, as if she's that much greater than he is.

The note on my cubby told me to see the headmaster. I had no idea for what. He had received complaints about my amorous displays on the town green. It was Willie that spring. The headmaster told me he didn't care what I did but that Casey Academy had a reputation to uphold in the town. He lowered his glasses on his nose. "We've got twenty acres of woods on this campus," he said. "Smooch with your boyfriend there."

Everybody'd get weekend permissions for different places then we'd all go to someone's house whose parents were away. Usually there'd be more boys than girls. We raided the liquor closet and smoked pot at the kitchen table and you'd never know who would end up where, or with whom. There were always disasters. Ceci got bombed and cracked her head open on the bannister and needed stitches. Then there was the time Wendel Blair walked through the picture window at the Lowe's and got slashed to ribbons.

He scared me. In bed, I didn't dare look at him. I lay back with my eyes closed, luxuriating because he knew all sorts of expert angles, his hands never fumbling, going over my whole body, pressing the hair up and off the back of my head, giving an extra hip shove, as if to say

There. I parted my eyes slightly, keeping the screen of my lashes low because it was too much to look at him, his mouth loose and pink and parted, his eyes looking through my forehead, or kneeling up, looking through my throat. I was ashamed but couldn't look him in the eye.

You wonder about things feeling a little off-kilter. You begin to feel like a piece of pounded veal.

At boarding school, everyone gets depressed. We go in and see the housemother, Mrs. Gunther. She got married when she was eighteen. Mr. Gunther was her high-school sweetheart, the only boyfriend she ever had.

"And you knew you wanted to marry him right off?" we ask her.

She smiles and says, "Yes."

"They always want something from you," says Jill, complaining about her boyfriend.

"Yeah," says Giddy. "You always feel like you have to deliver something."

"You do," says Mrs. Gunther. "Babies."

After sex, you curl up like a shrimp, something deep inside you ruined, slammed in a place that sickens at slamming, and slowly you fill up with an overwhelming sadness, an elusive gaping worry. You don't try to explain it, filled with the knowledge that it's nothing after all, everything filling up finally and absolutely with death. After the briskness of loving, loving stops. And you roll over with death stretched out alongside you like a feather boa, or a snake, light as air, and you . . . you don't even ask for anything or try to say something to him because it's obviously your own damn fault. You haven't been able to— to what? To open your heart. You open your legs but can't, or don't dare anymore, to open your heart.

It starts this way:

You stare into their eyes. They flash like all the stars are out. They look at you seriously, their eyes at a low burn and their hands no matter what starting off shy and with such a gentle touch that the only thing you can do is take that tenderness and let yourself be swept away. When, with one attentive finger they tuck the hair behind your ear, you—

You do everything they want.

Then comes after. After when they don't look at you. They scratch their balls, stare at the ceiling. Or if they do turn, their gaze is altogether changed. They are surprised. They turn casually to look at you, distracted, and get a mild distracted surprise. You're gone. Their black look tells you that the girl they were fucking is not there anymore. You seem to have disappeared.

1989

BHARATI MUKHERJEE

THE TENANT

Maya Sanyal has been in Cedar Falls, Iowa, less than two weeks. She's come, books and clothes and one armchair rattling in the smallest truck that U-Haul would rent her, from New Jersey. Before that she was in North Carolina. Before that, Calcutta, India. Every place has something to give. She is sitting at the kitchen table with Fran drinking bourbon for the first time in her life. Fran Johnson found her the furnished apartment and helped her settle in. Now she's brought a bottle of bourbon which gives her the right to stay and talk for a bit. She's breaking up with someone named Vern, a pharmacist. Vern's father is also a pharmacist and owns a drugstore. Maya has seen Vern's father on TV twice already. The first time was on the local news when he spoke out against the selling of painkillers like Advil and Nuprin in supermarkets and gas stations. In the matter of painkillers, Maya is a universalist. The other time he was in a barbershop quartet. Vern gets along all right with his father. He likes the pharmacy business, as business goes, but he wants to go back to graduate school and learn to make films. Maya is drinking her first bourbon tonight because Vern left today for San Francisco State.

"I understand totally," Fran says. She teaches Utopian Fiction and a course in Women's Studies and worked hard to get Maya hired. Maya has a Ph.D. in Comparative Literature and will introduce writers like R. K. Narayan and Chinua Achebe to three sections of sophomores at the University of Northern Iowa. "A person has to leave home. Try out his wings."

Fran has to use the bathroom. "I don't feel abandoned." She pushes her chair away from the table. "Anyway, it was a sex thing totally. We were good together. It'd be different if I'd loved him."

Maya tries to remember what's in the refrigerator. They need food. She hasn't been to the supermarket in over a week. She doesn't have a car yet and so she relies on a corner store—a longish walk—for milk, cereal, and frozen dinners. Someday these exigencies will show up as bad skin and collapsed muscle tone. No folly is ever lost. Maya pictures history as a net, the kind of safety net travelling trapeze artists of her childhood fell into when they were inattentive, or clumsy. Going to circuses in Calcutta with her father is what she remembers vividly. It is a banal memory, for her father, the owner of a steel company, is a complicated man.

Fran is out in the kitchen long enough for Maya to worry. They need food. Her mother believed in food. What is love, anger, inner peace, etc., her mother used to say, but the brain's biochemistry. Maya doesn't want to get into that, but she is glad she has enough stuff in the refrigerator to make an omelette. She realizes Indian women are supposed to be inventive with food, whip up exotic delights to tickle an American's palate, and she knows she should be meeting Fran's generosity and candor with some sort of bizarre and effortless counter-move. If there's an exotic spice store in Cedar Falls or in neighboring Waterloo, she hasn't found it. She's looked in the phone book for common Indian names, especially Bengali, but hasn't yet struck up culinary intimacies. That will come—it always does. There's a six-pack in the fridge that her landlord, Ted Suminski, had put in because she'd be thirsty after unpacking. She was thirsty, but she doesn't drink beer. She probably should have asked him to come up and drink the beer. Except for Fran she hasn't had anyone over. Fran is more friendly and helpful than anyone Maya has known in the States since she came to North Carolina ten years ago, at nineteen. Fran is a Swede, and she is tall, with blue eyes. Her hair, however, is a dull, darkish brown.

"I don't think I can handle anything that heavy-duty," Fran says when she comes back to the room. She means the omelette. "I have to go home in any case." She lives with her mother and her aunt, two women in their mid-seventies, in a drafty farmhouse. The farmhouse now has a computer store catty-corner from it. Maya's been to the farm. She's been shown photographs of the way the corner used to be. If land values ever rebound, Fran will be worth millions.

Before Fran leaves she says, "Has Rab Chatterji called you yet?"

"No." She remembers the name, a good, reliable Bengali name, from the first night's study of the phone book. Dr. Rabindra Chatterji teaches Physics.

"He called the English office just before I left." She takes car keys out of her pocketbook. She reknots her scarf. "I bet Indian men are more sensitive than Americans. Rab's a Brahmin, that's what people say."

A Chatterji has to be a Bengali Brahmin—last names give ancestral secrets away—but Brahminness seems to mean more to Fran than it does to Maya. She was born in 1954, six full years after India became independent. Her India was Nehru's[1] India: a charged, progressive place.

"All Indian men are wife beaters," Maya says. She means it and doesn't mean it. "That's why I married an American." Fran knows about the divorce, but nothing else. Fran is on the Hiring, Tenure, and Reappointment Committee.

Maya sees Fran down the stairs and to the car which is parked in the back in the spot reserved for Maya's car, if she had owned one. It will take her several months to save enough to buy one. She always pays cash, never borrows. She tells herself she's still recovering from the U-Haul drive halfway across the country. Ted Suminski is in his kitchen watching the women. Maya waves to him because waving to him, acknowledging him in that way, makes him seem less creepy. He seems to live alone though a sign, THE SUMINSKIS, hangs from a metal horse's head in the front yard. Maya hasn't seen Mrs. Suminski. She hasn't seen any children either. Ted always looks lonely. When she comes back from campus, he's nearly always in the back, throwing darts or shooting baskets.

"What's he like?" Fran gestures with her head as she starts up her car. "You hear these stories."

Maya doesn't want to know the stories. She has signed a year's lease. She doesn't want complications. "He's all right. I keep out of his way."

"You know what I'm thinking? Of all the people in Cedar Falls, you're the one who could understand Vern best. His wanting to try out his wings, run away, stuff like that."

"Not really." Maya is not being modest. Fran is being impulsively democratic, lumping her wayward lover and Indian friend together as headstrong adventurers. For Fran, a utopian and feminist, borders don't count. Maya's taken some big risks, made a break with her parents' ways. She's done things a woman from Ballygunge Park Road doesn't do, even in fantasies. She's not yet shared stories with Fran, apart from the divorce. She's told her nothing of men she picks up, the reputation she'd gained, before Cedar Falls, for "indiscretions." She has a job, equity, three friends she can count on for emergencies. She is an American citizen. But.

Fran's Brahmin calls her two nights later. On the phone he presents himself as Dr. Chatterji, not Rabindra or Rab. An old-fashioned

---

1. Jawaharlal Nehru (1889–1964), Indian statesman and prime minister.

Indian, she assumes. Her father still calls his closest friend, "Colonel." Dr. Chatterji asks her to tea on Sunday. She means to say no but hears herself saying, "Sunday? Fiveish? I'm not doing anything special this Sunday."

Outside, Ted Suminski is throwing darts into his garage door. The door has painted-on rings: orange, purple, pink. The bull's-eye is gray. He has to be fifty at least. He is a big, thick, lonely man about whom people tell stories. Maya pulls the phone cord as far as it'll go so she can look down more directly on her landlord's large, bald head. He has his back to her as he lines up a dart. He's in black running shoes, red shorts, he's naked to the waist. He hunches his right shoulder, he pulls the arm back; a big, lonely man shouldn't have so much grace. The dart is ready to cut through the September evening. But Ted Suminski doesn't let go. He swings on worn rubber soles, catches her eye in the window (she has to have imagined this), takes aim at her shadow. Could she have imagined the noise of the dart's metal tip on her windowpane?

Dr. Chatterji is still on the phone. "You are not having any mode of transportation, is that right?"

Ted Suminski has lost interest in her. Perhaps it isn't interest, at all; perhaps it's aggression. "I don't drive," she lies, knowing it sounds less shameful than not owning a car. She has said this so often she can get in the right degree of apology and Asian upper-class helplessness. "It's an awful nuisance."

"Not to worry, please." Then, "It is a great honor to be meeting Dr. Sanyal's daughter. In Calcutta business circles he is a legend."

On Sunday she is ready by four-thirty. She doesn't know what the afternoon holds; there are surely no places for "high tea"—a colonial tradition—in Cedar Falls, Iowa. If he takes her back to his place, it will mean he has invited other guests. From his voice she can tell Dr. Chatterji likes to do things correctly. She has dressed herself in a peach-colored nylon georgette sari, jade drop-earrings and a necklace. The color is good on dark skin. She is not pretty, but she does her best. Working at it is a part of self-respect. In the mid-seventies, when American women felt rather strongly about such things, Maya had been in trouble with her women's group at Duke. She was too feminine. She had tried to explain the world she came out of. Her grandmother had been married off at the age of five in a village now in Bangladesh. Her great-aunt had been burned to death over a dowry problem. She herself had been trained to speak softly, arrange flowers, sing, be pliant. If she were to seduce Ted Suminski, she thinks as she waits in the front yard for Dr. Chatterji, it would be minor heroism. She has broken with the past. But.

Dr. Chatterji drives up for her at about five ten. He is a hesitant driver. The car stalls, jumps ahead, finally slams to a stop. Maya has to tell him to back off a foot or so; it's hard to leap over two sacks of pruned branches in a sari. Ted Suminski is an obsessive pruner and gardener.

"My sincerest apologies, Mrs. Sanyal," Dr. Chatterji says. He leans across the wide front seat of his noisy, very old, very used car and unlocks the door for her. "I am late. But then, I am sure you're remembering that Indian Standard Time is not at all the same as time in the States." He laughs. He could be nervous—she often had that effect on Indian men. Or he could just be chatty. "These Americans are all the time rushing and rushing but where it gets them?" He moves his head laterally once, twice. It's the gesture made famous by Peter Sellers. When Peter Sellers did it, it had seemed hilarious. Now it suggests that Maya and Dr. Chatterji have three thousand years plus civilization, sophistication, moral virtue, over people born on this continent. Like her, Dr. Chatterji is a naturalized American.

"Call me Maya," she says. She fusses with the seat belt. She does it because she needs time to look him over. He seems quite harmless. She takes in the prominent teeth, the eyebrows that run together. He's in a blue shirt and a beige cardigan with the K-Mart logo that buttons tightly over the waist. It's hard to guess his age because he has dyed his hair and his moustache. Late thirties, early forties. Older than she had expected. "Not Mrs. Sanyal."

This isn't the time to tell about ex-husbands. She doesn't know where John is these days. He should have kept up at least. John had come into her life as a graduate student at Duke, and she, mistaking the brief breathlessness of sex for love, had married him. They had stayed together two years, maybe a little less. The pain that John had inflicted all those years ago by leaving her had subsided into a cozy feeling of loss. This isn't the time, but then she doesn't want to be a legend's daughter all evening. She's not necessarily on Dr. Chatterji's side is what she wants to get across early; she's not against America and Americans. She makes the story—of marriage outside the Brahminic pale, the divorce—quick, dull. Her unsentimentality seems to shock him. His stomach sags inside the cardigan.

"We've each had our several griefs," the physicist says. "We're each required to pay our karmic debts."

"Where are we headed?"

"Mrs. Chatterji has made some Indian snacks. She is waiting to meet you because she is knowing your cousin-sister who studied in Scottish Church College. My home is okay, no?"

Fran would get a kick out of this. Maya has slept with married men, with nameless men, with men little more than boys, but never with an Indian man. Never.

The Chatterjis live in a small blue house on a gravelly street. There are at least five or six other houses on the street; the same size but in different colors and with different front yard treatments. More houses are going up. This is the cutting edge of suburbia.

Mrs. Chatterji stands in the driveway. She is throwing a large plastic ball to a child. The child looks about four, and is Korean or Cambodian. The child is not hers because she tells it, "Chung-Hee, ta-ta, bye-bye. Now I play with guest," as Maya gets out of the car.

Maya hasn't seen this part of town. The early September light softens the construction pits. In that light the houses too close together, the stout woman in a striped cotton sari, the child hugging a pink ball, the two plastic lawn chairs by a tender young tree, the sheets and saris on the clothesline in the back, all seem miraculously incandescent.

"Go home now, Chung-Hee. I am busy." Mrs. Chatterji points the child homeward, then turns to Maya, who has folded her hands in traditional Bengali greeting. "It is an honor. We feel very privileged." She leads Maya indoors to a front room that smells of moisture and paint.

In her new, deliquescent mood, Maya allows herself to be backed into the best armchair—a low-backed, boxy Goodwill item draped over with a Rajasthani bedspread—and asks after the cousin Mrs. Chatterji knows. She doesn't want to let go of Mrs. Chatterji. She doesn't want husband and wife to get into whispered conferences about their guest's misadventures in America, as they make tea in the kitchen.

The coffee table is already laid with platters of mutton croquettes, fish chops, onion pakoras, ghugni with puris, samosas, chutneys. Mrs. Chatterji has gone to too much trouble. Maya counts four kinds of sweetmeats in Corning casseroles on an end table. She looks into a see-through lid; spongy, white dumplings float in rosewater syrup. Planets contained, mysteries made visible.

"What are you waiting for, Santana?" Dr. Chatterji becomes imperious, though not unaffectionate. He pulls a dining chair up close to the coffee table. "Make some tea." He speaks in Bengali to his wife, in English to Maya. To Maya he says, grandly, "We are having real Indian Green Label Lipton. A nephew is bringing it just one month back."

His wife ignores him. "The kettle's already on," she says. She wants to know about the Sanyal family. Is it true her great-grandfather was a member of the Star Chamber in England?

Nothing in Calcutta is ever lost. Just as her story is known to

Bengalis all over America, so are the scandals of her family, the grand-father hauled up for tax evasion, the aunt who left her husband to act in films. This woman brings up the Star Chamber, the glories of the Sanyal family, her father's philanthropies, but it's a way of saying, *I know the dirt.*

The bedrooms are upstairs. In one of those bedrooms an unseen, tormented presence—Maya pictures it as a clumsy ghost that strains to shake off the body's shell—drops things on the floor. The things are heavy and they make the front room's chandelier shake. Light bulbs, shaped like tiny candle flames, flicker. The Chatterjis have said nothing about children. There are no tricycles in the hallway, no small sandals behind the doors. Maya is too polite to ask about the noise, and the Chatterjis don't explain. They talk just a little louder. They flip the embroidered cover off the stereo. What would Maya like to hear? Hemanta Kumar? Manna Dey? Oh, that young chap, Manna Dey! What sincerity, what tenderness he can convey!

Upstairs the ghost doesn't hear the music of nostalgia. The ghost throws and thumps. The ghost makes its own vehement music. Maya hears in its voice madness, self-hate.

Finally the water in the kettle comes to a boil. The whistle cuts through all fantasy and pretense. Dr. Chatterji says, "I'll see to it," and rushes out of the room. But he doesn't go to the kitchen. He shouts up the stairwell. "Poltoo, kindly stop this nonsense straightaway! We're having a brilliant and cultured lady-guest and you're creating earth-quakes?" The kettle is hysterical.

Mrs. Chatterji wipes her face. The face that had seemed plump and cheery at the start of the evening now is flabby. "My sister's boy," the woman says.

So this is the nephew who has brought with him the cartons of Green Label tea, one of which will be given to Maya.

Mrs. Chatterji speaks to Maya in English as though only the alien language can keep emotions in check. "Such an intelligent boy! His father is government servant. Very highly placed."

Maya is meant to visualize a smart, clean-cut young man from south Calcutta, but all she can see is a crazy, thwarted, lost graduate student. Intelligence, proper family guarantee nothing. Even Brahmins can do self-destructive things, feel unsavory urges. Maya herself had been an excellent student.

"He was First Class First in B. Sc. from Presidency College," the woman says. "Now he's getting Master's in Ag. Science at Iowa State."

The kitchen is silent. Dr. Chatterji comes back into the room with a tray. The teapot is under a tea cozy, a Kashmiri one embroidered with the usual chinar leaves, loops, and chains. "*Her* nephew," he says. The dyed hair and dyed moustache are no longer signs of a man wishing to fight the odds. He is a vain man, anxious to cut losses. "Very unfortunate business."

The nephew's story comes out slowly, over fish chops and mutton croquettes. He is in love with a student from Ghana.

"Everything was A-Okay until the Christmas break. Grades, assistantship for next semester, everything."

"I blame the college. The office for foreign students arranged a Christmas party. And now, *haapre baap!*[2] Our poor Poltoo wants to marry a Negro Muslim."

Maya is known for her nasty, ironic one-liners. It has taken her friends weeks to overlook her malicious, un-American pleasure in others' misfortunes. Maya would like to finish Dr. Chatterji off quickly. He is pompous; he is reactionary; he wants to live and work in America but give back nothing except taxes. The confused world of the immigrant—the lostness that Maya and Poltoo feel—that's what Dr. Chatterji wants to avoid. She hates him. But.

Dr. Chatterji's horror is real. A good Brahmin boy in Iowa is in love with an African Muslim. It shouldn't be a big deal. But the more she watches the physicist, the more she realizes that "Brahmin" isn't a caste; it's a metaphor. You break one small rule, and the constellation collapses. She thinks suddenly that John Cheever—she is teaching him as a "world writer" in her classes, cheek-by-jowl with Africans and West Indians—would have understood Dr. Chatterji's dread. Cheever had been on her mind, ever since the late afternoon light slanted over Mrs. Chatterji's drying saris. She remembers now how full of a soft, Cheeverian light Durham had been the summer she had slept with John Hadwen; and how after that, her tidy graduate-student world became monstrous, lawless. All men became John Hadwen; John became all men. Outwardly, she retained her poise, her Brahminical breeding. She treated her crisis as a literary event; she lost her moral sense, her judgment, her power to distinguish. Her parents had behaved magnanimously. They had cabled from Calcutta: WHAT'S DONE IS DONE WE ARE CONFIDENT YOU WILL HANDLE NEW SITUATIONS WELL, ALL LOVE. But she knows more than do her parents. Love is anarchy.

Poltoo is Mrs. Chatterji's favorite nephew. She looks as though it is her fault that the Sunday has turned unpleasant. She stacks the empty platters methodically. To Maya she says, "It is the goddess who

2. Literal translation: "My father, my father" (Bengali). Idiomatic translation: "For heaven's sake."

pulls the strings. We are puppets. I know the goddess will fix it. Poltoo will not marry that African woman." Then she goes to the coat closet in the hall and staggers back with a harmonium, the kind sold in music stores in Calcutta, and sets it down on the carpeted floor. "We're nothing but puppets," she says again. She sits at Maya's feet, her pudgy hands on the harmonium's shiny, black bellows. She sings, beautifully, in a virgin's high voice, "Come, goddess, come, muse, come to us hapless peoples' rescue."

Maya is astonished. She has taken singing lessons at Dakshini Academy in Calcutta. She plays the sitar and the tanpur,[3] well enough to please Bengalis, to astonish Americans. But stout Mrs. Chatterji is a devotee, talking to God.

A little after eight, Dr. Chatterji drops her off. It's been an odd evening and they are both subdued.

"I want to say one thing," he says. He stops her from undoing her seat belt. The plastic sacks of pruned branches are still at the corner.

"You don't have to get out," she says.

"Please. Give me one more minute of your time."

"Sure."

"Maya is my favorite name."

She says nothing. She turns away from him without making her embarrassment obvious.

"Truly speaking, it is my favorite. You are sometimes lonely, no? But you are lucky. Divorced women can date, they can go to bars and discos. They can see mens, many mens. But inside marriage there is so much loneliness." A groan, low, horrible, comes out of him.

She turns back toward him, to unlatch the seat belt and run out of the car. She sees that Dr. Chatterji's pants are unzipped. One hand works hard under his Jockey shorts; the other rests, limp, penitential, on the steering wheel.

"Dr. Chatterji—*really!*" she cries.

The next day, Monday, instead of getting a ride home with Fran— Fran says she *likes* to give rides, she needs the chance to talk, and she won't share gas expenses, absolutely not—Maya goes to the periodicals room of the library. There are newspapers from everywhere, even from Madagascar and New Caledonia. She thinks of the periodicals room as an asylum for homesick aliens. There are two aliens already in the

3. Sitar: an Indian lute with a long neck and six or seven main playing strings. Tanpur: a four- or five-stringed guitarlike instrument that provides the background drone for a vocalist or sitar player.

room, both Orientals, both absorbed in the politics and gossip of their far off homes.

She goes straight to the newspapers from India. She bunches her raincoat like a bolster to make herself more comfortable. There's so much to catch up on. A village headman, a known Congress-Indira party worker, has been shot at by scooter-riding snipers. An Indian pugilist has won an international medal—in Nepal. A child drawing well water—the reporter calls the child "a neo-Buddhist, a convert from the now-outlawed untouchable caste"—has been stoned. An editorial explains that the story about stoning is not a story about caste but about failed idealism; a story about promises of green fields and clean, potable water broken, a story about bribes paid and wells not dug. But no, thinks Maya, it's about caste.

Out here, in the heartland of the new world, the India of serious newspapers unsettles. Maya longs again to feel what she had felt in the Chatterjis' living room: virtues made physical. It is a familiar feeling, a longing. Had a suitable man presented himself in the reading room at that instant, she would have seduced him. She goes on to the stack of *India Abroads*, reads through matrimonial columns, and steals an issue to take home.

Indian men want Indian brides. Married Indian men want Indian mistresses. All over America, "handsome, tall, fair" engineers, doctors, data processors—the new pioneers—cry their eerie love calls.

Maya runs a finger down the first column; her fingertip, dark with newsprint, stops at random.

Hello! Hi! Yes, you *are* the one I'm looking for. You are the new emancipated Indo-American woman. You have a zest for life. You are at ease in USA and yet your ethics are rooted in Indian tradition. The man of your dreams has come. Yours truly is handsome, ear-nose-throat specialist, well-settled in Connecticut. Age is 41 but never married, physically fit, sportsmanly, and strong. I adore idealism, poetry, beauty. I abhor smugness, passivity, caste system. Write with recent photo. Better still, call!!!.

Maya calls. Hullo, hullo, hullo! She hears immigrant lovers cry in crowded shopping malls. Yes, you who are at ease in both worlds, you are the one. She feels she has a fair chance.

A man answers. "Ashoke Mehta speaking."

She speaks quickly into the bright-red mouthpiece of her telephone. He will be in Chicago, in transit, passing through O'Hare. United counter, Saturday, two P.M. As easy as that.

"Good," Ashoke Mehta says. "For these encounters I, too, prefer a neutral zone."

On Saturday at exactly two o'clock the man of Maya's dreams floats toward her as lovers used to in shampoo commercials. The United counter is a loud, harrassed place but passengers and piled-up luggage fall away from him. Full-cheeked and fleshy-lipped, he is handsome. He hasn't lied. He is serene, assured, a Hindu god touching down in Illinois.

She can't move. She feels ugly and unworthy. Her adult life no longer seems miraculously rebellious; it is grim, it is perverse. She has accomplished nothing. She has changed her citizenship but she hasn't broken through into the light, the vigor, the *bustle* of the New World. She is stuck in dead space.

"Hullo, Hullo!" Their fingers touch.

Oh, the excitement! Ashoke Mehta's palm feels so right in the small of her back. Hullo, hullo, hullo. He pushes her out of the reach of anti-Khomeini Iranians, Hare Krishnas, American Fascists, men with fierce wants, and guides her to an empty gate. They have less than an hour.

"What would you like, Maya?"

She knows he can read her mind, she knows her thoughts are open to him. *You*, she's almost giddy with the thought, with simple desire. "From the snack bar," he says, as though to clarify. "I'm afraid I'm starved."

Below them, where the light is strong and hurtful, a Boeing is being serviced. "Nothing," she says.

He leans forward. She can feel the nap of his scarf—she recognizes the Cambridge colors—she can smell the wool of his Icelandic sweater. She runs her hand along the scarf, then against the flesh of his neck. "Only the impulsive ones call," he says.

The immigrant courtship proceeds. It's easy, he's good with facts. He knows how to come across to a stranger who may end up a lover, a spouse. He makes over a hundred thousand. He owns a house in Hartford, and two income properties in Newark. He plays the market but he's cautious. He's good at badminton but plays handball to keep in shape. He watches all the sports on television. Last August he visited Copenhagen, Helsinki and Leningrad. Once upon a time he collected stamps but now he doesn't have hobbies, except for reading. He counts himself an intellectual, he spends too much on books. Ludlum, Forsyth, MacInnes; other names she doesn't catch. She suppresses a smile, she's told him only she's a graduate student. He's not without his vices. He's a spender, not a saver. He's a sensualist: good food—all foods, but easy on the Indian—good wine. Some temptations he doesn't try to resist.

And I, she wants to ask, do I tempt?

"Now tell me about yourself, Maya." He makes it easy for her. "Have you ever been in love?"

"No."

"But many have loved you, I can see that." He says it not unkindly. It is the fate of women like her, and men like him. Their karmic duty, to be loved. It is expected, not judged. She feels he can see them all, the sad parade of need and demand. This isn't the time to reveal all.

And so the courtship enters a second phase.

When she gets back to Cedar Falls, Ted Suminski is standing on the front porch. It's late at night, chilly. He is wearing a down vest. She's never seen him on the porch. In fact there's no chair to sit on. He looks chilled through. He's waited around a while.

"Hi." She has her keys ready. This isn't the night to offer the six-pack in the fridge. He looks expectant, ready to pounce.

"Hi." He looks like a man who might have aimed the dart at her. What has he done to his wife, his kids? Why isn't there at least a dog? "Say, I left a note upstairs."

The note is written in Magic Marker and thumb-tacked to her apartment door. DUE TO PERSONAL REASONS, NAMELY REMARRIAGE, I REQUEST THAT YOU VACATE MY PLACE AT THE END OF THE SEMESTER.

Maya takes the note down and retacks it to the kitchen wall. The whole wall is like a bulletin board, made of some new, crumbly building-material. Her kitchen, Ted Suminski had told her, was once a child's bedroom. Suminski in love: the idea stuns her. She has misread her landlord. The dart at her window speaks of no twisted fantasy. The landlord wants the tenant out.

She gets a glass out of the kitchen cabinet, gets out a tray of ice, pours herself a shot of Fran's bourbon. She is happy for Ted Suminski. She is. She wants to tell someone how moved she'd been by Mrs. Chatterji's singing. How she'd felt in O'Hare, even about Dr. Rab Chatterji in the car. But Fran is not the person. No one she's ever met is the person. She can't talk about the dead space she lives in. She wishes Ashoke Mehta would call. Right now.

Weeks pass. Then two months. She finds a new room, signs another lease. Her new landlord calls himself Fred. He has no arms, but he helps her move her things. He drives between Ted Suminski's place and his twice in his station wagon. He uses his toes the way Maya uses her fingers. He likes to do things. He pushes garbage sacks full of Maya's clothes up the stairs.

"It's all right to stare," Fred says. "Hell, I would."

That first afternoon in Fred's rooming house, they share a Chianti. Fred wants to cook her pork chops but he's a little shy about Indians and meat. Is it beef, or pork? Or any meat? She says it's okay, any meat, but not tonight. He has an ex-wife in Des Moines, two kids in Portland, Oregon. The kids are both normal; he's the only freak in the family. But he's self-reliant. He shops in the supermarket like anyone else, he carries out the garbage, shovels the snow off the sidewalk. He needs Maya's help with one thing. Just one thing. The box of Tide is a bit too heavy to manage. Could she get him the giant size every so often and leave it in the basement?

The dead space need not suffocate. Over the months, Fred and she will settle into companionship. She has never slept with a man without arms. Two wounded people, he will joke during their nightly contortions. It will shock her, this assumed equivalence with a man so strikingly deficient. She knows she is strange, and lonely, but being Indian is not the same, she would have thought, as being a freak.

One night in spring, Fred's phone rings. "Ashoke Mehta speaking." None of this "do you remember me?" nonsense. The god has tracked her down. He hasn't forgotten. "Hullo," he says, in their special way. And because she doesn't answer back, "Hullo, hullo, hullo." She is aware of Fred in the back of the room. He is lighting a cigarette with his toes.

"Yes," she says, "I remember."

"I had to take care of a problem," Ashoke Mehta says. "You know that I have my vices. That time at O'Hare I was honest with you."

She is breathless.

"Who is it, May?" asks Fred.

"You also have a problem," says the voice. His laugh echoes. "You will come to Hartford, I know."

When she moves out, she tells herself, it will not be the end of Fred's world.

1988

ALICE MUNRO

WILD SWANS

Flo said to watch for White Slavers. She said this was how they operated: an old woman, a motherly or grandmotherly sort, made friends
while riding beside you on a bus or train. She offered you candy, which
was drugged. Pretty soon you began to droop and mumble, were in no
condition to speak for yourself. Oh, help, the woman said, my daughter
(granddaughter) is sick, please somebody help me get her off so that
she can recover in the fresh air. Up stepped a polite gentleman, pretending to be a stranger, offering assistance. Together, at the next stop,
they hustled you off the train or bus, and that was the last the ordinary
world ever saw of you. They kept you a prisoner in the White Slave
place (to which you had been transported drugged and bound so you
wouldn't even know where you were), until such time as you were
thoroughly degraded and in despair, your insides torn up by drunken
men and invested with vile disease, your mind destroyed by drugs, your
hair and teeth fallen out. It took about three years, for you to get to this
state. You wouldn't want to go home, then, maybe couldn't remember
home, or find your way if you did. So they let you out on the streets.

Flo took ten dollars and put it in a little cloth bag which she
sewed to the strap of Rose's slip. Another thing likely to happen was
that Rose would get her purse stolen.

Watch out, Flo said as well, for people dressed up as ministers.
They were the worst. That disguise was commonly adopted by White
Slavers, as well as those after your money.

Rose said she didn't see how she could tell which ones were dis-
guised.

Flo had worked in Toronto once. She had worked as a waitress in
a coffee shop in Union Station. That was how she knew all she knew.
She never saw sunlight, in those days, except on her days off. But she

403

saw plenty else. She saw a man cut another man's stomach with a knife, just pull out his shirt and do a tidy cut, as if it was a watermelon not a stomach. The stomach's owner just sat looking down surprised, with no time to protest. Flo implied that that was nothing, in Toronto. She saw two bad women (that was what Flo called whores, running the two words together, like badminton) get into a fight, and a man laughed at them, other men stopped and laughed and egged them on, and they had their fists full of each other's hair. At last the police came and took them away, still howling and yelping.

She saw a child die of a fit, too. Its face was black as ink.

"Well I'm not scared," said Rose provokingly. "There's the police, anyway."

"Oh, them! They'd be the first ones to diddle you!"

She did not believe anything Flo said on the subject of sex. Consider the undertaker.

A little bald man, very neatly dressed, would come into the store sometimes and speak to Flo with a placating expression.

"I only wanted a bag of candy. And maybe a few packages of gum. And one or two chocolate bars. Could you go to the trouble of wrapping them?"

Flo in her mock-deferential tone would assure him that she could. She wrapped them in heavy-duty white paper, so they were something like presents. He took his time with the selection, humming and chatting, then dawdled for a while. He might ask how Flo was feeling. And how Rose was, if she was there.

"You look pale. Young girls need fresh air." To Flo he would say, "You work too hard. You've worked hard all your life."

"No rest for the wicked," Flo would say agreeably.

When he went out she hurried to the window. There it was—the old black hearse with its purple curtains.

"He'll be after them today!" Flo would say as the hearse rolled away at a gentle pace, almost a funeral pace. The little man had been an undertaker, but he was retired now. The hearse was retired too. His sons had taken over the undertaking and bought a new one. He drove the old hearse all over the country, looking for women. So Flo said. Rose could not believe it. Flo said he gave them the gum and the candy. Rose said he probably ate them himself. Flo said he had been seen, he had been heard. In mild weather he drove with the windows down, singing, to himself or to somebody out of sight in the back.

> Her brow is like the snowdrift
> Her throat is like the swan

Flo imitated him singing. Gently overtaking some woman walking on a back road, or resting at a country crossroads. All compliments and courtesy and chocolate bars, offering a ride. Of course every woman who reported being asked said she had turned him down. He never pestered anybody, drove politely on. He called in at houses, and if the husband was home he seemed to like just as well as anything to sit and chat. Wives said that was all he ever did anyway but Flo did not believe it.

"Some women are taken in," she said. "A number." She liked to speculate on what the hearse was like inside. Plush. Plush on the walls and the roof and the floor. Soft purple, the color of the curtains, the color of dark lilacs.

All nonsense, Rose thought. Who could believe it, of a man that age?

Rose was going to Toronto on the train for the first time by herself. She had been once before, but that was with Flo, long before her father died. They took along their own sandwiches and bought milk from the vendor on the train. It was sour. Sour chocolate milk. Rose kept taking tiny sips, unwilling to admit that something so much desired could fail her. Flo sniffed it, then hunted up and down the train until she found the old man in his red jacket, with no teeth and the tray hanging around his neck. She invited him to sample the chocolate milk. She invited people nearby to smell it. He let her have some ginger ale for nothing. It was slightly warm.

"I let him know," Flo said looking around after he had left. "You have to let them know."

A woman agreed with her but most people looked out the window. Rose drank the warm ginger ale. Either that, or the scene with the vendor, or the conversation Flo and the agreeing woman now got into about where they came from, why they were going to Toronto, and Rose's morning constipation which was why she was lacking color, or the small amount of chocolate milk she had got inside her, caused her to throw up in the train toilet. All day long she was afraid people in Toronto could smell vomit on her coat.

This time Flo started the trip off by saying, "Keep an eye on her, she's never been away from home before!" to the conductor, then looking around and laughing, to show that was jokingly meant. Then she had to get off. It seemed the conductor had no more need for jokes than Rose had, and no intention of keeping an eye on anybody. He never spoke to Rose except to ask for her ticket. She had a window seat, and was soon extraordinarily happy. She felt Flo receding, West

Hanratty flying away from her, her own wearying self discarded as easily as everything else. She loved the towns less and less known. A woman was standing at her back door in her nightgown, not caring if everybody on the train saw her. They were traveling south, out of the snow belt, into an earlier spring, a tenderer sort of landscape. People could grow peach trees in their backyards.

Rose collected in her mind the things she had to look for in Toronto. First, things for Flo. Special stockings for her varicose veins. A special kind of cement for sticking handles on pots. And a full set of dominoes.

For herself Rose wanted to buy hair-remover to put on her arms and legs, and if possible an arrangement of inflatable cushions, supposed to reduce your hips and thighs. She thought they probably had hair-remover in the drugstore in Hanratty, but the woman in there was a friend of Flo's and told everything. She told Flo who bought hair dye and slimming medicine and French safes. As for the cushion business, you could send away for it but there was sure to be a comment at the Post Office, and Flo knew people there as well. She also planned to buy some bangles, and an angora sweater. She had great hopes of silver bangles and powder-blue angora. She thought they could transform her, make her calm and slender and take the frizz out of her hair, dry her underarms and turn her complexion to pearl.

The money for these things, as well as the money for the trip, came from a prize Rose had won, for writing an essay called "Art and Science in the World of Tomorrow." To her surprise, Flo asked if she could read it, and while she was reading it, she remarked that they must have thought they had to give Rose the prize for swallowing the dictionary. Then she said shyly, "It's very interesting."

She would have to spend the night at Cela McKinney's. Cela McKinney was her father's cousin. She had married a hotel manager and thought she had gone up in the world. But the hotel manager came home one day and sat down on the dining room floor between two chairs and said, "I am never going to leave this house again." Nothing unusual had happened, he had just decided not to go out of the house again, and he didn't, until he died. That had made Cela McKinney odd and nervous. She locked her doors at eight o'clock. She was also very stingy. Supper was usually oatmeal porridge, with raisins. Her house was dark and narrow and smelled like a bank.

The train was filling up. At Brantford a man asked if she would mind if he sat down beside her.

"It's cooler out than you'd think," he said. He offered her part of his newspaper. She said no thanks.

Then lest he think her rude she said it really was cooler. She went on looking out the window at the spring morning. There was no snow left, down here. The trees and bushes seemed to have a paler bark than they did at home. Even the sunlight looked different. It was as different from home, here, as the coast of the Mediterranean would be, or the valleys of California.

"Filthy windows, you'd think they'd take more care," the man said. "Do you travel much by train?"

She said no.

Water was lying in the fields. He nodded at it and said there was a lot this year.

"Heavy snows."

She noticed his saying *snows*, a poetic-sounding word. Anyone at home would have said *snow*.

"I had an unusual experience the other day. I was driving out in the country. In fact I was on my way to see one of my parishioners, a lady with a heart condition—"

She looked quickly at his collar. He was wearing an ordinary shirt and tie and a dark blue suit.

"Oh, yes," he said. "I'm a United Church minister. But I don't always wear my uniform. I wear it for preaching in. I'm off duty today."

"Well as I said I was driving through the country and I saw some Canada geese down on a pond, and I took another look, and there were some swans down with them. A whole great flock of swans. What a lovely sight they were. They would be on their spring migration, I expect, heading up north. What a spectacle. I never saw anything like it."

Rose was unable to think appreciatively of the wild swans because she was afraid he was going to lead the conversation from them to Nature in general and then to God, the way a minister would feel obliged to do. But he did not, he stopped with the swans.

"A very fine sight. You would have enjoyed them."

He was between fifty and sixty years old, Rose thought. He was short, and energetic-looking, with a square ruddy face and bright waves of gray hair combed straight up from his forehead. When she realized he was not going to mention God she felt she ought to show her gratitude.

She said they must have been lovely.

"It wasn't even a regular pond, it was only some water lying in a field. It was just luck the water was lying there and they came down and I came driving by at the right time. Just luck. They come in at the east end of Lake Erie, I think. But I never was lucky enough to see them before."

She turned by degrees to the window, and he returned to his

paper. She remained slightly smiling, so as not to seem rude, not to seem to be rejecting conversation altogether. The morning really was cool, and she had taken down her coat off the hook where she put it when she first got on the train, she had spread it over herself, like a lap robe. She had set her purse on the floor when the minister sat down, to give him room. He took the sections of the paper apart, shaking and rustling them in a leisurely, rather showy, way. He seemed to her the sort of person who does everything in a showy way. A ministerial way. He brushed aside the sections he didn't want at the moment. A corner of newspaper touched her leg, just at the edge of her coat.

She thought for some time that it was the paper. Then she said to herself, what if it is a hand? That was the kind of thing she could imagine. She would sometimes look at men's hands, at the fuzz on their forearms, their concentrating profiles. She would think about everything they could do. Even the stupid ones. For instance the driver-salesman who brought the bread to Flo's store. The ripeness and confidence of manner, the settled mixture of ease and alertness with which he handled the bread truck. A fold of mature belly over the belt did not displease her. Another time she had her eye on the French teacher at school. Not a Frenchman at all, really, his name was McLaren, but Rose thought teaching French had rubbed off on him, made him look like one. Quick and sallow; sharp shoulders; hooked nose and sad eyes. She saw him lapping and coiling his way through slow pleasures, a perfect autocrat of indulgences. She had a considerable longing to be somebody's object. Pounded, pleasured, reduced, exhausted.

But what if it was a hand? What if it really was a hand? She shifted slightly, moved as much as she could toward the window. Her imagination seemed to have created this reality, a reality she was not prepared for at all. She found it alarming. She was concentrating on that leg, that bit of skin with the stocking over it. She could not bring herself to look. Was there a pressure, or was there not? She shifted again. Her legs had been, and remained, tightly closed. It was. It was a hand. It was a hand's pressure.

Please don't. That was what she tried to say. She shaped the words in her mind, tried them out, then couldn't get them past her lips. Why was that? The embarrassment, was it, the fear that people might hear? People were all around them, the seats were full.

It was not only that.

She did manage to look at him, not raising her head but turning it cautiously. He had tilted his seat back and closed his eyes. There was his dark blue suit sleeve, disappearing under the newspaper. He had arranged the paper so that it overlapped Rose's coat. His hand was underneath, simply resting, as if flung out in sleep.

Now, Rose could have shifted the newspaper and removed her coat. If he was not asleep, he would have been obliged to draw back his hand. If he was asleep, if he did not draw it back, she could have whispered, *Excuse me*, and set his hand firmly on his own knee. This solution, so obvious and foolproof, did not occur to her. And she would have to wonder, why not? The minister's hand was not, or not yet, at all welcome to her. It made her feel uncomfortable, resentful, slightly disgusted, trapped and wary. But she could not take charge of it, to reject it. She could not insist that it was there, when he seemed to be insisting that it was not. How could she declare him responsible, when he lay there so harmless and trusting, resting himself before his busy day, with such a pleased and healthy face? A man older than her father would be, if he were living, a man used to deference, an appreciator of Nature, delighter in wild swans. If she did say *Please don't* she was sure he would ignore her, as if overlooking some silliness or impoliteness on her part. She knew that as soon as she said it she would hope he had not heard.

But there was more to it than that. Curiosity. More constant, more imperious, than any lust. A lust in itself, that will make you draw back and wait, wait too long, risk almost anything, just to see what will happen. *To see what will happen.*

The hand began, over the next several miles, the most delicate, the most timid, pressures and investigations. Not asleep. Or if he was, his hand wasn't. She did feel disgust. She felt a faint, wandering nausea. She thought of flesh: lumps of flesh, pink snouts, fat tongues, blunt fingers, all on their way trotting and creeping and lolling and rubbing, looking for their comfort. She thought of cats in heat rubbing themselves along the top of board fences, yowling with their miserable complaint. It was pitiful, infantile, this itching and shoving and squeezing. Spongy tissues, inflamed membranes, tormented nerve-ends, shameful smells; humiliation.

All that was starting. His hand, that she wouldn't ever have wanted to hold, that she wouldn't have squeezed back, his stubborn patient hand was able, after all, to get the ferns to rustle and the streams to flow, to waken a sly luxuriance.

Nevertheless, she would rather not. She would still rather not. Please remove this, she said out the window. Stop it, please, she said to the stumps and barns. The hand moved up her leg past the top of her stocking to her bare skin, had moved higher, under her suspender, reached her underpants and the lower part of her belly. Her legs were still crossed, pinched together. While her legs stayed crossed she could lay claim to innocence, she had not admitted anything. She could still believe that she would stop this in a minute. Nothing was going to happen, nothing more. Her legs were never going to open.

But they were. They were. As the train crossed the Niagara Escarpment above Dundas, as they looked down at the preglacial valley, the silver-wooded rubble of little hills, as they came sliding down to the shores of Lake Ontario, she would make this slow, and silent, and definite, declaration, perhaps disappointing as much as satisfying the hand's owner. He would not lift his eyelids, his face would not alter, his fingers would not hesitate, but would go powerfully and discreetly to work. Invasion, and welcome, and sunlight flashing far and wide on the lake water; miles of bare orchards stirring round Burlington.

This was disgrace, this was beggary. But what harm in that, we say to ourselves at such moments, what harm in anything, the worse the better, as we ride the cold wave of greed, of greedy assent. A stranger's hand, or root vegetables or humble kitchen tools that people tell jokes about; the world is tumbling with innocent-seeming objects ready to declare themselves, slippery and obliging. She was careful of her breathing. She could not believe this. Victim and accomplice she was borne past Glassco's Jams and Marmalades, past the big pulsating pipes of oil refineries. They glided into suburbs where bedsheets, and towels used to wipe up intimate stains, flapped leeringly on the clotheslines, where even the children seemed to be frolicking lewdly in the school-yards, and the very truckdrivers stopped at the railway crossings must be thrusting their thumbs gleefully into curled hands. Such cunning antics now, such popular visions. The gates and towers of the Exhibition Grounds came into view, the painted domes and pillars floated marvelously against her eyelids' rosy sky. Then flew apart in celebration. You could have had such a flock of birds, wild swans, even, wakened under one big dome together, exploding from it, taking to the sky.

She bit the edge of her tongue. Very soon the conductor passed through the train, to stir the travelers, warn them back to life.

In the darkness under the station the United Church minister, refreshed, opened his eyes and got his paper folded together, then asked if she would like some help with her coat. His gallantry was self-satisfied, dismissive. No, said Rose, with a sore tongue. He hurried out of the train ahead of her. She did not see him in the station. She never saw him again in her life. But he remained on call, so to speak, for years and years, ready to slip into place at a critical moment, without even any regard, later on, for husband or lovers. What recommended him? She could never understand it. His simplicity, his arrogance, his perversely appealing lack of handsomeness, even of ordinary grown-up masculinity? When he stood up she saw that he was shorter even than she had thought, that his face was pink and shiny, that there was something crude and pushy and childish about him.

Was he a minister, really, or was that only what he said? Flo had mentioned people who were not ministers, dressed up as if they were. Not real ministers dressed as if they were not. Or, stranger still, men who were not real ministers pretending to be real but dressed as if they were not. But that she had come as close as she had, to what could happen, was an unwelcome thing. Rose walked through Union Station feeling the little bag with the ten dollars rubbing at her, knew she would feel it all day long, rubbing its reminder against her skin.

She couldn't stop getting Flo's messages, even with that. She remembered, because she was in Union Station, that there was a girl named Mavis working here, in the Gift Shop, when Flo was working in the coffee shop. Mavis had warts on her eyelids that looked like they were going to turn into sties but they didn't, they went away. Maybe she had them removed, Flo didn't ask. She was very good-looking without them. There was a movie star in those days she looked a lot like. The movie star's name was Frances Farmer.

Frances Farmer. Rose had never heard of her.

That was the name. And Mavis went and bought herself a big hat that dipped over one eye and a dress entirely made of lace. She went off for the weekend to Georgian Bay, to a resort up there. She booked herself in under the name of Florence Farmer. To give everybody the idea she was really the other one, Frances Farmer, but calling herself Florence because she was on holiday and didn't want to be recognized. She had a little cigarette holder that was black and mother-of-pearl. She could have been arrested, Flo said. For the *nerve*.

Rose almost went over to the Gift Shop, to see if Mavis was still there and if she could recognize her. She thought it would be an especially fine thing, to manage a transformation like that. To dare it; to get away with it, to enter on preposterous adventures in your own, but newly named, skin.

1977

▪   ▪   ▪

JOYCE CAROL OATES

BAD GIRLS

That last year of the four of us—Marietta Murchison and her three teenaged daughters—if we'd known it was to be the last we'd have done things differently. But we didn't know, nor did we have a clue how happy (in spite of all our squabbling!) we were. So what came out was, I guess you could say, what had to.

Nor did we set out to destroy our mother's man friend Isaak Drumm, exactly.

How Icy, Orchid, and Crystal, sixteen years old, fifteen, and thirteen, confirmed the neighborhood's and our own relatives' judgment of us, that we were *bad*. And not only *bad* in ourselves but the cause of somebody else being *bad*, too.

But who would have thought we had that much power?

For in our lives, Momma with two ex-husbands and no child support let alone alimony, living on the south side of Yewville on Niagara Street where the old woodframe ratty-rotted houses look like they're about to slide downhill into the railroad yard and the river—we didn't have any power, at all. If what's meant by *power* is to control your own life and the lives of people you love and make them turn out well and happy. *That*, we sure didn't have.

Seeing us downtown after school, though, or at the East Hills Mall where the kids hang out, the three of us swinging along with our arms around one another's waists, in tight jeans and tank tops in summer, metal-stud jackets in cold weather and clattery boots, purple, maroon, and bright green dye-streaks in our hair—Icy with her gold nose ring and a half-dozen studs in each ear, and Orchid with her heavy-broody eyebrows and sassy mouth, and baby-girl Crystal in skin-tight jeans looking from the rear like a juicy honeydew melon sliced in half—people cut their eyes at us like we were threats to public safety.

Bad girls you could almost hear them thinking. *Bad girls!* some old pain-in-the-ass aunt of Momma's once hissed at us 'cause we were doing something she didn't like. Which is what adults mean by *bad*— you're doing something they don't like.

It's to hurt your feelings, too. Like Momma's aunt meaning to make a judgment on Momma as a mother. But look—anybody wants to hurt your feelings the smartest strategy is just to laugh in their face. That, Crystal and I learned from Icy. And it works.

Every time our mother fell in love it was like whichever apartment or house we lived in, the actual floors and walls would begin to lurch. Like the four of us were in a boat we weren't aware of in calm waters and then a storm comes up pitching and tossing us—causing sea-sickness, or worse. You're desperate clutching for something to keep from being thrown overboard. To keep from being drowned.

Momma's men! On the telephone asking for her they'd sound OK then she'd bring them home and it was all we could do, Icy, Orchid, and Crystal, to keep from laughing in their faces—even their names were weird. There was "John Calvin Penny" who was Momma's boss at Penny Realtors where she answered phones and did bookkeeping for a while till working conditions became, in Momma's words, "too tense." There was "Dr. Kenneth Nutt" who was our dentist—he first asked Momma for a date in the dentist's chair!—till Momma broke up with him. There was "Corky Silver" who passed himself off as a free-lance investment banker and who drove a lipstick-red MG and wore a wavy blond toupee so fake it was embarrassing—this creep in his fifties at least pretending to be Momma's age (thirty-six) and calling us all *"girls."* And for a while there was this class-A jerk we called "The Hulk." And this serial-killer type "Mouse Ears." And there was "Isaak Drumm."

The way Momma spoke of Drumm, only informing us after they'd gone out three times, almost stammering his name and her eyes clouding up not looking at us exactly, a single thought rushed through us like a warning—*This one might be serious.* Isaak Drumm, Momma informed us, worked for O'Mara's Construction Co., which was a well-known local name, and he'd been a U.S. Army sergeant for seven years having served—the goofy way Momma said "served"!—in Beirut, Lebanon. (Which was where? And who gives a damn?) "Isaak" had a Silver Star medal, Momma said, like she expected us to be impressed. He was thirty-nine years old and long ago married and divorced with no children—here Momma spoke rapidly not inviting questions—and a volunteer in the Niagara Christian Youth Aid which was one of those do-good organizations you yawn just to hear the name of. And "Isaak" was courteous, Momma said. And kind. And warm. And *funny*—a wonderful sense of humor. Momma talking fast trying not to see the three of us staring deadpan at her, taking all this in like it was gospel truth and not a variation of the crap we'd been hearing, in different words, a dozen times already. *Yeah sure Momma, we know this guy is terrific! Sure! We'll be real nice to him we'll be good girls you can trust us!*

What Momma neglected to tell us, and it's the first thing anybody would notice about Isaak Drumm, as soon as he approached us smiling and squinting and shifting his shoulders like his coat's too tight—and *limping* from his "war-wound" in his left knee—is the guy's *weird-looking.* Not ugly because actually Isaak Drumm wasn't ugly, you could almost see how somebody hopeful like our mother might imagine he was handsome, sort of—just *weird-looking.* His eyes were shiny-black like beetles' shells, staring at us so hard we all felt queasy. His skin was coarse and the cheeks pitted from old acne scars and a queer radish-color like it's been stewed. His head looked like a concrete block, so square, the jaw especially, and he had a bushy-droopy mustache that looked like it'd been soaked in peanut oil, and his thick black hair was oily too, a little pompadour up front then matted down with a full tube of Brylcreme to make him look like a Middle Eastern terrorist. Probably he'd been in great condition when he was younger, a body-builder maybe, but now he was thick-set in the torso and neck like a bull going to fat. Six feet tall and weighing, I'd guess, two hundred fifteen pounds. He was wearing a sport coat with a silvery sheen like plastic and a black silk shirt open at the neck showing frizzy iron-gray hairs and trousers flared at the knees and he was clumsy on his feet with that limp he tried to disguise, not walking so much as plunging forward, in a way that was swaggering but also self-conscious—like his sharp eyes were taking in the fact that the three of us were surprised by him, we were judging him and not too positively. And when he shook hands with us and repeated our names as Momma pronounced them—"Isabel!" (for Momma refused to call Icy "Icy")—"Orchid!"—"Crystal!"—we had all we could do not to duck away from this latest man friend of our mother's looming over us breathing hot in our faces and doused with enough cologne to kill mosquitoes on the wing and practically breaking our hands in his big ham-hand. That first evening Isaak Drumm emitted such a heat, he was so pushy and *hopeful* himself, like a car salesman on TV, we girls could hardly think of anything to say to him that didn't sound weak and stumbling. Even Icy, who'd gone against Momma's wishes and was wearing her nose ring, had to admit afterward Isaak Drumm sort of swept her away.

That night Drumm took us all out to the Friday All-You-Can-Eat Buffet at the Ramada Inn and the more he and Momma talked, the quieter Icy, Orchid, and Crystal were. Though hitting the buffet like starving refugees and nudging one another giggling at the attention we drew—what's there about teenagers with dye-streaked hair, not to mention ear-studs and nose-rings, that freaks "normal" people out? Wild! We basked in the attention and liked it fine but turned sullen when Momma scolded us for sampling so many desserts, and Isaak Drumm defended us saying, "Marietta, these are growing girls—" or some similar asshole remark. And him twirling his mustache around his fork, and laughing this phony-happy laugh like he was our favorite uncle or somebody, or our own Dad. Icy terminated the scene by reaching for a spoon and accidentally spilling The Mustache's beer stein into his lap.

That night, we're undressing for bed, Crystal and Orchid in one room and Icy nextdoor but hanging out with us peering out our window at the street where, in Drumm's car (a Mazda, creamy-yellow, looking like it was washed and Simonized for tonight), Drumm and Momma were sitting and talking, and Icy said, " 'Isaak Drumm'!—he's the scariest yet. You notice those eyes? I know psycho eyes when I see them. *Rapist* eyes. *Pederast.*"

In a single amazed voice Orchid and Crystal said, " 'Pederast'?—"

The words Icy came up with, sometimes you'd wonder if she invented them herself. Or flipped through the dictionary seeking strangeness.

Walking out of our room Icy tossed back over her shoulder, with a sneer, "Ask 'Isaak.' "

Three bad girls. In the neighborhoods we'd lived in on the south side of Yewville—Momma had to move a lot, one dumpy rental to another—and among our relatives, us Murchison girls were tough characters. This was a joke applied to Crystal who'd burst into tears if some asshole teacher made a sarcastic remark to her, but, with Icy and Orchid as models, she learned to hide the fact.

I'm Orchid. Momma always claimed she named me this because "it was the prettiest name I could think of" and I'd say, making a face, since if you're ugly the only strategy is to make yourself uglier by your own effort, "Geez Momma, too bad you couldn't make *me* pretty, not just my name." And Momma, being Momma, would protest, "Orchid, you *are* pretty!" like her words, earnest enough, could make it so.

Momma hadn't anything solid to trust in beyond the words she'd say to us all the time, with her bright forced smile and upturned eyes—

"We'll be just fine, as long as we're *together*." Icy said Momma's faith was like trying to keep warm in a freezing wind by calling to mind the memory of a heated, sheltered place.

Also, not to be critical of her, Marietta Murchison was so *hopeful* it brought out the sadist in you. And she'd contradict herself like her tongue got twisted and things came out the opposite of what she wanted to say—like insisting she was "fine" returning from the gynecologist, then adding, with that smile that meant she was scared stiff, "if God wills!" The kind of behavior you see a lot on TV and in the movies, good-looking woman not overly bright but *sexy*. I guess you could say, sort of, Marietta Murchison was *sexy*. With curly auburn hair, eyes a deeper green than Icy's, a smooth almost-unlined skin. And except when she got depressed, and over-ate, and drank, and could put on ten pounds in a week, her eyes seeming to shrink in her puffy face, she had a nice figure. Men did glance after her in the street, and in stores—we noticed that, all the time. And her man friends would smile at her indulging her dumb-bimbo remarks saying, "Just like a woman!"—like it was praise, and not an insult.

Icy used to say contemptuously, "Well, what can you expect?— our mother was born in a retrograde era."

Weird to think how long ago that was: Momma a little girl, and videos hadn't been invented yet! or VCRs! or computers! and Elvis Presley still living, and Marilyn Monroe! They'd invented the atomic bomb by then, and dropped it in Japan, but no nuclear warheads or space stations—Momma said when she was growing up the big question was, would the Russians blow us up, or would we blow them up first?

Like Icy said, *retrograde*.

Icy's actual name was "Isabel" which she hated, it was so prissy and *nice*. The one thing you don't want to be, the world's gonna walk over you if you are, is *nice*, Icy said. In ninth grade she named herself after Vanilla Ice the rap singer, later outgrew the jerk but kept "Icy"— it suited her. Probably still does.

Icy was sort of pretty and might have been popular at school but we moved around a lot and it was hard to get settled and even so, as Icy said, you can't trust other people—even the "nice" ones, the girls who invite you home with them, and want to be friends, betray your secrets. She did OK in school but her teachers never liked her—the deadpan way she'd stare at them, and refuse to laugh at their jokes, and wouldn't let herself be, as she said, "co-opted" by the Establishment. She'd started dyeing purple streaks in her hair, her junior year in high school, and got Orchid and Crystal to dye theirs; went to the mall to get her nose pierced, without informing Momma—*that* was a

wild scene, like something on "Roseanne" when Momma came home.
Momma, said, "My own daughter, looking like a *cannibal!*"

Crystal was named by her own mother, not Momma. She'd come
to live with us when she was nine and her mother died of some terrible
quick cancer when Momma and her second husband Wayne Murchison (who was Crystal's father) had only been married about a year. For
a while she wouldn't talk, or couldn't. Nor could she go to school,
where she was supposed to be in fourth grade. But Momma was real
nice to her, and in a few months she got better, though she was always
shy. (Shyest around her own father, for good reason as we learned.)
Unlike Icy and Orchid who were apt to take their mother for granted,
Crystal never did. So she was the most anxious about Momma's man
friends. After Momma and Crystal's father were divorced (that's
another story) there was a calm quiet interlude of eighteen months
when Momma lost fifteen pounds to fit into a size 9 dress, switched to
a new receptionist job and started dating men again and each one of
them she brought home, poor Crystal would go into a panic thinking
he'd take Momma away from us.

Even so, we were *not* jealous of Momma's man friends. Even
Crystal could see the logic of, how, if Momma married again, this time
a man who was worthy of her, we'd all be better off. A hell of a lot
better off. We'd move from the south side of Yewville uptown, transfer
to new schools where nobody knew us. We'd get a new car—maybe
two new cars. Momma could quit work if she wanted and anyway
would never again be made to grovel applying for county assistance
when she was between jobs.

Except—Momma never seemed to bring home a man who was
worthy. For sure, The Mustache wasn't him.

Like each of Momma's man friends she was serious about, Isaak
Drumm came to possess a mysterious power. Us girls could see this
clearly, and we didn't like it. Momma's emotional life was surrendered
to this guy we scarcely knew, this "U.S. Army sergeant" with the goofy
mustache and bad knee and gleaming black eyes like Dracula. *He* had
the power of making her happy like a little girl, hugging and kissing us
for no reason, or plunging her into worry and self-doubt. First thing in
the morning Momma might be singing, or she might be padding
around heavy-hearted and distracted squinting at her own daughters
like for a moment she didn't know who we were. As Icy observed, "It's
God-damned *insulting.*"

Isaak Drumm did make Momma cry, sometimes. Maybe he was
seeing another woman, or women?—we'd hear Momma on the phone
saying quietly, "Whatever you think is best, Isaak. I understand." Or, "I

was needing a little time to myself this weekend, too. As a matter of fact."

Then, a few days later, The Mustache would "happen to be in the neighborhood" around 6 P.M. bringing some dead-looking scentless red hothouse flowers "for all my girls" — except, in his mouth, the word came out "gur-rls." And every time, to our disgust, Momma's face lit up in welcome and she'd insist he eat supper with us.

Most times Drumm took Momma out, and always on her late-night at work, which was Fridays, and they'd be gone for hours. No regular dinner and movie date but obviously they were at his place — for hours. It was clear that Momma was *in love* with this latest man friend but not clear that he was *in love* with her and this hurt our pride, beyond just the fact of disliking him. Icy said, "Momma has become a desperate woman. Somebody's got to save her." We vowed we'd never be *women* if *women* means *weakness*.

Watching a cop show on TV one night when Momma and Drumm were out, Icy came up with her plan. "This is what we'll do: break in his place and collect the evidence."

Orchid and Crystal just stared at Icy. We'd been eating cold slices of pizza and a rubbery string of mozzarella hung down from Crystal's lip like a broken tusk. " 'Evidence' — ?"

"To use against him."

"Use against him *how?*"

Icy smiled pityingly at us, the way she would when she solved my algebra problems in her head without needing any steps to get the answer, or the way she'd finish Crystal's slow sentences for her. Like it was the most obvious thing in the world we should've thought of ourselves. "To make our deluded mother realize what a slimy bastard she's gotten involved with. Again."

Icy's and my father's name was Marvin H. Wilmer and he left us when I was two years old and I didn't remember him at all, it was like a blank whitewashed wall if I tried to remember him, and it still is.

Icy said, "Lucky you."

The Mustache was always making such a big deal of how his boss Mr. O'Mara counted on him to work long hours so we believed we'd be safe breaking into his place after school. Meaning after 4 P.M. which was the earliest we could get to where he lived—this "condominium village" called Brookside Manor, about three miles away, we had to take a city bus to get to. We'd seen the place from the outside once when Momma drove by saying in her moony voice, "That's where Isaak lives"—like it was the White House or something not some dumpy apartment building covered in aluminum siding glaring like tin. 9 Brookside Manor was Drumm's address, lucky for us at the far end of the building practically in a woods. Each of the units had its own front and rear entrance and a balcony that would've been cramped for a dwarf overlooking the "brook"—a greasy little ditch down a ravine littered with debris. So's not to be seen by anyone Icy led us along this route and it was depressing on a drizzly-windy day and the clouds overhead like bread mold and Icy saying, to spook Orchid and Crystal, "Brrr! This is the exact kind of place, the caption says 'Where the bodies were discovered, partly decomposed.' "

No cars were parked behind 9 Brookside. We crept up behind the garbagey-smelling dumpster, trying to avoid broken glass; tried the back door but naturally it was locked. Icy led the way up onto the balcony and that door was locked, too, but—this was Icy's luck!— beside the door was one of those narrow windows operated by a crank, and this Icy discovered was loose enough to pry open so she could force her hand, then her arm, inside, and crank it open as far as it would go. You'd see such a small window and figure nobody could squeeze through it, but this wasn't so.

Afterward we'd be asked if we broke in places habitually—if we were thieves, shoplifters—but I swear this wasn't so. Maybe a few things lifted from the 7-Eleven near our house, and Discount Drugs and Woolworth's, sometimes. Nothing major.

Icy crawled through the window supple and squirmy as a snake, nor had Orchid any trouble, being rail-thin too and wiry; Crystal with her soft hips might've gotten stuck, and panicked, if we hadn't tugged at her arms to yank her free. Poor Crystal flush-faced and panting like a dog and terrified clutching at her sisters' hands so we slapped her away, laughing and giddy. "Control yourself," Icy whispered. "This is it." But she was trembling, too. *For now we were in Isaak Drumm's apartment. In the place of the enemy.*

For the first ten minutes or so we drifted around staring like this was a weird dream. We'd bump into each other, like sleepwalkers. Not that The Mustache's living quarters were anything special, they were not. "Luxury units" the sign out front said but that was an exaggeration. The rooms were small and there wasn't much furniture and it was all cheap-slick and impersonal like in a motel room. Drawers and cupboards in the kitchen open, plates in the sink, burnt crud on the stove and a mixed smell of cooking odors and cologne—no mistaking who lived here. One of us collided with a chair and the others went "Shhh!" not knowing if we were scared to death or about the most excited we'd ever been, the three of us. Breaking into somebody's place there's a way your heart beats, like a hummingbird's whirring wings, and a sharp taste in your mouth you don't get anywhere anytime else!

On top of the TV set in the living room were framed photos of Drumm's family. Lots of them. We tried to pick Drumm out but weren't too sure, he had brothers, or cousins; all of them with those deep dark glistening eyes and thick black hair and square-built faces. Orchid said in surprise, "The Mustache has a *family!*" and Icy said, sneering, "So what? So's a rat." Of course, this was so.

If Isaak Drumm had been expecting visitors today, he'd have picked up a little. Or maybe, when Momma came over, *she* picked up for him—that'd be just like Momma. There were soiled T-shirts tossed around, and a pair of what looked like size XXX jogging shoes under the coffee table in the living room, and lots of old newspapers, magazines, *TV Guides*, paperback books, videos. Why anybody buys videos, not just rents them, *I* don't know. Drumm's taste was for sappy macho-action films—sci-fi horror—some of the stuff, in video stores, classified as "cult." Momma's taste was for romantic comedy—you had to wonder, if they watched videos together here, what they watched. Or maybe Momma pretended she liked Drumm's choices? That's part of being *sexy*, being a *hypocrite*.

The bedroom at the rear was the room we needed to search but we seemed reluctant to go into it. Even Icy. The thought came to us all—*what if he's in there, hiding? waiting for us?*

Crystal went suddenly into the kitchen where she opened the refrigerator and snatched up a can of Miller's Ale and, before we could stop her, opened it and took a large gulping swallow. "Crystal! Shit!" Icy grabbed the can from her but took a swallow herself, and so did Orchid. We shared the ale and it was gone in possibly thirty seconds. Then—*three bad girls* wiping our mouths and panting, shivering with excitement.

Ale or beer, drunk fast, when you're in a state of nerves, generates a glowing buzz at the back of the skull you can just about feel *vibrate*.

We took another Miller's figuring The Mustache wouldn't miss it, he had plenty in reserve. Or maybe we took two.

We felt braver poking around next in the bathroom noting the sink, the toilet, the shower stall weren't any too clean. Soap-scum in the sink, and tiny black hairs from shaving. And more hairs in the shower drain. "Look!" Icy pointed at the two shampoos side by side on the shower ledge: one of them Head & Shoulders Dandruff Control and the other Finesse for Fine, Thin, Permed Hair—Momma's shampoo. And in the medicine cabinet, the first thing we saw was Lady Speed Stick Deodorant—Momma's deodorant. The three of us just staring not saying anything.

Was *this* evidence?

We pushed into the bedroom where the smell of Drumm was

strongest. Cologne, hair oil, used sheets and clothes. And that low-grade stink of shoes in an unaired closet. At least, the bed was made—a shiny pumpkin-colored spread carelessly yanked up over the pillows. There was another TV on a bureau, and more paperbacks and videos. This room was darker than the front rooms overlooking the "brook"—though mainly the dumpster. The horrible thought came to us *Momma has been here, in that bed? is that possible!* but somehow it did not seem possible. We scared ourselves seeing our reflections in a mirror—how pale and *young* we looked. Those bright dye-streaks of color in our hair like somebody had swathed us with paint as a cruel joke.

We poked around in the closet, sniffing and giggling at Drumm's clothes. For a guy who worked construction he sure owned a lot of sport coats and fancy shirts. And shoes, including more jogging shoes. But what stopped us cold was a baby-blue flannel bathrobe of Momma's we'd given her for Christmas a few years before and we hadn't even realized it was missing from home! Crystal made a little mewing-hurt sound and we just stood there, staring. Like it was Momma her-self, her body, we'd discovered, hidden in Isaak Drumm's closet.

Evidence.

More evidence: in a drawer of Drumm's bedside table, a broken-open packet of condoms. And a much-squeezed tube of vaseline.

"Dis-gusting!" Icy said, her nostrils pinched, shutting the drawer quick.

"Well, what'd you think they did," Orchid asked meanly, "—watch videos every night?"

Crystal rushed off to be sick in the bathroom. We heard her choking and coughing, and the toilet flush. When she reappeared, wiping her mouth, her eyes were brimming with tears. "Oh, Icy, I want to go home, I'm *scared.*"

Icy and Orchid had checked into the kitchen again, came away with two more ales and a box of Frosties—sugary cereal you can eat in handfuls like candy. Crystal was moaning but shared the ale and ate Frosties anyway. Scared and excited, you eat like it's your last meal. There's no real taste but your jaws take pleasure in *grinding.*

Icy was searching Drumm's bureau drawers. No interrupting Icy. And whatever time it was we'd sort of lost awareness. As, in a dream, you have no awareness of time nor even that, like a fast-running river, time is rushing out of your control. "Look!"—Icy drew out from under a bunch of balled-up socks a snub-nosed bluish-gleaming handgun.

From TV and movies you see so many guns the real, actual thing doesn't seem much different. Except there's a part of your brain click-ing *Yes this is different! You can die!*

After this, things get confused.

The more we were questioned afterward, and talked about it again, again, again among ourselves, the more confused it was. But, for sure: Orchid and Crystal were so scared they practically wet themselves seeing this *gun* out of nowhere in Icy's hand—and her hand visibly trembling, though she tried to hide it.

Icy lifted the gun and stared at it, weighed it reverently in her hand, frowned at herself in the mirror, aimed it at the mirror. While Orchid begged, "Icy, no! It might be loaded!" Icy teased, "Y' want me to pull the trigger, and see?" It was like she was hypnotized. Her cheeks were warm and splotched and her glassy-green eyes were shining like cat's eyes.

Icy murmuring, with a level gaze at herself in the mirror, "I'm holding Death in my hand." Swinging the gun in a slow arc, always watching herself in the mirror, as Orchid and Crystal ducked. "This is Death, I'm holding in my hand."

Crystal was whimpering, "Oh Icy, please!" and Orchid was saying, "Hey, Icy, you're scaring us!" and Icy ignored them preening in front of the mirror and how long, how many actual minutes, this craziness went on, I don't know. Finally we got Icy to put back the gun, she made a fuss wiping her fingerprints off, the drawer was messed up so we tried to straighten it and we were laughing and hiccuping and getting in one another's way and we could tell it was getting darker outside, or a storm was coming up, and we were jumpy even before hearing a car pull up at the rear, and suddenly *the worst that can happen is happening: Isaak Drumm is home.*

We were frozen in place. Hearing a car door slam, and a few seconds later somebody is whistling at the back door, fitting a key in the lock.

What I believed happened was: Icy quick-shoved the gun back into the drawer. And herded us ahead of her, back to the window we'd crawled through. Except evidently Icy hadn't put the gun back at all, but shoved it into the belt of her jeans.

First went Crystal, panting and whimpering like a sick baby—her sisters saw to that, hoisting her up when she slipped, and pushing her hips through the narrow space; then Orchid, flushed with adrenaline, wiry-quick and unhesitating, though she would have fallen onto her head on the balcony if Crystal hadn't managed to catch her. Next was Icy at the window with a look of fierce concentration, biting her lower lip to draw blood, squeezing through too, almost she was going to make it—we had hold of her wrists—but this nightmare thing happens: Isaak Drumm comes up yelling behind her and grabs her ankles, her thighs, her shoulders, and yanks her back inside. Icy is screaming, and

Drumm is cursing, and Orchid and Crystal freak out completely jumping off the balcony and running to hide behind the dumpster.

Where, panting, crouched like hunted animals, staring terrified at each other and gripping each other's hand, they hear the gun go off, a single *crack!* of a shot, inside Isaak Drumm's apartment.

Afterward there would be so much confusion about what happened that day at 9 Brookside Manor, so many rumors!—what was truth, and what wasn't, soon got lost, like pieces of a shattered vase swept up with all kinds of other debris. But: taking in both Icy's and Drumm's testimonies, before they diverged, it's clear they were struggling at the window, and Icy had the gun (which was a .38-caliber Smith & Wesson holding six bullets), and Drumm tried to wrestle it from her, and Icy pulled the trigger or the trigger went off, and a bullet just missed Drumm's head—so close his scalp was singed!—and lodged in the ceiling.

Of course, out behind the dumpster, Orchid and Crystal didn't know this. We believed one of them was killed. Knowing Icy, how wired she'd been, we thought it would be Isaak Drumm. And Icy, our sister, would be arrested for murder!

We hugged each other, crying. Hiding there behind the smelly dumpster in the rain with no clue what was happening until, a while later, a Yewville city cop discovered us, as surprised to see us there as we were surprised to see him.

Nobody knew it at the time but that was the end, right then, of Momma and Isaak Drumm. Immediately when the gun went off, and the gunshot was heard, and a neighbor called the police.

If the police hadn't been called, and all of us questioned, and so much attention paid, things might have gone differently. Sure, Isaak Drumm was furious about us breaking into his apartment, and shocked at how Icy seemed to hate him, but he and Momma might have smoothed things out between them. And maybe they'd be together now—Momma might be Mrs. Isaak Drumm. Who knows?

Poor Momma. Her rotten luck with men. And us *bad girls* breaking her heart.

But there was so much fuss, fuss, fuss! and naturally Momma kept after Icy with questions, and finally after about forty-eight hours Icy freaked out and started sobbing like a little, hurt girl, lifting her shirt to show Momma the bruises on her breasts, midriff, and back, and lowering her jeans to show even uglier bruises on her thighs and buttocks. She was crying, choked, "You know what he did, Momma?—he assaulted me. Sexual assault! Tried to rape me!"

Momma almost fainted. Later she'd say this was her worst, her very worst nightmare come true: one of her daughters would be injured by a man she'd brought into our lives.

Right away Momma drove Icy who was hysterical now to the emergency room of the Yewville General Hospital. And there Icy was treated for her bruises, and given a pelvic examination, no she had not been raped but she repeated her story of how Isaak Drumm had assaulted her when he'd caught her in his apartment, and the hospital informed the police, and two police officers, one of them a woman, came to question Icy, and Icy repeated her story, and expanded it, encouraged to describe in detail how Drumm grabbed her and yanked her from the window, how he'd sworn at her, how he'd fondled her breasts, squeezed and pinched and slapped her, yanked her by the hair, pulled down her jeans and panties and spanked her as hard as he could, and kneaded her buttocks, and opened his pants and jabbed his penis against her like a maniac—"He said he'd strangle me if I told anyone," Icy said, "—so when the police came I didn't say anything. But now I'm scared he'll kill me anyway!"

There was no trace of semen on Icy's body for by then she'd taken several baths. And her clothes—thrown into the washer, and laundered.

Orchid and Crystal, when they heard their sister's story, which was an *official testimony* filed with the county district attorney's office, had to wonder—was this true? In the weeks that followed, sometimes they'd think one way; sometimes another. What was certain was, for Icy, once she found the words to tell the story and saw how adults believed her, not just Momma but strangers, people in authority, and how they felt such sympathy for her, it *was* true, for her.

Momma must have made a decision, like throwing a bolt to lock a door forever—*she* believed Icy. She would never waiver in believing Icy. Saying, "Nobody hurts my girls and gets away with it. Nobody so much as *touches* my girls and gets away with it."

Sure, Isaak Drumm tried to talk to her. In person, and, when she refused to let him in, over the phone. But she never would speak with him. Never again.

That very day Momma took Icy to the hospital, Drumm was served with a warrant for a "sexual felony committed against a minor" and arrested at a construction site, hauled off in a squad car handcuffed and astonished, his picture in the Yewville *Journal*, publicly shamed. Already Drumm was in trouble with the law for possession of an unlicensed handgun, and the kindness he'd done us—declining to press charges against us for unlawful entry of his home, passing off the incident as "just some kids playing around"—seemed to backfire on him. At police headquarters, Drumm lost his temper insisting he hadn't touched Icy at all; refused to call a lawyer because he didn't want to pay any God-damned lawyer when he was innocent; threatened the police with false arrest charges—which, I'm told, you don't want to do. And later he changed his story admitting yes maybe he'd spanked Icy, but not hard. But he hadn't pulled down her jeans and panties, no he had *not*.

SUSPECT ADMITS SPANKING GIRL got in the *Journal*, and it was all anybody talked about! In the end, the lawyer Isaak Drumm finally hired advised him to plead guilty to a reduced charge—a "sexual misdemeanor." If Drumm insisted he was innocent, and went to trial, he'd risk being found guilty of the more serious charge and wind up going to prison for as long as seven years. As it was, he was given two years' suspended sentence, and put on probation.

After this upset to all our lives, which was sort of like a death in the family, Momma has never regained her old, hopeful spirits. Nor her desire to meet the right man and remarry. So much rumor and gossip, she's had to move from Niagara Street, and she'd gained so much weight so fast, she lost her job as a receptionist; right now she's working check-out at a 7-Eleven. She's gotten religious, joined the Methodist Church. She tells me, "You get to feel God is testing you, and watching how you react. *That's* the important thing."

Icy soon left home. Quit high school, quarreled with her mother and her sisters and moved away. It's been four years since she left Yewville and at least a year since any of us, even Momma, have heard from her. The last was a postcard from Pensacola, Florida—saying she loves us, and misses us, but she's OK, she's planning to sign up with the U.S. Navy and would Momma make a copy of her birth certificate? But no further word.

Crystal is seventeen, still in school, and Momma's worried sick about *her*—Crystal and the guys she hangs out with.

As for Orchid—I'm nineteen, a second-year nursing student in Rochester. I'm not a *bad girl* now except sometimes in my thoughts.

What I think about a lot, and I'll never tell Momma, is: a few weeks ago I ran into Isaak Drumm here in Rochester. He'd just parked his car at a curb and I noticed him looking at me not recognizing him at first, then he got out, car keys in hand, and stared—and I stared back— neither of us sure who the other was. Isaak Drumm had changed a lot in four years, his hair not in a pompadour now but flat and graying, and his mustache vanished so his face looked raw and exposed, the skin coarser than I remembered, yet the eyes so *intense*. I realized I've been seeing those eyes, feeling that hurt liquidy *intense* stare, for a long time.

Hesitantly Drumm called out, "Orchid—?"

So seeing he recognized me, and there's no danger in it, out here on a public sidewalk, I admitted yes, I was Orchid Murchison. My face going hot, and my heart pounding so hard I believed I would faint.

But I didn't faint, I was OK. Though this conversation, the next five or ten minutes, passed by me in a roar.

I believe Isaak Drumm asked me would I like to have a cup of coffee with him and I must have said no thank you. He saw how nervous I was so he didn't press it and tried to smile to indicate he had no grudge against me, raising his voice to be heard over the street noises asking after Momma and I told him Momma was fine, he asked was she married and I said yes in fact she was, and he took that news sort of squinting and smiling harder. It was strange—he wasn't all that tall, only two or three inches taller than me. The limp wasn't that noticeable, or he was better practiced at disguising it. He was asking after Crystal, and me, and I told him we were fine, too, keeping it brief and polite as possible. I was surprised he remembered our names! I could see he was reluctant to ask after Icy—"Isabel"—so I volunteered she was a WAC and doing OK, we were proud of her. To all this Isaak Drumm listened inclining his head, as if he'd become hard of hearing in his left ear; or it pained him, to look me full in the face.

Then suddenly he was looking at me, and his eyes were shiny with tears, he was saying, "—I was hurt so bad, Orchid, the way it ended—like I was kicked in the stomach—" actually rubbing his stomach and his chest beneath his heart, wincing, "—it took me a long time to get over it—except I'm not, I guess. I had to leave Yewville, I was so shamed. I live here in Rochester now, I'm looking for work. Sometimes even now I can't believe it—how my life changed, in one hour. The way you all dumped me—so fast. Your mother—who I loved—believed that girl, the story that girl told, not even giving me a chance to talk to her. Your sister *was* lying—didn't you all know? You must've known! Didn't you *care?* Didn't any of you like me, or trust me? Jesus, I loved you so much. I was crazy about you all. I wanted to—you know—marry your mother, and—"

I just stood there, stunned. Here's the man we'd so feared would take Momma from us, and he's standing in front of me on a street corner just about crying confiding in me the most amazing thing I have ever heard. My thoughts are all in a buzz. I don't know what to think. *Can a man have such feelings, like a woman? Can a man be hurt? Is that possible?* My eyes were brimming with tears like Isaak

Drumm's and I was in a panic I'd start crying, and how would that end, right out here on the street where people were glancing at us. I hate being emotional, I'm not good at emotions and I avoid things I don't do well. So I mumbled something vague and apologetic and said I had to leave, I had a class to get to, and Isaak Drumm followed after me a bit but not too forcibly so it wouldn't look like here's a guy harassing this girl right out on the street, he was saying maybe we could get together sometime? maybe we could talk? would I pass along hello and best wishes to my mother?—"You remember my name, Orchid? 'Isaak Drumm'—I'm in the Rochester directory—if you could call me sometime—" I was walking quickly away. My head ached, and my eyes were stinging so I was in a fury wiping them with my fists. *Can a man love you? Can a man tell the truth?* I walked away without looking back and Isaak Drumm's voice was fading, lost in the traffic noises, becoming more and more remote like a voice inside my head or like the memory of something that once held my life together, that, now I'm grown up, I can't remember—like the one thing you vow you'll never lose turns into, in time, the one thing too painful to recall.

No, I'll never tell Momma. Even if I telephone Isaak Drumm, and hear more of this. Which I don't know if I want to do, exactly— I'm still debating.

1994

■   ■   ■

TIM O'BRIEN

THE THINGS THEY CARRIED

First Lieutenant Jimmy Cross carried letters from a girl named Martha, a junior at Mount Sebastian College in New Jersey. They were not love letters, but Lieutenant Cross was hoping, so he kept them folded in plastic at the bottom of his rucksack. In the late afternoon, after a day's march, he would dig his foxhole, wash his hands under a canteen, unwrap the letters, hold them with the tips of his fingers, and spend the last hour of light pretending. He would imagine romantic camping trips into the White Mountains in New Hampshire. He would some-times taste the envelope flaps, knowing her tongue had been there. More than anything, he wanted Martha to love him as he loved her, but the letters were mostly chatty, elusive on the matter of love. She was a virgin, he was almost sure. She was an English major at Mount Sebastian, and she wrote beautifully about her professors and room-mates and midterm exams, about her respect for Chaucer and her great affection for Virginia Woolf. She often quoted lines of poetry; she never mentioned the war, except to say, Jimmy, take care of yourself. The letters weighed ten ounces. They were signed "Love, Martha." but Lieutenant Cross understood that "Love" was only a way of signing and did not mean what he sometimes pretended it meant. At dusk, he would carefully return the letters to his rucksack. Slowly a bit dis-tracted, he would get up and move among his men, checking the perimeter, then at full dark he would return to his hole and watch the night and wonder if Martha was a virgin.

The things they carried were largely determined by necessity. Among the necessities or near necessities were P-38 can openers, pocket knives, heat tabs, wrist watches, dog tags, mosquito repellent, chewing gum, candy, cigarettes, salt tablets, packets of Kool-Aid, light-ers, matches, sewing kits, Military Payment Certificates, C rations, and two or three canteens of water. Together, these items weighed between fifteen and twenty pounds, depending upon a man's habits or rate of metabolism. Henry Dobbins, who was a big man, carried extra rations; he was especially fond of canned peaches in heavy syrup over pound cake. Dave Jensen, who practiced field hygiene, carried a toothbrush, dental floss, and several hotel-size bars of soap he'd stolen on R&R[1] in Sydney, Australia. Ted Lavender, who was scared, carried tranquilizers until he was shot in the head outside the village of Than Khe in mid-April. By necessity, and because it was SOP,[2] they all carried steel helmets that weighed five pounds including the liner and camouflage cover. They carried the standard fatigue jackets and trousers. Very few carried underwear. On their feet they carried jungle boots—2.1 pounds—and Dave Jensen carried three pairs of socks and a can of Dr. Scholl's foot powder as a precaution against trench foot. Until he was shot. Ted Lavender carried six or seven ounces of premium dope, which for him was a necessity. Mitchell Sanders, the RTO,[3] carried condoms. Norman Bowker carried a diary. Rat Kiley carried comic books. Kiowa, a devout Baptist, carried an illustrated New Testament that had been presented to him by his father, who taught Sunday school in Oklahoma City, Oklahoma. As a hedge against bad times, however, Kiowa also carried his grandmother's distrust of the white man, his grandfather's old hunting hatchet. Necessity dictated. Because the land was mined and booby-trapped, it was SOP for each man to carry a steel-centered, nylon-covered flak jacket, which weighed 6.7 pounds, but which on hot days seemed much heavier. Because you could die so quickly, each man carried at least one large compress bandage, usually in the helmet band for easy access. Because the nights were cold, and because the monsoons were wet, each carried a green plastic poncho that could be used as a raincoat or ground sheet or makeshift tent. With its quilted liner, the poncho weighed almost two pounds, but it was worth every ounce. In April, for instance, when Ted Lavender was shot, they used his poncho to wrap him up, then to carry him across the paddy, then to lift him into the chopper that took him away.

They were called legs or grunts.

To carry something was to "hump" it, as when Lieutenant Jimmy Cross humped his love for Martha up the hills and through the swamps. In its intransitive form, "to hump" meant "to walk," or "to march," but it implied burdens far beyond the intransitive.

1. Rest and rehabilitation leave.
2. Standard operating procedure.
3. Radio and telephone operator.

Almost everyone humped photographs. In his wallet, Lieutenant Cross carried two photographs of Martha. The first was a Kodachrome snapshot signed "Love," though he knew better. She stood against a brick wall. Her eyes were gray and neutral, her lips slightly open as she stared straight-on at the camera. At night, sometimes, Lieutenant Cross wondered who had taken the picture, because he knew she had boyfriends, because he loved her so much, and because he could see the shadow of the picture taker spreading out against the brick wall. The second photograph had been clipped from the 1968 Mount Sebastian yearbook. It was an action shot—women's volleyball—and Martha was bent horizontal to the floor, reaching, the palms of her hands in sharp focus, the tongue taut, the expression frank and competitive. There was no visible sweat. She wore white gym shorts. Her legs, he thought, were almost certainly the legs of a virgin, dry and without hair, the left knee cocked and carrying her entire weight, which was just over one hundred pounds. Lieutenant Cross remembered touching that left knee. A dark theater, he remembered, and the movie was *Bonnie and Clyde*, and Martha wore a tweed skirt, and during the final scene, when he touched her knee, she turned and looked at him in a sad, sober way that made him pull his hand back, but he would always remember the feel of the tweed skirt and the knee beneath it and the sound of the gunfire that killed Bonnie and Clyde, how embarrassing it was, how slow and oppressive. He remembered kissing her good night at the dorm door. Right then, he thought, he should've done something brave. He should've carried her up the stairs to her room and tied her to the bed and touched that left knee all night long. He should've risked it. Whenever he looked at the photographs, he thought of new things he should've done.

What they carried was partly a function of rank, partly of field specialty.

As a first lieutenant and platoon leader, Jimmy Cross carried a compass, maps, code books, binoculars, and a .45-caliber pistol that weighed 2.9 pounds fully loaded. He carried a strobe light and the responsibility for the lives of his men.

As an RTO, Mitchell Sanders carried the PRC-25 radio, a killer, twenty-six pounds with its battery.

As a medic, Rat Kiley carried a canvas satchel filled with morphine and plasma and malaria tablets and surgical tape and comic books and all the things a medic must carry, including M&Ms[4] for especially bad wounds, for a total weight of nearly twenty pounds.

---

4. Apparently this candy was used as a placebo since it would have no other medical value.

As a big man, therefore a machine gunner, Henry Dobbins carried the M-60, which weighed twenty-three pounds unloaded, but which was almost always loaded. In addition, Dobbins carried between ten and fifteen pounds of ammunition draped in belts across his chest and shoulders.

As PCFs or Specs 4s, most of them were common grunts and carried the standard M-16 gas-operated assault rifle. The weapon weighed 7.5 pounds unloaded, 8.2 pounds with its full twenty-round magazine. Depending on numerous factors, such as topography and psychology, the riflemen carried anywhere from twelve to twenty magazines, usually in cloth bandoliers, adding on another 8.4 pounds at minimum, fourteen pounds at maximum. When it was available, they also carried M-16 maintenance gear—rods and steel brushes and swabs and tubes of LSA oil—all of which weighed about a pound. Among the grunts, some carried the M-79 grenade launcher, 5.9 pounds unloaded, a reasonably light weapon except for the ammunition, which was heavy. A single round weighed ten ounces. The typical load was twenty-five rounds. But Ted Lavender, who was scared, carried thirty-four rounds when he was shot and killed outside Than Khe, and he went down under an exceptional burden, more than twenty pounds of ammunition, plus the flak jacket and helmet and rations and water and toilet paper and tranquilizers and all the rest, plus the unweighed fear. He was dead weight. There was no twitching or flopping. Kiowa, who saw it happen, said it was like watching a rock fall, or a big sandbag or something—just boom, then down—not like the movies where the dead guy rolls around and does fancy spins and goes ass over teakettle—not like that, Kiowa said, the poor bastard just flat-fuck fell. Boom. Down. Nothing else. It was a bright morning in mid-April. Lieutenant Cross felt the pain. He blamed himself. They stripped off Lavender's canteens and ammo, all the heavy things, and Rat Kiley said the obvious, the guy's dead, and Mitchell Sanders used his radio to report one U.S. KIA[5] and to request a chopper. Then they wrapped Lavender in his poncho. They carried him out to a dry paddy, established security, and sat smoking the dead man's dope until the chopper came. Lieutenant Cross kept to himself. He pictured Martha's smooth young face, thinking he loved her more than anything, more than his men, and now Ted Lavender was dead because he loved her so much and could not stop thinking about her. When the dust-off[6] arrived, they carried Lavender aboard. Afterward they burned Than Khe. They marched until dusk, then dug their holes, and that night Kiowa kept

5. Killed in action.
6. Helicopter.

explaining how you had to be there, how fast it was, how the poor guy just dropped like so much concrete. Boom-down, he said. Like cement.

In addition to the three standard weapons—the M-60, M-16, and M-79—they carried whatever presented itself, or whatever seemed appropriate as a means of killing or staying alive. They carried catch-as-catch-can. At various times, in various situations, they carried M-14s and CAR-15s and Swedish Ks and grease guns and captured AK-47s and Chi-Coms and RPGs and Simonov carbines and black-market Uzis and .38-caliber Smith & Wesson handguns and 66 mm LAWs and shotguns and silencers and blackjacks and bayonets and C-4 plastic explosives. Lee Strunk carried a slingshot; a weapon of last resort, he called it. Mitchell Sanders carried brass knuckles. Kiowa carried his grandfather's feathered hatchet. Every third or fourth man carried a Claymore antipersonnel mine—3.5 pounds with its firing device. They all carried fragmentation grenades—fourteen ounces each. They all carried at least one M-18 colored smoke grenade—twenty-four ounces. Some carried CS or tear-gas grenades. Some carried white-phosphorus grenades. They carried all they could bear, and then some, including a silent awe for the terrible power of the things they carried.

In the first week of April, before Lavender died, Lieutenant Jimmy Cross received a good-luck charm from Martha. It was a simple pebble, an ounce at most. Smooth to the touch, it was a milky-white color with flecks of orange and violet, oval-shaped, like a miniature egg. In the accompanying letter, Martha wrote that she had found the pebble on the Jersey shoreline, precisely where the land touched water at high tide, where things came together but also separated. It was this sepa-rate-but-together quality, she wrote, that had inspired her to pick up the pebble and to carry it in her breast pocket for several days, where it seemed weightless, and then to send it through the mail, by air, as a token of her truest feelings for him. Lieutenant Cross found this romantic. But he wondered what her truest feelings were, exactly, and what she meant by separate-but-together. He wondered how the tides and waves had come into play on that afternoon along the Jersey shore-line when Martha saw the pebble and bent down to rescue it from geology. He imagined bare feet. Martha was a poet, with the poet's sensibilities, and her feet would be brown and bare, the toenails unpainted, the eyes chilly and somber like the ocean in March, and though it was painful, he wondered who had been with her that after-noon. He imagined a pair of shadows moving along the strip of sand where things came together but also separated. It was phantom jeal-ousy, he knew, but he couldn't help himself. He loved her so much. On the march, through the hot days of early April, he carried the pebble in his mouth, turning it with his tongue, tasting sea salts and moisture. His mind wandered. He had difficulty keeping his attention on the war. On occasion he would yell at his men to spread out the column, to keep their eyes open, but then he would slip away into daydreams, just pretending, walking barefoot along the Jersey shore, with Martha, carrying nothing. He would feel himself rising. Sun and waves and gentle winds, all love and lightness.

What they carried varied by mission.

When a mission took them to the mountains, they carried mosquito netting, machetes, canvas tarps, and extra bug juice.

If a mission seemed especially hazardous, or if it involved a place they knew to be bad, they carried everything they could. In certain heavily mined AOs,[7] where the land was dense with Toe Poppers and Bouncing Betties, they took turns humping a twenty-eight-pound mine detector. With its headphones and big sensing plate, the equipment was a stress on the lower back and shoulders, awkward to handle, often useless because of the shrapnel in the earth, but they carried it anyway, partly for safety, partly for the illusion of safety.

On ambush, or other night missions, they carried peculiar little odds and ends. Kiowa always took along his New Testament and a pair of moccasins for silence. Dave Jensen carried night-sight vitamins high in carotin. Lee Strunk carried his slingshot; ammo, he claimed, would never be a problem. Rat Kiley carried brandy and M&Ms. Until he was shot, Ted Lavender carried the starlight scope, which weighed 6.3 pounds with its aluminum carrying case. Henry Dobbins carried his girlfriend's pantyhose wrapped around his neck as a comforter. They all carried ghosts. When dark came, they would move out single file across the meadows and paddies to their ambush coordinates, where they would quietly set up the Claymores and lie down and spend the night waiting.

Other missions were more complicated and required special equipment. In mid-April, it was their mission to search out and destroy the elaborate tunnel complexes in the Than Khe area south of Chu Lai. To blow the tunnels, they carried one-pound blocks of pentrite high explosives, four blocks to a man, sixty-eight pounds in all. They carried wiring, detonators, and battery-powered clackers. Dave Jensen carried earplugs. Most often, before blowing the tunnels, they were ordered by higher command to search them, which was considered bad news, but by and large they just shrugged and carried out orders. Because he was a big man, Henry Dobbins was excused from tunnel

7. Areas of operation.

duty. The others would draw numbers. Before Lavender died there were seventeen men in the platoon, and whoever drew the number seventeen would strip off his gear and crawl in head first with a flashlight and Lieutenant Cross's .45-caliber pistol. The rest of them would fan out as security. They would sit down or kneel, not facing the hole, listening to the ground beneath them, imagining cobwebs and ghosts, whatever was down there—the tunnel walls squeezing in—how the flashlight seemed impossibly heavy in the hand and how it was tunnel vision in the very strictest sense, compression in all ways, even time, and how you had to wiggle in—ass and elbows—a swallowed-up feeling—and how you found yourself worrying about odd things—will your flashlight go dead? Do rats carry rabies? If you screamed, how far would the sound carry? Would your buddies hear it? Would they have the courage to drag you out? In some respects, though not many, the waiting was worse than the tunnel itself. Imagination was a killer.

On April 16, when Lee Strunk drew the number seventeen, he laughed and muttered something and went down quickly. The morning was hot and very still. Not good, Kiowa said. He looked at the tunnel opening, then out across a dry paddy toward the village of Than Khe. Nothing moved. No clouds or birds or people. As they waited, the men smoked and drank Kool-Aid, not talking much, feeling sympathy for Lee Strunk but also feeling the luck of the draw. You win some, you lose some, said Mitchell Sanders, and sometimes you settle for a rain check. It was a tired line and no one laughed.

Henry Dobbins ate a tropical chocolate bar. Ted Lavender popped a tranquilizer and went off to pee.

After five minutes, Lieutenant Jimmy Cross moved to the tunnel, leaned down, and examined the darkness. Trouble, he thought—a cave-in maybe. And then suddenly, without willing it, he was thinking about Martha. The stresses and fractures, the quick collapse, the two of them buried alive under all that weight. Dense, crushing love. Kneeling, watching the hole, he tried to concentrate on Lee Strunk and the war, all the dangers, but his love was too much for him, he felt paralyzed, he wanted to sleep inside her lungs and breathe her blood and be smothered. He wanted her to be a virgin and not a virgin, all at once. He wanted to know her. Intimate secrets—why poetry? Why so sad? Why that grayness in her eyes? Why so alone? Not lonely, just alone—riding her bike across campus or sitting off by herself in the cafeteria. Even dancing, she danced alone—and it was the aloneness that filled him with love. He remembered telling her that one evening. How she nodded and looked away. And how, later, when he kissed her, she received the kiss without returning it, her eyes wide open, not afraid, not a virgin's eyes, just flat and uninvolved.

Lieutenant Cross gazed at the tunnel. But he was not there. He was buried with Martha under the white sand at the Jersey shore. They were pressed together, and the pebble in his mouth was her tongue. He was smiling. Vaguely, he was aware of how quiet the day was, the sullen paddies yet he could not bring himself to worry about matters of security. He was beyond that. He was just a kid at war, in love. He was twenty-two years old. He couldn't help it.

A few moments later Lee Strunk crawled out of the tunnel. He came up grinning, filthy but alive. Lieutenant Cross nodded and closed his eyes while the others clapped Strunk on the back and made jokes about rising from the dead.

Worms, Rat Kiley said. Right out of the grave. Fuckin' zombie.

The men laughed. They all felt great relief.

Spook City, said Mitchell Sanders.

Lee Strunk made a funny ghost sound, a kind of moaning, yet very happy, and right then, when Strunk made that high happy moaning sound, when he went *Ahhooooo*, right then Ted Lavender was shot in the head on his way back from peeing. He lay with his mouth open. The teeth were broken. There was a swollen black bruise under his left eye. The cheekbone was gone. Oh shit, Rat Kiley said, the guy's dead. The guy's dead, he kept saying, which seemed profound—the guy's dead. I mean really.

The things they carried were determined to some extent by superstition. Lieutenant Cross carried his good-luck pebble. Dave Jensen carried a rabbit's foot. Norman Bowker, otherwise a very gentle person, carried a thumb that had been presented to him as a gift by Mitchell Sanders. The thumb was dark brown, rubbery to the touch, and weighed four ounces at most. It had been cut from a VC corpse, a boy of fifteen or sixteen. They'd found him at the bottom of an irrigation ditch, badly burned, flies in his mouth and eyes. The boy wore black shorts and sandals. At the time of his death he had been carrying a pouch of rice, rifle, and three magazines of ammunition.

You want my opinion, Mitchell Sanders said, there's a definite moral here.

He put his hand on the dead boy's wrist. He was quiet for a time, as if counting a pulse, then he patted the stomach, almost affectionately, and used Kiowa's hunting hatchet to remove the thumb.

Henry Dobbins asked what the moral was.

Moral?

You know. *Moral.*

Sanders wrapped the thumb in toilet paper and handed it across to Norman Bowker. There was no blood. Smiling, he kicked the boy's

head, watched the flies scatter, and said, It's like with that old TV
show—Paladin. Have gun, will travel.
Henry Dobbins thought about it.
Yeah, well, he finally said. I don't see no moral.
There it *is*, man.
Fuck off.

They carried USO stationery and pencils and pens. They carried
Sterno, safety pins, trip flares, signal flares, spools of wire, razor blades,
chewing tobacco, liberated joss sticks and statuettes of the smiling Buddha, candles, grease pencils. *The Stars and Stripes*, fingernail clippers,
Psy Ops[8] leaflets, bush hats, bolos, and much more. Twice a week,
when the resupply choppers came in, they carried hot chow in green
Mermite cans and large canvas bags filled with iced beer and soda pop.
They carried plastic water containers, each with a two-gallon capacity.
Mitchell Sanders carried a set of starched tiger fatigues for special
occasions. Henry Dobbins carried Black Flag insecticide. Dave Jensen
carried empty sandbags that could be filled at night for added protection. Lee Strunk carried tanning lotion. Some things they carried in
common. Taking turns, they carried the big PRC-77 scrambler radio,
which weighed thirty pounds with its battery. They shared the weight
of memory. They took up what others could no longer bear. Often,
they carried each other, the wounded or weak. They carried infections.
They carried chess sets, basketballs, Vietnamese-English dictionaries,
insignia of rank, Bronze Stars and Purple Hearts, plastic cards
imprinted with the Code of Conduct. They carried diseases, among
them malaria and dysentery. They carried lice and ringworm and
leeches and paddy algae and various rots and molds. They carried the
land itself—Vietnam, the place, the soil—a powdery orange-red dust
that covered their boots and fatigues and faces. They carried the sky.
The whole atmosphere, they carried it, the humidity, the monsoons,
the stink of fungus and decay, all of it, they carried gravity. They moved
like mules. By daylight they took sniper fire, at night they were mor-
tared, but it was not battle, it was just the endless march, village to
village, without purpose, nothing won or lost. They marched for the
sake of the march. They plodded along slowly, dumbly, leaning forward against the heat, unthinking, all blood and bone, simple grunts,
soldiering with their legs, toiling up the hills and down into the paddies
and across the rivers and up again and down, just humping, one step
and then the next and then another, but no volition, no will, because
it was automatic, it was anatomy, and the war was entirely a matter of

8. Psychological Operations.

posture and carriage, the hump was everything, a kind of inertia, a kind of emptiness, a dullness of desire and intellect and conscience and hope and human sensibility. Their principles were in their feet. Their calculations were biological. They had no sense of strategy or mission. They searched the villages without knowing what to look for, not caring, kicking over jars of rice, frisking children and old men, blowing tunnels, sometimes setting fires and sometimes not, then forming up and moving on to the next village, then other villages, where it would always be the same. They carried their own lives. The pressures were enormous. In the heat of early afternoon, they would remove their helmets and flak jackets, walking bare, which was dangerous but which helped ease the strain. They would often discard things along the route of march. Purely for comfort, they would throw away rations, blow their Claymores and grenades, no matter, because by nightfall the resupply choppers would arrive with more of the same, then a day or two later still more, fresh watermelons and crates of ammunition and sunglasses and woolen sweaters—the resources were stunning—sparklers for the Fourth of July, colored eggs for Easter. It was the great American war chest—the fruits of science, the smokestacks, the canneries, the arsenals at Hartford, the Minnesota forests, the machine shops, the vast fields of corn and wheat—they carried like freight trains; they carried it on their backs and shoulders—for all the ambiguities of Vietnam, all the mysteries and unknowns, there was at least the single abiding certainty that they would never be at a loss for things to carry.

After the chopper took Lavender away, Lieutenant Jimmy Cross led his men into the village of Than Khe. They burned everything. They shot chickens and dogs, they trashed the village well, they called in artillery and watched the wreckage, then they marched for several hours through the hot afternoon, and then at dusk, while Kiowa explained how Lavender died, Lieutenant Cross found himself trembling.

He tried not to cry. With his entrenching tool, which weighed five pounds, he began digging a hole in the earth.

He felt shame. He hated himself. He had loved Martha more than his men, and as a consequence Lavender was now dead, and this was something he would have to carry like a stone in his stomach for the rest of the war.

All he could do was dig. He used his entrenching tool like an ax, slashing, feeling both love and hate, and then later, when it was full dark, he sat at the bottom of his foxhole and wept. It went on for a long while. In part, he was grieving for Ted Lavender, but mostly it was for

Martha, and for himself, because she belonged to another world, which was not quite real, and because she was a junior at Mount Sebastian College in New Jersey, a poet and a virgin and uninvolved, and because he realized she did not love him and never would.

Like cement, Kiowa whispered in the dark. I swear to God—boom-down. Not a word.

I've heard this, said Norman Bowker.

A pisser, you know? Still zipping himself up. Zapped while zipping.

All right, fine. That's enough.

Yeah, but you had to see it, the guy just—

I *heard*, man. Cement. So why not shut the fuck *up?*

Kiowa shook his head sadly and glanced over at the hole where Lieutenant Jimmy Cross sat watching the night. The air was thick and wet. A warm, dense fog had settled over the paddies and there was the stillness that precedes rain.

After a time Kiowa sighed.

One thing for sure, he said. The Lieutenant's in some deep hurt. I mean that crying jag—the way he was carrying on—it wasn't fake or anything, it was real heavy-duty hurt. The man cares.

Sure, Norman Bowker said.

Say what you want, the man does care.

We all got problems.

Not Lavender.

No, I guess not. Bowker said. Do me a favor, though.

Shut up?

That's a smart Indian. Shut up.

Shrugging, Kiowa pulled off his boots. He wanted to say more, just to lighten up his sleep, but instead he opened his New Testament and arranged it beneath his head as a pillow. The fog made things seem hollow and unattached. He tried not to think about Ted Lavender, but then he was thinking how fast it was, no drama, down and dead, and how it was hard to feel anything except surprise. It seemed un-Christian. He wished he could find some great sadness, or even anger, but the emotion wasn't there and he couldn't make it happen. Mostly he felt pleased to be alive. He liked the smell of the New Testament under his cheek, the leather and ink and paper and glue, whatever the chemicals were. He liked hearing the sounds of night. Even his fatigue, it felt fine, the stiff muscles and the prickly awareness of his own body, a floating feeling. He enjoyed not being dead. Lying there, Kiowa admired Lieutenant Jimmy Cross's capacity for grief. He wanted to share the man's pain, he wanted to care as Jimmy Cross cared. And yet when he closed his eyes, all he could think was Boom-down, and all he could feel was the pleasure of having his boots off and the fog curling in around him and the damp soil and the Bible smells and the plush comfort of night.

After a moment Norman Bowker sat up in the dark.

What the hell, he said. You want to talk, *talk.* Tell it to me.

Forget it.

No, man, go on. One thing I hate, it's a silent Indian.

For the most part they carried themselves with poise, a kind of dignity. Now and then, however, there were times of panic, when they squealed or wanted to squeal but couldn't, when they twitched and made moaning sounds and covered their heads and said Dear Jesus and flopped around on the earth and fired their weapons blindly and cringed and sobbed and begged for the noise to stop and went wild and made stupid promises to themselves and to God and to their mothers and fathers, hoping not to die. In different ways, it happened to all of them. Afterward, when the firing ended, they would blink and peek up. They would touch their bodies, feeling shame, then quickly hiding it. They would force themselves to stand. As if in slow motion, frame by frame, the world would take on the old logic—absolute silence, then the wind, then sunlight, then voices. It was the burden of being alive. Awkwardly, the men would reassemble themselves, first in private, then in groups, becoming soldiers again. They would repair the leaks in their eyes. They would check for casualties, call in dust-offs, light cigarettes, try to smile, clear their throats and spit and begin cleaning their weapons. After a time someone would shake his head and say, No lie, I almost shit my pants, and someone else would laugh, which meant it was bad, yes, but the guy had obviously not shit his pants, it wasn't that bad, and in any case nobody would ever do such a thing and then go ahead and talk about it. They would squint into the dense, oppressive sunlight. For a few moment, perhaps, they would fall silent, lighting a joint and tracking its passage from man to man, inhaling, holding in the humiliation. Scary stuff, one of them might say. But then someone else would grin or flick his eyebrows and say, Roger-dodger, almost cut me a new asshole, *almost.*

There were numerous such poses. Some carried themselves with a sort of wistful resignation, others with pride or stiff soldierly discipline on good humor or macho zeal. They were afraid of dying but they were even more afraid to show it.

They found jokes to tell.

They used a hard vocabulary to contain the terrible softness. *Greased,* they'd say. *Offed, lit up, zapped while zipping.* It wasn't cruelty, just stage presence. They were actors and the war came at them in 3-D. When someone died, it wasn't quite dying, because in a curious way it seemed scripted, and because they had their lines mostly memorized, irony mixed with tragedy, and because they called it by other names, as if to encyst and destroy the reality of death itself. They kicked corpses. They cut off thumbs. They talked grunt lingo. They told stories about Ted Lavender's supply of tranquilizers, how the poor guy didn't feel a thing, how incredibly tranquil he was.

There's a moral here, said Mitchell Sanders.

They were waiting for Lavender's chopper, smoking the dead man's dope.

The moral's pretty obvious, Sanders said, and winked. Stay away from drugs. No joke, they'll ruin your day every time.

Cute, said Henry Dobbins.

Mind-blower, get it? Talk about wiggy—nothing left, just blood and brains.

They made themselves laugh.

There it is, they'd say, over and over, as if the repetition itself were an act of poise, a balance between crazy and almost crazy, knowing without going. There it is, which meant be cool, let it ride, because oh yeah, man, you can't change what can't be changed, there it is, there it absolutely and positively and fucking well *is*.

They were tough.

They carried all the emotional baggage of men who might die. Grief, terror, love, longing—these were intangibles, but the intangibles had their own mass and specific gravity, they had tangible weight. They carried shameful memories. They carried the common secret of cowardice barely restrained, the instinct to run or freeze or hide, and in many respects this was the heaviest burden of all, for it could never be put down, it required perfect balance and perfect posture. They carried their reputations. They carried the soldier's greatest fear, which was the fear of blushing. Men killed, and died, because they were embarrassed not to. It was what had brought them to the war in the first place, nothing positive, no dreams of glory or honor, just to avoid the blush of dishonor. They died so as not to die of embarrassment. They crawled into tunnels and walked point and advanced under fire. Each morning, despite the unknowns, they made their legs move. They endured. They kept humping. They did not submit to the obvious alternative, which was simply to close the eyes and fall. So easy, really. Go limp and tumble to the ground and let the muscles unwind and not speak and not budge until your buddies picked you up and lifted you into the chopper that would roar and dip its nose and carry you off to the world.

A mere matter of falling, yet no one ever fell. It was not courage, exactly; the object was not valor. Rather, they were too frightened to be cowards.

By and large they carried these things inside, maintaining the masks of composure. They sneered at sick call. They spoke bitterly about guys who had found release by shooting off their own toes or fingers. Pussies, they'd say. Candyasses. It was fierce, mocking talk, with only a trace of envy or awe, but even so, the image played itself out behind their eyes.

They imagined the muzzle against flesh. They imagined the quick, sweet pain, then the evacuation to Japan, then a hospital with warm beds and cute geisha nurses.

They dreamed of freedom birds.

At night, on guard, staring into the dark, they were carried away by jumbo jets. They felt the rush of takeoff. *Gone!* they yelled. And then velocity, wings and engines, a smiling stewardess—but it was more than a plane, it was a real bird, a big sleek silver bird with feathers and talons and high screeching. They were flying. The weights fell off, there was nothing to bear. They laughed and held on tight, feeling the cold slap of wind and altitude, soaring, thinking *It's over, I'm gone!*— they were naked, they were light and free—it was all lightness, bright and fast and buoyant, light as light, a helium buzz in the brain, a giddy bubbling in the lungs as they were taken up over the clouds and the war, beyond duty, beyond gravity and mortification and global entanglements—*Sin loi!*[9] they yelled, *I'm sorry, motherfuckers, but I'm out of it, I'm goofed, I'm on a space cruise, I'm gone!*—and it was a restful, disencumbered sensation, just riding the light waves, sailing that big silver freedom bird over the mountains and oceans, over America, over the farms and great sleeping cities and cemeteries and highways and the golden arches of McDonald's. It was flight, a kind of fleeing, a kind of falling, falling higher and higher, spinning off the edge of the earth and beyond the sun and through the vast, silent vacuum where there were no burdens and were everything weighed exactly nothing. *Gone!* they screamed, *I'm sorry but I'm gone!* And so at night, not quite dreaming, they gave themselves to lightness, they were carried, they were purely borne.

On the morning after Ted Lavender died, First Lieutenant Jimmy Cross crouched at the bottom of his foxhole and burned Martha's letters. Then he burned the two photographs. There was a steady rain

9. "Sorry about that" (Vietnamese).

falling which made it difficult, but he used heat tabs and Sterno to build a small fire, screening it with his body, holding the photographs over the tight blue flame with the tips of his fingers.

He realized it was only a gesture. Stupid, he thought. Sentimental, too, but mostly just stupid.

Lavender was dead. You couldn't burn the blame.

Besides, the letters were in his head. And even now, without photographs, Lieutenant Cross could see Martha playing volleyball in her white gym shorts and yellow T-shirt. He could see her moving in the rain.

When the fire died out, Lieutenant Cross pulled his poncho over his shoulders and ate breakfast from a can.

There was no great mystery, he decided.

In those burned letters Martha had never mentioned the war except to say, Jimmy, take care of yourself. She wasn't involved. She signed the letters "Love," but it wasn't love, and all the fine lines and technicalities did not matter.

The morning came up wet and blurry. Everything seemed part of everything else, the fog and Martha and the deepening rain.

It was a war, after all.

Half smiling, Lieutenant Jimmy Cross took out his maps. He shook his head hard, as if to clear it, then bent forward and began planning the day's march. In ten minutes, or maybe twenty, he would rouse the men and they would pack up and head west, where the maps showed the country to be green and inviting. They would do what they had always done. The rain might add some weight, but otherwise it would be one more day layered upon all the other days.

He was realistic about it. There was that new hardness in his stomach.

No more fantasies, he told himself.

Henceforth, when he thought about Martha, it would be only to think that she belonged elsewhere. He would shut down the daydreams. This was not Mount Sebastian, it was another world, where there were no pretty poems or midterm exams, a place where men died because of carelessness and gross stupidity. Kiowa was right. Boomdown, and you were dead, never partly dead.

Briefly, in the rain, Lieutenant Cross saw Martha's gray eyes gazing back at him.

He understood.

It was very sad, he thought. The things men carried inside. The things men did or felt they had to do.

He almost nodded at her, but didn't.

Instead he went back to his maps. He was now determined to

perform his duties firmly and without negligence. It wouldn't help Lavender, he knew that, but from this point on he would comport himself as a soldier. He would dispose of his good-luck pebble. Swallow it, maybe, or use Lee Strunk's slingshot, or just drop it along the trail. On the march he would impose strict field discipline. He would be careful to send out flank security, to prevent straggling or bunching up, to keep his troops moving at the proper pace and at the proper interval. He would insist on clean weapons. He would confiscate the remainder of Lavender's dope. Later in the day, perhaps, he would call the men together and speak to them plainly. He would accept the blame for what had happened to Ted Lavender. He would be a man about it. He would look them in the eyes, keeping his chin level, and he would issue the new SOPs in a calm, impersonal tone of voice, an officer's voice, leaving no room for argument or discussion. Commencing immediately, he'd tell them, they would no longer abandon equipment along the route of march. They would police up their acts. They would get their shit together, and keep it together, and maintain it neatly and in good working order.

He would not tolerate laxity. He would show strength, distancing himself.

Among the men there would be grumbling, of course, and maybe worse, because their days would seem longer and their loads heavier, but Lieutenant Cross reminded himself that his obligation was not to be loved but to lead. He would dispense with love; it was not now a factor. And if anyone quarreled or complained, he would simply tighten his lips and arrange his shoulders in the correct command posture. He might give a curt little nod. Or he might not. He might just shrug and say Carry on, then they would saddle up and form into a column and move out toward the villages of Than Khe.

1990

■   ■   ■

JONATHAN PENNER

EMOTION RECOLLECTED IN TRANQUILLITY[1]

After I got out of the service, I moved back in with my mother. Our temple was teaching contract bridge, and my mother drafted me as her partner, at least one generation younger than anybody else in the room. No matter which of us was declarer, my mother played the hand (her card sense was amazing, I give her that) while I sat behind the dummy.

Mrs. Leonard was another regular, a huge woman who always toadied up to my mother. I was the reason why. "Tell Philly," she'd beg my mother, as though we had food and she were starving, "to give Diane a little phone call." Then she'd squeeze my arm or sometimes, under the bridge table, always frightening me, my thigh. She was terrified her daughter would marry Richard Dean, a Gentile whose pharmacist uncle had been heard to pass anti-Semitic remarks.

"In addition to which," she would tell me sadly, taking me aside afterward during coffee and cake, "the boy is AC-DC."

Though this was close enough to the truth, I was silent out of loyalty. Mrs. Leonard thought I hadn't understood. She narrowed her eyes. "Do I need to spell it out?" She puffed at her cigarette in the way she used to signal sophistication. "A switch-hitter."

What Mrs. Leonard didn't know was that Diane had been on my mind as far back as my memory went. I had felt for her, starting in kindergarten, an unforgettable hatred. Even then she was considered pretty, which I especially hated, because it drew attention to her, there-

---

1. Famous definition of poetry from the Preface to the *Lyrical Ballads*, by William Wordsworth (1770–1850), English poet.

444

fore to me. Back then, and through the first six grades, she and I were the only Jews in our class.

Diane was incredibly stupid, incredibly something—nobody minding the store, was how my mother put it. In class, teachers had to yell at her to pay attention. It was always the same. Her vagueness, her dreamy sweetness, made me want to hit her, but I was afraid to. And year after year, fat Mrs. Leonard, whenever we met, would reach out a hand to stroke my head, which I didn't dare lean away more than slightly. The smell of her sweat and perfume intoxicated me, and I watched in fascination as the flesh hanging from her upper arm swung like a water-filled balloon.

"Philly, let me take you home," she'd say. "You'll write a little poem for me." Her voice was so melodious, humorous, and inviting that I would nervously feel myself falling under her spell.

"You and Diane are some pair. A little bride and groom."

The idea of my marrying anyone was humiliating. When her mother maneuvered us face to face at temple "events," I stared at Diane expressionlessly, while she wore a simple-minded smile and tried to back away. At last she would escape to the temple's front steps and sit reading a book, whose title she would hide when she saw me looking at it, and I would join my friends in back of the building, humming rocks at the garbage cans with as vicious a sidearm whip as possible.

In high school, to her mother's despair, she hung around with a brotherhood of tough guys we all called—I never knew why—the Baldies. Their leader, Rodney Cooper, would take her to movies, and then, late at night, to a deserted golf course. Big Ones, he always called her, Big Ones, and she'd only smile. Her mother was right to worry. Loathsome as Rodney was, he made himself the love of her life. Maybe it was just his being the first. Diane was soft, and would have retained anyone's impress.

"Sucks and fucks," he claimed, standing with his friends on the baseball field, all of them smoking and strewing the ground with butts. "Shakespeare!" Seeing me on the fringe of the group he drew me apart and put his arm over my shoulder. "Jew girls are the best," he told me, as a compliment. "Right, Shakespeare?" I imagined myself dividing his grinning face into diamonds by pushing it through the chain-link backstop, but in a fight he would have destroyed me.

Oh, she loved him. He didn't go to college, so she didn't—she enrolled in Hammersmith Secretarial School, whose billboard showed a giant hammer striking a door marked GOOD JOB, HI PAY. When Mrs. Leonard saw me at temple, escorting my mother to a bar mitzvah, she stared reproachfully. At the reception afterward she cornered us, holding out a paper napkin laden with rugaluch.[2] "And you, Philly," she said bitterly. "What are your plans? Yale? Harvard? Brandeis?"

"I may go into the Army," I said.

She looked at my mother, who flushed but shrugged. Mrs. Leonard brightened. "A young man has time," she said, folding her napkin around the rugaluch and stuffing it into her pocketbook. "Are you still writing your lovely poems?"

"It's harder now."

"Explain to Mrs. Leonard about the Army," said my mother cruelly.

So I must have been able to explain my reasoning, then—I had to repeatedly, until the very day I left. But now don't ask me. It turned out I never wrote a poem about the Army. You see novels about the Army, but did you ever see a poem? They sent me to Germany—no poems about that, either. But once while I was there I got drunk and helped overturn some parked cars. And in jail I did write a poem, not about jail, but about Diane's face, which I remembered as too big, a pale floating target.

When I returned home she was working in a department store, going to the local college part-time. I enrolled there too. Rodney had gone to Texas to seek his fortune. Diane missed him badly, but was falling in love with someone new, the one her mother, squinting through cigarette smoke, called the switch-hitter, AC-DC.

This was unfair, but it was true that Richard Dean was (and God knows how Mrs. Leonard found out) a transvestite. Once a week or so he liked to go into the city dressed as a woman. Diane, who had taken to confiding in me (her oldest friend, she remarked sentimentally) about her love life, said it was the deception he liked. That and the whiff of danger.

"He knows he isn't a homo," she explained. Saying the word made her squirm. "He just likes to see if he can pass. Can you understand that a little?"

"Sure," I said, and I thought I could. "When I was small I liked to go around the house in my mother's heels."

Our temple had started a theater group, and my mother was there night after night for rehearsals. I usually stayed home alone. Though I met girls at college, they weren't right—that was all I would say whenever my mother raised the subject. To my surprise I'd turned out to be a serious, no, a gloomy person, and could hardly stand frivolity or even cheerfulness. Since getting out of the Army I'd had acceptances from

2. Pastry.

a few literary magazines, and was starting to think about a book of poems. If I could accumulate forty I liked, I'd try for the Yale Younger Poets Award. That was enough to dream about.

But, as though I were forever back in jail in Germany, seeing her pale face float before me, I was disturbed to find myself—after all these years—contracting Diane like a kind of disease. I might have become infected in childhood. Like leprosy, its stain could have taken decades to surface. In any case, the way Richard Dean would slide his hand around under her armpit—as though he were sticking it between two cushions—made me furious.

It was Diane's cowlike submissiveness to him that bothered me most. She was pitifully afraid of his leaving her, already afraid—something I could hardly believe, in such a luscious girl—of being single all her life, and alone in her old age. "If I looked younger," she said (she wasn't yet twenty-five), craning to peer in my car's rear-view mirror, stretching her face with her fingertips. Her sweater rode up, exposing an inch of white back.

Finally Richard told her she shouldn't talk to me so much. That amazed Diane.

"It's natural," I said, because I could understand his jealousy. Sometimes, after rehearsals, my mother was spending the night with her theater group's director, a retired actor. It wasn't the same, but upsetting enough. "I'd be nervous too," I said, "in Richard's position."

"You wouldn't if I were your girl," said Diane—protesting her loyalty to him, and not hinting at anything at all.

Her mindless subservience made me angry enough to think she was right, he was certain to leave her—who could be happy with her for long? But at night, waiting to fall asleep, I had visions of Richard Dean dying in a car accident—sometimes my mother was in the car too—visions so clear that I frightened myself, and beamed into my pillow the thought that I didn't mean it.

At other times I imagined myself catching him in a homosexual act, and beating him up in spite of his being dressed as a woman, and telling him never to see Diane again. But I knew I would never lift a finger to him. He said he was a karate expert, and once, in a sudden rage, had half-squatted into combat position, hands stiffened like hatchets. "I can break twelve of your bones in two seconds," he told me softly. I laughed and backed away. Though the Army had tried teaching me a little of that, I had failed to learn it. In a fight he would demolish me.

Ghazir—he was a Christian Lebanese, raised in France, but an Arab was all Mrs. Leonard ever saw—was twenty years older than we were, with enormous shoulders and a walrus mustache. Divorced, he lived in a cottage he had built out in the country. Less than a month after she met him, Diane was living with him.

What, she asked me with a hopeless little smile, could she tell her mother? I didn't know. When Mrs. Leonard saw me in the supermarket, she rose from the freezer bin, a quart of ice cream in each hand. "Philly," she said distractedly, pointing at me with one of the quarts, the pendulous flesh of her arm swaying, the look on her face telling the world—while I pretended not to see, hurrying to the checkout—that I, my stubbornness, disloyalty, unmanliness, was the cause of it all.

I guess there are periods in everyone's life, like childhood, that seem to last forever, but when you look back at them later they're collapsed as flat as packing cartons, and everything's squashed together. That's what it started to be like for me now. Diane lived with Ghazir and finally married him. I got a job distributing newspapers, and didn't win the Yale Younger Poets Award. I began to send my book of poems to little presses named after things like planets and trees. Diane and Ghazir fought, were divorced, but continued to live together—their trouble was her fault, she was too demanding, she told me. Mrs. Leonard died. I wept at her funeral, but when I saw Richard Dean there, crying too, a guy who knew she'd hated him, I dried right up. My mother, svelte leading lady, was there with her boy friend, the director of the Temple B'Nai Israel Players. "The weight this woman carried," said my mother, "she's got no kick coming."

Ghazir began to beat Diane. When I, drunk, tried to return the favor, he hugged me until one of my ribs cracked. I paid to have my book of poems published, and stacked the boxed copies in my bedroom. Ghazir was seeing other women, blaming Diane, who agreed that she was driving him crazy, she wanted so much to remarry him. My mother married her director, they bought a condo in Miami, and she gave me a hug and sold the house out from under me. "This is my chance for happiness," she explained. "Not so many years are left. What about you?" She made claws in the air. "When are you going to grab hold?"

I moved, then, to a furnished room nearer the university. My landlord was an old man who swept his sidewalk with painful care early each morning. He was completely deaf. I communicated with him in writing, but seldom, because my childish script irritated him. On a ledge in the dim downstairs hall, beside the disconnected telephone, lay a tract titled "What to Do in Time of Sorrow." It lay there, slowly growing a skin of dust, the three years I lived in that house.

Ghazir had been having an affair with a French girl who lived with a wealthy family as a baby-sitter. She met him at his cottage, often bringing the children, when Diane was at work. Diane knew about it. Ghazir vehemently denied that anything sexual was going on. But when the girl returned to France he was broken-hearted, and wept with his face pressed into Diane's lap, she told me. Then he said he was going to Europe.

His picture postcards arrived with decreasing frequency, with no return address and no mention of his coming back. Diane still lived at the cottage, where, every time I visited her, she would talk to me for hours about nothing but Ghazir. The surrounding vegetation grew wild. I attacked it with a sickle. Winter came, and Ghazir wrote that he was working in a bicycle shop, thinking of getting married. He had asked his cousin to look into selling the cottage.

And a sign, FOR SALE, did appear, hammered through the snow into the frozen ground. No buyers came. Ghazir stopped writing. The cold wind oozed in; each time I visited I tacked up more cardboard. I left my deaf old man and slept in Diane's front room. Evenings, we made a fire and talked about our childhood, which she, to my amazement, remembered as perfect. Spring came early. I pounded open the windows, bruising the heel of my palm, and patched the torn screens. On a night with a full moon and a scented breeze, Diane and I became lovers. As we lay together in the valley of Ghazir's mattress, as she slept in my arms, I beamed a promise into her damp forehead: to compensate her for every insult and betrayal.

We moved back to town, which had grown disturbingly since we were children, and rented a garden apartment in what I remembered as empty marshland. I got a job at an aerospace plant—it had to do with missile nosecones, they said, but I never learned how. I emptied boxes of head-sized plastic hunks into a hopper atop a machine. They came out at the bottom fist-sized, warm, and smelling like model airplane glue. Diane, who was working as a secretary at the telephone company, joined their Executive-in-Training Program. We bought chairs and a sofa, rough-hewn wood slung with leather, the style that year. New sets of everything that came in sets—linens, pots and pans, china, glasses, silverware. It was the nicest place I ever lived in.

Except when we were at our jobs, we were together, even if I was just taking a ten-minute trip to the drug store. "You don't think I'm too clingy?" she asked.

"I love it," I told her. "Don't use that word."

Diane knew from the start how badly I was going to fail her, and her difficult job was to teach me that. She started practically at once asking whether she disappointed me, whether I was upset with her, as though I were a doctor withholding news of fatal illness.

"You look nervous," she'd say, or "You look unhappy," when I wasn't aware of feeling those things. If I did tell her something was bothering me, a backache, or something from work, she was more upset than I was, as though the trouble were her fault. She saw things in my expression that I never meant to be there. She heard them in my voice. She heard them in my silence.

And at last it became maddening, when I had been thinking about something, to look up and see her little smile of guilty fear. "I wasn't being cold," I'd shout, before she had a chance to say it.

But now I began to criticize everything about her. I said she spent too much on clothes—her dresses filled her closet and half of mine, many more than my mother had owned.

"That's because she threw them out whenever the style changed," said Diane. And it was true, I had been unfair, most of Diane's clothes were old, I thought I could remember some from the days of Richard Dean—old and unflattering, tight around the stomach and rear. And how strangely somber. When I saw them by the dozen, packed together on hangers, I realized that she never wore anything vivid.

"You should try bright colors," I told her.

But she only looked worried and asked me, smiling a little, her voice as hopeless as though I'd suggested she leap the moon, "Do you think I should?"

Diane. I saw now that I was stuck with her, her with me, forever. We weren't unhappy. I shouted, but not often; she rarely cried. We bought a second car, used. She dyed her hair to conceal the white. I had an extra drink each evening. We bought a little outboard cruiser and moored it in the river. I hardly remembered, would barely have wanted, any other life.

And then one night—out for supper at Howard Johnson's—we saw someone who looked familiar. "It couldn't be," said Diane.

I doubted it too. But Rodney Cooper recognized us at once, grinned, waved, and came to join us in our booth. "Shakespeare," he laughed, squeezing my hand. His face was deeply tanned, his hair silver, his wrinkles full of sly good humor. He was just back for a visit, he said—he came every year to see his family. He'd done, oh, pretty well in Texas, had his own business, now. Contractor, laying pipe, starting to bid on some pretty big jobs. His lawyer and his accountant were both Jews, he told us, then grinned, showing us that he admired the sharpness and shadiness of our race. Diane, with an unconscious half-smile, was staring at him—trying to read his face, I knew, wondering what he was thinking of her. It was exactly the same as always. "Big Ones," said Rodney, as he reached for our checks, "I gotta ask. You two married, or what?" Diane and I shook our heads slowly, as though in time to the same music.

They live in Houston now—I know from the postmark on their Christmas card. It's the same card every year, the one his secretary must mail to his customers and suppliers. The signature, Rodney and Diane Cooper, is in red Old English type, within a wreath of green holly. I wonder how many others come to our town, whether he sends them to his grade school teachers in their retirement, or any of the old Baldies.

The missile nosecone business hasn't been good. But by the time the layoffs came, I had enough seniority to bump a younger man in what we call the Publications Division. Now I edit and mostly write *Inner Space,* a weekly that's distributed throughout the plant. News about the company, contracts we've been awarded, results from the bowling league, necrology—the Director of Publications lets me do whatever I want. Lately I've tried some light verse. I don't sign it, but the other publications people know who wrote it, and they say it's not bad. One of them is a woman, Lila. She hasn't been to where I live, but someday I think I'll open Diane's old closet and show her the boxes full of my book of poems.

Last week I saw Ghazir. He must be close to seventy, now. But he still has his swagger, and I stopped on the sidewalk to watch him. He emerged from a barbershop, thin hair and great mustache beautifully trimmed, and jaywalked across the street. I wanted to stop him there in the middle of traffic and ask when he'd gotten back from France. I'd have liked to know what he thought of his ex-wife's marriage, whether it would last or whether we'd see Diane back in town one of these years, alone in her old age as she'd always predicted. I wished we could go to a bar together, he and I, and have some drinks and talk about our lives. But Ghazir was across the street now. He hopped into an idling Thunderbird, where a young woman had just slid from the driver's seat to make room for him, and drove away with his arm around her.

And when I saw that, I knew it was good I hadn't spoken to him. I might have told him that he'd never loved Diane, none of them had, that they'd ruined her. If we'd gone to that bar and had those drinks I'd probably have cried and said that I was the only one in the world who had tried to save her. If even a shadow of mockery crossed his face I might have grabbed his thick neck and squeezed. And it would have been the same as always—no matter how I fought, old as he was, he would have crucified me.

1983

JAYNE ANNE PHILLIPS

SOUVENIR

Kate always sent her mother a card on Valentine's Day. She timed the mails from wherever she was so that the cards arrived on February 14th. Her parents had celebrated the day in some small fashion, and since her father's death six years before, Kate made a gesture of compensatory remembrance. At first, she made the cards herself: collage and pressed grass on construction paper sewn in fabric. Now she settled for art reproductions, glossy cards with blank insides. Kate wrote in them with colored inks, "You have always been my Valentine," or simply "Hey, take care of yourself." She might enclose a present as well, something small enough to fit into an envelope; a sachet, a perfumed soap, a funny tintype of a prune-faced man in a bowler hat.

This time, she forgot. Despite the garish displays of paper cupids and heart-shaped boxes in drugstore windows, she let the day nearly approach before remembering. It was too late to send anything in the mail. She called her mother long-distance at night when the rates were low.

"Mom? How are you?"

"It's you! How are *you?*" Her mother's voice grew suddenly brighter; Kate recognized a tone reserved for welcome company. Sometimes it took a while to warm up.

"I'm fine," answered Kate. "What have you been doing?"

"Well, actually I was trying to sleep."

"Sleep? You should be out setting the old hometown on fire."

"The old hometown can burn up without me tonight."

"Really? What's going on?"

"I'm running in-service training sessions for the primary teachers." Kate's mother was a school superintendent. "They're driving me batty. You'd think their brains were rubber."

"They are," Kate said. "Or you wouldn't have to train them. Think of them as a salvation, They create a need for your job."

"Some salvation. Besides, your logic is ridiculous. Just because someone needs training doesn't mean they're stupid."

"I'm just kidding. But *I'm* stupid. I forgot to send you a Valentine's card."

"You did? That's bad. I'm trained to receive one. They bring me luck."

"You're receiving a phone call instead," Kate said. "Won't that do?"

"Of course," said her mother, "but this is costing you money. Tell me quick, how are you?"

"Oh, you know. Doctoral pursuits. Doing my student trip, grooving with the professors."

"The professors? You'd better watch yourself."

"It's a joke, Mom, a joke. But what about you? Any men on the horizon?"

"No, not really. A married salesman or two asking me to dinner when they come through the office. Thank heavens I never let those things get started."

"You should do what you want to," Kate said.

"Sure," said her mother. "And where would I be then?"

"I don't know. Maybe Venezuela."

"They don't even have plumbing in Venezuela."

"Yes, but their sunsets are perfect, and the villages are full of dark passionate men in blousy shirts."

"That's your department, not mine."

"Ha," Kate said, "I wish it were my department. Sounds a lot more exciting than teaching undergraduates."

Her mother laughed. "Be careful," she said. "You'll get what you want. End up sweeping a dirt floor with a squawling baby around your neck."

"A dark baby," Kate said, "to stir up the family blood."

"Nothing would surprise me," her mother said as the line went fuzzy. Her voice was submerged in static, then surfaced. "Listen," she was saying. "Write to me. You seem so far away."

They hung up and Kate sat watching the windows of the neighboring house. The curtains were transparent and flowered and none of them matched. Silhouettes of the window frames spread across them like single dark bars. Her mother's curtains were all the same, white cotton hemmed with a ruffle, tiebacks blousing the cloth into identical shapes. From the street it looked as if the house was always in order.

Kate made a cup of strong Chinese tea, turned the lights off, and sat holding the warm cup in the dark. Her mother kept no real tea in the house, just packets of instant diabetic mixture which tasted of chemical sweetener and had a bitter aftertaste. The packets sat on the shelf next to her mother's miniature scales. The scales were white. Kate saw clearly the face of the metal dial on the front, its markings and trembling needle. Her mother weighed portions of food for meals: frozen broccoli, slices of plastic-wrapped Kraft cheese, careful chunks of roast beef. A dog-eared copy of *The Diabetic Diet* had remained propped against the salt shaker for the last two years.

Kate rubbed her forehead. Often at night she had headaches. Sometimes she wondered if there were an agent in her body, a secret in her blood making ready to work against her.

The phone blared repeatedly, careening into her sleep. Kate scrambled out of bed, naked and cold, stumbling, before she recognized the striped wallpaper of her bedroom and realized the phone was right there on the bedside table, as always. She picked up the receiver.

"Kate?" said her brother's voice. "It's Robert. Mom is in the hospital. They don't know what's wrong but she's in for tests."

"Tests? What's happened? I just talked to her last night."

"I'm not sure. She called the neighbors and they took her to the emergency room around dawn." Robert's voice still had that slight twang Kate knew was disappearing from her own. He would be calling from his insurance office, nine o'clock their time, in his thick glasses and wide, perfectly knotted tie. He was a member of the million-dollar club[1] and his picture, tiny, the size of a postage stamp, appeared in the Mutual of Omaha magazine. His voice seemed small too over the distance. Kate felt heavy and dull. She would never make much money, and recently she had begun wearing make-up again, waking in smeared mascara as she had in high school.

"Is Mom all right?" she managed now. "How serious is it?"

"They're not sure," Robert said. "Her doctor thinks it could have been any of several things, but they're doing X rays."

"Her doctor *thinks*? Doesn't he know? Get her to someone else. There aren't any doctors in that one-horse town."

"I don't know about that," Robert said defensively. "Anyway, I can't force her. You know how she is about money."

"Money? She could have a stroke and drop dead while her doctor wonders what's wrong."

"Doesn't matter. You know you can't tell her what to do."

1. I.e., has been honored by his employers for selling more than a million dollars worth of insurance.

"Could I call her somehow?"

"No, not yet. And don't get her all worried. She's been scared enough as it is. I'll tell her what you said about getting another opinion, and I'll call you back in a few hours when I have some news. Meanwhile, she's all right, do you hear?"

The line went dead with a click and Kate walked to the bathroom to wash her face. She splashed her eyes and felt guilty about the Valentine's card. Slogans danced in her head like reprimands. *For A Special One. Dearest Mother. My Best Friend.* Despite Robert, after breakfast she would call the hospital.

She sat a long time with her coffee, waiting for minutes to pass, considering how many meals she and her mother ate alone. Similar times of day, hundreds of miles apart. Women by themselves. The last person Kate had eaten breakfast with had been someone she'd met in a bar. He was passing through town. He liked his fried eggs gelatinized in the center, only slightly runny, and Kate had studiously looked away as he ate. The night before he'd looked down from above her as he finished and she still moved under him. "You're still wanting," he'd said. "That's nice." Mornings now, Kate saw her own face in the mirror and was glad she'd forgotten his name. When she looked at her reflection from the side, she saw a faint etching of lines beside her mouth. She hadn't slept with anyone for five weeks, and the skin beneath her eyes had taken on a creamy darkness.

She reached for the phone but drew back. It seemed bad luck to ask for news, to push toward whatever was coming as though she had no respect for it.

Standing in the kitchen last summer, her mother had stirred gravy and argued with her.

"I'm thinking of your own good, not mine," she'd said. "Thinking of what you put yourself through. And how can you feel right about it? You were born here, I don't care what you say." Her voice broke and she looked, perplexed, at the broth in the pan.

"But, hypothetically," Kate continued, her own voice unaccountably shaking, "if I'm willing to endure whatever I have to, do you have a right to object? You're my mother. You're supposed to defend my choices."

"You'll have enough trouble without choosing more for yourself. Using birth control that'll ruin your insides, moving from one place to another. I can't defend your choices. I can't even defend myself against you." She wiped her eyes on a napkin.

"Why do you have to make me feel so guilty?" Kate said, fighting tears of frustration. "I'm not attacking you."

"You're not? Then who are you talking to?"

"Oh Mom, give me a break."

"I've tried to give you more than that," her mother said. "I know what your choices are saying to me." She set the steaming gravy off the stove. "You may feel very differently later on. It's just a shame I won't be around to see it."

"Oh? Where will you be?"

"Floating around on a fleecy cloud."

Kate got up to set the table before she realized her mother had already done it.

The days went by. They'd gone shopping before Kate left. Standing at the cash register in an antique shop on Main Street, they bought each other pewter candle holders. "A souvenir," her mother said. "A reminder to always be nice to yourself. If you live alone you should eat by candlelight."

"Listen," Kate said, "I eat in a heart-shaped tub with bubbles to my chin. I sleep on satin sheets and my mattress has a built-in massage engine. My overnight guests are impressed. You don't have to tell me about the solitary pleasures."

They laughed and touched hands.

"Well," her mother said. "If you like yourself, I must have done something right."

Robert didn't phone until evening. His voice was fatigued and thin. "I've moved her to the university hospital," he said. "They can't deal with it at home."

Kate waited, saying nothing. She concentrated on the toes of her shoes. They needed shining. *You never take care of anything,* her mother would say.

"She has a tumor in her head." He said it firmly, as though Kate might challenge him.

"I'll take a plane tomorrow morning," Kate answered, "I'll be there by noon."

Robert exhaled. "Look," he said, "don't even come back here unless you can keep your mouth shut and do it my way."

"Get to the point."

"The point is they believe she has a malignancy and we're not going to tell her. I almost didn't tell you." His voice faltered. "They're going to operate but if they find what they're expecting, they don't think they can stop it."

For a moment there was no sound except an oceanic vibration of distance on the wire. Even that sound grew still. Robert breathed. Kate could almost see him, in a booth at the hospital, staring straight ahead at the plastic instructions screwed to the narrow rectangular body of the telephone. It seemed to her that she was hurtling toward him.

"I'll do it your way," she said.

The hospital cafeteria was a large room full of orange Formica tables. Its southern wall was glass. Across the highway, Kate saw a small park modestly dotted with amusement rides and bordered by a narrow band of river. How odd, to build a children's park across from a medical center. The sight was pleasant in a cruel way. The rolling lawn of the little park was perfectly, relentlessly green.

Robert sat down. Their mother was to have surgery in two days.

"After it's over," he said, "they're not certain what will happen. The tumor is in a bad place. There may be some paralysis."

"What kind of paralysis?" Kate said. She watched him twist the green-edged coffee cup around and around on its saucer.

"Facial. And maybe worse."

"You've told her this?"

He didn't answer.

"Robert, what is she going to think if she wakes up and—"

He leaned forward, grasping the cup and speaking through clenched teeth. "Don't you think I thought of that?" He gripped the sides of the table and the cup rolled onto the carpeted floor with a dull thud. He seemed ready to throw the table after it, then grabbed Kate's wrists and squeezed them hard.

"You didn't drive her here," he said. "She was so scared she couldn't talk. How much do you want to hand her at once?"

Kate watched the cup sitting solidly on the nubby carpet.

"We've told her it's benign," Robert said, "that the surgery will cause complications, but she can learn back whatever is lost."

Kate looked at him. "Is that true?"

"They hope so."

"We're lying to her, all of us, more and more." Kate pulled her hands away and Robert touched her shoulder.

"What do you want to tell her, Kate? You're fifty-five and you're done for'?"

She stiffened. "Why put her through the operation at all?"

He sat back and dropped his arms, lowering his head. "Because without it she'd be in bad pain. Soon." They were silent, then he looked up. "And anyway," he said softly, "we don't *know*, do we? She may have a better chance than they think."

Kate put her hands on her face. Behind her closed eyes she saw a succession of blocks tumbling over.

They took the elevator up to the hospital room. They were alone and they stood close together. Above the door red numerals lit up, flashing. Behind the illuminated shapes droned an impersonal hum of machinery.

Then the doors opened with a sucking sound. Three nurses stood waiting with a lunch cart, identical covered trays stacked in tiers. There was a hot bland smell, like warm cardboard. One of the women caught the thick steel door with her arm and smiled. Kate looked quickly at their rubber-soled shoes. White polish, the kind that rubs off. And their legs seemed only white shapes, boneless and two-dimensional, stepping silently into the metal cage.

She looked smaller in the white bed. The chrome side rails were pulled up and she seemed powerless behind them, her dark hair pushed back from her face and her forearms delicate in the baggy hospital gown. Her eyes were different in some nearly imperceptible way; she held them wider, they were shiny with a veiled wetness. For a moment the room seemed empty of all else; there were only her eyes and the dark blossoms of the flowers on the table beside her. Red roses with pine. Everyone had sent the same thing.

Robert walked close to the bed with his hands clasped behind his back, as though afraid to touch. "Where did all the flowers come from?" he asked.

"From school, and the neighbors. And Katie." She smiled.

"FTD," Kate said. "Before I left home. I felt so bad for not being here all along."

"That's silly," said their mother. "You can hardly sit at home and wait for some problem to arise."

"Speaking of problems," Robert said, "the doctor tells me you're not eating. Do I have to urge you a little?" He sat down on the edge of the bed and shook the silverware from its paper sleeve.

Kate touched the plastic tray. "Jell-O and canned cream of chicken soup. Looks great. We should have brought you something."

"They don't *want* us to bring her anything," Robert said. "This is a hospital. And I'm sure your comments make her lunch seem even more appetizing."

"I'll eat it!" said their mother in mock dismay. "Admit they sent you in here to stage a battle until I gave in."

"I'm sorry," Kate said. "He's right."

Robert grinned. "Did you hear that? She says I'm right. I don't believe it." He pushed the tray closer to his mother's chest and made a show of tucking a napkin under her chin.

"Of course you're right, dear." She smiled and gave Kate an obvious wink.

"Yeah," Robert said, "I know you two. But seriously, you eat this. I have to go make some business calls from the motel room."

Their mother frowned. "That motel must be costing you a fortune."

"No, it's reasonable," he said. "Kate can stay for a week or two and I'll drive back and forth from home. If you think this food is bad, you should see the meals in that motel restaurant." He got up to go, flashing Kate a glance of collusion. "I'll be back after supper."

His footsteps echoed down the hallway. Kate and her mother looked wordlessly at each other, relieved. Kate looked away guiltily. Then her mother spoke, apologetic. "He's so tired," she said. "He's been with me since yesterday."

She looked at Kate, then into the air of the room. "I'm in a fix," she said. "Except for when the pain comes, it's all a show that goes on without me. I'm like an invalid, or a lunatic."

Kate moved close and touched her mother's arms. "That's all right, we're going to get you through it. Someone's covering for you at work?"

"I had to take a leave of absence. It's going to take a while afterward—"

"I know. But it's the last thing to worry about, it can't be helped."

"Like spilt milk. Isn't that what they say?"

"I don't know what they say. But why didn't you tell me? Didn't you know something was wrong?"

"Yes . . . bad headaches. Migraines, I thought, or the diabetes getting worse. I was afraid they'd start me on insulin." She tightened the corner of her mouth. "Little did I know . . ."

They heard the shuffle of slippers. An old woman stood at the open door of the room, looking in confusedly. She seemed about to speak, then moved on.

"Oh," said Kate's mother in exasperation, "shut that door, please? They let these old women wander around like refugees." She sat up, reaching for a robe. "And let's get me out of this bed."

They sat near the window while she finished eating. Bars of moted yellow banded the floor of the room. The light held a tinge of spring which seemed painful because it might vanish. They heard the rattle of the meal cart outside the closed door, and the clunk-slide of patients with aluminum walkers. Kate's mother sighed and pushed away the half-empty soup bowl.

"They'll be here after me any minute. More tests. I just want to stay with you." Her face was warm and smooth in the slanted light, lines in her skin delicate, unreal; as though a face behind her face was now apparent after many years. She sat looking at Kate and smiled.

"One day when you were about four you were dragging a broom around the kitchen. I asked what you were doing and you told me that when you got old you were going to be an angel and sweep the rotten rain off the clouds."

"What did you say to that?"

"I said that when you were old I was sure God would see to it," Her mother laughed. "I'm glad you weren't such a smart aleck then," she said. "You would have told me my view of God was paternalistic."

"Ah yes," sighed Kate. "God, that famous dude. Here I am, getting old, facing unemployment, alone, and where is He?"

"You're not alone," her mother said, "I'm right here."

Kate didn't answer. She sat motionless and felt her heart begin to open like a box with a hinged lid. The fullness had no edges.

Her mother stood. She rubbed her hands slowly, twisting her wedding rings. "My hands are so dry in the winter," she said softly, "I brought some hand cream with me but I can't find it anywhere, my suitcase is so jumbled. Thank heavens spring is early this year. . . . They told me that little park over there doesn't usually open till the end of March . . ."

She's helping me, thought Kate, I'm not supposed to let her down.

". . . but they're already running it on weekends. Even past dusk. We'll see the lights tonight. You can't see the shapes this far away, just the motion . . ."

A nurse came in with a wheelchair. Kate's mother pulled a wry face. "This wheelchair is a bit much," she said.

"We don't want to tire you out," said the nurse.

The chair took her weight quietly. At the door she put out her hand to stop, turned, and said anxiously, "Kate, see if you can find that hand cream?"

It was the blue suitcase from years ago, still almost new. She's brought things she never used for everyday; a cashmere sweater, lace slips, silk underpants wrapped in tissue. Folded beneath was a stack of postmarked envelopes, slightly ragged, tied with twine. Kate opened one and realized that all the cards were there, beginning with the first of the marriage. There were a few photographs of her and Robert, baby pitchers almost indistinguishable from each other, and then Kate's homemade Valentines, fastened together with rubber bands. Kate stared. *What will I do with these things?* She wanted air; she needed to breathe. She walked to the window and put the bundled papers on the sill. She'd raised the glass and pushed back the screen when suddenly, her mother's clock radio went off with a flat buzz. Kate moved to switch it off and brushed the cards with her arm. Envelopes shifted and slid, scattering on the floor of the room. A few snapshots wafted silently out the window. They dipped and turned, twirling. Kate didn't try to reach them. They seemed only scraps, buoyant and yellowed, blown away, the faces small as pennies. Somewhere far-off there were sirens, almost musical, drawn out and carefully approaching.

The nurse came in with evening medication. Kate's mother lay in bed. "I hope this is strong enough," she said. "Last night I couldn't sleep at all. So many sounds in a hospital . . ."

"You'll sleep tonight," the nurse assured her.

Kate winked at her mother. "That's right," she said, "I'll help you out if I have to."

They stayed up for an hour, watching the moving lights outside and the stationary glows of houses across the distant river. The halls grew darker, were lit with night lights, and the hospital dimmed. Kate waited. Her mother's eyes fluttered and finally she slept. Her breathing was low and regular.

Kate didn't move. Robert had said he'd be back; where was he? She felt a sunken anger and shook her head. She'd been on the point of telling her mother everything. The secrets were a travesty. What if there were things her mother wanted done, people she needed to see? Kate wanted to wake her before these hours passed in the dark and confess that she had lied. Between them, through the tension, there had always been a trusted clarity. Now it was twisted. Kate sat leaning forward, nearly touching the hospital bed.

Suddenly her mother sat bolt upright, her eyes open and her face transfixed. She looked blindly toward Kate but seemed to see nothing. "Who are you?" she whispered. Kate stood, at first unable to move. The woman in the bed opened and closed her mouth several times, as though she were gasping. Then she said loudly, "Stop moving the table. Stop it this instant!" Her eyes were wide with fright and her body was vibrating.

Kate reached her. "Mama, wake up, you're dreaming." Her mother jerked, flinging her arms out. Kate held her tightly.

"I can hear the wheels," she moaned.

"No, no," Kate said. "You're here with me."

"It's not so?"

"No," Kate said. "It's not so."

She went limp. Kate felt for her pulse and found it rapid, then regular. She sat rocking her mother. In a few minutes she lay her back on the pillows and smoothed the damp hair at her temples, smoothed the sheets of the bed. Later she slept fitfully in a chair, waking repeatedly to assure herself that her mother was breathing.

Near dawn she got up, exhausted, and left the room to walk in the corridor. In front of the window at the end of the hallway she saw a man slumped on a couch; the man slowly stood and wavered before her like a specter. It was Robert.

"Kate?" he said.

Years ago he had flunked out of a small junior college and their mother sat in her bedroom rocker, crying hard for over an hour while Kate tried in vain to comfort her. Kate went to the university the next fall, so anxious that she studied frantically, outlining whole textbooks in yellow ink. She sat in the front rows of large classrooms to take voluminous notes, writing quickly in her thick notebook. Robert had gone home, held a job in a plant that manufactured business forms and worked his way through the hometown college. By that time their father was dead, and Robert became, always and forever, the man of the house.

"Robert," Kate said, "I'll stay. Go home."

After breakfast they sat waiting for Robert, who had called and said he'd arrive soon. Kate's fatigue had given way to an intense awareness of every sound, every gesture. How would they get through the day? Her mother had awakened from the drugged sleep still groggy, unable to eat. The meal was sent away untouched and she watched the window as though she feared the walls of the room.

"I'm glad your father isn't here to see this," she said. There was a silence and Kate opened her mouth to speak. "I mean," said her mother quickly, "I'm going to look horrible for a few weeks, with my head all shaved." She pulled an afghan up around her lap and straightened the magazines on the table beside her chair.

"Mom," Kate said, "your hair will grow back."

Her mother pulled the afghan closer. "I've been thinking of your father," she said. "It's not that I'd have wanted him to suffer. But if he had to die, sometimes I wish he'd done it more gently. That heart attack, so finished; never a warning. I wish I'd had some time to nurse him. In a way, it's a chance to settle things."

"Did things need settling?"

"They always do, don't they?" She sat looking out the window, then said softly, "I wonder where I'm headed."

"You're not headed anywhere." Kate said. "I want you right here to see me settle down into normal American womanhood."

Her mother smiled reassuringly. "Where are my grandchildren?" she said. "That's what I'd like to know."

"You stick around," said Kate, "and I promise to start working on it." She moved her chair closer, so that their knees were touching and they could both see out the window. Below them cars moved on the highway and the Ferris wheel in the little park was turning.

"I remember when you were one of the little girls in the parade at the country fair. You weren't even in school yet; you were beautiful in that white organdy dress and pinafore. You wore those shiny black patent shoes and a crown of real apple blossoms. Do you remember?"

"Yes." Kate said. "That long parade. They told me not to move and I sat so still my legs went to sleep. When they lifted me off the float I couldn't stand up. They put me under a tree to wait for you, and you came, in a full white skirt and white sandals, your hair tied back in a red scarf. I can see you yet."

Her mother laughed. "Sounds like a pretty exaggerated picture."

Kate nodded. "I was little. You were big."

"You loved the county fair. You were wild about the carnivals." They looked down at the little park. "Magic, isn't it?" her mother said.

"Maybe we could go see it," said Kate. "I'll ask the doctor."

They walked across a pedestrian footbridge spanning the highway. Kate had bundled her mother into a winter coat and gloves despite the sunny weather. The day was sharp, nearly still, holding its bright air like illusion. Kate tasted the brittle water of her breath, felt for the cool handrail and thin steel of the webbed fencing. Cars moved steadily under the bridge. Beyond a muted roar of motors the park spread green and wooded, its limits clearly visible.

Kate's mother had combed her hair and put on lipstick. Her mouth was defined and brilliant; she linked arms with Kate like an escort. "I was afraid they'd tell us no," she said. "I was ready to run away!"

"I promised I wouldn't let you. And we only have ten minutes, long enough for the Ferris wheel." Kate grinned.

"I haven't ridden one in years. I wonder if I still know how."

"Of course you do. Ferris wheels are genetic knowledge."

"All right, whatever you say." She smiled. "We'll just hold on."

They drew closer and walked quickly through the sounds of the highway. When they reached the grass it was ankle-high and thick, longer and more ragged than it appeared from a distance. The Ferris wheel sat squarely near a grove of swaying elms, squat and laboring, taller than trees. Its neon lights still burned, pale in the sun, spiraling from inside like an imagined bloom. The naked elms surrounded it, their topmost branches tapping. Steel ribs of the machine were graceful and slightly rusted, squeaking faintly above a tinkling music. Only a few people were riding.

"Looks a little rickety," Kate said.

"Oh, don't worry," said her mother.

Kate tried to buy tickets but the ride was free. The old man running the motor wore an engineer's cap and patched overalls. He stopped the wheel and led them on a short ramp to an open car. It dipped gently, padded with black cushions. An orderly and his children rode in the car above. Kate saw their dangling feet, the girls' dusty sandals and gray socks beside their father's shoes and the hem of his white pants. The youngest one swung her feet absently, so it seemed the breeze blew her legs like fabric hung on a line.

Kate looked at her mother. "Are you ready for the big sky?" They laughed. Beyond them the river moved lazily. Houses on the opposite bank seemed empty, but a few rowboats bobbed at the docks. The surface of the water lapped and reflected clouds, and as Kate watched, searching for a definition of line, the Ferris wheel jerked into motion. The car rocked. They looked into the distance and Kate caught her mother's hand as they ascended.

Far away the hospital rose up white and glistening, its windows catching the glint of the sun. Directly below, the park was nearly deserted. There were a few cars in the parking lot and several dogs chasing each other across the grass. Two or three lone women held children on the teeter-totters and a wind was coming up. The forlorn swings moved on their chains. Kate had a vision of the park at night, totally empty, wind weaving heavily through the trees and children's playthings like a great black fish about to surface. She felt a chill on her arms. The light had gone darker, quietly, like a minor chord.

"Mom," Kate said, "it's going to storm." Her own voice seemed distant, the sound strained through layers of screen or gauze.

"No," said her mother, "it's going to pass over." She moved her hand to Kate's knee and touched the cloth of her daughter's skirt.

Kate gripped the metal bar at their waists and looked straight ahead. They were rising again and she felt she would scream. She tried to breathe rhythmically, steadily. She felt the immense weight of the air as they moved through it.

They came almost to the top and stopped. The little car swayed back and forth.

"You're sick, aren't you," her mother said.

Kate shook her head. Below them the grass seemed to glitter coldly, like a sea. Kate sat wordless, feeling the touch of her mother's hand. The hand moved away and Kate felt the absence of the warmth.

They looked at each other levelly.

"I know all about it," her mother said, "I know what you haven't told me."

The sky circled around them, a sure gray movement. Kate swallowed calmly and let their gaze grow endless. She saw herself in her mother's wide brown eyes and felt she was falling slowly into them.

1979

▪   ▪   ▪

MARY ROBISON

COACH

The August two-a-day practice sessions were sixty-seven days away, Coach calculated. He was drying breakfast dishes. He swabbed a coffee cup and made himself listen to his wife, who was across the kitchen, sponging the stove's burner coils.

"I know I'm no Rembrandt," Sherry said, "but I have so damn much fun trying, and this little studio—this room—we can afford. I could get out of your way by going there and get you and Daphne out of my way. No offense."

"I'm thinking," Coach said.

His wife coasted from appliance to appliance. She swiped the face of the oven clock with her sponge. "You're thinking too slow. Your reporter's coming at nine and it's way after eight now. Should I give them a deposit on the studio or not? Yes or no?"

Coach was staring at the sink, at a thread of water that came from one of the taps. He thought of the lake place where they used to go in North Carolina. He saw green water being thickly sliced by a power boat; the boat towing Sherry, who was blonde and laughing on her skis, her rounded back strong, her suit shining red.

"Of course, of course, give them the money," he said.

Their daughter, Daphne, wandered into the kitchen. She was dark-haired, lazy-looking, fifteen. Her eyes were lost behind bangs. She drew open the enormous door of the refrigerator.

"Don't hang, Daphne, you'll unhinge things," her mother said. "What are you after?"

"Food mainly," Daphne said.

Sherry went away, to the little sun patio off the kitchen. Coach pushed the glass door sideways after her and it smacked shut.

"Eat and run," he said to Daphne. "I've got a reporter coming in

466

short order. Get dressed." He spoke firmly but in the smaller voice he always used for his child.

"Yes, sir," Daphne said. She broke into the freezer compartment and ducked to let its gate pass over head. "Looks bad. Nothing in here but Eggos."

"I ate Eggos. Just hustle up," Coach said.

"Can I be here for this guy?" Daphne asked.

"Who guy? The reporter? Nuh-uh. He's just from the college, Daph. Coming to see if the new freshman coach has three heads or just two."

Daphne was nodding at the food jars racked on the wide refrigerator door. "Hey, lookit," she said. She blew a breath in front of the freezer compartment and made a short jet of mist.

Coach remembered a fall night, a Friday-game night, long ago, when he had put Daphne on the playing field. It was during the ceremonies before his unbeaten squad had taken on Ignatius South High School. Parents' Night. He had laced shoulder pads on Daphne and draped the trainer's gag jersey—number 1/2—over her, and balanced Tim-somebody's helmet on her eight-year-old head. She was lost in the getup, a small pile of equipment out on the fifty-yard line. She had applauded when the loudspeaker announced her name, when the p.a. voice, garbled by amplification and echo, had rung out, "Daughter of our coach, Harry Noonan, and his wife—number one-half, Daphne Noonan!" She had stood in the bath of floodlights, shaking as the players and their folks strolled by—the players grim in their war gear, the parents tiny and apologetic-seeming in civilian clothes. The co-captain of the team, awesome in his pads and cleats and steaming from warm-up running, had palmed Daphne's big helmet and twisted it sideways. From behind, from the home stands, Coach had heard, "Haaa!" as Daphne turned circles of happy confusion, trying to right the helmet. Through the ear hole her left eye had twinkled, Coach remembered. He had heard, "God, that's funny," and "Coach's kid."

On the sun porch now, his wife was doing a set of tennis exercises. She was between Coach and the morning sun, framed by the glass doors. He could see through the careless weave of her caftan, enough to make out the white flesh left by her swimsuit.

"I knew you wouldn't let me," Daphne said. She had poured a glass of chocolate milk. She pulled open a chilled banana. "I bet Mom gets to be here."

"Daph, this isn't a big deal. We've been through it all before," Coach said.

"Not for a college paper," Daphne said. "Wait a minute, I'll be right back." She left the kitchen.

"I'll hold my breath and count the heartbeats," Coach said to the space she had left behind.

They were new to the little town, new to Pennsylvania. Coach was assuming charge of the freshman squad, in a league where freshmen weren't eligible for the varsity. He had taken the job, not sure if it was a step up for him or a serious misstep. The money was so-so. But he wanted the college setting for his family—especially for Daphne. She had been seeming to lose interest in the small celebrity they achieved in high-school towns. She had acted bored at the Noonans' Sunday spaghetti dinners for standout players. She had stopped fetching plates of food for the boys, who were too game-sore to get their own. She had even stopped wearing the charm bracelet her parents had put together for her—a silver bracelet with a tiny megaphone, the numerals 68—a league championship year—and, of course, a miniature football.

Coach took a seat at the kitchen table. He ate grapes from a bowl. He spilled bottled wheat germ into his palm. On the table were four chunky ring binders, their black leatherette covers printed with the college seal—which still looked strange to him. These were his playbooks, and he was having trouble getting the play tactics into his head.

"Will you turn off the radio?" he yelled.

The bleat from Daphne's upstairs bedroom ceased. A minute later she came down and into the kitchen. She had a cardboard folder and some textbooks with her. "Later on, would you look at this stuff and help me? Can you do these?" she asked Coach.

He glanced over one of her papers. It was penciled with algebra equations, smutty with erasures and scribbled-out parts. "I'd have to see the book, but no. Not now, not later. I don't want to and I don't have time."

"That's just great," Daphne said.

"Your mother and I got our Algebra homework done already, Daph. We turned ours in," Coach said. "This was in nineteen fifty-six."

"Mom!" Daphne said, pushing aside the glass door.

"Forget it," Sherry said.

2

Toby, the boy sent from *The Rooter* to interview Coach, was unshaven and bleary-eyed. He wore a rumpled cerise polo shirt and faded Levi's. He asked few questions, dragging his words. Now and then he grumbled of a hangover and no sleep. He yawned during Coach's answers. He took no notes.

"You're getting this now?" Coach said.

"Oh, yeah, it's writing itself, I'm such a pro," Toby said, and Coach wasn't certain if the boy was kidding.

"So, you've been here just a little while. Lucky you," Toby said. "Less than a month?"

"Is that like a question? It seems less than less than a month—less than a week—a day and a half," Coach said.

For the interview, he had put on white sports slacks and a maroon pullover with a gold collar—the college's colors. The pullover he had bought at Campus World. The clothes had a snug fit that flattered Coach and showed off his flat stomach and heavy biceps.

He and Toby were on either end of the sofa in the living room of the house, a wooden two-story Coach had found and would be paying off for decades, he was sure.

Toby said, "Well, believe it or not, I've got enough for a couple sticks, which is shoptalk among we press men for two columns. If you're going to be home tomorrow, there's a girl who'll come and take your picture—Marcia. She's a drag, I warn you."

"One thing about this town, there aren't any damn sidewalks, and the cars don't give you much room if you're jogging," Coach said, standing up.

"Hey, tell me about it. When I'm hitching, I wear an orange poncho and carry a red flag and paint a big X on my back. Of course, I'm probably just making a better target," the reporter said.

"I jog down at the track now. It's a great facility, comparable to a Big Ten's. I like the layout," Coach said.

"Okay, but the interview's over," Toby said.

"Well, I came from high schools, remember. In Indiana and Ohio—good schools with good budgets, mind you, but high schools, nonetheless."

"Yeah, I got where you're coming from," Toby said.

"Did you need to know what courses I'll be handling? Fall quarter, they've got me lined up for two things: The Atlantic World is the first one, and Colloquium on European Industrial Development, I think it is. Before, I always taught World History. P.O.D.,[1] once or twice."

"That three-eighty-one you're going to teach is a tit course, in case nobody's informed you. It's what we call lunch," Toby said.

"It's, in nature, a refresher class," Coach said.

"Yeah, or out of nature," Toby said.

Daphne came from the long hall steps into the living room. Her dark hair was brushed and lifting with static. Her eyes seemed to Coach larger than usual, and a little sooty around the lashes.

1. Problems of Democracy.

"You're just leaving, aren't you, buster?" Coach said to her.

"Retrieving a pencil," Daphne said.

"Is your name really Buster?" Toby asked.

"Get your pencil and scoot. This is Toby here. Toby, this is my daughter, Daphne," Coach said.

"Nice to meet you," Daphne said. She slipped into a deep chair at the far corner of the long living room.

"Can she hear us over in that country?" Toby said. "Do you read me?" he shouted.

Daphne smiled. Coach saw bangs and her very white teeth.

"Come on, Daph, hit the trail," he said.

"I've got a joke for her first," Toby said. "What's green and moves very fast?"

"Frog in a blender," Daphne said. "Dad? Some friends invited me to go swimming with them at the Natatorium. May I?"

"You've got to see the Nat. It's the best thing," Toby said.

"What about your class, though? She's in makeup school here, Toby, catching up on some algebra that didn't take the first time around."

Toby wrinkled his nose at Daphne. "At first, I thought you meant *makeup* school, like lipstick and rouge."

"I wish," Daphne said.

She slipped her left foot from her leather sandal and casually stroked the toes.

"She's a nut for swimming," Coach said.

"You'll be so bored here. Most nights, your options are either ordering a pizza or slashing your wrists," Toby told Daphne.

"Oh," she said, rolling her chin on her shoulder in a rather seductive way.

"Take it from Toby," he said.

Coach let Toby through the front door, and watched until he was down the street.

"He was nice," Daphne said.

"Aw, Daph. That's what you say about everybody. There's a lot better things you could say—more on-the-beam things."

"I guess you're mad," she said.

Coach went to the kitchen, to sit down with his playbooks again. Daphne came after him.

"Aren't you?" she said.

"I guess you thought he was cute," Coach said. He flapped through some mimeographed pages, turning them on the notebook's silver rings. "I don't mean to shock you about it, but you'd be wasting your time there, Daph. You'd be trying to start a fire with a wet match."

Daphne stared at her father. "That's sick!" she said.

"I'm not criticizing him for it. I'm just telling you," Coach said.

3

"This is completely wrong," Coach said sadly. He read further. "Oh, no," he said. He drowned the newspaper in his bath water and slogged the pages over into a corner by the commode.

His wife handed him a dry edition, one of the ten or twelve *Rooters* Daphne had brought home.

Sherry was parallel to Coach on the edge of the tub, sitting with her back braced against the wall. "Oh, cheer up," she said. "Nobody reads a free newspaper."

Coach quartered the dry *Rooter* into a package around Toby's article. "Well, I wasn't head coach at Elmgrove, and I sure wasn't Phi Beta Kappa. And look at this picture," Coach said.

"What's wrong with it?" Sherry said.

"Where did he get that you were at Mt. Holyoke? And I didn't bitch about the sidewalks this much."

"You didn't?" Sherry said. "That's almost too bad. I thought that was the best part of the article."

Coach slunk farther into the warm water until it crowded his chin. He kept the newspaper aloft. "Oh, come on, give me some credit here! Don't they have any supervision over in Journalism? I don't see how he could get away with this shit. It's an unbelievably sloppy job."

"It's just a dinky article in a handout paper, Coach. What do you care? It wouldn't matter if he said we were a bright-green family with scales," Sherry said.

"He didn't think of that or he would have. This breaks my heart," Coach said.

"Daph liked it," Sherry said.

Coach wearily chopped bath water with the side of his hand and threw a splash at the soap recess in the tiled wall. "I tell you, I'm going to be spending my whole first year here explaining how none of it's true."

"What difference does true make?" Sherry said.

4

Coach was seated awkwardly on an iron stool at a white table on the patio of the Dairy Frost. Daphne was across from him, fighting the early evening heat for her mocha-fudge cone. She tilted her head at the cone, lapping at it.

"You aren't saying anything," Coach said.

"Wait," Daphne said.

She worked on the cone.

"I've been waiting."

"If you two want to separate, it's none of my business," she said.

They were facing the busy parking lot when a new Pontiac turned in off the highway, glided easily onto the gravel, took a parking slot close by. In the driver's seat was a boy with built-up shoulders—a boy who looked very familiar to Coach. In back was a couple in their fifties—the boy's parents, Coach thought—both talking at once.

"Have I been spilling all this breath for nothing? *Not* a separation," Coach said. "Not anything like it."

"All right, not," Daphne said. She stopped in her attack on the cone long enough to watch the Pontiac boy step out. Dark brown ice cream streamed between her knuckles and down the inside of her wrist.

"You're losing it, honey," Coach said.

Daphne dabbed around the cone and her hand, making repairs.

"Hell, *real* trouble your father wouldn't tell you about at a *Dairy Frost.* This apartment your mom found is like an office or something. A studio for her to go to and get away every now and then. That kid's in my backfield. What the *hell's* his name?"

They watched as the young man took orders from his parents, then went inside the Dairy Frost. He looked both wider and taller than the other patrons, out of their scale. His rump and haunches were thick with muscle. His neck was fat but tight.

"Bobby Stark!" Coach said, and smiled very quickly at the parents in the Pontiac. He turned back to his daughter.

"She wants to get away from us," Daphne said.

"Definitely not. She gave me a list, is how this whole thing started. She's got stuff she wants to do, and you with your school problems and me with the team—we're too much for her, see? She could spend her entire day on us, if you think about it, and never have one second for herself. If you think about it fairly, Daphne, you'll agree."

Daphne seemed to consider. She was focused on the inside of the Dairy Frost building, and for a while she kept still.

"That guy looks dumb. One of the truly dumb," she said.

"My halfback? He's not. He was his class salutatorian," Coach said.

"He doesn't know *you.*"

"Just embarrassed," Coach said. "Can we stick to the point, Daph? And quit rocking the boat. Look what you're doing." Daphne's arm was on the table and she was violently swinging her legs under her chair.

She made a sigh and marched over to a trash can to deposit her slumping cone. Then she washed up at the children's drinking fountain and rejoined Coach, who had finished his Brown Cow but had kept the plastic spoon in his mouth.

"What was on this list of Mom's?" Daphne asked.

"Adult stuff," Coach said.

"Just give me an example."

Coach removed the plastic spoon and cracked it in half.

"Your mother's list is for five years. In that time, she wants to be speaking French regularly. She wants to follow up on her printmaking."

"This is adult stuff?" Daphne said.

Coach raised a hand to Bobby Stark. Stark had three malt cups in a cardboard carrier and he was moving toward the parking lot.

"Hey, those all for you?" Coach called out.

"I got a month to get fat, Coach. You'll have five months to beat it off me," the boy called back.

The people at some of the tables around Coach's lit up with grins. Bobby Stark's parents were grinning.

"Every hit of that junk takes a second off your time in the forty—just remember that!" Coach shouted.

Stark wagged his head ruefully, his cheeks blushing. He pretended to hide the malts behind his arm.

"Duh," Daphne said in a hoarse voice. "Which way to the door, Coach?"

"He can hear you," Coach said.

"Duh, kin I have a candy bar, Coach?" she rasped.

They faced Stark, who smiled a little crookedly at Daphne, and threw her a wink so dazzling, she went silent.

5

Coach was in the basement laundry room, both arms busy hugging a bundle of jogging clothes. He was waiting on the washer, waiting for Sherry to unload her clothes.

"The Cowboys are soaking their players in a sense-deprivation tub of warm saltwater," she said.

"We know," Coach said.

"If Dallas is doing it, I just thought you might want to consider it."

"We have. Hustle up a little with your stuff, will you?" Coach said.

"It's like my apartment," Sherry said. "A place apart."

Coach cut her off. "Don't go on about how much you love your apartment."

"I wasn't going to," Sherry said. She slung her wet slacks and blouses into the dryer.

Coach had just two weeks before the start of the heavy practices. His team would have him then, he knew, almost straight through the Christmas holidays.

"I like that," Coach said. "A place apart."

A half hour later, Coach and his wife were on the side patio. They could hear the tick of the clothes dryer downstairs. Sherry had changed into a halter top. She was taking sun on her back, adding to her tan.

"You know what's odd?" she said. "Daphne's popularity here. I don't mean it's odd."

"She's always done terrific with people, always gone over well," Coach said.

"*Your* people, though. These are hers," Sherry said. "Like that reporter."

"Yeah, they're like sisters," Coach said.

6

It was a week before the two-a-day practice sessions would begin. The sky was colorless and glazed, like milk glass. When Coach looked at the sun, his eyes ached, his head screamed.

He had run some wind sprints on the stadium field, and now he was doing an easy lap. A stopwatch on a noose of ribbon swung against his chest. He cut through the goalposts and trotted for the sidelines, for the twenty, where he had dumped his clipboard and a towel.

Someone called to him.

Blond Bobby Stark came out from under the stands. His football shoes were laced together and draped around his neck. He wore a midriff-cut T-shirt and shorts. He walked gingerly in white wool socks.

"Did everybody go? Or am I the first one here?" he called to Coach.

" 'Bout a half hour," Coach said, heaving.

Stark sat down to untangle his shoes, and Coach, sweating, stood over him.

Coach spat. He folded his arms in a way that pushed out his muscles. He sniffed, twisting his whole nose and mouth to the left. He said, "You know Stark, you were salutatorian for your class."

"High school," the boy said. He grinned up at Coach, an eye pinched against the glare.

"That counts, believe me. Maybe we can use you to help some of our slower players along—some of the linemen, maybe I'm thinking."

"What do you mean—tutor?" Stark said.

"Naw. Teach them to eat without biting off their fingers. How to tie a necktie. Some of your style," Coach said, and Stark bobbed his head.

Stark settled the fit of his right shoe. He said, "But there aren't any really dumb ones on our squad, because they'd just get flunked out. Recruiters won't touch them in this league. There wouldn't be any percentage in it."

"Then I'm greatly relieved," Coach said.

He planted his feet along a furrow of lime-eaten grass. He faced the open end of the stadium, where the enormous library building stood shimmering and uncertain behind sheets of heat that rose from the parking area.

Stark stood up and studied his shoes as he began jogging in place. He danced twenty yards down the field; loped back.

Other players were arriving for the informal session. Coach meant to time them in the mile, and in some dashes.

Stark looked jittery. He walked in semicircles, crowding Coach.

"What're you worried about?" Coach asked him. "Girl problems you got? You pull a muscle already?"

Stark glanced quickly around them. He said, "I live all my life two doors down from Coach Burton's house. My mom and Burton's wife are best friends, so I always know what's going on."

Burton had been the head coach of the varsity team for over a decade.

"You probably know about it already, anyway," Stark said. "Do you?"

"What the hell are you talking about, Stark?"

"You don't know? Typical. Burton's leaving, see? Like at the end of this year. His wife wants him out real bad, and the alumni want him out because they're tired of losing seasons. So what I heard was you were brought in because of it. And if we do okay this season, like you'll be varsity coach next year."

"That's conjecture," Coach said. But he was excited.

It was three o'clock, still hot. Coach was moving along a sidewalk with Bobby Stark, who was balanced on a racing bicycle, moving just enough to keep the machine upright.

"Three things," Coach said. "I've seen all the game films from last year, and I came here personally and witnessed the Tech game. No one lost because of the coaching. A coach can work miracles with a good team, but he is *helpless* if his personnel don't want it bad enough. That's the worst part about running a team—you can't climb down into your people's hearts and change them."

Some college girls in a large expensive car went past. They shrieked and whistled at Bobby Stark.

"Lifeguards at the pool," he explained.

"I don't know if Burton's leaving or not," Coach continued. "But if his wife wants him to go, he probably will. If you're ever thinking about a career in coaching someday, Bob, think about that. Your family's either with you or you've had it. And remember, whether you stay someplace or not depends completely on a bunch of *kids*. I swear, I'd give up a leg for a chance to get in a game myself—just one play, with what I know now."

Stark nodded. They went on a block, and he said, "I turn off here. You going to tell your daughter about the job?"

"My daughter?" Coach said, and smiled.

7

No one was home. A magnet under a plastic ladybug held a note to the face of the refrigerator. The note read:

Harry, I'm at my place. Daph's with Toby K. somewhere, fooling around. Be good now, Sherry Baby.

"Dope," Coach said.

He felt very good.

He took a beer upstairs and drank it while he showered. He cinched on a pair of sweat pants and, wearing only these, went back down and fetched another beer.

He watched some of a baseball game on cable. He thought over his conversation with Bobby Stark. "Boy, is that true!" Coach said, and then was not at all sure why he had said it.

He frowned, remembering that in his second year of college, the only year he had been on the varsity team, he had proved an indifferent player.

"Not now," he whispered. "Not anymore."

He squashed the shape out of his beer can and stood it on top of the television.

There was a thump over his head. The ceiling creaked.

"Someone came home while I was in the shower," he said to himself, and ran his hand over his belly, feeling for signs of bloat from the beer.

He took the stairs in three leaps, strode into the master bedroom, calling, "Sherry?"

The dark figure in the room surprised Coach.

He yelled, "Hey!"

Daphne was dancing in front of the full-length mirror. She had improvised a look—sweeping her hair over her right ear, and stretching the neck of her shirt until her right shoulder was bared. A thing by the Commodores shrieked from her transistor.

"Nothing," she said.

"You're not home. Aren't you with whoosis? You're supposed to be out. You are *beet* red," Coach said.

Daphne lowered her head and squared her shirt, which bagged around her small torso. "Okay, Dad," she said.

"No, but how did your audience like the show? I bet they loved it," Coach said. He smiled at himself in the mirror. "I'm just kidding you, Daph. You looked great."

"Come *on*, Dad," she said, and tried to pass.

Coach chimed in with the radio. He shuffled his feet. "Hey, Daph, you know what time it is?" he said.

"Let me out, please," Daphne said.

"It's monkey time" Coach did a jerky turn, keeping in the way of the exit door. "Do the shing-a-ling. Do the Daphne." He rolled his shoulder vampishly. He kissed his own hand. He sang along.

"Thanks a lot," Daphne said. She gave up on trying to get around him. She leaned over and snapped off her radio. "You've got to use a mirror so you don't look stupid," she said. "Everybody does."

"I was only kidding. Seriously. I know dancing is important," Coach said.

"May I go now? I've got algebra." Daphne brought her hair from behind her ear.

"Before that, you have to hear the news. Here's a news bulletin, flash extra."

"You're drunk. You and Mom are going to live in different cities," Daphne said. "Somebody shot somebody."

"No, this is good news. I'm going to be coach here of the varsity. Me." Coach pointed to his chest.

"Now let me out, please," Daphne said.

Coach let her pass. He followed her down the narrow hallway to her bedroom.

"More money," he said. "I'll even be on TV. I'll have my own show on Sundays. And I'll get written up in the press all the time. By *real* reporters. Hey! Why am I yelling at wood, here?"

8

Coach was drunk at the kitchen table. He was enjoying the largeness of the room, and he was making out a roster for his dream team. He had put the best kids from his fifteen years of coaching in the positions they had played for him. He was puzzling over the tight-end spot. "Jim Wyekoff or Jerry Kinney?" he said aloud. He penciled "Kinney" into his diagram.

He heard Daphne on the stairs. It occurred to him to clear the beer cans from the table. Instead, he snapped open a fresh can. "Daphne?" he called.

"Wait a second. What?" she said from the living room.

"Just wondered who else was alive besides me," Coach said. "Your mom's still not home."

Daphne entered the kitchen.

"You're sorry you were rude before? That's perfectly okay, honey, just forget it. All right, Father, but I really am ashamed of myself anyway," Coach said.

"You guzzled all those?" Daphne said.

"Hold still. What've you got on?" Coach asked her. He hauled his chair around so that he could see his daughter.

"Two, four, five," Daphne said, counting the cans.

She was wearing one of the fan shirts that Coach had seen on a few summer coeds. On the front, against a maroon field, in gold, was GO. Across the back was CRIFFINS.

"Now you're talking," Coach said.

"It was free. This guy I met—well, these two guys, really—who work at Campus World, they gave it to me. It's dumb, but I want you to see I care. I do care. Not just for you, but because I want to stay here. Do you think we can maybe? Do your people look any good this year?"

"Winners," Coach said.

"Yeah," Daphne said.

Coach skidded his chair forward. "Have a beer," he said "Sit down here and let me show you on paper the material they've given me to work with. Then maybe you'll be a believer. Now these guys are fast and big for once. I'm not overestimating them, either. I've seen what I've seen," Coach said.

A car crept into the drive, and then its engine noise filled the garage. Coach and Daphne were quiet until Sherry bustled down the short hall that connected the garage to the kitchen.

"Really late. Sorry, sorry," she said.

"It's a party in here, I warn you," Coach said.

"So I noticed." Sherry had a grocery sack, but it was almost empty. There were bright streaks of paint on her brown arms.

Daphne plucked a bag of Oreo cookies from the groceries.

"Shoot me one of those," Coach said.

"Is there any beer left for me?" Sherry said. "I want to drown my disappointment. I can't paint!"

"You *can* paint," Coach said.

"Let's face it," Sherry said. "An artist? The wife of a coach?"

1983

■   ■   ■

A M Y   T A N

RULES OF THE GAME

I was six when my mother taught me the art of invisible strength. It was a strategy for winning arguments, respect from others, and eventually, though neither of us knew it at the time, chess games.

"Bite back your tongue," scolded my mother when I cried loudly, yanking her hand toward the store that sold bags of salted plums. At home, she said, "Wise guy, he not go against wind. In Chinese we say, Come from South, blow with wind—poom!—North will follow. Strongest wind cannot be seen."

The next week I bit back my tongue as we entered the store with the forbidden candies. When my mother finished her shopping, she quietly plucked a small bag of plums from the rack and put it on the counter with the rest of the items.

My mother imparted her daily truths so she could help my older brothers and me rise above our circumstances. We lived in San Francisco's Chinatown. Like most of the other Chinese children who played in the back alleys of restaurants and curio shops, I didn't think we were poor. My bowl was always full, three five-course meals every day, beginning with a soup of mysterious things I didn't want to know the names of.

We lived on Waverly Place, in a warm, clean, two-bedroom flat that sat above a small Chinese bakery specializing in steamed pastries and dim sum. In the early morning, when the alley was still quiet, I could smell fragrant red beans as they were cooked down to a pasty sweetness. By daybreak, our flat was heavy with the odor of fried sesame balls and sweet curried chicken crescents. From my bed, I would listen as my father got ready for work, then locked the door behind him, one-two-three clicks.

At the end of our two-block alley was a small sandlot playground with swings and slides well-shined down the middle with use. The play area was bordered by wood-slat benches where old-country people sat cracking roasted watermelon seeds with their golden teeth and scattering the husks to an impatient gathering of gurgling pigeons. The best playground, however, was the dark alley itself. It was crammed with daily mysteries and adventures. My brothers and I would peer into the medicinal herb shop, watching old Li dole out onto a stiff sheet of white paper the right amount of insect shells, saffron-colored seeds, and pungent leaves for his ailing customers. It was said that he once cured a woman dying of an ancestral curse that had eluded the best of American doctors. Next to the pharmacy was a printer who specialized in gold-embossed wedding invitations and festive red banners.

Farther down the street was Ping Yuen Fish Market. The front window displayed a tank crowded with doomed fish and turtles struggling to gain footing on the slimy green-tiled sides. A hand-written sign informed tourists, "Within this store, is all for food, not for pet." Inside, the butchers with their bloodstained white smocks deftly gutted the fish while customers cried out their orders and shouted, "Give me your freshest," to which the butchers always protested, "All are freshest." On less crowded market days, we would inspect the crates of live frogs and crabs which we were warned not to poke, boxes of dried cuttlefish, and row upon row of iced prawns, squid, and slippery fish. The sanddabs made me shiver each time; their eyes lay on one flattened side and reminded me of my mother's story of a careless girl who ran into a crowded street and was crushed by a cab. "Was smash flat," reported my mother.

At the corner of the alley was Hong Sing's, a four-table café with a recessed stairwell in front that led to a door marked "Tradesmen." My brothers and I believed the bad people emerged from this door at night. Tourists never went to Hong Sing's, since the menu was printed only in Chinese. A Caucasian man with a big camera once posed me and my playmates in front of the restaurant. He had us move to the side of the picture window so the photo would capture the roasted duck with its head dangling from a juice-covered rope. After he took the picture, I told him he should go into Hong Sing's and eat dinner. When he smiled and asked me what they served, I shouted, "Guts and duck's feet and octopus gizzards!" Then I ran off with my friends, shrieking with laughter as we scampered across the alley and hid in the entryway grotto of the China Gem Company, my heart pounding with hope that he would chase us.

My mother named me after the street that we lived on: Waverly Place Jong, my official name for important American documents. But my family called me Meimei, "Little Sister." I was the youngest, the only daughter. Each morning before school, my mother would twist and yank on my thick black hair until she had formed two tightly wound pigtails. One day, as she struggled to weave a hard-toothed comb through my disobedient hair, I had a sly thought.

I asked her, "Ma, what is Chinese torture?" My mother shook her head. A bobby pin was wedged between her lips. She wetted her palm and smoothed the hair above my ear, then pushed the pin in so that it nicked sharply against my scalp.

"Who say this word?" she asked without a trace of knowing how wicked I was being. I shrugged my shoulders and said, "Some boy in my class said Chinese people do Chinese torture."

"Chinese people do many things," she said simply. "Chinese people do business, do medicine, do painting. Not lazy like American people. We do torture. Best torture."

My older brother Vincent was the one who actually got the chess set. We had gone to the annual Christmas party held at the First Chinese Baptist Church at the end of the alley. The missionary ladies had put together a Santa bag of gifts donated by members of another church. None of the gifts had names on them. There were separate sacks for boys and girls of different ages.

One of the Chinese parishioners had donned a Santa Claus costume and a stiff paper beard with cotton balls glued to it. I think the only children who thought he was the real thing were too young to know that Santa Claus was not Chinese. When my turn came up, the Santa man asked me how old I was. I thought it was a trick question; I was seven according to the American formula and eight by the Chinese calendar. I said I was born on March 17, 1951. That seemed to satisfy him. He then solemnly asked if I had been a very, very good girl this year and did I believe in Jesus Christ and obey my parents. I knew the only answer to that. I nodded back with equal solemnity.

Having watched the older children opening their gifts, I already knew that the big gifts were not necessarily the nicest ones. One girl my age got a large coloring book of biblical characters, while a less greedy girl who selected a smaller box received a glass vial of lavender toilet water. The sound of the box was also important. A ten-year-old boy had chosen a box that jangled when he shook it. It was a tin globe of the world with a slit for inserting money. He must have thought it was full of dimes and nickels, because when he saw that it had just ten pennies, his face fell with such undisguised disappointment that his mother slapped the side of his head and led him out of the church hall, apologizing to the crowd for her son who had such bad manners he couldn't appreciate such a fine gift.

As I peered into the sack, I quickly fingered the remaining presents, testing their weight, imagining what they contained. I chose a heavy compact one that was wrapped in shiny silver foil and a red satin ribbon. It was a twelve-pack of Life Savers and I spent the rest of the party arranging and rearranging the candy tubes in the order of my favorites. My brother Winston chose wisely as well. His present turned out to be a box of intricate plastic parts; the instructions on the box proclaimed that when they were properly assembled he would have an authentic miniature replica of a World War II submarine.

Vincent got the chess set, which would have been a very decent present to get at a church Christmas party, except it was obviously used and, as we discovered later, it was missing a black pawn and a white knight. My mother graciously thanked the unknown benefactor, saying, "Too good. Cost too much." At which point, an old lady with fine white, wispy hair nodded toward our family and said with a whistling whisper, "Merry, merry Christmas."

When we got home, my mother told Vincent to throw the chess set away. "She not want it. We not want it." she said, tossing her head stiffly to the side with a tight, proud smile. My brothers had deaf ears. They were already lining up the chess pieces and reading from the dog-eared instruction book.

I watched Vincent and Winston play during Christmas week. The chessboard seemed to hold elaborate secrets waiting to be untangled. The chessmen were more powerful than old Li's magic herbs that cured ancestral curses. And my brothers wore such serious faces that I was sure something was at stake that was greater than avoiding the tradesmen's door to Hong Sing's.

"Let me! Let me!" I begged between games when one brother or the other would sit back with a deep sigh of relief and victory, the other annoyed, unable to let go of the outcome. Vincent at first refused to let me play, but when I offered my Life Savers as replacements for the buttons that filled in for the missing pieces, he relented. He chose the flavors: wild cherry for the black pawn and peppermint for the white knight. Winner could eat both.

As our mother sprinkled flour and rolled out small doughy circles for the steamed dumplings that would be our dinner that night, Vincent explained the rules, pointing to each piece. "You have sixteen pieces and so do I. One king and queen, two bishops, two knights, two castles, and eight pawns. The pawns can only move forward one step, except on the first move. Then they can move two. But they can only take men by moving crossways like this, except in the beginning, when you can move ahead and take another pawn."

"Why?" I asked as I moved my pawn. "Why can't they move more steps?"

"Because they're pawns," he said.

"But why do they go crossways to take other men? Why aren't there any women and children?"

"Why is the sky blue? Why must you always ask stupid questions?" asked Vincent. "This is a game. These are the rules. I didn't make them up. See. Here in the book." He jabbed a page with a pawn in his hand. "Pawn. P-A-W-N. Pawn. Read it yourself."

My mother patted the flour off her hands. "Let me see book," she said quietly. She scanned the pages quickly, not reading the foreign English symbols, seeming to search deliberately for nothing in particular.

"This American rules," she concluded at last. "Every time people come out from foreign country, must know rules. You not know, judge say, Too bad, go back. They not telling you why so you can use their way go forward. They say, Don't know why, you find out yourself. But they knowing all the time. Better you take it, find out why yourself." She tossed her head back with a satisfied smile.

I found out about all the whys later. I read the rules and looked up all the big words in a dictionary. I borrowed books from the Chinatown library. I studied each chess piece, trying to absorb the power each contained.

I learned about opening moves and why it's important to control the center early on; the shortest distance between two points is straight down the middle. I learned about the middle game and why tactics between two adversaries are like clashing ideas; the one who plays better has the clearest plans for both attacking and getting out of traps. I learned why it is essential in the endgame to have foresight, a mathematical understanding of all possible moves, and patience; all weaknesses and advantages become evident to a strong adversary and are obscured to a tiring opponent. I discovered that for the whole game one must gather invisible strengths and see the endgame before the game begins.

I also found out why I should never reveal "why" to others. A little knowledge withheld is a great advantage one should store for future use. That is the power of chess. It is a game of secrets in which one must show and never tell.

I loved the secrets I found within the sixty-four black and white squares. I carefully drew a handmade chessboard and pinned it to the wall next to my bed, where I would stare for hours at imaginary battles. Soon I no longer lost any games or Life Savers, but I lost my adversaries. Winston and Vincent decided they were more interested in roaming the streets after school in their Hopalong Cassidy cowboy hats.

On a cold spring afternoon, while walking home from school, I detoured through the playground at the end of our alley. I saw a group of old men, two seated across a folding table playing a game of chess, others smoking pipes, eating peanuts, and watching. I ran home and grabbed Vincent's chess set, which was bound in a cardboard box with rubber bands. I also carefully selected two prized rolls of Life Savers. I came back to the park and approached a man who was observing the game.

"Want to play?" I asked him. His face widened with surprise and he grinned as he looked at the box under my arm.

"Little sister, been a long time since I play with dolls," he said, smiling benevolently. I quickly put the box down next to him on the bench and displayed my retort.

Lau Po, as he allowed me to call him, turned out to be a much better player than my brothers. I lost many games and many Life Savers. But over the weeks, with each diminishing roll of candies, I added new secrets. Lau Po gave me the names. The Double Attack from the East and West Shores. Throwing Stones on the Drowning Man. The Sudden Meeting of the Clan. The Surprise from the Sleeping Guard. The Humble Servant Who Kills the King. Sand in the Eyes of Advancing Forces. A Double Killing Without Blood.

There were also the fine points of chess etiquette. Keep captured men in neat rows, as well-tended prisoners. Never announce "Check" with vanity, lest someone with an unseen sword slit your throat. Never hurl pieces into the sandbox after you have lost a game, because then you must find them again, by yourself, after apologizing to all around you. By the end of the summer, Lau Po had taught me all he knew, and I had become a better chess player.

A small weekend crowd of Chinese people and tourists would gather as I played and defeated my opponents one by one. My mother would join the crowds during these outdoor exhibition games. She sat proudly on the bench, telling my admirers with proper Chinese humility, "Is luck."

A man who watched me play in the park suggested that my mother allow me to play in local chess tournaments. My mother smiled graciously, an answer that meant nothing. I desperately wanted to go, but I bit back my tongue. I knew she would not let me play among strangers. So as we walked home I said in a small voice that I didn't want to play in the local tournament. They would have American rules. If I lost, I would bring shame on my family.

"Is shame you fall down nobody push you," said my mother.

During my first tournament, my mother sat with me in the front row as I waited for my turn. I frequently bounced my legs to unstick them from the cold metal seat of the folding chair. When my name was called, I leapt up. My mother unwrapped something in her lap. It was her *chang*, a small tablet of red jade which held the sun's fire. "Is luck," she whispered, and tucked it into my dress pocket. I turned to my opponent, a fifteen-year-old boy from Oakland. He looked at me, wrinkling his nose.

As I began to play, the boy disappeared, the color ran out of the room, and I saw only my white pieces and his black ones waiting on the other side. A light wind began blowing past my ears. It whispered secrets only I could hear.

"Blow from the South," it murmured. "The wind leaves no trail." I saw a clear path, the traps to avoid. The crowd rustled. "Shhh! Shhh!" said the corners of the room. The wind blew stronger. "Throw sand from the East to distract him." The knight came forward ready for the sacrifice. The wind hissed, louder and louder. "Blow, blow, blow. He cannot see. He is blind now. Make him lean away from the wind so he is easier to knock down."

"Check," I said, as the wind roared with laughter. The wind died down to little puffs, my own breath.

My mother placed my first trophy next to a new plastic chess set that the neighborhood Tao society had given to me. As she wiped each piece with a soft cloth, she said, "Next time win more, lose less."

"Ma, it's not how many pieces you lose," I said. "Sometimes you need to lose pieces to get ahead."

"Better to lose less, see if you really need."

At the next tournament, I won again, but it was my mother who wore the triumphant grin.

"Lost eight piece this time. Last time was eleven. What I tell you? Better off lose less!" I was annoyed, but I couldn't say anything.

I attended more tournaments, each one farther away from home. I won all games, in all divisions. The Chinese bakery downstairs from our flat displayed my growing collection of trophies in its window, amidst the dust-covered cakes that were never picked up. The day after I won an important regional tournament, the window encased a fresh sheet cake with whipped-cream frosting and red script saying "Congratulations, Waverly Jong, Chinatown Chess Champion." Soon after that, a flower shop, headstone engraver, and funeral parlor offered to sponsor me in national tournaments. That's when my mother decided I no longer had to do the dishes. Winston and Vincent had to do my chores.

"Why does she get to play and we do all the work," complained Vincent.

"Is new American rules," said my mother. "Meimei play, squeeze all her brains out for win chess. You play, worth squeeze towel."

By my ninth birthday, I was a national chess champion. I was still some 429 points away from grand-master status, but I was touted as the Great American Hope, a child prodigy and a girl to boot. They ran a photo of me in *Life* magazine next to a quote in which Bobby Fischer said, "There will never be a woman grand master." "Your move, Bobby," said the caption.

The day they took the magazine picture I wore neatly plaited braids clipped with plastic barrettes trimmed with rhinestones. I was playing in a large high school auditorium that echoed with phlegmy coughs and the squeaky rubber knobs of chair legs sliding across freshly waxed wooden floors. Seated across from me was an American man, about the same age as Lau Po, maybe fifty. I remember that his sweaty brow seemed to weep at my every move. He wore a dark, malodorous suit. One of his pockets was stuffed with a great white kerchief on which he wiped his palm before sweeping his hand over the chosen chess piece with great flourish.

In my crisp pink-and-white dress with scratchy lace at the neck, one of two my mother had sewn for these special occasions, I would clasp my hands under my chin, the delicate points of my elbows poised lightly on the table in the manner my mother had shown me for posing for the press. I would swing my patent leather shoes back and forth like an impatient child riding on a school bus. Then I would pause, such in my lips, twirl my chosen piece in midair as if undecided, and then firmly plant it in its new threatening place, with a triumphant smile thrown back at my opponent for good measure.

I no longer played in the alley of Waverly Place. I never visited the playground where the pigeons and old men gathered. I went to school, then directly home to learn new chess secrets, cleverly concealed advantages, more escape routes.

But I found it difficult to concentrate at home. My mother had a habit of standing over me while I plotted out my games. I think she thought of herself as my protective ally. Her lips would be sealed tight, and after each move I made, a soft "Hmmmmph" would escape from her nose.

"Ma, I can't practice when you stand there like that," I said one day. She retreated to the kitchen and made loud noises with the pots and pans. When the crashing stopped, I could see out of the corner of my eye that she was standing in the doorway. "Hmmmmph!" Only this one came out of her tight throat.

My parents made many concessions to allow me to practice. One time I complained that the bedroom I shared was so noisy that I couldn't think. Thereafter, my brothers slept in a bed in the living room facing the street. I said I couldn't finish my rice; my head didn't work right when my stomach was too full. I left the table with half-finished bowls and nobody complained. But there was one duty I couldn't avoid. I had to accompany my mother on Saturday market days when I had no tournament to play. My mother would proudly walk with me, visiting many shops, buying very little "This my daughter Wave-ly Jong," she said to whoever looked her way.

One day after we left a shop I said under my breath, "I wish you wouldn't do that, telling everybody I'm your daughter." My mother stopped walking. Crowds of people with heavy bags pushed past us on the sidewalk, bumping into first one shoulder, than another.

"Aiii-ya. So shame be with mother?" She grasped my hand even tighter as she glared at me.

I looked down. "It's not that, it's just so obvious. It's just so embarrassing."

"Embarrass you be my daughter?" Her voice was cracking with anger.

"That's not what I meant. That's not what I said."

"What you say?"

I knew it was a mistake to say anything more, but I heard my voice speaking, "Why do you have to use me to show off? If you want to show off, then why don't you learn to play chess?"

My mother's eyes turned into dangerous black slits. She had no words for me, just sharp silence.

I felt the wind rushing around my hot ears. I jerked my hand out of my mother's tight grasp and spun around, knocking into an old woman. Her bag of groceries spilled to the ground.

"Aii-ya! Stupid girl!" my mother and the woman cried. Oranges and tin cans careened down the sidewalk. As my mother stooped to help the old woman pick up the escaping food, I took off.

I raced down the street, dashing between people, not looking back as my mother screamed shrilly, "Meimei! Meimei!" I fled down an alley, past dark, curtained shops and merchants washing the grime off their windows. I sped into the sunlight, into a large street crowded with tourists examining trinkets and souvenirs. I ducked into another dark alley, down another street, up another alley. I ran until it hurt and I realized I had nowhere to go, that I was not running from anything. The alleys contained no escape routes.

My breath came out like angry smoke. It was cold. I sat down on an upturned plastic pail next to a stack of empty boxes, cupping my chin with my hands, thinking hard. I imagined my mother, first walking briskly down one street or another looking for me, then giving up and returning home to await my arrival. After two hours, I stood up on creaking legs and slowly walked home.

The alley was quiet and I could see the yellow lights shining from our flat like two tiger's eyes in the night. I climbed the sixteen steps to the door, advancing quietly up each so as not to make any warning sounds. I turned the knob; the door was locked. I heard a chair moving, quick steps, the locks turning—click! click! click!—and then the door opened.

"About time you got home," said Vincent. "Boy, are you in trouble."

He slid back to the dinner table. On a platter were the remains of a large fish, its fleshy head still connected to bones swimming upstream in vain escape. Standing there waiting for my punishment, I heard my mother speak in a dry voice.

"We not concerning this girl. This girl not have concerning for us."

Nobody looked at me. Bone chopsticks clinked against the inside of bowls being emptied into hungry mouths.

I walked into my room, closed the door, and lay down on my bed. The room was dark, the ceiling filled with shadows from the dinnertime lights of neighboring flats.

In my head, I saw a chessboard with sixty-four black and white squares. Opposite me was my opponent, two angry black slits. She wore a triumphant smile. "Strongest wind cannot be seen," she said.

Her black men advanced across the plane, slowly marching to each successive level as a single unit. My white pieces screamed as they scurried and fell off the board one by one. As her men drew closer to my edge, I felt myself growing light. I rose up into the air and flew out the window. Higher and higher, above the alley, over the tops of tiled roofs, where I was gathered up by the wind and pushed up toward the night sky until everything below me disappeared and I was alone.

I closed my eyes and pondered my next move.

1989

HUNTER S. THOMPSON

A DEATH IN THE FAMILY

*"Throughout the centuries, the red fox has left a record symbolizing cun-
ningness, sagacity, and courage. . . . It has left a mark on the pages of
literature and legend, even to modern slang, which applies the name to
sly, sharp-witted people: for example, 'He is a foxy fellow,' or 'He out-
foxed me.' "*

—*New Hunters' Encyclopedia*, p. 147

Well, folks, let me tell you a story about the red fox, and how I came
to know him. It is a tale of treachery and violence and vengeance rarely
encountered in a family newspaper—or even by me, in my own life,
which has not been entirely free of these things.

But even dumb brutes can learn, and I have long since quit even
violence, which I used to enjoy as a sport (but that passed when I
realized that not everybody feels that way, and some people really want
to hurt you).

Vengeance went the same way. It was fun to plot and to talk about,
but the real thing required more time and energy than being saddled
with a terminal disease, and not even the best vengeance ever paid the
rent.

The English language is not crowded with words beginning with
the letter "v" that suggest anything but trouble. After violence and vengeance, there is also vulgar, vicious, victim, vermin, vain, vacant, vile,
vampire. . . . the list is long, with not a lot of smiles.

Right. And never mind these arcane drifts of language. We will
leave them to villains and vissmongers[1] like Edwin Newman and
Robin MacNeil.

What we are talking about now is the hideous death in life of a

---

1. Synthetic word that combines current and obsolete words into an epithet of contempt.

red fox, considered by many experts to be one of the smartest beasts in nature.

"The fox has a distinct personality. His exceptional cunning, amounting sometimes almost to genius, has been responsible for many exaggerated stories of his extreme resourcefulness."

—Ibid.

But not from me. There is a whole nest of those vicious little red buggers about 200 yards across the field from my front porch, and I am now in the process of killing them. I got the big one a few days ago and the others have gone into hiding.

They went all to pieces when the old man finally returned from his last trip across the field. He was blind in both eyes and covered with a hard crust of feathers and peacock dung, and he was leaving a trail of blood from the stumps of his hind legs.

It was midafternoon and the carrion birds were just beginning to think about feeding, but they were not in any hurry. There is no lack of food around here. The peacocks eat well—even at 20 below—and so do all the scavengers. There is always plenty of wheat, cracked corn and French fries.

But not a lot of *meat*, which is what they really like. . . . They will eat anything that bleeds, including their own kind, like sharks in a feeding frenzy. If one of them gets wounded, he will be quickly devoured by the others. They eat the eyes and entrails first, and then they get into the meat.

"Certain outdoorsmen consider it a sin to kill a red fox; such enthusiasts view it solely as a coursing animal and are content to let it remain such forever."

—Ibid.

On any market survey with a "chic scale" from one to ten, the red fox will run about eight. He is a very stylish little animal, with a neo-valuable pelt and a social cachet on the level of mean horses and fast dogs.

Even George Washington loved the red fox. He "spent many happy hours running foxhounds over the wooded areas of his Mount Vernon plantation."

On some farms they will settle for lesser prey, like the *grey* fox— one of the lower and uglier strains in the *Vulpes vulva* family; it has eyes like warts and hair like the spines of a sea urchin, and a brain like a chicken on speed.

There is also the coyote, which is hunted or at least chased now and then by gangs of *nouveau riche* huntsmen in places like Vail and Palm Springs. . . . But it is not quite the same, because the coyote always wins.

He is not a vain little punk like the red fox, with its bitchy little temper and its pampered way of life. The coyote is a mean, solitary meat eater who will eventually kill any dog who can follow it far enough.

But I have never had a problem with coyotes, although the valley is full of them. In 15 years of relentless coexistence, not even a rabid coyote has ever come up on my front porch and killed one of the family animals, or even chewed up one of the peacocks.

The red fox had a different attitude. He was arrogant and greedy and rude, and somewhere along the line he developed a taste for Salisbury steak. He also killed the family cat and took to roaming brazenly in the yard and even up on my porch in broad daylight, sniffing around the peacock cage.

The Hav-a-Hart trap is a heavy metal box about 4 feet long, with doors on both ends and a nice little food tray in the middle. When the animal gets far enough in to eat the Salisbury steak, both doors clang shut and lock firmly. Escape is impossible.

When I found the red fox in the cage I talked to him for a while as I prepared a mixture of feathers and peacock dung, which I then began shoveling through the bars and into the cage with him. The fox became hysterical as he thrashed around in the mess, trying to bite off the end of the shovel. Every once in a while I sprayed him with liquid glue and then a final shot of Mace in his eyes before I let him go.

He looked more like a raccoon than a fox at that point. The glue had set up quickly, producing a layered effect with the dung and the feathers. The beast dragged himself out of the cage, yapping and howling, and ran awkwardly across the field in the general direction of his den in the briar patch.

On his way across the field, the hideous, stinking, half-blind, brain-shattered animal had to pass between two yearling peacocks who were pecking around in the grass for bugs, paying no attention to this thing that they didn't even recognize as a fox. I was stunned, however, to see the fox veer off his course and make a kind of staggering dumb-vicious pass at one of the birds. So I shot him from behind with a load of double-0 buckshot to help him on his way. The last time I saw him he was covered with blood and two huge red-tailed hawks were circling overhead preparing to take him into the food chain.

1988

JOHN UPDIKE

THE OTHER

Rob Arnold met Priscilla Hunter at college in the fifties, and the fact that she was a twin seemed to matter as little as the fact she had been raised as an Episcopalian and he as a Baptist. How blissfully little did seem to matter in the fifties! Politics, religion, class—all beside the point. Young lives then, once Eisenhower had settled for a draw in Korea[1] and McCarthy had self-destructed like a fairy-tale goblin, seemed to be composed of timeless simplicities and old verities, of weather and works of art on opposite sides of a museum wall, of ancient professors, arrogant and scarcely audible from within the security of their tenure, lecturing from yellowing notes upon Dante and Kant while in the tall windows at their backs sunlight filtered through the feathery leaves of overarching elms. In those days Harvard Yard was innocent of Dutch-elm disease. And in those days a large and not laughable sexual territory existed within the borders of virginity, where physical parts were fed to the partner one at a time, beginning with the lips and hands. Strangely, Rob and Priscilla had been traversing this territory for several weeks before she confided to him that she was an identical twin. One of her breasts, clothed in an angora sweater and the underlying stiffness of a brassiere, was held in his hand at the time. Their faces were so close together that he could smell the mentholated tobacco in the breath of her confession. "Rob, I ought to tell you. I have a sister who looks just like me." Priscilla seemed to think it slightly shameful, and in fact it was exciting.

Her twin, the other, was named Susan, and attended the University of Chicago, though she, too, had been admitted to Radcliffe. Their

1. President Eisenhower brought the Korean War to a conclusion with a compromise. Senator Joseph McCarthy (1909–1957) was a notorious red-baiting politician.

parents—two Minneapolis lawyers, the father a specialist in corporation law and the mother in divorce and legal-aid work—had always encouraged the girls to be different; they had dressed them in different clothes from the start and had sent them to different private schools at an early age. A myth had been fostered in the family that Priscilla was the "artistic" one and Susan the more "practical" and "scientific," though to the twins themselves their interests and attitudes seemed close to identical. As children, they had succumbed simultaneously to the same diseases—chicken pox, mumps—and even when sent to different summer camps had a way, their conversations in September revealed, of undergoing the same trials and initiations. They learned to swim the same week, in widely separated lakes, and had let themselves be necked with in different forests. They fell in love with the same movie star (Montgomery Clift), had the same favorite song ("Two Loves Have I," as sung by Frankie Laine), and preferred the same Everly brother (Don, the darker and slicker-looking). Rob asked Priscilla if she missed her twin. She said, "No," but to have said otherwise might have been insulting, for she was lying entangled with him, mussed and overheated, in his fifth-floor room, with its single dormer window, in Winthrop House.

Rob was an only child, with a widowed mother, and asked, "What does it feel like, having a twin?"

Priscilla made a thoughtful mouth; prim little creases appeared in her pursed upper lip. "Nice," she answered, after a long pause that had dried the amorous moisture from her eyes. They were brown eyes, a delicious candy color, darker than caramel but paler than Hershey's kisses. "You have a backup, seeing the same things you do. A kind of insurance policy, in a funny way."

"Even when you're sent to different schools and all that?"

"That doesn't matter so much, it turns out. Suzie and I always knew we weren't the other and were going to have to lead different lives. It's just that when I'm with her there's so much less explaining to do. Maybe that's why I'm not much good at explaining things. Sorry," Priscilla said. Her face was still pink from the soft struggle they had been having on his bed.

"You're good enough," Rob said, and dropped the subject, for it had interrupted this slow journey they were making, bit by bit, into one another. He considered himself lucky to have landed her. She had, Priscilla, a lovely athletic figure, long-muscled and hippy and with wide sloping shoulders, yet narrowed to a fine firmness at the ankles and wrists; his pleasure at seeing her undressed at first disconcerted her in its intensity, and time passed before she could accept it as her due and, still a virgin, coolly give him, in his room, in the narrow space between his iron frame bed and standard oak desk, little one-woman "parades." Though they could not, for all those good fifties reasons (pregnancy, the social worth of female chastity), make love, he had talked her into this piece of display. She held her chin up bravely and slowly turned in mock-model style, showing all sides of herself; the sight was so glorious Rob had to avert his eyes, and saw how her bare feet, fresh from chilly boots and rimmed in pink, slowly pivoted on the oval rug of braided rags his mother had given him to make his room more cozy. When his minute of drinking in Priscilla was up, she would scramble, suddenly blushing and laughing at herself, into bed beside him, under rough blue blankets that Harvard issued in those days as if to soldiers or monks. They would try to read from the same book; they were taking a course together—Philosophy 10, Idealism from Plato to Whitehead.[2]

Once she had told him that she was a twin, he could not forget it, or quite forgive her. The monstrous idea flirted at the back of his head that she was half a person; there was something withheld, something hollowbacked and tinny about the figure she cut in his mind even as their courtship proceeded smoothly toward marriage. He wanted to become a lawyer; she was doubly the daughter of lawyers and in all things ideal, given the inevitable small differences between two individuals. She had been raised rather rich and he rather poor. His drab and pious upbringing embarrassed him. He had felt indignantly drowned on that absurd day when, dressed in a sleazy white gown, he had submitted to the shock of immersion, tipped backward and all the way under by the murderous hands of a minister wearing hip waders; whereas Priscilla kept in her room like a girlhood Teddy bear the embossed prayer book given her upon confirmation and sometimes carried it, in white-gloved hands, to services at the pretty little Church of New Jerusalem across from the Busch-Reisinger.[3] Both young people were for Stevenson in 1956, but she seemed secretly pleased when Eisenhower won again and Rob had wished Henry Wallace[4] were still running. He wanted to become a lawyer for a perverse reason: to avenge his father. His father, not yet fifty when he died of Hodgkin's disease, in the days before chemotherapy, had been an auto mechanic who had borrowed heavily to open a garage of his own, and it had been lawyers—lawyers for the bank and other creditors— who had briskly, with perfect legality, administered the financial

2. Alfred North Whitehead, British philosopher (1861–1947).
3. Museum on the Harvard campus.
4. American politician (1888–1965).

ruin and thwarted the dying man's attempts to divert money to his survivors.

None of this at the time seemed to matter; what mattered was her beauty and his ardor and gratitude and her cool appraisal of the future value of his gratitude as she dazzlingly, with a silver poise faintly resembling cruelty, displayed herself to him. The fact of her being a twin put a halo around her form, a shimmer of duplication, a suggestion, curiously platonic, that there was, somewhere else, unseen, another version of this reality, this body.

Priscilla's parents lived in St. Paul, in a big, cream-colored, many-dormered house a few blocks from the gorge holding the Mississippi, which was not especially wide this far north. Though Rob several times travelled there to display himself, in his best clothes, to his prospective in-laws, he did not meet Susan until the wedding. She had always been away—on a package tour of Europe or waitressing in Southern California, a part of the world where she had been led by some of her racier U. of C. friends. When Rob met her at last, she had come from Santa Barbara to be Priscilla's maid of honor. Though it was early June and cool in Minnesota, she had a surfer's deep tan and a fluffy haircut short as a boy's. A stranger to the family might not have spotted her, amid the welter of siblings and cousins, as the bride's twin. But Rob had been long alerted, and as he clasped her warm hand the current of identity stunned him to wordlessness. Her face was Priscilla's down to the protruding, determined cut of her upper lip and the slightly sad droop of the lashes at the outside corners of her eyes. He reddened, and imagined that Susan did, though her manner with him was instantly ironical—bantering and languid in perhaps the West Coast manner. Enclosed within Priscilla's body, the coolness of a stranger seemed rude, even hostile. Rob noted what seemed to be a ray or two less of caramel in her irises, a smoother consistency of chocolate. These darker eyes made her seem more passionate, more impudent and flitting, as she moved through her old home with none of a bride's responsibilities. And Susan was, Rob thought, appraising her repeatedly through the social flurry, distinctly bigger, if only by a centimetre and an ounce.

His impressions, Priscilla told him when they were alone, were wrong: Susan had expected to like him and did, very much. And though she had been the firstborn, she had never been, as often happens, the stronger or heavier. Their heights and weights had always been precisely the same. Priscilla thought that, indeed, Suzie had lost some weight, chasing around with that creepy crowd of beach bums out there. Their parents were up in arms because she had announced her intention to do graduate work in art history at U.C.L.A., where there really wasn't any art, when there was that entire wonderful Chester Dale collection at the Art Institute, along with everything else in Chicago. Or why not go East, like Priscilla? Their parents had hoped Susan would become a physicist, or at least a psychologist. Rob liked hearing Priscilla, not normally much of an explainer, run on this way about her sister; being near her twin did seem to embolden her, to loosen her tongue. He enjoyed the tumble of an extensive, ambitious family, amid whose many branches his own mother, their guest for the weekend, seemed a wan, doomed graft. The big house was loaded with pale padded furniture and vacation souvenirs; his mother found a safe corner in a little-used library and worked at a needlepoint footstool cover she had brought from North Carolina.

In church, the twins, the one majestic in white tulle and the other rather mousy in mauve taffeta, were vividly distinguishable. Rob, however, standing at the altar in a daze of high Episcopalianism, the musk of incense in his nostrils and a gold-leafed panel of apostles flickering off to the side, had a disquieting thrill of confusion, as if the mocking-eyed maid of honor might be his intimate from Winthrop House days and the mysterious figure on their father's arm a woman virtually unknown to him, tanned and crop-haired beneath her veil and garland of florets. Susan's voice was just a grain or two the huskier, so he knew it was Priscilla who, in a shy, true voice, recited the archaic vows with him. At the reception, amid all the kissing, he kissed his sister-in-law and was startled at the awkwardly averted, rather stubbornly downcast cheek; Rob had reflexively expected Priscilla's habituated frontal case. And when they danced, Susan was stiff in his arms. Yet none of this marred her fascination, the superior authenticity she enjoyed over the actual reality as the wedding night untidily proceeded through champagne and forced jollity to its trite, closeted climax. Susan was with them (her remembered stiffness, as if she and Rob had too much to say to dare a word, and her imagined slightly greater size and heft) during the botch of defloration, exciting him, urging him on through Priscilla's pain. Though he knew he had put an unfortunate crimp in this infant marriage, and had given his long-cherished ardor a bad name, he fell asleep with happy exhaustion, as if all his guilt were shifted onto the body of a twin of his own.

Rob was not accepted at Harvard Law School; but good-hearted Yale took him. It was all for the best, for if Cambridge in those years was the path to Washington, New Haven was closer to New York and Wall Street, where the real money was. After a few years in the city, the Arnolds settled in Greenwich and had children—a girl, a boy, and a girl. Having married a La Jolla builder of million-dollar homes,

Susan kept pace with a girl, a boy, and then another boy. This break in symmetry led them both, it seemed, to stop bearing children. Also, the Pill had come along and made birth control irresistible. Kennedy had been shot, and something called rock blasted from the radio however you twisted the dial. The twins, though, had their nests safely made. Susan's husband was named Jeb Herrera; he claimed descent from one of the old Spanish ranching families of Alta California, but in joying moods asserted that his great-great-grandfather had been a missionary's illegitimate son. He was a curly-haired, heavy, gracious, enthusiastic man, a bit too proclaimedly, for Rob's taste, in love with life. His small, even teeth looked piratical, when he smiled through the black curls of his beard. He was one of the first men Rob knew to wear a full beard and to own a computer—a tan metal box taller than a man, a freestanding broom closet that spat paper. Jeb had programmed it to respond to the children's questions with jokes in printout. His office was a made over wharf shed where dozens shuffled paper beside canted windows full of the Pacific. None of his employees wore neckties. Though the twins, as they eased into matronhood, might still be mistaken for one another, there was no mistaking the husbands. Susan, it would appear, had the artistic taste, and Priscilla had bet on practicality. Rob had become a specialist in tax law, saw his name enrolled in the list of junior partners on the engraved firm stationery, and forgot about avenging his father.

The growing families visited back and forth; there was something concordant about the homes, though one was white clapboard set primly on watered green lawn, and the other was redwood and stucco wedged into a hillside where fat little cactuses intricate as snowflakes flourished among expensively transplanted rocks. Both houses were cheerful for children, with back stairs and big windows and a certain sporty airiness. The Arnolds had a long sun room with a Ping-Pong table and, above it on the second floor, a sleeping porch with a hammock. As soon as they could afford it, they crowded a composition tennis court into the space between the garage and the line fence, where the lawn had always been scruffy anyway and the vegetable garden had gone to weeds every July. The La Jolla house, which overlooked the fifteenth fairway of a golf course, shuffled indoors and outdoors with its sliding glass doors and cantilevered deck and its family-sized hot tub out on the deck.

Rob first saw his wife's sister naked one warm evening in Christmas vacation when Susan let fall a large white towel behind her and slid her silent silhouette into this hot tub. Rob and his wife were already in, coping with the slithering, giggling bodies of their excited children; so the moment passed almost unnoticed amid the family tumble. Almost. Susan was distinctly not Priscilla; their skins had aged differently on the two different coasts. Priscilla's was dead pale this time of year, its summer tan long faded, whereas there was something thickened and delicately crinkled and permanently golden about Susan's. With an accustomed motion she had eased her weight from her buttocks into the steaming wide circle of water. Her expression looked solemn, dented by shadow. Rob remembered the same resolute, unfocussed expression on Priscilla's face in the days when she would grant him her little "parade" in the shadows of his narrow college room. Both sisters had brown eyes in deep sockets and noses that looked upturned, with long nostrils and sharp central dents in their upper lips. Both were wearing bangs that winter. Their heads and shoulders floated side by side; Susan's breasts seemed the whiter for the contrast with her year-round bathing-suit tan.

"How much do you do this sort of thing?" Priscilla asked her twin, a touch nervously, glancing toward Rob.

"Oh, now and then, with people you know, usually. You get used to it—it's a local custom. You sort of let yourself dissolve."

Yet she, too, gave Rob an alert glance. He had already passed into dissolution, his vapor of double love one with the heat, the steam, the abundant dinner wine, the scent of the eucalyptus trees brooding above the deck, the stars beyond them, the strangeness of this all being a few days before Christmas. Immersed, their bodies had become foreshortened stumps of flesh, comical blobs of mercury. Jeb appeared on the deck holding a naked baby—little Lucas—in one crooked arm and a fresh half gallon of Gallo Chablis in the other. Early in his thirties, Jeb had a pendulous belly. He descended to them like a hairy Neptune; the tub overflowed. When the water calmed, his penis drifted under Rob's eyes like a lead-colored fish swimming nowhere.

The families stopped travelling back and forth in complete units as the maturing children developed local attachments and summer jobs. The two oldest cousins, Karen and Rose, had been fast friends from the start, though there was no mistaking them for twins: Karen had become as washed-out and mild-faced a blonde as Rob's mother (now dead), and Rose was so dark that boys on the street catcalled to her in Spanish. The two older boys, Henry and Gabriel, made a more awkward matchup, the one burdened with all of Rob's allergies and a drowsy shyness all his own, and the other a macho little athlete with a wedge-shaped back and the unthinking cruelty of those whose bodies are perfectly connected to their wills. The girl and the boy that completed the sets, Jennifer and Lucas, claimed to detest each other, and, indeed, did squabble tediously, perhaps in defense against any notion that they would someday marry. The bigger the children became, the harder they pulled apart, and the more frayed the lines between their parents became. Once little Lucas became too big to hold in one arm and strike a pose with, Jeb's interest seemed to wander away from families and family get-togethers. There were late-night long-distance calls between the sisters, and secrets from the children.

Susan suddenly had more gray hair than Priscilla. Rob felt touched by her, and drawn in a new fashion, when she would visit them for a few weeks in the summer without Jeb, with perhaps an inscrutable Rose and a resentful Lucas in tow. More than once, Rob met the L.A. red-eye at LaGuardia and was kissed at the gate as if he were Susan's savior; there had been drunks on the plane, college kids, nobody could sleep, Lucas had insisted on watching a ghastly Jerry Lewis movie, Rose threw up over Nebraska somewhere, they had gone way north around some thunderheads, an old lech in an admiral's uniform kept trying to buy her drinks at three in the morning, my God, never again. As Rob gently swung the car up the summer-green curves of the Merritt Parkway, Susan nodded asleep, and seemed his wife. Priscilla's skin, too, now sagged in those defenseless puckers when she slept.

As a guest in their home, Susan slept on the upstairs porch. The swish of cars headed toward the railroad station, and the birds—so much more aggressive, she said, than those on the West Coast—awakened her too early; and then at night the Arnolds took her to too many parties. "How do you stand it?" she would ask her twin.

"Oh, it gets to be a habit. Try taking a nap in the afternoon. That's what I do."

"Jeb and I hardly go out at all anymore. We decided other people weren't helping our marriage." This was a clue, and far from the only one. There was a hungry boniness to her figure now. Like a sick person willing to try any cure, Susan drank only herbal tea—no caffeine, no alcohol—and ate as little meat as she politely could. Whereas Priscilla, who had once appeared so distinctly a centimetre smaller, now was relatively hefty. Broad of shoulder and hip, she moved through parties with a certain roll, a practiced cruiser who knew where the ports were—the confiding women and the unhappy men and the bar table in the corner. Sometimes after midnight Rob watched her undress in their bedroom and thought of all the Martinis and Manhattans, the celery sticks and devilled eggs that had gone into those haunches and upper arms.

"Other people don't help *it*," was Priscilla's answer to Susan. "But they might do something for *you*. You, a woman. Aren't you a woman, or are you only a part of a marriage?" She had never forgiven him, Rob feared, for that unideal wedding night.

Poor Susan seemed a vision of chastity whom they would discover each morning at the breakfast table, frazzled after another night's poor sleep, her hair drooping onto the lapels of a borrowed bathrobe, her ascetic breakfast of grapefruit and granola long eaten, the *Times* scattered about her in pieces read with a desperate thoroughness. Rob wanted to urge bacon and waffles upon her, and to make up good news to counteract the bad news that had been turning her hair gray. Priscilla knew what it was, but was no good at explaining. "Jeb's a bastard," she would say simply in their bedroom. "He always was. My parents knew it, but what could they do? She had to get married, once I did. And all men are bastards, more or less."

"My, you've gotten tough. He was always very dear with the kids, I thought. At least when they were little. And he builds those million-dollar houses."

"Not so much anymore he doesn't," she said. As she pivoted on their plush carpet, yellow calluses showed at her heels.

"What do you mean?"

"Ask *her*, if you're so interested."

But he never could. He could no more have asked Susan to confide her private life than he could have tiptoed onto the sleeping porch and looked down at—what he held so clearly in his mind—his wife's very face, transposed into another, chastened existence, fragilely asleep in this alien house, this alien climate and time zone. So magical a stranger might awake under the pressure of his regard. He would have trespassed. He would have spoiled something he was saving.

The 1973–75 recession gave Jeb's tottering, overextended business the last push it needed; everything coming undone at once, the Herreras began to divorce amid the liquidation. When Susan visited them in the bicentennial year, it was as a single woman, her thinness now whittled to a certain point, a renewed availability. But not, of course, available to Rob; the collapse of one marriage made the other doubly precious.

As in other summers, Rob was touched by Susan's zeal with the children, ushering as many as could be captured onto the train and into the city for a visit to the Museum of Natural History or to see the tall ships that beautiful hazy July day. Rose was not with her; the girl had drawn closer to her father in his distress, and was waitressing in a taco joint in San Diego. And Karen, now stunning with her flaxen hair and pale moonface above a slender body, was above everything except boys and ballet. One Saturday while Priscilla stayed home, having contracted for a lunch at the club with one of those similarly boozy women she called "girlfriends," Rob accompanied Susan on an excursion she had cooked up for the just barely willing Jennifer and Lucas, all the way to New Haven to see the Beinecke Library, with its translucent marble and the three Noguchis[5] so marvelously toylike and monumental in their sunken well. Rob had not see these wonders himself; they had come to Yale after his time. And he rather enjoyed these excursions with his sister-in-law; all that old tumble of family life had fallen to them to perpetuate. He let her drive his Mercedes and sat beside her, taking secret inventory of all the minute ways in which she differed from Priscilla—the slight extra sharpness to the thrust of her upper lip, the sea scallop of shallow wrinkles the sun had engraved at the corner of her eye, the hair or two more of bulk or wildness to her eyebrow on its crest of bone. The hair of her head, once shorter, then grayer, was now dyed too even a dark brown, with unnatural reddish lights. She turned to him for a second on a long straightaway. "You've never asked about me and Jeb," she said.

"What was to ask? Things speak for themselves."

"I loved that about you," Susan pronounced. Her verb alarmed him; "love" was a word he associated with the tacky sermons of his youth. "It's been a nightmare for years," she went on, and he realized that she was offering to present herself in a new way to him, as more than a strange ghost behind a familiar mask. She was in a sense naked. But he, after nearly two decades of playing the good husband, had discovered affairs, and had fallen in love locally. The image of his mistress—she was one of Priscilla's "girlfriends"—rose up, her head tipped back, her lipstick smeared, and deafened him to the woman he was with; without hearing the words, he saw Susan's mouth, that distinctive complicated mouth the sisters shared, making a pursy, careful expression, like a schoolteacher emphasizing a crucial point.

Lucas, in the back seat, was listening and cried out, "Mom, stop bitching about Dad to Uncle Rob—you do it to everybody!"

Jennifer said, "Oh listen to big man here, protecting his awful daddy," and there was a thump, and the girl sobbed in spite of her scorn.

"You make me barf, you know that?" Lucas told her, his own voice shakily full of tears. "You've always been the most god-awful germ, no kidding."

"Daddy," Jennifer said, with something of womanly aloofness. "This little spic just broke my arm."

The adult conversation was not resumed. Priscilla a few days later drove her sister back to LaGuardia, to begin a new life. Susan was

5. Isamu Noguchi (b. 1904), American sculptor.

planning to take her half of what money was left when the La Jolla house was sold and move with the two younger children to the Bay area and study ceramics at Berkeley.

"I told her she's crazy," Priscilla said to him. "There's nothing but gays in San Francisco."

"Maybe she's not as needful of male consolation as some."

"What's that supposed to mean? You're not above a little consolation yourself, from what I've been hearing."

"Easy, easy. The kids are upstairs."

"Karen isn't upstairs; she's in New York, letting that cradle robber she met at the club take her to the Alvin Ailey.[6] Wake up. You know what your trouble has always been? You're an only child. You never loved me, you just loved the idea of sneaking into a family. You loved my family, the idea of there being so many of us, rich and Episcopalian and all that."

"I didn't need the Episcopalian so much. I thought I was going to sneeze all through the wedding. Incense, I couldn't believe it."

"You poor little Baptist boy. You know what my father said at the time? I've never told you this."

"Then don't."

"He said, 'He'll never fit in. He's a guttersnipe, Prissy.' "

"Wow. Did he really say 'guttersnipe'? And fit into what—the St. Paul Order of the Moose? Gee, I always rather liked him, too. Especially early in the mornings, when you could catch him sober."

"He *despised* you. But then Sue picked Jeb, and he was so much worse."

"That *was* lucky."

"He made you look good, it's a crazy fact."

"Yes, and you make Sue look good, so it evens out. Come on, let's save this for midnight. Here comes Henry."

But the boy, six feet tall suddenly, was wearing earphones plugged into a satchel-sized radio; on his way to the porch he gave his parents a glassy, oblivious smile.

Any smugness the Arnolds may have felt in relation to the Herreras' disasters lasted less than a year. An ingenious tax shelter Rob had directed a number of clients into was ruled invalid by the I.R.S., and these clients suddenly owed the government hundreds of thousands of dollars, including tens of thousands in penalties. Though they had been duly cautioned and no criminal offense was charged, the firm could not keep him; his divorce soon followed. One of the men Pris-

6. A dance troupe.

cilla had been seeing had freed himself from his own wife and was prepared to take her on; Rob wondered what Priscilla did now, all hundred and fifty pounds of her, that was so wonderful. To think that he had started it all off with those formalized, chaste "parades."

She resettled with the children in Cos Cob. Having fouled his professional nest in the East, Rob accepted with gratitude the offer of a former colleague to join a firm in Los Angeles, as less than a junior partner. He had always been happy on their visits to Southern California and, though a one-bedroom condo in Westwood wasn't a redwood house overlooking a fairway in La Jolla, Old Man Hunter had been right: he fitted in better here. Southern California had a Baptist flavor and that helped him heal. The people mostly came from small Midwestern towns, and there was a naïveté in even the sin—the naked acts in the bars and the painted little-girl hookers in jogging shorts along Hollywood Boulevard. The great stucco movie theatres of the thirties had been given over to X-rated films; freckle-faced young couples watched them holding hands and eating popcorn. In this city where sex was a kind of official currency, Rob made up for the fun he had missed while catching the train and raising the children in Greenwich, and evened the score with his former wife. Los Angeles was like that earlier immersion, at the age of religious decision, which coincided with puberty; that bullying big hand had shoved him under and he had come up feeling, as well as indignant, cleansed and born again.

One day downtown on the escalator from Figueroa Street up to the Bonaventure,[7] he found himself riding behind a vivid black-haired girl whom he slowly recognized as his niece, Rose. He touched her naked shoulder and bought her a drink in the lobby lounge, amid all the noisy, curving pools. Rose was all of twenty-four now; he could hardly believe it. She told him her father had a job as foreman for another builder and had bought himself a stinkpot and kept taking weekend runs into Mexico; his dope-snorting friends that kept putting a move on her drove her crazy, so she had split. Now she worked as a salesgirl in a failing imported-leather-goods shop in the underground Arco Plaza while her chances of becoming an actress became geometrically smaller with each passing year. These days, she explained, if you haven't got your face somewhere by the time you're nineteen you're *finito*. And indeed, Rob thought, her face was unsubtle for a career of pretense; framed by a poodle cut of tight black curls, it had too much of Jeb's raw hopefulness, a shiny candor somehow coarse. Rob was

7. A large hotel in downtown Los Angeles.

excited by this disappointed young beauty, but women her age, with their round breasts and enormous pure eye whites, rather frightened him, like machines that are too new and expensive. He asked about her mother, and was given Susan's address. "She's doing real well," Rose warned him.

An exchange of letters followed; Susan's handwriting was a touch rounder than Priscilla's, but with the same "g"s that looked like "s"s and "t"s that had lost their crossings, like hats blown off by the wind. One autumn Saturday, he flew up to the Bay area. Three hundred miles of coast were cloudless and the hills had put on their inflammable tawny summer coats, that golden color the Californian loves as a New Englander loves the scarlet of turning maples. Berkeley looked surprisingly like Cambridge, once you ascended out of Oakland's slough: big homes built by a species of the middle class that had migrated elsewhere, and Xeroxed protest posters in many colors pasted to mailboxes and tacked to trees. Susan lived in the second-floor-back of a great yellow house that, but for its flaking paint and improvised outside stairways, reminded him of her ancestral home in St. Paul. She had been watching for him, and they kissed awkwardly halfway up her access stairs.

The apartment was dominated by old photos of her children and by examples of her own ceramics—crusty, oddly lovely things, with a preponderance of turquoise and muddy orange in the glazes. She was even selling a few, at a shop a friend of hers ran in Sausalito. A female friend. And she taught part time at a private elementary school. And still took classes—the other students called her Granny, but she loved them; their notions of what mattered were so utterly different from what ours were at that age. All this came out in a rapid voice, with a diffident stabbing of hands and a way of pushing her hair back from her ears as if to improve her hearing. Something in her manner implied that this was a slightly tiresome duty he had invented for them. He was an old relative, a page from the past. She was thinner than ever and had let her hair go back to gray, no longer just streaked but solidly gray, hanging down past the shoulders of a russet wool turtleneck sweater such as men wear in Scotch ads. He had never seen Priscilla look like this. In tight, spattered jeans and bare feet, Susan's skinniness was exciting; he wanted to seize her before she dwindled away entirely.

She took him for a drive, in her Mazda, just as if they still had children to entertain together. The golden slashed hills interwoven with ocean and lagoons, the curving paths full of cyclists and joggers and young parents with infants in backpacks looked idyllic, a vision of the future, an enchanted land not of perpetual summer, as where he lived, but of eternal spring. She had put on spike heels with her jeans and a vest of sheepskin patches over her sweater, and these additions made her startlingly stylish. They went out to eat at a local place where tabbouleh[8] followed artichoke soup. Unlike most couples on a first date, they had no lack of things to talk about. Reminiscence shied away from old grievances and turned to the six children, their varying and still uncertain fates; fates seemed so much slower to shape up than when they had been young. Priscilla was hardly mentioned. As the evening wore on, Priscilla became an immense hole in their talk, a kind of cave they were dwelling in, while their voices slurred and their table candle flickered. Was it that Susan was trying to spare him acknowledging what had been, after all, a great marital defeat; or was Rob trying not to cast upon her a shadow of comparison, an onus of being half a person? She took him back to her apartment; indeed, he had not arranged for anywhere else to go.

Suzie kicked off her shoes and turned on an electric heater and dragged a magnum of Gallo from the refrigerator. She was tired; he liked that, since he was, too, as though they had been pulling at the same load in tandem all these years. They sat on the floor, on opposite sides of a glass coffee table in whose surface her face was mirrored— the swinging witchy hair, the deep eye sockets and thoughtful upper lip. "You've come a long way," she announced, in that voice which had once struck him as huskier than another but that in this room felt as fragile as the pots blushing turquoise on the shelves.

"How do you mean?"

"To see me. Do you see me? Me, I mean."

"Who else? I've always liked you. Loved, should I say? Or would that be too much?"

"I think it would. Things between us have always been . . ."

"Complicated," Rob finished.

"Exactly. I don't want to be just a way of correcting a mistake."

He thought a long time, so long her face became anxious, before answering, "Why not?" He knew that most people, including Susan, had more options than he, but he had faith that in an affluent nation a need, honestly confessed, has a good chance of being met.

This being the eighties, she was nervous about herpes, and even after his reassurances was still nervous. She asked him to hold off for a while, until she really felt trust. Meanwhile, there were things they *could* do. Seeing her undress and move self-consciously, chin up, through a little parade in the room, he thought her majestic, for being

8. A Middle Eastern salad made with bulgur wheat.

nearly skeletal. Plato was wrong, what is is absolute.[9] The delay Susan imposed, the distances between them that could not be quickly changed, helped Rob grasp the blissful truth that she was only another woman.

1987

■   ■   ■

9. A somewhat garbled reference to Plato's doctrine that the apparent world is illusory while ideas are absolute.

GUY VANDERHAEGHE

GOING TO RUSSIA

"Another of your letters arrived at my house yesterday," the doctor announces. "That makes four now." He says this in a colourless, insipid voice, in the way he says most things.

It is only the significant pause which follows that alerts me I am expected to respond, and distracts my attention from the scene outside his office window. For several minutes I have been watching two children as they tramp stiffly off into the distance. They lead me to think of my daughter, and to wonder if she misses my visits.

Here, we are on the outskirts of the city, where the new suburbs dwindle into prairie, and prairie into winter sky. The children, stuffed into bulky snowsuits, totter along, their arms stiffly extended like tiny astronauts foraging on the frozen cinder of a spent star.

Suburban tots often come to explore these splendid spaces. I have navigated them too, in my imagination, warm behind a double pane of glass. I find it strange that this blank sweep of land terrifies some of my fellow inmates and that they feel the need to keep their blinds down night and day. I like it. It makes me think of Russia.

"Yes?" I say finally, a little late, but nevertheless meaning to politely encourage him.

"Mr. Caragan, I thought when we met last Wednesday we agreed there would be no more letters."

The man has me there. But I am an impulsive fellow and that was Wednesday. By Thursday I felt I owed him some kind of explanation as to what had moved me to write the first three letters.""That's true," I admit, "that was the understanding."

"But?"

I shrug.

Dr. Herzl spreads a sheet of paper on his desk. His fingers rub diligently at the fold marks. When he is satisfied everything is ship-shape, he begins to read to himself. I note a barely perceptible flicker in his upper lip. When he finishes, he looks up at me sharply. An old tactic that I recognize immediately. "This doesn't make much sense to me," he says.

"No?"

"Excuse me," he says, pausing. "I'm not a critic. . . ." The doctor smiles to signal me that this is an offering from his store of inexhaustible wit. "But I find your language rather . . . formal, stilted," he says at last, finding the words he wants. "As if you are under great strain, as if you are trying to keep a lid on your feelings when you write me these letters." He searches the page. "For instance, there's this: 'I answer in writing because my thought will thus be more fully expressed, and more distinctly perceived, like a sound amid silence.' Doesn't that sound a bit unusual to you?"

"There's quotation marks around that."

"Pardon?"

"I didn't write that. There's quotation marks around that."

"Oh." The doctor hesitates. "Who *did* write it then?"

"Mikhail Osipovich Gershenzon."[1]

A doubtful look passes over his face. He suspects me of pulling his leg. Dr. Herzl considers me a great joker, albeit an unbalanced, a lunatic one.

"It's true," I assure him.

"I am not familiar . . ."

"So who is? But then, you don't need to be," I say. "I explained it all in the letter. It's all in there. I used Gershenzon as an example. I was trying to help you see why I write—"

I am interrupted. "Yes, I'm sure. But you understand—fourteen pages in your tiny handwriting—I only skimmed it."

"Of course." I don't know whatever led me to believe he would profit from the story of the Corner-to-Corner Correspondence. Or that anyone else would, for that matter. When I told Janet, who is young, an artist, and believes herself to be in possession of a sensitive soul, about the series of letters exchanged between Gershenzon and Viacheslav Ivanovitch Ivanov[2] while they recuperated in a rest-home in Russia, she said: "I don't get it. What's a corner-to-corner correspondence?"

"It was called that because each of the correspondents was in opposite corners of the same room. That's why it was called the Cor-

1. Russian writer (1869–1925).
2. Russian writer (1866–1949).

ner-to-Corner Correspondence," I said, ending my obvious explanation
lamely.

"They couldn't talk? What was it, throat cancer?"

"No, as I said before, these guys were poets, philosophers, men of
letters. Remember?" I prodded. "It was just that they felt more comfortable, surer of themselves, when writing. They had time to reflect on
what they wanted to say, to test their ideas. To compose."

"That's the weirdest thing I ever heard—writing to someone in
the same room," she said. "That sort of thing just gets in the way of
real feelings. It's a kind of mask to hide who you really are, and what
you're all about."

That was her final judgment, and from Janet's considered deci-
sions there is no appeal, as I have learned to my sorrow. Still, I was
almost in love, and at that precarious point one imagines it is important
to be understood. So at our next planned meeting, two days later, I
took along with me a passage I had copied from one of Gershenzon's
letters. It was to demonstrate to her the subtleties which are the province of the written word, and, more importantly, to signal her what was
going on in my mind.

"You see, honey," I said, trying to explain what Gershenzon meant
to me, "he felt out of step with things going on around him. He might
have said to old Ivanov: 'Viacheslav, what's the matter with me? I don't
feel I belong. I don't feel right. Why is it I don't think what other
people think, or feel what other people say they feel?' He could have
put it that way. He could have, but he didn't. What he did do was
write:

> This is the life I lead by day. But on a deeper level of consciousness
> I lead a different life. There, an insistent, persistent, hidden voice has
> been saying for years: No, no, this is not it! Some other kind of will
> in me turns away in misery and distaste from all of culture, from all
> that is being said and done around me. It finds all this tedious and
> vain, like a struggle of phantoms flailing away in a void; it seems to
> know another world, to foresee a different life, not yet to be found on
> earth but which will come and cannot fail to come, for only then will
> true reality be achieved. To me this voice is the voice of my real self.
> I live like a foreigner acclimatized in an alien land; the natives like
> me and I like them, I diligently work for their good, share their sor-
> rows and rejoice in their joys, but at the same time I know that I am
> a stranger. I secretly long for the fields of my homeland, for its differ-
> ent spring, the smell of its flowers, and the way its women speak.
> Where is my homeland? I shall never see it, I shall die in foreign
> parts."

Of course, when I looked up from the page, it was only to discover that Janet had gone to the bathroom to apply her contraceptive foam.

"I hear that you're still refusing to see your wife," says Dr. Herzl, introducing a new topic.

"That's not entirely true. I said I wouldn't see her alone. If she brings our daughter with her, well, that's a different story?"

"Why won't you speak to your wife alone?"

"I explain that in my second letter—"

"Why don't you explain it to me now. Face to face, without the pretences of these letters." There is a measure of asperity in the good doctor's voice. From the very beginning I knew he didn't like me. I do not have a confessional nature and he holds that against me.

I stare back stolidly.

"Is it because you're ashamed? Is that why you won't allow your wife to visit?"

"Yes." There is little harm in agreeing with him. He has made up his mind on this point long ago.

"Ashamed of what? Your affair? Or what you did at the gallery?"

Why not? "Both," I affirm, blithely shouldering a double load, the tawdry fardels of sexual guilt.

"Speaking of the gallery," says Dr. Herzl, "your wife agrees with me. She believes that the depiction of the penis was what triggered the incident there."

"She does, does she?"

"She thinks you felt it was undersized. She says you're prone to read a disproportionate significance into that sort of thing."

This is so like Miriam that I offer no complaint against this pre-posterous interpretation of my actions. I had my reasons.

Dr. Herzl clears his throat. "How am I to understand your silence?"

"The suggestion is too silly to grace with a comment."

"How did you feel when you did it?"

"Cold."

"I see," says the doctor, letting his fingers wander through the paper on his desk. "Well, I believe we've made some progress. We've begun to talk to one another, at any rate. Now is as good a time to stop as any." He closes my file. Perhaps the fact that it bulges with my correspondence reminds him. "You do see that writing letters is a way of avoiding the problem?" he asks hopefully.

"I want to see my daughter. You tell Miriam to bring Cynthia here."

"I'm sorry," says Dr. Herzl. "Mrs. Caragan says that would be impossible."

In my room I lie down on my bed and speculate how Miriam is making out. I know she is not starving. I am on full salary while incapacitated. The teachers' federation knows how to negotiate a collective agreement, and insanity is paid its rich deserts.

As far as the other things go—the neighbours' whispers, the long, woeful faces of acquaintances—the proud prow of Miriam's clipper can cleave those mundane waters. And her real friends, the ones that never liked me, will be intent on keeping her busy, or, as they would prefer, "involved".

For a number of years, I was "involved" too. Miriam demanded it. She was terribly concerned that we didn't trade our ideals for a mortgage, that we didn't become ordinary people. The flight from ordinariness kept me on a pretty strenuous schedule. I'd get home from the high school where I teach something called social studies just in time to grab a cheese sandwich and receive a briefing while the paint dried on my placard. Then we'd all load into a Volkswagen van owned by a troll with a social conscience, a short, hairy guy who made pieces of knotty-pine furniture capacious and sturdy enough to stand up to hard use by the giants I assumed were his clients, and drive off to let our opinions be known.

But about four years ago, when Miriam and I were fighting about Cynthia, and I was drinking even more than I was just before I got tossed in here, I gave up being involved and began my own journey; and there is no way that I'm going to give Miriam the chance to coax me back to Canada, now that I'm safely here, on the borders of Russia.

There's an irony, too, in how my travels began. They commenced at one of Miriam's protest rallies. About a dozen lonely souls were picketing a Liberal Fund-Raising Dinner—the reason why I now fail to recollect. It was the usual dispirited occasion. I was a little drunk and bored. The cars kept pulling up to the front of the hotel and discharging Liberals who slunk tight-lipped through our righteous gauntlet. One particularly incensed woman of our number kept demanding to know whether the Liberals were dining on macaroni and cheese that night. "Are you?" she shrilled in their faces. "Are you eating macaroni and cheese tonight?" The implication being that her own feisty spirit was sustained solely on that starchy, plebeian fuel.

It was all going more or less our way until a large, ruddy, drunk, middle-aged Liberal turned a passionate eye on our assembly. He was very angry. He seemed to have missed the point about macaroni and cheese. He thought we were objecting to our country. "Hey, you bastards!" he bellowed, while his wife tried to drag him into the lobby, "I love my country! I love Canada!" he yelled, actually striking his chest with his fist. "And if you don't, why don't you get out! *Why don't you go to Russia if you don't like it here?"*

The poor man's obvious sincerity touched me as much as his logic bewildered me. Why did he presume those people had any interest in going to Russia? Didn't he know it was *Sweden* they wanted to get to? Volvos, guiltless sex, Bergman films, functional furniture. Hey, I wanted to shout back, these people would prefer Sweden! And realizing for the first time where my wife and her friends were bound, I admitted I didn't want to go along. I was the one the gentleman was addressing. Although at the time I didn't know my longing was for Russia.

Oh, not the Russia he meant. Not Soviet Russia. But nineteenth-century Russia, the Russia of Dostoevsky's saintly prostitutes and Alyosha; of Tolstoy's Pierre; and Aksionov, the sufferer in "God Sees The Truth But Waits".[3] A country where the characters in books were allowed to ask one another the questions: How must I live to be happy? What is goodness? Why does man suffer? What is to be done?

I had set a timid foot on that Eurasian continent years ago when, as a student in a course on European literature in translation, I had read some of the Russian masters. I returned because I was unhappy and because I sensed that only in Russia does unhappiness find a meaning. Like Aksionov, who suffered in place of the real murderer and thief, I felt a hundred times worse, a hundred times more guilt. I don't suppose I let it show much. I punished Miriam by putting our daughter's framed photograph on the end table, by drinking too much, and by being rude to people she wished desperately to impress.

Still, I was faithful to her in a purely technical sense until I met Janet several months ago. Janet is a young artist who supports herself as a substitute teacher; we met in the staffroom of my high school. At the end of that particular day, a bitterly cold one late in November, I spotted her waiting at the bus stop, looking hypothermic in the kind of tatty old fur coat creative people buy at Salvation Army thrift stores. I offered her a ride. She, in turn, when I had driven her home, offered me coffee.

I think it was the splendour of the drawings and paintings lending life to her old, decaying, high-ceilinged apartment that attracted me to her. Perhaps I felt she could salvage any wreck and breathe life into it, as she had that apartment. *Here,* I thought, gazing at the fire on her walls, *is a Russian soul.*

I asked if I could come back another day to make a purchase. She

---

3. A story by Tolstoy. Pierre appears in *War and Peace*; Alyosha, in *The Brothers Karamazov*.

assured me that I could, that she would be delighted. I returned, bought a drawing. Returned again and carried away a canvas. Simply put, one thing led to another. We became lovers. Regularly, on schooldays between three-thirty and four-thirty, P.M., she screwed me with clinical detachment. If I close my eyes I can see her hard little jockey-body rocking above me, muscles strained and taut (I could pluck the cords on her neck) as she mutely galloped me hither and thither, while I snorted away under her like old Dobbin.

That it was nothing more than a little equestrian exercise I lacked the courage to see.

Dr. Herzl makes a point of telling me how pleased he is that there have been no more letters since last we met. He sits behind his desk, bathed in pale March sunshine and self-assurance. I am struck by his aseptic smile and unlined face, hardly the face of a man privy to so many sorrows. More than most men, certainly.

Out of the blue he asks: "I think we're ready to talk about the Opening. And Janet. Don't you?"

"We could." I clear my throat and look at my hands. They're very soft. The therapists here have tried to encourage me to take up handi-crafts. However, if I cannot make boots like Tolstoy I will do nothing in that line.

"I'm interested to know the reasons why you posed for her. Particularly in light of what subsequently happened, it seems an odd thing for you to do."

"I didn't want to."

"But you did nevertheless."

"Obviously."

"Why?"

"Because she said she needed to sketch from life, and now that she wasn't a student she didn't get the opportunity. She couldn't afford to pay a model."

"So you wanted to help her with her work?"

"Yes." I knew how much it meant to her. Even then I knew what she was: a gifted, intense, ambitious girl, who was also a little bit stupid about things that had nothing to do with her art, and therefore did not concern her.

I can see by the look in the doctor's eyes that he is about to chance something. "Could it have been that modelling was a way of exposing yourself? Exposing yourself without having to fear consequences?"

"No."

He presses his hands together. "Why did you take such violent exception when you learned that the sketches were to be shown?" he asks softly.

"You can't be serious."

"Perfectly. I am perfectly serious. Tell me why."

"Because she didn't tell me," I say. I am unable to keep the anger out of my voice. "I saw it on a poster. 'Janet Markowsky: Studies in the Male Nude'."

"Any other reason?"

"Sure. This is a small city. I'm a teacher. Somebody would recognize me. How the hell could I walk into a classroom after every kid in the school had gone down to take a gander at old Caragan's wazoo?"

"You're exaggerating."

"And you don't know kids. Anyway, it was the principle of the thing. Don't you see?" My hands have begun to tremble, I trap them between my knees.

"Were you disturbed that there were drawings of other men?"

"No."

"Are you sure?"

"I went to Janet and I said, 'For God's sake, what are you doing to me? I can't take this right now. Please, take the sketches out of the show.' " It *was* a bad time for me. Cynthia's birthday was coming up and every year she gets older, the more her face haunts me.

"And?"

"She said she was very sorry but this opportunity had suddenly presented itself. A small gallery had an immediate opening because the artist slotted had decided to show in Calgary. Janet said she hadn't time to produce new work. She had to go with the drawings. With what she had. 'Janet,' I said, 'I'm a teacher, put a mustache on me. Anything!'

" 'I can't touch them,' she said. 'I could screw them up really badly. You can never tell what you'll do when you start mucking around with things.' "

"I phoned Ms. Markowsky yesterday and I asked her a question," says Herzl severely.

"What question?" I am surprised.

"I asked her if you wanted her to change the penises. It was just a hunch," he says, very much the clever, smug detective. "She said you did. She said you wanted them made bigger."

I put my head in my hands. I should have known it. The little bitch is the type to make sure she gets even. She won't forgive me for ruining her Opening. Herzl, the moron, gave her the clue she needed to do it. Not that I really mind. "I wanted a mustache," I say tiredly.

Herzl is really on a roll now. "Why did you take all your clothes off and walk through the gallery, Mr. Caragan? Did you think you would frighten people with your penis? Do you think it is menacing?"

"Because I'm crazy," I say. "Because I thought Life should imitate Art."

The hospital is silent at night. Nothing like I would have imagined—no dim cries, or the muffled sounds of sleepers dreaming bad dreams. Everyone has sunk into the opaque slumber of the correctly dosed and medicated. Except me. I hide my pills under my tongue and make a magnificent show of swallowing.

I hear the night-duty nurse go by. The moon is so bright tonight, so full and white and gleaming, that I can write my fifth letter to Dr. Herzl without showing a light under my door and risking detection at three o'clock in the morning.

On my shaky plastic desk my books are piled. I have Herzen, Dostoevsky, Gogol, Turgenev, Lermontov, Soloviev, Leontiev, Gorky, Chekhov, Pushkin, Tolstoy and Rozanov to keep me company in exile. Day by day I feel a little of my guilt subside as I share her sentence. Like her father, Cynthia sleeps in an institution.

The people who care for her tell me she doesn't remember me from visit to visit. That is why Miriam never goes to visit the child. *It is pointless,* she says *Cynthia is profoundly retarded, and nothing will ever change that. I refuse to feel guilt.*

But my daughter is four years old now. She is no longer a baby. She must remember me.

And whenever I look into her wise, calm eyes set like stones in their Asiatic folds, I sense the grandeur of Russia, the infinite, colossal steppes sleeping there.

1982

■   ■   ■

A L I C E   W A L K E R

EVERYDAY USE

for your grandmamma

I will wait for her in the yard that Maggie and I made so clean and wavy yesterday afternoon. A yard like this is more comfortable than most people know. It is not just a yard. It is like an extended living room. When the hard clay is swept clean as a floor and the fine sand around the edges lined with tiny, irregular grooves, anyone can come and sit and look up into the elm tree and wait for the breezes that never come inside the house.

Maggie will be nervous until after her sister goes: she will stand hopelessly in corners, homely and ashamed of the burn scars down her arms and legs, eying her sister with a mixture of envy and awe. She thinks her sister has held life always in the palm of one hand, that "no" is a word the world never learned to say to her.

You've no doubt seen those TV shows where the child who has "made it" is confronted, as a surprise, by her own mother and father, tottering in weakly from backstage. (A pleasant surprise, of course: What would they do if parent and child came on the show only to curse out and insult each other?) On TV mother and child embrace and smile into each other's faces. Sometimes the mother and father weep, the child wraps them in her arms and leans across the table to tell how she would not have made it without their help. I have seen these programs.

Sometimes I dream a dream in which Dee and I are suddenly brought together on a TV program of this sort. Out of a dark and soft-seated limousine I am ushered into a bright room filled with many people. There I meet a smiling, gray, sporty man like Johnny Carson who shakes my hand and tells me what a fine girl I have. Then we are on the stage and Dee is embracing me with tears in her eyes. She pins on my dress a large orchid, even though she has told me once that she thinks orchids are tacky flowers.

In real life I am a large, big-boned woman with rough, man-working hands. In the winter I wear flannel nightgowns to bed and overalls during the day. I can kill and clean a hog as mercilessly as a man. My fat keeps me hot in zero weather. I can work outside all day, breaking ice to get water for washing; I can eat pork liver cooked over the open fire minutes after it comes steaming from the hog. One winter I knocked a bull calf straight in the brain between the eyes with a sledge hammer and had the meat hung up to chill before nightfall. But of course all this does not show on television. I am the way my daughter would want me to be: a hundred pounds lighter, my skin like an uncooked barley pancake. My hair glistens in the hot bright lights. Johnny Carson has much to do to keep up with my quick and witty tongue.

But that is a mistake. I know even before I wake up. Who ever knew a Johnson with a quick tongue? Who can even imagine me looking a strange white man in the eye? It seems to me I have talked to them always with one foot raised in flight, with my head turned in whichever way is farthest from them. Dee, though. She would always look anyone in the eye. Hesitation was no part of her nature.

"How do I look, Mama?" Maggie says, showing just enough of her thin body enveloped in pink skirt and red blouse for me to know she's there, almost hidden by the door.

"Come out into the yard," I say.

Have you ever seen a lame animal, perhaps a dog run over by some careless person rich enough to own a car, sidle up to someone who is ignorant enough to be kind to him? That is the way my Maggie walks. She has been like this, chin on chest, eyes on ground, feet in shuffle, ever since the fire that burned the other house to the ground.

Dee is lighter than Maggie, with nicer hair and a fuller figure. She's a woman now, though sometimes I forget. How long ago was it that the other house burned? Ten, twelve years? Sometimes I can still hear the flames and feel Maggie's arms sticking to me, her hair smoking and her dress falling off her in little black papery flakes. Her eyes seemed stretched open, blazed open by the flames reflected in them. And Dee. I see her standing off under the sweet gum tree she used to dig gum out of; a look of concentration on her face as she watched the last dingy gray board of the house fall in toward the red-hot brick chimney. Why don't you do a dance around the ashes? I'd wanted to ask her. She had hated the house that much.

I used to think she hated Maggie, too. But that was before we raised the money, the church and me, to send her to Augusta to school. She used to read to us without pity; forcing words, lies, other folks' habits, whole lives upon us two, sitting trapped and ignorant underneath her voice. She washed us in a river of make-believe, burned us with a lot of knowledge we didn't necessarily need to know. Pressed us to her with the serious way she read, to shove us away at just the moment, like dimwits, we seemed about to understand.

Dee wanted nice things. A yellow organdy dress to wear to her graduation from high school; black pumps to match a green suit she'd made from an old suit somebody gave me. She was determined to stare down any disaster in her efforts. Her eyelids would not flicker for minutes at a time. Often I fought off the temptation to shake her. At sixteen she had a style of her own: and knew what style was.

I never had an education myself. After second grade the school was closed down. Don't ask me why: in 1927 colored asked fewer questions than they do now. Sometimes Maggie reads to me. She stumbles along good-naturedly but can't see well. She knows she is not bright. Like good looks and money, quickness passed her by. She will marry John Thomas (who has mossy teeth in an earnest face) and then I'll be free to sit here and I guess just sing church songs to myself. Although I never was a good singer. Never could carry a tune. I was always better at a man's job. I used to love to milk till I was hooked[1] in the side in '49. Cows are soothing and slow and don't bother you, unless you try to milk them the wrong way.

I have deliberately turned my back on the house. It is three rooms, just like the one that burned, except the roof is tin; they don't make shingle roofs any more. There are no real windows, just some holes cut in the sides, like the portholes in a ship, but not round and not square, with rawhide holding the shutters up on the outside. This house is in a pasture, too, like the other one. No doubt when Dee sees it she will want to tear it down. She wrote me once that no matter where we "choose" to live, she will manage to come see us. But she will never bring her friends. Maggie and I thought about this and Maggie asked me, "Mama, when did Dee ever *have* any friends?"

She had a few. Furtive boys in pink shirts hanging about on washday after school. Nervous girls who never laughed. Impressed with her they worshiped the well-turned phrase, the cute shape, the scalding humor that erupted like bubbles in lye. She read to them.

When she was courting Jimmy T she didn't have much time to pay to us, but turned all her faultfinding power on him. He *flew* to

---

1. I.e., by the horn of the cow being milked.

marry a cheap city girl from a family of ignorant flashy people. She hardly had time to recompose herself.

When she comes I will meet—but there they are!

Maggie attempts to make a dash for the house, in her shuffling way, but I stay her with my hand. "Come back here," I say. And she stops and tries to dig a well in the sand with her toe.

It is hard to see them clearly through the strong sun. But even the first glimpse of leg out of the car tells me it is Dee. Her feet were always neat-looking, as if God himself had shaped them with a certain style. From the other side of the car comes a short, stocky man. Hair is all over his head a foot long and hanging from his chin like a kinky mule tail. I hear Maggie suck in her breath. "Uhnnnh," is what it sounds like. Like when you see the wriggling end of a snake just in front of your foot on the road. "Uhnnnh."

Dee next. A dress down to the ground, in this hot weather. A dress so loud it hurts my eyes. There are yellows and oranges enough to throw back the light of the sun. I feel my whole face warming from the heat waves it throws out. Earrings gold, too, and hanging down to her shoulders. Bracelets dangling and making noises when she moves her arm up to shake the folds of the dress out of her armpits. The dress is loose and flows, and as she walks closer, I like it. I hear Maggie go "Uhnnnh" again. It is her sister's hair. It stands straight up like the wool on a sheep. It is black as night and around the edges are two long pigtails that rope about like small lizards disappearing behind her ears.

"Wa-su-zo-Tean-o!" she says, coming on in that gliding way the dress makes her move. The short stocky fellow with the hair to his navel is all grinning and he follows up with "Asalamalakim,[2] my mother and sister!" He moves to hug Maggie but she falls back, right up against the back of my chair. I feel her trembling there and when I look up I see the perspiration falling off her chin.

"Don't get up," says Dee. Since I am stout it takes something of a push. You can see me trying to move a second or two before I make it. She turns, showing white heels through her sandals, and goes back to the car. Out she peeks next with a Polaroid. She stoops down quickly and lines up picture after picture of me sitting there in front of the house with Maggie cowering behind me. She never takes a shot without making sure the house is included. When a cow comes nibbling around the edge of the yard she snaps it and me and Maggie *and* the

---

2. Phonetic rendering of a Muslim greeting. "Wa-su-zo-Tean-o" is a similar rendering of an African dialect salutation.

house. Then she puts the Polaroid in the back seat of the car, and comes up and kisses me on the forehead.

Meanwhile Asalamalakim is going through motions with Maggie's hand. Maggie's hand is as limp as a fish, and probably as cold, despite the sweat, and she keeps trying to pull it back. It looks like Asalamalakim wants to shake hands but wants to do it fancy. Or maybe he don't know how people shake hands. Anyhow, he soon gives up on Maggie.

"Well," I say. "Dee."

"No, Mama," she says. "Not 'Dee,' Wangero Leewanika Kemanjo!"

"What happened to 'Dee'?" I wanted to know.

"She's dead," Wangero said. "I couldn't bear it any longer, being named after the people who oppress me."

"You know as well as me you was named after your aunt Dicie," I said. Dicie is my sister. She named Dee. We called her "Big Dee" after Dee was born.

"But who was *she* named after?" asked Wangero.

"I guess after Grandma Dee," I said.

"And who was she named after?" asked Wangero.

"Her mother," I said, and saw Wangero was getting tired. "That's about as far back as I can trace it," I said. Though, in fact, I probably could have carried it back beyond the Civil War through the branches.

"Well," said Asalamalakim, "there you are."

"Uhnnnh," I heard Maggie say.

"There I was not," I said, "before 'Dicie' cropped up in our family, so why should I try to trace it that far back?"

He just stood there grinning, looking down on me like somebody inspecting a Model A car. Every once in a while he and Wangero sent eye signals over my head.

"How do you pronounce this name?" I asked.

"You don't have to call me by it if you don't want to," said Wangero.

"Why shouldn't I?" I asked. "If that's what you want us to call you, we'll call you."

"I know it might sound awkward at first," said Wangero.

"I'll get used to it," I said. "Ream it out again."

Well, soon we got the name out of the way. Asalamalakim had a name twice as long and three times as hard. After I tripped over it two or three times he told me to just call him Hakim-a-barber. I wanted to ask him was he a barber, but I didn't really think he was, so I didn't ask.

"You must belong to those beef-cattle peoples down the road," I said. They said "Asalamalakim" when they met you, too, but they didn't shake hands. Always too busy: feeding the cattle, fixing the fences, putting up salt-lick shelters, throwing down hay. When the white folks poisoned some of the herd the men stayed up all night with rifles in their hands. I walked a mile and a half just to see the sight.

Hakim-a-barber said, "I accept some of their doctrines, but farming and raising cattle is not my style." (They didn't tell me, and I didn't ask, whether Wangero (Dee) had really gone and married him.)

We sat down to eat and right away he said he didn't eat collards and pork was unclean. Wangero, though, went on through the chitlins and corn bread, the greens and everything else. She talked a blue streak over the sweet potatoes. Everything delighted her. Even the fact that we still used the benches her daddy made for the table when we couldn't afford to buy chairs.

"Oh, Mama!" she cried. Then turned to Hakim-a-barber. "I never knew how lovely these benches are. You can feel the rump prints," she said, running her hands underneath her and along the bench. Then she gave a sigh and her hand closed over Grandma Dee's butter dish. "That's it!" she said. "I knew there was something I wanted to ask you if I could have." She jumped up from the table and went over in the corner where the churn stood, the milk in it clabber by now. She looked at the churn and looked at it.

"This churn top is what I need," she said. "Didn't Uncle Buddy whittle it out of a tree you all used to have?"

"Yes," I said.

"Uh huh," she said happily. "And I want the dasher, too."

"Uncle Buddy whittle that too?" asked the barber.

Dee (Wangero) looked up at me.

"Aunt Dee's first husband whittled the dash," said Maggie so low you almost couldn't hear her. "His name was Henry, but they called him Stash."

"Maggie's brain is like an elephant's," Wangero said, laughing. "I can use the churn top as a centerpiece for the alcove table," she said, sliding a plate over the churn, "and I'll think of something artistic to do with the dasher."

When she finished wrapping the dasher the handle stuck out. I took it for a moment in my hands. You didn't even have to look close to see where hands pushing the dasher up and down to make butter had left a kind of sink in the wood. In fact, there were a lot of small sinks; you could see where thumbs and fingers had sunk into the wood. It was beautiful light yellow wood, from a tree that grew in the yard where Big Dee and Stash had lived.

After dinner Dee (Wangero) went to the trunk at the foot of my bed and started rifling through it. Maggie hung back in the kitchen over the dishpan. Out came Wangero with two quilts. They had been pieced by Grandma Dee and then Big Dee and me had hung them on the quilt frames on the front porch and quilted them. One was in the Lone Star pattern. The other was Walk Around the Mountain. In both of them were scraps of dresses Grandma Dee had worn fifty and more years ago. Bits and pieces of Grandpa Jarrell's Paisley shirts. And one teeny faded blue piece, about the size of a penny matchbox, that was from Great Grandpa Ezra's uniform that he wore in the Civil War.

"Mama," Wangero said sweet as a bird. "Can I have these old quilts?"

I heard something fall in the kitchen, and a minute later the kitchen door slammed.

"Why don't you take one or two of the others?" I asked. "These old things was just done by me and Big Dee from some tops your grandma pieced before she died."

"No," said Wangero. "I don't want those. They are stitched around the borders by machine."

"That'll make them last better," I said.

"That's not the point," said Wangero. "These are all pieces of dresses Grandma used to wear. She did all this stitching by hand. Imagine!" She held the quilts securely in her arms, stroking them.

"Some of the pieces, like those lavender ones, come from old clothes her mother handed down to her," I said, moving up to touch the quilts. Dee (Wangero) moved back just enough so that I couldn't reach the quilts. They already belonged to her.

"Imagine!" she breathed again, clutching them closely to her bosom.

"The truth is," I said, "I promised to give them quilts to Maggie, for when she marries John Thomas."

She gasped like a bee had stung her.

"Maggie can't appreciate these quilts!" she said. "She'd probably be backward enough to put them to everyday use."

"I reckon she would," I said. "God knows I been saving 'em for long enough with nobody using 'em. I hope she will!" I didn't want to bring up how I had offered Dee (Wangero) a quilt when she went away to college. Then she had told me they were old-fashioned, out of style.

"But they're *priceless!*" she was saying now, furiously; for she has a temper. "Maggie would put them on the bed and in five years they'd be in rags. Less than that!" "She can always make some more," I said. "Maggie knows how to quilt."

Dee (Wangero) looked at me with hatred. "You just will not understand. The point is these quilts, *these* quilts!"

"Well," I said, stumped. "What would *you* do with them?"

"Hang them," she said. As if that was the only thing you *could* do with quilts.

Maggie by now was standing in the door. I could almost hear the sound her feet made as they scraped over each other.

"She can have them, Mama," she said, like somebody used to never winning anything, or having anything reserved for her. "I can 'member Grandma Dee without the quilts."

I looked at her hard. She had filled her bottom lip with checkerberry snuff and it gave her face a kind of dopey, hangdog look. It was Grandma Dee and Big Dee who taught her how to quilt herself. She stood there with her scarred hands hidden in the folds of her skirt. She looked at her sister with something like fear but she wasn't mad at her. This was Maggie's portion. This was the way she knew God to work.

When I looked at her like that something hit me in the top of my head and ran down to the soles of my feet. Just like when I'm in church and the spirit of God touches me and I get happy and shout. I did something I never had done before: hugged Maggie to me, then dragged her on into the room, snatched the quilts out of Miss Wangero's hands and dumped them into Maggie's lap. Maggie just sat there on my bed with her mouth open.

"Take one or two of the others," I said to Dee.

But she turned without a word and went out to Hakim-a-barber.

"You just don't understand," she said, as Maggie and I came out to the car.

"What don't I understand?" I wanted to know.

"Your heritage," she said. And then she turned to Maggie, kissed her, and said, "You ought to try to make something of yourself, too, Maggie. It's really a new day for us. But from the way you and Mama still live you'd never know it."

She put on some sunglasses that hid everything above the tip of her nose and her chin.

Maggie smiled; maybe at the sunglasses. But a real smile, not scared. After we watched the car dust settle I asked Maggie to bring me a dip of snuff. And then the two of us sat there just enjoying, until it was time to go in the house and go to bed.

1973

TAKING CARE

I

Jones, the preacher, has been in love all his life. He is baffled by this because as far as he can see, it has never helped anyone, even when they have acknowledged it, which is not often. Jones' love is much too apparent and arouses neglect. He is like an animal in a traveling show who, through some aberration, wears a vital organ outside the skin, awkward and unfortunate, something that shouldn't be seen, certainly something that shouldn't be watched working. Now he sits on a bed beside his wife in the self-care unit of a hospital fifteen miles from their home. She has been committed here for tests. She is so weak, so tired. There is something wrong with her blood. Her arms are covered with bruises where they have gone into the veins. Her hip, too, is blue and swollen where they have drawn out samples of bone marrow. All of this is frightening. The doctors are severe and wise, answering Jones' questions in a way that makes him feel hopelessly deaf. They have told him that there really is no such thing as a disease of the blood, for the blood is not a living tissue but a passive vehicle for the transportation of food, oxygen and waste. They have told him that abnormalities in the blood corpucles, which his wife seems to have, must be regarded as symptoms of disease elsewhere in the body. They have shown him, upon request, slides and charts of normal and pathological blood cells which look to Jones like canapés. They speak (for he insists) of leukocytosis, myelocytes and megaloblasts. None of this takes into account the love he has for his wife! Jones sits beside her in this dim pleasant room, wearing a gray suit and his clerical collar, for when he leaves her he must visit other parishioners who are patients here. This part of the hospital is like a motel. One may wear one's regular clothes. The rooms have ice-buckets, rugs and colorful bedspreads. How he wishes that they were traveling and staying overnight, this night, in a motel. A nurse comes in with a tiny paper cup full of pills. There are three pills, or rather, capsules, and they are not for his wife but for her blood. The cup is the smallest of its type that Jones has ever seen. All perspective, all sense of time and scale seem abandoned in this hospital. For example, when Jones turns to kiss his wife's hair, he nicks the air instead.

II

Jones and his wife have one child, a daughter, who, in turn, has a single child, a girl, born one-half year ago. Jones' daughter has fallen in with the stars and is using the heavens, as Jones would be the first to admit, more than he ever has. It has, however, brought her only grief and confusion. She has left her husband and brought the baby to Jones. She has also given him her dog, a German shepherd. She is going to Mexico where soon, in the mountains, she will have a nervous breakdown. Jones does not know this, but his daughter has seen it in the stars and is going out to meet it. Jones quickly agrees to care for both the baby and the dog, as this seems to be the only thing his daughter needs from him. The day of the baby's birth is secondary to the position of the planets and the terms of houses, quadrants and gradients.[1] Her symbol is a bareback rider. To Jones, this is a graceful thought. It signifies audacity. It also means luck. Jones slips a twenty dollar bill in the pocket of his daughter's suitcase and drives her to the airport. The plane taxis down the runway and Jones waves, holding all their luck in his arms.

III

One afternoon, Jones had come home and found his wife sitting in the garden, weeping. She had been transplanting flowers, putting them in pots before the first frost came. There was dirt on her forehead and around her mouth. Her light clothes felt so heavy. Their weight made her body ache. Each breath was a stone she had to swallow. She cried and cried in the weak autumn sunshine. Jones could see the veins throbbing in her neck. "I'm dying," she said. "It's taking me months to die." But after he had brought her inside, she insisted that she felt better and made them both a cup of tea while Jones potted the rest of the plants and carried them down cellar. She lay on the sofa and Jones sat beside her. They talked quietly with one another. Indeed, they were almost whispering, as though they were in a public place surrounded by strangers instead of in their own house with no one present but themselves. "It's the season," Jones said. "In fall everything slows down,

1. Astrological terms.

retreats. I'm feeling tired myself. We need iron. I'll go to the druggist right now and buy some iron tablets." His wife agreed. She wanted to go with him, for the ride. Together they ride, through the towns, for miles and miles, even into the next state. She does not want to stop driving. They buy sandwiches and milkshakes and eat in the car. Jones drives. They have to buy more gasoline. His wife sits close to him, her eyes closed, her head tipped back against the seat. He can see the veins beating on in her neck. Somewhere there is a dreadful sound, almost audible. "First I thought it was my imagination," his wife said. "I couldn't sleep. All night I would stay awake, dreaming. But it's not in my head. It's in my ears, my eyes. They ache. Everything. My tongue. My hair. The tips of my fingers are dead." Jones pressed her cold hand to his lips. He thinks of something mad and loving better than he— running out of control, deeply in the darkness of his wife. "Just don't make me go to the hospital," she pleaded. Of course she will go there. The moment has already occurred.

IV

Jones is writing to his daughter. He received a brief letter from her this morning, telling him where she could be reached. The foreign post-mark was so large that it almost obliterated Jones' address. She did not mention either her mother or the baby, which makes Jones feel pecu-liar. His life seems increated[2] as his God's life, perhaps even imaginary. His daughter tells him about the town in which she lives. She does not plan to stay there long. She wants to travel. She will find out exactly what she wants to do and then she will come home again. The town is poor but interesting and there are many Americans there her own age. There is a zoo right on the beach. Almost all the towns, no matter how small, have little zoos. There are primarily eagles and hawks in the cages. And what can Jones reply to that? He writes *Everything is fine here. We are burning wood from the old apple tree in the fire place and its smells wonderful. Has the baby had her full series of polio shots? Take care.* Jones uses this expression constantly, usually in totally unwar-ranted situations, as when he purchases pipe cleaners or drives through toll booths. Distracted, Jones writes off the edge of the paper and onto the blotter. He must begin again. He will mail this on the way to the hospital. They have been taking X-rays for three days now but the pictures are cloudy. They cannot read them. His wife is now in a real sickbed with high metal sides. He sits with her while she eats her dinner. She asks him to take her good nightgown home and wash it with a bar of Ivory. They won't let her do anything now, not even wash out a few things. *You must take care.*

---

2. Existing without having been created.

V

Jones is driving down a country road. It is the first snowfall of the season and he wants to show it to the baby who rides beside him in a small foam-and-metal car seat all her own. Her head is almost on a level with his and she looks earnestly at the landscape, sometimes smiling. They follow the road that winds tightly between fields and deep pine woods. Everything is white and clean. It has been snowing all afternoon and is doing so still, but very very lightly. Fat snowflakes fall solitary against the windshield. Sometimes the baby reaches out for them. Sometimes she gives a brief kick and cry of joy. They have done their errands. Jones has bought milk and groceries and two yellow roses which lie wrapped in tissue and newspaper in the trunk, in the cold. He must buy two on Saturday as the florist is closed on Sunday. He does not like to do this but there is no alternative. The roses do not keep well. Tonight he will give one to his wife. The other he will pack in sugar water and store in the refrigerator. He can only hope that the bud will remain tight until Sunday when he brings it into the terrible heat of the hospital. The baby rocks against the straps of her small carrier. Her lips are pursed as she watches intently the fields, the gray stalks of crops growing out of the snow, the trees. She is warmly dressed and she wears a knitted orange cap. It is twenty-three years old, the age of her mother. Jones found it just the other day when he was looking for it. It has faded almost to pink on one side. At one time, it must have been stored in the sun. Jones, driving feels almost gay. The snow is so beautiful. Everything is white, even the hood of the car. Jones is an educated man. He has read Melville, who says that white[3] is the colorless all-color of atheism from which we shrink. Jones does not believe this. He sees a holiness in snow, a promise. He hopes that his wife will know that it is snowing even though she is separated from the window by a curtain. Jones sees something moving across the snow, a part of the snow itself, running. Although he is going slowly, he takes his foot completely off the accelerator. "Look, darling, a snowshoe rabbit." At the sound of his voice, the baby stretches open her mouth and narrows her eyes in soundless glee. The hare is splendid. So fast! It flows around invisible obstructions, something out of a kind dream. It flies across the ditch, its paws like paddles, faintly yellow, the color of raw wood. "Look, sweet," cries Jones, "how big he is!" But suddenly the hare is curved and falling, round as a ball, its feet and head tucked closely against its body. It strikes the road and skids upside down for several

3. The reference is to Chapter 42 of *Moby-Dick* by Herman Melville. The entire chapter is an imaginative discourse on *whiteness*. A typical passage: "This elusive quality it is, which causes the thought of whiteness, when divorced from its more kindly associations, and coupled with any object terrible in itself, to heighten that terror to its furthest bounds."

yards. The car passes around it, avoids it. Jones brakes and stops, amazed. He opens the door and trots back to the animal. The baby twists about in her seat as well as she can and peers after him. It is as though the animal had never been alive at all. Its head is broken in several places. Jones bends to touch its fur, but straightens again, not doing so. A man emerges from the woods, swinging a shotgun. He nods at Jones and picks the hare up by the ears. As he walks away, the hare's legs rub across the ground. There are small crystal stains on the snow. Jones returns to the car. He wants to apologize but he does not know to whom or for what. His life has been devoted to apologetics. It is his profession. He is concerned with both justification and remorse. He has always acted rightly, but nothing has ever come of it. He gets in the car, starts the engine. "Oh, sweet," he says to the baby. She smiles at him, exposing her tooth. At home that night, after the baby's supper, Jones reads a story to her. She is asleep, panting in her sleep, but Jones tells her the story of al-Boraq, the milkwhite steed of Mohammed, who could stride out of the sight of mankind with a single step.

VI

Jones sorts through a collection of records, none of which have been opened. They are still wrapped in cellophane. The jacket designs are subdued, epic. Names, instruments and orchestras are mentioned confidently. He would like to agree with their importance, for he knows that they have worth, but he is not familiar with the references. His daughter brought these records with her. They had been given to her by an older man, a professor she had been having an affair with. Naturally, this pains Jones. His daughter speaks about the men she has been involved with but no longer cares about. Where did these men come from? Where were they waiting and why have they gone? Jones remembers his daughter when she was a little girl, helping him rake leaves. What can he say? For years on April Fool's Day, she would take tobacco out of his humidor and fill it with Corn Flakes. Jones is full of remorse and astonishment. When he saw his daughter only a few weeks ago, she was thin and nervous. She had torn out almost all her eyebrows with her fingers from this nervousness. And her lashes. The roots of her eyes were white, like the bulbs of flowers. Her fingernails were crudely bitten, some bleeding below the quick. She was tough and remote, wanting only to go on a trip for which she had a ticket. What can he do? He seeks her in the face of the baby but she is not there. All is being both continued and resumed, but the dream is different. The dream cannot be revived. Jones breaks into one of the albums, blows the dust from the needle, plays a record. Outside it is dark. The parsonage is remote and the only buildings nearby are barns. The river cannot be seen. The music is Bruckner's *Te Deum*.[4] Very nice. Dedicated to God. He plays the other side. A woman, Kathleen Ferrier,[5] is singing in German. Jones cannot understand the words but the music stuns him. *Kindertotenlieder*,[6] It is devastating. In college he had studied only scientific German, the vocabulary of submarines, dirigibles and steam engines. Jones plays the record again and again, searching for his old grammar. At last he finds it. The wings of insects are between some of the pages. There are notes in pencil, written in his own young hand.

Render:
A. *Was the teacher satisfied with you today?*
B. *No, he was not. My essay was good but it was not copied well.*
C. *I am sorry you were not industrious this time for you generally are.*

These lessons are neither of life or death. Why was he instructed in them? In the hospital, his wife waits to be translated, no longer a woman, the woman whom he loves, but a situation. Her blood moves mysteriously as constellations. She is under scrutiny and attack and she has abandoned Jones. She is a swimmer waiting to get on with the drowning. Jones is on the shore. In Mexico, his daughter walks along the beach with two men. She is acting out a play that has become her life. Jones is on the mountaintop. The baby cries and Jones takes her from the crib to change her. The dog paws the door. Jones lets him out. He settles down with the baby and listens to the record. *Songs on the Deaths of Infants.* Controlled heartbreak. He still cannot make out many of the words. The baby wiggles restlessly on his lap. Her eyes are a foal's eyes, navy-blue. She has grown in a few weeks to expect everything from Jones. He props her on one edge of the couch and goes to her small toy box where he keeps a bear, a few rattles and balls. On the way, he opens the door and the dog immediately enters. His heavy coat is cold, fragrant with ice. He noses the baby and she squeals.

> Oft denk' ich, sie sind nur ausgegangen
> Bald werden sie wieder nach Hause gelangen[7]

Jones selects a bright ball and pushes it gently in her direction.

---

4. "Thou, Lord," by Anton Bruckner (1824–1896), Austrian composer.
5. English contralto (1912–1953).
6. *Songs of the Death of Children.*
7. "Often I think you have only gone out / Soon you will come into the house again."

VII

It is Sunday morning and Jones is in the pulpit. The church is very old but the walls of the sanctuary have recently been painted a pale blue. In the cemetery adjoining, some of the graves are three hundred years old. It has become a historical landmark and no one has been buried there since World War I. There is a new place, not far away, which the families now use. Plots are marked not with stones but with small tablets, and immediately after any burial, workmen roll grassed sod over the new graves so that there is no blemish on the grounds, not even for a little while. Present for today's service are seventy-eight adults, eleven children and the junior choir. Jones counts them as the offertory is received. The church rolls say that there are 350 members but as far as Jones can see, everyone is here today. This is the day he baptizes the baby. He has made arrangements with one of the ladies to hold her and bring her up to the font at the end of the first hymn. The baby looks charming in a lacy white dress. Jones has combed her fine hair carefully, slicking it in a curl with water, but now it has dried and it sticks up awkwardly like the crest of a kingfisher. Jones bought the dress in Mammoth Mart, an enormous store which has a large metal elephant dressed in overalls dancing on the roof. He feels foolish at buying it there but he had gone to several stores and that is where he saw the prettiest dress. He blesses the baby with water from the silver bowl. He says, *We are saved not because we are worthy. We are saved because we are loved.* It is a brief ceremony. The baby, looking curiously at Jones, is taken out to the nursery. Jones begins his sermon. He can't remember when he wrote it, but here it is, typed, in front of him. *There is nothing wrong in what one does but there is something wrong in what one becomes.* He finds this questionable but goes on speaking. He has been preaching for thirty-four years. He is gaunt with belief. But his wife has a red cell count of only 2.3 millions. It is not enough! She is not getting enough oxygen! Jones is giving his sermon. Somewhere he has lost what he was looking for. He must have known once, surely. The congregation sways, like the wings of a ray in water. It is Sunday and for patients it is a holiday. The doctors don't visit. There are no tests or diagnoses. Jones would like to leave, to walk down the aisle and out into the winter, where he would read his words into the ground. Why can't he remember his life! He finishes, sits down, stands up to present communion. Tiny cubes of bread lie in a slumped pyramid. They are offered and received. Jones takes his morsel, hacked earlier from a sliced enriched loaf with his own hand. It is so dry, almost wicked. The very thought now sickens him. He chews it over and over again, but it lies unconsumed, like a muscle in his mouth.

VIII

Jones is waiting in the lobby for the results of his wife's operation. Has there ever been a time before dread? He would be grateful even to have dread back, but it has been lost, for a long time, in rapid possibility, probability and fact. The baby sits on his knees and plays with his tie. She woke very early this morning for her orange juice and then gravely, immediately, spit it all up. She seems fine now, however, her fingers exploring Jones' tie. Whenever he looks at her, she gives him a dazzling smile. He has spent most of the day fiercely cleaning the house, changing the bedsheets and the pages of the many calendars that hang in the rooms, things he should have done a week ago. He has dusted and vacuumed and pressed all his shirts. He has laundered all the baby's clothes, soft small sacks and gowns and sleepers which froze in his hands the moment he stepped outside. And now he is waiting and watching his wristwatch. The tumor is precisely this size, they tell him, the size of his clock's face.

IX

Jones has the baby on his lap and he is feeding her. The evening meal is lengthy and complex. First he must give her vitamins, then, because she has a cold, a dropper of liquid aspirin. This is followed by a bottle of milk, eight ounces, and a portion of strained vegetables. He gives her a rest now so that the food can settle. On his hip, she rides through the rooms of the huge house as Jones turns lights off and on. He comes back to the table and gives her a little more milk, a half jar of strained chicken and a few spoonfuls of dessert, usually cobbler, buckle or pudding. The baby enjoys all equally. She is good. She eats rapidly and neatly. Sometimes she grasps the spoon, turns it around and thrusts the wrong end into her mouth. Of course there is nothing that cannot be done incorrectly. Jones adores the baby. He sniffs her warm head. Her birth is a deep error, an abstraction. Born in wedlock but out of love. He puts her in the playpen and tends to the dog. He fills one dish with water and one with horsemeat. He rinses out the empty can before putting it in the wastebasket. The dog eats with great civility. He eats a little meat and then takes some water, then meat, then water. When the dog has finished, the dishes are as clean as though they'd been washed. Jones now thinks about his own dinner. He opens the refrigerator. The ladies of the church have brought brownies, venison, cheese and apple sauce. There are turkey pies, pork chops, steak, haddock and sausage patties. A brilliant light exposes all this food. There is so much of it. It must be used. A crust has formed around the punctures in a can of Pet. There is a clear bag of chicken livers stapled shut. There are large brown eggs in a bowl. Jones stares unhappily at the beads of moisture on cartons and bottles, at the pearls of fat on the cold cooked stew. He sits down. The room is full of lamps and cords. He thinks of his wife, her breathing body deranged in tubes, and begins to shake. All objects here are perplexed by such grief.

X

Now it is almost Christmas and Jones is walking down by the river, around an abandoned house. The dog wades heavily through the snow, biting it. There are petals of ice on the tree limbs and when Jones lingers under them, the baby puts out her hand and her mouth starts working because she would like to have it, the ice, the branch, everything. His wife will be coming home in a few days, in time for Christmas. Jones has already put up the tree and brought the ornaments down from the attic. He will not trim it until she comes home. He wants very much to make a fine occasion out of opening the boxes of old decorations. The two of them have always enjoyed this greatly in the past. Jones will doubtlessly drop and smash a bauble, for he does every year. He tramps through the snow with his small voyager. She dangles in a shoulder sling, her legs wedged around his hip. They regard the rotting house seriously. Once it was a doctor's home and offices but long before Jones' time, the doctor, who was very respected, had been driven away because a town girl accused him of fathering her child. The story goes that all the doctor said was, "Is that so?" This incensed the town and the girl's parents, who insisted that he take the child as soon as it was born. He did and he cared for it very well even though his practice was ruined and no one had anything to do with him. A year later the girl told the truth—that the actual father was a young college boy who she was now going to marry. They wanted the child back, and the doctor willingly gave the infant to them, saying to their apology and confession only, "Is that so?" Of course it is a very old, important story. Jones has always appreciated it, but now he is annoyed at the man's passivity. His wife's sickness has changed everything for Jones. He will continue to accept but he will no longer surrender. Surely things are different for Jones now.

XI

For insurance purposes, Jones' wife is brought out to the car in a wheelchair. She is thin and beautiful. Jones is grateful and confused. He has a mad wish to tip the orderly. Have so many years really passed? Is this not his wife, his love, fresh from giving birth? Isn't everything about to begin? In Mexico, his daughter wanders disinterestedly through a jewelry shop where she picks up a small silver egg. It opens on a hinge and inside are two figures, a bride and groom. Jones puts the baby in his wife's arms. At first the baby is alarmed because she cannot remember this person very well and she reaches for Jones, whimpering. But soon she is soothed by his wife's soft voice and she falls asleep in her arms as they drive. Jones has readied everything carefully for his wife's homecoming. The house is clean and orderly. For days he has restricted himself to only one part of the house so that his clutter will be minimal. Jones helps his wife up the steps to the door. Together they enter the shining rooms.

1982

TOBIAS WOLFF

IN THE GARDEN OF THE
NORTH AMERICAN MARTYRS

When she was young, Mary saw a brilliant and original man lose his job because he had expressed ideas that were offensive to the trustees of the college where they both taught. She shared his views, but did not sign the protest petition. She was, after all, on trial herself—as a teacher, as a woman, as an interpreter of history.

Mary watched herself. Before giving a lecture she wrote it out in full, using the arguments and often the words of other, approved writers, so that she would not by chance say something scandalous. Her own thoughts she kept to herself, and the words for them grew faint as time went on; without quite disappearing they shrank to remote, nervous points, like birds flying away.

When the department turned into a hive of cliques, Mary went about her business and pretended not to know that people hated each other. To avoid seeming bland she let herself become eccentric in harmless ways. She took up bowling, which she learned to love, and founded the Brandon College chapter of a society dedicated to restoring the good name of Richard III.[1] She memorized comedy routines from records and jokes from books; people groaned when she rattled them off, but she did not let that stop her, and after a time the groans became the point of the jokes. They were a kind of tribute to Mary's willingness to expose herself.

In fact no one at the college was safer than Mary, for she was making herself into something institutional, like a custom, or a mascot—part of the college's idea of itself.

1. English king (1452–1485), generally regarded as ruthless and brutal.

535

Now and then she wondered whether she had been too careful. The things she said and wrote seemed flat to her, pulpy, as though someone else had squeezed the juice out of them. And once, while talking with a senior professor, Mary saw herself reflected in a window: she was leaning toward him and had her head turned so that her ear was right in front of his moving mouth. The sight disgusted her. Years, later, when she had to get a hearing aid, Mary suspected that her deafness was a result of always trying to catch everything everyone said.

In the second half of Mary's fifteenth year at Brandon the provost called a meeting of all faculty and students to announce that the college was bankrupt and would not open its gates again. He was every bit as much surprised as they; the report from the trustees had reached his desk only that morning. It seemed that Brandon's financial manager had speculated in some kind of futures and lost everything. The provost wanted to deliver the news in person before it reached the papers. He wept openly and so did the students and teachers, with only a few exceptions—some cynical upperclassmen who claimed to despise the education they had received.

Mary could not rid her mind of the word "speculate." It meant to guess, in terms of money to gamble. How could a man gamble a college? Why would he want to do that, and how could it be that no one stopped him? To Mary, it seemed to belong to another time; she thought of a drunken plantation owner gaming away his slaves.

She applied for jobs and got an offer from a new experimental college in Oregon. It was her only offer so she took it.

The college was in one building. Bells rang all the time, lockers lined the hallways, and at every corner stood a buzzing water fountain. The student newspaper came out twice a month on mimeograph paper which felt wet. The library, which was next to the band room, had no librarian and no books.

The countryside was beautiful, though, and Mary might have enjoyed it if the rain had not caused her so much trouble. There was something wrong with her lungs that the doctors couldn't agree on, and couldn't cure; whatever it was, the dampness made it worse. On rainy days condensation formed in Mary's hearing aid and shorted it out. She began to dread, talking with people, never knowing when she would have to take out her control box and slap it against her leg.

It rained nearly every day. When it was not raining it was getting ready to rain, or clearing. The ground glinted under the grass, and the light had a yellow undertone that flared up during storms.

There was water in Mary's basement. Her walls sweated, and she had found toadstools growing behind the refrigerator. She felt as though she were rusting out, like one of those old cars people thereabouts kept in their front yards, on pieces of wood. Mary knew that everyone was dying, but it did seem to her that she was dying faster than most.

She continued to look for another job, without success. Then, in the fall of her third year in Oregon, she got a letter from a woman named Louise who'd once taught in Brandon. Louise had scored a great success with a book on Benedict Arnold[2] and was now on the faculty of a famous college in upstate New York. She said that one of her colleagues would be retiring at the end of the year and asked whether Mary would be interested in the position.

The letter surprised Mary. Louise thought of herself as a great historian and of almost everyone else as useless; Mary had not known that she felt differently about her. Moreover, enthusiasm for other people's causes did not come easily to Louise, who had a way of sucking in her breath when familiar names were mentioned, as though she knew things that friendship kept her from disclosing.

Mary expected nothing, but sent a résumé and copies of her two books. Shortly after that Louise called to say that the search committee, of which she was chairwoman, had decided to grant Mary an interview in early November. "Now don't get your hopes *too* high," Louise said.

"Oh, no," Mary said, but thought: Why shouldn't I hope? They would not go to the bother and expense of bringing her to the college if they weren't serious. And she was certain that the interview would go well. She would make them like her, or at least give them no cause to dislike her.

She read about the area with a strange sense of familiarity, as if the land and its history were already known to her. And when her plane left Portland and climbed easily into the clouds, Mary felt like she was going home. The feeling stayed with her, growing stronger when they landed. She tried to describe it to Louise as they left the airport at Syracuse and drove toward the college, an hour or so away. "It's like *déjà vu*," she said.

"*Déjà vu*, is a hoax," Louise said. "It's just a chemical imbalance of some kind."

"Maybe so," Mary said, "but I still have this sensation."

"Don't get serious on me," Louise said. "That's not your long suit. Just be your funny, wisecracking old self. Tell me now—honestly—how do I look?"

It was night, too dark to see Louise's face well, but in the airport

2. U.S. general (1741–1801) in Revolutionary War, who became a traitor.

she had seemed gaunt and pale and intense. She reminded Mary of a description in the book she'd been reading, of how Iroquois[3] warriors gave themselves visions by fasting. She had that kind of look about her. But she wouldn't want to hear that. "You look wonderful," Mary said.

"There's a reason," Louise said. "I've taken a lover. My concentration has improved, my energy level is up, and I've lost ten pounds. I'm also getting some color in my cheeks, though that could be the weather. I recommend the experience highly. But you probably disapprove."

Mary didn't know what to say. She said that she was sure Louise knew best, but that didn't seem to be enough. "Marriage is a great institution," she added, "but who wants to live in an institution?"

Louise groaned. "I know you," she said, "and I know that right now you're thinking 'But what about Ted? What about the children?' The fact is, Mary, they aren't taking it well at all. Ted has become a nag." She handed Mary her purse. "Be a good girl and light me a cigarette, will you? I know I told you I quit, but this whole thing has been very hard on me, very hard, and I'm afraid I've started again."

They were in the hills now, heading north on a narrow road. Tall trees arched above them. As they topped a rise Mary saw the forest all around, deep black under the plum-colored sky. There were a few lights and these made the darkness seem even greater.

"Ted has succeeded in completely alienating the children from me," Louise was saying. "There is no reasoning with any of them. In fact, they refuse to discuss the matter at all, which is very ironical because over the years I have tried to instill in them a willingness to see things from the other person's point of view. If they could just *meet* Jonathan I know they would feel differently. But they won't hear of it. Jonathan," she said, "is my lover."

"I see," Mary said, and nodded.

Coming around a curve they caught two deer in the headlights. Their eyes lit up and their hindquarters tensed; Mary could see them trembling as the car went by. "Deer," she said.

"I don't know," Louise said, "I just don't know. I do my best and it never seems to be enough. But that's enough about me—let's talk about you. What did you think of my latest book?" She squawked and beat her palms on the steering wheel. "God, I love that joke," she said. "Seriously, though, what about you? It must have been a real shockeroo when good old Brandon folded."

"It was hard. Things haven't been good but they'll be a lot better if I get this job."

3. A tribe native to the lower Great Lakes region; war-loving by reputation.

"At least you have work," Louise said. "You should look at it from the bright side."

"I try."

"You seem so gloomy. I hope you're not worrying about the interview, or the class. Worrying won't do you a bit of good. Be happy."

"Class? What class?"

"The class you're supposed to give tomorrow, after the interview. Didn't I tell you? *Mea culpa*, hon, *mea maxima culpa*. I've been uncharacteristically forgetful lately."

"But what will I do?"

"Relax," Louise said. "Just pick a subject and wing it."

"Wing it?"

"You know, open your mouth and see what comes out. Extemporize."

"But I always work from a prepared lecture."

Louise sighed. "All right. I'll tell you what. Last year I wrote an article on the Marshall Plan[4] that I got bored with and never published. You can read that."

Parroting what Louise had written seemed wrong to Mary, at first; then it occurred to her that she had been doing the same kind of thing for many years, and that this was not the time to get scruples. "Thanks," she said. "I appreciate it."

"Here we are," Louise said, and pulled into a circular drive with several cabins grouped around it. In two of the cabins lights were on; smoke drifted straight up from the chimneys. "This is the visitors' center. The college is another two miles thataway." Louise pointed down the road. "I'd invite you to stay at my house, but I'm spending the night with Jonathan and Ted is not good company these days. You would hardly recognize him."

She took Mary's bags from the trunk and carried them up the steps of a darkened cabin. "Look," she said, "they've laid a fire for you. All you have to do is light it." She stood in the middle of the room with her arms crossed and watched as Mary held a match under the kindling. "There," she said. "You'll be snugaroo in no time. I'd love to stay and chew the fat but I can't. You just get a good night's sleep and I'll see you in the morning."

Mary stood in the doorway and waved as Louise pulled out of the drive, spraying gravel. She filled her lungs, to taste the air: it was tart and clear. She could see the stars in their figurations, and the vague streams of light that ran among the stars.

4. Plan for rehabilitating European economies devastated by W.W. II, formulated by George Catlett Marshall (1880–1959), U.S. chief of staff.

She still felt uneasy about reading Louise's work as her own. It would be her first complete act of plagiarism. It would change her. It would make her less—how much less, she did not know. But what else could she do? She certainly couldn't "wing it." Words might fail her, and then what? Mary had a dread of silence. When she thought of silence she thought of drowning, as if it were a kind of water she could not swim in.

"I want this job," she said, and settled deep into her coat. It was cashmere and Mary had not worn it since moving to Oregon, because people there thought you were pretentious if you had on anything but a Pendleton shirt or, of course, raingear. She rubbed her check against the upturned collar and thought of a silver moon shining through bare black branches, a white house with green shutters, red leaves falling in a hard blue sky.

Louise woke her a few hours later. She was sitting on the edge of the bed, pushing at Mary's shoulder and snuffling loudly. When Mary asked her what was wrong she said, "I want your opinion on something. It's very important. Do you think I'm womanly?"

Mary sat up. "Louise, can this wait?"

"No."

"Womanly?"

Louise nodded.

"You are very beautiful," Mary said, "and you know how to present yourself."

Louise stood and paced the room. "That son of a bitch," she said. She came back and stood over Mary. "Let's suppose someone said I have no sense of humor. Would you agree or disagree?"

"In some things you do. I mean, yes, you have a good sense of humor."

"What do you mean, 'in some things?' What kind of things?"

"Well, if you heard that someone had been killed in an unusual way, like by an exploding cigar, you would think that was funny."

Louise laughed.

"That's what I mean," Mary said.

Louise went on laughing. "Oh, Lordy," she said. "Now it's my turn to say something about you." She sat down beside Mary.

"Please," Mary said.

"Just one thing," Louise said.

Mary waited.

"You're trembling," Louise said. "I was just going to say—oh, forget it. Listen, do you mind if I sleep on the couch? I'm all in."

"Go ahead."

"Sure it's okay? You've got a big day tomorrow." She fell back on the sofa and kicked off her shoes. "I was just going to say, you should use some liner on those eyebrows of yours. They sort of disappear and the effect is disconcerting."

Neither of them slept. Louise chain-smoked cigarettes and Mary watched the coals burn down. When it was light enough that they could see each other Louise got up. "I'll send a student for you," she said. "Good luck."

The college looked the way colleges are supposed to look. Roger, the student assigned to show Mary around, explained that it was an exact copy of a college in England, right down to the gargoyles and stained-glass windows. It looked so much like a college that moviemakers sometimes used it as a set. *Andy Hardy Goes to College*[5] had been filmed there, and every fall they had an Andy Hardy Goes to College Day, with raccoon coats and goldfish-swallowing contests.

Above the door of the Founder's Building was a Latin motto which, roughly translated, meant "God helps those who help themselves." As Roger recited the names of illustrious graduates Mary was struck by the extent to which they had taken this precept to heart. They had helped themselves to railroads, mines, armies, states; to empires of finance with outposts all over the world.

Roger took Mary to the chapel and showed her a plaque bearing the names of alumni who had been killed in various wars, all the way back to the Civil War. There were not many names. Here too, apparently, the graduates had helped themselves. "Oh yes," Roger said as they were leaving, "I forgot to tell you. The communion rail comes from some church in Europe where Charlemagne[6] used to go."

They went to the gymnasium, and the three hockey rinks, and the library, where Mary inspected the card catalogue, as though she would turn down the job if they didn't have the right books. "We have a little more time," Roger said as they went outside. "Would you like to see the power plant?"

Mary wanted to keep busy until the last minute, so she agreed.

Roger led her into the depths of the service building, explaining things about the machine, which was the most advanced in the country. "People think the college is really old-fashioned," he said, "but it

5. Before and during W.W. II the series of Hardy Family films was extremely popular in the U.S. Andy Hardy was played by film star Mickey Rooney.
6. King of the Franks (742–814) and emperor of the Holy Roman Empire.

isn't. They let girls come here now, and some of the teachers are women. In fact, there's a statute that says they have to interview at least one woman for each opening. There it is."

They were standing on an iron catwalk above the biggest machine Mary had ever beheld. Roger, who was majoring in Earth Sciences, said that it had been built from a design pioneered by a professor in his department. Where before he had been gabby Roger now became reverent. It was clear that for him this machine was the soul of the college, that the purpose of the college was to provide outlets for the machine. Together they leaned against the railing and watched it hum.

Mary arrived at the committee room exactly on time for her interview, but the room was empty. Her two books were on the table, along with a water pitcher and some glasses. She sat down and picked up one of the books. The binding cracked as she opened it. The pages were smooth, clean, unread. Mary turned to the first chapter, which began, "It is generally believed that . . ." How dull, she thought.

Nearly twenty minutes later Louise came in with several men. "Sorry we're late," she said. "We don't have much time so we'd better get started." She introduced Mary to the men, but with one exception the names and faces did not stay together. The exception was Dr. Howells, the department chairman, who had a porous blue nose and terrible teeth.

A shiny-faced man to Dr. Howells's right spoke first. "So," he said, "I understand you once taught at Brandon College."

"It was a shame that Brandon had to close," said a young man with a pipe in his mouth. "There is a place for schools like Brandon." As he talked the pipe wagged up and down.

"Now you're in Oregon," Dr. Howells said. "I've never been there. How do you like it?"

"Not very much," Mary said.

"Is that right?" Dr. Howells leaned toward her. "I thought everyone liked Oregon. I hear it's very green."

"That's true," Mary said.

"I suppose it rains a lot," he said.

"Nearly every day."

"I wouldn't like that," he said, shaking his head. "I like it dry. Of course it snows here, and you have your rain now and then, but it's a *dry* rain. Have you ever been to Utah? There's a state for you. Bryce Canyon. The Mormon Tabernacle Choir."

"Dr. Howells was brought up in Utah," said the young man with the pipe.

"It was a different place altogether in those days," Dr. Howells said. "Mrs. Howells and I have always talked about going back when I retire, but now I'm not so sure."

"We're a little short on time," Louise said.

"And here I've been going on and on," Dr. Howells said. "Before we wind things up, is there anything you want to tell us?"

"Yes. I think you should give me the job." Mary laughed when she said this, but no one laughed back, or even looked at her. They all looked away. Mary understood then that they were not really considering her for the position. She had been brought here to satisfy a rule. She had no hope.

The men gathered their papers and shook hands with Mary and told her how much they were looking forward to her class. "I can't get enough of the Marshall Plan," Dr. Howells said.

"Sorry about that," Louise said when they were alone. "I didn't think it would be so bad. That was a real bitcheroo."

"Tell me something," Mary said. "You already know who you're going to hire, don't you?"

Louise nodded.

"Then why did you bring me here?"

Louise began to explain about the statute and Mary interrupted. "I know all that. But why me? Why did you pick *me?*"

Louise walked to the window. She spoke with her back to Mary. "Things haven't been going very well for old Louise," she said. "I've been unhappy and I thought you might cheer me up. You used to be so funny, and I was sure you would enjoy the trip—it didn't cost you anything, and it's pretty this time of year with the leaves and everything. Mary, you don't know the things my parents did to me. And Ted is no barrel of laughs either. Or Jonathan, the son of a bitch. I deserve some love and friendship but I don't get any." She turned and looked at her watch. "It's almost time for your class. We'd better go."

"I would rather not give it. After all, there's not much point, is there?"

"But you *have* to give it. That's part of the interview." Louise handed Mary a folder. "All you have to do is read this. It isn't much, considering all the money we've laid out to get you here."

Mary followed Louise down the hall to the lecture room. The professors were sitting in the front row with their legs crossed. They smiled and nodded at Mary. Behind them the room was full of students, some of whom had spilled over into the aisles. One of the professors adjusted the microphone to Mary's height, crouching down as he went to the podium and back as though he would prefer not to be seen.

Louise called the room to order. She introduced Mary and gave the subject of the lecture. But Mary had decided to wing it after all. Mary came to the podium unsure of what she would say; sure only that she would rather die than read Louise's article. The sun poured through the stained glass onto the people around her, painting their faces. Thick streams of smoke from the young professor's pipe drifted through a circle of red light at Mary's feet, turning crimson and twisting like flames.

"I wonder how many of you know," she began, "that we are in the Long House,[7] the ancient domain of the Five Nations of the Iroquois."

Two professors looked at each other.

"The Iroquois were without pity," Mary said. "They hunted people down with clubs and arrows and spears and nets, and blowguns made from elder stalks. They tortured their captives, sparing no one, not even the little children. They took scalps and practiced cannibalism and slavery. Because they had no pity they became powerful, so powerful that no other tribe dared to oppose them. They made the other tribes pay tribute, and when they had nothing more to pay the Iroquois attacked them."

Several of the professors began to whisper. Dr. Howells was saying something to Louise, and Louise was shaking her head.

"In one of their raids," Mary said, "they captured two Jesuit priests, Jean de Brébeuf and Gabriel Lalement.[8] They covered Lalement with pitch and set him on fire in front of Brébeuf. When Brébeuf rebuked them they cut off his lips and put a burning iron down his throat. They hung a collar of red-hot hatchets around his neck, and poured boiling water over his head. When he continued to preach to them they cut strips of flesh from his body and ate them before his eyes. While he was still alive they scalped him and cut open his breast and drank his blood. Later, their chief tore out Brébeuf's heart and ate it, but just before he did this Brébeuf spoke to them one last time. He said—"

"That's enough!" yelled Dr. Howells, jumping to his feet.

Louise stopped shaking her head. Her eyes were perfectly round

Mary had come to the end of her facts. She did not know what Brébeuf had said. Silence rose up around her; just when she thought she would go under and be lost in it she heard someone whistling in the hallway outside, trilling the notes like a bird, like many birds.

"Mend your lives." she said. "You have deceived yourselves in the pride of your hearts, and the strength of your arms. Though you soar

---

7. Communal Indian dwelling, in actuality a wooden frame covered with bark.
8. The two most famous martyrs among the Jesuit missionaries in North America. They were tortured and killed by the Iroquois in 1649.

aloft like the eagle, though your nest is set among the stars, thence I will bring you down, says the Lord.[9] Turn from power to love. Be kind. Do justice. Walk humbly."

Louise was waving her arms. "Mary!" she shouted.

But Mary had more to say, much more; she waved back at Louise, then turned off her hearing aid so that she would not be distracted again.

1981

■   ■   ■

9. Obadiah 1:4.

BIOGRAPHICAL SKETCHES

Alice Adams (b. 1926) Born in Virginia, Adams was raised near Chapel Hill, North Carolina, the setting for much of her fiction. Her novels include *Careless Love* (1966), *Listening to Billie* (1978), *Rich Rewards* (1980), *Superior Women* (1984), and *A Southern Exposure* (1996); her stories have been collected in *Beautiful Girl* (1979), *To See You Again* (1982), *Return Trips* (1985), and *After You've Gone* (1989).

Julia Alvarez (b. 1950) Born in the Dominican Republic, Alvarez emigrated to the United States in 1960 and currently teaches at Middlebury College. Her publications include a book of poetry, *Homecoming* (1984); a collection of stories, *How the Garcia Girls Lost Their Accents* (1991); and two novels, *In the Time of the Butterflies* (1995) and *¡YO!* (1997).

Margaret Atwood (b. 1939) A longtime resident of Toronto, Canada, Atwood is an internationally renowned novelist, short story writer, poet, and critic. Among her novels are *Surfacing* (1972), *The Handmaid's Tale* (1985), *The Robber Bride* (1993), and *Alias Grace* (1996); her story collections include *Dancing Girls* (1977), *Bluebeard's Egg* (1983), and *Wilderness Tips* (1991).

Donald Barthelme (1931–1989) Born in Philadelphia, raised in Houston, Texas, and a longtime resident of New York City, Barthelme is known for his short story collections *Come Back, Dr. Caligari* (1964), *Unspeakable Practices, Unnatural Acts* (1968), *City Life* (1970), *Amateurs* (1976), and *Sixty Stories* (1982); his novels are *Snow White* (1967) and *The Dead Father* (1975).

Charles Baxter (b. 1947) Born in Minneapolis, Baxter currently directs the writing program at the University of Michigan at Ann Arbor. He has published the short story collections *Harmony of the World* (1984), *Through the Safety Net* (1985), *A Relative Stranger* (1990), and *Believers* (1997); his novels are *First Light* (1987), *Imaginary Paintings* (1990), and *Shadow Play* (1993). A volume of his essays on fiction, *Burning Down the House*, is forthcoming in 1997.

Ann Beattie (b. 1947) Born in Washington, D.C., Beattie has taught at Harvard and the University of Virginia. Her many stories in *The New Yorker* have established her as a chronicler of contemporary lifestyles and manners. Among her story collections are *Distortions* (1976), *Secrets and Surprises* (1978), *The Burning House* (1982), and *Where You'll Find Me* (1986); her novels are *Chilly Scenes of Winter* (1976), *Falling in Place* (1980), *Love Always* (1985), and *Picturing Will* (1990).

T. Coraghessan Boyle (b. 1948) Born and raised in Peekskill, New York, now a resident of Montecito, California, Boyle has published his highly original short stories in a variety of periodicals, including *The Atlantic*, *Esquire*, *Harper's*, and

Penthouse. His stories are collected in Descent of Man (1979), Greasy Lake (1985), If the River Was Whiskey (1989), and Without a Hero (1994); his novels include World's End (1987), East Is East (1990), and The Tortilla Curtain (1995).

Ron Carlson (b. 1947) Born in Logan, Utah, Carlson currently teaches at Arizona State University. His novels are Betrayed by F. Scott Fitzgerald (1977) and Truants (1981); his short stories have been collected in The News of the World (1987), Plan B for the Middle Class (1992), and The Hotel Eden (1997).

Raymond Carver (1939–1988) Born in Oregon and raised in Yakima, Washington, Carver was one of the most highly acclaimed short story authors of postwar America. He chronicled the ordinariness of blue-collar life in a spare, poetic style that has often been compared to that of Hemingway. His four major short story collections are Will You Please Be Quiet Please? (1976), What We Talk About When We Talk About Love (1981), Cathedral (1983), and Where I'm Calling From (1988).

Sandra Cisneros (b. 1954) Born in Chicago and currently residing in San Antonio, Texas, Cisneros combines oral tradition, music, poetry, and prose in her work. She has published two collections of stories, The House on Mango Street (1985) and Woman Hollering Creek (1991); her books of poetry are Bad Boys (1980), My Wicked, Wicked Ways (1987), and Loose Woman (1994).

Robert Coover (b. 1932) Born in Iowa, Coover incorporates into his fiction a mixture of satire and slapstick, black humor and political badinage. His titles include the innovative collection Pricksongs & Descants (1969) and the novels The Origins of the Brunists (1966), The Universal Baseball Association, Inc., J. Henry Waugh, Prop. (1968), The Public Burning (1977), Gerald's Party (1987), and Pinocchio (1991).

Mark Costello (b. 1936) Born in Decatur, Illinois, Costello currently teaches in the writing program at the University of Illinois. He is admired for his first book, The Murphy Stories (1973), and its sequel, Middle Murphy (1991).

Andre Dubus (b. 1936) Born in Lake Charles, Louisiana, Dubus is widely regarded for his fiction, which portrays the decline of postwar America, and for his moral responsibility as an author. His titles include The Lieutenant (1967), a novel; We Don't Live Here Any More (1984), a collected trilogy of novellas; Separate Flights (1975), Land Where My Fathers Died (1984), The Last Worthless Evening (1986), and Dancing After Hours (1996), all short story collections; and Blood Vessels (1991), a book of personal essays.

Stuart Dybek (b. 1942) Born and raised in Chicago, Dybek lives in Kalamazoo, Michigan, where he teaches literature and writing at Western Michigan University. He has published two collections of short stories, Childhood and Other Neighborhoods (1980) and The Coast of Chicago (1990), and one book of poetry, Brass Knuckles (1979).

Louise Erdrich (b. 1954) Born in Little Falls, Minnesota, of German-American and Chippewa descent, Erdrich grew up in Wahpeton, North Dakota. She is known for her honest portrayal of native Americans in her novels *Love Medicine* (1984), *The Beet Queen* (1986), *Tracks* (1988), *The Bingo Palace* (1994), *Tales of Burning Love* (1996), and, co-authored with Michael Dorris, *The Columbus of Love* (1991). Erdrich has published two books of poems, *Jacklight* (1984) and *Baptism of Desire* (1989).

Richard Ford (b. 1944) Born in Jackson, Mississippi, and raised in Arkansas, Ford now divides his time between New Orleans, Louisiana, and Montana. His stories, which have been published in *Esquire*, *The New Yorker*, and *Granta*, are collected in *Rock Springs* (1987). His novels are *A Piece of My Heart* (1976), *The Ultimate Good Luck* (1981), *The Sportswriter* (1986), *Wildlife* (1990), and *Independence Day* (1995).

Gabriel García Márquez (b. 1928) Born in Aracataca, Columbia, Márquez is now a resident of Barcelona. Many of his short stories as well as his epic novel *One Hundred Years of Solitude* (1976) are set in the fictional town of Macondo— which some have seen as a counterpart to Faulkner's Yoknapatawpha County— and present several generations of one family in a series of interconnected narratives. His publications include *Collected Stories* (1984) as well as the novels *In an Evil Hour* (1962), *Leaf Storm* (1972), *Autumn of the Patriarch* (1975), and *Love in the Time of Cholera* (1987).

George Garrett (b. 1929) A poet, fiction writer, dramatist, biographer, and critic born in Orlando, Florida, Garrett teaches creative writing at the University of Virginia. Prominent in his later work is a trilogy of novels set in the Elizabethan period: *Death of the Fox* (1971), *The Succession* (1983), and *Entered from the Sun* (1990). Among his other novels are *Which Ones Are the Enemy?* (1961), *Do, Lord, Remember Me* (1965), and *The Magic Strip Tease* (1973); many of his short stories are collected in *A Wreath for Garibaldi* (1969) and *An Evening Performance* (1985).

William H. Gass (b. 1924) Born in Fargo, North Dakota, Gass is currently the director of the International Writers' Center at Washington University. He has published one volume of short stories, *In the Heart of the Heart of the Country* (1968), as well as considerable literary criticism. His novels are *Omensetter's Luck* (1966), *Willie Master's Lonesome Wife* (1968), and *The Tunnel* (1995).

C. S. Godshalk Born and raised in New York City, Godshalk is a former freelance journalist who began writing fiction in the early 1980s. Two of her stories have appeared in *The Best American Short Stories* and her novel *Kalimantaan* is forthcoming in 1998.

Tom Hawkins (b. 1946) Born in Park Ridge, Illinois, Hawkins intended to become a journalist before turning his hand to writing fiction. His story collection, *Paper Crown* (1989), contains pieces that have been published in a number of distinguished literary magazines.

Amy Hempel (b. 1951) Born in Chicago, Hempel has recently been writer-in-residence at Brown University. She has published two volumes of short stories, *Reasons to Live* (1985) and *At the Gates of the Animal Kingdom* (1990).

Pam Houston (b. 1962) Born in New Jersey, Houston traveled through Colorado and Montana before settling in Utah. Her first book of short stories is *Cowboys Are My Weakness* (1983), and she has edited *Women on Hunting* (1995), a collection of prose and poetry.

Charles Johnson (b. 1948) A novelist, short story writer, cartoonist, and critic born in Evanston, Illinois, Johnson teaches literature at the University of Washington. He is the author of the novels *Oxherding Tale* (1974), *Middle Passage* (1990), and *Dreamer* (1997), a fictionalized version of the life of Martin Luther King Jr. He has also published a story collection, *The Sorcerer's Apprentice* (1986); a book of cartoons, *Black Humor* (1970); and a critical study, *Being and Race* (1988).

Thom Jones (b. 1945) A former Marine and an amateur boxer, Jones currently teaches writing at the University of Iowa. He is the author of the highly regarded story collections *The Pugilist at Rest* (1993) and *Cold Snap* (1995).

Jamaica Kincaid (b. 1946) Born in St. Johns, Antigua, in the British West Indies, Kincaid is now a naturalized citizen of the United States and a staff writer for *The New Yorker*. She has been praised not only for her vivid portrayal of the island culture but also for the color and liveliness of her writing style. Kincaid has published the short story collection *At the Bottom of the River* (1983), the novels *Annie John* (1985), *Lucy* (1990), and *The Autobiography of My Mother* (1996) as well as the book-length essay *A Small Place* (1988).

William Kotzwinkle (b. 1938) Born in Scranton, Pennsylvania, Kotzwinkle is the author of two collections of short stories, *Elephant Bangs Train* (1971) and *Jewel of the Moon* (1986). His novels include *Hermes 3000* (1972), *Swimmer in the Secret Sea* (1975), and *Seduction in Berlin* (1985).

Ursula K. Le Guin (b. 1929) Born in Berkeley, California, and now residing in Portland, Oregon, Le Guin is the acclaimed author of science fiction that extends moral and ecological boundaries to explore new possibilities for human society. Her publications include a celebrated series of children's books—*A Wizard of Earthsea* (1968), *The Tombs of Autan* (1971), and *The Farthest Shore* (1972)—known as the Earthsea Trilogy; the novels *The Left Hand of Darkness* (1969), *The Dispossessed* (1974), *The Beginning Place* (1980), and *Always Coming Home* (1985), as well as the short story collections *The Wind's Twelve Quarters* (1975) and *Orsinian Tales* (1976).

David Madden (b. 1933) Born in Knoxville, Tennessee, Madden was writer-in-residence at Louisiana State University from 1968 to 1992; he served as director of the Creative Writing Program until 1994. He is known for his novels *The Beautiful Greed* (1961) and *Cassandra Singing* (1969) as well as his short story collections *The Shadow Knows* (1970) and *The New Orleans of Possibilities* (1982).

Bobbie Ann Mason (b. 1940) Born and raised in western Kentucky, Mason is highly regarded for her stories, many of which chronicle the ordinary details of working-class life. She has published two collections, *Shiloh and Other Stories* (1982) and *Love Life* (1989); her novels are *In Country* (1988), *Spence and Lila* (1988), and *Feather Crowns* (1993).

Susan Minot (b. 1956) Born in Boston, Minot is the author of the novels *Monkeys* (1986) and *Folly* (1992) as well as the short story collection *Lust and Other Stories* (1989).

Bharati Mukherjee (b. 1940) Born a Bengali Brahmin in India, Mukherjee has as an adult lived in Canada and the United States, and she currently teaches at the University of California at Berkeley. Her titles include the novels *The Tiger's Daughter* (1971), *Wife* (1975), and *Jasmine* (1989); and the story collections *Darkness* (1985) and *The Middleman* (1988). She has co-authored two books with her husband, Clark Blaise: *Days and Nights in Calcutta* (1977) and *The Sorrow and the Terror: The Haunting Legacy of the Air India Tragedy* (1987).

Alice Munro (b. 1931) Born in Wingham, Ontario, Munro is the highly acclaimed author of short stories that find the humanity in small-town life. She has published numerous volumes, including *Lives of Girls and Women* (1971), *Something I've Been Meaning to Tell You* (1974), *Who Do You Think You Are?* (1978; published in the United States as *The Beggar Maid*), *The Moons of Jupiter* (1982), *The Progress of Love* (1986), and the comprehensive collection *Selected Stories* (1996).

Joyce Carol Oates (b. 1938) Born in Lockport, New York, and highly regarded as a short story writer, novelist, dramatist, and critic, Oates currently teaches at Princeton University. She is the author of numerous story collections, including, most recently, *Heat* (1991), *Haunted: Tales of the Grotesque* (1994), and *Will You Always Love Me?* (1996); among her many novels are *them* (1969), *What I Lived For* (1994), and *We Were the Mulvaneys* (1996).

Tim O'Brien (b. 1946) Born in Austin, Minnesota, O'Brien served in Vietnam and emerged as one of its most important chroniclers. Though his work is characterized by a solid vein of realism, it is also influenced by the "magical realism" of contemporary South American novelists. O'Brien is the author of a war journal, *If I Die in a Combat Zone, Box Me Up and Ship Me Home* (1973), and the novels *Northern Lights* (1974), *Going after Cacciato* (1978), and *The Nuclear Age* (1985); his story collections are *In the Lake of the Woods* (1984) and *The Things They Carried* (1990).

Jonathan Penner (b. 1940) Born in Bridgeport, Connecticut, Penner has most recently taught at the University of Arizona. His publications include the novel *Going Blind* (1977), the novella *The Intelligent Traveler's Guide to Chiribosco* (1983), and the short story collection *Private Parties* (1983).

Jayne Anne Phillips (b. 1952) Born in Buckhannon, West Virginia, Phillips has published two novels, *Machine Dreams* (1984) and *Shelter* (1994); her highly regarded books of short stories are *Sweethearts* (1976), *Counting* (1978), *Black Tickets* (1978), and *Fast Lanes* (1987).

Mary Robison (b. 1949) Born in Washington, D.C., Robison has published extensively in *The New Yorker* and has taught at Harvard and the University of Houston. She is the author of three books of short stories, *Days* (1979), *An Amateur's Guide to the Night* (1983), and *Believe Them*; her novels are *Oh* (1981) and *Subtraction* (1991).

Amy Tan (b. 1952) Born in Oakland, California, after her parents emigrated from Beijing, Tan explores the relationship between Chinese immigrant women and their American-born daughters in her fiction. Her novels are *The Joy Luck Club* (1989), *The Kitchen God's Wife* (1991), and *The Hundred Secret Senses* (1995).

Hunter S. Thompson (b. 1937) Born in Kentucky and now residing in Colorado, Thompson is a prominent and often outrageous political journalist whose titles include *Hell's Angels* (1969), *Fear and Loathing in Las Vegas* (1971), and *Fear and Loathing on the Campaign Trail '72* (1973). He is known primarily for his four-volume *Gonzo Papers* series: *The Great Shark Hunt* (1979), *Generation of Swine* (1988), *Song of the Doomed* (1990), and *Better than Sex* (1994).

John Updike (b. 1932) A poet, novelist, and short story writer born in Shillington, Pennsylvania, Updike is primarily known for his *Rabbit* chronicles, including *Rabbit Is Rich* (1982) and *Rabbit at Rest* (1990). Among his other titles are story collections, including *Pigeon Feathers* (1962) and *Bech Is Back* (1982), and many novels, including *The Poorhouse Fair* (1959), *The Coup* (1978), *The Witches of Eastwick* (1984), and *Roger's Version* (1986).

Guy Vanderhaeghe (b. 1951) Born in Saskatchewan, Canada, where he continues to live, Vanderhaeghe is admired for his short stories collected in *Man Descending* (1982), *The Trouble with Heroes* (1983), and *Things As They Are* (1992). He has published two novels, *My Present Age* (1984) and *Homesick* (1989).

Alice Walker (b. 1944) Born in Eatonton, Georgia, and now residing in San Francisco, Walker is a novelist, short story writer, essayist, poet, civil rights activist, and teacher of African American literature. Her novels are *The Third Life of Grange Copeland* (1970), *Meridian* (1976), *The Color Purple* (1982), *The Temple of My Familiar* (1989), and *Possessing the Secret of Joy* (1992); her short stories are collected in *In Love & Trouble: Stories of Black Women* (1973) and *You Can't Keep a Good Woman Down* (1982). She has recently published a memoir, *The Same River Twice: Honoring the Difficult* (1996).

Joy Williams (b. 1944) Born in Massachusetts, Williams now resides in Florida. Among her novels are *State of Grace* (1973), *The Changeling* (1978), and *Breaking & Entering* (1988); her short story collections include *Taking Care* (1982) and *Escapes* (1990).

Tobias Wolff (b. 1945) Born in Alabama and raised in Washington State, Wolff has taught in the writing programs at Syracuse and Indiana universities. His novels include *Ugly Rumors: A Novel* (1975), *The Barracks Thief* (1984), *Back in the World* (1985), and the autobiographical *This Boy's Life* (1989). Many of his short stories are collected in *In the Garden of the North American Martyrs* (1981).

PERMISSIONS ACKNOWLEDGMENTS

Alice Adams: "Barcelona" from *Return Trips* by Alice Adams. Copyright © 1984 by Alice Adams. Reprinted by permission of Alfred A. Knopf, Inc.

Julia Alvarez: "The Rudy Elmenhurst Story" from *How the Garcia Girls Lost Their Accents*. Copyright © 1991 by Julia Alvarez. Published by Plume, an imprint of Dutton Signet, a division of Penguin Books USA, Inc. First published by Algonquin Books of Chapel Hill. Reprinted by permission of Susan Bergholz Literary Services, New York.

Margaret Atwood: "The Man from Mars" from *Dancing Girls and Other Stories* by Margaret Atwood. Copyright © 1977, 1981 by O. W. Toad Ltd. Reprinted with the permission of Simon and Schuster and McClelland and Stewart, Inc., Toronto, *The Canadian Publishers*.

Donald Barthelme: "The Indian Uprising" from *Unspeakable Practices. Unnatural Acts* by Donald Barthelme. Copyright © 1981 by Donald Barthelme. Reprinted by permission of The Wylie Agency, Inc.

Charles Baxter: "Snow" from *A Relative Stranger* by Charles Baxter. Copyright © 1990 by Charles Baxter. Reprinted by permission of W. W. Norton & Company, Inc.

Ann Beattie: "The Cinderella Waltz" from *The Burning House* by Ann Beattie. Copyright © 1982 by Ann Beattie. Reprinted by permission of Random House, Inc.

T. Coraghessan Boyle: "Descent of Man" from *Descent of Man* by T. Coraghessan Boyle, Copyright © 1974 by T. Coraghessan Boyle. Reprinted by permission of Georges Borchardt, Inc., on behalf of the author.

Ron Carlson: "Blazo" from *Plan B for the Middle Class* by Ron Carlson. Copyright © 1992 by Ron Carlson. Reprinted by permission of W. W. Norton & Company, Inc.

Raymond Carver: "Cathedral" from *Cathedral* by Raymond Carver. Copyright © 1981 by Raymond Carver. Reprinted by permission of Alfred A. Knopf, Inc.

Sandra Cisneros: "One Holy Night" from *Woman Hollering Creek* by Sandra Cisneros. Copyright © 1991 by Sandra Cisneros. Published by Vintage, a division of Random House, Inc., and in hardcover by Random House. Reprinted by permission of Susan Bergholz Literary Services, New York.

Robert Coover: "The Babysitter" from *Pricksongs and Descants* by Robert Coover. Copyright © 1969 by Robert Coover. Used by permission of Dutton Signet, a division of Penguin Books USA, Inc.

Mark Costello: "Murphy's Xmas" from *The Murphy Stories* by Mark Costello. Copyright © 1973 by Mark Costello. Used with the permission of the author and the University of Illinois Press.

Andre Dubus: "A Father's Story" from *The Times Are Never So Bad* by Andre Dubus. Copyright © 1983 by Andre Dubus. Reprinted by permission of David R. Godine, Publisher, Inc.

Stuart Dybek: "Pet Milk" from *The Coast of Chicago* by Stuart Dybek. Copyright © 1981 by Stuart Dybek. Reprinted by permission of International Creative Management, Inc.

Louise Erdrich: "Saint Marie" from the revised edition of *Love Medicine* by Louise Erdrich. First published in the *O'Henry Collection* and the *Atlantic Monthly*. Copyright © 1984, 1993 by Louise Erdrich. Reprinted by permission of Henry Holt & Co., Inc.

Richard Ford: "Rock Springs" from *Rock Springs* by Richard Ford. Copyright © 1987 by Richard Ford. Reprinted by permission of Grove / Atlantic, Inc.

Gabriel García Márquez: "A Very Old Man With Enormous Wings" from *Leaf Storm and Other Stories* by Gabriel García Márquez and translated by Gregory Rabassa. Copyright © 1971 by Gabriel García Márquez. Reprinted by permission of HarperCollins Publishers, Inc.

George Garrett: "An Evening Performance" from *An Evening Performance* by George Garrett. Copyright © 1985 by George Garrett. Used by permission of Doubleday, a division of Bantam Doubleday Dell Publishing Group, Inc.

William H. Gass: "In the Heart of the Heart of the Country" from *In the Heart of the Heart of the Country* by William Gass. Copyright © 1968 by William H. Gass. Reprinted by permission of International Creative Management, Inc.

C. S. Godshalk: "The Wizard" by C. S. Godshalk, published by the *Agni Review*. Copyright © 1989 by C. S. Godshalk. Reprinted by permission of the Ellen Levine Literary Agency.

Tom Hawkins: "Putting A Child to Bed" from *Paper Crown* by Tom Hawkins. Copyright © 1989. Reprinted by permission of the author and BkMk Press.

Amy Hempel: "In the Cemetery Where Al Jolson is Buried" from *Reasons to Live* by Amy Hempel. Copyright © 1985 by Amy Hempel. Reprinted by permission of the Darhansoff & Verrill Literary Agency on behalf of the author.

Pam Houston: "Cowboys Are My Weakness" from *Cowboys Are My Weakness* by Pam Houston. Copyright © 1992 by Pam Houston. Reprinted by permission of W. W. Norton & Company, Inc.

Charles Johnson: "Kwoon." Copyright © 1991 by Charles Johnson. Reprinted by permission of Georges Borchardt, Inc., for the author. Originally appeared in *Playboy*.

Thom Jones: "The Black Lights" from *The Pugilist at Rest* by Thom Jones. Copyright © 1993 by Thom Jones. Reprinted by permission of Little, Brown and Company.

Jamaica Kincaid: "Girl" from *At the Bottom of the River* by Jamaica Kincaid. Copyright © 1983 by Jamaica Kincaid. Reprinted by permission of Farrar, Straus & Giroux, Inc.

William Kotzwinkle: "Follow the Eagle" from *Elephant Bangs Train* by William Kotzwinkle. Copyright © 1971 by William Kotzwinkle. Reprinted by permission of Harold Ober Associates.

Ursula K. Le Guin: "The New Atlantis" from *The New Atlantis* by Ursula K. LeGuin. Copyright © 1975 by Ursula K. LeGuin. Reprinted by permission of the author and the author's agent, Virginia Kidd.

David Madden: "No Trace" from *The Shadow Knows*. Copyright © 1970 by Louisiana State University Press. "No Trace" originally appeared in *The Southern Review*. Reprinted by permission of David Madden.

Bobbie Ann Mason: "Love Life." Copyright © 1990 by Bobbie Ann Mason. Reprinted by permission of HarperCollins Publishers, Inc.

Susan Minot: "Lust" from *Lust and Other Stories* by Susan Minot. Copyright © 1989 by Susan Minot. Reprinted by permission of Houghton Mifflin Co. / Seymour Lawrence. All rights reserved.

Bharati Mukherjee: "The Tenant" from *The Middleman and Other Stories* by Bharati Mukherjee. Copyright © 1988 by Bharati Mukherjee. Reprinted by permission of Grove / Atlantic and Penguin Books Canada Ltd.

Alice Munro: "Wild Swans" from *The Beggar Maid* (Canadian title: *Who Do You Think You Are?*) by Alice Munro. Copyright © 1977, 1978 by Alice Munro. Reprinted by permission of Alfred A. Knopf, Inc., and Macmillan Canada.

Joyce Carol Oates: "Bad Girls" from *Boulevard*. Copyright © 1994 by *The Ontario Review Inc.* Reprinted by permission of the author.

Tim O'Brien: "The Things They Carried" from *The Things They Carried* by Tim O'Brien. Copyright © 1990 by Tim O'Brien. Reprinted by permission of International Creative Management, Inc.

Jonathan Penner: "Emotion Recollected in Tranquillity" from *Private Parties* by Jonathan Penner. Copyright © 1983. Reprinted by permission of the University of Pittsburgh Press.

Jayne Anne Phillips: "Souvenir" from *Black Tickets* by Jayne Anne Phillips. Copyright © 1979 by Jayne Anne Phillips. Used by permission of Delacorte Press / Seymour Lawrence, a division of Bantam Doubleday Dell Publishing Group, Inc.

Mary Robison: "Coach" from *An Amateur's Guide to the Night* by Mary Robison. Copyright © 1983 by Mary Robison. Reprinted by permission of Alfred A. Knopf, Inc.

Amy Tan: "Rules of the Game" from *The Joy Luck Club* by Amy Tan. Copyright © 1989 by Amy Tan. Reprinted by permission of G. P. Putnam's Sons.

Hunter S. Thompson: "A Death in the Family" from *Generation of Swine* by Hunter S. Thompson. Copyright © 1988 by Hunter S. Thompson. Reprinted with the permission of Simon & Schuster.

John Updike: "The Other" from *Trust Me* by John Updike. Copyright © 1987 by John Updike. Reprinted by permission of Alfred A. Knopf, Inc.

Guy Vanderhaeghe: "Going to Russia" from *Man Descending* by Guy Vanderhaeghe. Copyright © 1982 by Guy Vanderhaeghe. Reprinted by permission of Ticknor & Fields / Houghton Mifflin Company and Macmillan Canada. All rights reserved.

Alice Walker: "Everyday Use" from *In Love & Trouble: Stories of Black Women* by Alice Walker. Copyright © 1973 by Alice Walker. Reprinted by permission of Harcourt Brace & Company.

Joy Williams: "Taking Care" from *Taking Care* by Joy Williams. Copyright © 1982 by Joy Williams. Reprinted by permission of Random House, Inc.

Tobias Wolff: "In the Garden of the North American Martyrs" from *In the Garden of the North American Martyrs* by Tobias Wolff. Copyright © 1981 by Tobias Wolff. First published by Ecco Press. Reprinted by permission.